MBA精选教材·英文影印版

A FRAMEWORK FOR MARKETING MANAGEMENT

[第4版]

营销管理架构

〔美〕Philip Kotler
Kevin Lane Keller 著

北京大学出版社
PEKING UNIVERSITY PRESS

北京市版权局著作权合同登记号　图字:01-2009-7100

图书在版编目(CIP)数据

营销管理架构:第4版:英文/(美)科特勒(Kotler,P.)等著. —影印本. —北京:北京大学出版社,2012.10

(MBA精选教材·英文影印版)

ISBN 978-7-301-21243-1

Ⅰ.①营… Ⅱ.①科… Ⅲ.①市场营销学-研究生-教材-英文 Ⅳ.①F713.50

中国版本图书馆CIP数据核字(2012)第219792号

Original edition, entitled A FRAMEWORK FOR MARKETING MANAGEMENT 4th Edition, 0-13-602660-5 by PHILIP KOTLER, KEVIN LANE KELLER, published by Pearson Education, Inc., publishing as Prentice Hall. Copyright © 2009.

All rights reserved. No part of this book may be reproduced or transmitted in any form or by any means, electronic or mechanical, including photocopying, recording or by any information storage retrieval system, without permission from Pearson Education, Inc.

本书原版书名为《营销管理架构》(第4版),作者科特勒、凯勒,书号0-13-602660-5,由培生教育出版集团2009年出版。

版权所有,盗印必究。未经培生教育出版集团授权,不得以任何形式、任何途径,生产、传播和复制本书的任何部分。

China edition published by PEARSON EDUCATION ASIA LTD., and PEKING UNIVERSITY PRESS Copyright © 2012.

This edition is manufactured in the People's Republic of China and is authorized for sale only in the People's Republic of China excluding Hong Kong, Macao SARs and Taiwan.

本书英文影印版由北京大学出版社和培生教育亚洲有限公司2012年出版发行。

此版本在中华人民共和国境内生产,被授权在中华人民共和国境内(不包括中国香港、澳门特别行政区及中国台湾地区)销售。

书　　　名:营销管理架构(第4版)
著作责任者:〔美〕Philip Kotler　Kevin Lane Keller　著
责 任 编 辑:仙　妍
标 准 书 号:ISBN 978-7-301-21243-1/F·3338
出 版 发 行:北京大学出版社
地　　　址:北京市海淀区成府路205号　100871
网　　　址:http://www.pup.cn　电子信箱:em@pup.pku.edu.cn
电　　　话:邮购部 62752015　发行部 62750672　编辑部 62752926　出版部 62754962
印 刷 者:北京鑫海金澳胶印有限公司
经 销 者:新华书店
　　　　　850毫米×1168毫米　16开本　25印张　487千字
　　　　　2012年10月第1版　2016年12月第3次印刷
印　　　数:8001—12000册
定　　　价:49.00元

未经许可,不得以任何方式复制或抄袭本书之部分或全部内容。
版权所有,侵权必究
举报电话:010-62752024　电子邮箱:fd@pup.pku.edu.cn

院长寄语

北京大学光华管理学院秉承北大悠久的人文传统、深邃的学术思想和深厚的文化底蕴,经过多年努力,目前已经站在中国经济发展与企业管理研究的前列,以向社会提供具有国际水准的管理教育为己任,并致力于帮助国有企业、混合所有制企业和民营企业实现经营管理的现代化,以适应经济全球化趋势。

光华MBA项目旨在为那些有才华的学员提供国际水准的管理教育,为工商界培养熟悉现代管理理念、原理和技巧的高级经营管理人才,使我们的MBA项目成为企业发展壮大之源,为学员创造迅速成长和充分发挥优势的条件和机会。

为了适应现代人才需求模式和建立中国的一流商学院,同时也为了配合北大MBA教育工作的展开,光华管理学院与北京大学出版社联合推出本套《MBA精选教材·英文影印版》,并向国内各兄弟院校及工商界人士推荐本套丛书。相信我们这些尝试将会得到社会的支持。而社会对我们的支持,一定会使光华MBA项目越办越好,越办越有特色。

北京大学光华管理学院名誉院长 厉以宁

出版者序言

自 2001 年 12 月加入世界贸易组织以来,中国进一步加强了与世界各国的政治、经济、文化各方面的交流与合作,这一切都注定中国将在未来世界经济发展中书写重要的一笔。

然而,中国经济的发展正面临着前所未有的人才考验,在许多领域都面临着人才匮乏的问题,特别是了解国际贸易规则、能够适应国际竞争需要的国际管理人才,更是中国在未来国际竞争中取胜的决定性因素。因此,制定和实施人才战略,培养大批优秀人才,是我们在新一轮国际竞争中赢得主动的关键。

工商管理硕士(MBA)1910 年首创于美国哈佛大学,随后 MBA 教育历经百年风雨不断完善,取得了令世人瞩目的成绩。如今,美国 MBA 教育已经为世界企业界所熟知,得到社会的广泛承认和高度评价。MBA 教育在我国虽起步较晚,但在过去十余年里,我国的 MBA 教育事业发展非常迅速,也取得了相当显著的成绩。

目前,国内的 MBA 教育市场呈现一片繁荣景象,但繁荣的背后却隐藏着种种亟待解决的问题。其中一个就是教材的问题。目前,国内市场上国外引进版教材在一定程度上还存在新旧好坏参差不齐的现象,这就需要读者在使用引进版教材时进行仔细的甄别。

北京大学出版社推出的《MBA 精选教材·英文影印版》弥补了国内 MBA 教材市场的缺憾,给国内 MBA 教材市场注入了一股新鲜的血液。全套丛书基本覆盖了北京大学 MBA 的主修课程,包括:管理学、营销学、战略管理、管理信息系统、运作管理、人力资源管理、商务沟通、国际金融、金融管理、决策分析、货币银行学、会计学等。另外,在十几门主课的基础上又增加了几门高级选修课程,包括:国际会计学、组织行为学、投资学、商务学、财务报表解析、管理会计、管理沟通、商业伦理学、企业家精神等。

本套丛书的筛选大体上本着以下几点原则:(1)出"新"。克服以往教材知识陈旧、落后的弊端,大部分教材都与国外原版书同步出版。(2)出"好"。本套丛书收入了美国哈佛大学、斯坦福大学、麻省理工学院等著名院校所采用的教材,如《管理学》、《营销管理架构》、《管理信息系统》、《人力资源管理》、《财务会计》、《管理会计》、《面向管理的数量分析》等;本套丛书还收入了著名学术界宗师包括斯蒂芬·罗宾斯(《管理学基础》)、菲利普·科特勒(《营销管理架构》)、查尔斯·霍恩格伦(《财务会计》)等人的学术巨著。(3)出"精"。大多数教材都是再版多次,经过不断的修改和完善而成的。

本套《MBA 精选教材·英文影印版》集合了美国经济学界和管理学界各个学科领域专家的权威巨著,该丛书经过北京大学光华管理学院及其他著名高校知名学者的精心选编,包括了大量精深的理论指导和丰富的教学案例,真正称得上是一套优中选精的 MBA 教材。

致谢

本套教材是我社与国外一流专业出版公司合作出版的,是从大量外版教材中选出的最优秀的一部分。在选书的过程中我们得到了很多专家学者的支持和帮助,可以说每一本书都经过处于教学一线的专家、学者们的精心审定,北京大学出版社英文影印版教材的顺利出版离不开他们

的无私帮助,在此,我们对审读并对本套图书提出过宝贵意见的老师们表示衷心的感谢,他们是:

北京大学光华管理学院:符国群、李东、梁钧平、陆正飞、王建国、王其文、杨岳全、于鸿君、张国有、张圣平、张志学、朱善利

中央财经大学会计系:孟焰

本套丛书的顺利出版还得到了培生教育出版集团(Pearson Education)北京办事处的大力支持,对他们的付出我们也致以深深的谢意。

教辅材料说明

教材,顾名思义教学之材料,它和普通的书籍有一个很大的区别,就是必须"方便教师教学"。所以,好的教材更需有完备的教学辅助材料相匹配,且每一本教材都要有教辅材料,只有配备了齐全的辅助材料才能称其为完整的教材。《MBA精选教材·英文影印版》系北京大学出版社获全球最大的教育出版集团——美国培生教育出版集团(Pearson Education)独家授权之英文影印版本。培生教育出版集团旗下的国际知名教育图书出版公司Prentice Hall/Addison Wesley/Longman出版的高品质的经济管理类出版物,已成为全美乃至全球高校采用率最高的教材,享誉全球教育界、工商界。我社在选择此套教材的过程中,尽量选择了教辅材料齐全的教材,这些教辅材料包括:教学指导用书、教学提纲、测试题、解答题、课堂演示文稿等,以书、幻灯片、CD、CD-ROM等形式出现。同时,这些材料还可通过访问培生教育出版集团的相关网址:http://www.prenhall.com、http://www.pearsoned.com、http://www.aw.com 免费下载。

欲获得相关教辅材料的教师烦请填写每本书后面所附的《教学支持说明》,以确保此教辅材料仅为教师获得。

出版声明

本套丛书是对国外原版教材的直接影印,由于各个国家政治、经济、文化背景的不同,原书中出版者和作者所持观点及结论尚需商榷,请广大读者在阅读过程中加以认真分析和鉴别。我们希望本套丛书的出版能够促进中外文化学术交流,推进国内经济与管理专业的教学,为中国经济走向世界作出一份贡献。

我们欢迎所有关心中国MBA教育的专家学者对我们的工作进行指导,欢迎每一位读者给我们提出宝贵的意见和建议。

北京大学出版社
经济与管理图书事业部
2006年1月

关于本书

适用对象

本书适用于 MBA 以及本科生和研究生的营销管理和营销战略课程,也可用作企业管理人员的培训教材和参考书。

内容简介

本书是营销学大师科特勒所著的最畅销教材《营销管理》(第 13 版)的精缩版。全书由七部分组成:第 1 部分是了解营销管理;第 2 部分是与顾客相联系;第 3 部分是塑造强大的品牌;第 4 部分是打造市场供应品;第 5 部分是提供价值;第 6 部分是传播价值;第 7 部分是实现成功的长期增长。

作者简介

菲利普·科特勒,西北大学凯洛格管理学院终身教授,被誉为"现代营销之父"。凯文·莱恩·凯勒,达特茅斯大学塔克商学院营销学教授。

本书特色

本书是营销学大师科特勒所著的最畅销教材《营销管理》(第 13 版)的精缩版,对当今营销管理实践作出了权威性介绍,而且篇幅适中,教师在授课过程中可以根据需要自行加入案例、模拟和项目练习,本书与其以前版本一样,旨在帮助公司、社会团体和个人调整自身的营销战略和管理以适应 21 世纪的营销现状。

本版更新

- 新主题——本版强调创新的作用以及技术发展对营销的影响。
- 新思想——本书加入相关学术研究取得的新概念和新思想。
- 新案例——本书加入大量现实生活中的最新案例。

教辅资源

- 教师手册
- 教学用 PPT
- 试题库
- 试卷生成软件

上述教辅资源教师可通过填写并邮寄本书后的《教学支持说明》免费获取。

简明目录

前言 xv

第 1 部分　了解营销管理 1
  第 1 章　定义 21 世纪的营销 1
  第 2 章　制定并实施营销战略和计划 21
  第 3 章　了解市场、市场需求和营销环境 40

第 2 部分　与顾客相联系 63
  第 4 章　建立顾客价值、满意和忠诚 63
  第 5 章　消费者市场分析 83
  第 6 章　企业市场分析 101
  第 7 章　确定细分市场和目标市场 116

第 3 部分　塑造强大的品牌 135
  第 8 章　创建品牌资产 135
  第 9 章　定位与竞争 154

第 4 部分　打造市场供应品 177
  第 10 章　制定产品战略及产品生命周期不同阶段的营销 .. 177
  第 11 章　服务的设计与管理 200
  第 12 章　制定定价战略和计划 217

第 5 部分　提供价值 239
  第 13 章　设计和管理价值网络与营销渠道 239
  第 14 章　零售、批发和物流的管理 259

第 6 部分　传播价值 278
  第 15 章　整合营销传播的设计和管理 278
  第 16 章　大众传播管理 294
  第 17 章　人员传播管理 313

第 7 部分　实现成功的长期增长 331
  第 18 章　在全球经济中对营销进行管理 331

术语表 347
索引 353

Brief Contents

Preface xvi

Part I UNDERSTANDING MARKETING MANAGEMENT 1
1. Defining Marketing for the Twenty-First Century 1
2. Developing and Implementing Marketing Strategies and Plans 20
3. Understanding Markets, Market Demand, and the Marketing Environment 38

Part II CONNECTING WITH CUSTOMERS 59
4. Creating Customer Value, Satisfaction, and Loyalty 59
5. Analyzing Consumer Markets 76
6. Analyzing Business Markets 94
7. Identifying Market Segments and Targets 110

Part III BUILDING STRONG BRANDS 128
8. Creating Brand Equity 128
9. Crafting the Brand Positioning and Dealing with Competition 147

Part IV SHAPING THE MARKET OFFERINGS 168
10. Setting Product Strategy and Marketing through the Life Cycle 168
11. Designing and Managing Services 191
12. Developing Pricing Strategies and Programs 209

Part V DELIVERING VALUE 230
13. Designing and Managing Integrated Marketing Channels 230
14. Managing Retailing, Wholesaling, and Logistics 248

Part VI COMMUNICATING VALUE 265
15. Designing and Managing Integrated Marketing Communications 265
16. Managing Mass Communications 282
17. Managing Personal Communications 302

Part VII CREATING SUCCESSFUL LONG-TERM GROWTH 323
18. Managing Marketing in the Global Economy 323

Glossary 341

Index 347

Contents

Preface xvi

Part I   UNDERSTANDING MARKETING MANAGEMENT   1

1. **Defining Marketing for the Twenty-First Century   1**

   The Importance of Marketing   2
   The Scope of Marketing   2
        What Is Marketing?   2
        What Is Marketed?   3
        What Is a Market?   4
        Who Markets?   5
        How Is Marketing Done?   5
   Core Marketing Concepts   6
        Needs, Wants, and Demands   6
        Target Markets, Positioning, and Segmentation   7
        Offerings and Brands   7
        Value and Satisfaction   8
        Marketing Channels   8
        Supply Chain   8
        Competition   8
        Marketing Environment   9
   The New Marketing Realities   9
        Major Societal Forces   9
        New Consumer Capabilities   10
        New Company Capabilities   10
   Company Orientation Toward the Marketplace   10
        The Production Concept   10
        The Product Concept   11
        The Selling Concept   11
        The Marketing Concept   11
        The Holistic Marketing Concept   12
   Marketing Management Tasks   16
   Executive Summary   17
   Notes   18

2. Developing and Implementing Marketing Strategies and Plans 20

Marketing and Customer Value 21
    The Value Delivery Process 21
    The Value Chain 22
    Core Competencies 23
    A Holistic Marketing Orientation and Customer Value 23
    The Central Role of Strategic Planning 25

Corporate and Division Strategic Planning 26
    Defining the Corporate Mission 26
    Defining the Business 27
    Assigning Resources to SBUs 28
    Assessing Growth Opportunities 28
    Organization, Organizational Culture, and Innovation 29

Business Unit Strategic Planning 29
    Business Mission 29
    SWOT Analysis 30
    Goal Formulation 31
    Strategy Formulation 31
    Program Formulation and Implementation 32
    Feedback and Control 32

The Marketing Plan and Marketing Performance 33
    Contents of a Marketing Plan 33
    Measuring Marketing Performance 33

Executive Summary 35
Notes 36

3. Understanding Markets, Market Demand, and the Marketing Environment 38

Marketing Information, Intelligence, and Research 39
    Internal Records 39
    Marketing Intelligence System 40
    Marketing Research System 40

Forecasting and Demand Measurement 46
    Which Market to Measure? 46
    Demand Measurement 47
    Company Demand and Sales Forecast 48
    Estimating Current Demand 48
    Estimating Future Demand 50

Macroenvironmental Trends and Forces 50
Demographic Environment 51
Economic Environment 53
Social-Cultural Environment 53
Natural Environment 54
Technological Environment 55
Political-Legal Environment 56
Executive Summary 56
Notes 57

Part II CONNECTING WITH CUSTOMERS 59

4. Creating Customer Value, Satisfaction, and Loyalty 59

Building Customer Value and Satisfaction 60
Customer Perceived Value 60
Total Customer Satisfaction 62
Monitoring Satisfaction 62
Product and Service Quality 64
Maximizing Customer Lifetime Value 64
Customer Profitability 64
Measuring Customer Lifetime Value 66
Cultivating Customer Relationships 67
Attracting and Retaining Customers 67
Building Loyalty 68
Customer Databases and Database Marketing 70
Data Warehouses and Datamining 71
The Downside of Database Marketing and CRM 72
Executive Summary 72
Notes 73

5. Analyzing Consumer Markets 76

What Influences Consumer Behavior? 77
Cultural Factors 77
Social Factors 77
Personal Factors 79
Key Psychological Processes 81
Motivation: Freud, Maslow, Herzberg 81
Perception 82
Learning 83
Memory 83

The Buying Decision Process: The Five-Stage Model   85
    Problem Recognition   85
    Information Search   85
    Evaluation of Alternatives   87
    Purchase Decisions   88
    Postpurchase Behavior   88
Executive Summary   90
Notes   90

6. Analyzing Business Markets   94

What Is Organizational Buying?   95
    The Business Market versus the Consumer Market   95
    Institutional and Organizational Markets   95
    Buying Situations   97
    Systems Buying and Selling   98
    Participants in the Business Buying Process   98
    The Buying Center   98
    Buying Center Influences   99
    Buying Center Targeting   100
Stages in the Buying Process   101
    Problem Recognition   101
    General Need Description and Product Specification   101
    Supplier Search   102
    Proposal Solicitation   103
    Supplier Selection   103
    Order-Routine Specification   104
    Performance Review   104
    Building Business Relationships   104
Executive Summary   106
Notes   107

7. Identifying Market Segments and Targets   110

Levels of Market Segmentation   111
    Segment Marketing   111
    Niche Marketing   111
    Local Marketing   112
    Individual Marketing   112
Segmenting Consumer and Business Markets   113
    Bases for Segmenting Consumer Markets   114
    Bases for Segmenting Business Markets   119

Market Targeting   120
   Effective Segmentation Criteria   121
   Evaluating and Selecting Market Segments   122
   Additional Considerations   124
Executive Summary   125
Notes   125

Part III BUILDING STRONG BRANDS   128

8. Creating Brand Equity   128

What is Brand Equity?   129
   The Role of Brands   129
   The Scope of Branding   129
   Defining Brand Equity   130
   Brand Equity as a Bridge   131
Building Brand Equity   131
   Choosing Brand Elements   132
   Designing Holistic Marketing Activities   133
   Leveraging Secondary Associations   134
Measuring and Managing Brand Equity   135
   Brand Audits and Brand Tracking   135
   Brand Valuation   136
   Managing Brand Equity   136
Brand Strategy and Customer Equity   137
   Branding Decisions   138
   Brand Extensions   139
   Brand Portfolios   140
   Customer Equity   141
Executive Summary   142
Notes   142

9. Crafting the Brand Positioning and Dealing with Competition   147

Developing and Communicating a Positioning Strategy   148
   Competitive Frame of Reference   149
   Points-of-Parity and Points-of-Difference   149
   Establishing Category Membership   150
   Choosing POPs and PODs   151
   Creating POPs and PODs   151

Differentiation Strategies 152
   Product Differentiation 152
   Services Differentiation 153
   Other Dimensions of Differentiation 154
Competitive Forces and Competitors 154
   Identifying Competitors 155
   Industry and Market Views of Competition 155
Analyzing Competitors 157
   Strategies 157
   Objectives 158
   Strengths and Weaknesses 158
   Selecting Competitors 158
Competitive Strategies 159
   Market-Leader Strategies 159
   Other Competitive Strategies 161
   Balancing Customer and Competitor Orientations 163
Executive Summary 164
Notes 165

Part IV SHAPING THE MARKET OFFERINGS 168

10. Setting Product Strategy and Marketing through the Life Cycle 168

Product Characteristics and Classifications 169
   Product Levels 169
   Product Classifications 170
Product and Brand Relationships 171
   Product-Line Analysis 172
   Product-Line Length 172
   Line Modernization, Featuring, and Pruning 172
   Co-Branding and Ingredient Branding 173
Packaging, Labeling, Warranties, and Guarantees 173
   Packaging 173
   Labeling 174
   Warranties and Guarantees 174
Managing New Products 175
   Why New Products Fail—and Succeed 175
   New Product Development 175

    The Consumer Adoption Process 181
     Stages in the Adoption Process 182
     Factors Influencing Adoption 182
    Marketing Through the Product Life Cycle 183
     Product Life Cycles 183
     Marketing Strategies: Introduction Stage
      and the Pioneer Advantage 184
     Marketing Strategies: Growth Stage 184
     Marketing Strategies: Maturity Stage 185
     Marketing Strategies: Decline Stage 185
     Critique of the Product Life-Cycle Concept 186
    Executive Summary 187
    Notes 187

11. Designing and Managing Services 191
    The Nature of Services 192
     Categories of Service Mix 192
     Distinctive Characteristics of Services 193
    Marketing Strategies for Service Firms 194
     A Shifting Customer Relationship 195
     Holistic Marketing for Services 196
    Managing Service Quality 198
     Customer Expectations 198
     Best Practices of Service-Quality Management 200
    Managing Service Brands 202
     Differentiating Services 202
     Developing Brand Strategies for Services 202
    Managing Product Support Services 203
     Identifying and Satisfying Customer Needs 203
     Post-Sale Service Strategy 204
    Executive Summary 204
    Notes 205

12. Developing Pricing Strategies and Programs 209
    Understanding Pricing 210
     A Changing Pricing Environment 210
     How Companies Price 210
     Consumer Psychology and Pricing 211
    Setting The Price 212
     Step 1: Selecting the Pricing Objective 212

    Step 2: Determining Demand 213
    Step 3: Estimating Costs 214
    Step 4: Analyzing Competitors' Costs, Prices, and Offers 216
    Step 5: Selecting a Pricing Method 216
    Step 6: Selecting the Final Price 221
  Adapting the Price 221
    Geographical Pricing 222
    Price Discounts and Allowances 222
    Promotional Pricing 222
    Differentiated Pricing 223
    Product-Mix Pricing 224
  Initiating and Responding to Price Changes 225
    Initiating Price Cuts 225
    Initiating Price Increases 225
    Responding to Competitors' Price Changes 226
  Executive Summary 227
  Notes 227

Part V   DELIVERING VALUE 230

13. Designing and Managing Integrated Marketing Channels 230

  Marketing Channels and Value Networks 231
    The Importance of Channels 231
    Value Networks 232
  The Role of Marketing Channels 232
    Channel Functions and Flows 232
    Channel Levels 234
    Service Sector Channels 235
  Channel-Design Decisions 235
    Analyzing Customers' Desired Service Output Levels 235
    Establishing Objectives and Constraints 235
    Identifying Major Channel Alternatives 236
    Evaluating the Major Alternatives 237
  Channel-Management Decisions 238
    Selecting Channel Members 238
    Training and Motivating Channel Members 238
    Evaluating Channel Members 238
    Modifying Channel Arrangements 239

Channel Integration and Systems 240
    Vertical Marketing Systems 240
    The New Competition in Retailing 241
    Conflict, Cooperation, and Competition 241
    Legal and Ethical Issues in Channel Relations 243
E-Commerce Marketing Practices 244
    Pure-Click Companies 244
    Brick-and-Click Companies 245
    M-Commerce 245
Executive Summary 245
Notes 246

14. Managing Retailing, Wholesaling, and Logistics 248

Retailing 249
    Types of Retailers 249
    The New Retail Environment 250
    Retailer Marketing Decisions 251
Private Labels 254
    House Brands 254
    The Private Label Threat 255
Wholesaling 255
    Trends in Wholesaling 257
    Strengthening Channel Relationships 257
Market Logistics 257
    Integrated Logistics Systems 258
    Market-Logistics Objectives 259
    Market-Logistics Decisions 260
    Market Logistics Lessons 262
Executive Summary 262
Notes 263

Part VI COMMUNICATING VALUE 265

15. Designing and Managing Integrated Marketing Communications 265

The Role of Marketing Communications 266
    The Changing Marketing Communications Environment 266
    Marketing Communications, Brand Equity, and Sales 267
    Communications Process Models 267

Developing Effective Communications   268
- *Identify the Target Audience*   270
- *Determine the Communications Objectives*   270
- *Design the Communications*   271
- *Select the Communications Channels*   272
- *Establish the Total Marketing Communications Budget*   274

Deciding on the Marketing Communications Mix   275
- *Characteristics of the Marketing Communications Mix*   275
- *Factors in Setting the Marketing Communications Mix*   276
- *Measuring Communication Results*   277

Managing the Integrated Marketing Communications Process   277
- *Coordinating Media*   278
- *Implementing IMC*   278

Executive Summary   279
Notes   279

16. Managing Mass Communications   282

Developing and Managing an Advertising Program   283
- *Setting the Objectives*   283
- *Deciding on the Advertising Budget*   284
- *Developing the Advertising Campaign*   284
- *Deciding on Media and Measuring Effectiveness*   285

Sales Promotion   289
- *Sales Promotion Objectives*   289
- *Advertising versus Promotion*   290
- *Major Decisions*   290

Events and Experiences   293
- *Events Objectives*   293
- *Major Sponsorship Decisions*   294
- *Creating Experiences*   294

Public Relations   295
- *Marketing Public Relations*   295
- *Major Decisions in Marketing PR*   296

Executive Summary   297
Notes   297

17. Managing Personal Communications 302

Direct Marketing 303
    The Benefits of Direct Marketing 303
    Direct Mail 303
    Catalog Marketing 304
    Telemarketing 304
    Other Media for Direct-Response Marketing 305
    Public and Ethical Issues in Direct Marketing 305
Interactive Marketing 305
Word-of-Mouth 308
    Buzz and Viral Marketing 308
    Opinion Leaders 308
    Blogs 310
    Measuring the Effects of Word-of-Mouth 311
Personal Selling and the Sales Force 311
    Personal Selling and Relationship Marketing 311
    Designing the Sales Force 312
    Sales Force Objectives and Strategy 313
    Sales Force Structure 313
    Sales Force Size 314
    Sales Force Compensation 314
Managing the Sales Force 314
    Recruiting and Selecting Sales Representatives 315
    Training and Supervising Sales Representatives 315
    Sales Rep Productivity 316
    Motivating Sales Representatives 316
    Evaluating Sales Representatives 317
Executive Summary 317
Notes 318

Part VII CREATING SUCCESSFUL LONG-TERM GROWTH 323

18. Managing Marketing in the Global Economy 323

Competing on a Global Basis 324
    Deciding Whether to Go Abroad 325
    Deciding Which Markets to Enter 325
    Deciding How to Enter the Market 326
    Deciding on the Marketing Program 327
    Country-of-Origin Effects 328

Internal Marketing 329
    Organizing the Marketing Department 329
    Relations with Other Departments 331
Managing the Marketing Process 331
    Evaluation and Control 331
    The Marketing Audit 333
Socially Responsible Marketing 334
    Ethical, Legal, and Social Responsibility Behavior 334
    Cause-Related Marketing 334
    Sustainability 335
Executive Summary 335
Notes 336

Glossary 341
Index 347

Preface

A *Framework for Marketing Management* is a concise paperback adapted from Philip Kotler and Kevin Lane Keller's number-one text, *Marketing Management, Thirteenth Edition*. Its streamlined approach will appeal to those professors who want an authoritative account of current marketing management practices and theory plus a text that is short enough to allow the incorporation of outside cases, simulations, and projects. Like previous editions, *A Framework for Marketing Management, Fourth Edition* is dedicated to helping companies, groups, and individuals adapt their marketing strategies and management to the marketplace of the twenty-first century.

FEATURES OF THE FOURTH EDITION

Major Themes

Building on the broad theme of holistic marketing, this new edition explores the vital role of creativity and innovation in successful marketing. Other major themes include customer value creation, marketing ethics and social responsibility, and marketing accountability. Another key theme is the impact of technology on contemporary marketing, driving developments as diverse as podcasts and marketing dashboards. And in updating every chapter, we have incorporated the latest concepts and ideas drawn from recent academic research studies.

Major Features

This edition is filled with numerous real-world examples of marketing management in action at a wide variety of companies, from Amazon.com to Zara.

- *Marketing Management at . . .* chapter-openers examine the challenges and opportunities faced by marketers of all kinds of goods and services, from health care (Mayo Clinic) and entertainment (ESPN) to coffee (Starbucks) and consumer electronics (Royal Philips).
- *Breakthrough Marketing* boxes highlight the innovative and insightful marketing accomplishments of such well-known businesses as IKEA, Nike, UPS, Ideo, Tesco, GE, eBay, Ocean Spray, Samsung, and Yahoo!
- *Marketing Skills* boxes discuss how marketers can develop skills they need to succeed in today's marketing environment, such as spotting trends (Chapter 3); finding new product ideas (Chapter 10); and starting a buzz fire (Chapter 17).

The Teaching and Learning Package
Marketing Management Cases

Through Prentice Hall Custom Business, instructors can create Custom Coursepacks or CustomCaseBooks for each course. Resources include top-tier cases from Darden, Harvard, Ivey, NACRA, and Thunderbird, plus full access to a database of articles. For details on how to order these value-priced packages, contact your local rep or visit the Prentice Hall Custom Business Web site at www.prenhall.com/custombusiness. To aid in your case selection, we have provided the following list of cases from our custom business Web site:

9-583-151	National Chemical Corp.: Tiger-Tread	Richard N. Cardozo	General Marketing	Harvard Business School Publishing
9-396-264	Virtual Vineyards	Jeffrey F. Rayport, Alvin J. Silk, Thomas A. Gerace, Lisa R. Klein	Marketing Strategy	Harvard Business School Publishing
9-593-064	Colgate-Palmolive Co.: The Precision Toothbrush	John A. Quelch, Nathalie Laidler	Marketing Strategy	Harvard Business School Publishing
9-504-009	XM Satellite Radio (A)	David B. Godes, Elie Ofek	Marketing Strategy	Harvard Business School Publishing
9-501-021	Freeport Studio	Rajiv Lal, James B. Weber	Market Research	Harvard Business School Publishing
9-501-002	Omnitel Pronto Italia	Rajiv Lal, Carin-Isabel Knoop, Suma Raju	Market Research	Harvard Business School Publishing
9-593-082	Bayerische Motoren Werke AG (BMW)	Robert J. Dolan	Market Research	Harvard Business School Publishing
9-703-516	Ice-Fili	Michael G. Rukstad, Sasha Mattu, Asya Petinova	Market Research	Harvard Business School Publishing
9-599-113	The Coop: Market Research	Ruth Bolton, Youngme Moon	Market Research	Harvard Business School Publishing
9-500-024	The Brita Products Co	John Deighton	Customer Retention	Harvard Business School Publishing
9-501-050	Customer Value Measurement at Nortel Networks—Optical Networks Division	Das Narayandas	Customer Retention	Harvard Business School Publishing
9-582-026	CIBA-GEIGY Agricultural Division	Benson P. Shapiro, Anne T. Pigneri, Roy H. Schoeman	Consumer Marketing	Harvard Business School Publishing
9-595-035	Nestle Refrigerated Foods: Contadina Pasta & Pizza (A)	V. Kasturi Rangan, Marie Bell	Consumer Marketing	Harvard Business School Publishing
9-500-052	Webvan: Groceries on the Internet	John Deighton, Kayla Bakshi	Consumer Marketing	Harvard Business School Publishing
9A99A009	Augat Electronics, Inc.	Adrian Ryans	Business-to-Business Marketing	Ivey
9-500-041	VerticalNet (www.verticalnet.com)	Das Narayandas	Business-to-Business Marketing	Harvard Business School Publishing
9-598-056	L'Oreal of Paris: Bringing "Class to Mass" with Plenitude	Robert J. Dolan	Market Segmentation	Harvard Business School Publishing
9-594-001	American Airlines' Value Pricing (A)	Alvin J. Silk, Steven C. Michael	Market Segmentation	Harvard Business School Publishing
9-596-036	Land Rover North America, Inc.	Susan Fournier	Brands	Harvard Business School Publishing
9-591-133	Barco Projection Systems (A): Worldwide Niche Marketing	Rowland T. Moriarty Jr., Krista McQuade	Product Lines	Harvard Business School Publishing
9-594-074	Planet Reebok (A)	John A. Quelch, Jamie Harper	Advertising	Harvard Business School Publishing
2069	Mountain Man Brewing Company: Bringing the Brand to Light	Heide Abelli	Marketing Strategy	Harvard Business School Publishing
9-500-024	The Brita Products Co.	John Deighton	Marketing Strategy	Harvard Business School Publishing
9-582-103	Sealed Air Corp.	Robert J. Dolan	Market Positioning	Harvard Business School Publishing
9-594-023	Mary Kay Cosmetics: Asian Market Entry	John A. Quelch, Nathalie Laidler	Market Positioning	Harvard Business School Publishing
9-596-076	Dewar's (A): Brand Repositioning in the 1990s	Alvin J. Silk, Lisa R. Klein	Brands	Harvard Business School Publishing
2086	Saxonville Sausage	Kate Moore	Product Positioning	Harvard Business School Publishing
9-593-064	Colgate-Palmolive Co.: The Precision Toothbrush	John A. Quelch, Nathalie Laidler	Product Positioning	Harvard Business School Publishing

9-500-070	Priceline.com: Name Your Own Price	Robert J. Dolan	Marketing Strategy	Harvard Business School Publishing
SAW007	TiVo: Changing the Face of Television	Mohanbir Sawhney	Product Positioning	Kellogg
9-592-035	Calyx and Corolla	Walter J. Salmon, David Wylie	Services Management	Harvard Business School Publishing
9-388-064	ServiceMaster Industries, Inc.	James L. Heskett	Services Management	Harvard Business School Publishing
9-597-063	Computron, Inc. – 1996	John A. Quelch	Pricing Strategy	Harvard Business School Publishing
M284A	Value Pricing at Procter & Gamble	Rajiv Lal, Mitchell Kristofferson	Pricing Strategy	Harvard Business School Publishing
9-598-109	FreeMarkets Online	V. Kasturi Rangan	Pricing Strategy	Harvard Business School Publishing
9-575-060	Southwest Airlines (A)	Christopher H. Lovelock	Pricing Strategy	Harvard Business School Publishing
9-595-001	RCI Master Distributor: The Evolution of Supplier Relationships	V. Kasturi Rangan	Distribution Channels	Harvard Business School Publishing
9-500-015	Autobytel.com	Youngme Moon	Distribution Channels	Harvard Business School Publishing
9-800-305	Staples.com	Joanna Jacobson, Thomas Eisenmann, Gillian Morris	Distribution Channels	Harvard Business School Publishing
9-503-004	GolfLogix: Measuring the Game of Golf	John T. Gourville, Jerry N. Conover	Strategic Planning	Harvard Business School Publishing
9-799-158	Matching Dell	Jan W. Rivkin, Michael E. Porter	Strategic Planning	Harvard Business School Publishing
9-593-094	MathSoft, Inc. (A)	V. Kasturi Rangan, Gordon Swartz	Strategic Planning	Harvard Business School Publishing
9-585-019	Suave (C)	Mark S. Albion	Marketing Communications	Harvard Business School Publishing
2066	MedNet.com Confronts 'Click-Through' Competition	Allegra Young	Marketing Communications	Harvard Business School Publishing
9-594-051	Northern Telecom (A): Greenwich Investment Proposal (Condensed)	Robert J. Dolan	Marketing Strategy	Harvard Business School Publishing
9-593-104	Northern Telecom (B): The Norstar Launch	Robert J. Dolan	Marketing Strategy	Harvard Business School Publishing
UVA-M-0340	Reagan-Bush '84 (A)	John Norton	Marketing Strategy	Darden
9-584-012	Milford Industries (A)	Benson P. Shapiro, Robert J. Dolan	Marketing Communications	Harvard Business School Publishing
9-584-013	Milford Industries (B)	Benson P. Shapiro, Robert J. Dolan	Marketing Communications	Harvard Business School Publishing
9-504-009	XM Satellite Radio (A)	David B. Godes, Elie Ofek	International Markets	Harvard Business School Publishing
9-598-150	Biopure Corp.	John T. Gourville	International Markets	Harvard Business School Publishing
9-595-026	Citibank: Launching the Credit Card in Asia-Pacific (A)	V. Kasturi Rangan	International Markets	Harvard Business School Publishing
9A99A016	Rougemont Fruit Nectar: Distributing in China	Tom Gleave, Paul Beamish	International Markets	Ivey
9-505-056	Unilever in India: Hindustan Lever's Project Shakti—Marketing FMCG to the Rural Consumer	V. Kasturi Rangan, Rohithari Rajan	International Markets	Harvard Business School Publishing

Instructor's Manual

This component contains chapter overviews and teaching objectives, plus suggested lecture outlines—providing structure for class discussions around key issues. A listing of key contemporary articles is included, along with synopses and ideas for class/course utilization of the materials. Harvard case analyses are also provided, integrating the current topic areas.

Test Item File

The Test Item File includes more than 70 questions per chapter, consisting of multiple-choice, true/false, essay, and mini-cases. Page references and suggested answers are provided for each question. Prentice-Hall's TestGen test-generating software is also available (online only) for this edition and is easily customizable for individual needs.

PowerPoint Basic

This simple presentation consists of basic outlines and key points from each chapter. No animation or forms of rich media are integrated, which makes the total file size manageable and easier to share online or via email.

PowerPoint Media Rich

This presentation includes basic outlines and key points from each chapter, plus art from the text, discussion questions, and Web links.

Marketing Management Video Gallery

Make your classroom "newsworthy." Using today's popular newsmagazine format, students are taken on location and behind closed doors. Each news story profiles a well-known company leading the way in its industry. Highlighting various companies, the issue-focused footage includes interviews with top executives and objective reporting by real news anchors, industry research analysts, and marketing and advertising experts. A video guide, including synopses and discussion questions, is available. The video library is offered on DVD, and instructors can choose to have it shrink-wrapped with this text.

Companion Web Site

The companion Web site, available at www.prenhall.com/kotler, offers students valuable resources, including two quizzes per chapter. The Concept Check Quiz is to be administered prior to reviewing the chapter, in order to assess students' initial understanding. The Concept Challenge Quiz is to be administered after studying the chapter, allowing students to determine the areas they need to review further. Also featured is the text glossary, as well as a link to Case Pilot. Case Pilot is a one-of-a-kind interactive tool that helps students develop the fundamentals of case study analysis. Three sample cases from the high-technology, service, and consumer-product sectors enable students to write problem statements, identify key marketing issues, perform SWOT analysis, and develop solutions.

Instructor's Resource Center (IRC)

The IRC is available online at www.prenhall.com/kotler, where instructors can access an array of teaching materials, consisting of the Instructor's Manual, Test Item File, TestGen, Video Guide, and Basic PowerPoint slides. These materials are also available on CD-ROM (except TestGen), where the Media Rich PowerPoint slides and an Image Library can be found as well.

The Marketing Plan Handbook, 3rd edition with Marketing Plan Pro

Marketing Plan Pro is a highly rated commercial software program that guides students through the entire marketing plan process. The software is totally interactive and features ten sample marketing plans, step-by-step guides, and customizable charts. Customize your marketing plan to fit your marketing needs by following easy-to-use plan wizards. Follow the clearly outlined steps from strategy to implementation. Click to print, and your text, spreadsheet, and charts come together to create a powerful marketing plan. The new *The Marketing Plan Handbook*, by Marian Burk Wood, supplements the in-text marketing plan material with an in-depth guide to what student marketers really need to know. A structured learning process leads to a complete and actionable marketing plan. Also included are timely, real-world examples that illustrate key points, sample marketing plans, and Internet resources. The Handbook and Marketing Plan Pro software are available as value-pack items at a discounted price. Contact your local Prentice Hall representative for more information.

We've partnered for you.

Texts from Prentice Hall.
Simulations from Interpretive.
Value for your students.

When you adopt a Prentice Hall textbook packaged *with* an Interpretive simulation, each new textbook purchased will contain an access code that will give you immediate access to your simulation online from Interpretive.

To ensure your students receive textbooks that contain access codes, make sure your bookstore orders the appropriate value-package ISBN. Your local Prentice Hall representative will be happy to assist.

INTERPRETIVE SIMULATIONS AT-A-GLANCE

PharmaSim

Predominantly used in: Marketing Management, Brand Management, and Marketing Strategy.

Take the role of a Brand Manager in the over-the-counter cold medicine market.

This leading marketing management online simulation drives home the Four P's of Marketing: Pricing, Promotion, Product, and Place (distribution), while introducing students to the concepts of brand equity and marketing planning for multiple product lines.

In PharmaSim, students take the role of a Brand Manager in the over-the-counter pharmaceutical industry and manage 'Allround,' the leading multi-symptom cold medicine. Over the course of up to 10 simulated periods, students may reformulate their brand, introduce a line extension, and launch a new product. PharmaSim is modeled from a brand management perspective, but the issues raised apply to marketers in any industry.

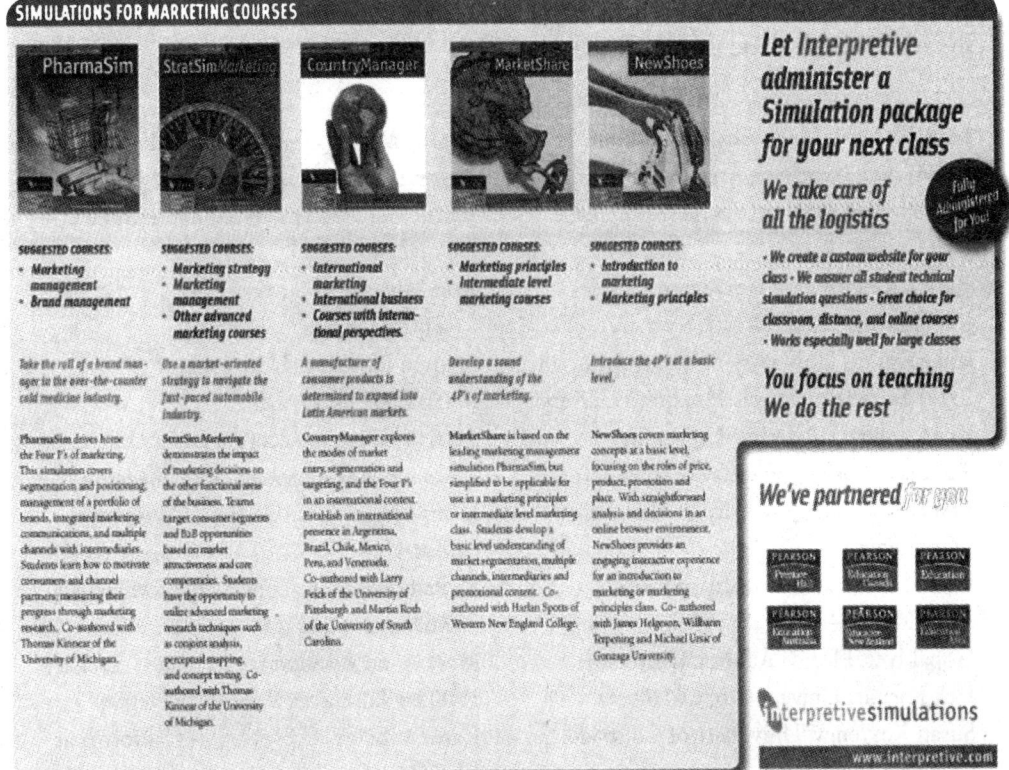

StratSim

Predominantly used in: Marketing Strategy, Marketing Management, and other advanced marketing courses.

Use a market-oriented strategy to navigate the fast-paced automobile industry.

This competitive marketing strategy simulation allows teams to target consumer segments and B2B opportunities based on market attractiveness and core competencies. Students have the opportunity to utilize advanced marketing research techniques such as conjoint analysis, perceptual mapping, and concept testing to enhance their understanding of the environment and consumers.

StratSim*Marketing* also highlights the importance of integrated decision-making by demonstrating the impact of marketing decisions on other functional areas of the business such as operations and finance.

ACKNOWLEDGMENTS

This edition of *A Framework for Marketing Management* bears the imprint of many people who have contributed to the previous edition of this text and to *Marketing Management, Thirteenth Edition*. We are sincerely grateful to Marian Burk Wood for her development and editorial work. Many thanks also to the professional editorial and production teams at Prentice Hall. We gratefully acknowledge the many reviewers who helped shape this book over the years.

John H. Antil, University of Delaware
Bill Archer, Northern Arizona University
Timothy W. Aurand, Northern Illinois University
Ruth Clottey, Barry University
Jeff Conant, Texas A&M University
Mike Dailey, University of Texas, Arlington
Brian Engelland, Mississippi State University
Brian Gibbs, Vanderbilt University
Thomas Gruca, University of Iowa
Mark Houston, University of Missouri, Columbia
Nicole Howatt, University of Central Florida
Gopal Iyer, Florida Atlantic University
Jack Kasulis, University of Oklahoma
Susan Keaveney, University of Colorado, Denver
Bob Kent, University of Delaware
Robert Kuchta, Lehigh University
Jack K. H. Lee, City University of New York Baruch College
Ning Li, University of Delaware
Steven Lysonski, Marquette University
Naomi Mandel, Arizona State University
Ajay K. Manrai, University of Delaware
Denny McCorkle, Southwest Missouri State University
James McCullough, Washington State University
Ron Michaels, University of Central Florida
George R. Milne, University of Massachusetts, Amherst
Marian Chapman Moore, Duke University
Steve Nowlis, Arizona State University
Louis Nzegwu, University of Wisconsin, Platteville
K. Padmanabhan, University of Michigan, Dearborn
Mary Anne Raymond, Clemson University
William Robinson, Purdue University
Carol A. Scott, University of California at Los Angeles
Stanley F. Slater, Colorado State University
Robert Spekman, University of Virginia
Edwin Stafford, Utah State University
Vernon Stauble, California State Polytechnic
Mike Swenson, Brigham Young University
Kimberly A. Taylor, Florida International University
Bronis J. Verhage, Georgia State University

Philip Kotler
S. C. Johnson & Son Distinguished Professor of International Marketing
Kellogg School of Management
Northwestern University
Evanston, Illinois

Kevin Lane Keller
E.B. Osborn Professor of Marketing
Tuck School of Business
Dartmouth College
Hanover, New Hampshire

PART I Understanding Marketing Management

CHAPTER 1

Defining Marketing for the Twenty-First Century

> In this chapter, we will address the following questions:
>
> 1. Why is marketing important?
> 2. What is the scope of marketing?
> 3. What are some fundamental marketing concepts and new marketing realities?
> 4. What are the tasks necessary for successful marketing management?

MARKETING MANAGEMENT AT STARBUCKS

Two teenage girls walk into their local Starbucks, which happens to be in Shanghai. While one orders peppermint lattés, the other sits at a table and opens her Lenovo ThinkPad notebook computer. She quickly connects to the Internet, courtesy of Starbucks' deal to provide wireless access through China Mobile, and uses the Chinese search engine Baidu.com to search for information about online games from China's Shanda Interactive. Her friend returns with the lattés, checks her Motorola cell phone for messages, and settles back to enjoy the chic coffeehouse ambience. Switch a few of the brand names—T-Mobile provides wireless access in the U.S. outlets, for example—and this would be a typical scene in nearly any Starbucks worldwide.

These days, Starbucks is really pouring on the marketing in China, where it sees huge profit potential. As a luxury brand, Starbucks appeals to status-conscious Chinese customers who are drawn to its "coffee culture" image. The company encourages coffee sales in a nation of tea drinkers by customizing its beverages to local tastes and offering free samples to both employees and customers. Starbucks already operates 500 coffeehouses in China and plans to open hundreds more, with the goal of making its lattes part of the daily routine for tens of millions of customers throughout the country.¹

As Starbucks knows, good marketing has become an increasingly vital ingredient for business success. It is both an "art" and a "science"—there's a constant tension between its formulated side and its creative side. It's easier to learn the formulated side, which will occupy most of our attention in this book, but we will also describe how real innovation, creativity, and passion operate in many companies. In this chapter, we lay the foundation for our study by reviewing a number of important marketing concepts, tools, frameworks, and issues.

THE IMPORTANCE OF MARKETING

Financial success often depends on marketing ability. Finance, operations, accounting, and other business functions will not really matter if there isn't sufficient demand for goods and services so the company can make a profit. There must be a top line for there to be a bottom line. Many companies have created a Chief Marketing Officer (CMO) position to put marketing on a more equal footing with other C-level executives such as the Chief Executive Officer (CEO) and Chief Financial Officer (CFO).

Marketing is tricky, however, and it has been the Achilles' heel of many formerly prosperous companies. Large, well-known businesses such as Sears, Levi's, Sony, General Motors, Kodak, and Xerox have confronted newly empowered customers and new competitors, and have had to rethink their business models. Even market leaders such as Intel, Microsoft, and Wal-Mart recognize that they cannot afford to relax as their leadership is challenged.

Xerox, for example, has had to become more than just a copier company. It now sports the world's broadest array of imaging products and dominates the market for high-end printing systems. And it's making a huge transition to digital systems and color printing. Having been slow at one time to respond to the emergence of Canon and the small copier market, Xerox is doing everything it can to stay ahead of the game.²

The companies at greatest risk are those that fail to carefully monitor their customers and competitors and to continuously improve their value offerings. They take a short-term, sales-driven view of their business and, ultimately, they fail to satisfy their stockholders, their employees, their suppliers, and their channel partners. Skillful marketing is a never-ending pursuit.

THE SCOPE OF MARKETING

To prepare to be a marketer, you need to understand what marketing is, how it works, what is marketed, and who does the marketing.

What Is Marketing?

Marketing is about identifying and meeting human and social needs. One of the shortest good definitions of marketing is "meeting needs profitably." When eBay recognized that people were unable to locate some of the items they desired most, it created an online auction clearinghouse. When IKEA noticed that people wanted good furniture at a substantially lower price, it created knock-down furniture. These two firms demonstrated marketing savvy and turned a private or social need into a profitable business opportunity.

The American Marketing Association offers the following formal definition: Marketing is *an organizational function and a set of processes for creating, communicating, and delivering value to customers and for managing customer relationships in ways that benefit the organization and its stakeholders.*[3] We see **marketing management** as *the art and science of choosing target markets and getting, keeping, and growing customers through creating, delivering, and communicating superior customer value.*

Managers sometimes think of marketing as "the art of selling products," but selling is *not* the most important part of marketing. Peter Drucker, a leading management theorist, says that "the aim of marketing is to make selling superfluous. The aim of marketing is to know and understand the customer so well that the product or service fits him and sells itself. Ideally, marketing should result in a customer who is ready to buy. All that should be needed then is to make the product or service available."[4] When Apple launched its iPod digital music player and when Toyota introduced its Prius hybrid automobile, these companies were swamped with orders because they had designed the "right" product based on careful marketing homework.

What Is Marketed?

Marketing people market 10 types of entities: goods, services, experiences, events, persons, places, properties, organizations, information, and ideas.

- *Goods.* Physical goods constitute the bulk of most countries' production and marketing effort. Each year, U.S. companies alone market billions of fresh, canned, bagged, and frozen food products and other tangible items. Thanks in part to the Internet, even individuals can effectively market goods.
- *Services.* As economies advance, a growing proportion of their activities are focused on the production of services. The U.S. economy today consists of a 70–30 services-to-goods mix. Services include the work of airlines, hotels, car rental firms, barbers and beauticians, maintenance and repair people, as well as professionals working within or for companies, such as accountants and programmers. Many market offerings consist of a variable mix of goods and services, as when a restaurant offers both food and service.
- *Events.* Marketers promote time-based events, such as major trade shows, artistic performances, and company anniversaries. Global sporting events such as the Olympics and the World Cup are promoted aggressively to both companies and fans.
- *Experiences.* By orchestrating several services and goods, a firm can create, stage, and market experiences. Walt Disney World's Magic Kingdom represents this kind of experiential marketing, allowing customers to visit a fairy kingdom, a pirate ship, or a haunted house. There is also a market for customized experiences, such as spending a few days at a baseball camp playing with retired baseball greats.[5]
- *Persons.* Celebrity marketing is a major business. Artists, musicians, CEOs, physicians, high-profile lawyers and financiers, and other professionals all get help from celebrity marketers.[6]
- *Places.* Cities, states, regions, and whole nations compete to attract tourists, factories, company headquarters, and new residents.[7] Place marketers include economic development specialists, real estate agents, commercial banks, business associations, and

advertising and public relations agencies. For example, the Las Vegas Convention & Tourism Authority has spent about $80 million on its "What Happens Here, Stays Here" ad campaign, with the goal of attracting 43 million visitors by 2009.[8]

- *Properties.* Properties are intangible rights of ownership of either real property (real estate) or financial property (stocks and bonds). Properties are bought and sold through the marketing efforts of real estate agents, investment companies, and banks.
- *Organizations.* Organizations actively work to build a strong, favorable, and unique image in the minds of their target publics. Tesco's "Every Little Bit Helps" marketing program has vaulted it to the top of the supermarket chains in the United Kingdom. Universities, museums, performing arts organizations, and nonprofits use marketing to boost their public images and compete for audiences and funds.
- *Information.* Schools and universities essentially produce and distribute information at a price to parents, students, and communities. Books, magazines, and newspapers also market information. One of our society's major industries is the production, packaging, and distribution of information.[9] Even companies that sell physical products add value through the use of information. The CEO of Siemens Medical Systems, for instance, says the firm's product "is not necessarily an X-ray or an MRI, but information. Our business is really healthcare information, and our end product is really an electronic patient record: information on lab tests, pathology, and drugs as well as voice dictation."[10]
- *Ideas.* Every market offering includes a basic idea. For instance, social marketers are busy promoting such ideas as "Friends Don't Let Friends Drive Drunk" and "A Mind Is a Terrible Thing to Waste."

What Is a Market?

Traditionally, a market was a physical place where buyers and sellers gathered to buy and sell goods. Economists describe a market as a collection of buyers and sellers who transact over a particular product or product class (such as the housing market). Marketers often use the term **market** to cover groupings of customers. They view the sellers as constituting the industry and buyers as constituting the market. They talk about need markets (the diet-seeking market), product markets (the shoe market), demographic markets (the youth market), and geographic markets (the French market); or other types of markets, such as voter markets, labor markets, and donor markets. Marketers may serve consumer markets, business markets, global markets, nonprofit markets, government markets, or some combination of these.

Figure 1.1 illustrates the relationship between the industry and the market. Sellers send goods, services, and communications (ads, direct mail) to the market; in return they receive money and information (customer attitudes, sales data). The inner loop shows an exchange of money for goods and services; the outer loop shows an exchange of information.

The *marketplace* is physical, such as a store you shop in, whereas the *marketspace* is digital, as when you shop on the Internet.[11] Mohan Sawhney has proposed the concept of a *metamarket* to describe a cluster of complementary goods and services that are closely related in the minds of consumers but are spread across a diverse set of industries. The automobile metamarket consists of automobile manufacturers, new car and used car dealers, financing companies, insurance companies, mechanics,

FIGURE 1.1 A Simple Marketing System

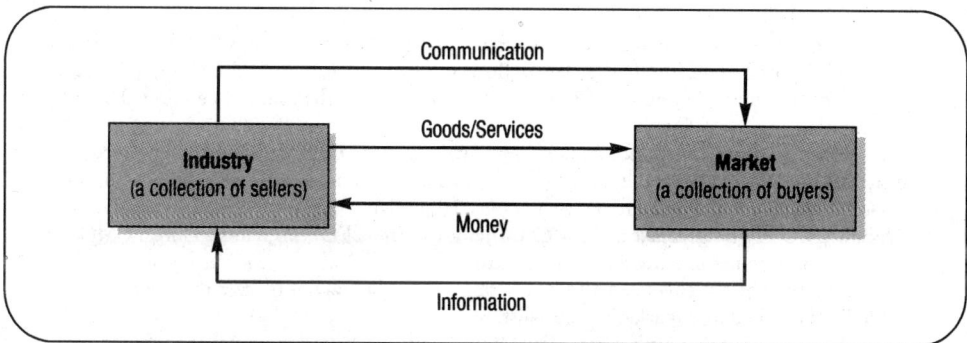

spare parts dealers, service shops, auto magazines, classified auto ads in newspapers, and auto sites on the Internet.

Car buyers can get involved in many parts of this metamarket. This has created an opportunity for *metamediaries* to assist buyers to move seamlessly through these groups, although they are disconnected in physical space. One example is Edmund's (www.edmunds.com), where buyers can find the features and prices of different vehicles and search for the lowest-price dealer, for financing, for car accessories, and for used cars at bargain prices. Metamediaries can also serve other metamarkets, such as the home ownership market and the wedding market.[12]

Who Markets?

A **marketer** is someone who seeks a response (attention, a purchase, a vote, a donation) from another party, called the **prospect**. If two parties are seeking to sell something to each other, both are marketers. Marketers must have diverse quantitative and qualitative skills, entrepreneurial attitudes, and keen understanding of how marketing can create value within their organizations.[13]

The CMO has five key functions: (1) strengthening the brands; (2) measuring marketing effectiveness; (3) driving new product development based on customer needs; (4) gathering meaningful customer insights; and (5) utilizing new marketing technology. Harvard's John Quelch and Gail McGovern note that there is tremendous variability in the responsibilities and job descriptions for CMOs.[14] They offer eight ways to improve CMO success (see Figure 1.2).

How Is Marketing Done?

In practice, marketing follows a logical process. The marketing planning process consists of analyzing marketing opportunities; selecting target markets; designing marketing strategies; developing marketing programs; and managing the marketing effort. In highly competitive marketplaces, marketing planning is more fluid and is continually refreshed.

Increasingly, marketing is *not* done only by the marketing department. Marketing needs to affect every aspect of the customer experience, all possible touch points—store layouts, package designs, product functions, employee training, and shipping and logistics methods. Marketing must also be heavily involved in key management activities

FIGURE 1.2 Improving CMO Success

1. *Make the mission and responsibilities clear.* Be certain that the case for having a CMO is strong and the mission is well understood by leaders in the organization, particularly the CEO, the board, and line management. Without a clear need (real or perceived), the role will be rejected by the organization.
2. *Fit the role to the marketing culture and structure.* Avoid having a CMO in a marketing-led company that has many individual brands rather than a single corporate umbrella—unless the person appointed to the position is a well-connected insider.
3. *Choose a CMO who is compatible with the CEO.* Beware of the CEO who wants to hire a CMO but doesn't want to relinquish any marketing control. Find a CEO who recognizes his or her responsibility to be the cheerleader for marketing and the brand, but realizes the need to be guided and coached by a marketing specialist.
4. *Remember that show people don't succeed.* The CMO should work hard to ensure the CEO is successful at being the principal cheerleader for the brand.
5. *Match the personality with the CMO type.* Be certain that the chief marketer has the right skills and personality for whichever of the three CMO models he or she might fill (VP of Marketing Services, Classic CMO, or "Super" CMO). There is little tolerance for on-the-job training.
6. *Make line managers marketing heroes.* By stretching their marketing budgets, CMOs can improve a division's marketing productivity and help business unit leaders increase their top-line revenues.
7. *Infiltrate the line organization.* Have the CMO support the placement of marketing professionals from the corporate marketing department into divisional marketing roles. Provide input from the CMO into the annual reviews of line marketers.
8. *Require right-brain and left-brain skills.* The most successful CMO will have strong creative and technical marketing expertise, be politically savvy, and have the interpersonal skills to be a great leader and manager.

Source: Gail McGovern and John A. Quelch, "The Fall and Rise of the CMO," *Strategy & Business,* Winter 2004. Reprinted by permission of Booz Allen Hamilton.

such as product innovation and new business development. In creating a strong marketing organization, marketers must think like executives in other departments, and executives in other departments must think more like marketers.[15]

CORE MARKETING CONCEPTS

To understand the marketing function, we need to understand the following core concepts.

Needs, Wants, and Demands

Needs are the basic human requirements. People need food, air, water, clothing, and shelter to survive. People also have strong needs for recreation, education, and entertainment. These needs become *wants* when they are directed to specific objects that might satisfy the need. An American needs food but may want a hamburger, French fries, and a soft drink. A person in Mauritius needs food but may want a mango, rice, lentils, and beans. Wants are shaped by one's society. *Demands* are wants for specific products backed by an ability to pay. Many people want a Mercedes; only a few are willing and able to buy one. Companies must measure not only how many people want their product but also how many would actually be willing and able to buy it.

These distinctions shed light on the frequent criticism that "marketers create needs" or "marketers get people to buy things they don't want." Marketers do not create needs: Needs preexist marketers. Marketers, along with other societal factors, influence wants. Marketers might promote the idea that a Mercedes would satisfy a person's need for social status. They do not, however, create the need for social status.

Understanding customer needs and wants is not always simple. Some customers have needs of which they are not fully conscious, or they cannot articulate these needs, or they use words that require some interpretation. Consider the customer who says he wants "an inexpensive car." A marketer may distinguish among five types of needs in this case:

1. *Stated needs:* The customer wants an inexpensive car.
2. *Real needs:* The customer wants a car with a low operating cost, not a low initial price.
3. *Unstated needs:* The customer expects good service from the dealer.
4. *Delight needs:* The customer wants the dealer to include an onboard navigation system.
5. *Secret needs:* The customer wants to be seen by friends as a savvy consumer.

Responding only to the stated need may shortchange the customer, because sometimes consumers do not know what they want in a product, especially breakthrough products such as the first cellular phone. Simply giving customers what they want isn't enough any more—to gain an edge, companies must help customers learn what they want.

Target Markets, Positioning, and Segmentation

A marketer can rarely satisfy everyone in a market. Not everyone likes the same cereal, automobile, college, or movie. Therefore, marketers identify and profile distinct groups of buyers who might prefer or require varying product and service mixes by examining demographic, psychographic, and behavioral differences among buyers. The marketer then decides which segments present the greatest opportunity—which are its *target markets*.

For each target market, the firm develops a *market offering* that it *positions* in the minds of the target buyers as delivering some central benefit(s). For example, Volvo develops its cars for buyers who are concerned about automobile safety. Volvo, therefore, positions its car as the safest a customer can buy. Companies do best when they choose their target market(s) carefully and prepare tailored marketing programs.

Offerings and Brands

Companies address needs by putting forth a **value proposition**, a set of benefits they offer to satisfy customers' needs. The intangible value proposition is made physical by an *offering*, which can be a combination of products, services, information, and experiences. A *brand* is an offering from a known source. A brand such as McDonald's carries many associations in people's minds that make up the brand image: hamburgers, fun, children, fast food, convenience, and golden arches. All companies strive to build a strong, favorable, and unique brand image.

Value and Satisfaction

The offering will be successful if it delivers value and satisfaction to the target buyer. The buyer chooses between offerings on the basis of which is perceived to deliver the most value. *Value* reflects the sum of the perceived tangible and intangible benefits and costs to customers. It's primarily a combination of quality, service, and price, called the "customer value triad." Value increases with quality and service and decreases with price, although other factors can also play an important role in perceptions of value.

Value is a central marketing concept. Marketing can be seen as the identification, creation, communication, delivery, and monitoring of customer value. *Satisfaction* reflects a person's comparative judgment of a product's perceived performance (or outcome) in relation to expectations. If product performance falls short of expectations, the customer is dissatisfied and disappointed. If it matches expectations, the customer is satisfied—and if it exceeds expectations, the customer is delighted.

Marketing Channels

To reach a target market, the marketer uses three kinds of marketing channels. *Communication channels*, which deliver and receive messages from target buyers, include newspapers, magazines, radio, television, mail, telephone, billboards, posters, CDs, and the Internet. And, just as people convey messages by facial expressions and clothing, firms communicate through the look of their stores, the appearance of their Web sites, and in other ways. Marketers are increasingly adding dialogue channels, including e-mail and blogs, to familiar monologue channels such as ads.

The marketer uses *distribution channels* to display, sell, or deliver the physical product or service(s) to the buyer or user. These include distributors, wholesalers, retailers, and agents. The marketer also uses *service channels* such as warehouses, transportation firms, banks, and insurance companies to carry out transactions with potential buyers. Marketers clearly face a design problem in choosing the best mix of communication, distribution, and service channels for their offerings.

Supply Chain

The supply chain is a longer channel stretching from raw materials to components to final products that are carried to final buyers. The supply chain for women's purses starts with hides and moves through tanning operations, cutting operations, manufacturing, and the marketing channels bringing products to customers. Each company captures only a certain percentage of the total value generated by the supply chain's value delivery system. When a company acquires competitors or moves upstream or downstream, its aim is to capture a higher percentage of supply chain value.

Competition

Competition includes all the actual and potential rival offerings and substitutes that a buyer might consider. Suppose an automobile company is planning to buy steel for its cars. There are several possible levels of competitors. The manufacturer can buy from U.S. Steel, from a foreign firm in Japan or Korea, or from a mini-mill such as Nucor.

Other alternatives are to buy aluminum for certain parts to lighten the car's weight or to buy engineered plastics instead of steel for bumpers. Clearly, U.S. Steel would be thinking too narrowly of competition if it thought only of other integrated steel companies. In fact, U.S. Steel is more likely to be hurt in the long run by substitute products than by other steel companies.

Marketing Environment

The marketing environment consists of the task environment and the broad environment. The *task environment* includes the immediate actors involved in producing, distributing, and promoting the offering, such as the company, suppliers, distributors, dealers, and the target customers. In the supplier group are material suppliers and service suppliers such as marketing research agencies, advertising agencies, banks and insurance companies, transportation companies, and telecommunications companies. Distributors and dealers include agents, brokers, manufacturer representatives, and others who facilitate finding and selling to customers.

The *broad environment* consists of six components: demographic environment, economic environment, physical environment, technological environment, political-legal environment, and social-cultural environment. Marketers must pay close attention to the trends and developments in these environments and make timely adjustments to their marketing strategies.

THE NEW MARKETING REALITIES

Marketers today must attend and respond to a number of significant developments, including major societal forces, new consumer capabilities, and new company capabilities.

Major Societal Forces

New behaviors, opportunities, and challenges are emerging as a result of a variety of major and sometimes interlinking societal forces. Network information technology promises more accurate levels of production, more targeted communications, and more relevant pricing. Globalization—specifically advances in transportation, shipping, and communication—makes it easier to market in other countries and easier for consumers to buy from marketers in other countries. Deregulation has increased competition and growth opportunities in many nations, even as privatization in some countries has put public firms in private hands.

Brand manufacturers face intense competition from domestic and foreign brands; at the same time, many strong brands are becoming mega-brands with considerable presence. Industry convergence is increasing as companies discover new opportunities at the intersection of multiple industries. Meanwhile, more consumers are resisting marketing efforts. Retailing is being transformed as small retailers succumb to the power of giant retailers and "category killers" and store-based retailers meet competition from non-store retailers. Finally, online businesses such as Amazon created *disintermediation* by intervening in the traditional flow of goods through distribution channels. In response, many firms engaged in *reintermediation* and added online services to their existing offerings.

New Consumer Capabilities

Customers now perceive fewer real product differences and show less brand loyalty, while becoming more price- and quality-sensitive in their search for value. In fact, consumers have substantially increased their buying power because of the Internet and can choose from a greater variety of available goods and services. They have access to a huge amount of information about practically anything—and they can more easily interact, place, and receive orders from home, office, or mobile phone. Social networking sites bring together buyers with a common interest and allow them to compare notes on offerings. And the Internet gives consumers an amplified voice to influence peer and public opinion through MySpace, YouTube, and other sites.

New Company Capabilities

New forces are generating a new set of capabilities for companies, starting with the use of the Internet as a powerful information and sales channel that augments marketers' geographical reach. Researchers can collect fuller and richer data about markets, customers, prospects, and competitors. Internal communication is faster and easier with today's technology. Also, companies are facilitating and speeding communication among customers by creating "buzz" through brand advocates and user communities.

Target marketing and two-way communication are easier, thanks to the proliferation of special-interest magazines, TV channels, and Internet technology. Marketers can now send ads, coupons, samples, and information to customers who have requested them or given permission to have them sent. Companies can reach consumers on the move with mobile marketing. Firms can produce individually differentiated goods because of advances in factory customization, computers, the Internet, and database software. Managers can improve purchasing, recruiting, training, and internal and external communications. Finally, corporate buyers can save by comparing sellers' prices online and purchasing at auction or posting their own buying terms.

COMPANY ORIENTATION TOWARD THE MARKETPLACE

What philosophy should guide a company's marketing efforts? Marketers have operated under the production concept, product concept, selling concept, and marketing concept; increasingly, they are operating under the holistic marketing concept.

The Production Concept

The production concept, one of the oldest concepts in business, holds that consumers will prefer products that are widely available and inexpensive. Managers of production-oriented businesses concentrate on achieving high production efficiency, low costs, and mass distribution. This orientation makes sense in developing countries such as China, where the largest PC manufacturer, Lenovo, takes advantage of the huge inexpensive labor pool to dominate the market.[16] This orientation is also used when a company wants to expand the market.

The Product Concept

The product concept proposes that consumers favor those products that offer the most quality, performance, or innovative features. Managers in these organizations focus on making superior products and improving them over time. However, these managers are sometimes caught up in love affairs with their products. Although they may believe that "a better mousetrap" will lead people to beat paths to their doors, new or improved products will not necessarily be successful unless they are priced, distributed, advertised, and sold properly.

The Selling Concept

The selling concept holds that consumers and businesses, if left alone, won't buy enough of the organization's products. The organization must, therefore, undertake an aggressive selling and promotion effort. As Coca-Cola's former vice president, Sergio Zyman, once observed: "The purpose of marketing is to sell more stuff to more people more often for more money in order to make more profit."[17]

The selling concept is practiced most aggressively with unsought goods, goods that buyers normally do not think of buying, such as insurance, encyclopedias, and funeral plots. Most firms practice the selling concept when they have overcapacity, aiming to sell what they make rather than making what the market wants. However, marketing based on hard selling carries high risks. It assumes that customers who are coaxed into buying a product will like it; and that if they do not, they not only won't return it or bad-mouth it or complain to consumer organizations, but they might even buy it again.

The Marketing Concept

The marketing concept emerged in the mid-1950s when business shifted to a customer-centered, "sense-and-respond" philosophy.[18] The job is not to find the right customers for your products, but to find the right products for your customers. Under the marketing concept, the key to achieving organizational goals is being more effective than competitors in creating, delivering, and communicating superior customer value to your target markets.

Theodore Levitt of Harvard drew a perceptive contrast between the selling and marketing concepts: Selling focuses on the needs of the seller; marketing on the needs of the buyer. Selling is preoccupied with the seller's need to convert his or her product into cash; marketing with the idea of satisfying the needs of the customer by means of the product and the whole cluster of things associated with creating, delivering and finally consuming it.[19]

Several scholars have found that companies that embrace the marketing concept achieve superior performance.[20] This was first demonstrated by companies practicing a *reactive market orientation*—understanding and meeting customers' expressed needs. Some critics say this means companies develop only low-level innovations. Narver and his colleagues argue that more advanced, high-level innovation is possible if the focus is on customers' latent needs. He calls this a *proactive marketing orientation*.[21] Companies such as 3M, Hewlett-Packard, and Motorola have made a practice of researching latent needs through a "probe-and-learn" process. Firms that practice both reactive and proactive marketing orientations are implementing *total market orientation* and are likely to be the most successful.

FIGURE 1.3 Holistic Marketing Dimensions

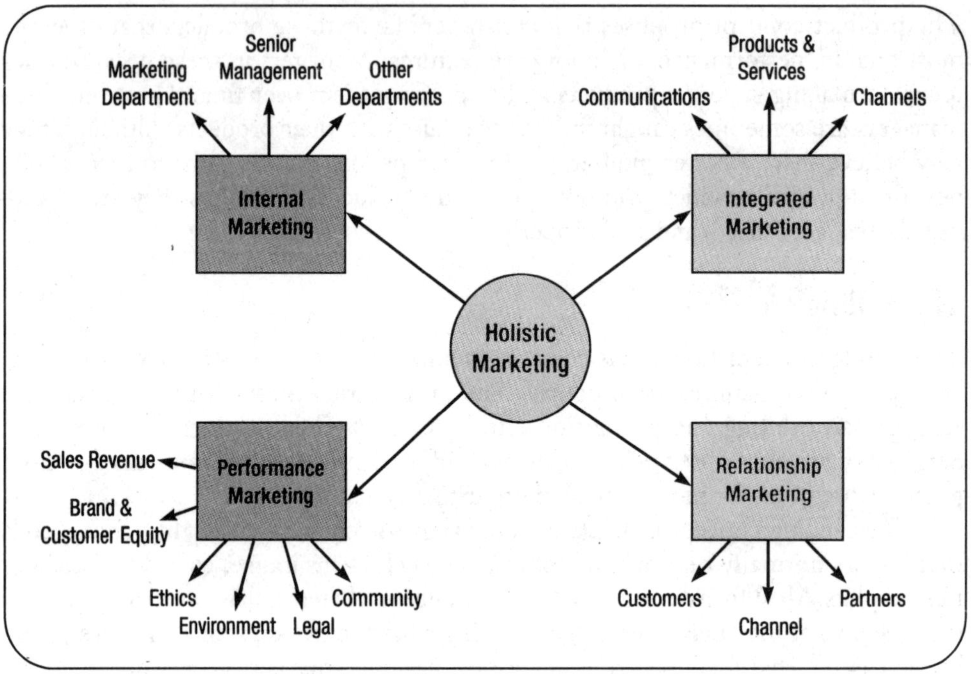

[Diagram showing Holistic Marketing at center, connected to four components:]
- *Internal Marketing* (Marketing Department, Senior Management, Other Departments)
- *Integrated Marketing* (Communications, Products & Services, Channels)
- *Performance Marketing* (Sales Revenue, Brand & Customer Equity, Ethics, Environment, Legal, Community)
- *Relationship Marketing* (Customers, Channel, Partners)

The Holistic Marketing Concept

Today's best marketers recognize the need for a more complete, cohesive approach that goes beyond traditional applications of the marketing concept. The **holistic marketing concept** is based on the development, design, and implementation of marketing programs, processes, and activities that recognize their breadth and interdependencies. Holistic marketing recognizes that "everything matters" with marketing—and that a broad, integrated perspective is often necessary. Holistic marketing is thus an approach to marketing that attempts to recognize and reconcile the scope and complexities of marketing activities. Figure 1.3 is a schematic overview of four broad components characterizing holistic marketing, themes that will appear throughout this book: relationship marketing, integrated marketing, internal marketing, and performance marketing.

Successful companies apply holistic marketing to keep their programs and activities changing with the changes in their marketplace and marketspace. "Breakthrough Marketing: Nike" shows how the company has done this to maintain its market leadership over the years.

Relationship Marketing Relationship marketing aims to build mutually satisfying long-term relationships with key constituents in order to earn and retain their business.[22] Four key constituents for relationship marketing are customers, employees, marketing partners (channels, suppliers, distributors, dealers, agencies), and members of the financial community (shareholders, investors, analysts).

The ultimate outcome of relationship marketing is the building of a unique company asset called a marketing network. A **marketing network** consists of the company and its supporting stakeholders (customers, employees, suppliers, distributors, retailers, ad agencies, university scientists, and others) with whom it has built

> ### BREAKTHROUGH MARKETING: NIKE
>
> Nike hit the ground running in 1962. Originally known as Blue Ribbon Sports, the company focused on high-quality running shoes designed especially for athletes by athletes. Understanding that customer choices are influenced by top athletes' preferences and behavior, Nike's marketing has always featured winning athletes. In 1988, Nike aired the first ads in its landmark "Just Do It" campaign, inspiring a generation of athletic enthusiasts to pursue their goals.
>
> As Nike began expanding internationally, however, it found that its ads were seen as too aggressive overseas. Nike had to "authenticate" its brand the way it had in the United States by building credibility and relevance in European sports, particularly soccer (known outside the United States as football). Nike began to sponsor youth leagues, local clubs, and national teams. The big break came in 1994, when the Brazilian team (the only national team for which Nike had any real sponsorships) won the World Cup. That victory helped Nike succeed in major markets such as China. Moving into new markets and new product categories has propelled Nike to the top, making it the world's leading athletic apparel, footwear, and equipment manufacturer.[23]

mutually profitable business relationships. The operating principle is simple: Build an effective network of relationships with key stakeholders, and profits will follow.[24]

A growing number of companies are also shaping separate offers, services, and messages for individual customers, based on information about past transactions, demographics, psychographics, and media and distribution preferences. By focusing on their most profitable customers, products, and channels, these firms hope to achieve profitable growth by capturing a larger share of each customer's expenditures, building high loyalty and customer lifetime value. Such activities fall under the umbrella of "customer centricity."[25] Note that marketers must conduct partner relationship management as well as customer relationship management.

Integrated Marketing With *integrated marketing*, the marketer's task is to devise marketing activities and assemble fully integrated marketing programs that create, communicate, and deliver value for consumers. Marketing activities come in all forms.[26] McCarthy classified these activities as *marketing mix* tools of four broad kinds, which he called *the four Ps* of marketing: product, price, place, and promotion (see Figure 1.4).[27]

The firm can change its price, sales force size, and advertising expenditures in the short run. It can develop new products and modify its distribution channels only in the long run. Thus the firm typically makes fewer period-to-period marketing-mix changes in the short run than the number of marketing-mix decision variables might suggest.

The four Ps represent the sellers' view of the marketing tools available for influencing buyers. From a buyer's point of view, each marketing tool is designed to deliver a customer benefit. A complementary breakdown of marketing activities has been proposed, centering on the customer questions that the four dimensions (SIVA) are designed to answer:[28]

1. *Solution:* How can I solve my problem?
2. *Information:* Where can I learn more about it?

FIGURE 1.4 The Four P Components of the Marketing Mix

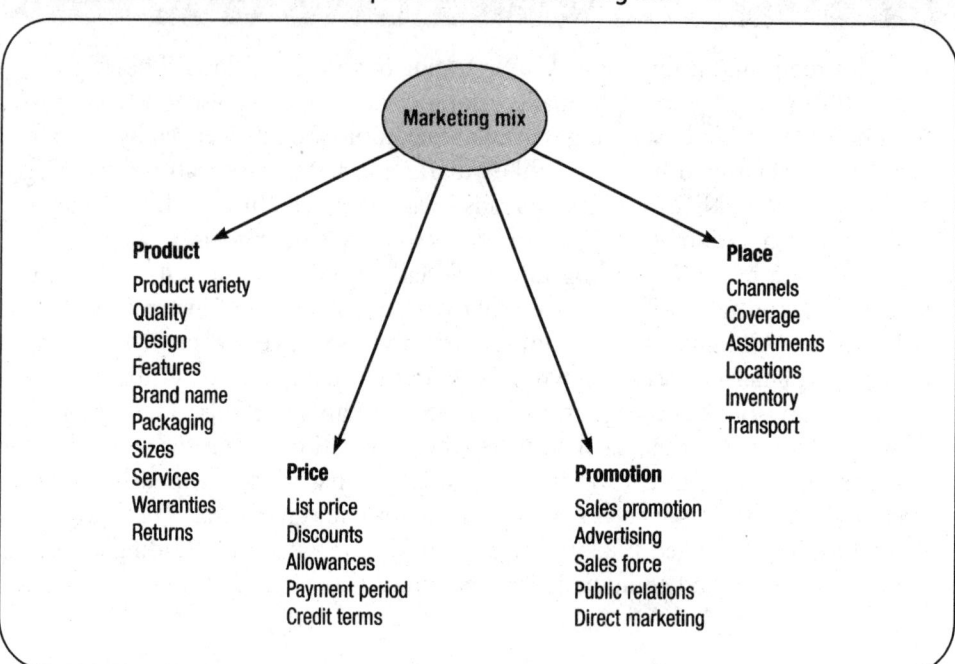

3. *V*alue: What is my total sacrifice to get this solution?
4. *A*ccess: Where can I find it?

Two key themes of integrated marketing are that (1) many different marketing activities communicate and deliver value; and (2) when coordinated, marketing activities maximize their joint effects. In other words, marketers should design and implement any one marketing activity with all other activities in mind.

Internal Marketing Holistic marketing incorporates *internal marketing*, ensuring that everyone in the organization embraces appropriate marketing principles, especially senior management. Internal marketing is the task of hiring, training, and motivating able employees who want to serve customers well. Smart marketers recognize that internal marketing activities can be as important as, or even more important than external marketing activities. It makes no sense to promise excellent service before the company's staff is ready to provide it (see "Marketing Skills: Internal Marketing").

Internal marketing must take place on two levels. At one level, the various marketing functions—sales force, advertising, customer service, product management, marketing research—must work together and be coordinated from the customer's point of view. At the second level, other departments must embrace marketing and must "think customer." Marketing is not a department so much as a company orientation.[29]

The bottom-line importance of internal marketing was highlighted in a recent study by Booz Allen Hamilton and the Association of National Advertisers, in conjunction with *Brandweek* magazine. The researchers identified six types of marketing organizations: Growth Champions, Marketing Masters, Senior Counselors, Best Practice Advisors, Brand Builders, and Service Providers. Marketing heavily influenced all aspects of the organization in the most successful type, Growth

MARKETING SKILLS: INTERNAL MARKETING

One of the most valuable skills marketers can have is the ability to select, educate, and rally people inside the organization to build mutually satisfying long-term relationships with stakeholders. Internal marketing starts with the selection of managers and employees who have positive attitudes toward the company, its products, and its customers. The next step is to train, motivate, and empower the entire staff so that they have the knowledge, tools, and authority to provide value to customers. After establishing standards for employee performance, the final step is to monitor employee actions, then reward and reinforce good performance.

Internal marketing is a key strength at Southwest Airlines. Top managers constantly visit different Southwest facilities, thank staff members for their efforts, send birthday cards to employees, and share customer comments with employees. Southwest's employees deliver superior service with a smile, and they are so dedicated that some have worked without pay to keep the airline's costs down during difficult periods. Clearly, Southwest's managers are good role models for learning the critical skill of internal marketing.[30]

Champions—and this type was 20% more likely to deliver revenue growth and profitability than the other types.[31]

Performance Marketing Holistic marketing incorporates performance marketing and understanding the business returns from marketing activities and programs, as well as addressing broader concerns and their legal, ethical, social, and environmental effects. Top management is going beyond sales revenue to examine the marketing scorecard and interpret what is happening to market share, customer loss rate, customer satisfaction, product quality, and other measures.

- *Financial accountability.* Marketers are increasingly asked to justify their investments to top management in financial and profitability terms, as well as in terms of building the brand and growing the customer base.[32] Therefore, they're using a variety of financial measures to assess the direct and indirect value of their marketing efforts. They're also recognizing that much of their firms' market value comes from intangible assets such as their brands, customers, employees, and distributor and supplier relations.
- *Social responsibility marketing.* Marketers must consider the ethical, environmental, legal, and social context of their activities. Under the *societal marketing concept*, the company's task is to determine the needs, wants, and interests of target markets so it can satisfy customers more effectively and efficiently than competitors while preserving or enhancing customers' and society's long-term well-being.[33] Sustainability has become a major concern in the face of challenging environmental forces. For example, McDonald's strives for a "socially responsible supply system" encompassing everything from healthy fisheries to redesigned packaging.[34] Some firms use social responsibility to differentiate themselves, build consumer preference, and improve sales and profits. Table 1.1 displays some different types of corporate social initiatives, illustrated by McDonald's.[35]

TABLE 1.1 Corporate Social Initiatives

Type	Description	Example
Corporate social marketing	Supporting behavior change campaigns	McDonald's promotion of a statewide childhood immunization campaign in Oklahoma
Cause marketing	Promoting social issues through efforts such as sponsorships, licensing agreements, and advertising	McDonald's sponsorship of Forest (a gorilla) at Sydney's Zoo—a 10-year sponsorship commitment, aimed at preserving this endangered species
Cause-related marketing	Donating a percentage of revenues to a specific cause based on the revenue occurring during the announced period of support	McDonald's earmarking of $1 for Ronald McDonald Children's Charities from the sale of every Big Mac and pizza sold on McHappy Day
Corporate philanthropy	Making gifts of money, goods, or time to help nonprofit organizations, groups, or individuals	McDonald's contributions to Ronald McDonald House Charities
Corporate community involvement	Providing in-kind or volunteer services in the community	McDonald's catering meals for firefighters in the December 1997 bushfires in Australia
Socially responsible business practices	Adapting and conducting business practices that protect the environment, and human and animal rights	McDonald's requirement that suppliers increase the amount of living space for laying hens on factory farms

Source: Philip Kotler and Nancy Lee, "Corporate Social Responsibility: Doing the Most Good for Your Company and Your Cause" (Wiley, December 2004). Reprinted by permission.

MARKETING MANAGEMENT TASKS

With holistic marketing as a backdrop, we can identify a specific set of tasks that make up successful marketing management and marketing leadership.

- *Developing marketing strategies and plans.* The first task is to identify the organization's potential long-run opportunities, given its market experience and core competencies. Chapter 2 discusses this process in detail.
- *Capturing marketing insights.* Marketers must understand what is happening inside and outside the organization by monitoring the marketing environment and conducting marketing research to assess buyer needs and behavior, as well as actual and potential market size. Chapter 3 looks at marketing research, demand, and the marketing environment.
- *Connecting with customers.* The firm must determine how to best create value for its chosen target markets and how to develop strong, profitable, long-term relationships with consumers and business customers, as discussed in Chapter 4. Chapters 5 and Chapter 6 explore the analysis of consumer and business markets. Next, marketers identify major market segments, evaluate each, and target those that the firm can serve most effectively, as discussed in Chapter 7.
- *Building strong brands.* Now marketers need to understand how customers perceive their brands' strengths and weaknesses—the subject of Chapter 8. Because brands

never exist in a vacuum, marketers must not only deal with the competitive situation, they must develop and communicate appropriate positioning. Chapter 9 explains how to do this.

- *Shaping market offerings.* At the heart of the marketing program is the product—the firm's tangible offering to the market, which includes the product quality, design, features, and packaging, all explored in Chapter 10. Marketers may also include services as part of the market offering, as discussed in Chapter 11; in addition, pricing is a key element, as shown in Chapter 12.
- *Delivering value.* Here, marketers determine how to deliver the offering's value to the target market by identifying, recruiting, and linking with marketing facilitators such as retailers, wholesalers, and physical-distribution firms. Marketing channels are examined in Chapter 13; retailing, wholesaling, and logistics are covered in Chapter 14.
- *Communicating value.* Now the firm must convey the value embodied by the offering to the target market through an integrated marketing communication program that maximizes the individual and collective contribution of all communication activities. Chapter 15 discusses the design and management of integrated marketing communications; Chapter 16 explores mass communications such as advertising and sales promotions, while Chapter 17 looks at personal communications such as direct marketing and personal selling.
- *Creating long-term growth.* The company's marketing strategy must take into account changing global opportunities and challenges. Moreover, management must put in place a marketing organization capable of implementing the marketing plan. See Chapter 18 for more detail.

EXECUTIVE SUMMARY

Marketing is an organizational function and a set of processes for creating, communicating, and delivering value to customers and for managing customer relationships in ways that benefit the organization and its stakeholders. Marketing management is the art and science of choosing target markets and getting, keeping, and growing customers through creating, delivering, and communicating superior customer value. Marketers are involved in marketing 10 types of entities: goods, services, events, experiences, persons, places, properties, organizations, information, and ideas. They operate in four different customer markets: consumer, business, global, and nonprofit.

Marketers today must attend and respond to a number of significant developments, including major societal forces, new consumer capabilities, and new company capabilities. Over the years, organizations have operated under the production concept, product concept, selling concept, and marketing concept. Increasingly, they operate under the holistic marketing concept, based on the development, design, and implementation of marketing programs, processes, and activities that recognize their breadth and interdependencies. Four components of holistic marketing are relationship marketing, integrated marketing, internal marketing, and performance marketing (both financial accountability and social responsibility marketing).

Successful marketing managers must accomplish these tasks: develop marketing strategies and plans, capture marketing insights, connect with customers, build strong brands, shape the market offerings, deliver value, communicate value, and create successful long-term growth.

NOTES

1. "Starbucks to Rely on China, Shed Trans Fats in N. America," *Nation's Restaurant News*, May 21, 2007, p. 12; Janet Adamy, "Different Brew: Eyeing a Billion Tea Drinkers, Starbucks Pours It on in China," *Wall Street Journal*, November 29, 2006, p. A1.
2. Sandra Ward, "Warming up the Copier," *Barron's*, May 1, 2006, pp. 19, 21.
3. American Marketing Association, 2004.
4. Peter Drucker, *Management: Tasks, Responsibilities, Practices* (New York: Harper and Row, 1973), pp. 64–65.
5. Philip Kotler, "Dream Vacations: The Booming Market for Designed Experiences," *The Futurist* (October 1984): 7–13; B. Joseph Pine II and James Gilmore, *The Experience Economy* (Boston: Harvard Business School Press, 1999); Bernd Schmitt, *Experience Marketing* (New York: Free Press, 1999); Mark Hyman, "The Family That Fields Together," *Business Week*, February 9, 2004, p. 92.
6. Irving J. Rein, Philip Kotler, and Martin Stoller, *High Visibility* (Chicago: NTC Publishers, 1998); H. Lee Murphy, "New Salton Recipe: Celeb Chefs," *Crain's Chicago Business*, April 4, 2005, p. 4.
7. Philip Kotler, Irving J. Rein, and Donald Haider, *Marketing Places: Attracting Investment, Industry, and Tourism to Cities, States, and Nations* (New York: Free Press, 1993); Philip Kotler, Christer Asplund, Irving Rein, and Donald H. Haider, *Marketing Places in Europe* (London: Financial Times Prentice-Hall, 1999).
8. Michael McCarthy, "Vegas Goes Back to Naughty Roots," *USA Today*, April 11, 2005; Julie Dunn, "Vegas Hopes for Payoff with Denverites," *The Denver Post*, June 16, 2005; John M. Broder, "The Pied Piper of Las Vegas Seems to Have Perfect Pitch," *The New York Times*, June 4, 2004.
9. Carl Shapiro and Hal R. Varian, "Versioning: The Smart Way to Sell Information," *Harvard Business Review* (November–December 1998): 106–114.
10. John R. Brandt, "Dare to Be Different," *Chief Executive*, May 2003, pp. 34–38.
11. Jeffrey Rayport and John Sviokla, "Managing in the Marketspace," *Harvard Business Review* (November–December 1994): 141–150. Also see their "Exploring the Virtual Value Chain," *Harvard Business Review* (November–December 1995): 75–85.
12. Mohan Sawhney, *Seven Steps to Nirvana* (New York: McGraw-Hill, 2001).
13. Richard Rawlinson, "Beyond Brand Management," *Strategy & Business*, Summer 2006.
14. Gail McGovern and John A. Quelch, "The Fall and Rise of the CMO," *Strategy+Business*, Winter 2004.
15. Constantine von Hoffman, "Armed with Intelligence," *Brandweek*, May 29, 2006, pp. 17–20.
16. Jane Spencer and Geoffrey A. Fowler, "Lenovo Goes for Its Own Olympic Medal," *Wall Street Journal*, March 27, 2007, p. B4.
17. Bruce I. Newman, ed., *Handbook of Political Marketing* (Thousand Oaks, CA: Sage Publications, 1999); and Bruce I. Newman, *The Mass Marketing of Politics* (Thousand Oaks, CA: Sage Publications, 1999).
18. John B. McKitterick, "What Is the Marketing Management Concept?" in Frank M. Bass, ed. *The Frontiers of Marketing Thought and Action* (Chicago: American Marketing Association, 1957), pp. 71–82; Fred J. Borch, "The Marketing Philosophy as a Way of Business Life," *The Marketing Concept: Its Meaning to Management* (Marketing series, no. 99) (New York: American Management Association, 1957), pp. 3–5; Robert J. Keith, "The Marketing Revolution," *Journal of Marketing* (January 1960): 35–38.
19. Theodore Levitt, "Marketing Myopia," *Harvard Business Review*, July–August 1960, p. 50.
20. Ajay K. Kohli and Bernard J. Jaworski, "Market Orientation: The Construct, Research Propositions, and Managerial Implications," *Journal of Marketing* (April 1990): 1–18; John C. Narver and Stanley F. Slater, "The Effect of a Market Orientation on Business Profitability," *Journal of Marketing* (October 1990): 20–35; Stanley F. Slater and John C. Narver, "Market Orientation, Customer Value, and Superior Performance," *Business Horizons* (March–April 1994): 22–28; A. Pelham and D. Wilson, "A Longitudinal Study of the Impact of Market Structure, Firm Structure, Strategy and Market Orientation Culture on Dimensions of Business Performance," *Journal of the Academy of Marketing Science* 24, no. 1 (1996): 27–43; Rohit Deshpande and John U. Farley, "Measuring Market Orientation: Generalization and Synthesis," *Journal of Market-Focused Management* 2 (1998): 213–232.
21. John C. Narver, Stanley F. Slater, and Douglas L. MacLachlan, "Total Market Orientation, Business Performance, and Innovation," Working Paper Series, Journal of Marketing Science Institute, Report No. 00-116, 2000, pp. 1–20. See also Ken Matsuno and John T. Mentzer, "The Effects of

Strategy Type on the Market Orientation–Performance Relationship," *Journal on Marketing* (October 2000): 1–16.
22. Evert Gummesson, *Total Relationship Marketing* (Boston: Butterworth-Heinemann, 1999); Regis McKenna, *Relationship Marketing* (Reading, MA: Addison-Wesley, 1991); Martin Christopher, Adrian Payne, and David Ballantyne, *Relationship Marketing: Bringing Quality, Customer Service, and Marketing Together* (Oxford, U.K.: Butterworth-Heinemann, 1991).
23. Paula L. Stepankowsky, "Nike Tries to Catch Up to Trend," *Wall Street Journal*, May 29, 2007, p. B3D; Justin Ewers and Tim Smart, "A Designer Swooshes In," *U.S. News & World Report*, January 26, 2004, p. 12; "10 Top Non Traditional Campaigns," *Advertising Age*, December 22, 2003, p. 24; Chris Zook and James Allen, "Growth Outside the Core," *Harvard Business Review* (December 2003): 66(8).
24. James C. Anderson, Hakan Hakansson, and Jan Johanson, "Dyadic Business Relationships within a Business Network Context," *Journal of Marketing* (October 15, 1994): 1–15.
25. Larry Selden and Yoko S. Selden, "Profitable Customer: The Key to Great Brands," *Advertising Age*, July 10, 2006, p. S7.
26. Neil H. Borden, "The Concept of the Marketing Mix," *Journal of Advertising Research* 4 (June 1964): 2–7. For another framework, see George S. Day, "The Capabilities of Market-Driven Organizations," *Journal of Marketing* 58, no. 4 (October 1994): 37–52.
27. E. Jerome McCarthy and William D. Perreault, *Basic Marketing: A Global-Managerial Approach*, 14th ed. (Homewood, IL: McGraw-Hill Irwin, 2002).
28. Chekitan S. Dev and Don E. Schultz, "A Customer-Focused Approach Can Bring the Current Marketing Mix into the 21st Century," (*Marketing Management* 14 (January/February 2005).
29. Christian Homburg, John P. Workman Jr., and Harley Krohmen, "Marketing's Influence Within the Firm," *Journal of Marketing* (January 1999): 1–15.
30. "Using Positive Four-Letter Words: Southwest Airlines Incorporates Myers-Briggs Personality Test into Training Program," *Employee Benefit News*, April 1, 2007; Barney Gimbel, "Southwest's New Flight Plan," *Fortune*, May 16, 2005, pp. 93+; Jane Lewis, "The Leaders Who Changed HR," *Personnel Today*, January 22, 2002, pp. 2+.
31. *Booz Allen Hamilton/Assn. of National Advertisers Marketing Profiles*, in conjunction with *Brandweek*, from Constantine von Hoffman, "Armed with Intelligence," *Brandweek*, May 29, 2006, pp. 17–20.
32. Robert Shaw and David Merrick, *Marketing Payback: Is Your Marketing Profitable?* (London, UK: Pearson Education, 2005).
33. Rajendra Sisodia, David Wolfe, and Jagdish Sheth, *Firms of Endearment: How World Class Companies Profit from Passion* (Upper Saddle River, NJ: Wharton School Publishing, 2007).
34. John Ehernfield, "Feeding the Beast," *Fast Company*, December 2006/January 2007, pp. 41–43.
35. If choosing to develop a strategic corporate social responsibility program, see Michael E. Porter and Mark R. Kramer, "Strategy and Society: The Link between Competitive Advantage and Corporate Social Responsibility," *Harvard Business Review* (December 2006): 78–92.

CHAPTER 2

Developing and Implementing Marketing Strategies and Plans

In this chapter, we will address the following questions:

1. How does marketing affect customer value?
2. How is strategic planning carried out at different levels of the organization?
3. What does a marketing plan include?
4. How can management assess marketing performance?

MARKETING MANAGEMENT AT SIEMENS

Siemens AG is one of the world's largest global electronics and engineering firms, with sales of $117 billion and employees in 190 countries. Based in Germany, Siemens has been growing organically through innovation as it pursues profitable business opportunities amid high demand for infrastructure improvements. The company has also been investing heavily in research and development to create new products such as low-emissions power generation systems. And it has made strategic acquisitions in the areas of medical imaging, clean-coal technology, pollution control, wind power, and water technologies.

To prepare for profitable long-term growth, Siemens has fixed up, sold, or closed a number of problem businesses. For instance, it sold its money-losing cellular handset unit to Taiwan's BenQ Corp. and turned its ailing telecommunications network equipment unit into a successful joint venture with Nokia, the giant global handset maker. As a result of all these strategic changes, Siemens is well prepared to meet the needs of business and government customers with a coordinated set of state-of-the-art market offerings.[1]

Developing the right marketing strategy over time requires a blend of insight, creativity, discipline, and flexibility. Firms must stick to a strategy but must also find new ways to constantly improve marketing activities at every level and in every business unit, as Siemens has done. This chapter opens by examining some of the strategic marketing implications of creating customer value. Next, we explore strategic planning on four levels, including how to prepare a formal marketing plan. We'll close with a look at how firms can measure marketing performance.

MARKETING AND CUSTOMER VALUE

Marketing is about satisfying customers' needs and wants. In a hypercompetitive economy where buyers are faced with abundant choices, a company can win profits only by fine-tuning the value delivery process and choosing, providing, and communicating superior value.

The Value Delivery Process

The traditional view of marketing is that the firm makes something and then, once it has been produced, sells it. Companies that subscribe to this view have the best chance of succeeding in economies marked by goods shortages where consumers are not fussy about quality, features, or style—for example, basic staple goods in developing markets. In economies where people face abundant choices, however, the "mass market" is splintering into numerous micromarkets, each with its own wants, perceptions, preferences, and buying criteria.

The smart competitor must design and deliver offerings for well-defined target markets. This realization has inspired a new view of business processes in which marketing is at the *beginning* of planning. Instead of emphasizing making and selling, companies now see themselves as part of a value delivery process.

The value creation and delivery sequence actually consists of three phases. In the first phase, *choosing the value*, marketers segment the market, select the appropriate market target, and develop the offering's value positioning for the chosen market target(s). The formula "segmentation, targeting, positioning (STP)" is the essence of strategic marketing.

The second phase is *providing the value* through specific product features, service development, pricing, sourcing and making the offering, and distributing and serving it. The third task is *communicating the value* through the sales force, advertising, and other communication tools to announce and promote the product. In other words, the value creation and delivery process begins before there is a product and continues while it is being developed and after it is available to the target market

London Business School's Nirmalya Kumar has put forth a "3 Vs" approach to marketing: (1) define the *value segment* or customers (and their needs); (2) define the *value proposition*; and (3) define the *value network* to deliver promised service.[2] Dartmouth's Frederick Webster views marketing in terms of: (1) *value-defining processes* like market research; (2) *value-developing processes* including new-product development, sourcing strategy, and vendor selection; and (3) *value-delivering processes* such as advertising and managing distribution.[3]

The Value Chain

Michael Porter of Harvard has proposed the **value chain** as a tool for identifying ways to create more customer value (see Figure 2.1).[4] According to this model, every firm is a synthesis of activities performed to design, produce, market, deliver, and support its product. The value chain identifies nine strategically relevant activities—five primary and four support activities—that create value and cost in a specific business.

The firm's task is to examine its costs and performance in each value-creating activity and look for ways to improve. In addition to estimating its competitors' costs and performances as *benchmarks* against which to compare its own costs and performances, the firm should also study the "best of class" practices of the world's best companies.[5] The firm's success depends not only on how well each department performs its work but also how well the company coordinates various departmental activities to manage these five *core business processes*.[6]

1. *The market sensing process:* All the activities involved in gathering market intelligence, disseminating it within the firm, and acting on it
2. *The new offering realization process:* All the activities involved in researching, developing, and launching new, high-quality offerings quickly and within budget
3. *The customer acquisition process:* All the activities involved in defining target markets and prospecting for new customers

FIGURE 2.1   The Generic Value Chain

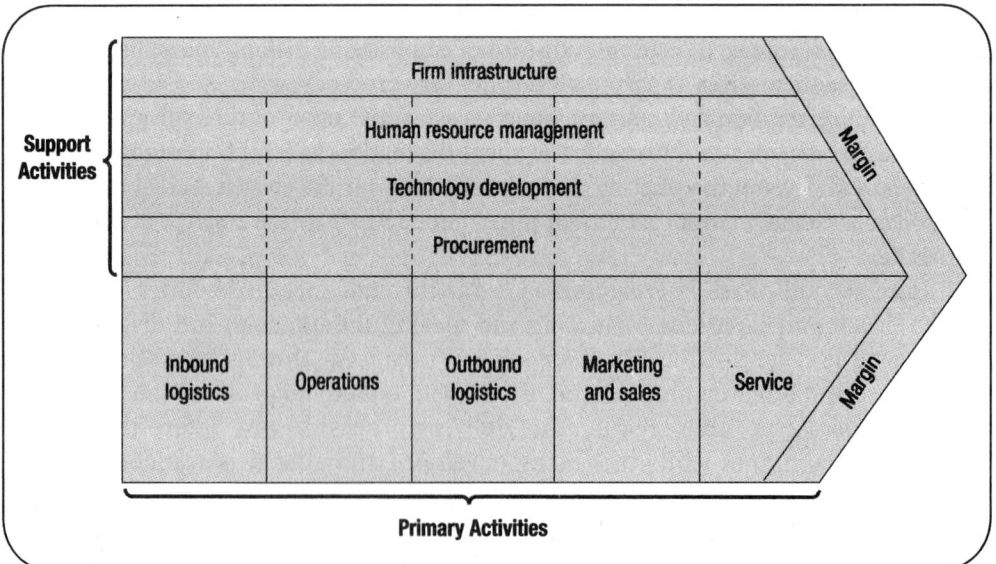

Source: Reprinted with the permission of The Free Press, an imprint of Simon & Schuster, from Michael E. Porter, "Competitive Advantage, Creating and Sustaining Superior Performance." Copyright 1985 by Michael E. Porter.

4. *The customer relationship management process:* All the activities involved in building deeper understanding of, relationships with, and offerings to individual customers
5. *The fulfillment management process:* All the activities involved in receiving and approving orders, shipping the goods on time, and collecting payment

A successful firm looks for competitive advantages beyond its own operations, into the value chains of suppliers, distributors, and customers. Many companies today partner with specific suppliers and distributors to create a superior **value delivery network** (also called a **supply chain**).

Core Competencies

Although firms traditionally owned and controlled most of the resources that entered their businesses—labor power, materials, machines, information, and energy—this situation is changing. Now many firms outsource less-critical resources if they can obtain better quality or lower cost.

The key, then, is to own and nurture the resources and competencies that make up the *essence* of the business. Nike, for example, does not manufacture its own shoes, because certain Asian manufacturers are more competent in this task; instead, Nike nurtures its superiority in shoe design and shoe merchandising, its two core competencies. A **core competency** has three characteristics: (1) It is a source of competitive advantage in that it makes a significant contribution to perceived customer benefits; (2) it has applications in a wide variety of markets; and (3) it is difficult for competitors to imitate.[7]

Competitive advantage also accrues to companies that possess distinctive capabilities. Whereas core competencies refer to areas of special technical and production expertise, *distinctive capabilities* describe excellence in broader business processes. Competitive advantage ultimately derives from how well the company has fitted its core competencies and distinctive capabilities into tightly interlocking "activity systems." Competitors find it hard to imitate companies such as Google or IKEA because they are unable to copy their activity systems.

Wharton's George Day sees market-driven organizations as excelling in three distinctive capabilities: market sensing, customer linking, and channel bonding.[8] In terms of market sensing, Day says opportunities and threats often begin as "weak signals" from the "periphery" of a business.[9] He offers a systematic process for developing peripheral vision and building "vigilant organizations" attuned to environmental changes by asking questions in three categories (see Table 2.1).

A Holistic Marketing Orientation and Customer Value

A holistic marketing orientation can also help capture customer value. One view of holistic marketing sees it as "integrating the value exploration, value creation, and value delivery activities with the purpose of building long-term, mutually satisfying relationships and co-prosperity among key stakeholders."[10] With a superior value chain to deliver a high level of product quality, service, and speed, the holistic marketer can achieve profitable growth by expanding customer share, building loyalty, and capturing customer lifetime value. Figure 2.2, a holistic marketing framework, shows how the interaction between relevant actors and value-based activities helps to create, maintain, and renew customer value.

TABLE 2.1 Becoming a Vigilant Organization

- *Learning from the past*
  - What have been our past blind spots?
  - What instructive analogies do other industries offer?
  - Who in the industry is skilled at picking up weak signals and acting on them?
- *Evaluating the present*
  - What important signals are we rationalizing away?
  - What are our mavericks, outliers, complainers, and defectors telling us?
  - What are our peripheral customers and competitors really thinking?
- *Envisioning the future*
  - What future surprises could really hurt or help us?
  - What emerging technologies could change the game?
  - Is there an unthinkable scenario that might disrupt our business?

Source: George S. Day and Paul J. H. Schoemaker, *Peripheral Vision: Detecting the Weak Signals That Will Make or Break Your Company* (Boston: Harvard Business School Press, 2006).

FIGURE 2.2 A Holistic Marketing Framework

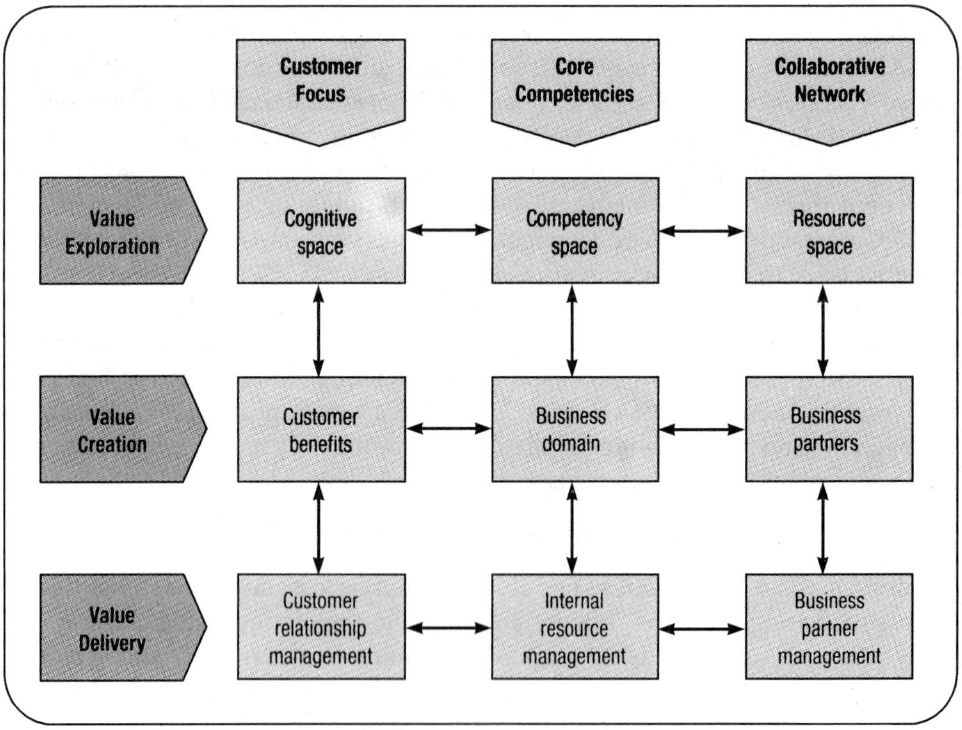

	Customer Focus	Core Competencies	Collaborative Network
Value Exploration	Cognitive space	Competency space	Resource space
Value Creation	Customer benefits	Business domain	Business partners
Value Delivery	Customer relationship management	Internal resource management	Business partner management

Source: P. Kotler, D. C. Jain and S. Maesincee, "Formulating a Market Renewal Strategy," in Marketing Moves (Part 1), Fig. 1-1 (Boston: Harvard Business School Press, 2002), p. 29.

The holistic marketing framework addresses three key management questions:

1. *Value exploration: How can a company identify new value opportunities?* This requires an understanding of the customer's *cognitive space*, existing and latent needs and dimensions such as the need for participation, stability, freedom, and change.[11] The company's *competency space* can be described in terms of breadth and depth. The collaborator's *resource space* includes partnerships forged to exploit market opportunities and serve value creation.
2. *Value creation: How can a company efficiently create more promising new value offerings?* Here, marketers must identify new customer benefits from the customer's perspective, utilize core competencies, and partner effectively with firms in its collaborative networks.
3. *Value delivery: How can a company use its capabilities and infrastructure to deliver the new value offerings more efficiently?* The company must become proficient at customer-relationship management by understanding its customers and responding accordingly. Effective response depends on internal resource management and business partnership management.

"Breakthrough Marketing: Intel" describes how that company created customer value and built a brand in a category for which most people thought branding impossible.

The Central Role of Strategic Planning

Successful marketing thus requires companies to have capabilities such as understanding customer value, creating customer value, delivering customer value, capturing customer value, and sustaining customer value. To plan and execute the right activities, marketers must give priority to strategic planning in three key areas: managing a company's businesses as an investment portfolio, assessing each business's strength, and establishing a strategy. For each business, the company must develop a game plan for achieving its long-run objectives.

Most large companies consist of four organizational levels: the corporate level, division level, business unit level, and product level. Corporate headquarters is

BREAKTHROUGH MARKETING: INTEL

Intel makes the advanced microprocessors that power 80% of the world's personal computers. Yet in the early days, Intel had difficulty convincing consumers to pay more for its high-performance products because they were hidden inside PCs. In response, the company launched its historic "Intel Inside" marketing campaign to build brand awareness and get its name outside the PC and into the minds of consumers. Intel helped pay for advertising if computer makers included Intel's logo in their ads; it also gave manufacturers a rebate on Intel products if they placed an "Intel Inside" sticker on the outside of their PCs and laptops.

The long-running "Intel Inside" campaign was a major success and set the stage for the recent "Leap Ahead" campaign to promote Intel's latest microprocessor products. Today, Intel's branding efforts target four key markets: users of digital home and entertainment products; the digital health care industry; businesses; and the mobile technology market. The company continues to research customer needs, develop new microprocessors, leverage its channel partnerships, and utilize marketing communications as it explores, creates, and delivers value.[12]

responsible for designing a corporate strategic plan to guide the whole enterprise; it makes decisions on the amount of resources to allocate to each division, as well as on which businesses to start or eliminate. Each division establishes a plan covering the allocation of funds to each business unit within the division. Each business unit develops a strategic plan to carry that business unit into a profitable future. Moreover, each product level (product line, brand) within a business unit develops a marketing plan for achieving its objectives in its market.

The **marketing plan** is the central instrument for directing and coordinating the marketing effort. The marketing plan operates at two levels: strategic and tactical. The **strategic marketing plan** lays out the firm's target markets and value proposition, based on the best market opportunities. The **tactical marketing plan** specifies the marketing tactics, including product features, promotion, pricing, and service. Managers implement these plans at the appropriate levels of the organization, monitor results, and take necessary corrective action. The complete planning, implementation, and control cycle is shown in Figure 2.3.

CORPORATE AND DIVISION STRATEGIC PLANNING

All corporate headquarters undertake four planning activities: (1) defining the corporate mission; (2) establishing strategic business units; (3) assigning resources to each unit; and (4) assessing growth opportunities.

Defining the Corporate Mission

An organization exists to accomplish something: to make cars, lend money, provide a night's lodging, and so on. Over time, the mission may change, to take advantage of new opportunities or respond to new market conditions. Amazon.com changed its mission from being the world's largest online bookstore to becoming the world's largest online store.

To define its mission, the company should address Peter Drucker's classic questions:[13] What is our business? Who is the customer? What is of value to the customer? What will our business be? What should our business be? Successful companies continuously raise and answer these questions thoughtfully and thoroughly.[14]

FIGURE 2.3 The Strategic Planning, Implementation, and Control Process

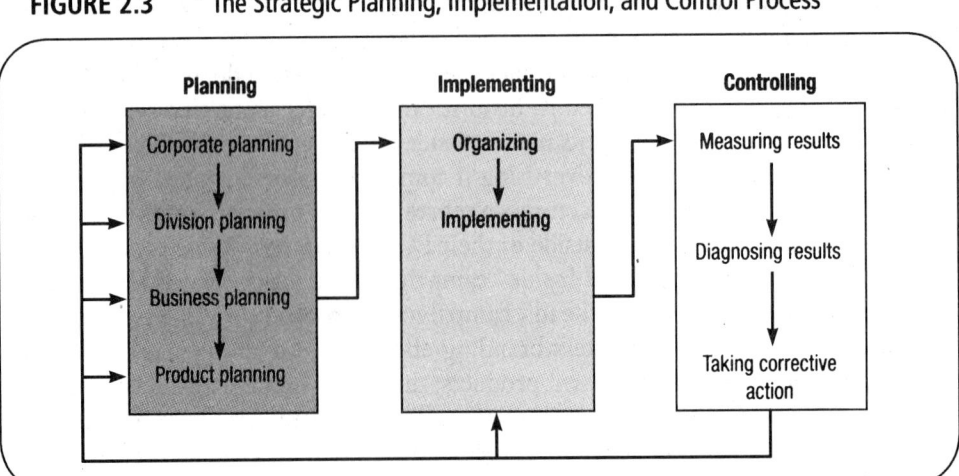

An organization develops a **mission statement** to share with managers, employees, and customers. A clear, thoughtful mission statement provides employees with a shared sense of purpose, direction, and opportunity. Good mission statements focus on a limited number of goals, stress the company's major policies and values, and define the company's major competitive spheres. These include:

- *Industry.* Some firms will operate in only one industry, some in a set of related industries, and some in any industry. For example, DuPont prefers to operate in the industrial market, whereas Dow operates in both the industrial and consumer markets.
- *Products and applications.* Firms define the range of products and applications they will supply. St. Jude Medical aims to "serve physicians worldwide with high-quality products for cardiovascular care."
- *Competence.* The firm identifies the range of technological and other core competencies it will master and leverage. Japan's NEC has built its core competencies in computing, communications, and components to support production of laptop computers, television receivers, and handheld telephones.
- *Market-segment.* The type of market or customers a company will serve is the market segment. For example, Gerber serves primarily the baby market.
- *Vertical.* The vertical sphere is the number of channel levels from raw material to final product and distribution in which a company will participate. At one extreme are firms with a large vertical scope; at the other extreme are firms with low or no vertical integration that outsource functions such as design, manufacture, marketing, and distribution.
- *Geographical.* The range of regions or countries in which a company operates defines its geographical sphere. Some companies operate in a specific city or state. Others are multinationals such as Unilever and Caterpillar, which operate in almost every country in the world.

A mission statement should be short, memorable, and as meaningful as possible. It also should be enduring, revised only when it ceases to be relevant. However, a company must make changes if its mission has lost credibility or no longer defines an optimal course.

Defining the Business

A business can be defined in terms of three dimensions: customer groups, customer needs, and technology.[15] Consider a company that defines its business as designing incandescent lighting systems for television studios. Its customer group is television studios; its customer need is lighting; and the technology is incandescent lighting. In line with Levitt's argument that *market definitions* of a business are superior to product definitions,[16] these three dimensions describe the business in terms of a customer-satisfying process, not a goods-producing process. Products are transient, but basic needs and customer groups endure forever. Transportation is a need; the horse and carriage, the automobile, the railroad, and the airline are products that meet that need.

Viewing businesses in terms of customer needs can suggest additional growth opportunities. A *target market definition* tends to focus on selling a product to a current market. Pepsi could define its target market as everyone who drinks cola beverages; its competitors would therefore be cola companies. A *strategic market definition*, however, focuses also on the potential market. If Pepsi considered everyone who might drink something to quench his or her thirst, its competition would also include non-cola soft drinks, bottled water, fruit juices, tea, and coffee. To better compete, Pepsi might decide to sell additional beverages with promising growth rates.

Large companies normally manage quite different businesses, each requiring its own strategy. A **strategic business unit (SBU)** has three characteristics: (1) It is a single business or collection of related businesses that can be planned separately from the rest of the company; (2) it has its own set of competitors; and (3) it has a manager responsible for strategic planning and profit performance who controls most of the factors affecting profit.

Assigning Resources to SBUs

The purpose of identifying the company's strategic business units is to develop separate strategies and assign appropriate funding. Senior management knows that the portfolio of businesses usually includes a number of "yesterday's has-beens" as well as "tomorrow's breadwinners."[17] Many executives therefore make decisions about assigning resources to units based on shareholder value analysis and whether the company's market value is greater with an SBU or without it. These value calculations assess the potential of a business based on potential growth opportunities from global expansion, repositioning or retargeting, and strategic outsourcing.[18]

Assessing Growth Opportunities

Assessing growth opportunities includes planning new businesses, downsizing, or terminating older businesses. A company's options for higher sales and profits include intensive growth, integrative growth, and diversification growth.

- *Intensive growth*. One useful framework for identifying intensive growth opportunities is a "product-market expansion grid."[19] The company first considers whether it could gain market share with its current products in current markets (market-penetration strategy) by encouraging current customers to buy more, attracting competitors' customers, or convincing nonusers to start buying its products. Next it considers whether it can find or develop new markets for its current products (market-development strategy). Then it considers whether it can develop new products for its current markets (product-development strategy). Later it will also review opportunities to develop new products for new markets (diversification strategy).
- *Integrative growth*. Often growth can be achieved through backward integration (acquiring a supplier), forward integration (acquiring a distributor), or horizontal integration (acquiring a competitor). If these sources do not deliver the desired results, the company must consider diversification.
- *Diversification growth*. This makes sense when good opportunities exist outside the present businesses. Three types of diversification are possible. The company could seek new products that have technological or marketing synergies with existing product lines, though the new products themselves may appeal to a different group of customers (concentric diversification strategy). Second, the company might search for new products that appeal to its current customers but are technologically unrelated to the current product line (horizontal diversification strategy). Finally, the

company might seek new businesses that have no relationship to the company's current technology, products, or markets (conglomerate diversification strategy).

Weak businesses require a disproportionate amount of managerial attention. Companies must carefully prune, harvest, or divest tired, old businesses in order to release needed resources and reduce costs in preparation for growth.

Organization, Organizational Culture, and Innovation

Strategic planning occurs within the context of the organization. A company's **organization** consists of its structures, policies, and corporate culture, all of which can become dysfunctional in a rapidly changing business environment. **Corporate culture** has been defined as "the shared experiences, stories, beliefs, and norms that characterize an organization." A customer-centric culture can affect all aspects of an organization. In the words of one expert: "The question is, do you see consumers as the driving life force of your company for as long as it exists, or do you see them as simply a hungry group of people that needs to be satisfied so your business will grow in the short term?"[20]

Sometimes corporate culture develops organically and is transmitted directly from the CEO's personality and habits to employees. Mike Lazaridis, president and co-CEO of Blackberry producer Research in Motion, hosts a weekly, innovation-centered "Vision Series" to focus on new research and company goals. As he states: "I think we have a culture of innovation here, and [engineers] have absolute access to me. I live a life that tries to promote innovation."[21]

Innovation in marketing is critical. The traditional view is that senior management hammers out the strategy and hands it down. Gary Hamel offers the contrasting view that imaginative ideas on strategy exist in many places within a company.[22] Management should encourage fresh ideas from three groups often underrepresented in strategy making: employees with youthful perspectives; employees far removed from company headquarters; and employees new to the industry.

Firms develop strategy by identifying and selecting among different views of the future. The Royal Dutch/Shell Group has pioneered **scenario analysis**, developing plausible representations of a firm's possible future based on different assumptions about forces driving the market and different uncertainties. The point is to ask: "What will we do if it happens?" Managers then adopt one scenario as the most probable and watch for signs that might confirm or disconfirm it.[23]

BUSINESS UNIT STRATEGIC PLANNING

The business unit strategic-planning process consists of the eight steps shown in Figure 2.4. We examine each step in the sections that follow.

Business Mission

Each business unit needs to define its specific mission within the broader company mission. Thus, a television studio-lighting-equipment company might define its mission as: "To target major television studios and become their vendor of choice for lighting technologies that represent the most advanced and reliable studio lighting arrangements."

FIGURE 2.4 The Business Unit Strategic-Planning Process

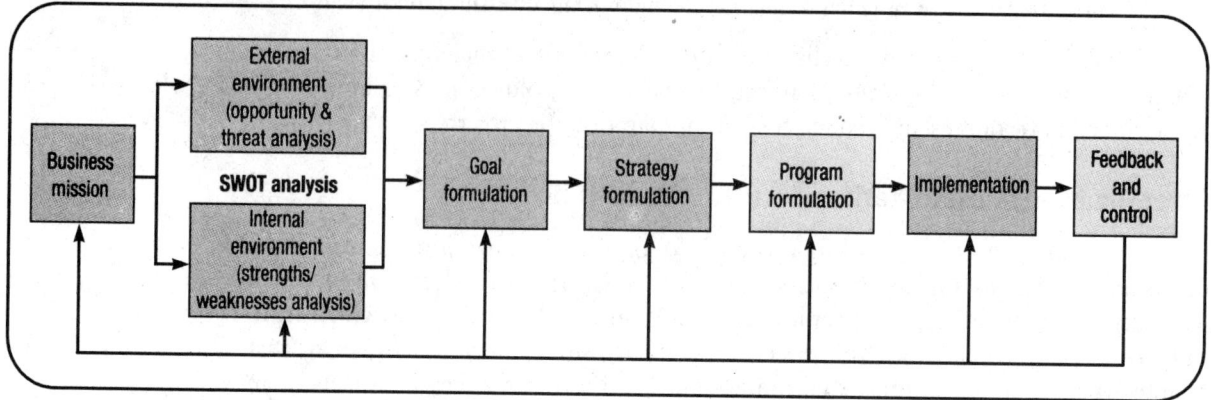

SWOT Analysis

The overall evaluation of a business's strengths, weaknesses, opportunities, and threats is called *SWOT analysis*. It's a way of monitoring the external and internal environments.

External Environment (Opportunity and Threat) Analysis A business unit has to monitor key *macroenvironment forces* and *microenvironment actors* that affect its ability to earn profits. Management should track trends and important developments as well as any related opportunities and threats.

A **marketing opportunity** is an area of buyer need and interest that a company has a high probability of profitably satisfying. There are three main sources of market opportunities.[24] The first source is to supply something that is in short supply. The second is to supply an existing product or service in a new or superior way by asking consumers for their suggestions (*problem detection method*), asking consumers to imagine an ideal version of the offering (*ideal method*), or asking consumers to chart their steps in acquiring, using, and disposing of a product (*consumption chain method*). The third source often leads to a totally new offering.

The company applies **market opportunity analysis (MOA)** to determine the attractiveness and success probability of each opportunity by asking questions like:

1. Can we articulate the benefits convincingly to the defined target market(s)?
2. Can we locate the target markets and reach them with cost-effective media and trade channels?
3. Do we have access to the capabilities and resources needed to deliver the customer benefits?
4. Can we deliver the benefits better than any actual or potential competitors?
5. Will the financial rate of return meet or exceed our required threshold for investment?

An **environmental threat** is a challenge posed by an unfavorable trend or development that would lead, in the absence of defensive marketing action, to lower sales or profit. Threats should be classified according to seriousness and probability of occurrence. Minor threats can be ignored; somewhat more serious threats must be carefully monitored; and major threats require the development of contingency plans.

Internal Environment (Strengths and Weaknesses) Analysis It's one thing to find attractive opportunities, and another to be able to take advantage of them. Each business needs to evaluate its internal strengths and weaknesses in marketing, finance, manufacturing, and organizational capabilities. Clearly, the business does not have to correct all its weaknesses nor should it gloat about all its strengths. The big question is whether the business should limit itself to those opportunities in which it possesses the required strengths or consider opportunities that might require it to acquire or develop new strengths.

Goal Formulation

After performing a SWOT analysis, marketers develop specific goals for the planning period, in a process called **goal formulation**. Goals are objectives that are specific with respect to magnitude and time. To be effective, goals must be (1) arranged hierarchically (from most to least important); (2) quantitative whenever possible; (3) realistic; and (4) consistent. Other important trade-offs include: short-term profit versus long-term growth; deep penetration of existing markets versus developing new markets; profit goals versus nonprofit goals; and high growth versus low risk. Each choice calls for a different marketing strategy.

Strategy Formulation

Goals indicate what a business unit wants to achieve; **strategy** is the game plan for getting there. Every business strategy consists of a *marketing strategy* plus a compatible *technology strategy* and *sourcing strategy*. Porter has proposed three generic strategies that form a good starting point for strategic thinking: overall cost leadership, differentiation, and focus.[25]

- *Overall cost leadership.* The business works to achieve the lowest production and distribution costs so it can price lower than competitors and win a large market share. Firms pursuing this strategy need less skill in marketing. The problem is that rivals will usually compete with still lower costs and hurt the firm that rested its whole future on cost.
- *Differentiation.* The business concentrates on uniquely achieving superior performance in an important customer benefit area valued by a large part of the market.
- *Focus.* The business focuses on one or more narrow market segments, getting to know these segments intimately and pursuing either cost leadership or differentiation within each.

Firms pursuing the same strategy directed to the same target market constitute a **strategic group**. The firm that carries off that strategy best will make the most profits. Porter draws a distinction between operational effectiveness and strategy. A company has a strategy when it "performs different activities from rivals or performs similar activities in different ways."[26]

Even giant companies such as Siemens often cannot achieve leadership, either nationally or globally, without alliances with domestic or multinational companies that complement or leverage their capabilities and resources. Marketing alliances may involve products or services (licensing or jointly marketing a product); promotions (promoting a complementary offering); logistics (delivering or distributing a complementary product); or pricing (offering mutual price discounts). Corporations have begun developing organizational structures to support these alliances and have come to view the ability to form and manage partnerships as a core skill called **Partner Relationship Management (PRM)**.[27]

Program Formulation and Implementation

Once goals and strategies are set, management must formulate and implement appropriate programs. For example, if the business strives for technological leadership, its managers must strengthen the R&D department, gather technological intelligence, develop leading-edge products, train the technical sales force, and communicate technological leadership to the target market. The marketing people must also estimate each program's costs and returns. Activity-based cost (ABC) accounting can help determine whether each marketing program is likely to produce sufficient results to justify the cost.[28]

According to McKinsey & Company, strategy is only one of seven elements in business success, all of which start with the letter "s."[29] The first three—strategy, structure, and systems—are the "hardware" of success. The next four—style (how employees think and behave), skills (to carry out the strategy), staff (able people who are properly trained and assigned), and shared values (values that guide employees' actions)—are the "software." When these elements are present, companies are usually more successful at strategy implementation.[30]

Another study of management practices found that superior performance over time depends on a clear and focused strategy, flawless execution, a corporate culture based on aiming high, and a flexible, responsive culture.[31] In the end, the greatest strategy or program can be sabotaged by poor implementation. (See "Marketing Skills: Managing Implementation" for more about how marketing managers can handle this vital process.)

Feedback and Control

A company's strategic fit with the environment will inevitably erode because the market environment changes faster than the company's 7 Ss. Thus, a company might

---

MARKETING SKILLS: MANAGING IMPLEMENTATION

Creative implementation can translate a good marketing strategy into great profits. First, marketers have to break every program down into its component activities, identify the needed resources and their associated costs, estimate how long each activity should last and who should handle it, and set up measures to monitor results. Second, they must enlist the support of other departments to enhance creativity and prepare for potential problems. Third, marketers should be flexible enough to find workable options when dealing with unexpected twists such as late delivery of materials. Finally, they need to instill a sense of urgency about implementing every phase of every program, day in and day out.

Consider what managers at 20th Century Fox Home Entertainment do to ensure successful implementation of their strategy for marketing movies on DVD. Before every release, they develop appropriate marketing programs and a detailed schedule for activities such as advertising, online games, and giveaways. They choose a release date to take advantage of buying patterns and avoid conflicts with competing DVD releases. Finally, they work closely with retailers to have new DVDs prominently displayed. Good implementation helped the company generate sales of $100 million from the DVD of *Night at the Museum* during its first week in stores.[32]

remain efficient while losing effectiveness. Peter Drucker pointed out that it is more important to "do the right thing" (effectiveness) than "to do things right" (efficiency). The most successful companies excel at both. Once a firm fails to respond to a changed environment, it becomes increasingly hard to recapture its lost position.

THE MARKETING PLAN AND MARKETING PERFORMANCE

Working within the plans set by the levels above them, product managers come up with a marketing plan for individual products, lines, brands, channels, or customer groups. Each product level (line or brand) must develop a marketing plan for achieving its goals. A **marketing plan** is a written document that summarizes what the marketer has learned about the marketplace, what objectives are to be achieved through marketing, and how.[33]

Marketing plans are becoming more customer- and competitor-oriented, and better reasoned and more realistic than in the past as companies seek high marketing performance. Moreover, they are an integral part of what has become a continuous planning process that allows a firm to respond to rapidly changing market conditions.

Contents of a Marketing Plan

A typical marketing plan includes these basic sections:

- *Executive summary and table of contents*. The plan should open with a brief summary of the main goals and recommendations, followed by a table of contents.
- *Situation analysis*. This section presents relevant background data on sales, costs, profits, the market, competitors, and the macroenvironment. How is the market defined, how big is it, how fast is it growing, and what are the critical trends and issues? All this information is used to carry out a SWOT (strengths, weaknesses, opportunities, threats) analysis.
- *Marketing strategy*. Here the product manager defines the mission, the marketing and financial objectives, and groups and needs that the offerings are intended to satisfy. This section establishes the product line's competitive positioning and explains how objectives will be achieved. All this requires inputs from other organizational areas, such as purchasing, sales, finance, and human resources.
- *Financial projections*. In this section, management includes a sales forecast (by month and product), an expense forecast (marketing costs broken down into finer categories), and a break-even analysis (how many units must be sold to offset fixed costs and average per-unit variable costs).
- *Implementation controls*. The final section outlines controls for monitoring and adjusting plan implementation. Typically, it spells out the goals and budget for each month or quarter so management can review results and take corrective action as needed. Some firms include contingency plans for handling specific environmental developments (such as price wars).

Measuring Marketing Performance

How do companies know whether their marketing plans are achieving the marketing and financial objectives that have been set? More than ever, senior managers are holding marketers accountable for marketing investments and asking that marketing expenditures be justified.[34] One survey of top U.S. marketers revealed that approximately half were not satisfied with their ability to measure the return on their marketing investments.[35] Another study revealed that 63% of senior managers were dissatisfied with their firm's marketing performance measurement system and wanted marketing to supply estimates of the impact of marketing programs.[36] Therefore, more firms are measuring and tracking results using marketing metrics and marketing dashboards, analyses of marketing plan performance, and profitability analysis.

Marketing Metrics and Marketing Dashboards Marketers employ a wide variety of measures to assess marketing effects.[37] **Marketing metrics** is the set of measures that helps them quantify, compare, and interpret their marketing performance. Brand managers apply marketing metrics to design marketing programs; senior managers use marketing metrics to determine financial allocations. Marketers who are able to estimate the dollar contribution of marketing activities can better justify the value of marketing investments to senior management.[38] Marketing metrics can be used to evaluate both short-term results (such as sales turnover) and changes in brand equity (including measures such as customer loyalty).[39] Management may also monitor metrics internal to the company. For example, 3M tracks the proportion of sales resulting from its recent innovations.

Management can assemble a summary set of relevant internal and external measures in a *marketing dashboard* for synthesis and interpretation. Like the instrument panel in a car, a marketing dashboard visually displays real-time indicators to ensure proper functioning. An effective dashboard will focus management thinking, improve internal communications, and reveal where marketing investments are paying off and where they aren't.[40]

As input to the marketing dashboard, companies can prepare two market-based scorecards that reflect performance and possible early warning signals. A **customer performance scorecard** records how well the company is doing year after year on such customer-based measures as the percentage of new customers to average number of customers and the percentage of targeted customers who have brand awareness or recall. A **stakeholder-performance scorecard** shows the satisfaction of various constituencies who have a critical interest in and impact on the company's performance: employees, suppliers, banks, distributors, retailers, stockholders. Management should set norms for each measure and take action when actual results get out of bounds or one or more groups register increased levels of dissatisfaction.[41]

Marketing Plan Performance Four ways to measure key aspects of the marketing plan's performance are sales analysis, market share analysis, marketing expense-to-sales analysis, and financial analysis. **Sales analysis** consists of measuring and evaluating actual sales in relation to goals. With **sales-variance analysis**, management measures the relative contribution of different factors to a gap in sales performance. With **microsales analysis**, management looks at specific products, territories, and other factors that failed to produce the expected sales levels.

To understand how the company is performing relative to competitors, management needs to track market share, which can be measured in three ways. **Overall market share** is the firm's sales expressed as a percentage of total market sales. **Served market share** is its sales expressed as a percentage of the total sales to its served market. Its **served market** is all the buyers who are able and willing to buy its product.

Note that served market share is always larger than overall market share. A firm could capture 100% of its served market and yet have a relatively small share of the total market. **Relative market share** can be expressed as market share in relation to its largest competitor. A relative market share over 100% indicates a market leader; a relative market share of exactly 100% means that the company is tied for the lead. A rise in relative market share means a company is gaining on its leading competitor.

Managers can check whether the company is overspending to achieve sales goals by examining the *marketing expense-to-sales* ratio. The company should investigate fluctuations outside the normal range of such ratios and examine the behavior of successive observations within even the upper and lower control limits to catch potential problems early. The expense-to-sales ratios should be analyzed in an overall financial framework to determine how and where the company is making its profits. For instance, companies use financial analysis to identify the factors that affect the company's *rate of return on net worth*.[42] This ratio is the product of the company's *return on assets* and its *financial leverage*. To improve return on net worth, the company must increase its ratio of net profits to assets or increase the ratio of its assets to net worth.

Also, the company should analyze the composition of its assets (i.e., cash, accounts receivable, inventory, and plant and equipment) to see if it can improve its asset management. The return on assets is the product of two ratios, the *profit margin* and the *asset turnover*. Companies can improve return on assets in two ways: (1) increase the profit margin by increasing sales or cutting costs; and (2) boost the asset turnover by increasing sales or reducing assets (e.g., inventory, receivables) that are held against a given level of sales.[43]

Profitability Analysis By measuring the profitability of their products, territories, customer groups, segments, trade channels, and order sizes, companies can determine whether any should be changed or eliminated. Managers first identify the expenses for each marketing function (such as advertising and delivery) and assign these costs to marketing entities (such as each type of channel). Next, they prepare a profit-and-loss statement for each marketing entity. Then they can determine whether corrective action is needed to improve the relative profitability of different marketing entities.

Companies are showing a growing interest in using marketing-profitability analysis or its broader version, activity-based cost accounting (ABC), to quantify the true profitability of different activities.[44] Managers can then examine options such as reducing the resources required to perform various activities; making the resources more productive or acquiring them at lower cost; or raising prices.

EXECUTIVE SUMMARY

The value delivery process involves choosing (or identifying), providing (or delivering), and communicating superior value. The value chain is a tool for identifying key activities that create value and costs in a specific business, including the core processes of marketing sensing, new offering realization, customer acquisition, customer relationship management, and fulfillment management. Managing these processes effectively means creating a network in which the company partners with firms in the production and distribution chain.

Holistic marketing maximizes value exploration by understanding the interaction between relevant actors (customers, company, and collaborators) and value-based activities (value exploration, value creation, and value delivery). Market-oriented strategic planning is the managerial process of developing and maintaining a viable fit between the organization's objectives, skills, and resources and its changing market opportunities. Strategic planning occurs at four levels: corporate, division, business unit, and product.

Corporate-level planning includes: defining the mission; establishing SBUs; assigning resources to SBUs; and assessing growth opportunities. The company's structure, policies, and corporate culture can all affect strategic planning and implementation. In each business unit, strategic planning covers the business mission; SWOT analysis; goal, strategy, and program formulation; implementation; and feedback and control. On the product level, the marketing plan summarizes what the firm knows about the marketplace, what marketing expects to accomplish, and how. The firm can assess marketing performance by using marketing metrics and a marketing dashboard, analyzing marketing plan performance, and applying profitability analysis.

NOTES

1. William Boston, "Siemens Goes Mega," *Time*, May 14, 2007; Jack Ewing, "Siemen's Tough Guy Gets Going," *BusinessWeek*, June 27, 2005; Jack Ewing, "Nokia, Siemens Plan to Join and Conquer," *Business Week*, June 20, 2006; Abraham Lustgarten, "Remaking a German Giant With American-Style Tactics," *Fortune*, August 7, 2006.
2. Nirmalya Kumar, *Marketing As Strategy: The CEO's Agenda for Driving Growth and Innovation* (Boston: Harvard Business School Press, 2004).
3. Frederick E. Webster Jr., "The Future Role of Marketing in the Organization," in *Reflections on the Futures of Marketing*, edited by Donald R. Lehmann and Katherine Jocz (Cambridge, MA: Marketing Science Institute, 1997), pp. 39–66.
4. Michael E. Porter, *Competitive Advantage: Creating and Sustaining Superior Performance* (New York: Free Press, 1985).
5. Robert Hiebeler, Thomas B. Kelly, and Charles Ketteman, *Best Practices: Building Your Business with Customer-Focused Solutions* (New York: Simon and Schuster, 1998).
6. Michael Hammer and James Champy, *Reengineering the Corporation* (New York: Harper Business, 1993).
7. C. K. Prahalad and Gary Hamel, "The Core Competence of the Corporation," *Harvard Business Review* (May–June 1990): 79–91.
8. George S. Day, "The Capabilities of Market-Driven Organizations," *Journal of Marketing* (October 1994): 38.
9. George S. Day and Paul J. H. Schoemaker, *Peripheral Vision: Detecting the Weak Signals That Will Make or Break Your Company* (Boston, MA: Harvard Business School Press, 2006).
10. *Pew Internet and American Life Project Survey*, November–December 2000.
11. Kasuaki Ushikubo, "A Method of Structure Analysis for Developing Product Concepts and Its Applications," *European Research* 14, no. 4 (1986): 174–175.
12. Erik Sherman, "Shifting Markets the Right Way; It Takes Tact," *Advertising Age*, April 9, 2007, p. 18; Don Clark, "Intel to Overhaul marketing in Bid to Go Beyond PCs," *Wall Street Journal*, December 30, 2005; Cliff Edwards, "Intel Everywhere?" *BusinessWeek*, March 8, 2004, pp. 56–62; "How to Become a Superbrand," *Marketing*, January 8, 2004, p. 15; Heather Clancy, "Intel Thinking Outside the Box," *Computer Reseller News*, November 24, 2003, p. 14.
13. Peter Drucker, *Management: Tasks, Responsibilities and Practices* (New York: Harper & Row, 1973), ch. 7.
14. Ralph A. Oliva, "Nowhere to Hide," *Marketing Management*, July/August 2001, pp. 44–46.
15. Derek Abell, *Defining the Business: The Starting Point of Strategic Planning* (Upper Saddle River, NJ: Prentice Hall, 1980), ch. 3.
16. Theodore Levitt, "Marketing Myopia," *Harvard Business Review* (July–August 1960): 45–56.
17. Tilman Kemmler, Monika Kubicová, Robert Musslewhite, and Rodney Prezeau, "E-Performance II—The Good, the Bad, and the Merely Average," an exclusive to *mckinseyquarterly.com*, 2001.
18. This section is based on Robert M. Grant, *Contemporary Strategy Analysis*, 5th ed. (Malden, MA: Blackwell Publishing, 2005), Chapter 16.
19. The same matrix can be expanded into nine cells by adding modified products and modified markets.

See S. J. Johnson and Conrad Jones, "How to Organize for New Products," *Harvard Business Review* (May–June 1957): 49–62.
20. "The Consumer-Centric Marketer As Guru of Exponential Growth: Kelly Styring," *KNOW*, Spring/Summer 2006, www.knowledgenetworks.com.
21. Jena McGregor, "The World's Most Innovative Companies," *BusinessWeek*, April 24, 2006, pp. 63–74.
22. E. Jerome McCarthy, *Basic Marketing: A Managerial Approach*, 12th ed. (Homewood, IL: Irwin, 1996).
23. Paul J. H. Shoemaker, "Scenario Planning: A Tool for Strategic Thinking," *Sloan Management Review* (Winter 1995): 25–40.
24. Philip Kotler, *Kotler on Marketing* (New York: Free Press, 1999).
25. Michael E. Porter, *Competitive Strategy: Techniques for Analyzing Industries and Competitors* (New York: Free Press, 1980), ch. 2.
26. Michael E. Porter, "What Is Strategy?" *Harvard Business Review* (November–December 1996): 61–78.
27. For more on strategic alliances, see Peter Lorange and Johan Roos, *Strategic Alliances: Formation, Implementation and Evolution* (Cambridge, MA: Blackwell, 1992); Jordan D. Lewis, *Partnerships for Profit: Structuring and Managing Strategic Alliances* (New York: The Free Press, 1990); John R. Harbison and Peter Pekar Jr., *Smart Alliances: A Practical Guide to Repeatable Success* (San Francisco: Jossey-Bass, 1998); *Harvard Business Review on Strategic Alliances* (Boston, MA: Harvard Business School Press, 2002).
28. Robin Cooper and Robert S. Kaplan, "Profit Priorities from Activity-Based Costing," *Harvard Business Review* (May–June 1991): 130–135.
29. Thomas J. Peters and Robert H. Waterman, Jr., *In Search of Excellence: Lessons from America's Best-Run Companies* (New York: Harper & Row, 1982) pp. 9–12.
30. Terrence E. Deal and Allan A. Kennedy, *Corporate Cultures: The Rites and Rituals of Corporate Life* (Reading, MA: Addison-Wesley, 1982); "Corporate Culture," *BusinessWeek*, October 27, 1980, pp. 148–160; Stanley M. Davis, *Managing Corporate Culture* (Cambridge, MA: Ballinger, 1984); and John P. Kotter and James L. Heskett, *Corporate Culture and Performance* (New York: Free Press, 1992).
31. Nitin Nohria, William Joyce, and Bruce Roberson, "What Really Works," *Harvard Business Review* 81, No. 7 (2003): 42–53.
32. Thomas K. Arnold, "'Museum' Opens with Double Win," *Hollywood Reporter*, May 3, 2007, p. 14; Miles Hanson, "Fresh Ideas Are Nothing Without Implementation," *Marketing*, March 21, 2002, p. 1; Elaine Dutka, "Coming Soon to a Store Near You: Fox Executives," *Los Angeles Times*, April 19, 2005, p. E1.
33. Marian Burk Wood, *The Marketing Plan Handbook*, 3d ed. (Upper Saddle River, NJ: Pearson Prentice Hall, 2008), p. 3.
34. John McManus, "Stumbling into Intelligence," *American Demographics*, April 2004, pp. 22–25.
35. Lisa Sanders, "Measuring ROI Eludes Half of Top Marketers," *Marketing News*, July 7, 2006, p. 4.
36. Tim Ambler, *Marketing and the Bottom Line: The New Metrics of Corporate Wealth* (London: FT Prentice Hall, 2000).
37. Paul Farris, Neil T. Bendle, Phillip E. Pfeifer, and David J. Reibstein, *Marketing Metrics: 50+ Metrics Every Executive Should Master* (Upper Saddle River, NJ: Pearson Education, 2006); John Davis, *Magic Numbers for Consumer Marketing: Key Measures to Evaluate Marketing Success* (Singapore: John Wiley & Sons, 2005).
38. Bob Donath, "Employ Marketing Metrics with a Track Record," *Marketing News*, September 15, 2003, p. 12.
39. Kusum L. Ailawadi, Donald R. Lehmann, and Scott A. Neslin, "Revenue Premium as an Outcome Measure of Brand Equity," *Journal of Marketing*, October 2003, pp. 1–17.
40. Richard Karpinski, "Making the Most of a Marketing Dashboard," *B to B*, March 13, 2006, p. 18; Patrick LaPointe, *Marketing by the Dashboard Light* (New York: Association of National Advertisers, 2005).
41. Robert S. Kaplan and David P. Norton, *The Balanced Scorecard* (Boston: Harvard Business School Press, 1996).
42. Alternatively, companies need to focus on factors affecting shareholder value. The goal of marketing planning is to increase shareholder value, which is the present value of the future income stream created by the company's present actions. Rate-of-return analysis usually focuses on only one year's results. See Alfred Rapport, *Creating Shareholder Value*, rev. ed. (New York: The Free Press, 1997).
43. For more on financial analysis, see Peter L. Mullins, *Measuring Customer and Product Line Profitability* (Washington, DC: Distribution Research and Education Foundation, 1984).

CHAPTER 3

Understanding Markets, Market Demand, and the Marketing Environment

> In this chapter, we will address the following questions:
>
> 1. What are the components of a modern marketing information system?
> 2. How can marketers use intelligence systems and marketing research?
> 3. How can demand be more accurately measured and forecasted?
> 4. What are some important macroenvironmental developments?

MARKETING MANAGEMENT AT WAL-MART

The world's largest retailer wants to become known for its eco-friendly business practices as well as its low prices. Wal-Mart is investing $500 million in a variety of sustainability projects to achieve aggressive environmental goals. The company wants to increase the efficiency of its vehicle fleet by 25% over the next three years and double it in ten years; eliminate 30% of the energy used in stores; and reduce solid waste from U.S. stores by 25% within three years. It's also promoting energy-efficient compact fluorescent light bulbs for consumer use and pushing its 66,000 suppliers to cut excess packaging.

Even small decisions can make a big difference for Wal-Mart. By eliminating some of the packaging on its private label toys, the retailer will save $2.4 million a year in shipping costs, 3,800 trees, and one million barrels of oil. By using a polymer wrapping derived from corn instead of oil, it will save as much as 800,000 gallons of gas. Although environmental groups are pleased, Wal-Mart still faces criticism from activists and union leaders about employee wages and benefits, gender discrimination, and treatment of local competition. In response, the company points to its progress on these issues—and to its leadership in green initiatives.[1]

To provide insight and inspiration for marketing decisions, Wal-Mart—like other companies—needs comprehensive, up-to-date information about macro trends (such as changes in the natural environment) and the micro effects particular to its business. Holistic marketers recognize the importance of continuously monitoring and adapting to the marketing environment, which constantly presents new opportunities and threats. This chapter considers processes and systems for gathering information, identifying trends, and conducting marketing research. It also examines key macroenvironmental forces that can affect the company, its markets, and its competitors.

MARKETING INFORMATION, INTELLIGENCE, AND RESEARCH

Although every manager in an organization needs to observe the outside environment, the major responsibility for identifying and interpreting marketplace changes falls to the company's marketers. Marketers have two advantages: They have disciplined methods for collecting information, and they spend more time than anyone else interacting with customers and observing competition and other outside firms and groups.

Marketing managers must have a continuous flow of information to understand and track changes in customer needs, wants, preferences, and consumption patterns. A **marketing information system (MIS)** consists of people, equipment, and procedures to gather, sort, analyze, evaluate, and distribute needed, timely, and accurate information to marketing decision makers. This system relies on internal company records, marketing intelligence, and marketing research.

Internal Records

Marketing managers rely on data from internal reports about orders, sales, prices, costs, inventory levels, receivables, payables, and so on. By analyzing this information, they can spot important opportunities and problems. The heart of the internal records system is the order-to-payment cycle. Sales representatives, dealers, and customers dispatch orders to the firm. The sales department prepares invoices, transmits copies to various departments, and back-orders out-of-stock items. Shipped items generate shipping and billing documents for various departments. Companies need to perform these steps quickly and accurately, because customers favor firms that can promise timely delivery.

Marketing managers require timely and accurate reports on current sales. Wal-Mart, for example, operates a sales and inventory data warehouse that captures data on every item, for every store, every day and refreshes it every hour. The retailer also transmits nightly orders to its many suppliers for new shipments of replacement stock, even entrusting some companies such as Procter & Gamble to handle its inventory management for certain product categories.[2]

Today companies organize information into databases—customer databases, product databases, salesperson databases—and then combine data from the different databases. A customer database typically contains every customer's name, address, past transactions, and sometimes even demographics and psychographics (activities, interests, and opinions). Companies warehouse these data and make them easily accessible to decision makers. In addition, analysts skilled in statistical methods can "mine" the data—*datamining*—to garner fresh insights into neglected customer segments, recent customer trends, and other useful information.

As an example, Best Buy created a database with information about 75 million households by capturing every transaction and interaction—from phone calls and mouse clicks to delivery and rebate-check addresses. It has also segmented its market into specific categories and applied a model to measure transaction profitability, factoring in consumer behaviors that either increase or decrease the value of the relationship. Now Best Buy can use precision marketing, improve store layout to boost sales, and increase response rates to incentive programs.[3]

Marketing Intelligence System

The internal records system supplies *results* data, but the marketing intelligence system supplies *happenings* data. A **marketing intelligence system** is the set of procedures and sources used by managers to obtain everyday information about developments in the marketing environment. Managers collect marketing intelligence by reading books, newspapers, and trade publications; talking to customers, suppliers, and distributors; monitoring online "social media" such as blogs, discussion groups, and e-mailing lists; and meeting with other company managers. A company can take several steps to improve the quality of its marketing intelligence (see Table 3.1).

Marketing Research System

Marketing managers often commission formal marketing studies of specific problems and opportunities, such as a market survey, a product-preference test, a sales forecast by region, or an advertising evaluation. **Marketing insights** provide diagnostic information about how and why certain effects are observed in the marketplace, and what that means to marketers.[4] **Marketing research** is the systematic design, collection, analysis, and reporting of data and findings relevant to a specific marketing situation facing the company.

A company can obtain marketing research in a number of ways. Most large companies have their own marketing research departments. Procter & Gamble's Consumer & Market Knowledge (CMK) marketing research function has a centralized team plus dedicated groups working for specific P&G businesses to improve brand strategies and program execution. At much smaller companies, everyone carries out marketing research—including customers, in some cases.

Companies normally budget marketing research at 1% to 2% of company sales. Much of this budget is spent with outside research firms, which fall into three categories. Syndicated-service research firms such as Nielsen Media Research gather

Chapter 3 Understanding Markets, Market Demand, and the Marketing Environment

TABLE 3.1 Improving the Quality of Marketing Intelligence

Action	Example
Train and motivate the sales force to spot and report new developments that may be missed by other means.	Have sales representatives observe how customers use the firm's products in innovative ways, which can lead to new product ideas.
Motivate distributors, retailers, and other intermediaries to pass along important intelligence.	Use mystery shoppers to identify service problems that can be addressed by revamping processes and retraining employees.
Network externally to gather data in legal and ethical ways.	Read competitors' published reports, examine rivals' Web sites and ads, and watch the competition in the field where appropriate.
Establish a customer advisory panel.	Invite the largest or the most representative, outspoken, or sophisticated customers to provide feedback.
Take advantage of government data resources.	Check U.S. Census data to learn more about population swings, demographic groups, regional migrations, and changing family structure.
Buy information from outside suppliers at a lower cost than collecting it internally.	Obtain supermarket scanner data from Information Resources, Inc. or data on television audiences from Nielsen Media Research.
Use online customer feedback systems to collect competitive intelligence.	Check chat rooms, blogs, customer complaint forums, and Web sites such as Bizrate.com to learn more about the competition.

consumer and trade information, which they sell for a fee. Custom marketing research firms design studies, carry them out, and report the findings. Specialty-line marketing research firms provide specialized services such as field interviewing. Smaller companies can hire a marketing research firm or conduct research in creative and affordable ways. For instance, they can engage students or professors to design and carry out projects; they can use the Internet; and they can visit their competitors.[5]

Effective marketing research involves the six steps shown in Figure 3.1. We illustrate these steps with the following situation: Assume that American Airlines is reviewing new ideas for serving its customers, especially to cater to its first-class passengers on very long flights, mainly businesspeople whose high-priced tickets pay most of the freight.[6] Among these ideas are (1) an Internet connection with limited access to Web pages and e-mail; (2) 24 channels of satellite cable TV; and (3) a 50-CD audio system that lets passengers customize in-flight play lists. The marketing research manager is assigned to find out how first-class passengers would rate these services—particularly the Internet connection—and the price they would pay for each. According to one estimate, airlines might realize revenues of $70 billion over the next decade from in-flight Internet access if enough first-class passengers were willing to pay $25 for this service. Making the connection available would cost AA $90,000 per plane.[7]

Step 1: Define the Problem, Decision Alternatives, and Research Objectives

Marketing management must be careful not to define the problem too broadly or narrowly for the researcher. American's marketing manager and marketing researcher defined the problem this way: "Will offering an in-flight Internet service create enough incremental preference and profit to justify its cost against other possible investments in service enhancements that American Airlines might make?" They agreed on five research objectives: (1) What types of first-class passengers would respond most to an in-flight Internet service? (2) How many first-class passengers are likely to use this service at different price levels? (3) How many extra first-class

FIGURE 3.1 The Marketing Research Process

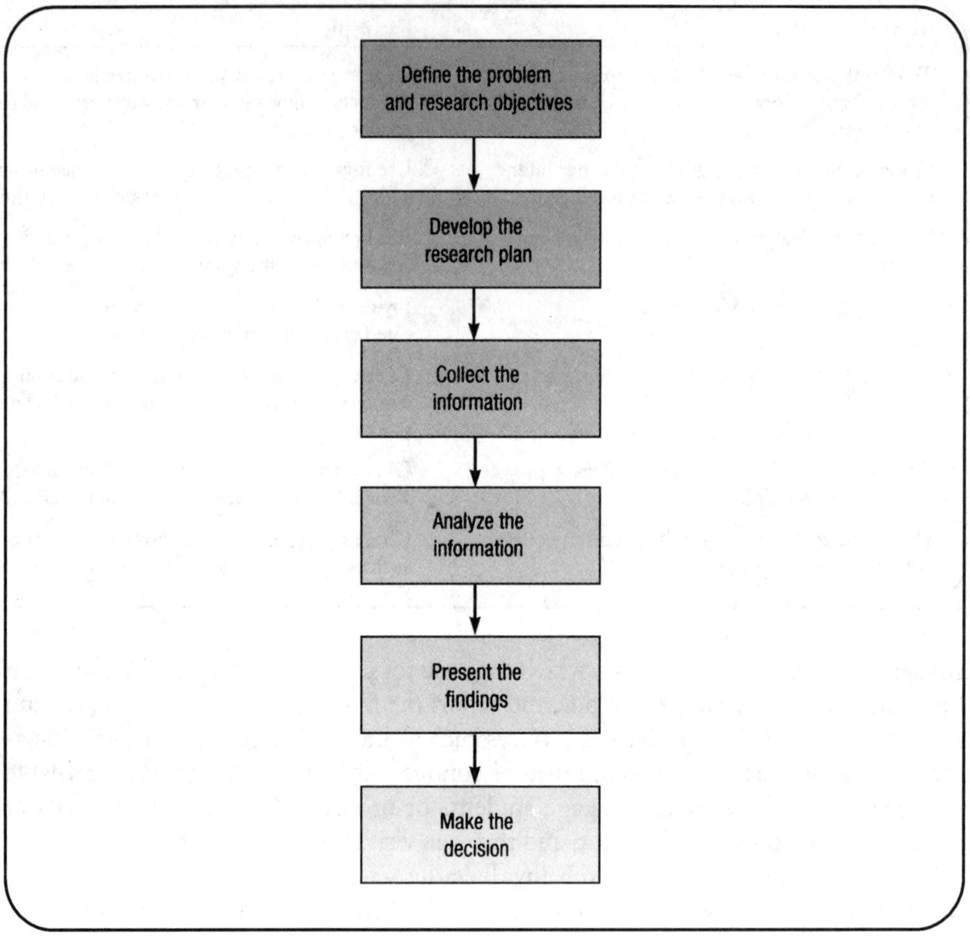

```
Define the problem
and research objectives
        ↓
Develop the
research plan
        ↓
Collect the
information
        ↓
Analyze the
information
        ↓
Present the
findings
        ↓
Make the
decision
```

passengers might choose American because of this new service? (4) How much long-term goodwill will this service add to American Airlines' image? (5) How important is this service to first-class passengers relative to providing other services such as enhanced entertainment?

Not all research projects are this specific. Some research is *exploratory*, to shed light on the real nature of the problem and suggest possible solutions or new ideas. Some research is *descriptive*, to ascertain certain magnitudes, such as how many first-class passengers would buy in-flight Internet access at $25. Some research is *causal*, to test a cause-and-effect relationship.

Step 2: Develop the Research Plan The second step calls for designing an efficient, affordable research plan for gathering the needed information. This entails decisions about data sources, research approaches, research instruments, sampling plan, and contact methods.

DATA SOURCES The researcher can gather secondary data, primary data, or both. *Secondary data* are data that were collected for another purpose and that already exist somewhere. *Primary data* are freshly gathered for a specific purpose or a specific research project. Researchers usually start by examining secondary data to see whether

Chapter 3 Understanding Markets, Market Demand, and the Marketing Environment

the problem can be partly or wholly solved without collecting costlier primary data. When the needed data do not exist or are dated, inaccurate, incomplete, or unreliable, primary data will have to be collected.

RESEARCH APPROACHES   Marketers can collect primary data in five main ways: by observation, focus groups, surveys, behavioral data, and experiments.

- *Observational research.* Fresh data can be gathered by observing the relevant actors and settings. **Ethnographic research** is an observational research approach that uses concepts and tools from anthropology and other social science disciplines to provide deep understanding of how people live and work.[8] The American Airlines researchers might meander around first-class lounges in airports to hear travelers talk about different carriers or fly on competitors' planes to observe in-flight service.

- *Focus-group research.* A **focus group** is a gathering of six to ten people who are carefully selected based on certain demographic, psychographic, or other considerations and brought together to discuss at length various topics of interest, assisted by a professional research moderator. In the American Airlines research, the moderator might ask a broad question such as "How do you feel about first-class air travel?" and discuss different airlines and proposed services such as Internet access.

- *Survey research.* Using surveys, companies can learn about people's knowledge, beliefs, preferences, and satisfaction, and can measure these magnitudes in the general population. American Airlines researchers might prepare their own questions, add questions to a larger survey, survey an ongoing consumer panel, or survey people in a shopping mall.

- *Behavioral data.* Customers leave traces of their purchasing behavior in store scanning data, catalog and online purchase records, and customer databases. Marketers can learn much by analyzing these data. Customers' purchases reflect their preferences and often are more reliable than their statements to researchers. This is because people often report preferences for popular brands, yet they actually buy other brands. American Airlines can analyze ticket purchase records and online behavior to obtain useful information about passengers.

- *Experimental research.* The most scientifically valid research is experimental research. Its purpose is to capture cause-and-effect relationships by eliminating competing explanations of the observed findings. American Airlines might experiment by introducing Internet access on one of its regular international flights at a price of $25 one week and only $15 the next week. If the plane carried the same number of first-class passengers each week, and particular weeks made no difference, any significant difference in the number of people using the service could be related to price.

RESEARCH INSTRUMENTS   Marketing researchers have a choice of three main research instruments in collecting primary data: questionnaires, qualitative measures, and technological devices. A **questionnaire** consists of a set of questions presented to respondents. Because of its flexibility, the questionnaire is by far the most common instrument used to collect primary data. Questionnaires need to be carefully developed, tested, and debugged before they are administered on a large scale. The form, wording, and sequence of questions can all influence the response. Closed-end questions specify all of the possible answers, so they are easy to interpret and tabulate. Open-end questions allow respondents to answer in their own words.

They are especially useful in exploratory research, where the researcher is looking for insight into how people think rather than measuring how many people think a certain way.

Some marketers prefer more qualitative methods for gauging consumer opinion because consumer actions do not always match their answers to survey questions. *Qualitative research techniques* are relatively unstructured measurement approaches that permit a range of possible responses, and they are a creative means of ascertaining consumer perceptions that may otherwise be difficult to uncover. Mobiltec, a California company that offers content-management software for wireless service providers, researches what teens want on their cell phones in terms of media, ring tones, games, music and TV. In one study, it asked teenagers on its global research panel to buy and download four mobile games, then rate the download experiences and the prices so Mobiltec could analyze their reactions.[9]

Technological devices are occasionally used in marketing research. Galvanometers measure the interest or emotions aroused by exposure to a specific ad or picture. Eye cameras study respondents' eye movements to see where their eyes land first, how long they linger on a given item, and so on. Technology now allows marketers to use devices like skin sensors, brain wave scanners, and full body scanners to gauge consumer responses. The term "neuromarketing" has been used to describe brain research on the effect of marketing stimuli.[10]

SAMPLING PLAN After deciding on the research approach and instruments, the marketing researcher must design a sampling plan, based on three decisions:

1. *Sampling unit: Who should we survey?* In the American Airlines survey, should the sampling unit be only first-class business travelers, first-class vacation travelers, or both? Once the sampling unit is determined, a sampling frame must be developed so that everyone in the target population has an equal or known chance of being sampled.
2. *Sample size: How many people should we survey?* Large samples give more reliable results than small samples. However, samples of less than 1% of a population can be reliable with a credible sampling procedure.
3. *Sampling procedure: How should we choose the respondents?* Probability sampling allows researchers to calculate confidence limits for sampling error and make the sample more representative. When the cost or time involved in probability sampling is too high, marketing researchers use nonprobability sampling.

CONTACT METHODS Now the marketing researcher must decide how to contact subjects: by mail, by telephone, in person, or online. The advantages and disadvantages of these methods are summarized in Table 3.2.

Step 3: Collect the Information The data collection phase of marketing research is generally the most expensive and the most prone to error. In the case of surveys, four major problems arise. Respondents who are not at home must be recontacted or replaced. Other respondents will not cooperate. Still others will give biased or dishonest answers. Finally, some interviewers will be biased or dishonest.

Getting the right respondents is critical. For example, MarketTools Inc. has recruited more than 100,000 participants, through online and offline methods, for its Hispanic-targeted research panel. MarketTools also works with a direct marketing agency to reach offline parties and make sure the panel represents the varying degrees of Hispanic acculturation in the United States. Hispanics who are relatively unacculturated,

TABLE 3.2 Marketing Research Contact Methods

Contact Method	Advantages	Disadvantages
Mail questionnaire	Best for reaching people who would not give personal interviews or whose responses might be biased or distorted by the interviewers.	Response rate is usually low or slow.
Telephone interview	Best for gathering information quickly and clarifying questions respondents do not understand; higher response rate than mail questionnaires.	Interviews must be short and not too personal; contact getting more difficult because of consumers' growing antipathy toward being called at home and the federal "Do Not Call" registry.
Personal interview	Most versatile because researcher can ask more questions and record additional observations about respondents, such as dress and body language.	Most expensive contact method; requires more planning and supervision; is subject to interviewer bias.
Online interview	Researcher can post questions on the Web; place a banner, sponsor a chat room, or use other techniques to quickly, easily recruit and survey participants. Inexpensive and versatile; respondents tend to be more honest online.	Samples can be small and skewed. Also, online research is prone to technological problems and inconsistencies.

such as seniors, are almost impossible to reach online; therefore, their offline responses are blended with the online ones.[11]

Step 4: Analyze the Information The next step in the process is to extract findings by tabulating the data and developing frequency distributions. The researchers now compute averages and measures of dispersion for the major variables and apply statistical techniques and decision models in the hope of discovering additional findings. They may test different hypotheses and theories, applying sensitivity analysis to test assumptions and the strength of the conclusions.

Step 5: Present the Findings Now the researcher presents findings relevant to the major marketing decisions facing management. Some researchers try to bring data to life for the people in the organization.[12] For example, Delta Airlines created a video of its primary business customers, personified in a character called "Ted," and showed it to flight attendants and airport personnel. In the American Airlines case, findings show that passengers would use in-flight Internet service to surf the Web and exchange e-mail messages. Passengers would charge the service and be repaid by their companies. About five first-class passengers out of every ten would use the service at $25; about six would use it at $15. Thus, a charge of $15 would produce less revenue ($90 = 6 × $15) than $25 ($125 = 5 × $25). By charging $25, AA would collect $125 a flight. Assuming that the same flight takes place 365 days a year, AA would annually collect $45,625 ($125 × 365). Since the investment is $90,000, AA would break even in about two years. Also, in-flight Internet service would boost AA's image as an innovator, bring in new passengers, and build goodwill.

Step 6: Make the Decision The managers who commission the research need to weigh the evidence. If American Airlines' managers have little confidence in the

BREAKTHROUGH MARKETING: IDEO

As the largest U.S. industrial-design firm, IDEO has created some of the most recognizable design icons of the technology age: the first laptop computer; the first mouse (for Apple); and the Treo mobile phone. The company has also designed household items such as the Swiffer Sweeper and the Crest Neat Squeeze toothpaste tube, both for Procter & Gamble. Its diverse roster of clients includes AT&T, Caterpillar, Lufthansa, Marriott, Nike, Prada, and the Mayo Clinic.

IDEO's goal is to design products that offer consumers a superior experience. Over the years, it has used a variety of methods to research how people purchase, interact with, use and even dispose of products. It often uses observation to conduct "deep dives" into consumer research by shadowing consumers, taking pictures or videos as they buy or use a product, and then interviewing them for more insights. It has also used "camera journals," asking consumers to record their visual impressions of a given product or category, and "storytelling," asking consumers to share personal narratives about their experiences with a product or service. IDEO's consumer-led approach to design has led to countless success stories for clients and for the firm itself.[13]

findings, they may decide against introducing the in-flight Internet service. If they are predisposed to launching the service, the findings support their inclination. They may even decide to do more research. The decision is theirs, but the research will have provided some insight into the problem.[14]

"Breakthrough Marketing: IDEO" shows how that company has used marketing research to come up with innovative product and service designs.

FORECASTING AND DEMAND MEASUREMENT

One major reason for using marketing research is to identify market opportunities. Once the research is complete, marketers must measure and forecast the size, growth, and profit potential of each market opportunity. Sales forecasts, based on demand estimates, are used by finance departments to plan for the needed cash for investment and operations; by manufacturing to establish capacity and output levels; by purchasing to acquire the right amount of supplies; and by human resources to hire the needed number of workers. The first step is to determine which market to measure.

Which Market to Measure?

The size of a market hinges on the number of buyers who might exist for a particular market offer. The **potential market** is the set of consumers who have sufficient interest in a market offer. However, interest is not enough to define a market unless consumers also have sufficient income and access to the product. The **available market** is the set of consumers who have interest, income, and access to a particular offer. The **target market** is the part of the *qualified available market* (those with the interest, income, access, and qualifications for a particular offer) that the company decides to pursue. Finally, the **penetrated market** is the set of consumers who are buying the company's product.

These market definitions are useful tools for market planning. If the company is not satisfied with its current sales, it can try to attract more buyers from its target market; lower the qualifications of potential buyers; expand its available market by adding distribution or lowering price; or reposition itself in the minds of customers.

Demand Measurement

The next step in evaluating marketing opportunities is to estimate market demand. **Market demand** for a product is the total volume that would be bought by a defined customer group in a defined geographical area in a defined time period in a defined marketing environment under a defined marketing program. Market demand is not fixed but rather a function of the stated conditions. For this reason, it can be called the *market demand function*.

Figure 3.2a shows how total market demand depends on underlying conditions. The horizontal axis depicts possible levels of industry marketing expenditure in a given time period. The vertical axis shows the resulting demand level. The curve represents the estimated market demand associated with varying levels of industry marketing expenditure. Some base sales (called the *market minimum*, labeled Q_1) would take place without any expenditures. Higher levels of industry marketing expenditures would yield higher levels of demand, first at an increasing rate, then at a decreasing rate. Marketing expenditures beyond a certain level would not stimulate much further demand, suggesting an upper limit called the *market potential* (labeled Q_2).

The total size of an *expansible market* is much affected by the level of industry marketing spending. In Figure 3.2a, the distance between Q_1 and Q_2 is relatively large. However, in a *nonexpansible market*—one not much affected by the level of marketing expenditures—the distance between Q_1 and Q_2 would be relatively small. Organizations that sell in a nonexpansible market must accept the market's size (the level of *primary demand* for the product class) and try to win a larger **market share** (the level of *selective demand* for the company's product).

FIGURE 3.2 Market Demand Functions

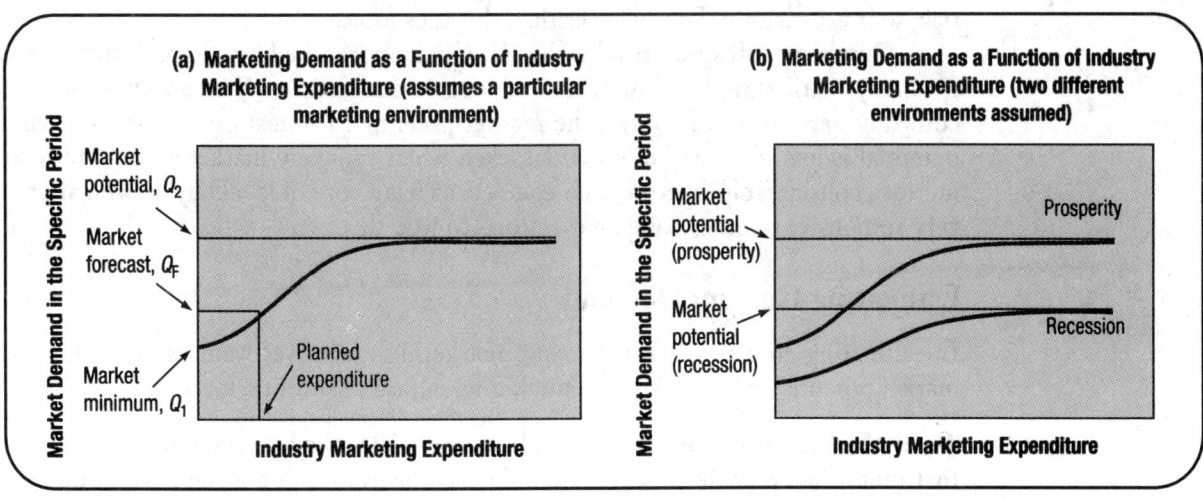

The market demand curve shows alternative current forecasts of market demand associated with possible levels of industry marketing effort. Only one level of industry marketing expenditure will actually occur; the market demand at this level is the **market forecast**. This forecast shows expected market demand, not maximum market demand.

Market potential is the limit approached by market demand as industry marketing expenditures approach infinity for a given marketing environment. The phrase "for a given marketing environment" is crucial. The market potential for many products is higher during prosperity than during recession, as illustrated in Figure 3.2b. Companies can't do anything about the position of the market demand function, which is determined by the marketing environment, but their marketing spending can influence their location on the function.

Company Demand and Sales Forecast

Company demand is the company's estimated share of market demand at alternative levels of company marketing effort in a given time period. It depends on how the firm's products, services, prices, and communications are perceived relative to the competitors'. If other things were equal, the company's share will depend on the size and effectiveness of its market expenditures. Marketing model builders have developed sales-response functions to measure how a company's sales are affected by its marketing expenditures, marketing mix, and marketing effectiveness.[15]

Once marketers have estimated company demand, they next choose a level of marketing effort to produce an expected level of sales. The **company sales forecast** is the expected level of company sales based on a chosen marketing plan and an assumed marketing environment. The company sales forecast is graphed with company sales on the vertical axis and company marketing effort on the horizontal axis, as in Figure 3.2. Note that the sales forecast is the result of an assumed marketing expenditure plan.

A **sales quota** is the sales goal set for a product line, company division, or sales representative. It is primarily a managerial device for defining and stimulating sales effort. Generally, sales quotas are set slightly higher than estimated sales to stretch the sales force's effort. A **sales budget** is a conservative estimate of the expected sales volume and is used primarily for making current purchasing, production, and cash flow decisions. The sales budget is based on the sales forecast and avoidance of excessive risk, so it is generally slightly lower than the sales forecast.

Company sales potential is the sales limit approached by company demand as company marketing effort increases relative to competitors. The absolute limit of company demand is, of course, the market potential. In most cases, company sales potential is less than market potential, even when company marketing expenditures increase considerably, because each competitor has a core of loyal buyers who are not very responsive to other companies' efforts to woo them.

Estimating Current Demand

In estimating current market demand, marketing executives want to examine total market potential, area market potential, total industry sales, and market shares.

Total Market Potential **Total market potential** is the maximum number of sales that might be available to all of the industry's firms during a given period, under a given level of industry marketing effort and environmental conditions. A common way to estimate total market potential is to multiply the potential number of buyers by the average quantity each purchases times the price. If 100 million people buy books each year, and the average book buyer buys three books a year, and the average price of a book is $20, the total market potential for books is $6 billion (100 million × 3 × $20).

The most difficult component to estimate is the number of buyers for the specific product or market. Companies can start with a total population, eliminate groups that obviously would not buy the product, and do research to eliminate groups without interest or money to buy. This leaves a pool of prospects that companies can include in the calculation of total market potential.

Area Market Potential Because companies must allocate their marketing budget optimally among their best territories, they need to estimate the market potential of different cities, states, and nations. Business marketers primarily use the market-buildup method, whereas consumer marketers primarily use the multiple-factor index method.

The **market-buildup method** calls for identifying all of the potential buyers in an area and estimating their potential purchases. This works well if firms have a list of all potential buyers and a good estimate of what each will buy—data that can be difficult to gather. For efficiency, some firms start with the *North American Industry Classification System (NAICS)*, a six-digit industry classification code that provides statistics comparable across the United States, Canada, and Mexico.[16] To use the NAICS, a lathe manufacturer would first determine the six-digit NAICS codes that represent products whose manufacturers are likely to require lathe machines. Then the manufacturer determines an appropriate base for estimating the number of lathes that will be used, such as customer industry sales. Once the company estimates the rate of lathe ownership relative to the customer industry's sales, it can compute the market potential.

Consumer companies also estimate area market potentials, but because their customers are too numerous to be listed, they often use the index method. A drug marketer, for example, might assume that the market potential for drugs is directly related to population size. If Virginia has 2.28% of the U.S. population, the company might assume that state will account for 2.28% of all drugs sold. In reality, drug sales are also influenced by other factors. Thus, it makes sense to develop a multiple-factor index with each factor assigned a specific weight. For example, if Virginia has 2.00% of the U.S. disposable personal income, 1.96% of U.S. retail sales, and 2.28% of U.S. population, with respective weights of 0.5, 0.3, and 0.2, the buying-power index for drugs in Virginia would be:

$$0.5 (2.00) + 0.3 (1.96) + 0.2 (2.28) = 2.04$$

In addition to estimating total market potential and area potential, a company needs to know the actual industry sales in its market. This means identifying its competitors and estimating their sales. Some information may be available from trade associations and marketing research firms, although not for individual competitors. Because distributors typically will not supply information about how much of competitors' products they are selling, business-goods marketers operate with less knowledge of their market share results.

TABLE 3.3 Sales Forecast Methods

Forecast Method	Description	Use
Survey of buyers' intentions	Survey consumers or businesses about purchase probability, future finances, and expectations about the economy.	To estimate demand for industrial products, consumer durables, purchases requiring advance planning, and new products.
Composite of sales force opinions	Have sales representatives estimate their future sales.	To gather detailed forecast estimates broken down by product, territory, customer, and sales rep
Expert opinion	Obtain forecasts from experts such as dealers, distributors, suppliers, consultants, and trade associations; can be purchased from economic-forecasting firms.	To gather estimates from knowledgeable specialists who may offer good insights.
Past-sales analysis	Use time-series analysis, exponential smoothing, statistical demand analysis, or econometric analysis to analyze past sales.	To project future demand on the basis of an analysis of past demand.
Market-test method	Conduct a direct-market test to understand customer response and estimate future sales.	To better forecast sales of new products or sales in a new area.

Estimating Future Demand

Forecasting is the art of anticipating what buyers are likely to do under a given set of conditions. The few offerings that lend themselves to easy forecasting generally enjoy an absolute level of demand or fairly constant demand and competition that is either nonexistent (public utilities) or stable (pure oligopolies). In most markets, in contrast, good forecasting is a key factor in success.

Companies commonly prepare a macroeconomic forecast first, then an industry forecast and a company sales forecast. The macroeconomic forecast projects inflation, unemployment, interest rates, consumer spending, business investment, government spending, net exports, and other variables. The result is a forecast of gross national product, which is used, along with other indicators, to forecast industry sales. Finally, the company derives its sales forecast by assuming it will win a certain market share. Methods for sales forecasting are shown in Table 3.3.

MACROENVIRONMENTAL TRENDS AND FORCES

Marketers find many opportunities by identifying trends in the macroenvironment. A **trend** is a direction or sequence of events that has some momentum and durability. In contrast, a **fad** is "unpredictable, short-lived, and without social, economic, and political significance."[17] A new product or marketing program is likely to be more successful if it is in line with strong trends rather than opposed to them. This is why marketers have to develop their trend-spotting skills (see "Marketing Skills: Spotting Trends"). Still, detecting a new market opportunity does not guarantee its success, even if it is technically feasible.

Chapter 3 Understanding Markets, Market Demand, and the Marketing Environment

MARKETING SKILLS: SPOTTING TRENDS

Marketers need good trend-spotting skills so they can take action in time to turn a change into a profitable opportunity rather than a dangerous threat. Trend-spotting requires "splatter vision," the ability to look at the entire environment without becoming too focused on one factor. Marketers can also use their mental models of future expectations—based on sales or industry forecasts—to scan for and explain deviations that could affect marketing performance. In the ever-changing technology industry, experts use a combination of five approaches: seeing the future as an extension of the past; searching for cycles and patterns; analyzing the actions of customers and other stakeholders; monitoring technical and social events as they unfold; and discerning trends from the interaction of these four approaches.

For example, Herman Miller, which manufactures office furniture, has one employee surfing the Web full-time to collect breaking information about the business world, design, retailing, and other issues, and then summarize the results in a daily e-mail to management. In addition, the president always carries a digital camera to capture images that suggest new design trends. Thanks to the firm's trend-spotting ability, it has also identified opportunities for expanding into new product categories, such as display units that retailers can move quickly and easily to reallocate floor space when needs change.[18]

Companies and their suppliers, marketing intermediaries, customers, and competitors all operate in a macroenvironment of forces and trends that shape opportunities and pose threats. Within the rapidly changing global picture, six major forces represent "noncontrollables" which the company must monitor and to which it must respond: demographic, economic, social-cultural, natural, technological, and political-legal. Although these forces will be described separately, marketers must pay attention to their interactions, because these set the stage for new opportunities as well as threats.

Demographic Environment

Marketers monitor *population* trends because people make up markets. Marketers are keenly interested in the size and growth rate of the population in cities, regions, and nations; age distribution and ethnic mix; educational levels; household patterns; and regional characteristics and movements.

Worldwide Population Growth The world population stands at over 6.3 billion and is expected to exceed 7.9 billion by 2025.[19] Population growth is a source of concern, in part because it is highest in areas that can least afford it. The less-developed regions of the world currently account for 76% of the world population and are growing at 2% per year, whereas the population in the more developed countries is growing at only 0.6% per year. Taking care of children by feeding, clothing, and educating them can help raise the standard of living, yet this is difficult in less-developed regions. For businesses, a growing population does not mean growing markets unless these markets have sufficient purchasing power. Nonetheless, firms that carefully analyze their markets can find opportunities.

Population Age Mix National populations vary in their age mix, although there is a global trend toward an aging population.[20] A population can be subdivided into six age groups: preschool, school-age children, teens, young adults age 25 to 40, middle-aged adults age 40 to 65, and older adults age 65 and up. Some marketers like to focus on **cohorts**, groups of individuals who are born during the same time period and travel through life together, such as the "baby boomers" born between 1946 and 1964 and Generation X, people born between 1965 and 1976.

Ethnic Markets Countries also vary in ethnic and racial makeup. Major groups within the U.S. population include whites, African Americans, Hispanics (with major subgroups of Mexican, Puerto Rican, and Cuban descent), and Asian Americans (with subgroups of Chinese, Filipino, Japanese, Asian Indian, and Korean descent). Moreover, nearly 25 million people living in the United States—more than 9% of the population—were born in another country. Each group has certain specific needs, wants, and buying habits that marketers need to understand. Yet marketers must be careful not to overgeneralize about ethnic groups. Within each ethnic group are consumers who are quite different from each other.

Educational Groups The population in any society falls into five educational groups: illiterates, high school dropouts, high school degrees, college degrees, and professional degrees. Over two-thirds of the world's 785 million illiterate adults are found in eight countries (India, China, Bangladesh, Pakistan, Nigeria, Ethiopia, Indonesia, and Egypt).[21] However, 36% of the U.S. population is college educated, one of the world's highest percentages; high education fuels demand for quality books, magazines, and travel.

Household Patterns The "traditional household" consists of a husband, wife, and children (and sometimes grandparents). Yet, by 2010, only one in five U.S. households will consist of married couples with children under the age of 18.[22] Other household compositions include single live-alones, adult live-togethers of one or both sexes, single-parent families, childless married couples and empty nesters, and living with non-relatives only. More people are divorcing or separating, not marrying, marrying later, or marrying without the intention to have children. Each group has a distinctive set of needs and buying habits. For example, single, separated, widowed, or divorced people need smaller apartments, smaller appliances and furniture, and food packaged in smaller sizes.

Marketers must increasingly consider the special needs of nontraditional households, because they are now growing more rapidly than traditional households. Compared to the average American, respondents who classify themselves as gay are more than 10 times as likely to be in professional jobs, almost twice as likely to own a vacation home, eight times more likely to own a notebook computer, and twice as likely to own individual stocks.[23] Companies such as Absolut, American Express, IKEA, Procter & Gamble, and Subaru have recognized the potential of this market and the nontraditional household market as a whole.

Geographical Shifts in Population This is a period of great migratory movements between and within countries. Although the United States experienced a rural rebound in the 1990s when nonmetropolitan counties attracted large numbers of urban refugees, urban markets now are growing more rapidly due to a higher birth rate, a lower death rate, and foreign immigration to U.S. cities.[24]

Location makes a difference in goods and service preferences. As an example, almost one in two people over the age of five (120 million) moved at least once between 1995 and 2000—with many moving to the Sunbelt states and away from the Midwest and Northeast.[25] As a result, demand for warm clothing and home heating equipment is decreasing while demand for air conditioning is increasing. And nearly 40 million Americans work out of their homes, fueling demand for electronic conveniences like computers and cell phones.

Economic Environment

The available purchasing power in an economy depends on current income, savings, debt, and credit availability. Marketers must pay careful attention to trends affecting purchasing power because these can have a strong impact on business, especially for companies offering products geared to high-income and price-sensitive consumers.

Income Distribution There are four types of industrial structures: *subsistence economies*, which offer few marketing opportunities; *raw-material-exporting economies* like Zaire (copper) and Saudi Arabia (oil), good markets for equipment, tools, and luxury goods for the rich; *industrializing economies* like India and the Philippines, where the rich and the middle class demand new types of goods; and *industrial economies* like those in Western Europe, good markets for all sorts of goods.

Marketers often distinguish countries with five different income-distribution patterns: (1) very low incomes; (2) mostly low incomes; (3) very low, very high incomes; (4) low, medium, high incomes; and (5) mostly medium incomes. From 1973 to 1999, the income of the wealthiest 5% of the U.S. population grew by 65%, while the income for the middle fifth households grew only 11%. This is leading to a two-tier U.S. market, with affluent people buying expensive goods and working-class people shopping at discount stores and buying less expensive store brands. Conventional retailers who offer medium-price goods are the most vulnerable to these changes. Companies can prosper if they respond to this trend by tailoring their products and pitches to these two very different Americas.[26]

Savings, Debt, and Credit Availability Consumer savings, debt, and credit availability affect consumer expenditures. U.S. consumers have a high debt-to-income ratio, which may slow down further expenditures on housing and large-ticket items. Credit is readily available in the United States, but lower-income borrowers pay fairly high interest rates. An economic issue of increasing importance to many unemployed U.S. consumers is the migration of manufacturers and service jobs off shore.

Social-Cultural Environment

Society shapes the beliefs, values, and norms that largely define consumer preferences. People absorb, almost unconsciously, a world view that defines their relationship to themselves, others, organizations, society, nature, and the universe.

- *Views of themselves.* In the United States during the 1960s and 1970s, "pleasure seekers" sought fun and escape while others sought "self-realization." Today, some people are adopting more conservative behaviors and ambitions.

- *Views of others.* People are concerned about the homeless, crime and victims, and other social problems. At the same time, they seek out "their own kind" for long-lasting relationships and avoid strangers. These trends portend a growing market for offerings that promote direct relations among human beings (such as health clubs) and for "social surrogates" (such as home video games).
- *Views of organizations.* After a wave of company downsizings and scandals, there has been an overall decline in organizational loyalty.[27] Companies need to find new ways to win back consumer and employee confidence through honesty and good corporate citizenship.[28]
- *Views of society.* Some people defend society, some run it, some take what they can from it, some want to change it, some look for something deeper, and some want to leave it.[29] Consumption patterns often reflect social attitude; those who want to change it, for example, may drive more fuel-efficient cars and live more frugally.
- *Views of nature.* People have awakened to nature's fragility and finite resources. Businesses are responding to increased consumer interest in experiencing nature by camping and other outdoor activities by producing wider varieties of offerings such as boots and tents.
- *Views of the universe.* Most U.S. citizens are monotheistic, although religious conviction and practice have varied through the years. Certain evangelical movements are reaching out to bring people back into organized religion.

High Persistence of Core Values The people living in a particular society hold many *core beliefs* that are passed on from parents to children and reinforced by major social institutions—schools, churches, business, and government. *Secondary beliefs* and values are more open to change. Marketers may change secondary values but have little chance of changing core values. For instance, the nonprofit organization Mothers Against Drunk Driving (MADD) does not try to stop the sale of alcohol, but it does promote more limited operating hours for businesses permitted to sell alcohol. Although core values are fairly persistent, cultural swings do take place.

Existence of Subcultures Each society contains **subcultures**, groups with shared values, beliefs, preferences, and behaviors emerging from their special life experiences or circumstances. There are sometimes unexpected rewards in targeting subcultures. For instance, marketers love teenagers because they are trendsetters in fashion, music, entertainment, and attitudes. Marketers know that if they attract someone as a teen, there's a good chance they will keep that customer for years. Frito-Lay, which draws 15% of its sales from teens, has seen more chip-snacking by grown-ups. "We think it's because we brought them in as teenagers," says a Frito-Lay marketing director.[30]

Natural Environment

The deterioration of the natural environment is a major global problem. In Western Europe, "green" parties have pressed for public action to reduce industrial pollution. However, new regulations protecting the natural environment have hit certain industries very hard. Steel companies have had to invest in expensive pollution-control equipment and earth-friendly fuels; the soap industry has increased its products' biodegradability.

Corporate environmentalism is the recognition of the importance of environmental issues facing the firm and the integration of those issues into the firm's strategic plans.[31] In general, marketers need to be aware of four environmental trends: the shortage of raw materials, the increased cost of energy, increased pollution levels, and the changing role of governments.

- The earth's raw materials consist of the infinite, the finite renewable, and the finite nonrenewable. *Finite nonrenewable resources* such as oil pose a particularly serious problem as the point of depletion approaches. Firms making products that require these resources face substantial cost increases; meanwhile, firms engaged in research and development have excellent opportunities to create substitute materials.
- One finite nonrenewable resource, oil, has created serious problems for the world economy. As oil prices have soared, companies are searching for practical means to harness alternative energy forms such as solar, nuclear, and wind.
- Some industrial activity will inevitably damage the natural environment. A large market has been created for pollution-control solutions, opening the way for alternative production and packaging methods.
- Governments vary in their concern and efforts to promote a clean environment. Many poor nations are doing little about pollution because they lack the funds or the political will. It is in the richer nations' interest to help the poorer nations control their pollution, but even the richer nations today lack the necessary funds.

Companies that mount "green programs" can face two main problems: consumers may believe the product is of inferior quality as a result of being green and consumers may feel the product is not really that green to begin with. Successful green products overcome these concerns by showing how they serve consumers' and society's interests at the same time (such as with energy-efficient appliances that cost less to run). Jacquelyn Ottman and her colleagues refer to the tendency to overly focus on a product's greenness as "green marketing myopia."[32]

Technological Environment

One of the most dramatic forces shaping people's lives is technology. New technology can lead to product breakthroughs, yet it is also a force for "creative destruction." Autos hurt the railroads, and television hurt the newspapers. Instead of moving into the new technologies, many old industries fought or ignored them, and their businesses declined. Also, technological progress can be sporadic; for example, railroads sparked investment, and then investment petered out until the auto industry emerged. In the time between major innovations, an economy can stagnate, despite minor innovations that fill the gap.

Marketers must monitor these trends in technology: the pace of change, the opportunities for innovation, varying R&D budgets, and increased regulation.

- *Accelerating pace of technological change.* More new ideas than ever are in the works, and the time between the appearance of new ideas and their successful implementation is all but disappearing. So is the time between introduction and peak production.
- *Unlimited opportunities for innovation.* Some of the most exciting work today is taking place in biotechnology, computers, microelectronics, telecommunications, and robotics. Biotech research is creating new medical cures, new foods, and new materials; robotic experts are designing robots for firefighting and home nursing.
- *Varying R & D budgets.* A growing portion of U.S. R&D spending is going into development rather than research, raising concerns about whether the country can

maintain its lead in basic science. Many firms are content to put their money into copying competitors' products and making minor feature and style improvements. Even basic research companies such as DuPont are proceeding cautiously, and more consortiums than single companies are directing their research efforts toward major breakthroughs.

- *Increased regulation of technological change.* Government has expanded its agencies' powers to investigate and ban potentially unsafe products. In the United States, the Federal Food and Drug Administration must approve all drugs before they can be sold. Safety and health regulations have also increased in the areas of food, automobiles, clothing, electrical appliances, and construction.

Political-Legal Environment

The political and legal environment consists of laws, government agencies, and pressure groups that influence and limit organizations and individuals. Sometimes these laws also create new opportunities for business. Mandatory recycling laws, for example, have spurred companies to make new products from recycled materials. Two major trends deal with business legislation and special interest groups.

Increase in Business Legislation Business legislation is intended to (1) protect firms from unfair competition; (2) protect consumers from unfair business practices; (3) protect society from unbridled business behavior; and (4) charge businesses with the social costs created by their products or processes. The European Community has laws that cover competitive behavior, product standards and liability, and commercial transactions; the United States has laws covering issues such as competition, product safety and liability, fair trade, and packaging and labeling.[33] Although each new law may have a legitimate rationale, it may also have the unintended effect of sapping initiative and retarding economic growth. Companies generally establish legal review procedures and set ethical standards to guide their marketing managers.

Growth of Special-Interest Groups Political-action committees (PACs) lobby government officials and pressure businesses to pay more attention to consumer rights, women's rights, senior citizens' rights, minority rights, and gay rights. Many companies have public affairs departments to deal with these groups and issues. An important force affecting business is the **consumerist movement**—an organized movement of citizens and government to strengthen the rights and powers of buyers in relationship to sellers. Consumerists have won many rights, including the right to know a loan's true interest cost and a product's true benefits. Yet new laws and pressure from special-interest groups continue to add more restraints, moving many private marketing transactions into the public domain.

EXECUTIVE SUMMARY

A marketing information system (MIS) consists of people, equipment, and procedures to gather, sort, analyze, evaluate, and distribute needed, timely, and accurate information to marketing decision makers. This system covers internal records with data about the order-to-payment cycle and sales; a marketing intelligence system to obtain everyday information about developments in the marketing environment; and marketing

Chapter 3 Understanding Markets, Market Demand, and the Marketing Environment

research for the systematic design, collection, analysis, and reporting of data and findings relevant to a particular marketing situation.

The marketing research process consists of: defining the problem, alternatives, and objectives; developing the research plan; collecting the information; analyzing the information; presenting the findings to management; and making the decision. In conducting research, firms must decide whether to collect primary data, secondary data, or both. They must also decide which research approach (observation, focus groups, surveys, behavioral data, or experiments) and which research instrument (questionnaire, qualitative measure, or technological device) to use. In addition, they must select a sampling plan and contact methods. One purpose of marketing research is to discover market opportunities that are then evaluated on the basis of sales forecasts of market and company demand.

Marketers must monitor six major environmental forces. In the demographic environment, they must look at population growth; changes in age, ethnic composition, and educational levels; household patterns; and geographic population shifts. In the economic environment, they should focus on income distribution, savings, debt, and credit availability. In the social-cultural arena, they must understand people's views of themselves, others, organizations, society, nature, and the universe; the role of core and secondary values; and the needs of subcultures. In the natural environment, they need to be aware of the public's increased concern about the health of the environment. In the technological environment, they should note the faster pace of change, innovation opportunities, varying R&D budgets, and increased governmental regulation. In the political-legal environment, marketers must work within the laws regulating business practices and with special-interest groups.

NOTES

1. Claudia H. Deutsch, "Incredible Shrinking Packages," *New York Times*, May 12, 2007, pp. C1, C9; John Carey, "Big Strides to Become the Jolly Green Giant," *BusinessWeek*, January 29, 2007, p. 57; Marc Gunther, "Wal-Mart Sees Green," *Fortune*, August 7, 2006, pp. 42–57; "Wal-Mart Goes Crunchy," *The Economist*, June 10, 2006, p. 60; Jerry Adler, "Going Green," *Newsweek*, July 17, 2006, pp. 43–52.
2. Charles Babcock, "Data, Data Everywhere," *InformationWeek*, January 9, 2006; Charles Fishman, "The Wal-Mart You Don't Know," *Fast Company*, December 2003, pp. 68–80.
3. "Jeff Zabin, "The Importance of Being Analytical," *Brandweek*, July 24, 2006, p. 21; Richard H. Levey, "Best Buy Uses Data to Place Products," *Direct*, January 1, 2006.
4. See Robert Schieffer, *Ten Key Customer Insights: Unlocking the Mind of the Market* (Mason, OH: Thomson, 2005) for more on how to generate customer insights to drive business results.
5. Melanie Haiken, "Tuned In to Crowdcasting," *Business 2.0* (November 2006): 66–68.
6. "Would You Fly in Chattering Class?" *The Economist*, September 9, 2006, p. 63.
7. For background information on in-flight Internet service, see "In-Flight Dogfight," *Business 2.0* (January 9, 2001): 84–91; John Blau, "In-Flight Internet Service Ready for Takeoff," *IDG News Service*, June 14, 2002; "Boeing In-Flight Internet Plan Goes Airborne," *Associated Press*, April 18, 2004.
8. For a detailed review of relevant academic work, see Eric J. Arnould and Amber Epp, "Deep Engagement with Consumer Experience," in the *Handbook of Marketing Research*, Rajiv Grover and Marco Vriens (Thousand Oaks, CA: Sage Publications, 2006). For practical tips, see Richard Durante and Michael Feehan, "Leverage Ethnography to Improve Strategic Decision Making," *Marketing Research*, Winter 2005. For additional academic discussion, see "Can Ethnography Uncover Richer Consumer Insights?" *Journal of Advertising Research*, 46 (September 2006).
9. Georgia Mullen, "Teens Talk Back to Mobile Industry," *Telecommunications America*, September 2006, p. 14.

10. Richard A. Friedman, "What's the Ultimate? Scan a Male Brain," *New York Times*, October 25, 2006, p. G10; Roger D. Blackwell, James S. Hensel, Michael B. Phillips, and Brian Sternthal, *Laboratory Equipment for Marketing Research* (Dubuque, IA: Kendall/Hunt, 1970); Gerald Zaltman, "Rethinking Market Research: Putting People Back In," *Journal of Marketing Research* 34, no. 4 (November 1997): 424–437; Andy Raskin, "A Face Any Business Can Trust," *Business 2.0* (December 2003): 58–60; and Louise Witt, "Inside Intent," *American Demographics* (March 2004): 34–39.
11. Allison Enright, "Make the Connection," *Marketing News*, April 1, 2006, p. 21.
12. Dale Buss, "Reflections of Reality," *Point*, June 2006, pp. 10–11; Todd Wasserman, "Unilever, Whirlpool Get Personal with Personas," *Brandweek*, September 18, 2006, p. 13.
13. Lisa Chamberlain, "Going Off the Beaten Path for New Design Ideas," *New York Times*, March 12, 2006, p. C1; Scott Morrison, "Sharp Focus Gives Design Group the Edge," *Financial Times*, February 18, 2005, *Business Life* p. 8.
14. Kevin J. Clancy and Peter C. Krieg, *Counterintuitive Marketing: How Great Results Come from Uncommon Sense* (New York: The Free Press, 2000).
15. For further discussion, see Gary L. Lilien, Philip Kotler, and K. Sridhar Moorthy, *Marketing Models* (Upper Saddle River, NJ: Prentice Hall, 1992).
16. See www.naics.com and www.census.gov/epcd/naics02.
17. Gerald Celente, *Trend Tracking* (New York: Warner Books, 1991).
18. "Herman Miller Sees Growth in Technology," *Associated Press*, June 7, 2005, www.forbes.com; Riza Cruz, "This Design Exec Manages 31 People Spread Over Two States," *Business 2.0*, April 2002, p. 115; Cynthia G. Wagner, "Top 10 Reasons to Watch Trends," *The Futurist*, March-April 2002, pp. 68+; Wayne Burkan, "Developing Your Wide-Angle Vision," *The Futurist*, March 1998, pp. 35+; Edward Cornish, "How We Can Anticipate Future Events," *The Futurist*, July 2001, pp. 26+; "Techniques for Forecasting," *The Futurist*, March 2001, p. 56.
19. Donald G. McNeil Jr., "Demographic 'Bomb' May Only Go 'Pop!'" *New York Times*, August 29, 2004, sec. 4, p. 1; "Survey: Forever Young," *The Economist*, March 27, 2004, pp. 53–54.
20. Sebastian Moffett, "Senior Moment: Fast-Aging Japan Keeps Its Elders on the Job Longer," *Wall Street Journal*, June 15, 2005, pp. A1+.
21. *The Central Intelligence Agency's World Factbook*.
22. "Population of the Number of Households and Families in the United States: 1995–2010," P25–1129, U.S. Department of Commerce.
23. Laura Koss-Feder, "Out and About," *Marketing News*, May 25, 1998, pp. 1, 20.
24. "Rural Population and Migration: Overview," Economic Research Service, U.S. Department of Agriculture.
25. Christopher Reynolds, "Magnetic South," *Forecast*, September 2003, p. 6.
26. David Leonhardt, "Two-Tier Marketing," *BusinessWeek*, March 17, 1997, pp. 82–90; Robert H. Franc, "Yes, the Rich Get Richer, but There's More to the Story," *Columbia Journalism Review*, November 1, 2000.
27. Pamela Paul, "Corporate Responsibility," *American Demographics*, May 2002, pp. 24–25.
28. Stephen Baker, "Wiser about the Web," *BusinessWeek*, March 27, 2006, pp. 53–57.
29. Paul Wenske, "You Too Could Lose $19,000!" *Kansas City Star*, October 31, 1999; "Clearing House Suit Chronology," *Associated Press*, January 26, 2001.
30. Laura Zinn, "Teens: Here Comes the Biggest Wave Yet," *BusinessWeek*, April 11, 2004, pp. 76–86.
31. Subhabrata Bobby Banerjee, Easwar S. Iyer, and Rajiv K Kashyap, "Corporate Environmentalism: Antecedents and Influence of Industry Type," *Journal of Marketing*, 67 (April 2003): 106–122.
32. Jacquelyn A. Ottman, Edwin R. Stafford, and Cathy L. Hartman, "Avoiding Green Marketing Myopia," *Environment* (June 2006): 22–36.
33. See Dorothy Cohen, *Legal Issues on Marketing Decision Making* (Cincinnati: South-Western, 1995).

PART II Connecting with Customers

CHAPTER 4

Creating Customer Value, Satisfaction, and Loyalty

> In this chapter, we will address the following questions:
>
> 1. How can companies deliver customer value, satisfaction, and loyalty?
> 2. What is the lifetime value of a customer, and why is it important to marketers?
> 3. How can companies cultivate strong customer relationships?
> 4. What is the role of database marketing in customer relationship management?

MARKETING MANAGEMENT AT RITZ-CARLTON

The Ritz-Carlton hotel chain, owned by Marriott International, is known throughout the world for its singular focus on providing exceptional service and luxurious amenities. This customer-centered approach is expressed by the company's motto: "We are ladies and gentlemen serving ladies and gentlemen." Guests at any of the 62 Ritz-Carlton hotels in 21 countries notice the brand's famed personal touch immediately upon checking in, when they are greeted by name.

Ritz-Carlton creates a daily "Service Quality Index"(SQI) at each of its locations, so employees can continually monitor key guest service processes and swiftly address any potential problems. At corporate headquarters in Maryland, management can check the SQIs of all Ritz-Carlton hotels and instantly analyze each location's performance. Other customer service initiatives include the CLASS (Customer Loyalty Anticipation Satisfaction System) database that contains the preferences and requirements of repeat Ritz-Carlton guests, and the CARE (Clean and Repair Everything) room maintenance system that ensures all guestrooms are checked and free of defects every 90 days. Such initiatives helped Ritz-Carlton become the only service company to win the Malcolm Baldrige National Quality Award twice. And they've enabled Ritz-Carlton to forge long-lasting customer relationships, as evidenced by the hotel's Top 20 ranking on the Brand Keys 2006 Customer Loyalty Index.[1]

Today, companies face their toughest competition ever. Moving from a product and sales philosophy to a holistic marketing philosophy, however, gives them a better chance of outperforming the competition. And the cornerstone of a well-conceived marketing orientation is strong customer relationships. In this chapter, we discuss how companies can win customer loyalty and improve profits by doing a better job of meeting or exceeding customer expectations. We also discuss the use of database marketing for customer relationship management.

BUILDING CUSTOMER VALUE AND SATISFACTION

Consumers are more educated and informed than ever, and they have the tools to verify companies' claims and seek out superior alternatives.[2] How then do they ultimately make choices? Customers tend to be value-maximizers, within the bounds of search costs and limited knowledge, mobility, and income. They estimate which offer will deliver the most perceived value and act on it. Whether the offer lives up to expectation affects customer satisfaction and the probability that the customer will purchase the product again.

Customer Perceived Value

Customer perceived value (CPV) is the difference between the prospective customer's evaluation of all the benefits and all the costs of an offering and the perceived alternatives (see Figure 4.1). **Total customer value** is the perceived monetary value of the bundle of economic, functional, and psychological benefits customers expect from a given market offering because of the products, services, personnel, and image involved. **Total customer cost** is the perceived bundle of costs that customers expect to incur in evaluating, obtaining, using, and disposing of the given market offering, including monetary, time, energy, and psychic costs.

    Suppose the buyer for a residential construction company wants to buy a tractor from either Caterpillar or Komatsu. After evaluating the two tractors, he decides that Caterpillar has greater product benefits, based on perceived reliability, durability, performance, and resale value. He also decides that Caterpillar's personnel are more knowledgeable and perceives that the company will provide better services, such as maintenance. Finally, he places higher value on Caterpillar's corporate image. He adds up all the benefits from these four sources—product, services, personnel, and image—and perceives Caterpillar as delivering greater customer benefits.

    The buyer also examines his total cost of transacting with Caterpillar versus Komatsu, including money plus the time, energy, and psychic costs expended in product acquisition, usage, maintenance, ownership, and disposal. Then the buyer compares Caterpillar's total customer cost to its total customer benefits and Komatsu's total customer cost to its total customer benefits. In the end, the buyer will buy from the source he thinks delivers the highest perceived value.

FIGURE 4.1 Determinants of Customer-Perceived Value

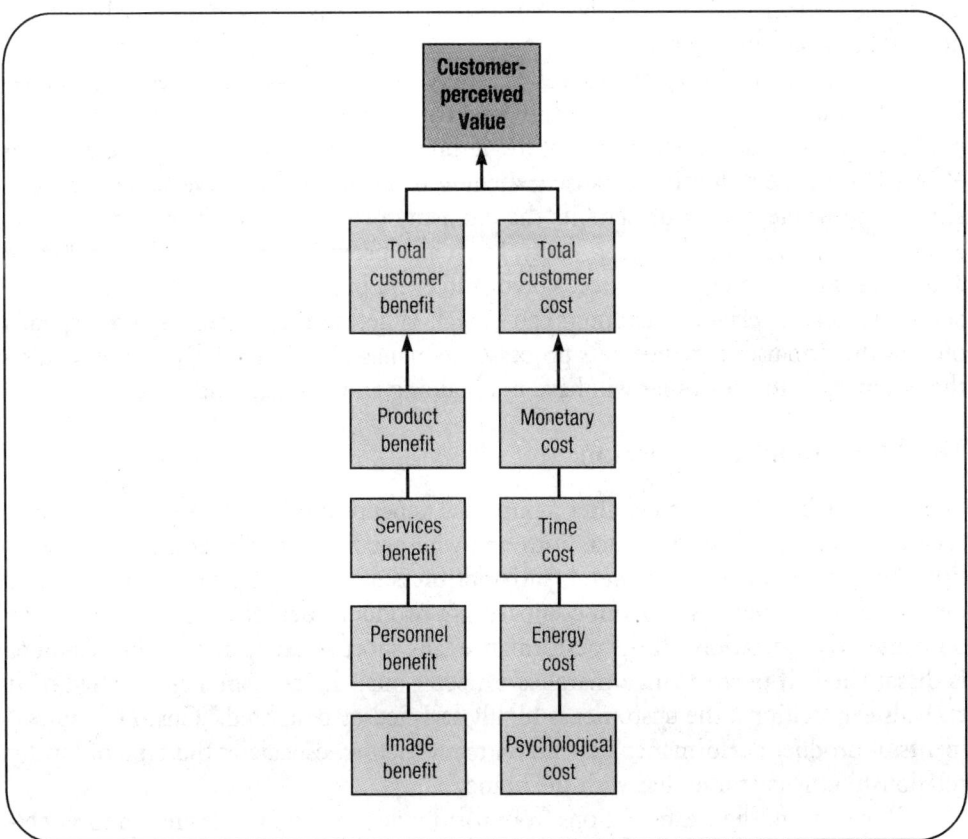

Caterpillar can make this sale by improving its offer and delivering more customer-perceived value than Komatsu. First, it can increase total customer benefit by improving economic, functional, and psychological benefits of its product, services, personnel, and/or image. Second, it can reduce the buyer's nonmonetary costs by reducing the time, energy, and psychic costs. Third, it can reduce its product's monetary cost.[3]

Some marketers might argue that this process is too rational. Suppose the customer chooses the Komatsu tractor. How can we explain this choice? Three possibilities are:

1. *The buyer might be under orders to buy at the lowest price.* To win this sale, Caterpillar must convince the buyer's manager that buying on price alone will result in lower long-term profits and customer value.
2. *The buyer will retire before the company realizes that the Komatsu tractor is more expensive to operate.* To win this sale, Caterpillar must convince other people in the buyer's company that it delivers greater long-term value.
3. *The buyer enjoys a long-term friendship with the Komatsu salesperson.* Here, Caterpillar must show the buyer that the Komatsu tractor will draw complaints from the tractor operators when they discover its high fuel cost and need for frequent repairs.

Customer perceived value is a useful framework that applies to many situations and yields rich insights. Here are its implications: First, the marketer must assess the total customer benefit and total customer cost associated with each competitor's offer to know how his or her offer rates in the buyer's mind. Second, the marketer who is at a customer-perceived-value disadvantage can try to increase total customer benefit or decrease total customer cost.[4]

Consumers have varying degrees of loyalty to specific brands, stores, and companies. Oliver defines **loyalty** as "A deeply held commitment to re-buy or re-patronize a preferred product or service in the future despite situational influences and marketing efforts having the potential to cause switching behavior."[5] The *value proposition* consists of the whole cluster of benefits the company promises to deliver. For example, Volvo's core positioning has been safety, but it also promises other benefits, including a long-lasting car and good service. Volvo (and every brand) must represent a promise about the total experience customers can expect. Whether the promise is kept depends on how the firm uses core business processes to manage its **value-delivery system**, all the experiences the customer will have in obtaining and using the offering.[6]

Total Customer Satisfaction

Whether the buyer is satisfied after a purchase depends on the offer's performance in relationship to the buyer's expectations and whether the buyer interprets any deviations between the two.[7] In general, **satisfaction** is a person's feelings of pleasure or disappointment that result from comparing a product's perceived performance (or outcome) to expectations. If the performance falls short of expectations, the customer is dissatisfied. If performance matches expectations, the customer is satisfied; if it exceeds expectations, the customer is highly satisfied or delighted.[8] Customer assessments of product performance depend on many factors, especially the type of loyalty relationship the customer has with the brand.[9]

Buyers form their expectations from past buying experience; friends' and associates' advice; and marketers' and competitors' information and promises. If marketers raise expectations too high, the buyer is likely to be disappointed. However, if the company sets expectations too low, it won't attract enough buyers (although it will satisfy those who do buy).[10] Some of today's most successful companies are raising expectations and delivering performance to match. Korean automaker Kia has been successful in the U.S. market by offering low-priced, high-quality cars reliable enough to be backed by 10-year warranties.

However, high customer satisfaction is not the ultimate goal. If the company increases customer satisfaction by lowering its price or increasing its services, the result may be lower profits. The company might be able to increase its profitability by means other than increased satisfaction (for example, by improving manufacturing processes). Also, the company has many stakeholders, including employees, dealers, suppliers, and stockholders. Spending more to increase customer satisfaction might divert funds from increasing the satisfaction of other "partners." Ultimately, the company must try to deliver a high level of customer satisfaction subject to delivering acceptable levels of satisfaction to the other stakeholders, given its total resources.[11]

Monitoring Satisfaction

Many companies are systematically monitoring how well they treat their customers, identifying the factors that shape customer satisfaction, and making changes in their operations and marketing as a result.[12] A highly satisfied customer generally stays loyal longer, buys more as the firm introduces new products and upgrades existing products, talks favorably to others about the firm and its products, pays less attention to competing brands and is less sensitive to price, offers product or service ideas to the firm, and costs less to serve than new customers because transactions become routine.[13] Greater customer satisfaction has also been linked to higher stock-market returns and lower market risk.[14]

The link between satisfaction and loyalty, however, is not proportional. Suppose customer satisfaction is rated on a scale from one to five. At a very low level of customer satisfaction (level one), customers are likely to abandon the company and even bad-mouth it. At levels two to four, customers are fairly satisfied but still find it easy to switch when a better offer comes along. At level five, the customer is very likely to repurchase and even spread good word of mouth about the company. High satisfaction or delight creates an emotional bond with the brand or company, not just a rational preference. Xerox's executives found out that their "completely satisfied" customers were six times more likely to repurchase Xerox products over the following 18 months than their "very satisfied" customers.[15]

When customers rate their satisfaction with an element of the firm's performance—say, delivery—they may vary in how they define good performance. Two customers can report being "highly satisfied" for different reasons. One may be easily satisfied most of the time and the other might be hard to please but was pleased on this occasion.[16] Marketers can monitor customer satisfaction in a number of ways.[17] Bain's Frederick Reichheld suggests that perhaps only one question really matters: "How likely is it that you would recommend this product or service to a friend or colleague?" According to Reichheld, a willingness to recommend is based on how well the customer is treated by front-line employees, which in turn is determined by all the functional areas that contribute to a customer's experience.[18] For more on monitoring satisfaction, see "Marketing Skills: Gauging Customer Satisfaction."

MARKETING SKILLS: GAUGING CUSTOMER SATISFACTION

The vital skill of gauging customer satisfaction requires a working knowledge of marketing research coupled with a sensitivity for customer concerns. Marketers start by defining their specific research goals as they relate to customer satisfaction. Next, they build on their knowledge of customer behavior and attitudes to design the study and encourage participation. After gathering and analyzing data, marketers should communicate the findings internally to highlight good news, act on bad news, and plan new ways of satisfying customers. Finally, continuously surveying customers or repeating research at regular intervals allows marketers to follow satisfaction trends and determine the effect of changes.

McAlister's Deli, a 220-unit restaurant chain based in Mississippi, prints a satisfaction survey invitation on every receipt. Customers who call in and respond to a five-minute automated telephone survey receive a $3 discount on their next purchase. CEO Phil Friedman says that making changes based on this research has definitely made a difference in the chain's financial results: "Satisfaction equals loyalty equals increased checks."[19]

Product and Service Quality

Satisfaction will also depend on product and service quality. What exactly is quality? Various experts have defined it as "fitness for use," "conformance to requirements," and "freedom from variation." We will use the American Society for Quality Control's customer-centered definition: **Quality** (or grade) is the totality of features and characteristics of a product or service that bear on its ability to satisfy stated or implied needs.[20] The seller has delivered quality whenever the product or service meets or exceeds the customers' expectations. It is important to distinguish between *conformance* quality and *performance* quality. A Lexus provides higher performance quality than a Hyundai: The Lexus rides smoother, goes faster, and lasts longer. Yet both a Lexus and a Hyundai deliver the same conformance quality if all the units deliver their respective promised quality.

Studies have shown a high correlation between relative product quality and company profitability.[21] Total quality is everyone's job, just as marketing is everyone's job. Marketers play six roles in helping their companies define and deliver high-quality goods and services to target customers. First, they bear the major responsibility for correctly identifying customers' needs and requirements. Second, they must communicate customer expectations properly to product designers. Third, they must be sure that orders are filled correctly and on time. Fourth, they must provide customers with proper instructions, training, and technical assistance. Fifth, they must stay in touch with customers after the sale to ensure ongoing satisfaction. Sixth, they must gather customer ideas for product and service improvements and convey them to the appropriate departments. When marketers do all this, they're making substantial contributions to product and service quality, customer satisfaction, customer profitability, and company profitability.

MAXIMIZING CUSTOMER LIFETIME VALUE

Ultimately, marketing is the art of attracting and keeping profitable customers. Yet every firm loses money on some of its customers. The well-known 20–80 rule says that the top 20% of the customers often generates 80% or more of the firm's profits. In some cases the profit distribution may be more extreme—the most profitable 20% of customers (on a per capita basis) may contribute as much as 150% to 300% of profitability. The least profitable 10% to 20% of customers, on the other hand, can actually reduce profits of 50% to 200% per account, with the middle 60% to 70% breaking even.[22] The implication is that a firm could improve its profits by "firing" its worst customers.

The largest customers don't always yield the most profit, because these customers can demand considerable service and receive the deepest discounts. The smallest customers pay full price and receive minimal service, but transaction costs reduce their profitability. The midsize customers who receive good service and pay nearly full price are often the most profitable.

Customer Profitability

What makes a customer profitable? A **profitable customer** is a person, household, or company that over time yields a revenue stream that exceeds by an acceptable amount the company's cost stream for attracting, selling, and servicing that customer. Note that the emphasis is on the *lifetime* stream of revenue and cost, not on one transaction's profitability. Marketers can assess customer profitability individually, by market segment, or by channel.

Although many firms measure customer satisfaction, most fail to measure individual customer profitability. Banks say this is because a customer uses different banking services and the transactions are logged in different departments. However, banks that have succeeded in linking customer transactions are appalled by the number of unprofitable customers in their customer base. Some report losing money on over 45% of their customers.[23] More marketers are recognizing the need to manage customer portfolios, made up of different groups of customers defined in terms of their loyalty, profitability, and other factors.[24] One perspective is that a firm's portfolio consists of a combination of "acquaintances," "friends," and "partners" that are constantly changing.[25]

Figure 4.2 shows a useful type of profitability analysis.[26] Customers are arrayed along the columns and products are arrayed along the rows. Each cell contains a symbol representing the profitability of selling that product to that customer. Customer 1 is very profitable, buying three profitable products. Customer 2 represents mixed profitability, buying one profitable and one unprofitable product. Customer 3 is a losing customer, buying one profitable and two unprofitable products. What can the company do about customers 2 and 3? It can either (1) raise the price of its less profitable products or eliminate them; or (2) try to sell customers 2 and 3 its profitable products. In fact, the firm should encourage unprofitable customers to switch to competitors.

Customer profitability analysis (CPA) is best conducted with an accounting technique called Activity-Based Costing (ABC). The company estimates all revenue coming from the customer, less all costs (including production, distribution, and all company resources that go into serving that customer). This helps classify customers into different profit tiers. Table 4.1 shows how a firm can classify its customers in terms of which are valuable and vulnerable; each of the four segments suggests different marketing and competitive activities.[27]

FIGURE 4.2 Customer-Product Profitability Analysis

		Customers			
		C_1	C_2	C_3	
Products	P_1	+	+	+	Highly profitable product
	P_2	+			Profitable product
	P_3		–	–	Losing product
	P_4	+		–	Mixed-bag product
		High-profit customer	Mixed-bag customer	Losing customer	

TABLE 4.1 Customer Selection Grid

	Vulnerable	Not Vulnerable
Valuable	These customers are profitable but not completely happy with the company. Find out and address their sources of vulnerability to **retain them**.	These customers are loyal and profitable. Don't take them for granted, but **maintain margins** and reap the benefits of their satisfaction.
Not Valuable	These customers are likely to defect. Let them go or even **encourage their departure**.	These unprofitable customers are happy. Try to **make them valuable or vulnerable**.

Source: John H. Roberts, "Defensive Marketing: How a Strong Incumbent Can Protect Its Position," Harvard Business Review (November 2005), p. 156.

TABLE 4.2 A Hypothetical Example to Illustrate CLV Calculations

	Year 0	Year 1	Year 2	Year 3	Year 4	Year 5	Year 6	Year 7	Year 8	Year 9	Year 10
Number of Customers	100	90	80	72	60	48	34	23	12	6	2
Revenue per Customer		100	110	120	125	130	135	140	142	143	145
Variable Cost per Customer		70	72	75	76	78	79	80	81	82	83
Margin per Customer		30	38	45	49	52	56	60	61	61	62
Acquisition Cost per Customer	40										
Total Cost or Profit	−4000	2700	3040	3240	2940	2496	1904	1380	732	366	124
Present Value	−4000	2454.55	2512.40	2434.26	2008.06	1549.82	1074.76	708.16	341.48	155.22	47.81

Source: Sunil Gupta and Donald R. Lehmann, "Models of Customer Value," in Handbook of Marketing Decision Models, ed. Berend Wierenga (Springer Science & Business Media), 2007.

Measuring Customer Lifetime Value

The case for maximizing long-term customer profitability is captured in the concept of customer lifetime value.[28] **Customer lifetime value (CLV)** describes the net present value of the stream of future profits expected over the customer's lifetime purchases. The company must subtract from its expected revenues the expected costs of attracting, selling, and servicing that customer's account, applying the appropriate discount rate (say, between 10% and 20%, depending on cost of capital and risk attitudes). Lifetime value calculations for a particular offering can be tens of thousands of dollars or even more.[29]

Many methods exist to measure customer lifetime value.[30] Don Lehmann and Sunil Gupta illustrate their approach by calculating the CLV of 100 customers over a 10-year period (see Table 4.2). In this example, the firm acquires 100 customers with an acquisition cost per customer of $40. Therefore, in year 0, it spends $4,000. Some of these customers defect each year. The present value of the profits from this cohort of customers over 10 years is $13,286.52. The net CLV (after deducting acquisition costs) is $9,286.52 or $92.87 per customer.

CULTIVATING CUSTOMER RELATIONSHIPS

Maximizing customer value means cultivating long-term customer relationships. Companies are now moving away from wasteful mass marketing to precision marketing designed to build strong customer relationships.[31] **Customer relationship management (CRM)** is the process of carefully managing detailed information about individual customers and all customer "touch points" to maximize customer loyalty. A *customer touch point* is any occasion on which a customer encounters the brand and product—from actual experience to personal or mass communications to casual observation. The touch points for a hotel include reservations, check-in and checkout, frequent-stay programs, room service, business services, exercise facilities, and restaurants.

Customer relationship management enables companies to provide excellent real-time customer service through the effective use of individual account information. Based on what they know about each valued customer, companies can customize market offerings, services, programs, messages, and media. CRM is important because a major driver of company profitability is the aggregate value of the company's customer base.[32] Peppers and Rogers outline a four-step framework for one-to-one marketing that can be adapted to CRM marketing as follows:[33]

1. *Identify your prospects and customers.* Don't go after everyone. Build, maintain, and mine a rich customer database with information derived from all the channels and customer touch points.
2. *Differentiate customers in terms of (1) their needs and (2) their value to your company.* Spend proportionately more effort on the most valuable customers. Calculate customer lifetime value and estimate net present value of all future profits coming from purchases, margin levels, and referrals, less customer-specific servicing costs.
3. *Interact with individual customers to improve your knowledge about their individual needs and to build stronger relationships.* Facilitate customer/company interaction through the company contact center and Web site.
4. *Customize products, services, and messages to each customer.* Formulate customized offerings that can be communicated in a personalized way.

A firm can improve the value of its customer base by reducing the rate of customer defection; increasing the longevity of the customer relationship; enhancing the growth potential of each customer through "share of wallet," cross-selling, and up-selling; making low-profit customers more profitable or terminating them; and treating high-value customers in a special way.[34]

Attracting and Retaining Customers

Companies seeking to expand their profits and sales have to spend considerable time and resources searching for new customers. To generate leads, they use advertising, direct mail, telemarketing, trade shows, and other methods to reach possible new prospects. Different types of acquisition methods can yield different types of customers with varying CLVs. One study showed that customers acquired through the offer of a 35% discount had about one-half the long-term value of customers acquired without any discount.[35]

It is not enough, however, to attract new customers; the company must keep them and increase their business.[36] Too many companies suffer from high **customer churn**, or defection. Many cellular carriers and cable TV operators, for example, lose 25% of their subscribers each year at an estimated cost of $2 billion to $4 billion. To reduce churn, the firm must first define and measure its retention rate; distinguish the causes of customer attrition and identify those that can be managed better; and compare the lost profit equal to the customer's lifetime value from a lost customer to the cost of lowering the defection rate. If the cost to discourage defection is lower than the lost profit, the firm should spend to retain the customer.

Figure 4.3 shows the main steps in attracting and retaining customers. The starting point is everyone who might conceivably buy the product or service (*potentials*). From these the company determines good *prospects*, people or organizations with the motivation, ability and opportunity to buy. The firm uses marketing to convert prospects into *first-time customers*, then into *repeat customers*, and then into *clients*, whom the company treats as special. The next challenge is to turn clients into *members* by starting a program that offers benefits to customers who join and then into *advocates* who recommend the company and its offerings to others. The ultimate challenge is to turn advocates into *partners*.

More companies are recognizing the benefits of satisfying and retaining current customers. Remember, acquiring new customers can cost five times more than the cost of satisfying and retaining current customers. On average, companies lose 10% of their customers each year. Yet by reducing the customer defection rate by 5%, companies can increase profits by 25% to 85%, depending on the industry. Also, the customer profit rate tends to increase over the life of the retained customer, due to increased purchases, referrals, price premiums, and reduced servicing costs.[37]

Building Loyalty

Companies that want to form strong customer bonds need to attend to a number of different considerations (see Figure 4.4). One set of researchers sees retention-building activities as adding financial benefits, social benefits, or structural ties.[38] Interacting with customers, developing loyalty programs, personalizing marketing, and creating institutional ties are four key marketing activities that companies are using to build customer loyalty.

Interacting with Customers Listening to customers is crucial to customer relationship management. Some companies have created an ongoing mechanism that keeps senior managers permanently plugged in to front-line customer feedback. For example, Chicken of the Sea has 80,000 members in its Mermaid Club, a core-customer group treated to coupons and special offers. In return, club members provide valuable feedback on what the company is doing and is thinking of doing. When the company considered introducing canned whitefish, members emphatically rejected the idea and the company chose not to introduce it.[39]

Listening is only part of the story. It's also important to be a customer advocate and, as much as possible, take the customers' side on issues, understanding their point of view.[40] *Customer evangelists* are an especially valuable group because, say authors Ben

FIGURE 4.3 The Customer Development Process

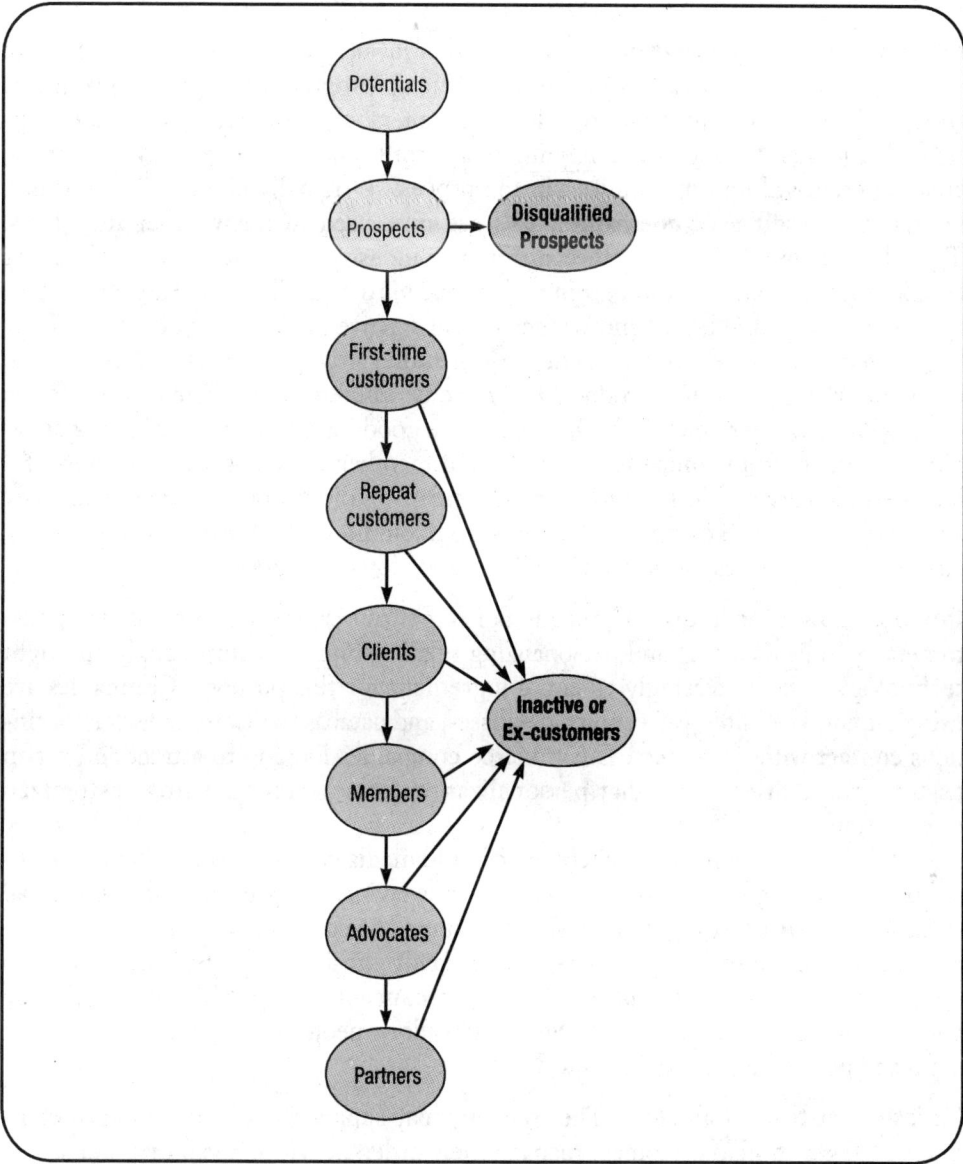

Source: Jill Griffin, "Customer Loyalty: How to Earn It, How to Keep It." (New York: Lexington Books, 1995), p. 36. Reprinted by permission.

FIGURE 4.4 Forming Strong Customer Bonds

- Create superior products, services, and experiences for the target market.
- Get cross-departmental participation in planning and managing the customer satisfaction and retention process.
- Integrate the "voice of the customer" to capture stated and unstated needs or requirements in all business decisions.
- Organize and make accessible a database of information on individual customer needs, preferences, contacts, purchase frequency, and satisfaction.
- Make it easy for customers to reach appropriate company personnel and express their needs, perceptions, and complaints.
- Assess potential of frequency programs and club marketing programs.
- Run award programs recognizing outstanding employees.

McConnell and Jackie Huba, these customers not only buy a company's offerings but also voluntarily spread the word, recruiting friends and colleagues on the company's behalf.[41]

Developing Loyalty Programs Two customer loyalty programs that companies can offer are frequency programs and club membership programs. **Frequency programs (FPs)** are designed to provide rewards to customers who buy frequently and in substantial amounts.[42] They can help build long-term loyalty with high CLV customers, creating cross-selling opportunities in the process. Originally pioneered by airlines, hotels, and credit card companies, FPs are now used in many other industries. Typically, the first firm to introduce an FP in an industry gains the most benefit. After competitors respond, FPs can become a financial burden to all the offering companies, although some marketers are more efficient and creative in managing FPs.

Many companies have created **club membership programs**, either open to everyone who purchases a product or service or limited to an affinity group (or to those willing to pay a small fee). Open clubs are good for building a database or snagging customers from competitors, yet limited membership clubs are more powerful long-term loyalty builders. Fees and membership conditions prevent those with only a fleeting interest in a company's products from joining while attracting and retaining customers who are responsible for the largest portion of business.

Personalizing Marketing Company personnel can create strong bonds with customers by individualizing and personalizing relationships. Not surprisingly, the right technology is an increasingly essential ingredient for this purpose. Companies are using e-mail, Web sites, call centers, databases, and database software to foster continuous contact with customers. E-commerce companies looking to attract and retain customers are discovering that personalization goes beyond creating customized information.

Even the BBC, British archetype of an old media company, is reaping the benefits of customizing its offerings, a practice that is taking it well beyond its commercial rivals in UK broadcasting. Its Web site, backstage.bbc.co.uk, provides data, resources, and support for Internet developers and designers—inside and outside the BBC—to share so they can build prototypes of new concepts using BBC material. One consumer-created prototype called Sport Map allows people to find the nearest soccer team and get that team's latest news.[43]

Creating Institutional Ties The company may supply special equipment or computer linkages to help customers manage their orders, payroll, inventory, and so on. Customers are less inclined to switch to another supplier when this would involve high capital costs, high search costs, or the loss of loyal-customer discounts. A good example is McKesson Corporation, a leading pharmaceutical wholesaler, which invested millions of dollars in electronic capabilities to help independent pharmacies manage inventory, order entry processes, and shelf space.

CUSTOMER DATABASES AND DATABASE MARKETING

Marketers must know their customers.[44] And in order to know the customer, the firm must collect information and store it in a database for database marketing. A **customer database** is an organized collection of comprehensive information about individual customers or prospects that is current, accessible, and actionable for such marketing purposes as lead generation, lead qualification, sale of a product or service, or maintenance of customer relationships. **Database marketing** is the process of building, maintaining, and using customer databases and other databases (products, suppliers, resellers) to make contact, facilitate transactions, and build customer relationships.

A customer database contains much more information than a *customer mailing list*, which is simply a set of names, addresses, and telephone numbers. Ideally, a customer database would contain the consumer's past purchases, demographics (age, income, family members, birthdays), psychographics (activities, interests, and opinions), mediagraphics (preferred media), and other useful information. A **business database** should contain past purchases of business customers; past volumes, prices, and profits; buyer team member names (and their ages, birthdays, hobbies, and favorite foods); status of current contracts; an estimate of the supplier's share of the customer's business; competitive suppliers; assessment of competitive strengths and weaknesses in selling and servicing the account; and buying practices, patterns, and policies. "Breakthrough Marketing: Tesco" describes how the U.K. supermarket giant has used its database to attract and engage customers.

Data Warehouses and Datamining

Savvy companies capture data every time a customer comes into contact with any of their departments. Touch points include a customer purchase, a customer-requested service call, an online query, or a mail-in rebate card. The information is collected by the company's contact center and organized into a **data warehouse** where marketers can capture, query, and analyze it to draw inferences about an individual customer's needs and responses. This allows the company's customer service reps or telemarketers to respond to customer inquiries based on a total picture of the customer relationship. Through **datamining**, marketing statisticians can extract useful information

BREAKTHROUGH MARKETING: TESCO

In the early 1980s, the U.K. supermarket chain Tesco had a reputation as a "pile it high and sell it cheap" mass-market retailer. By 1990, to gain share against Sainsbury's, the more upscale market leader, Tesco was upgrading its stores, improving the shopping experience, and adding new products. A new image campaign highlighted these customer-friendly changes and Tesco's commitment to "doing right by the customer." The result: More than a million new customers and an increase in revenues that, by 1995, allowed Tesco to surpass Sainsbury's as the market leader.

Tesco then introduced the initiative that made it a world-class example of how to build lasting relationships with customers: the Tesco Clubcard. A loyalty card with discounts and special offers tailored to individual shoppers, the Clubcard is also a powerful tool for building a comprehensive customer database. Based on their shopping habits, Tesco customers receive one of 4 million different variations of the quarterly Clubcard statement with targeted promotions. Analyzing Clubcard purchases helps Tesco do a better job of pricing products and scheduling promotions, at a $500 million savings. The Clubcard has helped Tesco expand in Europe, Asia, and beyond, including new stores in California, Arizona, and Nevada, bringing its total annual sales to $85 billion.[45]

about individuals, trends, and segments from the mass of data. Datamining uses sophisticated statistical and mathematical techniques such as cluster analysis, automatic interaction detection, predictive modeling, and neural networking.[46]

In general, companies can use their databases to (1) identify the best prospects by sorting through responses to marketing efforts; (2) match a specific offer with a specific customer as a way to sell, cross-sell, and up-sell; (3) deepen customer loyalty by remembering customer preferences and offering relevant incentives and information; (4) reactivate customer purchasing through reminders or timely promotions; and (5) avoid serious mistakes such as sending a customer two offers for the same product but at different prices.

The Downside of Database Marketing and CRM

Four problems can prevent a firm from effectively using database marketing for CRM. The first is the large investment in computer hardware, database software, analytical programs, communication links, and skilled personnel as well as the difficulty in collecting the right data during all company interactions with customers. Thus, building a customer database would not be worthwhile when the product is a once-in-a-lifetime purchase (e.g., a grand piano); when customers show little brand loyalty; when the unit sale is very small (e.g., a candy bar); and when the cost of gathering data is too high.

The second problem is the difficulty of getting everyone in the company to be customer oriented and use the available information for CRM rather than carrying on traditional transaction marketing. The third problem is that not all customers want an ongoing relationship with a company and may resent having their personal data collected and stored. Marketers must be concerned about customer attitudes toward privacy and security; online businesses in particular would be smart to explain their privacy policies and allow consumers to avoid having their information stored in a database.

A fourth problem is that the assumptions behind CRM may not always hold true.[47] For example, it may not cost less to serve more loyal customers. High-volume customers often know their value and can extract premium service and/or price discounts; loyal customers may expect and demand more from the firm and resent the company charging full or higher prices. One consulting firm reported that 70% of companies found little or no improvement from implementing a CRM system. The reasons are many: the system was poorly designed, it became too expensive, employees didn't make much use of it or report much benefit, and collaborators ignored the system. Each company must therefore determine how much and where to invest in building and using database marketing to manage its customer relationships.

EXECUTIVE SUMMARY

Customers are value maximizers. They form an expectation of value and act on it. Buyers will buy from the firm that they perceive to offer the highest customer-delivered value, defined as the difference between total customer benefits and total customer cost. A buyer's satisfaction is a function of the product's perceived performance and the buyer's expectations. Recognizing that high satisfaction leads to high customer loyalty, many companies today are aiming for total customer satisfaction. For such companies, customer satisfaction is both a goal and a marketing tool. Satisfaction also depends on quality, the totality of features and characteristics of a product or service that bear on its ability to satisfy stated or implied needs.

Companies need to understand which customers are profitable and calculate each customer's lifetime value. They must also determine how to increase the value of the customer base. Losing profitable customers can dramatically affect a firm's profits. The key to retention is customer relationship marketing (CRM), the process of managing detailed information about individual customers and managing all customer touch points to maximize loyalty. Customer relationship management often requires building a customer database and using datamining to detect trends, segments, and individual needs.

NOTES

1. Kirby Lee Davis, "Ritz-Carlton Executive Speaks on Building Quality Work Force at Seminar in Tulsa," *Journal Record (Oklahoma City)*, April 10, 2007; www.ritzcarlton.com; www.brandkeys.com.
2. Glen L. Urban, "The Emerging Era of Customer Advocacy," *MIT Sloan Management Review*, Winter 2004, pp. 77–82.
3. Irwin P. Levin and Richard D. Johnson, "Estimating Price-Quality Tradeoffs Using Comparative Judgments," *Journal of Consumer Research* (June 11, 1984): 593–600. Customer perceived value can be measured as a difference or as a ratio. If total customer value is $20,000 and total customer cost is $16,000, then the customer perceived value is $4,000 (measured as a difference) or 1.25 (measured as a ratio). Ratios that are used to compare offers are often called *value-price ratios*.
4. For more on customer perceived value, see David C. Swaddling and Charles Miller, *Customer Power* (Dublin, Ohio: The Wellington Press, 2001).
5. Gary Hamel, "Strategy as Revolution," *Harvard Business Review* (July–August 1996): 69–82.
6. Vikas Mittal, Eugene W. Anderson, Akin Sayrak, and Pandu Tadilamalla, "Dual Emphasis and the Long-Term Financial Impact of Customer Satisfaction," *Marketing Science*, 24 (Fall 2005): 544–555; Michael J. Lanning, *Delivering Profitable Value* (Oxford, U.K.: Capstone, 1998).
7. Michael Tsiros, Vikas Mittal, William T. Ross Jr., "The Role of Attributions in Customer Satisfaction: A Reexamination," *Journal of Consumer Research* (September 2004): 476–483.
8. For some provocative analysis, see Susan Fournier and David Glenmick, "Rediscovering Satisfaction," *Journal of Marketing* (October 1999): 5–23 and Praveen K. Kopalle and Donald R. Lehmann, "Setting Quality Expectations When Entering a Market: What Should the Promise Be?" *Marketing Science*, 25 (January-February, 2006): 8–24.
9. Jennifer Aaker, Susan Fournier, and S. Adam Brasel, "When Good Brands Do Bad," *Journal of Consumer Research*, 31 (June, 2004): 1–16; Pankaj Aggrawal, "The Effects of Brand Relationship Norms on Consumer Attitudes and Behavior," *Journal of Consumer Research*, 31 (June, 2004): 87–101.
10. For an interesting analysis of the effects of different types of expectations, see William Boulding, Ajay Kalra, and Richard Staelin, "The Quality Double Whammy," *Marketing Service* 18, no. 4 (1999): 463–484.
11. For in-depth discussion, see Michael D. Johnson and Anders Gustafsson, *Improving Customer Satisfaction, Loyalty, and Profit* (San Francisco, CA: Jossey-Bass, 2000).
12. Neil A. Morgan, Eugene W. Anderson, and Vikas Mittal, "Understanding Firms' Customer Satisfaction Information Usage," *Journal of Marketing*, 69 (July, 2005): 131–151.
13. See, for example, Christian Homburg, Nicole Koschate, and Wayne D. Hoyer, "Do Satisfied Customers Really Pay More? A Study of the Relationship between Customer Satisfaction and Willingness to Pay," *Journal of Marketing*, 69 (April, 2005): 84–96.
14. Claes Fornell, Sunil Mithas, Forrest V. Morgeson III, and M. S. Krishnan, "Customer Satisfaction and Stock Prices: High Returns, Low Risk," *Journal of Marketing*, 70 (January 2006): 3–14. See also: Eugene W. Anderson, Claes Fornell, and Sanal K. Mazvancheryl, "Customer Satisfaction and Shareholder Value," *Journal of Marketing*, 68 (October 2004): 172–185; Thomas S. Gruca and Lopo L. Rego, "Customer Satisfaction, Cash Flow, and Shareholder Value," *Journal of Marketing*, 69 (July 2005): 115–130.
15. Thomas O. Jones and W. Earl Sasser Jr., "Why Satisfied Customers Defect," *Harvard Business Review* (November–December 1995): 88–99.

16. Note that managers and salespeople can manipulate customer satisfaction ratings: They can be especially nice to customers just before the survey; they can also try to exclude unhappy customers. Another danger is that if customers know the company will go out of its way to please them, some may express high dissatisfaction in order to receive more concessions.

17. For an empirical comparison of methods for measuring customer satisfaction, see Neil A. Morgan and Lopo Leotto Rego, "The Value Different Customer Satisfaction and Loyalty Metrics in Predicting Business Performance," *Marketing Science*, 25 (September-October 2006): 426–439.

18. Matthew Creamer, "Do You Know Your Score?" *Advertising Age*, July 3, 2006, pp. 1–24; Frederick K. Reichheld, "The One Number You Need to Grow," *Harvard Business Review* (December 2003): 46–54.

19. "Humble Beginning to Major Player: McAlister's Deli Has Over 220 Units with Franchise Commitments for 200 More Over the Next Five Years," *Nation's Restaurant News*, December 11, 2006, p. S40; Christine Zimmerman, "Consumer Reports: Web-Based Results from Customer Surveys Give McAlister's Solutions for Satisfaction," *Chain Leader*, April 2005, pp. 48+; Jack Hayes, "Industry Execs: Best Customer Feedback Info Is 'Real' Thing," *Nation's Restaurant News*, March 18, 2002, pp. 4+; Leslie Wood and Michael Kirsch, "Performing Your Own Satisfaction Survey," *Agency Sales Magazine*, February 2002, p. 26.

20. Cyndee Miller, "U.S. Firms Lag in Meeting Global Quality Standards," *Marketing News*, February 15, 1993.

21. Robert D. Buzzell and Bradley T. Gale, *The PIMS Principles: Linking Strategy to Performance* (New York: The Free Press, 1987), ch. 6.

22. Lerzan Aksoy, Timothy L. Keiningham, and Terry G. Vavra, "Nearly Everything You Know About Loyalty Is Wrong," *Marketing News*, October 1, 2005, pp. 20–21; Timothy L. Keiningham, Terry G. Vavra, Lerzan Aksoy, and Henri Wallard, Loyalty Myths (Hoboken, NJ: John Wiley & Sons Inc., 2005).

23. Rakesh Niraj, Mahendra Gupta, and Chakravarthi Narasimhan, "Customer Profitability in a Supply Chain," *Journal of Marketing* (July 2001): 1–16.

24. Michael D. Johnson, and Fred Selnes, "Diversifying Your Customer Portfolio," *MIT Sloan Management Review*, Spring 2005, 46 (3), 11–14.

25. Michael D. Johnson, and Fred Selnes, "Customer Portfolio Management, *Journal of Marketing*, 68 (2) (April 2004): 1–17.

26. Thomas M. Petro, "Profitability: The Fifth P of Marketing," *Bank Marketing*, September 1990, pp. 48–52; "Who Are Your Best Customers?" *Bank Marketing*, October 1990, pp. 48–52.

27. These taxonomy come from the writings of John H. Roberts, "Defensive Marketing: How a Strong Incumbent Can Protect Its Position," *Harvard Business Review* (November 2005): 150–157; John Roberts, Charlie Nelson, and Pamela Morrison, "Defending the Beachhead: Telstra vs. Optus," *Business Strategy Review*, 12 (2001): 19–24.

28. Sunil Gupta, Donald R. Lehmann, and Jennifer Ames Stuart, "Valuing Customers," *Journal of Marketing Research*, 61 February 2004, pp. 7–18; Rajkumar Venkatesan and V. Kumar, "A Customer Lifetime Value Framework for Customer Selection and Resource Allocation Strategy," *Journal of Marketing*, 68 (October 2004): 106–125; V. Kumar, "Customer Lifetime Value," in the *Handbook of Marketing Research*, Rajiv Grover and Marco Vriens, eds. (Thousand Oaks, CA: Sage Publications, 2006), pp. 602–627.

29. V. Kumar, "Profitable Relationships, *Marketing Research*, 18 (Fall 2006): 41–46.

30. For some recent analysis and discussion, see Peter S. Fader, Bruce G. S. Hardie, and Ka Lok Lee, "RFM and CLV: Using Iso-Value Curves for Customer Base Analysis," *Journal of Marketing Research*, 62 (November 2005): 415–430; Michael Haenlein, Andreas M. Kaplan, and Detlef Schoder, "Valuing the Real Option of Abandoning Unprofitable Customers When Calculating Customer Lifetime Value, *Journal of Marketing*, 70 (July 2006): 5–20; and Teck-Hua Ho, Young-Hoon Park, and Yong-Pin Zhou, "Incorporating Satisfaction into Customer Value Analysis: Optimal Investment in Lifetime Value," *Marketing Science*, 25 (May-June 2006): 260–277.

31. Nicole E. Coviello, Roderick J. Brodie, Peter J. Danaher, and Wesley J. Johnston, "How Firms Relate to Their Markets: An Empirical Examination of Contemporary Marketing Practices," *Journal of Marketing* 66 (July 2002): 33–46.

32. Lanning, *Delivering Profitable Value*.

33. Don Peppers and Martha Rogers, *The One-to-One Future: Building Relationships One Customer at a Time* (New York: Doubleday, 1993); Don Peppers and Martha Rogers, *Enterprise One to One: Tools for Competing in the Interactive Age* (New York: Currency, 1997); Don Peppers and Martha Rogers, *The One-to-One Manager: Real-World Lessons in Customer Relationship Management* (New York:

Doubleday, 1999); Don Peppers, Martha Rogers, and Bob Dorf, *The One-to-One Fieldbook: The Complete Toolkit for Implementing a One-to-One Marketing Program* (New York: Bantam, 1999); Don Peppers and Martha Rogers, *One-to-One B2B: Customer Development Strategies for the Business-to-Business World* (New York: Doubleday, 2001).

34. Alan W. H. Grant and Leonard A. Schlesinger, "Realize Your Customer's Full Profit Potential," *Harvard Business Review* (September–October 1995): 59–72; Tom Ostenon, *Customer Share Marketing* (Upper Saddle River, NJ: Prentice-Hall, 2002).

35. Michael Lewis, "Customer Acquisition Promotions and Customer Asset Value," *Journal of Marketing Research*, 63 (May 2006): 195–203.

36. Werner Reinartz, Jacquelyn S. Thomas, and V. Kumar, "Balancing Acquisition and Retention Resources to Maximize Customer Profitability," *Journal of Marketing*, 69 (January 2005): 63–79.

37. Frederick F. Reichheld, *The Loyalty Effect* (Boston: Harvard Business School Press, 1996).

38. Leonard L. Berry and A. Parasuraman, *Marketing Services: Competing through Quality* (New York: The Free Press, 1991), pp. 136–142. For an academic examination in a business-to-business context, see Robert W. Palmatier, Srinath Gopalakrishna, and Mark B. Houston, "Returns on Business-to-Business Relationship Marketing Investments: Strategies for Leveraging Profits," *Marketing Science*, 25 (September–October 2006): 477–493.

39. Jim Edwards, "Broken Promises," *Brandweek*, May 22, 2006, pp. 23–28

40. Utpal M. Dholakia, "How Consumer Self-Determination Influences Relational Marketing Outcomes: Evidence from Longitudinal Field Studies," *Journal of Marketing Research*, 43 (February 2006), pp. 109–120.

41. Ben McConnell and Jackie Huba, "Learning to Leverage the Lunatic Fringe," *Point*, July/August 2006, pp. 14–15; Michael Krauss, "Work to Convert Customers into Evangelists," *Marketing News*, December 15, 2006, p. 6; Ben McConnell and Jackie Huba, *Creating Customer Evangelists: How Loyal Customers Become a Loyal Sales Force* (Chicago, IL: Kaplan Business, 2003).

42. For a review, see Grahame R. Dowling and Mark Uncles, "Do Customer Loyalty Programs Really Work?" *Sloan Management Review* 38, no. 4 (1997): 71–82.

43. Kerry Capell, "BBC: Step Right into the Telly," *Business Week*, July 24, 2006, p. 52; http://backstage.bbc.co.uk.

44. V. Kumar, Rajkumar Venkatesan, Werner Reinartz, "Knowing What to Sell, When and to Whom," *Harvard Business Review*, March 2006, pp. 131–137.

45. Sources: Cecilie Rohwedder, "Boss Talk: Tesco Studies Hard for U.S. Debut," *Wall Street Journal*, June 28, 2007, p. B1; Ashleye Sharpe and Joanna Bamford, "Tesco Stores Ltd." (paper presented at Advertising Effectiveness Awards, 2000); Hamish Pringle and Marjorie Thompson, *Brand Spirit* (New York: John Wiley, 1999); Elizabeth Rigby, "Prosperous Tesco Takes Retailing to a New Level," *Financial Times*, September 21, 2005, p. 23; Richard Fletcher, "Leahy Shrugs Off Talk of a 'Brain Drain,'" *Sunday Times (London)*, January 29, 2006, p. 7; Laura Cohn, "A Grocery War That's Not About Food," *BusinessWeek*, October 20, 2003, p. 30.

46. James Lattin, Doug Carroll, and Paul Green, *Analyzing Multivariate Data* (Florence, KY: Thomson Brooks/Cole, 2003); Christopher R. Stephens and R. Sukumar, "An Introduction to Data Mining," in the *Handbook of Marketing Research*, Rajiv Grover and Marco Vriens, eds. (Thousand Oaks, CA: Sage Publications, 2006), pp. 455–486.

47. Werner Reinartz and V. Kumar, "The Mismanagement of Customer Loyalty," *Harvard Business Review* (July 2002): 86–94; Susan M. Fournier, Susan Dobscha, and David Glen Mick, "Preventing the Premature Death of Relationship Marketing," *Harvard Business Review* (January–February 1998): 42–51.

CHAPTER 5

Analyzing Consumer Markets

> In this chapter, we will address the following questions:
>
> 1. How do consumer characteristics influence buying behavior?
> 2. What major psychological processes influence consumer responses to marketing?
> 3. How do marketers analyze consumer decision making?

MARKETING MANAGEMENT AT PROCTER & GAMBLE

With over 2.6 billion cell phone subscribers worldwide—more than 200 million in the United States alone—mobile marketing represents a major opportunity to reach consumers on the "third screen" (after the TV and the computer). That's why the household products giant Procter & Gamble, with global sales of $68 billion annually, is experimenting with a variety of mobile marketing programs.

For example, P&G combined guerilla marketing with mobile marketing in a promotion for its Crest Whitening Plus Scope Extreme Toothpaste. Consumers were prompted by ads on bar napkins and club bathroom signs to text the letters "IQ" to a specific number and have a chance to test their "Irresistibility IQ." As another example, when P&G held a mobile marketing sweepstakes for its Max Factor cosmetics brand, more than 250,000 people used their cell phones to enter. From this small start, the mobile advertising industry is expected to grow rapidly and reach $11 billion in revenues by 2011, according to Informa Telecoms & Media.[1]

Successful marketing requires that companies cultivate a connection with their customers. This is why firms like P&G look for customer trends that suggest new marketing opportunities. Adopting a holistic marketing orientation means understanding customers—gaining a 360-degree view of their daily lives and the changes that occur during their lifetimes so that the right products are marketed to the right customers in the right way. This chapter explores individual consumer buying dynamics; the next chapter explores the buying dynamics of businesses.

WHAT INFLUENCES CONSUMER BEHAVIOR?

Consumer behavior is the study of how individuals, groups, and organizations select, buy, use, and dispose of goods, services, ideas, or experiences to satisfy their needs and desires.[2] Marketers must fully understand both the theory and reality of consumer behavior. A consumer's buying behavior is influenced by cultural, social, and personal factors. Cultural factors exert the broadest and deepest influence.

Cultural Factors

Culture, subculture, and social class are particularly important influences on consumer buying behavior. **Culture** is the most fundamental determinant of a person's wants and behavior. Through family and other institutions, a child growing up in the United States is exposed to these cultural values: achievement and success, activity, efficiency and practicality, progress, material comfort, individualism, freedom, external comfort, humanitarianism, and youthfulness.[3]

Each culture consists of smaller *subcultures* that provide more specific identification and socialization for their members. Subcultures include nationalities, religions, racial groups, and geographic regions. When subcultures grow large and affluent enough, companies often design specialized marketing programs to serve them. *Multicultural marketing* grew out of careful marketing research, which revealed that ethnic and demographic niches did not always respond favorably to mass-market advertising. Now companies have capitalized on well-thought-out multicultural marketing strategies. For example, the retail chain David's Bridal targets Latino consumers with a Spanish-language Web site and special dresses for the Quinceañera, a celebration of a girls' transition to womanhood on her fifteenth birthday.[4]

Social classes are relatively homogeneous and enduring divisions in a society. They are hierarchically ordered and their members share similar values, interests, and behavior. One classic depiction of social classes in the United States defined seven ascending levels, as follows: (1) lower lowers, (2) upper lowers, (3) working class, (4) middle class, (5) upper middles, (6) lower uppers, and (7) upper uppers.[5]

Those within each class tend to behave more alike in dress, speech patterns, and recreational preferences than persons from different social classes. Also, persons are perceived as occupying inferior or superior positions according to social class. Note that social class is indicated by a cluster of variables—such as occupation, income, and education—rather than by any single variable. Finally, individuals can move up or down the social-class ladder during their lifetime. Marketers need to be aware that social classes show distinct product, brand, and media differences; because of language differences, they also must use advertising copy and dialogue that ring true to the targeted class.

Social Factors

In addition to cultural factors, a consumer's behavior is influenced by such social factors as reference groups, family, and social roles and statuses.

Reference Groups **Reference groups** consist of all of the groups that have a direct (face-to-face) or indirect influence on a person's attitudes or behavior. Groups having a direct influence on a person are called **membership groups**. Some *primary groups* are family, friends, neighbors, and co-workers, with whom individuals interact fairly continuously and informally. *Secondary groups*, such as professional and religious groups, tend to be more formal and require less continuous interaction. Reference groups expose people to new behaviors and lifestyles, influence attitudes and self-concept, and create pressures for conformity that may affect product and brand choices. People are also influenced by groups to which they do not belong. **Aspirational groups** are those a person hopes to join; **dissociative groups** are those whose values or behavior an individual rejects.

Where reference group is strong, marketers must determine how to reach and influence the group's opinion leaders. An **opinion leader** is the person who offers informal advice or information about a specific product or product category, such as which of several brands is best.[6] Marketers try to reach opinion leaders by identifying their demographic and psychographic characteristics, identifying their preferred media, and directing messages at them. In the United States, the hottest trends in teenage music, language, and fashion often start in the inner cities. Therefore, clothing companies like Hot Topic carefully monitor urban opinion leaders' style and behavior.

Family The family is the most important consumer buying organization in society—and its members are the most influential primary reference group.[7] The **family of orientation** consists of parents and siblings. From parents, we acquire our orientation toward religion, politics, and economics, as well as a sense of personal ambition, self-worth, and love.[8] A more direct influence on the everyday buying behavior of adults is the **family of procreation**—namely, one's spouse and children.

Marketers are interested in how the roles, behavior, and influence of family members affect purchasing for a variety of offerings.[9] For example, firms are realizing that women buy more technology than men do. This is why savvy stores are heeding women's complaints of being ignored, patronized, or offended by salespeople. The RadioShack chain began actively recruiting female store managers so that now a woman manages about one out of every seven stores.[10]

Children and teens wield considerable influence over family purchases. Children ages 4 to 12 directly or indirectly influence an estimated $700 billion in annual household purchases.[11] Direct influence describes children's hints, requests, and demands; indirect influence means that parents know the brands and product preferences of their children without hints or outright requests. By the time children are around two years old, they can often recognize characters, logos, and specific brands. Marketers are tapping into that audience with product tie-ins, placed at a child's eye level, on just about everything—from Scooby Doo vitamins to Elmo juice.[12] Further, research shows that teenagers are more active than ever before in helping parents choose cars, home entertainment equipment, or vacation spots.[13]

Roles and Statuses A person participates in many groups, such as family, clubs, and organizations. The person's position in each group can be defined in terms of role and status. A **role** consists of the activities a person is expected to perform. Each role carries a **status**. A Supreme Court justice has more status than a sales manager, and a sales manager has more status than an office clerk. An individual will choose products that communicate his or her role and actual or desired status in society. Thus, marketers must be aware of the status symbol potential of their products and brands.

Personal Factors

Consumers' buying decisions are also influenced by personal characteristics, including the buyer's age and stage in the life cycle; occupation and economic circumstances; personality and self-concept; and lifestyle and values.

Age and Stage in the Life Cycle   Our taste in clothes, furniture, and recreation is often related to our age. Consumption is also shaped by the *family life cycle* and the number, age, and gender of people in the household at any point in time. In addition, *psychological* life-cycle stages may matter, with adults experiencing certain "passages" or "transformations" in life.[14] Marketers should consider *critical life events or transitions*—marriage, childbirth, illness, divorce, widowhood—as giving rise to new needs that influence consumption behavior.

Occupation and Economic Circumstances   Occupation is another influence on consumption patterns. A blue-collar worker will buy work clothes, while a company president will buy dress suits and a country club membership. Marketers try to identify the occupational groups that have above-average interest in their offerings and even tailor their products for certain occupations. Software manufacturers, for example, design special programs for engineers, lawyers, physicians, and other occupational groups.

Product choice is greatly affected by a consumer's economic circumstances: spendable income (level, stability, and time pattern), savings and assets (including the percentage that is liquid), debts, borrowing power, and attitude toward spending and saving. Luxury-goods makers such as Gucci and Prada can be vulnerable to an economic downturn. If a recession is likely, marketers can redesign, reposition, and reprice their products—or introduce or emphasize discount brands—to continue to offer value to target customers.

Personality and Self-Concept   Each person has personality characteristics that influence buying behavior. **Personality** refers to the distinguishing psychological traits that lead to relatively consistent and enduring responses to environmental stimuli (including buying behavior). Personality is often described in terms of such traits as self-confidence, dominance, autonomy, deference, sociability, defensiveness, and adaptability.[15]

Personality can be useful in analyzing consumer behavior. The idea is that brands also have personalities and that consumers are likely to choose brands whose personalities match their own. **Brand personality** is the specific mix of human traits that we can attribute to a particular brand. Jennifer Aaker's research has identified five brand personality traits: sincerity, excitement, competence, sophistication, and ruggedness.[16] Cross-cultural studies have found that some of these traits—but not all—apply in other countries.[17]

Consumers often choose and use brands that have a brand personality consistent with their own *actual self-concept* (how we view ourselves), although the match may instead be based on the consumer's *ideal self-concept* (how we would like to view ourselves) or even on *others' self-concept* (how we think others see us).[18] These effects may be more pronounced for publicly consumed products as compared to privately consumed goods.[19] On the other hand, consumers who are sensitive to how others see them are more likely to choose brands whose personalities fit the consumption situation.[20] Often consumers have multiple aspects of self (serious professional, caring family member, active fun-lover) that may be evoked differently in different situations or around different types of people.

Lifestyle and Values People from the same subculture, social class, and occupation may actually lead quite different lifestyles. A **lifestyle** is a person's pattern of living as expressed in activities, interests, and opinions. Lifestyle portrays the "whole person" interacting with his or her environment. Marketers search for relationships between their products and lifestyle groups. For example, a computer manufacturer might find that most computer buyers are achievement-oriented and then aim its brand more clearly at the achiever lifestyle. As another example, organic food manufacturers are among the growing number of marketers targeting consumers in LOHAS segments—an acronym for *lifestyles of health and sustainability*, consumers who worry about the environment, are interested in sustainability, and spend money to advance their health and potential (see Table 5.1).

Lifestyles are shaped partly by whether consumers are *money constrained* or *time constrained*. Companies aiming to serve money-constrained consumers will create lower-cost offerings; those aiming to serve time-constrained consumers will create convenient offerings. "Breakthrough Marketing: IKEA" outlines IKEA's success in appealing to price-conscious shoppers.

Consumer decisions are also influenced by **core values**, the belief systems that underlie consumer attitudes and behaviors. Core values go much deeper than behav-

TABLE 5.1 LOHAS Market Segments

LOHAS Market Segments	
Sustainable Economy	**Alternative Healthcare**
Green building and industrial goods	Health and wellness solutions
Renewable energy	Acupuncture, homeopathy, naturopathy, etc.
Resource-efficient products	Holistic disease prevention
Socially responsible investing	Complementary medicine
Alternative transportation	*US Market—$30.7 billion*
Environmental management	
US Market—$76.47 billion	
Healthy Lifestyles	**Personal Development**
Natural, organics; nutritional products	Mind, body, and spirit products such as CDs, books, tapes, seminars
Food and beverage	Yoga, fitness, weight loss
Dietary supplements	Spiritual products and services
Personal care	*US Market—$10.63 billion*
US Market—$30 billion	
Ecological Lifestyles	
Ecological home and office products	
Organic/recycled fiber products	
Environmentally friendly appliances	
Eco-tourism and travel	
US Market—$81.19 billion	

Source: Based on http://www.lohas.com/

> **BREAKTHROUGH MARKETING: IKEA**
>
> IKEA, founded in 1943 by a 17-year-old Swede named Ingvar Kamprad, initially sold pens, Christmas cards, and seeds from a shed on Kamprad's family farm. Decades later, it has become a worldwide retail titan in home furnishings. In addition to selling affordably priced sofas, chairs, and other types of furniture, IKEA even sells Scandinavian-inspired pre-fabricated homes in some markets. The company can offer low prices in part because most items come boxed and require complete assembly at home, meaning they are easier to transport, take up less shelf space, and seldom require delivery, which reduces costs.
>
> IKEA's marketing is predicated on founder Kamprad's statement that "People have very thin wallets. We should take care of their interests." In fact, the firm aims to cut prices by 2% to 3% every year. Recently the company introduced a line of better-quality furniture that requires less at-home assembly and is priced slightly higher than other IKEA furniture. The retailer hasn't veered from its focus on value, however, as annual revenues top $18 billion and margins reach 10%, higher than key competitors like Target and Pier 1 Imports.[21]

ior or attitude and determine, at a basic level, people's choices and desires over the long term. Marketers who target consumers on the basis of their values believe that with appeals to people's inner selves, it is possible to influence their outer selves—their purchase behavior.

KEY PSYCHOLOGICAL PROCESSES

The starting point for understanding consumer behavior is the stimulus-response model shown in Figure 5.1. Marketing and environmental stimuli enter the consumer's consciousness, and a set of psychological processes combine with certain consumer characteristics to result in decision processes and purchase decisions. The marketer's task is to understand what happens in the consumer's consciousness between the arrival of the outside marketing stimuli and the ultimate purchase decisions. Four key psychological processes—motivation, perception, learning, and memory—fundamentally influence consumer responses.[22]

Motivation: Freud, Maslow, Herzberg

We all have many needs at any given time. Some needs are *biogenic*; they arise from physiological states of tension such as hunger, thirst, and discomfort. Other needs are *psychogenic*; they arise from psychological states of tension such as the need for recognition, esteem, or belonging. A need becomes a **motive** when it is aroused to a sufficient level of intensity to drive us to act. Three of the best known theories of human motivation—those of Sigmund Freud, Abraham Maslow, and Frederick Herzberg—carry quite different implications for consumer analysis and marketing strategy.

Sigmund Freud assumed that the psychological forces shaping people's behavior are largely at the subconscious level and that people cannot fully understand their own motivations. Consumers react not only to the stated capabilities of specific brands, but also to other less-conscious cues like shape, size, weight, material, color, and brand name. A technique called *laddering* lets us trace a person's motivations from the stated

FIGURE 5.1   Model of Consumer Behavior

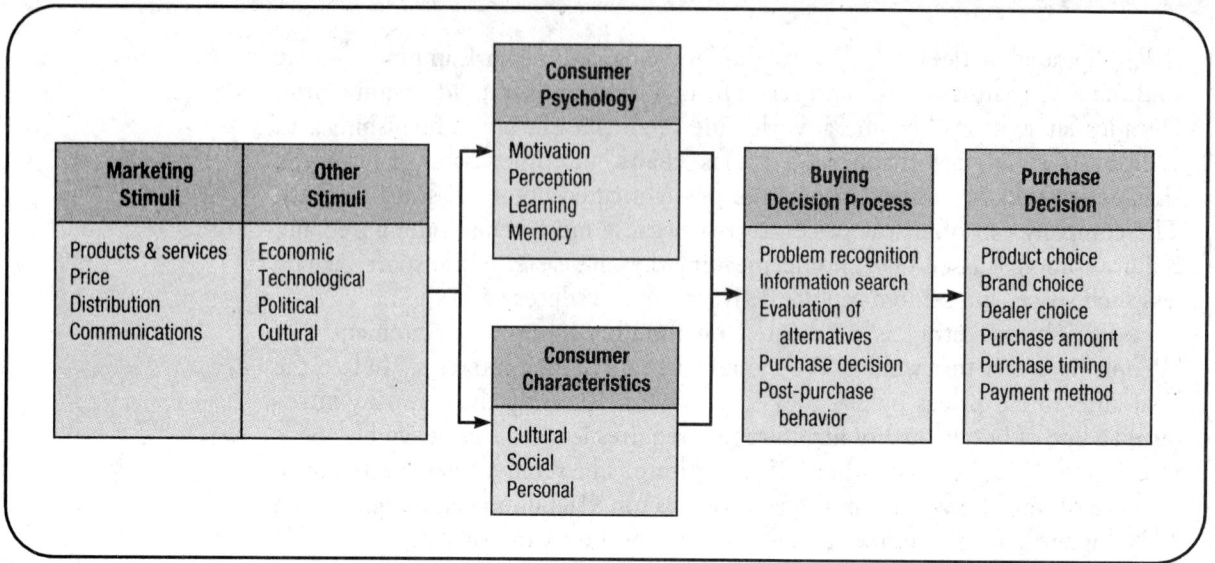

instrumental ones to the more terminal ones. Then the marketer can decide at what level to develop the message and appeal.[23]

Abraham Maslow sought to explain why people are driven by particular needs at particular times.[24] His answer is that human needs are arranged in a hierarchy from most to least pressing—physiological, safety, social, esteem, and self-actualization needs. A person will try to satisfy the most important need first; when that need is satisfied, he will try to satisfy the next most pressing need.

Frederick Herzberg developed a two-factor theory that distinguishes *dissatisfiers* (factors that cause dissatisfaction) from *satisfiers* (factors that cause satisfaction).[25] The absence of dissatisfiers is not enough to motivate a purchase; satisfiers must be present. For example, a computer that does not include a warranty would be a dissatisfier. Yet the presence of a product warranty would not act as a satisfier or motivator of a purchase, because it's not a source of intrinsic satisfaction. Ease of use would, however, be a satisfier. In line with this theory, marketers should avoid dissatisfiers that might "unsell" their products. They should also identify the major satisfiers or motivators of purchase in the market and then supply them.

Perception

A motivated person is ready to act, yet how she acts is influenced by her perception of the situation. **Perception** is the process by which we select, organize, and interpret information inputs to create a meaningful picture of the world.[26] Perception depends on physical stimuli as well as the stimuli's relationship to the surrounding field and conditions within each of us. In marketing, perceptions are more important than the reality, because perceptions affect consumers' actual behavior. People can emerge with different perceptions of the same object because of three perceptual processes: selective attention, selective distortion, and selective retention.

Although we're exposed to thousands of ads and other stimuli every day, we screen most of them out—a process called **selective attention**. The result is that marketers must work hard to attract consumers' attention. However, research shows that people are more likely to notice stimuli that relate to a current need; this is why car shoppers notice car ads but not appliance ads. Also, people are more likely to notice stimuli they anticipate, such as laptops displayed in a computer store. And people are more likely to notice stimuli whose deviations are large in relation to the normal size of the stimuli, such as an ad offering a $100 discount (not just $5).

Even noticed stimuli don't always come across the way that marketers intend. *Selective distortion* is the tendency to interpret information in a way that fits our preconceptions. Consumers will often distort information to be consistent with prior product and brand beliefs and expectations.[27] Selective distortion can work to the advantage of marketers with strong brands when consumers distort neutral or ambiguous brand information to make it more positive. In other words, beer may seem to taste better, or a car may seem to drive more smoothly, depending on the particular brands involved.

Most of us don't remember much information to which we're exposed, but we do retain information that supports our attitudes and beliefs. Because of *selective retention*, we're likely to remember good points mentioned about a product we like and forget good points about competing products. Selective retention again works to the advantage of strong brands; it also explains why marketers repeat messages to ensure that the information is not overlooked.

Learning

When we act, we learn. **Learning** induces changes in our behavior arising from experience. Most human behavior is learned, although much learning is incidental. Theorists believe that learning is produced through the interplay of drives, stimuli, cues, responses, and reinforcement. A **drive** is a strong internal stimulus that impels action. **Cues** are minor stimuli that determine when, where, and how a person responds.

Suppose you buy a Hewlett-Packard computer. If your experience is rewarding, your response to computers and HP will be positively reinforced. Later, when you want to buy a printer, you may assume that because HP makes good computers, it also makes good printers. You have now generalized your response to similar stimuli. A countertendency to generalization is *discrimination*, in which we've learned to recognize differences in sets of similar stimuli and adjust our responses accordingly. Applying learning theory, marketers can build up demand for a product by associating it with strong drives, using motivating cues, and providing positive reinforcement.

Memory

All the information and experiences we encounter as we go through life can end up in our long-term memory. Cognitive psychologists distinguish between *short-term memory (STM)*—a temporary and limited repository of information—and *long-term memory (LTM)*—a more permanent, essentially unlimited repository.

Most widely accepted views of long-term memory structure assume we form some kind of associative model.[28] For example, the **associative network memory model** views LTM as a set of nodes and links. *Nodes* are stored information connected by *links* that vary in strength. Any type of information can be stored in the memory network, including verbal, visual, abstract, and contextual. A spreading activation process from node to node determines how much we retrieve and what information we can actually recall in any given situation. When a node becomes activated because we're encoding external information (when we read or hear a word or phrase) or we're retrieving internal information from LTM (when we think about some concept), other nodes are also activated if they're strongly enough associated with that node.

In this model, we can think of consumer brand knowledge as a node in memory with a variety of linked associations. The strength and organization of these associations will be important determinants of the information we can recall about the brand. **Brand associations** consist of all brand-related thoughts, feelings, perceptions, images, experiences, beliefs, attitudes, and so on, that become linked to the brand node. Some companies create mental maps that depict consumers' knowledge of a particular brand in terms of the key associations that are likely to be triggered by marketing and their relative strength, favorability, and uniqueness to consumers. Figure 5.2 displays a simple mental map highlighting brand beliefs for a hypothetical consumer of State Farm insurance.

Memory Encoding *Memory encoding* describes how and where information gets into memory. The strength of the resulting association depends on how much we process the information at encoding (how much we think about it, for instance) and in what way. In general, the more attention placed on the meaning of information during encoding, the stronger the resulting associations in memory will be.[29] It's also easier for consumers to create an association to new information when extensive, relevant knowledge structures already exist in memory. Repeated exposures provide greater opportunity for processing and the potential for stronger associations. However, high

FIGURE 5.2   Hypothetical Mental Map

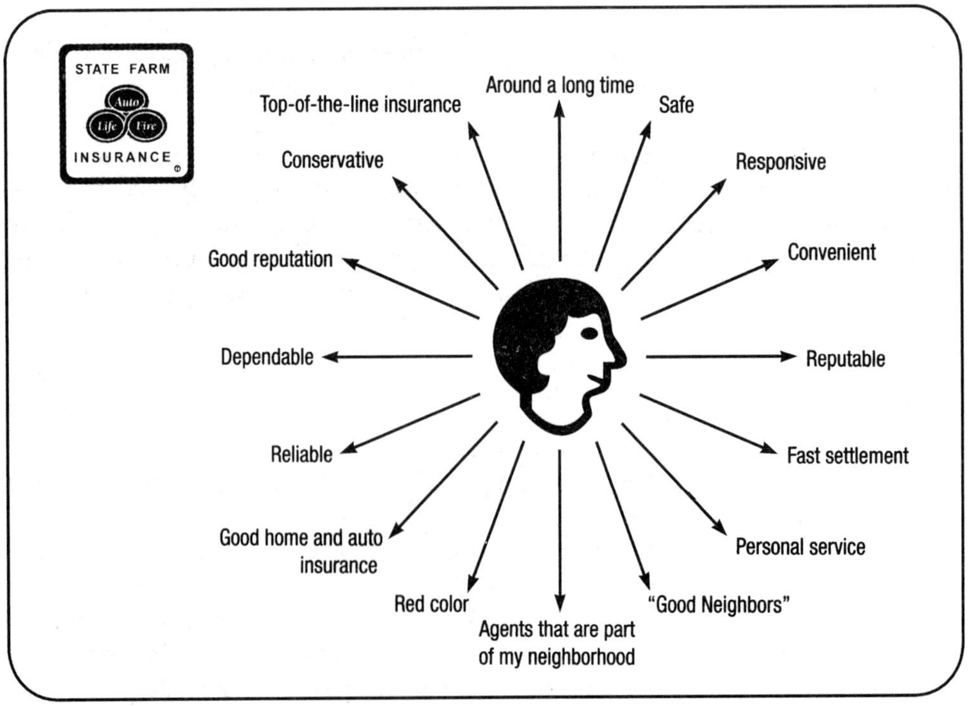

levels of repetition for an uninvolving, unpersuasive ad are unlikely to have as much sales impact as lower levels of repetition for an involving, persuasive ad.[30]

Memory Retrieval *Memory retrieval* is the way information gets out of memory. According to the associative network memory model, a strong brand association is both more accessible and more easily recalled by "spreading activation." Our successful recall of brand information depends on more than the initial strength of that information in memory. Three factors are particularly important. First, *other* product information in memory can produce interference effects, causing us to overlook or confuse new data. Second, the time between exposure to information and encoding matters: the longer the time delay, the weaker the association.

Finally, information may be *available* in memory but not be *accessible* (able to be recalled) without the proper retrieval cues or reminders. The particular associations that come to mind for a brand depend on the context in which we consider it. The more cues linked to a piece of information, however, the greater the likelihood that we can recall it. Thus, in-store marketing efforts such as product packaging are particularly critical because the information they contain and the reminders they provide of information conveyed outside the store will be prime determinants of consumer decision making.

THE BUYING DECISION PROCESS: THE FIVE-STAGE MODEL

Smart marketers try to fully understand the customers' buying decision process—all their experiences in learning about, choosing, using, and even disposing of a product.[31] Figure 5.3 shows a five-stage model of this process. Starting with problem recognition, the consumer passes through the stages of information search, evaluation of alternatives, purchase decision, and postpurchase behavior. Clearly, the buying process starts long before the actual purchase and has consequences long afterward.[32] Note that consumers don't always pass sequentially through all five stages in buying a product; they may skip or reverse some stages. The model provides a good frame of reference, however, because it captures the full range of considerations that arise when a consumer faces a highly involving new purchase.[33]

Problem Recognition

The buying process starts when the buyer recognizes a problem or need, triggered by internal stimuli (such as feeling hunger or thirst) or external stimuli (such as seeing an ad), that then becomes a drive. Marketers need to identify the circumstances that trigger a particular need by gathering information from a number of consumers. They can then develop marketing strategies that trigger consumer interest and lead to the second stage in the buying process.

Information Search

Surprisingly, consumers often search for limited amounts of information. Surveys have shown that for durables, half of all consumers look at only one store, and only 30% look at more than one brand of appliances. We can distinguish between two levels of involvement with search. At the milder search state of *heightened attention*, a person simply becomes more receptive to information about a product. At the *active information*

FIGURE 5.3 Five-Stage Model of the Consumer Buying Process

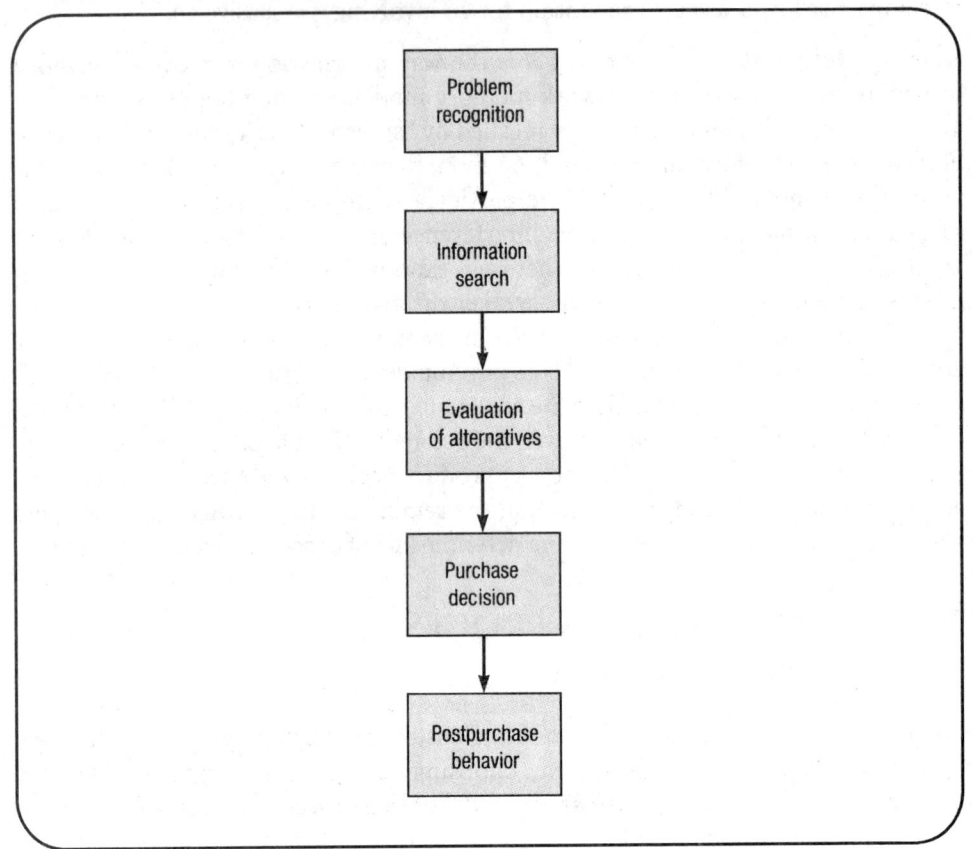

search level, a person talks with friends, searches online, and visits stores to learn about the product.

Information sources for consumers fall into four groups: personal (family, friends, neighbors, acquaintances), commercial (advertising, Web sites, salespersons, dealers, packaging, displays), public (mass media, consumer-rating organizations), and experiential (handling, examining, using the product). The consumer usually receives the most information from commercial (marketer-dominated) sources, although the most influential information comes from personal sources or public sources that are independent authorities.

Through gathering information, the consumer learns about competing brands and their features. The first box in Figure 5.4 shows the *total set* of brands available to the consumer. The individual consumer will come to know only a subset of these brands (*awareness set*). Some brands will meet initial buying criteria (*consideration set*). As the consumer gathers more information, only a few brands will remain as strong contenders (*choice set*). The consumer makes a final choice from this set.[34]

Figure 5.4 makes it clear that a company must strategize to get its brand into the prospect's awareness, consideration, and choice sets. The company must also identify the other brands in the consumer's choice set so it can plan appropriate competitive appeals. In addition, the company should identify the consumer's information sources and evaluate their relative importance so it can prepare effective communications for the target market.

FIGURE 5.4 Successive Sets Involved in Consumer Decision Making

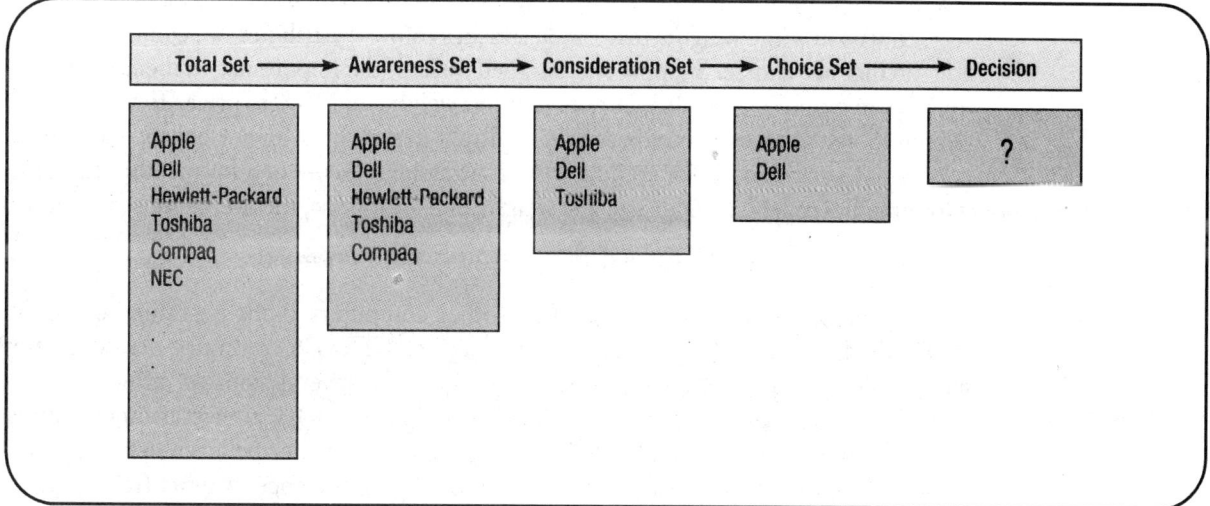

Evaluation of Alternatives

How does the consumer process competitive brand information and make a final judgment? There are several evaluation processes, and the most current models see the consumer forming judgments largely on a conscious and rational basis.

Some basic concepts underlie consumer evaluation processes. First, the consumer is trying to satisfy a need. Second, the consumer is looking for certain benefits from the product solution. Third, the consumer sees each product as a bundle of attributes with varying abilities for delivering the benefits to satisfy this need. The attributes of interest to buyers vary by product. For example, the attributes sought in a hotel might be location, cleanliness, atmosphere, and price. Knowing that consumers pay the most attention to attributes that deliver the sought-after benefits, marketers can segment their markets according to attributes that are most important to different consumer groups.

Through experience and learning, people acquire beliefs and attitudes that, in turn, influence buying behavior. A **belief** is a descriptive thought that a person holds about something. Just as important are **attitudes,** a person's enduring favorable or unfavorable evaluations, emotional feelings, and action tendencies toward some object or idea. People have attitudes toward almost everything: religion, politics, clothes, music, food. Because attitudes economize on energy and thought, they can be very difficult to change. A company is well advised to fit its product into existing attitudes rather than try to change attitudes.

The consumer arrives at attitudes toward various brands through an attribute evaluation procedure.[35] He or she develops a set of beliefs about where each brand stands on each attribute. The **expectancy-value model** of attitude formation posits that consumers evaluate products and services by combining their brand beliefs—the positives and negatives—according to importance.

Suppose, for example, that Linda has narrowed her choice set to four laptop computers (A, B, C, D) on the basis of memory capacity, graphics capability, size and weight, and price. If one computer laptop dominated the others on all the criteria, we could predict that Linda would choose it. However, her choice set consists of laptops that vary in their appeal: She sees that A has the best memory capacity, B has the best graphics capability, C has the best size and weight, and D has the best price.

If we knew the weights that Linda attaches to these attributes, we could more reliably predict her choice. Suppose she assigned 40% of the importance to memory capacity, 30% to graphics capability, 20% to size and weight, and 10% to price. To find Linda's perceived value for each computer, we multiply her weights by her beliefs about each computer's attributes. So for computer A, if she assigns a score of 8 for memory capacity, 9 for graphics capability, 6 for size and weight, and 9 for price, the overall score would be:

$$0.4(8) + 0.3(9) + 0.2(6) + 0.1(9) = 8.0$$

Calculating the scores for all of the other computers Linda is evaluating would show which one has the highest perceived value.[36] Thus, a computer manufacturer who knows how buyers form preferences might take several steps to influence consumer decisions: redesign the computer (real repositioning); alter consumer beliefs about the brand (psychological repositioning); alter consumer beliefs about competitors' brands (competitive depositioning); alter the importance weights (to persuade buyers to attach more importance to attributes in which the brand excels); call attention to neglected attributes (such as styling); or shift the buyer's ideals (to persuade buyers to change their ideal levels for one or more attributes).[37]

Purchase Decisions

In the fourth stage, the consumer forms preferences among brands in the choice set and may also form an intention to buy the most preferred brand. Two factors can intervene between the purchase intention and decision.[38] The first is the *attitudes of others*. The extent to which another person's attitude reduces our preferred alternative depends on (1) the intensity of the other person's negative attitude toward our preferred alternative and (2) our motivation to comply with the other person's wishes.[39] The more intense the other person's negativism and the closer the other person is to us, the more we'll adjust our purchase intention. The converse is also true.

The second factor is *unanticipated situational factors* that may erupt to change the purchase intention. A consumer could lose his or her job, some other purchase might become more urgent, or a store salesperson may offend the consumer, which is why preferences and purchase intentions are not completely reliable predictors of purchase behavior.

A consumer's decision to modify, postpone, or avoid a purchase decision is heavily influenced by *perceived risk*.[40] The amount of perceived risk varies with the amount of money at stake; attribute uncertainty; and consumer self-confidence. Consumers develop routines for reducing the uncertainty and the negative consequences of risk. These include decision avoidance, information gathering from friends, and preference for national brand names and warranties. Marketers must understand the factors that provoke a feeling of risk in consumers and then provide information and support to reduce the perceived risk.

Postpurchase Behavior

After the purchase, the consumer might experience dissonance stemming from noticing certain disquieting features or hearing favorable things about other brands and will be alert to information that supports his or her decision. Thus, the marketer's job doesn't end with the purchase. Marketers must monitor postpurchase satisfaction, postpurchase actions, and postpurchase product uses.

As discussed in Chapter 4, satisfaction is a function of the closeness between expectations and the product's perceived performance.[41] If the consumer is satisfied, he or she is more likely to purchase the product again and will tend to say good things about the brand to others. On the other hand, dissatisfied consumers may abandon or return the product; take public action by complaining to the company, going to lawyers, complaining to government agencies and other groups; or take private action such as not buying the product or warning friends.[42] ("Marketing Skills: Winning Back Customers" suggests how marketers can reverse this situation.)

Marketers can use postpurchase communications to reduce product returns and order cancellations.[43] Computer companies, for example, might send messages to new buyers congratulating them on having selected a fine computer, place ads showing satisfied customers, solicit suggestions for improvements, and provide channels for speedy resolution of customer complaints.

Also, marketers should monitor how buyers use and dispose of the product after purchase (see Figure 5.5). A key driver of sales frequency is product consumption rate—the more quickly buyers consume a product, the sooner they may be back in the market to repurchase it. One opportunity to increase frequency of product use occurs when consumers' perceptions of product usage differ from reality. Consumers may fail to replace products with relatively short life spans soon enough because they overestimate product life.[44] Here, marketers can speed up replacement by linking repurchasing to a certain holiday, event, or time of year. If consumers throw the product away, the marketer needs to know how they dispose of it, especially if—like certain batteries, beverage containers, and electronic equipment—it can hurt the environment.

MARKETING SKILLS: WINNING BACK LOST CUSTOMERS

Customers may defect because they are dissatisfied, have new needs, or simply lose interest in certain offerings. The road to winning back customers starts with an understanding of when, why, and how customers decide to leave. Companies that bill monthly learn quickly when a customer leaves, as do companies that receive complaints or cancellations; those with unscheduled or infrequent customer contact may not notice for some time. Marketers can also use informal contacts (such as phone calls from sales reps) or formal research (such as an exit interview) to learn why customers defect. The goal is to reveal sources of dissatisfaction or internal problems that can be addressed to win back and retain customers—and to demonstrate that the firm is listening and responding.

At Tumbleweed Southwest Grill, CEO Terry Smith has publicly promised to answer all customer complaints, an unusual approach that has helped the restaurant chain win back dissatisfied customers and reinforce customer loyalty. Hundreds of customers contact Smith each month, some with complaints but others with praise. The CEO responds to customers within 24 hours and then has the local restaurant manager follow up to resolve specific customer issues. This is "by far one of the best things we have ever done in achieving guest satisfaction," Smith says, adding that sales rose more than 10% during the first four months of the program.[45]

FIGURE 5.5 How Customers Use or Dispose of Products

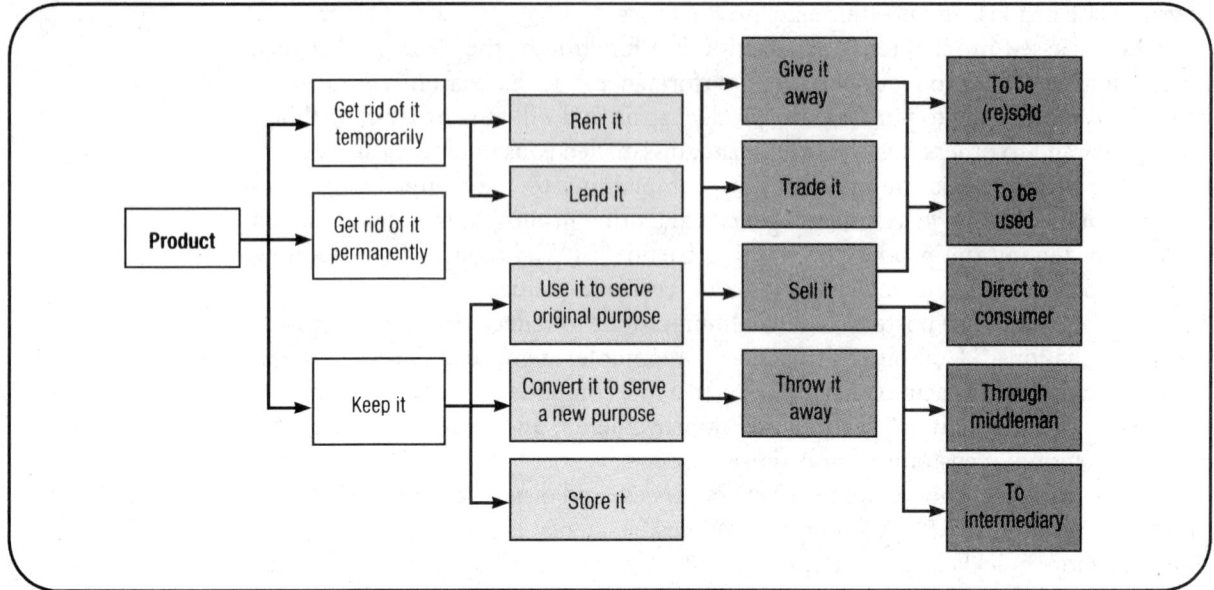

Source: From Jacob Jacoby, Carol K. Berning, and Thomas J. Dietvorst, "What about Disposition?" Journal of Marketing (July 1977): p. 23. Reprinted with permission of the American Marketing Association.

EXECUTIVE SUMMARY

Consumer behavior is influenced by three factors: cultural (culture, subculture, and social class), social (reference groups, family, and social roles and statuses), and personal (age and stage in the life cycle; occupation and economic circumstances; personality and self-concept; and lifestyle and values). The four psychological processes of motivation, perception, learning, and memory also influence consumer behavior. Research into all of these factors can provide marketers with clues to reaching and satisfying consumers more effectively.

The five-stage model of the consumer buying process consists of problem recognition, information search, evaluation of alternatives, purchase decision, and postpurchase behavior. The marketer's job is to understand the buyer's behavior at each stage. Consumers' evaluations of a product, based on attitudes and beliefs acquired through learning and experience, will affect their purchase decisions. The attitudes of others, unanticipated situational factors, and perceived risk may also affect the buying decision, as will consumers' postpurchase satisfaction, the company's postpurchase actions, and consumers' use and disposal of the product.

NOTES

1. "US Mobile Players Congregate to Propel the Sector Forward," *New Media Age*, July 28, 2007, p. 15; Emily Steel, "Grabbing Older Consumers via Cellphone," *Wall Street Journal*, January 31, 2007, p. B3; Alice Cuneo, "P&G Tries Out Mobile Marketing," *Advertising Age*, June 19, 2006, p. 2; Alice Cuneo, "Dot-com vs. Dot-mobi Debate Divides Industry," *Advertising Age*, June 19, 2006, p. 10.

2. Input on this chapter from Duke University's Jim Bettman and John Lynch and Stanford University's Itamar Simonson is gratefully acknowledged. For an academic overview of consumer research, see Itamar Simonson, Ziv Carmon, Ravi Dhar, Aimee Drolet, Stephen M. Nowlis, "Consumer Research: In Search of Identity," *Annual Review of Psychology*, 52, 2001, pp. 249–275.

3. See Leon G. Schiffman and Leslie Lazar Kanuk, *Consumer Behavior*, 9th ed. (Upper Saddle River, NJ: Prentice Hall, 2006).
4. Rob Walker, "The Princess Buy," *The New York Times Magazine*, Oct 15, 2006, www.nytimes.com.
5. Richard P. Coleman, "The Continuing Significance of Social Class to Marketing," *Journal of Consumer Research* (December 1983): 265–280; Richard P. Coleman and Lee P. Rainwater, *Social Standing in America: New Dimension of Class* (New York: Basic Books, 1978).
6. Schiffman and Kanuk, *Consumer Behavior*.
7. Rosann L. Spiro, "Persuasion in Family Decision Making," *Journal of Consumer Research* (March 1983): 393–402; David J. Burns, "Husband-Wife Innovative Consumer Decision Making: Exploring the Effect of Family Power," *Psychology & Marketing* (May–June 1992): 175–189; Robert Boutilier, "Pulling the Family's Strings," *American Demographics* (August 1993): 44–48; Elizabeth S. Moore, William L. Wilkie, and Richard J. Lutz, "Passing the Torch: Intergenerational Influences as a Source of Brand Equity," *Journal of Marketing* (April 2002): 17–37. For cross-cultural comparisons of husband–wife buying roles, see John B. Ford, Michael S. LaTour, and Tony L. Henthorne, "Perception of Marital Roles in Purchase-Decision Processes: A Cross-Cultural Study," *Journal of the Academy of Marketing Science* (Spring 1995): 120–131.
8. Kay M. Palan and Robert E. Wilkes, "Adolescent-Parent Interaction in Family Decision Making," *Journal of Consumer Research* 24, no. 2 (1997): 159–169; Sharon E. Beatty and Salil Talpade, "Adolescent Influence in Family Decision Making: A Replication with Extension," *Journal of Consumer Research* 21 (1994): 332–341.
9. Chenting Su, Edward F. Fern, and Keying Ye, "A Temporal Dynamic Model of Spousal Family Purchase-Decision Behavior," *Journal of Marketing Research*, 40 (August 2003): 268ff; Hillary Chura, "Failing to Connect: Marketing Messages for Women Fall Short," *Advertising Age*, September 23, 2002, pp. 13–14.
10. "Retailers Learn That Electronics Shopping Isn't Just a Guy Thing," *Wall Street Journal*, January 15, 2004, p. D3.
11. "Trillion-Dollar Kids," *The Economist*, December 2, 2006, p. 66.
12. Courtney Kane, "TV and Movie Characters Sell Children's Snacks," *New York Times*, December 8, 2003, p. C7.
13. Jennifer Bayot, "The Teenage Market; Young, Hip and Looking for a Bargain," *New York Times*, December 1, 2003, p. C8.
14. Rex Y. Du and Wagner A. Kamakura, "Household Life Cycles and Lifestyles in the United States," *Journal of Marketing Research*, 48 (February 2006), pp. 121–132; Lawrence Lepisto, "A Life Span Perspective of Consumer Behavior," in *Advances in Consumer Research*, vol. 12, ed. Elizabeth Hirshman and Morris Holbrook (Provo, UT: Association for Consumer Research, 1985), p. 47. Also see Gail Sheehy, *New Passages: Mapping Your Life Across Time* (New York: Random House, 1995).
15. Harold H. Kassarjian and Mary Jane Sheffet, "Personality and Consumer Behavior: An Update," in *Perspectives in Consumer Behavior*, eds. Harold H. Kassarjian and Thomas S. Robertson (Glenview, IL: Scott Foresman, 1981), pp. 160–180.
16. Jennifer Aaker, "Dimensions of Measuring Brand Personality," *Journal of Marketing Research* 34 (August 1997): 347–356.
17. Yongjun Sung and Spencer F. Tinkham, "Brand Personality Structures in the United States and Korea: Common and Culture-Specific Factors," *Journal of Consumer Psychology*, 15 (4) (2005): 334–350; Jennifer L. Aaker, Veronica Benet-Martinez, and Jordi Garolera, "Consumption Symbols as Carriers of Culture: A Study of Japanese and Spanish Brand Personality Constructs," *Journal of Personality and Social Psychology* 81, no. 3 (2001): 492–508.
18. M. Joseph Sirgy, "Self Concept in Consumer Behavior: A Critical Review," *Journal of Consumer Research* 9 (December 1982): 287–300.
19. Timothy R. Graeff, "Consumption Situations and the Effects of Brand Image on Consumers' Brand Evaluations," *Psychology & Marketing* 14, no. 1 (1997): 49–70; Timothy R. Graeff, "Image Congruence Effects on Product Evaluations: The Role of Self-Monitoring and Public/Private Consumption," *Psychology & Marketing* 13, no. 5 (1996): 481–499.
20. Jennifer L. Aaker, "The Malleable Self: The Role of Self-Expression in Persuasion," *Journal of Marketing Research* 36, no. 2 (1999): 45–57.
21. Marianne Rohrlich, "Ikea for the Post-Collegiate Crowd," *New York Times*, April 26, 2007, p. F3; Kerry Capell, "IKEA: How the Swedish Retailer Became a Global Cult Brand," *BusinessWeek*, November 14, 2005, p. 96; "Need a Home to Go with That Sofa?" *BusinessWeek*, November 14, 2005, p. 106; www.ikea.com.

22. For a review of current academic research on consumer behavior, see "Consumer Psychology: Categorization, Inferences, Affect, and Persuasion," *Annual Review of Psychology*, 57, 2006, pp. 453–495. To learn more about how consumer behavior theory can be applied to policy decisions, see "Special Issue on Helping Consumers Help Themselves: Improving the Quality of Judgments and Choices," *Journal of Public Policy & Marketing*, Spring 2006, p. 25.

23. Thomas J. Reynolds and Jonathan Gutman, "Laddering Theory, Method, Analysis, and Interpretation," *Journal of Advertising Research* (February–March 1988): 11–34.

24. Abraham Maslow, *Motivation and Personality* (New York: Harper & Row, 1954) pp. 80–106.

25. Frederick Herzberg, *Work and the Nature of Man* (Cleveland, OH: William Collins, 1966); and Henk Thierry and Agnes M. Koopman-Iwerna, "Motivation and Satisfaction," in *Handbook of Work and Organizational Psychology*, ed. P. J. Drenth (New York: John Wiley, 1984), pp. 141–142.

26. Bernard Berelson and Gary A. Steiner, *Human Behavior: An Inventory of Scientific Findings* (New York: Harcourt Brace Jovanovich, 1964), p. 88.

27. J. Edward Russo, Margaret G. Meloy, and T. J. Wilks, "The Distortion of Product Information During Brand Choice," *Journal of Marketing Research* 35 (1998): 438–452.

28. John R. Anderson, *The Architecture of Cognition* (Cambridge, MA: Harvard University Press, 1983); Robert S. Wyer Jr. and Thomas K. Srull, "Person Memory and Judgment," *Psychological Review* 96, no. 1 (1989): 58–83.

29. Fergus I. M. Craik and Robert S. Lockhart, "Levels of Processing: A Framework for Memory Research," *Journal of Verbal Learning and Verbal Behavior* 11 (1972): 671–684; Fergus I. M. Craik and Endel Tulving, "Depth of Processing and the Retention of Words in Episodic Memory," *Journal of Experimental Psychology* 104, no. 3 (1975): 268–294; Robert S. Lockhart, Fergus I. M. Craik, and Larry Jacoby, "Depth of Processing, Recognition, and Recall," in *Recall and Recognition*, ed. John Brown (New York: John Wiley & Sons, 1976).

30. Leonard M. Lodish, Magid Abraham, Stuart Kalmenson, Jeanne Livelsberger, Beth Lubetkin, Bruce Richardson, and Mary Ellen Stevens, "How T.V. Advertising Works: A Meta Analysis of 389 Real World Split Cable T.V. Advertising Experiments," *Journal of Marketing Research* 32 (May 1995): 125–139.

31. Benson Shapiro, V. Kasturi Rangan, and John Sviokla, "Staple Yourself to an Order," *Harvard Business Review* (July–August 1992): 113–122. See also Carrie M. Heilman, Douglas Bowman, and Gordon P. Wright, "The Evolution of Brand Preferences and Choice Behaviors of Consumers New to a Market," *Journal of Marketing Research* (May 2000): 139–155.

32. Marketing scholars have developed several models of the consumer buying process. See John A. Howard and Jagdish N. Sheth, *The Theory of Buyer Behavior* (New York: Wiley, 1969); James F. Engel, Roger D. Blackwell, and Paul W. Miniard, *Consumer Behavior*, 8th ed. (Fort Worth, TX: Dryden, 1994); Mary Frances Luce, James R. Bettman, and John W. Payne, *Emotional Decisions: Tradeoff Difficulty and Coping in Consumer Choice* (Chicago: University of Chicago Press, 2001).

33. William P. Putsis, Jr. and Narasimhan Srinivasan, "Buying or Just Browsing? The Duration of Purchase Deliberation," *Journal of Marketing Research* (August 1994): 393–402.

34. Chem L. Narayana and Rom J. Markin, "Consumer Behavior and Product Performance: An Alternative Conceptualization," *Journal of Marketing* (October 1975): 1–6. See also Wayne S. DeSarbo and Kamel Jedidi, "The Spatial Representation of Heterogeneous Consideration Sets," *Marketing Science* 14, no. 3, pt. 2 (1995): 326–342; and Lee G. Cooper and Akihiro Inoue, "Building Market Structures from Consumer Preferences," *Journal of Marketing Research* 33, no. 3 (August 1996): 293–306.

35. Paul E. Green and Yoram Wind, *Multiattribute Decisions in Marketing: A Measurement Approach* (Hinsdale, IL: Dryden, 1973), ch. 2; Leigh McAlister, "Choosing Multiple Items from a Product Class," *Journal of Consumer Research* (December 1979): 213–224; Richard J. Lutz, "The Role of Attitude Theory in Marketing," in eds. Kassarjian and Robertson, *Perspectives in Consumer Behavior*, pp. 317–339.

36. This expectancy-value model was originally developed by Martin Fishbein, "Attitudes and Prediction of Behavior," in *Readings in Attitude Theory and Measurement*, ed. Martin Fishbein (New York: John Wiley, 1967), pp. 477–492. For a critical review, see Paul W. Miniard and Joel B. Cohen, "An Examination of the Fishbein-Ajzen Behavioral-Intentions Model's Concepts and Measures," *Journal of Experimental Social Psychology* (May 1981): 309–339.

37. Michael R. Solomon, *Consumer Behavior: Buying, Having and Being*, 7th ed. (Upper Saddle River, NJ: Prentice Hall, 2007).

38. Jagdish N. Sheth, "An Investigation of Relationships Among Evaluative Beliefs, Affect, Behavioral Intention, and Behavior," in *Consumer Behavior: Theory and Application*, ed. John U. Farley, John A. Howard, and L. Winston Ring (Boston: Allyn & Bacon, 1974), pp. 89–114.
39. Fishbein, "Attitudes and Prediction of Behavior."
40. Raymond A. Bauer, "Consumer Behavior as Risk Taking," in *Risk Taking and Information Handling in Consumer Behavior*, ed. Donald F. Cox (Boston: Division of Research, Harvard Business School, 1967); James W. Taylor, "The Role of Risk in Consumer Behavior," *Journal of Marketing* (April 1974): 54–60; Grahame R. Dowling (1986), "Perceived Risk: The Concept and Its Measurement," *Psychology and Marketing*, 3 (Fall): 193–210; Grahame R. Dowling, "Perceived Risk," in *The Elgar Companion to Consumer Research and Economic Psychology*, ed. Peter E. Earl and Simon Kemp (Cheltenham, UK: Edward Elgar, 1999), pp. 419–424; Margaret C. Campbell and Ronald C. Goodstein, "The Moderating Effect of Perceived Risk on Consumers' Evaluations of Product Incongruity: Preference for the Norm," *Journal of Consumer Research*, 28 (December 2001): 439–449.
41. Richard L. Oliver, "Customer Satisfaction Research," in the *Handbook of Marketing Research*, Rajiv Grover and Marco Vriens, eds. (Thousand Oaks, CA: Sage Publications, 2006), pp. 569–587.
42. Albert O. Hirschman, *Exit, Voice, and Loyalty* (Cambridge, MA: Harvard University Press, 1970).
43. James H. Donnelly Jr. and John M. Ivancevich, "Post-Purchase Reinforcement and Back-Out Behavior," *Journal of Marketing Research* (August 1970): 399–400.
44. John D. Cripps, "Heuristics and Biases in Timing the Replacement of Durable Products," *Journal of Consumer Research* 21 (September 1994): 304–318.
45. Gregg Cebrzynski, "Tumbleweed's Sales Spike After CEO Vows to Field Complaints Personally," *Nation's Restaurant News*, April 9, 2007, p. 4; Jay Kassing, "Increasing Customer Retention: Profitability Isn't a Spectator Sport," *Financial Services Marketing* (March–April 2002): 32+; Jill Griffin and Michael W. Lowenstein, "Winning Back a Lost Customer," *Direct Marketing* (July 2001): 49+; John D. Cimperman, "Win-Back Starts Before Customer Is Lost," *Multichannel News*, February 19, 2001, pp. 53+.

CHAPTER 6

Analyzing Business Markets

> **In this chapter, we will address the following questions:**
>
> 1. What is the business market, and how does it differ from the consumer market?
> 2. What buying situations do organizational buyers face?
> 3. Who participates in the business-to-business buying process, and how are buying decisions made?
> 4. How can marketers build strong relationships with business customers?

MARKETING MANAGEMENT AT CISCO

Cisco, the leading manufacturer of switches and routers that direct communications traffic on the Internet, has grown by targeting small- and medium-sized business (SMB) customers. Its marketers define the SMB market as firms with fewer than 250 employees, an attractive market yet traditionally underserved. Cisco recently conducted research so its marketers could segment the SMB market into four tiers according to networking expenditure and buying patterns. Tier-1 and tier-2 firms, which view networking as the core of their business, make up 30% of the market but account for 75% of the expenditures. Tier-3 and tier-4 firms make up 70% of the market, but they're hesitant to invest heavily in networking technology.

Equipped with this knowledge, Cisco increased its R&D budget for the SMB market to $2 billion and directed 40% of its total marketing budget toward these segments. Next, its marketers developed a program called the "Smart Business Roadmap," which matches common business issues faced by SMB customer types with long-term technology solutions that Cisco can provide. Since launching this program, Cisco's revenues from SMB customers have grown 22%.[1]

Business organizations do not only sell; they also buy vast quantities of raw materials, manufactured components, plant and equipment, supplies, and business services. Some of the world's most valuable brands belong to business marketers: Cisco, Caterpillar, DuPont, FedEx, GE, Hewlett-Packard, IBM, Intel, and Siemens, to name a few. Although businesses need to embrace holistic marketing principles, such as building strong customer relationships, they also face some unique considerations in selling to other businesses, institutions, and government agencies. This chapter highlights some key similarities and differences for marketing in business markets.[2]

WHAT IS ORGANIZATIONAL BUYING?

Webster and Wind define **organizational buying** as the decision-making process by which formal organizations establish the need for purchased products and services and identify, evaluate, and choose among alternative brands and suppliers.[3] Organizational buying occurs within the business market, which differs from the consumer market in a number of significant ways.

The Business Market versus the Consumer Market

The **business market** consists of all the organizations that acquire goods and services used in the production of other products or services that are sold, rented, or supplied to other customers. The major industries making up the business market are agriculture, forestry, and fisheries; mining; manufacturing; construction; transportation; communication; public utilities; banking, finance, and insurance; distribution; and services. More dollars and items change hands in sales to business buyers than to consumers. Consider the process of producing and selling a pair of shoes. Hide dealers must sell hides to tanners, who sell leather to shoe manufacturers, who sell shoes to wholesalers, who sell shoes to retailers, who finally sell them to consumers. Each party in the supply chain also has to buy many other goods and services to support its operations.

From the number and size of buyers to geographical location, demand, and buying behaviors, business markets have a number of characteristics that contrast sharply with those of consumer markets. These characteristics are described in Table 6.1.

Institutional and Organizational Markets

The overall business market includes institutional and government organizations in addition to profit-seeking companies. However, the buying goals, needs, and methods of these two organizational markets generally differ from those of businesses, something firms must keep in mind when planning their business marketing strategies.

The Institutional Market The **institutional market** consists of schools, hospitals, nursing homes, prisons, and other institutions that provide goods and services to people in their care. Many of these organizations have low budgets and captive clienteles. For example, hospitals have to decide what quality of food to buy for patients. The buying objective here is not profit, because the food is provided as part of the total service package; nor is cost minimization the sole objective, because poor food will cause patients to complain and hurt the hospital's reputation. The hospital purchasing agent has to search for institutional food vendors whose quality meets or exceeds a certain

TABLE 6.1 Characteristics of Business Markets

Characteristic	Description
Fewer, larger buyers	Business marketers normally deal with far fewer, much larger buyers than do consumer marketers.
Close supplier-customer relationship	Because of the smaller customer base and the importance and power of the larger customers, suppliers often must customize offerings to individual business customer needs.
Professional purchasing	Trained purchasing agents follow formal policies, requirements, and constraints when buying. Many of the buying instruments—such as proposals and purchase contracts—are not typical of consumer buying.
Multiple buying influences	More people influence business buying decisions; buying committees are common in major purchases. Firms must send knowledgeable sales representatives and teams to deal with well-trained buyers.
Multiple sales calls	Because more people are involved in the process, it takes multiple sales calls to win most business orders, and the sales cycle can take years.
Derived demand	Demand for business goods is ultimately derived from demand for consumer goods, so business marketers must monitor the buying patterns of ultimate consumers.
Inelastic demand	Total demand for many business goods and services is inelastic and not much affected by price changes, especially in the short run, because producers cannot make quick production changes.
Fluctuating demand	Demand for business products tends to be more volatile than demand for consumer products. An increase in consumer demand can lead to a much larger increase in demand for plant and equipment needed to produce the additional output.
Geographically concentrated buyers	More than half of U.S. business buyers are concentrated in seven states—New York, California, Pennsylvania, Illinois, Ohio, New Jersey, and Michigan—which helps to reduce selling costs.
Direct purchasing	Business buyers often buy directly from manufacturers rather than through intermediaries, especially items that are technically complex or expensive.

minimum standard and whose prices are low. Knowing this, many food vendors set up a separate division and make special efforts to meet the needs of institutional buyers.

Consider Aramark Corp., which provides food services for stadiums, campuses, businesses, schools, and prisons. Where it once merely selected products from lists provided by potential suppliers, the firm now collaborates with suppliers to create products customized for individual segments. In the prison segment, for instance, quality has historically been sacrificed to meet stringent pricing considerations. "When you go after business in the corrections field, you are making bids that are measured in hundredths of a cent," says the head of Aramark's Food & Support Services, "so any edge we can gain on the purchasing side is extremely valuable." After Aramark arranged with suppliers to source a series of unique protein products, it was able to cut food costs by up to nine cents per meal while maintaining or even improving quality.[4]

The Government Market In most countries, government organizations are a major buyer of goods and services. The U.S. government, for example, buys goods and services valued at $200 billion, making it the largest customer in the world. The number of individual purchases is equally staggering: Over 20 million individual contract actions are processed every year. Although the cost of most items purchased is between $2,500 and $25,000, the government also makes purchases in the billions of dollars, often for technology.

Government organizations typically require suppliers to submit bids, and they normally award the contract to the lowest bidder. In some cases, they take into account a supplier's superior quality or reputation for on-time performance. Because their spending decisions are subject to public review, government agencies require considerable documentation from suppliers, who often complain about excessive paperwork, bureaucracy, regulations, decision-making delays, and shifts in procurement personnel. Fortunately for business marketers, the U.S. government has been working to simplify the contracting procedure and make bidding more attractive and more efficient.

Buying Situations

The business buyer faces many decisions in making a purchase. The number of decisions depends on the buying situation: complexity of the problem being solved, newness of the buying requirement, number of people involved, and time required. Three types of buying situations are the straight rebuy, the modified rebuy, and the new task.[5]

- *Straight rebuy.* The purchasing department reorders supplies like bulk chemicals on a routine basis, choosing from suppliers on an approved list. These suppliers make an effort to maintain product and service quality and often propose automatic reordering systems to save time. "Out-suppliers" attempt to offer something new or to exploit dissatisfaction with a current supplier. Their goal is to get a small order and then enlarge their purchase share over time.
- *Modified rebuy.* The buyer wants to modify product specifications, prices, delivery requirements, or other terms. The modified rebuy usually involves additional participants on both sides. The in-suppliers become nervous and have to protect the account; the out-suppliers see an opportunity to gain some business by proposing a better offer.
- *New task.* A purchaser buys a product or service for the first time (an office building, new security system). The greater the cost or risk, the larger the number of decision participants and the greater their information gathering—and, therefore, the longer the time to a decision.[6]

The business buyer makes the fewest decisions in the straight rebuy situation and the most in the new-task situation. Over time, new-buy tasks become straight rebuys and routine purchase behavior.

New-task buying passes through several stages: awareness, interest, evaluation, trial, and adoption.[7] Mass media can be most important during the initial awareness stage; salespeople have their greatest impact at the interest stage; and technical sources are key during the evaluation stage. In the new-task situation, the buyer has to determine product specifications, price limits, delivery terms and times, service terms, payment terms, order quantities, acceptable suppliers, and the selected supplier. Different participants influence each decision and the order in which they make these decisions can vary.

Because of the complicated selling involved in new-task situations, many companies use a *missionary sales force* consisting of their best salespeople. The brand promise and the manufacturer's brand name recognition will be important in establishing trust and the customer's willingness to consider change.[8] The marketer also tries to reach as many key participants as possible and provide helpful information and assistance.

Systems Buying and Selling

Many business buyers prefer to buy a total solution to their problem from one seller. Called *systems buying*, this practice originated with government purchases of major weapons and communication systems. The government solicited bids from *prime contractors*, who assembled the package or system. The winning contractor then bid out and assembled the system from subcomponents purchased from other contractors. Thus, the prime contractor was providing a *turnkey solution*, so-called because the buyer simply turns one key to get the job done.

Sellers have increasingly recognized that buyers like to purchase in this way, and many have adopted systems selling as a marketing tool. One variant of systems selling is *systems contracting*, where a single supplier provides the buyer with all required MRO supplies (maintenance, repair, and operating supplies). The buyer benefits from less time spent on supplier selection, lower procurement and management costs, and price protection during the contract period. The seller benefits from lower operating costs because of steady demand and reduced paperwork.

Systems selling is a key industrial marketing strategy in bidding to build large-scale industrial projects such as dams, steel factories, and pipelines. Project engineering firms must compete on price, quality, reliability, and other attributes to win these contracts. For example, when the Indonesian government requested bids to build a cement factory near Jakarta, a U.S. firm made a proposal that included choosing the site, designing the cement factory, hiring the construction crews, assembling the materials and equipment, and turning over the finished factory to the Indonesian government. The Japanese bidder's proposal included all of these services, plus hiring and training the factory workers, exporting the cement, and using the cement to build roads and offices in Jakarta. Although the Japanese proposal was more costly, it won. This is true system selling: The firm took the broadest view of its customer's needs.

Participants in the Business Buying Process

Who buys the trillions of dollars' worth of goods and services needed by business organizations? Purchasing agents are influential in straight-rebuy and modified-rebuy situations, whereas other personnel are more influential in new-buy situations. Engineering personnel carry the most influence in selecting product components, and purchasing agents dominate in selecting suppliers.[9]

The Buying Center

Webster and Wind call the decision-making unit of a buying organization the **buying center**. It consists of "all those individuals and groups who participate in the purchasing decision-making process, who share some common goals and the risks arising from the decisions."[10] The buying center includes organizational members who play any of seven roles in the purchase decision process:[11]

1. *Initiators:* Users or others who request that something be purchased
2. *Users:* Those who will use the product or service; often, users initiate the buying proposal and help define product requirements.

3. *Influencers:* People who influence the buying decision, including technical personnel; they often help define specifications and provide information for evaluating alternatives.
4. *Deciders:* Those who decide on product requirements or suppliers.
5. *Approvers:* People who authorize the proposed actions of deciders or buyers.
6. *Buyers:* People who have formal authority to select the supplier and arrange the purchase terms, including high-level managers. Buyers may help shape product specifications, but their major role is selecting vendors and negotiating.
7. *Gatekeepers:* People with the power to prevent sellers or information from reaching buying center members; examples are purchasing agents, receptionists, and telephone operators.

Several individuals can occupy a given role such as user or influencer, and one person may occupy multiple roles.[12] A purchasing manager, for example, often occupies the roles of buyer, influencer, and gatekeeper simultaneously: he or she can determine which sales reps can call on other people in the organization; what budget and other constraints to place on the purchase; and which firm will actually get the business, even though others (deciders) might select two or more potential vendors who can meet the company's requirements. The typical buying center has a minimum of five or six members and often has dozens, including people outside the organization, such as government officials, technical advisors, and members of the marketing channel.[13]

Buying Center Influences

Buying centers usually include several participants with differing interests, authority, status, and persuasiveness and sometimes very different decision criteria. For example, engineering personnel may want to maximize product performance; production personnel may want ease of use and reliability of supply; financial personnel may focus on the purchase's economics; purchasing may be concerned with operating and replacement costs; union officials may emphasize safety issues.

Business buyers also have personal motivations, perceptions, and preferences, which are influenced by their age, income, education, job position, personality, attitudes toward risk, and culture (for more about dealing with cultural influences in international business marketing, see "Marketing Skills: Marketing Across Cultures"). Buyers definitely exhibit different buying styles. Some prefer to conduct rigorous analyses of competitive proposals before choosing a supplier; others are "toughies" from the old school who pit competing sellers against one another.

Webster cautions that ultimately, individuals, not organizations, make purchasing decisions.[14] Individuals are motivated by their own needs and perceptions in attempting to maximize organizational rewards (pay, advancement, recognition, and feelings of achievement). Personal needs motivate the behavior of individuals but organizational needs legitimize the buying decision process and its outcomes. People aren't buying products; they're buying solutions to two problems: the organization's economic and strategic problem and their own personal need for individual achievement and reward. In this sense, industrial buying decisions are both "rational" and "emotional," as they serve both the organization's and the individual's needs.[15]

In principle, business buyers seek to obtain the highest benefit package (economic, technical, service, and social) in relation to a market offering's costs. To make

> ### MARKETING SKILLS: MARKETING ACROSS CULTURES
>
> All people are *not* basically alike. This is just one premise to keep in mind when developing the skill of marketing across cultures. Language differences aside, marketers must assume that people from other cultures have different customs, beliefs, preferences, and values, at least until they can confirm similarities with their own cultures. It's important to research the other culture and learn how to act in business and social settings, because many cultures value a good buyer–seller relationship more than they value price or other aspects of the offer. Just as important, find out how people in the other culture prefer to communicate and how they make decisions—and be ready to adapt to these differences throughout the course of the marketing relationship.
>
> Consider the skills needed by marketers and managers at Digital River, a Minnesota-based firm that designs and operates online stores for technology companies such as Skype. Digital River studied business needs and buying influences in Japan for more than a year before partnering with a local firm to facilitate its market entrance. The partner helps with Digital River's B2B Web site, a key marketing tool that must be relevant and appealing to Japanese decision makers and influencers. Using Japanese translators and graphic designers, Digital River's CEO says, ensures "not only that they get the words right, but that they get the culture right."[16]

comparisons, they will try to translate all costs and benefits into monetary terms. A business buyer's incentive to purchase will be a function of the difference between perceived benefits and perceived costs.[17] The marketer's task is to construct a profitable offering that delivers superior customer value to the target buyers.

Recognizing all these influences on business buying, more industrial firms have put greater emphasis on the corporate brand. At one time, Emerson Electric, global provider of power tools, compressors, electrical equipment and engineering solutions, was a conglomerate of 60 autonomous—and sometimes anonymous—companies. Then a new CMO aligned all companies under an overall brand architecture and identity, allowing Emerson to achieve a broader presence so it could sell locally while leveraging its brand globally. Record sales soon followed.[18]

Buying Center Targeting

To target their efforts properly, business marketers have to figure out: Who are the major decision participants? What decisions do they influence? What is their level of influence? What evaluation criteria do they use? The marketer is unlikely to know exactly what kind of group dynamics take place during the decision process, although information about personalities and interpersonal factors is useful.

Small sellers concentrate on reaching the *key buying influencers*. Larger sellers go for *multilevel in-depth selling* to reach as many participants as possible. Their salespeople virtually "live" with high-volume customers. Companies will have to rely more heavily on their communications programs to reach hidden buying influences and keep current customers informed.[19]

STAGES IN THE BUYING PROCESS

Business buying passes through eight stages called *buyphases*, as identified by Robinson and associates in the *buygrid* framework shown in Table 6.2.[20] In modified-rebuy or straight-rebuy situations, some stages are compressed or bypassed. For example, in a straight-rebuy situation, the buyer normally has a favorite supplier or a ranked list of suppliers and can skip the search and proposal solicitation stages. Following are some important considerations in each of the eight stages.

Problem Recognition

The buying process begins when someone in the company recognizes a problem or need that can be met by acquiring a good or service. The recognition can be triggered by internal or external stimuli. Internal stimuli might be that the firm decides to develop a new product and needs new equipment and materials; a machine breaks down and requires new parts; purchased material turns out to be unsatisfactory and the firm is looking for another supplier, lower prices, or better quality. Externally, the buyer may get new ideas at a trade show, see an ad, browse a Web site, or receive a call from a sales representative offering a better product or lower price. Business marketers can stimulate problem recognition by direct mail, telemarketing, Internet communications, and calling on prospects.

General Need Description and Product Specification

Next, the buyer has to determine the needed item's general characteristics and required quantity. For standard items, this is simple. For complex items, the buyer will work with others—engineers, users—to define characteristics like reliability, durability, or price. Marketers can help by describing how their products meet or even exceed the buyer's needs.

The buying organization now develops the item's technical specifications. Often, the company will use *product value analysis (PVA)*, a cost-reduction approach in

TABLE 6.2 Buygrid Framework: Major Stages (Buyphases) of the Industrial Buying Process in Relation to Major Buying Situations (Buyclasses)

		Buyclasses		
		New Task	Modified Rebuy	Straight Rebuy
BUYPHASES	1. Problem recognition	Yes	Maybe	No
	2. General need description	Yes	Maybe	No
	3. Product specification	Yes	Yes	Yes
	4. Supplier search	Yes	Maybe	No
	5. Proposal solicitation	Yes	Maybe	No
	6. Supplier selection	Yes	Maybe	No
	7. Order-routine specification	Yes	Maybe	No
	8. Performance review	Yes	Yes	Yes

Source: Adapted from Patrick J. Johnson, Charles W. Faris, and Yoram Wind, *Industrial Buying and Creative Marketing* (Boston: Allyn & Bacon, 1967), p. 14.

which components are studied to determine if they can be redesigned, standardized, or made by cheaper production methods. The PVA team will identify overdesigned product components, for example, that last longer than the product itself. Tightly written specifications will allow the buyer to refuse components that are too expensive or fail to meet the specified standards. Suppliers can also use product value analysis as a tool for positioning themselves to win an account.

Supplier Search

The buyer now tries to identify the most appropriate suppliers through trade directories, contacts with other companies, trade advertisements, trade shows, and the Internet.[21] The move to Internet purchasing has far-reaching implications for suppliers and will change the shape of purchasing for years to come.[22] Companies that purchase over the Internet are utilizing electronic marketplaces in a number of forms (see Table 6.3). Purchasing Web sites are organized around two types of e-hubs: *vertical hubs* centered on industries (plastics, steel, chemicals, paper) and *functional hubs* (logistics, media buying, advertising, energy management).

The supplier's task is to ensure it is considered when customers are—or could be—in the market and searching for a supplier. Identifying good leads and converting them to sales requires marketing and sales personnel to work in a coordinated, multichannel approach as trusted advisors to prospective customers. To proactively generate leads, suppliers need to know about their customers. For background information, they can turn to vendors such as Dun & Bradstreet and infoUSA or information-sharing Web sites such as Jigsaw.[23]

Suppliers that lack capacity or have a poor reputation will be rejected, while those who qualify may be visited by the buyer's agents, who will examine their facilities and meet their personnel. After evaluating each company, the buyer will end up with a short list of qualified suppliers.

TABLE 6.3 Electronic Marketplaces for Business Buying

- *Catalog sites*. Companies can order thousands of items through electronic catalogs distributed by e-procurement software, such as Grainger's.
- *Vertical markets*. Companies buying industrial products such as plastics or services such as media can search for the best prices among thousands of suppliers on specialized Web sites such as Plastics.com.
- *"Pure play" auction sites*. Online marketplaces such as eBay facilitate auction transactions between buyers and sellers (businesses as well as consumers).
- *Spot (or exchange) markets*. On spot electronic markets, prices change by the minute. ChemConnect.com is a successful exchange for buyers and sellers of bulk chemicals such as benzene.
- *Private exchanges*. Hewlett-Packard, IBM, and Wal-Mart operate private exchanges to link with specially invited groups of suppliers and partners over the Web.
- *Barter markets*. In barter markets, participants offer to trade goods or services.
- *Buying alliances*. Several companies buying the same types of goods join together to form purchasing consortia and gain deeper discounts on volume purchases.

Proposal Solicitation

The buyer next invites qualified suppliers to submit proposals. If the item is complex or expensive, the buyer will require a detailed written proposal from each qualified supplier. After evaluating the proposals, the buyer will invite a few suppliers to make formal presentations. Business marketers must be skilled in researching, writing, and presenting proposals. Their written proposals should be marketing documents that describe value and benefits in customer terms. Oral presentations must inspire confidence and position the company's capabilities and resources so they stand out from the competition.

Supplier Selection

Before selecting a supplier, the buying center will specify desired supplier attributes and indicate their relative importance. It will then rate each supplier on these attributes to identify the most attractive one. Business marketers need to do a better job of understanding how business buyers arrive at their valuations.[24] Researchers studying how business marketers assess customer value found eight different *customer value assessment (CVA)* methods. Companies tended to use the simpler methods, although the more sophisticated ones promise a more accurate picture of customer perceived value.

Developing a Compelling Value Proposition To command price premiums in competitive B-to-B markets, a firm must create compelling customer value propositions. The first step is to learn more about the customer using a productive research method such as: internal engineering assessment; field value-in-use assessment; focus-group value assessment; direct survey questions; conjoint analysis; benchmarks; compositional approach; or importance ratings. The next step is to specify the customer value proposition, clearly substantiating value claims by demonstrating the differences between the company's offerings and competitors' offerings on the dimensions that matter most to the customer. The firm should also document how the offering has actually added value or cut costs for existing customers. Finally, the firm must fully implement the value proposition, supported by appropriate employee training and rewards.[25]

Overcoming Price Pressures Despite moves toward strategic sourcing, partnering, and participation in cross-functional teams, buyers still spend a lot of time haggling over price and terms before making a final selection. However, the number of price-oriented buyers can vary by country.[26] Marketers can counter a buyer's request for a lower price in several ways. They may be able to show that the "life-cycle cost" of using their product is lower than that of competitors' products. They can also cite the value of the services the buyer now receives, especially if the services are superior to those offered by competitors. Service support and personal interactions, as well as a supplier's know-how and ability to improve customers' time to market, can be useful differentiators in achieving key-supplier status.[27] Some firms handle price-oriented buyers by setting a lower price with restrictive conditions: (1) limited quantities; (2) no refunds; (3) no adjustments; and (4) no services.[28]

Determining How Many Suppliers to Use As part of the supplier selection process, buying centers must decide how many suppliers to use. In the past, many firms preferred a large supplier base to ensure adequate supplies and to obtain price concessions. Out-suppliers would try to get in the door by offering low prices. Increasingly, however, companies are reducing the number of suppliers. Companies such as Ford,

Motorola, and AlliedSignal have cut the number of suppliers by anywhere from 20% to 80%. The suppliers who remain are responsible for larger component systems, for achieving continuous quality and performance improvements, and for lowering prices annually by a given percentage. There is even a trend toward single sourcing.

Order-Routine Specification

After selecting suppliers, the buyer negotiates the final order, listing the technical specifications, the quantity needed, the delivery schedule, and so on. In the case of MRO items, buyers are moving toward blanket contracts rather than periodic purchase orders. A blanket contract establishes a long-term relationship in which the supplier promises to resupply the buyer as needed at agreed-upon prices over a specified period. Because the seller holds the stock, blanket contracts are sometimes called *stockless purchase plans*. The buyer's computer automatically sends an order to the seller when stock is needed. Out-suppliers have difficulty breaking into such an arrangement unless the buyer becomes dissatisfied with the in-supplier's prices, quality, or service.

Companies that fear a shortage of key materials are willing to buy and hold large inventories and sign long-term supply contracts to ensure a steady flow of materials. DuPont, Ford, and several other major companies regard long-term supply planning as a major responsibility of their purchasing managers. For example, General Motors wants to buy from fewer suppliers who are willing to locate close to its plants and produce high-quality components. In addition, firms are setting up extranets to make ordering faster, easier, and less expensive. Some companies even shift ordering responsibility to their suppliers, in systems called *vendor-managed inventory*. These suppliers are privy to the customer's inventory levels and are responsible for replenishing it automatically through *continuous replenishment programs*.

Performance Review

The buyer periodically reviews the performance of the chosen supplier(s) using one of three methods. The buyer may contact the end users and ask for their evaluations; the buyer may rate the supplier on several criteria using a weighted score method; or the buyer might aggregate the cost of poor supplier performance to come up with adjusted costs of purchase, including price. The performance review may lead the buyer to continue, modify, or end a supplier relationship.

Building Business Relationships

To improve effectiveness and efficiency, business suppliers and their customers are exploring different ways to manage their relationships.[29] Cultivating the right business relationships is paramount for any holistic marketing program.[30] "Breakthrough Marketing: GE" shows that company's expertise in building strong business relationships.

Corporate Credibility and Trust Knowledge that is specific and relevant to a relationship partner is an important factor in the strength of inter-firm ties between partners.[31] In particular, trust is a key prerequisite to healthy long-term relationships (see Figure 6.1). *Corporate credibility* is the extent to which customers believe that a firm can design and deliver offerings that satisfy their needs and wants. It reflects the

BREAKTHROUGH MARKETING: GENERAL ELECTRIC

General Electric is so large (its annual revenues exceed $168 billion) that if each of its six business units were ranked separately, all would appear in the *Fortune* 500. It became the acknowledged pioneer in business-to-business marketing in the 1950s and 1960s when its tagline was "Live Better Electrically." As the company diversified into medical devices, financial services, and other offerings, it created new campaigns, including "Progress for People," "We Bring Good Things to Life," "Imagination at Work," and—more recently—"Ecomagination," highlighting its environmental commitment. It spends $150 million yearly on advertising that features the core GE brand. The result? "Research indicates GE is now being associated with attributes such as being high-tech, leading-edge, innovative, contemporary, and creative," says GE's general manager for global advertising and branding.

Another key to GE's success is its ability to put itself in the shoes of its customers. Consider its approach to pricing aircraft engines. GE knows that a large aircraft engine is a major purchase ($21 million). It also knows that customers (airlines) face substantial maintenance costs to meet regulatory guidelines and ensure engine reliability. That's why GE pioneered a pricing plan called "Power by the Hour," which allows customers to pay a fixed fee each time they run the engine. In return, GE performs all the maintenance and guarantees the engine's reliability. No wonder GE's customer relationships are both profitable and enduring.[32]

FIGURE 6.1 Trust Dimensions

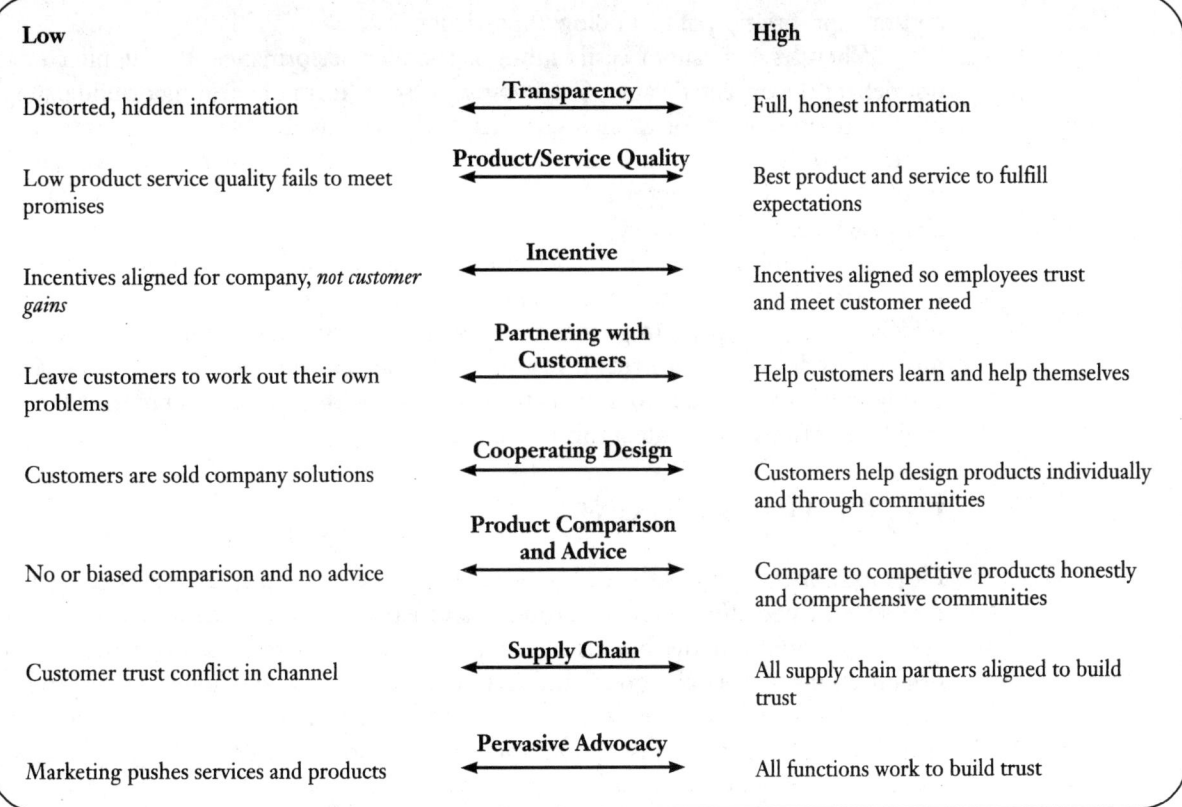

Source: Glen Urban, "Where Are You Positioned On the Trust Dimensions?" *Don't Just Relate—Advocate. A Blueprint for Profit in the Era of Customer Power*, Wharton School Publishers, 2005, p. 99. Reprinted by permission.

firm's reputation in the marketplace and is the foundation for a strong relationship. Corporate credibility depends on three factors:[33]

- *Corporate expertise.* The extent to which a company is seen as able to make and sell products or conduct services
- *Corporate trustworthiness.* The extent to which a company is seen as motivated to be honest, dependable, and sensitive to customer needs
- *Corporate likability.* The extent to which a company is seen as likable, attractive, prestigious, dynamic, and so on

Risks and Opportunism Researchers have noted that establishing a customer–supplier relationship creates tension between safeguarding and adaptation. Vertical coordination between customers and suppliers can facilitate stronger ties but may also increase the risk to the customer's and supplier's specific investments. *Specific investments* are those expenditures tailored to a particular company and value-chain partner (investments in company-specific training, equipment, and operations).[34] Specific investments help firms grow profits and achieve their positioning.[35] Yet they also entail considerable risk to both customer and supplier. Transaction theory from economics maintains that because these investments are partially sunk, they lock the firms into a particular relationship. Sensitive cost and process information may need to be exchanged. A buyer may be vulnerable to holdup because of switching costs; a supplier may be more vulnerable to holdup in future contracts because of dedicated assets and/or expropriation of technology/knowledge.[36]

When buyers cannot easily monitor supplier performance, the supplier might not deliver the expected value. *Opportunism* is "some form of cheating or undersupply relative to an implicit or explicit contract."[37] It may involve blatant self-interest and deliberate misrepresentation that violates contractual agreements. A more passive form of opportunism might involve a refusal or unwillingness to adapt to changing circumstances.

Opportunism is a concern because firms must devote resources to control and monitoring that otherwise could be allocated to more productive purposes. Contracts may become inadequate to govern transactions when supplier opportunism becomes difficult to detect; when firms invest in assets they cannot use elsewhere; and when contingencies are harder to anticipate. A supplier with a good reputation will try to avoid opportunism to protect this valuable asset.

EXECUTIVE SUMMARY

Organizational buying is the decision-making process by which formal organizations establish the need for purchased products and services and then identify, evaluate, and choose among alternative brands and suppliers. The business market consists of all the organizations that acquire goods and services used in the production of other products or services that are sold, rented, or supplied to others. The institutional market consists of schools and other institutions that provide goods and services to people in their care. Government organizations also are major buyers of goods and services.

Compared to consumer markets, business markets have fewer and larger buyers, closer customer–supplier relationships, and more geographically concentrated buyers. Demand in the business market is derived from demand in the consumer market and fluctuates with the business cycle. Organizations face three types of buying situations: the straight re-buy, the modified re-buy, and the new task. The buying center consists of initiators, users, influencers, deciders, approvers, buyers, and gatekeepers. To influence these parties, marketers must be aware of environmental, organizational, interpersonal, and individual factors.

The buying process consists of eight buyphases: (1) problem recognition; (2) general need description; (3) product specification; (4) supplier search; (5) proposal solicitation; (6) supplier selection; (7) order-routine specification; and (8) performance review. Business marketers must form strong relationships with their customers, maintain corporate credibility, and deliver the value that organizational buyers expect.

NOTES

1. David Raikow, "Cisco: Thinking Small," *VAR Business*, June 11, 2007, p. 96; Kate Maddox, "BMA Conference Showcases Innovation," *B to B*, June 12, 2006, p. 3.
2. For a comprehensive review of the topic, see James C. Anderson and James A. Narus, *Business Market Management: Understanding, Creating and Delivering Value*, 2nd edition (Upper Saddle River, NJ: Prentice Hall, 2004). Comments on a draft of this chapter from Northwestern University's Jim Anderson and University of Wisconsin's Jan Heide are gratefully acknowledged.
3. Frederick E. Webster Jr. and Yoram Wind, *Organizational Buying Behavior* (Upper Saddle River, NJ: Prentice Hall, 1972), p. 2. For a review of recent academic literature on the topic, see Håkan Håkansson and Ivan Snehota, "Marketing in Business Markets," in *Handbook of Marketing*, eds., Bart Weitz and Robin Wensley (London: Sage Publications, 2002), pp. 513–526.
4. Paul King, "Purchasing: Keener Competition Requires Thinking Outside the Box," *Nation's Restaurant News*, August 18, 2003, p. 87.
5. Patrick J. Robinson, Charles W. Faris, and Yoram Wind, *Industrial Buying and Creative Marketing* (Boston: Allyn & Bacon, 1967).
6. See Daniel H. McQuiston, "Novelty, Complexity, and Importance as Causal Determinants of Industrial Buyer Behavior," *Journal of Marketing* (April 1989), pp. 66–79; and Peter Doyle, Arch G. Woodside, and Paul Mitchell, "Organizational Buying in New Task and Rebuy Situations," *Industrial Marketing Management*, February 1979, pp. 7–11.
7. Urban B. Ozanne and Gilbert A. Churchill, Jr., "Five Dimensions of the Industrial Adoption Process," *Journal of Marketing Research* (August 1971), pp. 322–328.
8. To learn how business-to-business firms can improve their branding, see Philip Kotler and Waldemar Pfoertsch, *B2B Brand Management* (Berlin-Heidelberg: Springer, 2006).
9. See Donald W. Jackson Jr., Janet E. Keith, and Richard K. Burdick, "Purchasing Agents' Perceptions of Industrial Buying Center Influence: A Situational Approach," *Journal of Marketing* (Fall 1984): 75–83. Jeffrey E. Lewin and Naveen Donthu, "The Influence of Purchase Situation on Buying Center Structure and Involvement: A Select Meta-Analysis of Organizational Buying Behavior Research," *Journal of Business Research* 58 (October 2005), pp. 1381–1390; R. Venkatesh and Ajay K. Kohli, "Influence Strategies in Buying Centers," *Journal of Marketing* 59 (October 1995), pp. 71–82.
10. Webster and Wind, *Organizational Buying Behavior*, p. 6.
11. Ibid., pp. 78–80.
12. James C. Anderson and James A. Narus, *Business Market Management: Understanding, Creating and Delivering Value*, 2nd edition (Upper Saddle River, NJ: Prentice Hall, 2004); Frederick E. Webster Jr. and Yoram Wind, "A General Model for Understanding Organizational Buying Behavior," *Journal of Marketing* 36 (April 1972), pp. 12–19; Webster and Wind, *Organizational Buying Behavior*.
13. Allison Enright, "It Takes a Committee to Buy into B-to-B," *Marketing News*, February 15, 2006, pp. 12–13.
14. Frederick E. Webster Jr. and Kevin Lane Keller, "A Roadmap for Branding in Industrial Markets," *Journal of Brand Management* 11 (May 2004), pp. 388–402.
15. Scott Ward and Frederick E. Webster Jr., "Organizational Buying Behavior," in *Handbook of*

Consumer Behavior, Tom Robertson and Hal Kassarjian, eds. (Upper Saddle River, NJ: Prentice Hall, 1991), ch. 12, pp. 419–458.
16. "Skype Relaunches Online Shop for US Consumers," *Internet Business News*, March 16, 2007; Beckey Bright, "How Do You Say 'Web'?" *Wall Street Journal*, May 23, 2005, p. R11; Betsy Cummings, "Selling Around the World," *Sales & Marketing Management*, May 2001, p. 70; Rhonda Coast, "Understanding Cultural Differences Is a Priority," *Pittsburgh Business Times*, February 11, 2000, p. 13; John V. Thill and Courtland L. Bovée, *Excellence in Business Communication*, 5th ed. (Upper Saddle River, NJ: Prentice Hall, 2002), ch. 3.
17. James C. Anderson, James A. Narus, and Wouter van Rossum, "Customer Value Proposition in Business Markets," *Harvard Business Review*, March 2006, pp. 2–10; James C. Anderson, "From Understanding to Managing Customer Value in Business Markets," in *Rethinking Marketing: New Marketing Tools*, H. Håkansson, D. Harrison, and A. Waluszewski, eds. (London: John Wiley & Sons, 2004), pp. 137–159.
18. Michael Krauss, "Warriors of the Heart," *Marketing News*," February 1, 2006, p. 7.
19. Webster and Wind, *Organizational Buying Behavior*, p. 6.
20. Robinson, Faris, and Wind, *Industrial Buying and Creative Marketing*.
21. Rajdeep Grewal, James M. Comer, and Raj Mehta, "An Investigation into the Antecedents of Organizational Participation in Business-to-Business Electronic Markets," *Journal of Marketing* 65 (July 2001), pp. 17–33.
22. Knowledge@Wharton, "Open Sesame? Or Could the Doors Slam Shut for Alibaba.com?" July 27, 2005; Olga Kharif, "B2B, Take 2," *BusinessWeek*, November 25, 2003; George S. Day, Adam J. Fein, and Gregg Ruppersberger, "Shakeouts in Digital Markets: Lessons from B2B Exchanges," *California Management Review* 45, no. 2 (Winter 2003), pp. 131–151; Julia Angwin, "Top Online Chemical Exchange Is Unlikely Success Story," *Wall Street Journal*, January 8, 2004, p. A15.
23. Enright, "It Takes a Committee to Buy into B-to-B."
24. Daniel J. Flint, Robert B. Woodruff, and Sarah Fisher Gardial, "Exploring the Phenomenon of Customers' Desired Value Change in a Business-to-Business Context," *Journal of Marketing* 66 (October 2002), pp. 102–117.
25. James C. Anderson, James A. Narus, and Wouter van Rossum, "Customer Value Propositions in Business Markets," *Harvard Business Review*, March 2006, pp. 2–10; James C. Anderson and James A. Narus, "Business Marketing: Understanding What Customers Value," *Harvard Business Review*, November 1998, pp. 53–65; James C. Anderson and James A. Narus, "Capturing the Value of Supplementary Services," *Harvard Business Review*, January 1995, pp. 75–83; James C. Anderson, Dipak C. Jain, and Pradeep K. Chintagunta, "A Customer Value Assessment in Business Markets: A State-of-Practice Study," *Journal of Business-to-Business Marketing* 1, no. 1 (1993), pp. 3–29.
26. Ruth N. Bolton and Matthew B. Myers, "Price-Based Global Market Segmentation for Services," *Journal of Marketing* 67 (July 2003), pp. 108–128.
27. Wolfgang Ulaga and Andreas Eggert, "Value-Based Differentiation in Business Relationships: Gaining and Sustaining Key Supplier Status," *Journal of Marketing*, 70 (January), 2006, pp. 119–136.
28. Nirmalya Kumar, *Marketing As Strategy: Understanding the CEO's Agenda for Driving Growth and Innovation* (Boston: Harvard Business School Press, 2004).
29. For foundational material, see Lloyd M. Rinehart, James A. Eckert, Robert B. Handfield, Thomas J. Page, Jr., and Thomas Atkin, "An Assessment of Buyer-Seller Relationships," *Journal of Business Logistics*, 25 (1), 2004, pp. 25–62; Barbara Bund Jackson, *Winning & Keeping Industrial Customers: The Dynamics of Customer Relations* (Lexington, MA: D. C. Heath and Company, 1985); F. Robert Dwyer, Paul Schurr, and Sejo Oh, "Developing Buyer-Supplier Relationships," *Journal of Marketing*, 51 (April 1987), pp. 11–28.
30. Arnt Buvik and George John, "When Does Vertical Coordination Improve Industrial Purchasing Relationships?" *Journal of Marketing* 64 (October 2000), pp. 52–64.
31. Robert W. Palmatier, Rajiv P. Dant, Dhruv Grewal and Kenneth R. Evans, "Factors Influencing the Effectiveness of Relationship Marketing: A Meta-Analysis," *Journal of Marketing*, 70 (October 2006), pp. 136–153; Patricia M. Doney and Joseph P. Cannon, "An Examination of the Nature of Trust in Buyer–Seller Relationships," *Journal of Marketing* 61 (April 1997), pp. 35–51; Jean L. Johnson, Ravipreet S. Sohli, and Rajdeep Grewal, "The Role of Relational Knowledge Stores in Interfirm Partnering, *Journal of Marketing* 68 (July 2004), pp. 21–36; Fred Selnes and James Sallis, "Promoting Relationship Learning," *Journal of Marketing*, 67 (July 2003), pp. 80–95; Shankar

Ganesan, "Determinants of Long-Term Orientation in Buyer–Seller Relationships," *Journal of Marketing* 58 (April 1994), pp. 1–19.

32. Nelson D. Schwartz, "Is G.E. Too Big for Its Own Good?" *New York Times*, July 22, 2007, sec. 3, pp. 1, 8; Richard Siklos, "A Soft Sell with Cold, Hard Cash in Mind," *New York Times*, April 15, 2007, sec. 3, p. 6; John J. Fialka and Kathryn Kranhold, "As It Polishes Green Image, GE Fights EPA," *Wall Street Journal*, February 13, 2007, p. A1; Kathryn Kranhold, "The Immelt Era, Five Years Old, Transforms GE," *Wall Street Journal*, September 11, 2006; Geoffrey Colvin, "What Makes GE Great?" *Fortune*, March 6, 2006, pp. 90–104; Daniel Fisher, "GE Turns Green," *Forbes*, August 15, 2005, pp. 80–85; John A. Byrne, "Jeff Immelt," *Fast Company*, July 2005, pp. 60–65.

33. Bob Violino, "Building B2B Trust," *Computerworld*, June 17, 2002, p. 32; Robert M. Morgan and Shelby D. Hunt, "The Commitment–Trust Theory of Relationship Marketing," *Journal of Marketing* 58, no. 3 (1994), pp. 20–38; Christine Moorman, Rohit Deshpande, and Gerald Zaltman, "Factors Affecting Trust in Market Research Relationships," *Journal of Marketing* 57 (January 1993), pp. 81–101; Kevin Lane Keller and David A. Aaker, "Corporate-Level Marketing: The Impact of Credibility on a Company's Brand Extensions," *Corporate Reputation Review* 1 (August 1998), pp. 356–378; Richard E. Plank, David A. Reid, and Ellen Bolman Pullins, "Perceived Trust in Business-to-Business Sales: A New Measure," *Journal of Personal Selling and Sales Management* 19, no. 3 (Summer 1999): 61–72.

34. Akesel I. Rokkan, Jan B. Heide, and Kenneth H. Wathne, "Specific Investment in Marketing Relationships: Expropriation and Bonding Effects," *Journal of Marketing Research* 40 (May 2003), pp. 210–224.

35. Mrinal Ghosh and George John, "Governance Value Analysis and Marketing Strategy," *Journal of Marketing* 63 (Special Issue, 1999), pp. 131–145.

36. Buvik and John, "When Does Vertical Coordination Improve Industrial Purchasing Relationships?"

37. Kenneth H. Wathne and Jan B. Heide, "Opportunism in Interfirm Relationships: Forms, Outcomes, and Solutions," *Journal of Marketing* 64 (October 2000), pp. 36–51.

CHAPTER 7

Identifying Market Segments and Targets

In this chapter, we will address the following questions:

1. What are the different levels of market segmentation?
2. How can a company identify the segments that make up a market?
3. How should a company choose the most attractive target markets?

MARKETING MANAGEMENT AT SIGNATURE CYCLES

Who buys a custom-made $8,000 bicycle? At Signature Cycles in New York City, buyers range from a real estate developer who likes triathlon racing to an advertising executive who wants to stay fit in style. The main market for custom-made bicycles is affluent baby boomers (the 76 million U.S. consumers born between 1946 and 1964) who're feeling the physical effects of aging but want to keep riding—on their own terms. Signature Cycle's customers arrive by appointment to be measured, observed, and custom-fit for a bicycle built specifically for their needs. "People don't come to buy the product," explains the owner, Paul Levin. "They come for the benefit that the product can provide. So I need to know their goals and aspirations, not just their physical dimensions and limitations."

Customers can choose from an array of special options such as $3,000 carbon-fiber wheels and personalized paint schemes. The final price can be as much as $15,000, with delivery in two to twelve months. Although Signature Cycles sells only 200 custom bikes per year, its total revenues are approaching $2 million. And competition is on the rise as a growing number of elite bicycle retailers also target the lucrative baby-boomer market for custom bikes.[1]

To compete more effectively, companies such as Signature Cycles are embracing target marketing. Instead of scattering their marketing efforts, they're focusing on understanding and targeting those consumers they have the greatest chance of satisfying. Target marketing requires that marketers (1) identify and profile distinct groups of buyers who differ in their needs and preferences (market segmentation); (2) select one or more segments to enter (market targeting); and (3) establish and communicate the offering's distinctive benefit(s) to each target segment (market positioning). This chapter focuses on the first two steps; Chapter 9 will discuss positioning.

LEVELS OF MARKET SEGMENTATION

Sellers that use **mass marketing** engage in the mass production, distribution, and promotion of one product for all buyers. Henry Ford epitomized this strategy when he offered the Model T Ford in one color, black. Coca-Cola also used mass marketing when it sold only one kind of Coke in a 6.5-ounce bottle.

The argument for mass marketing is that it creates the largest potential market, which leads to the lowest costs, which in turn can lead to lower prices or higher margins. However, critics point to increased splintering of the market and the proliferation of media and distribution channels, which make it increasingly difficult to reach a mass audience. Some claim that mass marketing is dying. Most companies are turning to *micromarketing* at one of four levels: segments, niches, local areas, and individuals.

Segment Marketing

A *market segment* consists of a group of customers who share a similar set of needs and wants. Rather than creating the segments, the marketer's task is to identify them and decide which one(s) to target. Segment marketing offers key benefits over mass marketing. The company can often better design, price, disclose, and deliver the product or service and also can fine-tune the marketing program and activities to better deflect competitors' marketing.

However, even a segment is partly a fiction, in that not everyone wants exactly the same thing. Anderson and Narus urge marketers to present flexible market offerings to all members of a segment.[2] A **flexible market offering** consists of a *naked solution* containing the product and service elements that all segment members value, and *discretionary options* that some members value (perhaps for an additional charge). For example, Siemens Electrical Apparatus Division sells metal-clad boxes to small manufacturers at prices that include free delivery and a warranty, but it also offers installation and communication peripherals as extra-cost options.

We can characterize market segments in different ways. One way is to identify *preference segments*. **Homogeneous preferences** exist when all consumers have roughly the same preferences; the market shows no natural segments. At the other extreme are consumers with **diffused preferences,** who vary greatly in their preferences. Finally, **clustered preferences** result when natural market segments emerge from groups of consumers with shared preferences.

Niche Marketing

A *niche* is a more narrowly defined customer group seeking a distinctive mix of benefits. Marketers usually identify niches by dividing a segment into subsegments.

For example, while Avis and other firms provide airport rental cars for travelers, Enterprise has attacked the low-budget, insurance-replacement market by renting to customers whose cars have been wrecked or stolen.

A niche is attractive when its customers have a distinct set of needs; it is fairly small but has size, profit, and growth potential and is unlikely to attract many other competitors; its customers will pay a premium to the firm that best satisfies their needs; and the *nicher* gains certain economies through specialization. Note that as marketing efficiency increases, niches that were seemingly too small may become more profitable.[3]

Larger companies, such as IBM, have lost pieces of their market to nichers: these confrontations have been labeled "guerrillas against gorillas."[4] This is also happening online to the two big social-networking sites, MySpace and Facebook. Both rely on advertising revenue to survive and risk losing out by trying to be all things to all people while upstart nichers try to capitalize on the social networking phenomenon. For instance, 1Up.com is a content-heavy social site where online gaming fanatics can trade tips and opinions; Gather.com serves the so-called NPR crowd: people in the prime of their careers who have disposable income to burn.[5] The low cost of Internet marketing has led to many small start-ups aimed at niches. The recipe for Internet niching success: Choose a hard-to-find product that customers don't need to see and touch.

Niche marketers aim to understand their customers' needs so well that the customers willingly pay a premium. Tom's of Maine was acquired by Colgate-Palmolive for $100 million in part because its all-natural personal care products and charitable donation programs appeal to consumers who have been turned off by big businesses. The brand commands a 30% premium as a result.[6]

Local Marketing

Target marketing is leading to marketing programs tailored to the needs and wants of local customer groups in particular trading areas, neighborhoods, even individual stores. Citibank, for instance, adjusts its banking services in each branch depending on neighborhood demographics; Costco tailors its merchandise assortment to local tastes and buying patterns.[7]

Local marketing reflects a growing trend toward *grassroots marketing*, concentrating on getting as close and personally relevant to individual customers as possible. Much of Nike's initial success has been attributed to engaging target consumers through grassroots marketing such as sponsorship of local school teams and expert-conducted clinics. "Breakthrough Marketing: HSBC" profiles another success story.

Those who favor local marketing see national advertising as wasteful because it fails to address local needs. Opponents argue that local marketing drives up manufacturing and marketing costs by reducing economies of scale and magnifying logistical problems. A brand's overall image might be diluted if the product and message vary in different localities.

Individual Marketing

The ultimate level of segmentation leads to "segments of one," "customized marketing," or "one-to-one marketing."[8] Today customers are taking more individual initiative in determining what and how to buy. They search the Internet; look up information about

BREAKTHROUGH MARKETING: HSBC

London-based HSBC wants to be known as the "world's local bank." This tagline reflects HSBC's positioning as a globe-spanning financial institution specializing in serving local markets. Originally the Hong Kong and Shanghai Banking Corporation Limited, it's now the second-largest bank in the world, with over 100 million customers and 9,500 branches in 79 countries. Yet its marketing strategy is to remain close to its customers: "Our position as the world's local bank enables us to approach each country uniquely, blending local knowledge with a worldwide operating platform," states HSBC's chairman.

HSBC demonstrates its local knowledge with carefully targeted communications and products. For example, during a major expansion in New York City, the bank's multimedia campaign included a "New York City's Most Knowledgeable Cabbie" contest. The winning cabbie got paid to drive an HSBC BankCab full-time for a year—and any customer with a bankcard, checkbook, or bank statement from HSBC could ride for free. In researching new products, HSBC marketers discovered that the pet-insurance market is growing at 125% a year, so they began offering this insurance through the HSBC Insurance agency. In Malaysia, HSBC targeted students with no-frills credit cards and high-value customers with special "Premium Centers" branches. In Canada, it began offering free ATM withdrawals and deposits to customers in fast-growing cities such as Toronto. Local and global: HSBC's winning combination.[9]

and evaluations of offers; contact suppliers, users, and product critics; and in many cases, design the product they want.[10]

Wind and Rangaswamy see a movement toward "customerizing" the firm.[11] **Customerization** combines operationally driven mass customization with customized marketing in a way that empowers consumers to design the product and service offering of their choice. The firm no longer requires prior information about the customer, nor does it need to own manufacturing. The firm provides a platform and tools and "rents" out to customers the means to design their own products. A company is customerized when it is able to respond to individual customers by customizing its products, services, and messages on a one-to-one basis.[12]

Customization is certainly not for every company.[13] It may be difficult to implement for complex products such as automobiles, and it can raise the cost of goods by more than the customer is willing to pay. Moreover, customers don't always know what they want until they see actual products, yet they cannot cancel their orders after the company has started to work on the products. Despite these difficulties, some companies (including Signature Cycles, profiled at the start of the chapter) have been successful with customization.

SEGMENTING CONSUMER AND BUSINESS MARKETS

Because of the inherent differences between consumer and business markets, marketers cannot use exactly the same variables to segment both. Instead, they use one broad group of variables as the basis for consumer markets and another broad group for business markets.

Bases for Segmenting Consumer Markets

In consumer markets, some researchers try to form segments by looking at descriptive characteristics: geographic, demographic, and psychographic. Then they examine whether these customer segments exhibit different needs or product responses. Other researchers try to define segments by looking at behavioral considerations, such as responses to benefits, use occasions, or brands. Next, the researcher sees whether different characteristics are associated with each consumer-response segment. Regardless of which segmentation scheme is used, the key is adjusting the marketing program to customer differences. The major segmentation variables—geographic, demographic, psychographic, and behavioral—are summarized in Table 7.1.

Geographic Segmentation Geographic segmentation calls for dividing the market into different geographical units such as nations, states, regions, counties, cities, or neighborhoods. The company can operate in one or a few geographic areas or operate in all but pay attention to local variations. For example, Hilton Hotels customizes rooms and lobbies according to location: Northeastern hotels are sleek and cosmopolitan; Southwestern hotels are more rustic. National retailers such Bed Bath & Beyond allow store managers to cater to local tastes when they choose merchandise.[14]

More and more, regional marketing means marketing right down to a specific zip code.[15] Some approaches combine geographic data with demographic data to yield even richer descriptions of consumers and neighborhoods. Claritas Inc. has developed a geoclustering approach called PRIZM (Potential Rating Index by Zip Markets) NE that classifies over half a million U.S. residential neighborhoods into 14 distinct groups and 66 distinct lifestyle segments called PRIZM Clusters.[16] The groupings take into consideration 39 factors in five broad categories: (1) education and affluence; (2) family life cycle; (3) urbanization; (4) race and ethnicity; and (5) mobility. The clusters have descriptive titles such as *Blue Blood Estates*, *Young Digerati*, *Beltway Boomers*, *Latino America*, and *Shotguns and Pickups*. The inhabitants in a cluster tend to lead similar lives, drive similar cars, have similar jobs, and read similar magazines.

Demographic Segmentation In demographic segmentation, we divide the market into groups on the basis of age and the other variables. One reason demographic variables are so popular with marketers is that consumer wants, preferences, and usage rates are often associated with demographic variables. Another reason is these variables are easy to measure. Even as we describe the target market in non-demographic terms, such as by personality type, we may need the link back to demographic characteristics to estimate the size of the target market and the media that can be used to reach it.

Here's how demographic variables can be used to segment consumer markets:

- *Age and life-cycle stage*. Consumer wants and abilities change with age. Toothpaste brands such as Crest and Colgate offer three main lines of products to target kids, adults, and older consumers. Age segmentation can be even more refined. Pampers divides its market into prenatal, new baby (0–5 months), baby (6–12 months), toddler (13–23 months), and preschooler (24 months plus). However, age and life cycle can be tricky variables.[17]
- *Life stage*. People in the same part of the life cycle may differ in their life stage. **Life stage** defines a person's major concern, such as going through a divorce, going into a

TABLE 7.1 Major Segmentation Variables for Consumer Markets

Geographic region	Pacific, Mountain, West North Central, West South Central, East North Central, East South Central, South Atlantic, Middle Atlantic, New England
City or Metro size	Under 5,000; 5,000–20,000; 20,000–50,000; 50,000–100,000; 100,000–250,000; 250,000–500,000; 500,000–1,000,000; 1,000,000–4,000,000; 4,000,000 or over
Density	Urban, suburban, rural
Climate	Northern, southern
Demographic age	Under 6, 6–11, 12–19, 20–34, 35–49, 50–64, 65+
Family size	1–2, 3–4, 5+
Family life cycle	Young, single; young, married, no children; young, married, youngest child under 6; young, married, youngest child 6 or over; older, married, with children; older, married, no children under 18; older, single; other
Gender	Male, female
Income	Under $10,000; $10,000–$15,000; $15,000–$20,000; $20,000–$30,000; $30,000–$50,000; $50,000–$1,000,000; $1,000,000 and over
Occupation	Professional and technical; managers, officials, and proprietors; clerical; sales; craftspeople; forepersons; operatives; farmers; retired; students; homemakers; unemployed
Education	Grade school or less; some high school; high school graduate; some college; college graduate
Religion	Catholic, Protestant, Jewish, Muslim, Hindu, other
Race	White, Black, Asian, Hispanic
Generation	Baby boomers, Generation Xers
Nationality	North American, South American, British, French, German, Italian, Japanese
Social class	Lower lowers, upper lowers, working class, middle class, upper middles, lower uppers, upper uppers
Psychographic lifestyle	Culture-oriented, sports-oriented, outdoor-oriented
Personality	Compulsive, gregarious, authoritarian, ambitious
Behavioral occasions	Regular occasion, special occasion
Benefits	Quality, service, economy, speed
User status	Nonuser, ex-user, potential user, first-time user, regular user
Usage rate	Light user, medium user, heavy user
Loyalty status	None, medium, strong, absolute
Reading stage	Unaware, aware, informed, interested, desirous, intending to buy
Attitude toward product	Enthusiastic, positive, indifferent, negative, hostile

second marriage, taking care of an older parent, deciding to cohabit with another person, deciding to buy a new home, and so on. These life stages present opportunities for marketers who can help people cope with their major concerns. For instance, JC Penney has identified "Starting Outs" as one of its two major customer groups.[18]

- *Gender.* Men and women have different attitudes and behave differently, based partly on genetic makeup and partly on socialization. For example, research shows that men often need to be invited to touch a product, while women are likely to pick it up without prompting.[19] Gender segmentation has long been applied in clothing, cosmetics, and magazines. Now the automobile industry is recognizing gender segmentation and changing the way cars are designed and sold.[20] Women shop differently for cars than men; they are more interested in environmental impact, care more about interior than exterior styling, and view safety in terms of features that help survive an accident rather than handling to avoid an accident.[21]

- *Income.* Income segmentation is a long-standing practice in such categories as automobiles, boats, clothing, cosmetics, and travel. However, income does not always predict the best customers for a given product. Many firms are deliberately going after lower-income groups, in some cases discovering less competitive pressure or greater consumer loyalty.[22] Increasingly, companies are finding that their markets are "hourglass-shaped" as middle-market Americans migrate toward discount products and simultaneously trade up to premium products.[23]

- *Generation.* Each generation is profoundly influenced by the times in which it grows up—the music, movies, politics, and events of that period. Demographers call these generational groups *cohorts*. Because members share the same experiences and have similar outlooks and values, effective marketing appeals should use the icons and images prominent in their experiences. One key cohort is Generation Y, 78 million consumers born between 1977 and 1994 who have combined annual spending power of $187 billion. They grew up amid economic abundance followed by recession, in a world disrupted by events like Columbine and 9/11. They've been "wired" almost from birth—playing computer games, surfing the Web, downloading music, using instant messaging and mobile phones. And many are turned off by traditional, overt marketing.[24]

- *Social class.* Social class strongly influences preference in cars, clothing, home furnishings, leisure activities, reading habits, and retailers, which is why many firms design products for specific classes. However, the tastes of social classes change over time. The 1990s were about ostentation for the upper classes; affluent tastes are now more conservative, although Tiffany and other luxury goods makers still successfully sell to those seeking the good life.[25]

Psychographic Segmentation **Psychographics** is the science of using psychology and demographics to better understand consumers. In *psychographic segmentation*, buyers are divided into different groups on the basis of psychological/personality traits, lifestyle, or values. People within the same demographic group can exhibit very different psychographic profiles.

One of the most popular commercially available classification systems based on psychographic measurements is SRI Consulting Business Intelligence's (SRIC-BI) VALS™ framework. The VALS (values and lifestyles) system classifies U.S. adults into eight primary groups based on demographics and attitudes; it's updated with new data from more than 80,000 surveys per year (see Figure 7.1).[26]

FIGURE 7.1 The VALS Segmentation System

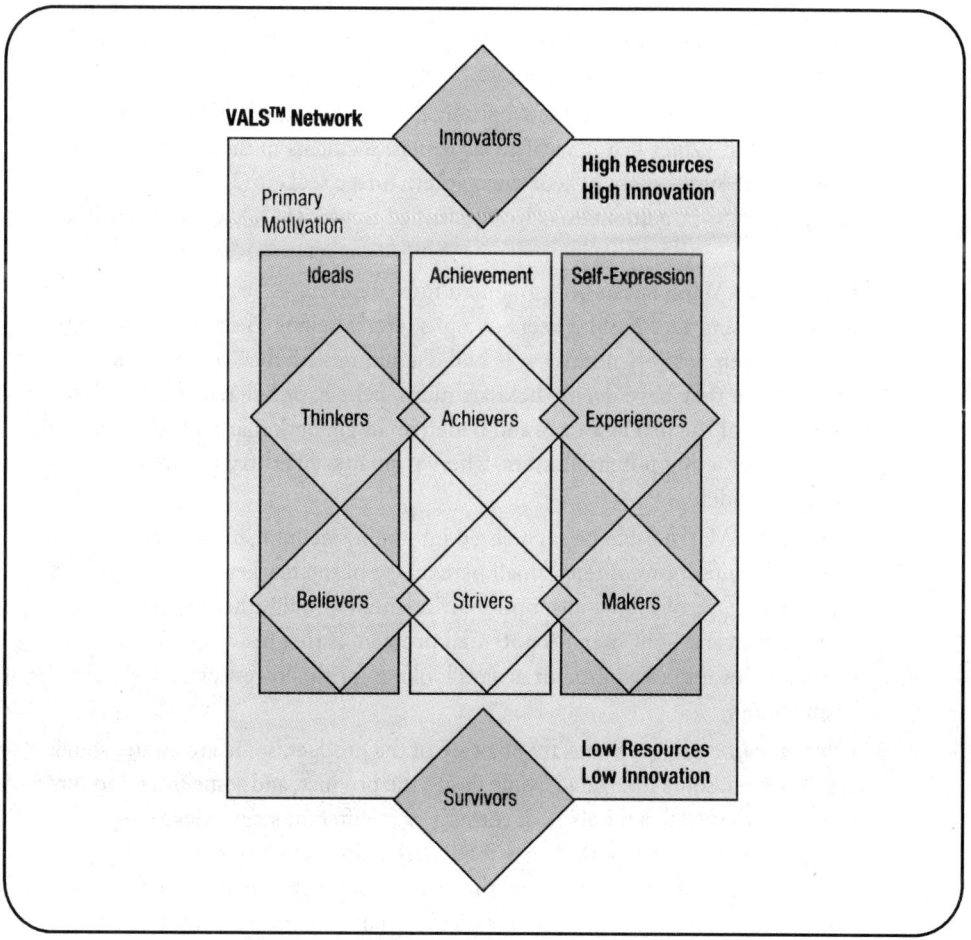

Source: © 2004 by SRI Consulting Business Intelligence. All Rights Reserved. Printed by permission.

Behavioral Segmentation In behavioral segmentation, marketers divide consumers into groups on the basis of their knowledge of, attitude toward, use of, or response to a product. Decision roles are one such variable. People play five roles in a buying decision: *Initiator, Influencer, Decider, Buyer,* and *User.* For example, assume a wife initiates a purchase by requesting a new treadmill for her birthday. The husband may then seek information from many sources, including a friend who has a treadmill and is a key influencer in what models to consider. After presenting the alternative choices to his wife, he then purchases her preferred model, which, as it turns out, ends up being used by the entire family. Different people are playing different roles, but all are crucial in the decision process and ultimate consumer satisfaction.

Many marketers believe that behavioral variables—occasions, benefits, user status, usage rate, loyalty status, buyer-readiness stage, and attitude—are the best starting points for segmentation.

- *Occasions.* We can distinguish buyers according to the occasions when they develop a need and purchase or use a product. For example, air travel is triggered by business, vacation, or family occasions. Occasion segmentation can help expand product usage. Thus, while Christmas, Mother's Day, and Valentine's Day are the three major gift-giving holidays, other occasions for gift-giving are birthdays, weddings, anniversaries, housewarmings, and new babies.[27]

- *Benefits.* Not everyone who buys a product wants the same benefits from it. Constellation Wines U.S. identified six benefit segments in the premium wine market: enthusiast (12% of the market); image seekers (20%), savvy shoppers (15%), traditionalists (16%), satisfied sippers (14%), and overwhelmed (23%).[28]

- *User status.* Markets can be segmented into nonusers, ex-users, potential users, first-time users, and regular users of a product. The key to attracting potential users, or even possibly nonusers, is understanding why they're not using a product. Do they have deeply held attitudes, beliefs, or behaviors or do they lack knowledge of the product or brand benefits? In general, market leaders tend to focus on attracting potential users, whereas smaller firms try to lure users away from the leader.

- *Usage rate.* Markets can be segmented into light, medium, and heavy product users. Heavy users are often a small percentage of the market but account for a high percentage of total consumption. Marketers would rather attract one heavy user than several light users. A potential problem is that heavy users either are extremely loyal to one brand or always looking for the lowest price and never loyal to any brand.

- *Buyer-readiness stage.* Some are unaware of the product, some are aware, some are informed, some interested, some desire the product, and some intend to buy. Note that the relative numbers of consumers at different stages make a big difference in planning marketing activities. To help characterize how many people are at different stages and how well the firm has converted people from one stage to another, some marketers employ a marketing funnel. Figure 7.2 displays a funnel for

FIGURE 7.2 Brand Funnel

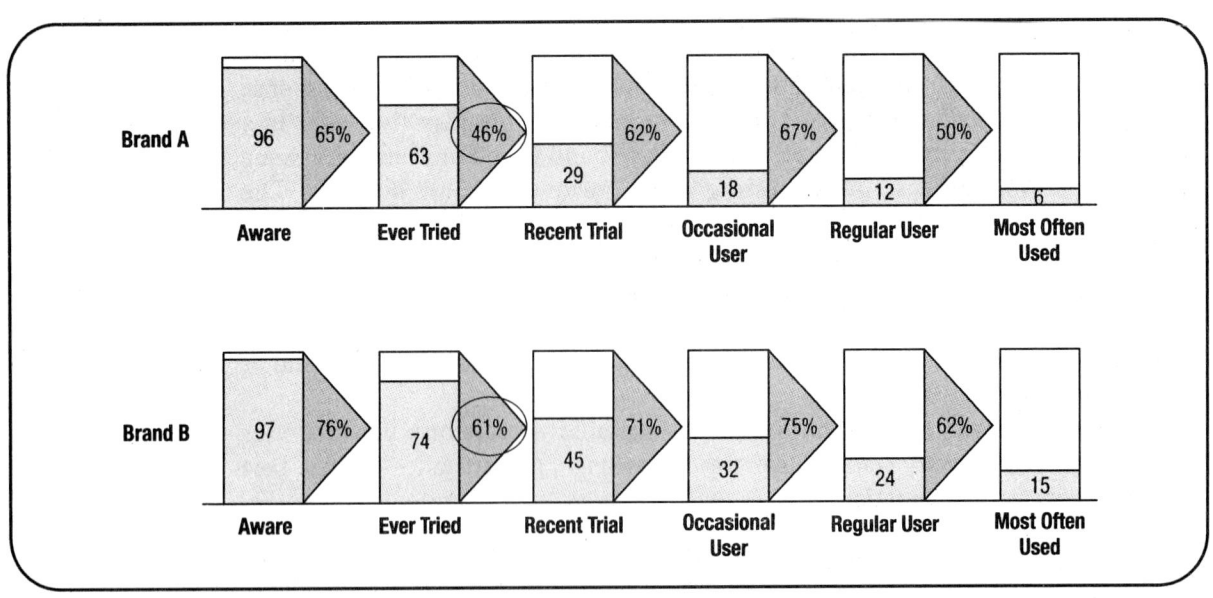

two hypothetical brands, A and B. Brand B performs poorly compared to Brand A at converting one-time triers to more recent triers (only 46% convert for Brand A as compared to 61% for Brand B).

- *Loyalty status.* Marketers usually envision four groups based on brand loyalty status: hard-core loyals (always buy one brand), split loyals (loyal to two or three brands), shifting loyals (shift from one brand to another), and switchers (no loyalty to any brand).[29] By studying its hard-core loyals, a company can identify its products' strengths; by studying its split loyals, the company can see which brands are most competitive with its own. By looking at customers shifting away from its brand, the company can learn about its marketing weaknesses and attempt to correct them. One caution: What appears to be brand loyalty may actually reflect habit, indifference, a low price, a high switching cost, or the unavailability of other brands.

- *Attitude.* Five attitudes about products: enthusiastic, positive, indifferent, negative, and hostile. So, for example, workers in a political campaign use the voter's attitude to determine how much time to spend with that voter. They thank enthusiastic voters and remind them to vote, reinforce those who are positively disposed, try to win the votes of indifferent voters, and spend no time trying to change the attitudes of negative and hostile voters.

The Conversion Model measures the strength of the consumers' psychological commitment to brands and their openness to change.[30] To determine how easily a consumer can be converted to another choice, the model assesses commitment based on factors such as consumer attitudes toward and satisfaction with current brand choices in a category and the importance of the brand-selection decision in the category.[31] Finally, a related behavioral segmentation method has recently been proposed that looks more at the expectations a consumer brings to a particular kind of transaction and locates those expectations on a "Gravity of Decision Spectrum." Focusing on consumers' relationships and involvement with products and categories can often reveal clues to where and how the firm should market to each segment.[32]

Bases for Segmenting Business Markets

We can segment business markets with some of the same variables used in consumer market segmentation, such as geography, benefits sought, and usage rate. Yet business marketers can also use several other variables (see Table 7.2). The demographic variables are the most important, followed by the operating variables—down to the personal characteristics of the buyer. A company should first decide which industries it wants to serve. Then, within a chosen industry, the company can further segment by company size (possibly setting up separate operations for selling to large and small customers) and by purchase criteria.

Business marketers generally identify segments through a sequential process. Consider an aluminum company: First it undertook macrosegmentation, looking at which end-use market to serve (automobile, residential, or beverage containers). It chose the residential market, and then needed to determine the most attractive product application (semifinished material, building components, or aluminum mobile homes). Deciding to focus on building components, it considered the best customer size and chose large customers. The second stage consisted of microsegmentation.

TABLE 7.2 Major Segmentation Variables for Business Markets

Demographic

1. *Industry:* Which industries should we serve?
2. *Company size:* What size companies should we serve?
3. *Location:* What geographical areas should we serve?

Operating Variables

4. *Technology:* What customer technologies should we focus on?
5. *User or nonuser status:* Should we serve heavy users, medium users, light users, or nonusers?
6. *Customer capabilities:* Should we serve customers needing many or few services?

Purchasing Approaches

7. *Purchasing-function organization:* Should we serve companies with highly centralized or decentralized purchasing organizations?
8. *Power structure:* Should we serve companies that are engineering dominated, financially dominated, and so on?
9. *Nature of existing relationships:* Should we serve companies with which we have strong relationships or simply go after the most desirable companies?
10. *General purchase policies:* Should we serve companies that prefer leasing? Service contracts? Systems purchases? Sealed bidding?
11. *Purchasing criteria:* Should we serve companies that are seeking quality? Service? Price?

Situation Factors

12. *Urgency:* Should we serve companies that need quick and sudden delivery or service?
13. *Specific application:* Should we focus on certain applications of our product rather than all applications?
14. *Size or order:* Should we focus on large or small orders?

Personal Characteristics

15. *Buyer-seller similarity:* Should we serve companies whose people and values are similar to ours?
16. *Attitudes toward risk:* Should we serve risk-taking or risk-avoiding customers?
17. *Loyalty:* Should we serve companies that show high loyalty to their suppliers?

Source: Adapted from Thomas V. Bonoma and Benson P. Shapiro, *Segmenting the Industrial Market* (Lexington, MA: Lexington Books, 1983). Reprinted by permission.

The company distinguished among customers buying on price, service, or quality. Because the aluminum company had a high-service profile, it decided to concentrate on the service-motivated segment.

MARKET TARGETING

There are many statistical techniques for developing market segments.[33] Once the firm has identified its market-segment opportunities, it has to decide how many and which ones to target. Marketers are increasingly combining several variables in an effort to identify smaller, better-defined target groups. Thus, a bank may not only identify a group of wealthy retired adults, but also within that group distinguish several segments depending on current income, assets, savings, and risk preferences.

TABLE 7.3 Steps in the Segmentation Process

	Description
1. Needs-Based Segmentation	Group customers into segments based on similar needs and benefits sought by customer in solving a particular consumption problem.
2. Segment Identification	For each needs-based segment, determine which demographics, lifestyles, and usage behaviors make the segment distinct and identifiable (actionable)
3. Segment Attractiveness	Using predetermined segment attractiveness criteria (such as market growth, competitive intensity, and market access), determine the overall attractiveness of each segment.
4. Segment Profitability	Determine segment profitability.
5. Segment Positioning	For each segment, create a "value proposition" and product-price positioning strategy based on that segment's unique customer needs and characteristics.
6. Segment "Acid Test"	Create "segment storyboards" to test the attractiveness of each segment's positioning strategy.
7. Marketing-Mix Strategy	Expand segment positioning strategy to include all aspects of the marketing mix: product, price, promotion, and place.

Source: Adapted from Robert J. Best, *Market-Based Management* (Upper Saddle River, NJ: Prentice Hall, 2000). Reprinted by permission.

This has led some experts to advocate a *needs-based market segmentation approach*. Roger Best proposed the seven-step approach shown in Table 7.3.

Effective Segmentation Criteria

Not all segmentation schemes are useful. For example, table salt buyers could be divided into blond and brunette customers, but hair color is undoubtedly irrelevant to the purchase of salt. Furthermore, if all salt buyers buy the same amount of salt each month, believe all salt is the same, and would pay only one price for salt, this market would be minimally segmentable from a marketing viewpoint.

To be useful, market segments must rate favorably on five key criteria:

1. *Measurable.* The size, purchasing power, and characteristics of the segments can be measured.
2. *Substantial.* The segments are large and profitable enough to serve; each should be the largest possible homogeneous group worth going after with a tailored marketing program.
3. *Accessible.* The segments can be effectively reached and served.
4. *Differentiable.* The segments are conceptually distinguishable and respond differently to different marketing-mix elements and programs. If two segments respond identically to an offer, they are not separate segments.
5. *Actionable.* Effective programs can be formulated for attracting and serving the segments.

Evaluating and Selecting Market Segments

In evaluating different market segments, the firm must look at two factors; the segment's overall attractiveness and the company's objectives and resources. How well does a potential segment score on the five criteria? Does a potential segment have characteristics that make it generally attractive, such as size, growth, profitability, scale economies, and low risk? Does investing in the segment make sense given the firm's objectives, competencies, and resources? Some attractive segments may not mesh with the company's long-run objectives, or the company may lack one or more necessary competencies to offer superior value (see "Marketing Skills: Evaluating Segments").

Having evaluated different segments, the company can consider five patterns of target market selection, as shown in Figure 7.3 and discussed next.

Single-Segment Concentration Through concentrated marketing, a firm can gain a thorough understanding of the chosen segment's needs and achieve a strong market presence, the way Porsche has by targeting the sports car market. Furthermore, the firm will enjoy operating economies through specializing in its production, distribution, and promotion; if it gains leadership, it can earn a high return on investment. However, concentrated marketing involves risks: The segment may turn sour because

MARKETING SKILLS: EVALUATING SEGMENTS

Because choosing the wrong segment(s) can waste money and divert attention from more profitable segments, marketers must be skilled in evaluating segments. To start, they establish criteria for weighing a segment's attractiveness. These may be market measures such as size and growth potential; competitive measures such as number of competitors and ease of market entry; and access measures such as channel availability and fit with company resources and competencies. Also they establish criteria for screening out unsuitable segments, such as illegal, controversial, or highly risky segments. The final step is to estimate the likely sales and profits from the remaining segments and use these figures, along with the attractiveness criteria, to rank the segments. Some marketers determine the order of entry by calculating a total score for each segment, then giving priority to the highest-scoring segments.

For example, Time Warner Cable has been using consumer segmentation in its marketing activities for digital phone service. In central Texas, the firm initially sent all residents a direct-mail package promoting the price advantages of digital phone service. For the second round of communications, however, marketers identified and targeted five particularly promising segments: high-tech households (who want the latest gadgets); trend-setters (who want to save money on phone service so they can buy other trendy products); financially savvy parents (who want to save money to put toward their children's college tuition); new parents (who want to talk about the new baby); and budget-conscious consumers (who can save money by bundling digital phone service with other cable services). Selecting the segments most likely to respond allowed Time Warner Cable to increase its digital-phone subscriptions by 45%.[34]

FIGURE 7.3 Five Patterns of Target Market Selection

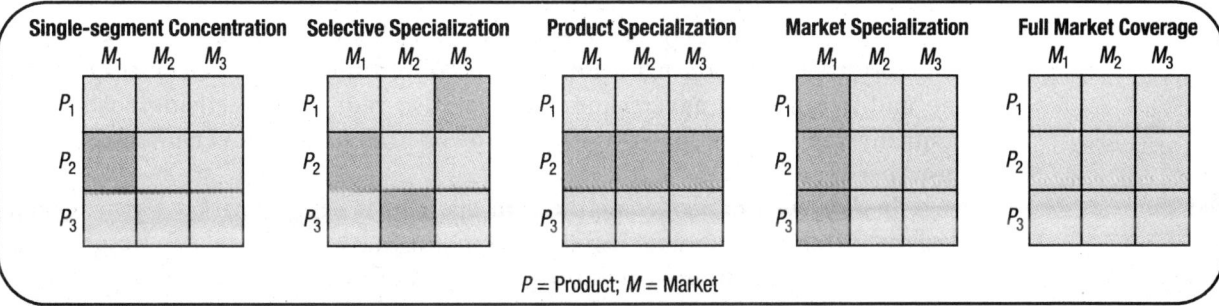

Source: Aadapted from Derek F. Abell, "Defining the Business: The Starting Point of Strategic Planning" (Upper Saddle River, NJ: Prentice Hall,1980), ch. 8, pp. 192–196. Reprinted by permission.

of changes in buying patterns or new competition. For these reasons, many companies prefer to operate in more than one segment.

Companies can try to operate in supersegments rather than in isolated segments. A **supersegment** is a set of segments sharing some exploitable similarity. For example, many symphony orchestras target people who have broad cultural interests, rather than only those who regularly attend concerts.

Selective Specialization A firm selects a number of segments, each objectively attractive and appropriate. There may be little or no synergy among the segments, but each segment promises to be a moneymaker. This strategy has the advantage of diversifying the firm's risk. When Procter & Gamble launched Crest Whitestrips, initial target segments included newly engaged women, brides-to-be, and gay males.

Product Specialization Another approach is to specialize in making a certain product for several segments. A microscope manufacturer, for instance, sells to university, government, and commercial laboratories. The firm makes different microscopes for different customer groups and builds a strong reputation in the specific product area. The downside risk is that the product may be supplanted by an entirely new technology.

Market Specialization The firm concentrates on serving many needs of a particular customer group. For example, a firm can sell an assortment of products only to university laboratories. The firm gains a strong reputation in serving this customer group and becomes a channel for further products the customer group can use. The downside risk is that the customer group may suffer budget cuts or shrink in size.

Full Market Coverage The firm attempts to serve all customer groups with all the products they might need. Only very large firms such as Microsoft (software market) and General Motors (vehicle market) can undertake a full market coverage strategy. Large firms can cover a whole market through undifferentiated marketing or differentiated marketing.

In *undifferentiated marketing*, the firm ignores segment differences and goes after the whole market with one market offer. It designs a product and a marketing program that will endow the product with a superior image and appeal to the broadest number of buyers, and it relies on mass distribution and advertising. The narrow product line keeps down costs of research and development, production, inventory, transportation, marketing research, advertising, and product management; the undifferentiated advertising program also reduces advertising costs. The company can turn its lower costs into lower prices to win over price-sensitive customers.

In *differentiated marketing*, the firm operates in several market segments and designs different programs for each segment. Starwood Hotels & Resorts, for example, is differentiating its hotels along emotional, experiential lines. At its upscale Westin Hotels, the key definition is "renewal," so guests are welcomed with herbal drinks, candles, and soft music. Four Points by Sheraton is a more value-oriented chain that emphasizes "comfort," with ads featuring apple pies and "the comforts of home."[35]

Because differentiated marketing leads to both higher sales and higher operating costs, we can't generalize about this strategy's profitability. Companies should be cautious about oversegmenting their markets. If this happens, they may want to use *countersegmentation* to broaden their customer base. As an example, Smith Kline Beecham launched its Aquafresh toothpaste to attract three benefit segments simultaneously: those seeking fresh breath, whiter teeth, and cavity protection.

Additional Considerations

Two other considerations in evaluating and selecting segments are segment-by-segment invasions and ethical choice of market targets.

Segment-by-Segment Invasions A company should enter one segment at a time and avoid letting rivals know what segment(s) will be next. Unfortunately, many companies fail to develop a long-term invasion plan. PepsiCo is an exception, attacking Coca-Cola first in the grocery market, then in the vending-machine market and other markets. A company facing blocked markets can apply **megamarketing**, the strategic coordination of economic, psychological, political, and public relations skills to gain the cooperation of a number of parties in order to enter or operate in a given market. Pepsi did this to enter India after Coca-Cola left. First, it worked with a local business group to gain government approval for its entry over the objections of domestic competitors and anti-multinational legislators. Pepsi also offered to help India export agricultural products to cover the cost of importing soft-drink concentrate and promised economic development for some rural areas. Pepsi's bundle of benefits won the support of the key interest groups.

Ethical Choice of Market Targets Market targeting sometimes generates public controversy.[36] Consumers become concerned when marketers take unfair advantage of vulnerable groups (such as children) or disadvantaged groups (such as poor people), or promote potentially harmful products. The cereal industry has been criticized for marketing to children. Critics worry that high-powered appeals presented through the mouths of animated characters will lead children to eat too much sugared cereal or poorly balanced breakfasts. Not all attempts to target children, minorities, or other special segments draw criticism. Colgate-Palmolive's Colgate Junior toothpaste has special features designed to get children to brush longer and more often. Thus the issue is not who is targeted, but rather how and for what purpose. Socially responsible marketing calls for targeting and positioning that serve not only the company's interests but also the interests of the targeted segments.

EXECUTIVE SUMMARY

Target marketing includes three activities: market segmentation, market targeting, and market positioning. Markets can be targeted at four levels: segments, niches, local areas, and individuals. Market segments are large, identifiable groups within a market. A niche is a more narrowly defined group. Marketers appeal to local markets through grassroots marketing for trading areas, neighborhoods, and even individual stores. More marketers now practice individual marketing and mass customization.

Two bases for segmenting consumer markets are characteristics and responses. The major segmentation variables for consumer markets are geographic, demographic, psychographic, and behavioral, used singly or in combination. Business marketers use all of these variables along with operating variables, purchasing approaches, and situational factors. To be useful, market segments must be measurable, substantial, accessible, differentiable, and actionable.

A firm has to evaluate the various segments and decide how many and which ones to target: a single segment, several segments, a specific product, a specific market, or the full market. In targeting the full market, it can use either differentiated or undifferentiated marketing. Firms also need to create segment-by-segment invasion plans and choose target markets in a socially responsible manner.

NOTES

1. Michael Frank, "Dream Rides," *Portfolio.com*, July 5, 2007, www.portfolio.com; Steve Friedman, "You Paid How Much for That Bike?" *New York Times*, November 9, 2006, p. G10; Loren Mooney, "By Appointment Only: Paul Levine's Exclusive, Custom Shop Guarantees Perfection," *Bicycling*, August, 2006, www.bicycling.com/article/0,6610,s1-1-3-14792-1,00.html.
2. James C. Anderson and James A. Narus, "Capturing the Value of Supplementary Services," *Harvard Business Review* (January–February 1995): 75–83.
3. Robert Blattberg and John Deighton, "Interactive Marketing: Exploiting the Age of Addressability," *Sloan Management Review* 33, no. 1 (1991): 5–14.
4. See Tevfik Dalgic and Maarten Leeuw, "Niche Marketing Revisited: Concept, Applications, and Some European Cases," *European Journal of Marketing* 28, no. 4 (1994): 39–55.
5. "Why Facebook Works Solo," *Wall Street Journal*, July 11, 2007, p. C12; Robert D. Hof, "There's Not Enough 'Me' in MySpace," *BusinessWeek*, December 4, 2006, p. 40; Abbey Klaassen, "Niche-targeted Social Networks Find Audiences," *Advertising Age*, November 6, 2006, p. 15.
6. Jerry Harkavy, "Colgate Buying Control of Tom's of Maine for $100 Million," *Associated Press*, March 21, 2006, www.boston.com; Ian Zack, "Out of the Tube," *Forbes*, November 26, 2001, p. 200.

7. Dale Buss, "Brands in the Hood," *Point*, December 2005, pp. 1924.
8. Don Peppers and Martha Rogers, *One to One B2B: Customer Development Strategies for the Business-to-Business World* (New York: Doubleday, 2001); Mark Rechtin, "Aston Martin Woos Customers One By One," *Automotive News*, March 28, 2005.
9. Colin Campbell, "The Little Bank That Could—Maybe," *Maclean's*, June 11, 2007, p. 35; Kate Nicholson, "HSBC Aims To Appear Global Yet Approachable," *Campaign*, December 2, 2005, p. 15; Deborah Orr, "New Ledger," *Forbes*, March 1, 2004, pp. 72–73; "Now Your Customers Can Afford to Take Fido to the Vet," *Bank Marketing*, December 2003, p. 47; Kenneth Hein, "HSBC Bank Rides the Coattails of Chatty Cabbies," *Brandweek*, December 1, 2003, p. 30; Sir John Bond and Stephen Green, "HSBC Strategic Overview," presentation to investors, November 27, 2003; "HSBC Enters the Global Branding Big League," *Bank Marketing International*, August 2003, pp. 1–2; www.hsbc.com.
10. Adrian J. Slywotzky and David J. Morrison, *How Digital Is Your Business?* (New York: Crown Business, 2000), p. 39.
11. Jerry Wind and A. Rangaswamy, "Customerization: The Second Revolution in Mass Customization," Wharton School Working Paper, June 1999.
12. Anderson and Narus, "Capturing the Value of Supplementary Services," pp. 75–83.
13. Itamar Simonson, "Determinants of Customers' Responses to Customized Offers: Conceptual Framework and Research Propositions," *Journal of Marketing*, 69 (January 2005): 32–45.
14. Nanette Byrnes, "What's Beyond for Bed Bath & Beyond?" *BusinessWeek*, January 19, 2004, pp. 45–50.
15. Kate Kane, "It's a Small World," *Working Woman*, October 1997, p. 22.
16. By visiting the company's sponsored site, MyBestSegments.com, you can enter in a ZIP Code and discover the top five clusters for that area. Another leading supplier of geodemographic data is ClusterPlus (Strategic Mapping).
17. Michael J. Weiss, "To Be about to Be," *American Demographics* (September 2003): 29–36.
18. Sarah Allison and Carlos Tejada, "Mr., Mrs., Meet Mr. Clean," *Wall Street Journal*, January 30, 2003, pp. B1, B3.
19. Jim Rendon, "Rear Window," *Business 2.0*, August 2003, p. 72.
20. Dawn Klingensmith, "Marketing Gurus Try to Read Women's Minds," *Chicago Tribune*, April 2006.
21. Marti Barletta, "Who's Really Buying That Car? Ask Her." *Brandweek*, September 4, 2006, p. 20; Robert Craven, Kiki Maurey and John Davis, "What Women Really Want," *Critical Eye*, 15, 2006, pp. 50–53.
22. Constantine Van Hoffman, "For Some Marketers, Low Income Is Hot," *Brandweek*, September 11, 2006, p. 6.
23. Michael J. Silverstein and Neil Fiske, *Trading Up: The New American Luxury* (New York: Portfolio, 2003); Michael J. Silverstein, *Treasure Hunt: Inside the Mind of the New Consumer* (New York: Portfolio, 2006); Jeff Cioletti, "Movin' on Up," *Beverage World*, June 2006, p. 20; Gregory L. White and Shirley Leung, "Middle Market Shrinks as Americans Migrate toward the Higher End," *Wall Street Journal*, March 29, 2002, pp. A1, A8.
24. M. Wilson, "Defining Gen Y," *Chain Store Age*, March 2007, pp. 35+; Weiss, "To Be about to Be;" Kelly Pate, "Not 'X,' but 'Y' Marks the Spot: Young Generation a Marketing Target," *Denver Post*, August 17, 2003, p. K1; Bruce Horovitz, "Gen Y: A Tough Crowd to Sell," *USA Today*, April 22, 2002, pp. 1B–2B.
25. Andrew E. Serwer, "42,496 Secrets Bared," *Fortune*, January 24, 1994, pp. 13–14; Kenneth Labich, "Class in America," *Fortune*, February 7, 1994, pp. 114–126.
26. www.sric-bi.com.
27. Pam Danziger, "Getting More for V-Day," *Brandweek*, February 9, 2004, p. 19.
28. Andrew Kaplan, "A Fruitful Mix," *BeverageWorld*, May 2006, pp. 28–36.
29. This classification was adapted from George H. Brown, "Brand Loyalty—Fact or Fiction?" *Advertising Age*, June 1952–January 1953, a series. See also Peter E. Rossi, R. McCulloch, and G. Allenby, "The Value of Purchase History Data in Target Marketing," *Marketing Science* 15, no. 4 (1996): 321–340.
30. Chip Walker, "How Strong Is Your Brand?" *Marketing Tools*, January/February 1995, pp. 46–53.
31. www.conversionmodel.com.
32. Daniel Yankelovich and David Meer, "Rediscovering Market Segmentation," *Harvard Business Review*, February 2006.
33. For a review of many of the methodological issues in developing segmentation schemes, see William R. Dillon and Soumen Mukherjee, "A Guide to the Design and Execution of Segmentation Studies," in the *Handbook of Marketing Research*, eds. Rajiv Grover and

Marco Vriens (Thousand Oaks, CA: Sage Publications, 2006); Michael Wedel and Wagner A. Kamakura, *Market Segmentation: Conceptual and Methodological Foundations* (Boston: Kluwer, 1997).

34. Linda Haugsted, "Segmenting Rings Up Phone Additions," *Multichannel News*, December 18, 2006, p. 18; Roger J. Best, *Market-Based Management*, 2d ed. (Upper Saddle River, NJ: Prentice Hall, 2000), pp. 111–114; Marian Burk Wood, *The Marketing Plan Handbook*, 3d ed. (Upper Saddle River, NJ: Pearson Prentice Hall, 2008), pp. 63–65.
35. Christopher Hosford, "A Transformative Experience," *Sales and Marketing Management*, June 2006, pp. 32–36.
36. See Bart Macchiette and Roy Abhijit, "Sensitive Groups and Social Issues," *Journal of Consumer Marketing* 11, no. 4 (1994): 55–64.

PART III Building Strong Brands

CHAPTER 8

Creating Brand Equity

In this chapter, we will address the following questions:

1. What is a brand, and how does branding work?
2. What is brand equity, and how is it built, measured, and managed?
3. What are the important decisions in developing a branding strategy?

MARKETING MANAGEMENT AT ESPN

ESPN (the Entertainment and Sports Programming Network) started in 1978 with a single satellite, broadcasting regional sports and obscure sports contents such as the "World's Strongest Man." Today, through its singular focus on sports programming and news, ESPN has become, as its slogan says, the "Worldwide Leader in Sports"—the sports authority with a youthful, slightly irreverent personality. Its strategy is to be wherever fans watch, read, and discuss sports. The ESPN brand covers a total of 10 cable channels, a Web site, a magazine, a restaurant chain, more than 600 local radio affiliates, original movies and television series, book publishing, a sports merchandise catalog and online store, and more.

The core ESPN cable channel is distributed on 99% of U.S. cable systems and commands a monthly per-subscriber license fee higher than any other cable channel. Building on this foundation, ESPN wants to expand its brand in many directions. Although a brief foray into the competitive cell phone market failed, ESPN quickly launched Web-based programming specifically for cell-phone viewing. Its mobile-content site already attracts 9 million visitors monthly. Owned by the Walt Disney Company, ESPN earns $5 billion a year in revenue, but perhaps the greatest tribute to its brand power came from the mouth of one male focus group respondent: "If ESPN was a woman, I'd marry her."[1]

The heart of a successful brand is a great offering backed by careful planning, long-term commitment, and creative marketing that encourages intense consumer loyalty. *Strategic brand management* combines the design and implementation of marketing activities and programs to build, measure, and manage brands to maximize their value. This process involves (1) identifying and establishing brand positioning; (2) planning and implementing brand marketing; (3) measuring and interpreting brand performance; and (4) growing and sustaining brand value. Chapter 9 deals with brand positioning and competition. The remaining topics are discussed in this chapter.

WHAT IS BRAND EQUITY?

The American Marketing Association defines a **brand** as "a name, term, sign, symbol, or design, or a combination of them, intended to identify the goods or services of one seller or group of sellers and to differentiate them from those of competitors." A brand adds dimensions that differentiate the offering in some way from other offerings designed to satisfy the same need. These differences may be functional, rational, or tangible—related to the brand's product performance. They may also be more symbolic, emotional, or intangible—related to what the brand represents.

The Role of Brands

Brands identify the source or maker of a product and allow consumers—either individuals or organizations—to assign responsibility for its performance to a particular manufacturer or distributor. Consumers may evaluate the identical product differently depending on how it's branded. They learn about brands through past experiences with the product and its marketing program, finding out which brands do and don't satisfy their needs. As consumers' lives become more complicated, rushed, and time-starved, the ability of a brand to simplify decision making and reduce risk is invaluable.[2]

Brands also perform valuable functions for firms.[3] Not only do they simplify product handling or tracing, they also help organize inventory and accounting records and offer the firm legal protection for unique product features or elements.[4] The brand name can be protected through registered trademarks; manufacturing processes can be protected through patents; and packaging can be protected through copyrights and designs. Intellectual property rights ensure that the firm can safely invest in the brand and reap the benefits of a valuable asset, as ESPN has done.

Brands signal a certain level of quality so that satisfied buyers can easily choose the product again.[5] Brand loyalty provides predictability and security of demand for the firm and creates barriers to entry that make it difficult for other firms to enter the market. Loyalty also can translate into a willingness to pay a higher price—often 20% to 25% more than competing brands.[6] Although competitors may easily duplicate manufacturing processes and product designs, they can't easily match the lasting impressions left in customers' minds by years of marketing activity and product experience. Branding can be a powerful means to secure a competitive advantage.[7]

"Breakthrough Marketing: Procter & Gamble" describes that firm's mastery of branding.

The Scope of Branding

Branding is endowing products and services with the power of a brand. It's all about creating differences between products. Marketers need to teach consumers "who" the product is—by giving it a name and using other brand elements to identify it—as

BREAKTHROUGH MARKETING: PROCTER & GAMBLE

With total annual sales of nearly $70 billion, Procter & Gamble (P&G) markets 16 billion-dollar global brands. How does P&G do it? First, it studies customers through more than 10,000 formal research projects every year, plus three million e-mail and phone contacts supplemented by visits to homes and stores. Second, P&G is a product innovator, devoting $1.8 billion to research and development and applying for thousands of patents, year after year, to launch new and improved products. These efforts have paid off in recent blockbuster brands such as Swiffer and Febreze.

Third, P&G produces its brands in multiple sizes and forms to gain more shelf space and prevent competitors from moving in to satisfy unmet market needs. For example, the Febreze brand now appears on an array of "freshness" products from room sprays to scented candles. Fourth, P&G markets several brands in the same product category, such as Luvs and Pampers diapers and Oral-B and Crest toothbrushes. Moreover, when it acquired Gillette, P&G became the largest U.S. advertiser, with a $5 billion annual ad budget that includes stronger emotional appeals for deeper consumer connections. Finally, each brand category is headed by a category manager with volume and profit responsibility, which sharpens the focus on consumer needs and category competition.[8]

well as what the product does and why consumers should care. Branding creates mental structures that help consumers organize their knowledge about products and services in a way that clarifies their decision making and, in the process, provides value to the firm.

For branding strategies to be successful and brand value to be created, consumers must be convinced there are meaningful differences among brands in the product or service category. It's possible to brand a physical good (Pantene shampoo), a service (Singapore Airlines), a store (Safeway supermarket), a person (Tony Hawk), a place (state of Texas), an organization (American Automobile Association), or an idea (freedom of speech).[9]

Defining Brand Equity

Brand equity is the added value endowed on products and services, reflected in how consumers think, feel, and act with respect to the brand, as well as in the prices, market share, and profitability the brand commands for the firm. Marketers and researchers use various perspectives to study brand equity.[10] **Customer-based brand equity** is the differential effect that brand knowledge has on consumer response to that brand's marketing.[11] A brand has positive customer-based brand equity when consumers react more favorably to a product and its marketing when the brand is *identified* than when it's not identified. A brand has negative customer-based brand equity if consumers react less favorably to the brand's marketing activity under the same circumstances.

Customer-based brand equity has three key ingredients. First, brand equity arises from differences in consumer response. If no differences occur, then the brand name product is essentially a commodity or generic version of the product and competition will probably be based on price. Second, differences in response are a result of

TABLE 8.1 Marketing Advantages of Strong Brands

> Improved Perceptions of Product Performance
> Greater Loyalty
> Less Vulnerability to Competitive Marketing Actions
> Less Vulnerability to Marketing Crises
> Larger Margins
> More Inelastic Consumer Response to Price Increases
> More Elastic Consumer Response to Price Decreases
> Greater Trade Cooperation and Support
> Increased Marketing Communications Effectiveness
> Possible Licensing Opportunities
> Additional Brand Extension Opportunities

consumer's **brand knowledge,** all the thoughts, feelings, images, experiences, beliefs, and so on that become associated with the brand. Brands must create strong, favorable, and unique brand associations with customers, as have Volvo (*safety*) and Harley-Davidson (*adventure*). Third, the differential response by consumers that makes up brand equity is reflected in perceptions, preferences, and behavior related to all aspects of the brand's marketing—and stronger brands lead to greater revenue.[12] Table 8.1 summarizes some of the key benefits of brand equity.

Brand Equity as a Bridge

Brand equity provides marketers with a vital strategic "bridge" from their past to their future.[13] From the perspective of brand equity, all the marketing dollars spent on offerings are actually investments in consumer brand knowledge. The *quality* of the investment in brand building is the critical factor, not necessarily the *quantity*, beyond some minimal threshold amount. It's actually possible to overspend on brand building if money isn't spent wisely. At the same time, the brand knowledge created by marketing investments dictates appropriate future directions for the brand. Consumers will decide, based on what they think and feel about the brand, where and how they believe the brand should go and grant or deny permission to any marketing action or program.

A **brand promise** is the marketer's vision of what the brand must be and do for consumers. Yet a brand's true value and future prospects rest with consumers, their knowledge about the brand, and their likely response to marketing activity as a result of this knowledge. Understanding consumer brand knowledge—all the different things that become linked to the brand in the minds of consumers—is of paramount importance because it is the foundation of brand equity.

BUILDING BRAND EQUITY

Marketers build brand equity by creating the right brand knowledge structures with the right consumers. This process depends on *all* brand-related contacts—whether marketer initiated or not. From a marketing management perspective, there are three main sets of *brand equity drivers*:

1. *The initial choices for the brand elements or identities making up the brand (brand names, URLs, logos, symbols, characters, spokespeople, slogans, jingles, packages, and signage)*. Method built annual sales beyond $32 million by creating a unique line of nontoxic household cleaning products with bright colors and sleek designs. Given its limited advertising budget, the company believes its attractive packaging and innovative products have to work harder to express the brand positioning.[14]

2. *The product and service and all accompanying marketing activities and supporting marketing programs*. Liz Claiborne's fastest growing brand is Juicy Couture, edgy, contemporary clothing positioned as an affordable luxury with a strong lifestyle appeal.[15]

3. *Other associations indirectly transferred to the brand by linking it to some other entity (a person, place, or thing)*. The brand name of New Zealand vodka 42 Below refers to a latitude that runs through New Zealand and the percentage of its alcohol content. The packaging and other cues are designed to leverage the country's perceived purity while communicating the brand's positioning.[16]

Choosing Brand Elements

Brand elements are those trademarkable devices that serve to identify and differentiate the brand. For example, Nike has the distinctive "swoosh" logo and the "Nike" name based on the winged goddess of victory. The test of the brand-building ability of these elements is what consumers would think or feel about the product *if* the brand element were all they knew. A brand element that enhances brand equity conveys certain valued associations or responses. So, based on its name alone, a consumer might expect ColorStay lipsticks to be long lasting.

Brand Element Choice Criteria There are six main criteria in choosing brand elements. As shown in Table 8.2, the first three (memorable, meaningful, and likeable) are "brand building." The other three (transferable, adaptable, and protectible) are "defensive," dealing with how to leverage and preserve a brand element's equity in the face of opportunities and constraints.

TABLE 8.2 Criteria for Choosing Brand Elements

For Building the Brand	For Defending the Brand
Memorable: Is the element easily recalled and recognized at both purchase and consumption? Example: Tide	*Transferable*: Can the element introduce new products in the same category or other categories? Does it add brand equity across geographic boundaries and segments? Example: Amazon
Meaningful: Is the element credible and suggestive of the corresponding category? Does it suggest something about an ingredient or a brand user? Example: Lean Cuisine	*Adaptable*: Can the element be adapted and updated? Example: Betty Crocker image
Likeable: Is the element aesthetically appealing and inherently likeable visually, verbally, and in other ways? Example: Thunderbird	*Protectible*: Is the element legally and competitively protectible? Can the firm retain trademark rights? Example: Yahoo!

Developing Brand Elements Brand elements can play a number of brand-building roles.[17] If consumers don't examine much information in making their product decisions, brand elements should be easy to recognize and recall, and inherently descriptive and persuasive. The likeability and appeal of brand elements may also play a critical role in awareness and associations leading to brand equity.[18] The Keebler elves reinforce home-style baking quality and a sense of magic and fun for their line of cookies.

Brand names aren't the only important brand element. Often, the less concrete brand benefits are, the more important it is that brand elements capture the brand's intangible characteristics. Many insurance firms use symbols of strength (such as the stag for Hartford). Slogans also are an efficient means to build brand equity, functioning as "hooks" or "handles" to help consumers grasp what the brand is and what makes it special. However, choosing a name with inherent meaning creates less flexibility, making it harder to add a different meaning or update the positioning.[19]

Designing Holistic Marketing Activities

Brands are not built by advertising alone. Customers come to know a brand through a range of contacts and touch points: personal observation and use, word of mouth, interactions with company personnel, online or telephone experiences, and payment transactions. A **brand contact** is any information-bearing experience a customer or prospect has with the brand, product category, or market that relates to the firm's product or service.[20] The company must put as much effort into managing these experiences as it puts into producing its ads.[21]

Holistic marketers emphasize three key themes in designing brand-building marketing programs: personalization, integration, and internalization.

Personalization *Personalizing marketing* means ensuring that the brand and its marketing are as relevant as possible to as many customers as possible—a challenge, given that no two customers are identical. The Internet is not the only way to personalize marketing. To adapt to the increased consumer desire for personalization, marketers have embraced concepts such as experiential marketing, one-to-one marketing, permission marketing, and participatory marketing as they create an intense, active relationship with consumers (see "Marketing Skills: Building a Cult Brand").

Integration **Integrating marketing** is about mixing and matching marketing activities to maximize their individual and collective effects.[23] To achieve it, firms need a variety of different marketing activities that reinforce the brand promise. As much as possible, there should be a match among certain communication options so that the effects of any one option are enhanced by the presence of another, making the whole greater than the sum of the parts.

Marketers should judge how effectively and efficiently all integrated marketing activities affect brand awareness and create, maintain, or strengthen brand image. Whereas *brand identity* is the way a firm aims to identify or position itself or its product, *brand image* is the way the public actually perceives the firm or its product. It's important to employ a mix of marketing activities, each playing a specific role in building or maintaining brand equity.

> ### MARKETING SKILLS: BUILDING A CULT BRAND
>
> Building a cult brand can significantly increase sales and profits without expensive promotions and without appealing to a mass market, making this skill particularly important for marketers launching unconventional or niche products. Several competencies contribute to this skill. First is the ability to create a "buzz" among opinion leaders and personalize the brand experience without diluting the effect. Next, marketers need to enhance the product's appeal through supply and distribution. A new product that is readily available everywhere will seem less special. Marketers can also provide a framework for brand-based communities; bringing enthusiasts together for special events makes the brand experience more personal and relevant.
>
> Entrepreneur Peter van Stolk honed his skills making Jones Soda a cult hit. After struggling to obtain shelf space in food stores, van Stolk placed his products in outlets such as surfboard stores and music stores that cater to 12-to-24-year-old consumers. Soon customers began asking for the sodas in other stores, paving the way for wider distribution. The firm cultivates a personal connection by inviting consumers to submit photos for possible use on bottle labels and the brand's Web site. It also sends the Jones RV to U.S. and Canadian cities to give away samples and stay in touch with customers. Still a cult brand, Jones Soda's annual sales top $50 million.[22]

Internalization Marketers must adopt an *internal* perspective to be sure that employees and marketing partners appreciate and understand basic branding notions and know how they can help—or hurt—brand equity.[24] **Internal branding** consists of activities and processes that inform and inspire employees.[25] It's critical for service companies and retailers that all employees have an up-to-date, deep understanding of the brand and its promise. Holistic marketers must go even further, training and encouraging distributors and dealers to serve their customers well.

Brand bonding occurs when customers experience the company as delivering on its brand promise. All the customers' contacts with company employees and communications must be positive.[26] *The brand promise will not be delivered unless everyone in the company lives the brand.* Disney is so successful at internal branding and having employees support its brand that it holds seminars on the "Disney Style" for employees from other companies.

Leveraging Secondary Associations

The third way to build brand equity is, in effect, to "borrow" it by linking the brand to other information in memory that conveys meaning to consumers (see Figure 8.1). These "secondary" brand associations can link to sources such as the company itself (through branding strategies), countries or other geographical regions (through identification of product origin), and channels of distribution (through channel strategy). Also, they may be linked to other brands (through co-branding or ingredient branding), characters (through licensing), spokespeople (through endorsements), sporting or cultural events (through sponsorship), or some other third-party sources (through awards or reviews).

FIGURE 8.1 Secondary Sources of Brand Knowledge

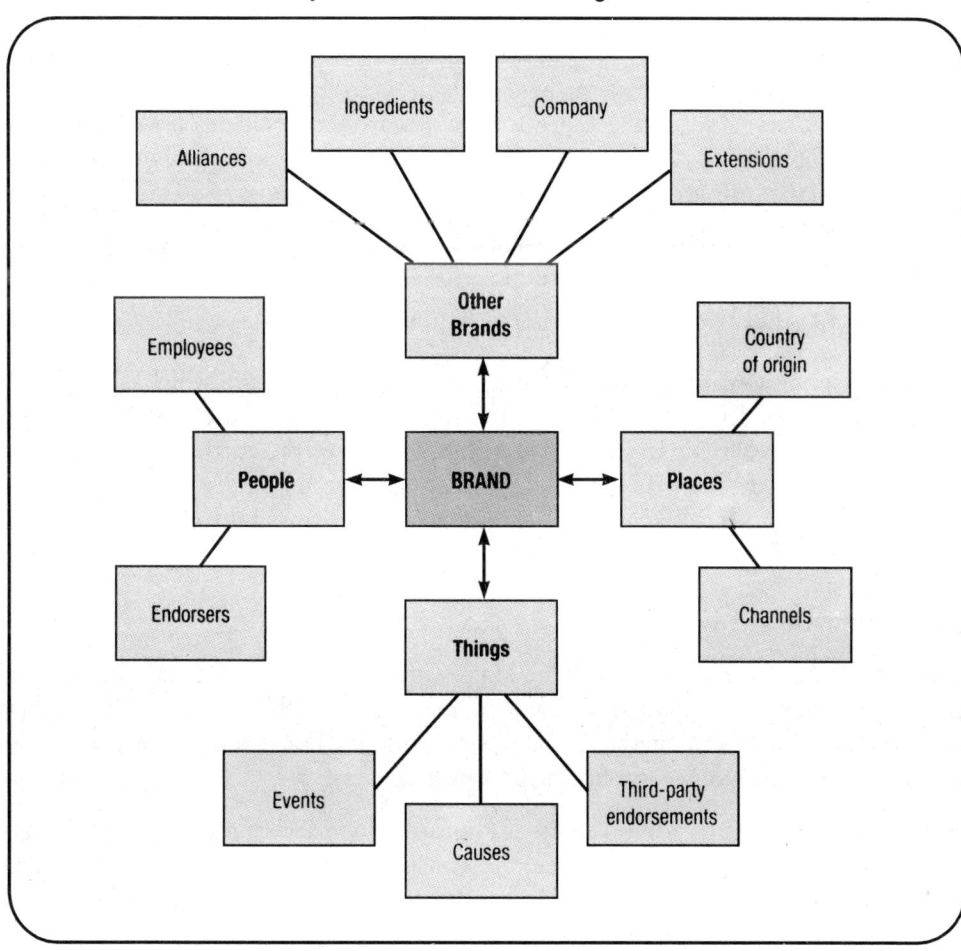

MEASURING AND MANAGING BRAND EQUITY

Given that the power of a brand resides in the minds of consumers and the way it changes their response to marketing, brand equity must be carefully measured. There are two basic approaches to measuring brand equity. An *indirect* approach assesses potential sources of brand equity by identifying and tracking consumer brand knowledge structures.[27] A *direct* approach assesses the actual impact of brand knowledge on consumer response to different aspects of the marketing.

For brand equity to perform a useful strategic function and guide marketing decisions, marketers should fully understand (1) the sources of brand equity and how they affect outcomes of interest, as well as (2) how these sources and outcomes change, if at all, over time. Brand audits are important for the former; brand tracking is important for the latter.

Brand Audits and Brand Tracking

A **brand audit** is a consumer-focused exercise that involves a series of procedures to assess the health of the brand, uncover its sources of brand equity, and suggest ways to improve and leverage its equity. Marketers should conduct a brand audit whenever they're considering important shifts in strategic direction. Conducting brand audits on a regular basis, such as annually, allows marketers to keep their fingers on the pulse of their brands so they can manage them more proactively and responsively.

Brand tracking studies collect quantitative data from consumers on a routine basis over time to provide marketers with consistent, baseline information about how their brands and marketing programs are performing on key dimensions. Tracking studies can help show where, how much, and in what ways brand value is being created, to facilitate day-to-day decision making.

Brand Valuation

Marketers should distinguish brand equity from **brand valuation,** which is the job of estimating the total financial value of the brand. At well-known companies such as Coca-Cola and Nokia, brand value is typically over half the total company market capitalization.[28] Although U.S. companies don't list brand equity on their balance sheets because of the arbitrariness of the estimate, some firms in the United Kingdom, Hong Kong, and Australia give brand equity a value.

Managing Brand Equity

Effective brand management requires a long-term view of marketing actions. Because consumer responses to marketing activity depend on what they know and remember about a brand, short-term marketing actions, by changing brand knowledge, necessarily increase or decrease long-term future marketing success.

Brand Reinforcement Brand equity is reinforced by marketing actions that consistently convey the meaning of the brand to consumers in terms of (1) what products the brand represents; what core benefits it supplies; and what needs it satisfies; as well as (2) how the brand makes those products superior and which strong, favorable, and unique brand associations should exist in the minds of consumers.[29] Nivea, one of Europe's strongest brands, has expanded its scope from a skin-cream brand to a skin-care and personal-care brand through carefully designed and implemented brand extensions reinforcing the Nivea brand promise of "mild," "gentle," and "caring" in a broader arena.

Reinforcing brand equity requires innovation and relevance throughout the marketing program. The brand must always be moving forward, but always in the right direction, with compelling new offerings and new marketing. Brands that fail to do so—such as Oldsmobile—find that their market leadership dwindles or even disappears. Without consistent and appropriate marketing support to reinforce the brand, brand awareness and image may weaken.

Many tactical changes may be necessary to maintain the brand's strategic thrust and direction. Unless there is some environmental change, however, there is little need to deviate from a successful positioning. Further, marketers must recognize the trade-offs between activities that fortify the brand and reinforce its meaning, such as a well-received product improvement or a creative ad campaign, and those that leverage or borrow from existing brand equity to reap some financial benefit, such as a short-term promotional discount that just emphasizes the lower price.[30]

Brand Revitalization Changes in consumer tastes and preferences, the emergence of new competitors or new technology, or any new development in the marketing environment can affect the fortunes of a brand. In virtually every product category, once prominent and admired brands—such as Smith Corona, Zenith, and TWA—have fallen on hard times or even disappeared.[31] Nevertheless, a number of brands have made comebacks recently; for instance, Dr. Scholl's has begun breathing new life into its customer franchise and reviving its brand fortune.

Often, the first thing to do in revitalizing a brand is to understand the original sources of brand equity. Are positive associations losing their strength or uniqueness? Have negative associations become linked to the brand? Then decide whether to retain the same positioning or create a new positioning, and, if so, which positioning to adopt. Sometimes the actual marketing program is the source of the problem, because it fails to deliver on the brand promise. Then a "back to basics" strategy may make sense.

In the continuum of revitalization strategies, pure "back to basics" is at one end, pure "reinvention" is at the other, and there are many combinations in between. Reinvention is necessary when the old positioning is no longer viable. For instance, Mountain Dew overhauled its brand image to become a soft-drink powerhouse by appealing to young men. With an action-oriented slogan ("Do the Dew"), ads stressing associations to extreme sports, plus new flavors and packaging, Mountain Dew passed Diet Pepsi to become one of the top-selling soft drinks.[32]

BRAND STRATEGY AND CUSTOMER EQUITY

A firm's **branding strategy** reflects the number and nature of both common and distinctive brand elements it applies to the products it sells. Deciding how to brand new products is especially critical. When introducing a new product, the firm has three main choices: (1) develop new brand elements for the new product; (2) apply some of its existing brand elements; (3) use a combination of new and existing brand elements (see definitions in Table 8.3).

TABLE 8.3 Branding New Products

Concept	Definition
Brand extension	Using an established brand to launch a new product
Subbrand	Combining a new brand with an existing brand
Parent brand	An existing brand that gives birth to a brand extension or sub-brand
Family brand	A parent brand that is associated with multiple brand extensions
Line extension	Using a parent brand on a new product within the segment it currently serves (such as with new flavors or colors)
Category extension	Using a parent brand to enter a different product category from the one it currently serves
Brand line	All products sold under a particular brand
Brand mix	The set of all brand lines that a firm offers to buyers (also known as brand assortment)
Branded variants	Specific brand lines supplied to particular retailers or channels
Licensed product	Using the brand name licensed from one firm on a product made by another firm

Branding Decisions

Today, branding is such a strong force that hardly anything goes unbranded. Assuming a firm decides to brand its offerings, it must choose which brand names to use. Four general strategies are:

1. *Individual names.* General Mills uses individual names like Gold Medal flour and Old El Paso Mexican foods. A major advantage is that the company's reputation is not tied to the products' reputations. If the product fails or seems low quality, the company's name or image is not hurt. Firms often use different brands for different quality lines within the same product class.
2. *Blanket family names.* Heinz and General Electric use their corporate brand across their range of products.[33] Development costs are lower because there is no need for "name" research or expensive advertising to create name recognition. New-product sales are likely to be strong if the manufacturer's name is good. Corporate-image associations of innovativeness, expertise, and trustworthiness have been shown to directly influence consumer evaluations.[34] Finally, a corporate branding strategy leads to greater intangible value for the firm.[35]
3. *Separate family names for all products.* Sears uses this strategy (Kenmore for appliances, Craftsman for tools). If a company offers quite different products like these, one blanket name is often not desirable. Swift and Company developed separate family names for its hams (Premium) and fertilizers (Vigoro).
4. *Corporate name combined with individual product names.* Kellogg combines corporate and individual names in Kellogg's Rice Krispies and Kellogg's Raisin Bran. The company name legitimizes the product and the individual name individualizes it.

Individual names and blanket family names are sometimes referred to as a "house of brands" and a "branded house," respectively, and they represent two ends of a brand relationship continuum. Separate family names fall between the two ends of the continuum, and corporate-plus-individual names combine them. Note that not every company follows one strategy. For instance, when FedEx acquired the copier chain Kinko's, the branding decision was trickier. Kinko's had enough brand equity that FedEx didn't want to throw the name out. After numerous focus groups, management co-branded the chain with the name FedEx Kinko's.[36]

Although firms rarely adopt a pure example of any of the four strategies, deciding which general strategy to emphasize depends on several factors, as evidenced by Table 8.4.

TABLE 8.4 Selecting a Brand Relationship Spectrum Position

Toward a Branded House	Toward a House of Brands
Does the parent brand contribute to the offering by adding:	Is there a compelling need for a separate brand because it will:
—Associations enhancing the value proposition?	—Create and own an association?
—Credibility through organizational associations?	—Represent a new, different offering?
—Visibility?	—Retain/capture customer/brand bond?
—Communication efficiencies?	—Deal with channel conflict?
Will the master brand be strengthened by associating with the new offering?	Will the business support a new brand name?

Source: Adapted from David A. Aaker and Erich Joachimsthaler, *Brand Leadership* (New York: Free Press, 2000), Figure 4.6, p. 120.

Brand Extensions

Many firms have decided to leverage their most valuable asset by introducing new products under their strongest brand names. Most new products are in fact line extensions—typically 80% to 90% in any one year. Moreover, many of the most successful new products are extensions, although numerous new products are introduced as new brands (Mini Cooper automobile).

Advantages of Brand Extensions One advantage of brand extensions is that they improve the odds of new-product success. Consumers can make inferences and form expectations about the likely composition and performance of a new product based on what they already know about the parent brand itself and the extent to which they feel this information is relevant to the new product.[37] By setting up positive expectations, extensions reduce risk.[38] It also may be easier to convince retailers to stock and promote a brand extension because of increased customer demand. From a marketing communications perspective, an introductory campaign for an extension doesn't have to create awareness of both the brand *and* the new product but instead can concentrate on the new product itself.[39]

Thus, brand extensions can reduce the cost of the launch campaign, which is important given that establishing a new brand name in the U.S. marketplace for a mass-consumer-packaged good can cost $100 million! Extensions also can avoid the difficulty—and expense—of coming up with a new name. In addition, they allow for packaging and labeling efficiencies and, if coordinated properly, more prominence in the retail store by creating a "billboard" effect. With a portfolio of brand variants within a product category, consumers who need a change can switch to a different product type without leaving the brand family.

A second advantage is that brand extensions can provide feedback benefits.[40] Extensions can help clarify a brand's meaning and its core values or improve consumer loyalty and perceptions of the credibility of the company behind the extension.[41] Thus, through brand extensions, Crayola means "colorful crafts for kids" and Weight Watchers means "weight loss and maintenance." Line extensions can renew interest in and liking for the brand as well as benefiting the parent brand by expanding market coverage. A successful extension may also serve as the basis for subsequent extensions.[42]

Disadvantages of Brand Extensions On the downside, line extensions may cause the brand name to be less strongly identified with any one product.[43] Ries and Trout call this the "line-extension trap."[44] By linking its brand to mainstream food products such as mashed potatoes, powdered milk, and soups, Cadbury ran the risk of losing its more specific meaning as a chocolates and candy brand.[45] **Brand dilution** occurs when consumers no longer associate a brand with a specific product or highly similar products and start thinking less of the brand.

If a firm launches extensions consumers deem inappropriate, they may question the brand's integrity or become confused and perhaps even frustrated: Which version is the "right one" for them? Retailers reject many new products and brands because they don't have the shelf or display space for them. And the company itself may become overwhelmed.

The worst possible scenario is for an extension not only to fail, but also to harm the parent brand image in the process. Fortunately, such events are rare. "Marketing failures," where insufficient consumers were attracted to a brand, are typically much less damaging than "product failures," where the brand fundamentally fails to live up to its promise. Even then, product failures dilute brand equity only when the extension is seen as very similar to the parent brand.

Even if sales of a brand extension are high and meet targets, the revenue may be coming from consumers switching to the extension from existing parent-brand offerings, *cannibalizing* the parent brand. Intrabrand shifts in sales may not necessarily be so undesirable if they're a form of *preemptive cannibalization*. Consumers who might have switched to a competing brand instead choose the line extension. Tide laundry detergent enjoys the same market share now as it had 50 years ago because of the sales contributions of its line extensions (scented and unscented powder, tablet, liquid, and other forms). One final disadvantage of brand extensions is that the firm forgoes the chance to create a new brand with its own unique image and equity. Consider the advantages to Disney of having introduced more adult-oriented Touchstone films, for example.

Success Characteristics Marketers must judge each potential brand extension by how effectively it leverages existing brand equity from the parent brand as well as how effectively the extension enhances the parent brand's equity.[46] Crest White Strips leveraged the strong reputation of Crest and dental care to provide reassurance in the teeth-whitening arena while reinforcing its dental authority image.

The most important consideration with brand extensions is the "fit" in the mind of the consumer, based on common physical attributes, usage situations, or user types. One major mistake in evaluating extension opportunities is focusing on one or a few brand associations as a potential basis of fit rather than considering *all* of the consumer's brand knowledge structures.

Brand Portfolios

All brands have boundaries—a brand can only be stretched so far, and all the segments the firm would like to target may not view the same brand equally favorably. Multiple brands are often necessary to pursue multiple market segments. Other reasons for introducing multiple brands in a category include:[47]

1. To increase shelf presence and retailer dependence in the store;
2. To attract consumers seeking variety who may otherwise have switched to another brand;
3. To increase internal competition within the firm; and
4. To yield economies of scale in advertising, sales, merchandising, and physical distribution.

The **brand portfolio** is the set of all brands and brand lines a particular firm offers for sale to buyers in a particular category or market segment. The hallmark of an optimal brand portfolio is the ability of each brand in it to maximize equity in combination with all other brands in it. If profits can be increased by dropping brands, a portfolio is too big; if profits can be increased by adding brands, a portfolio is not big enough. The basic principle is to *maximize market coverage*, so that no potential customers are being ignored, but to *minimize brand overlap*, so brands are not competing for customer approval. Each brand should be clearly differentiated and appealing to a sizable enough segment to justify its marketing and production costs.[48]

Brands can also play a number of specific roles within a brand portfolio:

- *Flankers.* Flanker or "fighter" brands are positioned with respect to competitors' brands so that more important (and more profitable) *flagship brands* retain their desired positioning. As an example, Procter & Gamble markets Luvs diapers in a way that flanks the more premium Pampers. Fighter brands must not be so attractive that they take sales away from their higher-priced comparison brands. Yet if a fighter brand is seen as connected to other brands in the portfolio in any way (say, by virtue of a common branding strategy), then it can't be designed so cheaply that it reflects poorly on the other brands.
- *Cash cows.* Some brands may be retained despite dwindling sales because they still manage to hold onto enough customers and maintain their profitability with virtually no marketing support. Firms can "milk" these "cash cow" brands by capitalizing on the existing brand equity. For example, even though technological advances have moved much of its market to the Mach III brand of razors, Gillette still sells the older Trac II, Atra, and Sensor brands. Because withdrawing them may not necessarily move customers to another Gillette brand, it may be more profitable for Gillette to keep them in the portfolio.
- *Low-end entry level.* The role of a relatively low-priced brand in the portfolio may be to attract customers to the brand franchise. Retailers feature these entry-level products because they are able to "trade up" customers to a higher-priced brand.
- *High-end prestige.* A relatively high-priced brand is often used to add prestige and credibility to the entire portfolio. For example, one analyst argued that the real value of Chevrolet's Corvette high performance sports car was "its ability to lure curious customers into showrooms and at the same time help improve the image of other Chevrolet cars. It does not mean a hell of a lot for GM profitability, but there is no question that it is a traffic builder."[49] The Corvette image and prestige cast a halo over the entire Chevrolet line.

Customer Equity

Finally, we can relate brand equity to one other important marketing concept, **customer equity.** The aim of customer relationship management (CRM) is to produce high customer equity.[50] Although we can calculate it in different ways, one definition of customer equity is "the sum of lifetime values of all customers."[51] As discussed in Chapter 4, customer lifetime value is affected by revenue and cost considerations related to customer acquisition, retention, and cross-selling.[52]

- *Acquisition* is affected by the number of prospects, the acquisition probability of a prospect, and acquisition spending per prospect.
- *Retention* is influenced by the retention rate and retention spending level.
- *Add-on spending* is a function of the efficiency of add-on selling, the number of add-on selling offers given to existing customers, and the response rate to new offers.

The brand equity and customer equity perspectives share many common themes.[53] Both emphasize the importance of customer loyalty and the notion that value is created by having as many customers as possible pay as high a price as possible. In practice, however, customer equity focuses on bottom-line financial value and offers limited guidance for go-to-market strategies and brand-building. It doesn't always fully account for competitive moves and counter-moves, social network effects, word-of-mouth, and customer-to-customer recommendations.

Brand equity, on the other hand, emphasizes strategic issues in managing brands and in creating and leveraging brand awareness and image, providing much practical guidance for specific marketing activities. Even with a focus on brands, managers don't always develop detailed customer analyses in terms of the brand equity they achieve or the long-term profitability they create.[54] Brand equity approaches could benefit from sharper segmentation schemes afforded by customer-level analyses, and more consideration of how to develop personalized, customized marketing programs for individual customers.

Nevertheless, both brand equity and customer equity matter. Brands serve as the "bait" that retailers and other channel intermediaries use to attract customers from whom they extract value. Customers serve as the tangible profit engine for brands to monetize their brand value.

EXECUTIVE SUMMARY

A brand is a name, term, sign, symbol, or design, or some combination of these elements, intended to identify the offerings of one seller or group of sellers and to differentiate them from those of competitors. The different components of a brand—brand names, logos, symbols, package designs, and so on—are brand elements. Brands offer a number of benefits to customers and firms and, as valuable intangible assets, must be managed carefully. The key to branding is that consumers perceive differences among brands in a product category.

Brand equity should be defined in terms of marketing effects uniquely attributable to a brand. Building brand equity depends on: (1) the initial choices for the brand elements or identities making up the brand; (2) the way the brand is integrated into the supporting marketing program; and (3) the associations indirectly transferred to the brand through a link to another entity. Brand equity needs to be measured in order to be managed well. Brand audits measure "where the brand has been;" tracking studies measure "where the brand is now" and whether marketing programs are having the intended effects.

A branding strategy identifies which brand elements a firm chooses to apply across its various products. In a brand extension, a firm uses an established brand name to introduce a new product. Brands can play a number of different roles within the brand portfolio, such as to expand coverage, to provide protection, or to extend an image. Customer equity is a complementary concept to brand equity that reflects the sum of lifetime values of all customers for a brand.

NOTES

1. Louise Story, "Yes, the Screen Is Tiny, But the Plans Are Big," *New York Times*, June 17, 2007, sec. 2, p. 1; Tom Lowry, "ESPN's Cell-Phone Fumble," *BusinessWeek*, October 30, 2006, p. 26.
2. Rajneesh Suri and Kent B. Monroe, "The Effects of Time Pressure on Consumers' Judgments of Prices and Products," *Journal of Consumer Research* 30 (June 2003): 92–104.
3. *The Economist on Branding*, Rita Clifton and John Simmons (eds.), (New York: Bloomberg Press, 2004); Rik Riezebos, *Brand Management: A Theoretical and Practical Approach* (Essex, England: Pearson Education, 2003); Paul Temporal, *Advanced Brand Management: From Vision to Valuation* (Singapore: John Wiley & Sons, 2002).

4. Constance E. Bagley, *Managers and the Legal Environment: Strategies for the 21st Century*, 2d ed. (Cincinnati, OH: West Publishing, 1995). For a marketing academic point of view of some important legal issues, see Judith Zaichkowsky, *The Psychology Behind Trademark Infringement and Counterfeiting* (LEA Publishing, 2006) and Maureen Morrin and Jacob Jacoby, "Trademark Dilution: Empirical Measures for an Elusive Concept," *Journal of Public Policy & Marketing* 19 (2), 2000: 265–276.

5. Tulin Erdem, "Brand Equity as a Signaling Phenomenon," *Journal of Consumer Psychology* 7, no. 2 (1998): 131–157.

6. Scott Davis, *Brand Asset Management: Driving Profitable Growth Through Your Brands* (San Francisco: Jossey-Bass, 2000); D. C. Bello and M. B. Holbrook, "Does an Absence of Brand Equity Generalize Across Product Classes?" *Journal of Business Research* 34 (1996): 125–131; Mary W. Sullivan, "How Brand Names Affect the Demand for Twin Automobiles," *Journal of Marketing Research* 35 (1998): 154–165; Adrian J. Slywotzky and Benson P. Shapiro, "Leveraging to Beat the Odds: The New Marketing Mindset," *Harvard Business Review* (September–October 1993): 97–107.

7. The power of branding is not without its critics, however, some of whom reject the commercialism associated with branding activities. See Naomi Klein, *No Logo: Taking Aim at the Brand Bullies* (New York: Picador, 2000).

8. Ellen Byron, "P&G Rekindles an Old Flame," *Wall Street Journal*, June 5, 2007, p. B6; "A Post-Modern Proctoid," *The Economist*, April 15, 2006, p. 68; *P&G Fact Sheet*, December 2006; John Galvin, "The World on a String," *Point*, February 2005, pp. 13–24; Jack Neff, "P&G Kisses Up to the Boss: Consumers," *Advertising Age*, May 2, 2005, p. 18; Robert Berner, "Detergent Can Be So Much More," *BusinessWeek*, May 1, 2006, pp. 66–68; <www.pg.com>.

9. For an academic discussion of how consumers become strongly attached to people as brands, see Matthew Thomson, "Human Brands: Investigating Antecedents to Consumers' Stronger Attachments to Celebrities," *Journal of Marketing* 70 (July 2006): 104–119. For practical branding tips from the world of rock and roll, see Roger Blackwell and Tina Stephan, *Brands That Rock* (Hoboken, NJ: John Wiley & Sons, 2004); and for tips from the world of sports, see Irving Rein, Philip Kotler, and Ben Shields, *The Elusive Fan: Reinventing Sports in a Crowded Marketplace* (New York: McGraw-Hill, 2006).

10. Other approaches are based on economic principles of signaling (e.g., Tulin Erdem, "Brand Equity as a Signaling Phenomenon," *Journal of Consumer Psychology* 7, no. 2 (1998): 131–157); or more of a sociological, anthropological, or biological perspective (e.g., Grant McCracken, *Culture and Consumption II: Markets, Meaning, and Brand Management* (Bloomington, IN: Indiana University Press, 2005)); or Susan Fournier, "Consumers and Their Brands: Developing Relationship Theory in Consumer Research," *Journal of Consumer Research* 24, (September 1998): 343–373.

11. Kevin Lane Keller, *Strategic Brand Management*, 3rd ed. (Upper Saddle River, NJ: Pearson Prentice Hall, 2008).

12. Kusum Ailawadi, Donald R. Lehmann, and Scott Neslin, "Revenue Premium as an Outcome Measure of Brand Equity," *Journal of Marketing* 67 (October 2003): 1–17.

13. Jon Miller and David Muir, *The Business of Brands* (West Sussex, England: John Wiley & Sons, 2004).

14. "Marketers of the Next Generation," *Brandweek*, April 17, 2006, p. 30.

15. Rachel Dodes, "From Tracksuits to Fast Track," *Wall Street Journal*, September 13, 2006, pp. B1–B2.

16. "42 Below," www.betterbydesign.org.nz.

17. Alina Wheeler, *Designing Brand Identity* (Hoboken, NJ: John Wiley & Sons, 2003).

18. Pat Fallon and Fred Senn, *Juicing the Orange: How to Turn Creativity into a Powerful Business Advantage* (Boston: Harvard Business School Press, 2006).

19. Kevin Lane Keller, Susan Heckler, and Michael J. Houston, "The Effects of Brand Name Suggestiveness on Advertising Recall," *Journal of Marketing* 62 (January 1998): 48–57; John R. Doyle and Paul A. Bottomly, "Dressed for the Occasion: Font-Product Congruity in the Perception of Logotype," *Journal of Consumer Psychology*, 16 (2), 2006:112–123. For an in-depth examination of how brand names get developed, see Alex Frankel, *Wordcraft: The Art of Turning Little Words Into Big Business* (New York: Crown Publishers, 2004).

20. Don E. Schultz, Stanley I. Tannenbaum, and Robert F. Lauterborn, *Integrated Marketing Communications* (Lincolnwood, IL: NTC Business Books, 1993); Don Schultz and Heidi Schultz, *IMC: The Next Generation* (New York: McGraw-Hill, 2003).

21. Mohanbir Sawhney, "Don't Harmonize, Synchronize," *Harvard Business Review*, July–August 2001: 101–108.

22. Christopher C. Williams, "Sales Pressures Could Take the Fizz Out of Jones Soda," *Wall Street Journal*, June 3, 2007, p. A3; Gene G. Marcial, "Inside Wall Street: Sip a Bohemian Raspberry from Jones Soda," *BusinessWeek Online*, July 4, 2005, www.businessweek.com; Bruce Horovitz, "Gen Y: A Tough Crowd to Sell," *USA Today*, April 22, 2002, p. B1; Melanie Wells, "Cult Brands," *Forbes*, April 16, 2001, pp. 150+.

23. Dawn Iacobucci and Bobby Calder, eds., *Kellogg on Integrated Marketing* (New York: John Wiley & Sons, 2003).

24. Scott Davis and Michael Dunn, *Building the Brand-Driven Business* (New York: John Wiley & Sons, 2002); Michael Dunn and Scott Davis, "Building Brands From the Inside, *Marketing Management*, May/June 2003, pp. 32–37.

25. Stan Maklan and Simon Knox, *Competing on Value* (Upper Saddle River, NJ: Financial Times Prentice Hall, 2000).

26. Coeli Carr, "Seeking to Attract Top Prospects, Employers Brush Up On Brands," *New York Times*, September 10, 2006.

27. Deborah Roedder John, Barbara Loken, Kyeong-Heui Kim, and Alokparna Basu Monga, "Brand Concept Maps: A Methodology for Identifying Brand Association Networks," *Journal of Marketing Research* 43 (November 2006): 549–563.

28. "The Best Global Brands," *BusinessWeek*, August 7, 2006, ranks and critiques the 100 best global brands in 2004, using the valuation method developed by Interbrand. For more discussion on brand winners and losers, see Matt Haig, *Brand Royalty: How the Top 100 Brands Thrive and Survive* (London: Kogan Page, 2004); and Matt Haig, *Brand Failures: The Truth About the 100 Biggest Branding Mistakes of All Time* (London: Kogan Page, 2003). For an academic discussion of valuing brand equity, see V. Srinivasan, Chan Su Park, and Dae Ryun Chang, "An Approach to the Measurement, Analysis, and Prediction of Brand Equity and Its Sources," *Management Science* 51 (September 2005): 1433–1448.

29. For an up-to-date discussion of what factors determine long-term branding success, see Allen P. Adamson, *Brand Simple* (New York: Palgrave Macmillan, 2006).

30. Natalie Mizik and Robert Jacobson, "Trading Off Between Value Creation and Value Appropriation: The Financial Implications of Shifts in Strategic Emphasis," *Journal of Marketing* 67 (January 2003): 63–76.

31. Mark Speece, "Marketer's Malady: Fear of Change," *Brandweek*, August 19, 2002, p. 34.

32. Betsy McKay, "Coke, Pepsi Are Slow to Revive Growth in Core Soda Brands," *Wall Street Journal*, March 9, 2007, p. B3; Kenneth Hein, "Dew Sports Street Smarts, Woos Urban Influences," *Brandweek*, June 6, 2005, p. 18.

33. For comprehensive corporate branding guidelines, see James R. Gregory, *The Best of Branding: Best Practices in Corporate Branding* (New York: McGraw-Hill, 2004). For some international perspectives, see *The Expressive Organization: Linking Identity, Reputation and Corporate Brand*, edited by Majken Schultz, Mary Jo Hatch, and Mogens Holten Larsen (Oxford, UK: Oxford University Press, 2000) and *Corporate Branding: Purpose, People, and Process*, edited by Majken Schultz, Yun Mi Antorini, and Fabian F. Csaba (Denmark: Copenhagen Business School Press, 2005).

34. Zeynep Gürhan-Canli and Rajeev Batra, "When Corporate Image Affects Product Evaluations: The Moderating Role of Perceived Risk," *Journal of Marketing Research* 41 (May 2004): 197–205; Thomas J. Brown and Peter Dacin (1997), "The Company and the Product: Corporate Associations and Consumer Product Responses," *Journal of Marketing* 61 (January): 68–84; Kevin Lane Keller and David A. Aaker (1998), "Corporate-Level Marketing: The Impact of Credibility on a Company's Brand Extensions," *Corporate Reputation Review* 1 (August): 356–378; Guido Berens, Cees B.M. van Riel, and Gerrit H. van Bruggen, "Corporate Associations and Consumer Product Responses: The Moderating Role of Corporate Brand Dominance," *Journal of Marketing* 69 (July 2005): 35–48.

35. Vithala R. Rao, Manoj K. Agarwal, and Denise Dalhoff (2004), "How Is Manifest Branding Strategy Related to the Intangible Value of a Corporation?" *Journal of Marketing* 68 (October 2004): 126–141. For an examination of the financial impact of brand portfolio decisions, see Neil A. Morgan and Lopo L. Rego, "The Marketing and Financial Performance Consequences of Firms' Brand Portfolio Strategy," working paper, Kelley School of Business, Indiana University, 2006.

36. William J. Holstein, "The Incalculable Value of Building Brands," *Chief Executive*, April/May 2006, pp. 52+.

37. Byung-Do Kim and Mary W. Sullivan, "The Effect of Parent Brand Experience on Line Extension Trial

and Repeat Purchase," *Marketing Letters* 9 (April 1998): 181–193.
38. Kevin Lane Keller and David A. Aaker, "The Effects of Sequential Introduction of Brand Extensions," *Journal of Marketing Research* 29 (February 1992): 35–50; John Milewicz and Paul Herbig, "Evaluating the Brand Extension Decision Using a Model of Reputation Building," *Journal of Product & Brand Management* 3, no. 1 (1994): 39–47.
39. Daniel C. Smith, "Brand Extension and Advertising Efficiency: What Can and Cannot Be Expected," *Journal of Advertising Research* (November/December 1992): 11–20; Daniel C. Smith and C. Whan Park, "The Effects of Brand Extensions on Market Share and Advertising Efficiency," *Journal of Marketing Research* 29 (August 1992): 296–313; Valarie A. Taylor and William O. Bearden, "Ad Spending on Brand Extensions: Does Similarity Matter?" *Journal of Brand Management* 11 (September 2003): 63–74; Sheri Bridges, Kevin Lane Keller, and Sanjay Sood, "Communication Strategies for Brand Extensions: Enhancing Perceived Fit By Establishing Explanatory Links," *Journal of Advertising* 29 (Winter 2000): 1–11.
40. Subramanian Balachander and Sanjoy Ghose, "Reciprocal Spillover Effects: A Strategic Benefit of Brand Extensions," *Journal of Marketing* 67, no. 1 (January 2003): 4–13.
41. Bharat N. Anand and Ron Shachar, "Brands as Beacons: A New Source of Loyalty to Multi-Product Firms," *Journal of Marketing Research* 41 (May 2004): 135–150.
42. Kevin Lane Keller and David A. Aaker, "The Effects of Sequential Introduction of Brand Extensions," *Journal of Marketing Research* 29 (February 1992): 35–50. For consumer processing implications, see Huifung Mao and H. Shanker Krishnan, "Effects of Prototype and Exemplar Fit on Brand Extension Evaluations: A Two-Process Contingency Model," *Journal of Consumer Research* 33 (June 2006): 41–49.
43. John A. Quelch and David Kenny, "Extend Profits, Not Product Lines," *Harvard Business Review* (September–October 1994): 153–160; Perspectives from the Editors, "The Logic of Product-Line Extensions," *Harvard Business Review* (November–December 1994): 53–62; J. Andrews and G. S. Low, "New But Not Improved: Factors That Affect the Development of Meaningful Line Extensions," Working Paper Report No. 98–124 (Cambridge, MA: Marketing Science Institute, November 1998); Maureen Morrin, "The Impact of Brand Extensions on Parent Brand Memory Structures and Retrieval Processes," *Journal of Marketing Research* 36, no. 4 (1999): 517–525.
44. Al Ries and Jack Trout, *Positioning: The Battle for Your Mind* (New York: McGraw-Hill, 1981).
45. David A. Aaker, *Brand Portfolio Strategy: Creating Relevance, Differentiation, Energy, Leverage, and Clarity* (New York: Free Press, 2004).
46. See Franziska Völckner and Henrik Sattler, "Drivers of Brand Extension Success," *Journal of Marketing* 70 (April 2006): 1–17; Chris Pullig, Carolyn Simmons, and Richard G. Netemeyer, "Brand Dilution: When Do New Brands Hurt Existing Brands?" *Journal of Marketing* 70 (April 2006): 52–66; Barbara Loken and Deborah Roedder John, "Diluting Brand Beliefs: When Do Brand Extensions Have a Negative Impact?" *Journal of Marketing* (July 1993): 71–84; Deborah Roedder John, Barbara Loken, and Christopher Joiner, "The Negative Impact of Extensions: Can Flagship Products Be Diluted?" *Journal of Marketing* (January 1998):19–32; Susan M. Broniarcyzk and Joseph W. Alba, "The Importance of the Brand in Brand Extension," *Journal of Marketing Research* (May 1994): 214–228 (this entire issue of *JMR* is devoted to brands and brand equity); R. Ahluwalia and Z. Gürhan-Canli, "The Effects of Extensions on the Family Brand Name: An Accessibility-Diagnosticity Perspective," *Journal of Consumer Research* 27 (December 2000): 371–381; Z. Gürhan-Canli and M. Durairaj, "The Effects of Extensions on Brand Name Dilution and Enhancement," *Journal of Marketing Research* 35 (1998): 464–473; S. J. Milberg, C. W. Park, and M. S. McCarthy, "Managing Negative Feedback Effects Associated with Brand Extensions: The Impact of Alternative Branding Strategies," *Journal of Consumer Psychology* 6 (1997): 119–140.
47. Philip Kotler and Kevin Lane Keller, *Marketing Management*, 12th ed. (Upper Saddle River, NJ: Prentice Hall, 2006); Patrick Barwise and Thomas Robertson, "Brand Portfolios," *European Management Journal* 10, no. 3 (September 1992): 277–285.
48. Jack Trout, *Differentiate or Die: Survival in Our Era of Killer Competition* (New York: John Wiley, 2000).
49. Paul W. Farris, "The Chevrolet Corvette," Case UVA-M-320, The Darden Graduate Business School Foundation, University of Virginia, Charlottesville, Virginia.
50. Roland T. Rust, Valerie A. Zeithaml, and Katherine A. Lemon, "Measuring Customer Equity and

Calculating Marketing ROI," in the *Handbook of Marketing Research*, Rajiv Grover and Marco Vriens, eds. (Thousand Oaks, CA: Sage Publications, 2006): 588–601; Roland T. Rust, Valerie A. Zeithaml, and Katherine A. Lemon, *Driving Customer Equity* (New York: Free Press, 2000).

51. Robert C. Blattberg and John Deighton, "Manage Marketing by the Customer Equity Test," *Harvard Business Review* (July-August 1996): 136–144.

52. Robert C. Blattberg, Gary Getz, and Jacquelyn S. Thomas, *Customer Equity: Building and Managing Relationships As Valuable Assets* (Boston: Harvard Business School Press, 2001); Robert C. Blattberg and Jacquelyn S. Thomas, "Valuing, Analyzing, and Managing the Marketing Function Using Customer Equity Principles," in *Kellogg on Marketing*, edited by Dawn Iacobucci (New York: John Wiley & Sons, 2002).

53. Much of this section is based on: Robert Leone, Vithala Rao, Kevin Lane Keller, Man Luo, Leigh McAlister, Rajendra Srivatstava (2006), "Linking Brand Equity to Customer Equity," *Journal of Service Research* 9 (November): 125–138. This special issue is devoted to customer equity and has a number of thought-provoking articles.

54. Niraj Dawar, "What Are Brands Good For?" *MIT Sloan Management Review* (Fall 2004): 31–37.

CHAPTER 9

Crafting the Brand Positioning and Dealing with Competition

In this chapter, we will address the following questions:

1. How can a firm choose and communicate an effective positioning?
2. How are brands and offerings differentiated?
3. How can a firm identify its primary competitors and analyze their strategies, objectives, strengths, and weaknesses?
4. How can market leaders, challengers, followers, and nichers compete effectively?

MARKETING MANAGEMENT AT PROGRESSIVE INSURANCE

When it was still a fairly minor player in the auto insurance industry, Progressive Insurance specialized in a small niche that most other insurers ignored: "non-standard" insurance for motorists with less-than-perfect driving records. Progressive used its core competence in data analysis to learn the exact cost of serving various types of customers and how to make a profit serving lucrative high-risk customers no other insurer wanted to cover.

But Progressive gained its truly sustainable competitive advantage in the mid-1990s, when it became one of the first to sell auto insurance directly to consumers via the Internet. It provides free online quotes for its own policies as well as quotes from up to three competitors, information that previously had been available only through insurance agents. In this way, Progressive saves consumers time and money by showing that, in many cases, its policies are more competitively priced. Later, if a customer has an accident, one of Progressive's 12,000 claims adjusters speeds to the scene and often cuts a check right on the spot. Customers can bring damaged vehicles to one of Progressive's 62 service centers for repair and pick up a rental car on the spot. Thanks to its competitive savvy and top-quality service, today the company serves 12 million customers and has become the third-biggest U.S. auto insurer, up from 48th in 1980.[1]

No company can succeed if its products and services resemble every other product and offering. Leaders such as Progressive capture and keep market share through careful positioning and differentiation, ensuring that each offering represents a distinctive big idea in the mind of the target market. In addition, to effectively devise and implement the best brand positioning strategies, companies must pay keen attention to their competitors. Markets have become too competitive to focus on the customer alone. This chapter explores how companies can effectively position and differentiate their offerings for competitive advantage. It also examines the role of competition and how marketers can manage brands depending on their market position.[2]

DEVELOPING AND COMMUNICATING A POSITIONING STRATEGY

All marketing strategy is based on STP—segmentation, targeting, and positioning. A company discovers different needs and groups in the marketplace, targets those that it can satisfy in a superior way, and then positions its product or service so that the target market recognizes the company's distinctive offering and image.

Positioning is the act of designing the company's offering and image to occupy a distinctive place in the minds of the target market.[3] The goal is to locate the brand in the minds of consumers to maximize the potential benefit to the firm. A good brand positioning helps guide marketing strategy by clarifying the brand's essence, what goals it helps the consumer achieve, and how it does so in a unique way. The result of positioning is the successful creation of a *customer-focused value proposition*, a cogent reason why the target market should buy the product. Table 9.1 shows how three companies—Perdue, Volvo, and Domino's—have defined their value proposition, given their target customers, benefits, and prices.

TABLE 9.1 Examples of Value Propositions Demand States and Marketing Tasks

Company and Product	Target Customers	Benefits	Price	Value Proposition
Perdue (chicken)	Quality-conscious consumers of chicken	Tenderness	10% premium	More tender golden chicken at a moderate premium price
Volvo (station wagon)	Safety-conscious "upscale" families	Durability and safety	20% premium	The safest, most durable wagon in which your family can ride
Domino's (pizza)	Convenience-minded pizza lovers	Delivery speed and good quality	15% premium	A good hot pizza, delivered to your door within 30 minutes of ordering, at a moderate price

BREAKTHROUGH MARKETING: UPS

The United Parcel Service was founded in 1907 to fill a gap in the shipping market: local parcel deliveries. As the first and largest national package delivery company, UPS dominated the shipping industry for decades. Its market leadership was challenged in the early 1980s, when upstart Federal Express (as it was then called) began offering a unique "triple play": overnight service, shipment tracking, and volume discounts. UPS launched its next-day service in 1982; by 1990, next-day service accounted for 21% of its business. Through international acquisitions, UPS positioned itself as the "provider of the broadest range of package distribution services and solutions in the world" with numerous air and ground shipping options.

Next, UPS acquired the nationwide franchise chain of Mail Boxes Etc. shipping stores, later changing the brand to The UPS Store. FedEx mirrored UPS's move by acquiring Kinko's and establishing FedEx Kinko's joint-branded stores. Recently, UPS addressed an area where it was perceived to lag behind FedEx: speed. By advertising its "fast lane" initiative (speedier shipments between major U.S. cities) and its "expanded early AM" program (delivery before 7 AM), UPS highlighted key benefits that customers seek. Now UPS delivers nearly 16 million packages daily and enjoys a commanding 65% share of the domestic package delivery market.[4]

To craft a positioning, marketers must determine a frame of reference by identifying the target market and the competition as well as the ideal points-of-parity and points-of-difference brand associations. "Breakthrough Marketing: UPS" chronicles how UPS has successfully positioned itself against a formidable opponent, FedEx.

Competitive Frame of Reference

A starting point in defining a competitive frame of reference for a brand positioning is to determine **category membership**—the products or sets of products with which a brand competes and which function as close substitutes. As discussed later in this chapter, competitive analysis considers a whole host of factors—including the resources, capabilities, and likely intentions of various other firms—in choosing those markets where consumers can be profitably served.

Deciding to target a particular type of consumer can define the nature of competition because certain firms have targeted that segment in the past (or plan to do so in the future), or because consumers in that segment may already look to certain brands in their purchase decisions. To determine the proper competitive frame of reference, marketers need to understand consumer behavior and the consideration sets consumers use in making brand choices. In the United Kingdom, for example, the Automobile Association has positioned itself as the fourth "emergency service"—along with police, fire, and ambulance—to convey greater credibility and urgency.

Points-of-Parity and Points-of-Difference

Once marketers have fixed the competitive frame of reference for positioning by defining the target market and nature of the competition, they can define the appropriate points-of-difference and points-of-parity associations.[5] **Points-of-difference (PODs)** are attributes or benefits that consumers strongly associate with a brand, positively evaluate, and believe they couldn't find to the same extent with a competitive brand. Associations that make up PODs may be based on virtually any type of attribute or benefit. Examples are Apple (*design*) and Lexus (*quality*). Creating strong, favorable, and unique brand associations is challenging but essential for competitive brand positioning.

Points-of-parity (POPs) are associations that aren't necessarily unique to the brand but may in fact be shared with other brands.[6] Two basic forms are category and competitive points-of-parity. *Category points-of-parity* are associations consumers view as necessary to a legitimate and credible offering within a certain category, although perhaps not sufficient for brand choice. Consumers might not consider a travel agency truly a travel agency unless it can make air and hotel reservations and provide advice about leisure packages. Category points-of-parity may change over time due to technological advances, legal developments, or consumer trends.

Competitive points-of-parity are associations designed to *negate* competitors' points-of-difference. If a brand can "break even" in those areas where the competitors are trying to find an advantage and can achieve advantages in other areas, the brand should be in a strong—and perhaps unbeatable—competitive position. For an offering to achieve a point-of-parity (POP) on a particular attribute or benefit, a sufficient number of consumers must believe that the brand is "good enough" on that dimension. Often, the key to positioning is not so much in achieving a point-of-difference (POD) as in achieving points-of-parity.

Establishing Category Membership

Target customers are aware that Maybelline is a leading brand of cosmetics; Accenture is a leading consulting firm; and so on. Often, however, marketers must inform consumers of a brand's category membership, especially when the category membership isn't apparent (as when a new product is introduced). This uncertainty can be a special problem for high-tech products. There are also situations where consumers know a brand's category membership but may not be convinced that the brand is a valid member of the category. For example, consumers may know that Hewlett-Packard makes digital cameras but may not be certain whether Hewlett-Packard cameras are in the same class as Sony, Olympus, and Kodak. Thus, HP might find it useful to reinforce category membership.

Brands are sometimes affiliated with categories in which they don't hold membership. This is one way to highlight a brand's point-of-difference, providing that consumers know the brand's actual membership. However, it's important that consumers understand what the brand stands for and not just what it's *not*. The typical approach to positioning is to inform consumers of a brand's membership before stating its point-of-difference. Presumably, consumers need to know what a product is and what function it serves before deciding whether it dominates the brands against which it competes.

There are three main ways to convey a brand's category membership:

1. *Announcing category benefits.* To reassure consumers that a brand will deliver on the fundamental reason for using a category, marketers frequently use benefits to announce category membership. Thus, a brownie mix might attain membership in the baked desserts category by claiming the benefit of great taste and support this claim through high-quality ingredients (performance).
2. *Comparing to exemplars.* Well-known, noteworthy brands can also be used to specify category membership. When Tommy Hilfiger was an unknown, advertising

announced his membership as a great American designer by associating him with recognized category members such as Geoffrey Beene and Calvin Klein.

3. *Relying on the product descriptor.* The product descriptor that follows the brand name is often a concise means of conveying category origin. The Sony Portable Reader, for example, conveys the benefit of portability while using the Sony brand to communicate its membership in the electronics category.

Choosing POPs and PODs

Points-of-parity are driven by the needs of category membership (to create category POPs) and the necessity of negating competitors' PODs (to create competitive POPs). In choosing points-of-difference, two important considerations are that consumers find the POD desirable and that the firm has the capabilities to deliver on it. Table 9.2 shows three consumer desirability criteria and three key deliverability criteria for PODs.

Research has shown, however, that brands can sometimes be successfully differentiated on seemingly irrelevant attributes *if* consumers infer the proper benefit.[7] Procter & Gamble differentiates its Folger's instant coffee by its "flaked coffee crystals," created through a "unique patented process." In reality, the shape of the coffee particles is irrelevant because the crystals immediately dissolve in the hot water.

Creating POPs and PODs

One common difficulty in creating a strong, competitive positioning is that many of the attributes or benefits that make up the points-of-parity and points-of-difference are negatively correlated. For example, it might be difficult to position a brand as "inexpensive" and at the same time assert that it is "of the highest quality." Moreover, individual attributes and benefits often have positive *and* negative aspects. A long-lived brand seen as having a great deal of heritage might be associated with experience, wisdom, and expertise. On the other hand, it could also imply being old-fashioned and not up-to-date. Therefore, the best approach is to develop an offering that performs well on both dimensions, the way Gore-Tex overcame the seemingly conflicting product image of "breathable" and "waterproof" through technological advances.

Some marketers have adopted other approaches to address attribute or benefit trade-offs: launching two different marketing campaigns, each devoted to a different brand attribute or benefit; linking the brand to any entity (person, place, or thing) that

TABLE 9.2   Key Criteria for Points-of-Difference

Desirability Criteria	Deliverability Criteria
■ *Relevance.* The POD must be personally relevant and important to consumers.	■ *Feasibility.* The product design and marketing offering must support the desired association.
■ *Distinctiveness.* Target consumers must find the POD distinctive and superior.	■ *Communicability.* Consumers must be given a compelling reason and understandable rationale as to why the brand can deliver the desired benefit.
■ *Believability.* Target consumers must find the POD believable and credible.	■ *Sustainability.* The firm must be committed and willing to devote enough resources to create an enduring positioning.

possesses the right kind of equity as a means to establish an attribute or benefit as a POP or POD; and even attempting to convince consumers that the negative relationship between attributes and benefits, if they consider it differently, is in fact positive.

DIFFERENTIATION STRATEGIES

Marketers must start with the belief that any offering can be differentiated. **Competitive advantage** is a company's ability to perform in one or more ways that competitors can't or won't match. Few competitive advantages are sustainable, although a *leverageable advantage* can be used as a springboard to new advantages, much as Microsoft has leveraged its operating system to Microsoft Office and other applications. To endure, a firm must continuously invent new advantages.

It's important that customers see any competitive advantage as a *customer advantage*. For example, if a company delivers faster than its competitors, it won't be a customer advantage if customers don't value speed. If companies focus on building customer advantages, they'll deliver high customer value and satisfaction, which leads to repeat purchasing and ultimately to high company profitability.[8] In general, the obvious means of differentiation, and often the most compelling for consumers, relate to aspects of the product and service.

Product Differentiation

Products can be differentiated in a number of ways:[9]

- *Form*. **Form** refers to the product's size, shape, or physical structure. For example, aspirin can be differentiated by dosage size, shape, coating, or action time.
- *Features*. Characteristics that supplement the product's basic function are its **features**. Marketers can identify and select new features by researching customer needs and calculating *customer value* versus *company cost* for each potential feature. They should also consider how many customers want each feature, how long they need to launch it, and how easily rivals can copy it. To avoid "feature fatigue," marketers also must prioritize those features that are included and find unobtrusive ways to provide information about how consumers can use and benefit from the feature.[10]
- *Customization*. With **mass customization,** the firm meets each customer's requirements, on a mass basis, by individually designing products, services, programs, and communications.[11]
- *Performance quality*. **Performance quality** is the level at which the product's primary characteristics operate. Firms should design a performance level appropriate to the target market and competitors' performance levels, while managing performance quality through time.
- *Conformance quality*. Buyers expect products to have a high **conformance quality**, the degree to which all the produced units are identical and meet the promised specifications. If a product has low conformance quality, it will disappoint some buyers.
- *Durability*. **Durability**, a measure of the product's expected operating life under natural or stressful conditions, is vital for products such as appliances. However, the extra price must not be excessive, and the product must not be subject to rapid technological obsolescence.

- *Reliability*. Buyers normally will pay a premium for high *reliability*, a measure of the probability that a product will not malfunction or fail within a specified period. Maytag, for instance, has an outstanding reputation for reliable home appliances.
- *Repairability*. How easily can a product be fixed when it malfunctions or fails? Ideal repairability would exist if users could fix the product themselves with little cost in money or time.
- *Style*. **Style** describes the product's look and feel to the buyer. Aesthetics have played a key role in such brands as Apple computers.[12] Style can create distinctiveness that is difficult to copy; however, strong style doesn't always mean high performance.
- *Design*. As competition intensifies, design offers a potent way to differentiate and position a company's products and services.[13] **Design** is the totality of features that affect how a product looks, feels, and functions in terms of customer requirements. The designer has to figure out how much to invest in form, feature development, performance, conformance, durability, reliability, repairability, and style. To the company, a well-designed product is one that is easy to manufacture and distribute. To the customer, a well-designed product is one that is pleasant to look at and easy to open, install, use, repair, and dispose.

Services Differentiation

When the physical product can't be differentiated easily, the key to competitive success may lie in adding valued services and improving their quality. The main service differentiators are:

- *Ordering ease*. How easy is it for the customer to place an order with the company?
- *Delivery*. How well is the offering delivered to the customer? This covers speed, accuracy, and care throughout the process. Mexico's Cemex promises to deliver concrete faster than pizza. With technology, it can track each of its trucks, and it promises that if delivery is more than 10 minutes late, the customer gets a 20% discount.[14]
- *Installation*. This refers to the work done to make a product operational in its planned location. Buyers of heavy equipment expect good installation service. Differentiation by installation is particularly important for companies that offer complex products.
- *Customer training*. Training the customer's employees to use products properly and efficiently is a key differentiator. General Electric not only sells and installs X-ray equipment in hospitals, but also trains users.
- *Customer consulting*. The seller can provide data, information systems, and advising services that meet buyers' needs. For example, the furniture company Herman Miller works with Future Industrial Technologies to show business customers how to get the full ergonomic benefit from office furnishings.[15]
- *Maintenance and repair*. What is the service program for helping customers keep products in good working order? This is an important consideration for many products.
- *Returns*. Returns are an unavoidable reality of doing business, especially with online purchases.[16] Costco's generous return policy allows returns for any reason at any time—except for electronics and computers, which now must be returned within three to six months, a policy change that saves Costco millions of dollars each year.[17]

Other Dimensions of Differentiation

Among the many other dimensions a company can use to differentiate its market offerings are:

- *Personnel differentiation.* Companies can gain an advantage by having better-trained employees. Singapore Airlines is well regarded in large part because of its flight attendants.
- *Channel differentiation.* Companies can more effectively and efficiently design their distribution channels' coverage, expertise, and performance. The European no-frills airline easyJet emphasizes online booking to keep costs low so it can keep airfares low.
- *Image differentiation.* Companies can craft powerful and distinctive images. For instance, such unique brand names as Turbodog and Purple Haze contribute to the not-mass-produced image of ales and beers from Louisiana microbrewery Abita Brewing Co.[18]

COMPETITIVE FORCES AND COMPETITORS

Michael Porter has identified five forces that determine the intrinsic, long-run profit attractiveness of a market or market segment: industry competitors, potential entrants, substitutes, buyers, and suppliers (see Figure 9.1). The threats these forces pose are:

1. *Threat of intense segment rivalry.* A segment is unattractive if it already contains numerous, strong, or aggressive competitors. It's even more unattractive if the segment

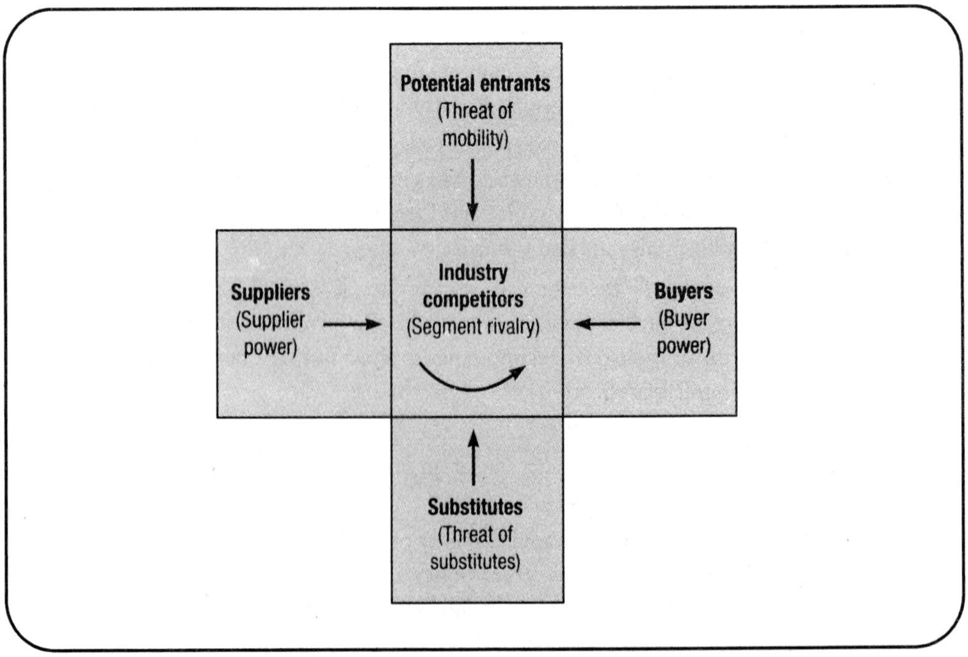

FIGURE 9.1 Five Forces That Determine Market Attractiveness

is stable or declining, if plant capacity must be added, if fixed costs or exit barriers are high, or if rivals have high stakes in staying in the segment. These conditions will lead to frequent price wars, advertising battles, and new-product introductions—making competition more expensive.

2. *Threat of new entrants.* The most attractive segment has high entry barriers and low exit barriers, so few new firms can enter, while poor-performing firms can exit easily.[19] Profit potential is high when both entry and exit barriers are high, but firms face more risk because poorer-performing firms stay and fight. When entry and exit barriers are both low, firms enter and leave easily, and the returns are stable and low. The worst case is when entry barriers are low and exit barriers are high. Firms can enter during good times but find it hard to leave during bad times, which results in chronic overcapacity and depressed earnings for all.

3. *Threat of substitute products.* A segment is unattractive when there are actual or potential substitutes for the product. Substitutes place a limit on prices and on the profits that a segment can earn. If technology advances or competition increases in these substitute industries, prices and profits in the segment are likely to fall.

4. *Threat of buyers' growing bargaining power.* A segment is unattractive if the buyers possess strong or growing bargaining power. Buyers' bargaining power grows when they become more concentrated or organized, when the product represents a significant fraction of the buyers' costs, when the product is undifferentiated, when the buyers' switching costs are low, when buyers are price sensitive, or when they can integrate upstream. To protect themselves, sellers might select buyers with the least power to negotiate or switch suppliers; a better defense is to develop superior offers that strong buyers can't refuse.

5. *Threat of suppliers' growing bargaining power.* A segment is unattractive if the company's suppliers are able to raise prices or reduce quantity supplied. Suppliers tend to be powerful when they are concentrated or organized, when there are few substitutes, when the supplied product is an important input, when the costs of switching suppliers are high, and when suppliers can integrate downstream. The best defenses are to build win–win relations with suppliers or use multiple supply sources.

Identifying Competitors

It would seem a simple task for a company to identify its competitors. PepsiCo knows that Coca-Cola's Dasani is a major bottled-water competitor for its Aquafina brand; Sony knows that Microsoft's Xbox competes with the Sony PlayStation. However, the range of a company's actual and potential competitors can be much broader than the obvious. A company is more likely to be hurt by emerging competitors or new technologies than by current competitors.

In recent years, for instance, a number of "emerging giants" have arisen from developing countries as nimble competitors not only competing with multinationals on their home turf but also becoming global forces in their own right. They have gained competitive advantage by exploiting their knowledge of local resources to build world-class businesses. In India, for example, Tata Consultancy Services and Infosys Technologies are successfully competing with multinationals like Accenture and EDS by catering to the global demand for software and services.[20]

Industry and Market Views of Competition

We can examine competition from both an industry and a market point of view.[21] An **industry** is a group of firms that offers a product or class of products that are close substitutes for each other. Marketers classify industries according to number of sellers; degree of product differentiation; presence or absence of entry, mobility, and exit barriers; cost structure; degree of vertical integration; and degree of globalization.

Using the market approach, competitors are companies that satisfy the same customer need. For example, a customer who buys word-processing software really wants "writing ability"—a need that can be satisfied by pencils, pens, or typewriters. The market concept of competition reveals a broader set of actual and potential competitors. Marketers must overcome "marketing myopia" and stop defining competition in traditional category and industry terms.[22] Coca-Cola, focused on its soft-drink business, missed seeing the growing market for coffee bars and fresh-fruit-juice bars that cut into sales of its carbonated beverages.

The market concept of competition reveals a broader set of actual and potential competitors than competition defined in just product category terms. Rayport and Jaworski suggest profiling a company's direct and indirect competitors by mapping the buyer's steps in obtaining and using the product. This type of analysis highlights a company's opportunities and its challenges.[23]

INSEAD professors W. Chan Kim and Renée Mauborgne recommend that companies engage in "blue ocean thinking" by creating offerings for which there are no direct competitors. Instead of searching within the conventional boundaries of industry competition, managers should look beyond to find unoccupied market positions that represent real value innovation.[24] Figure 9.2 summarizes their principles for successful formulation and execution of blue ocean strategy.

FIGURE 9.2   Key Principles of Blue Ocean Strategy

FORMULATION PRINCIPLES

a) Reconstruct market boundaries
  - Look across alternative industries
  - Look across strategic groups within industries
  - Look across chain of buyers
  - Look across complementary product and service offerings
  - Look across functional or emotional appeal to buyers
  - Look across time
b) Focus on the big picture, not the numbers
c) Reach beyond existing demand
d) Get the strategic sequence right
  - Is there buyer utility?
  - Is the price acceptable?
  - Can we attain target cost?
  - What are the adoption challenges?

EXECUTION PRINCIPLES

a) Overcome key organizational hurdles
  - Cognitive hurdle
  - Resource hurdle
  - Motivational hurdle
  - Political hurdle
b) Build execution into strategy

Source: W. Chan Kim and Renée Mauborgne, *Blue Ocean Strategy: How to Create Uncontested Market Space and Make the Competition Irrelevant* (Boston MA: Harvard Business School Press, 2005). Reprinted by permission.

Chapter 9 Crafting the Brand Positioning and Dealing with Competition

ANALYZING COMPETITORS

Once a company identifies its main competitors, it must ascertain their strategies, objectives, strengths, and weaknesses.[25]

Strategies

A group of firms following the same strategy in a given target market is a **strategic group**.[26] Suppose a company wants to enter the major appliance industry. What is its strategic group? It develops the chart shown in Figure 9.3 and discovers four strategic groups based on product quality and level of vertical integration. Group A has one competitor (Maytag); group B has three (General Electric, Whirlpool, and Sears); group C has four; and group D has two. This approach offers important insights. First, the height of the entry barriers differs for each group. Second, if the company successfully enters a group, the members of that group become its key competitors.

FIGURE 9.3   Strategic Groups in the Major Appliance Industry

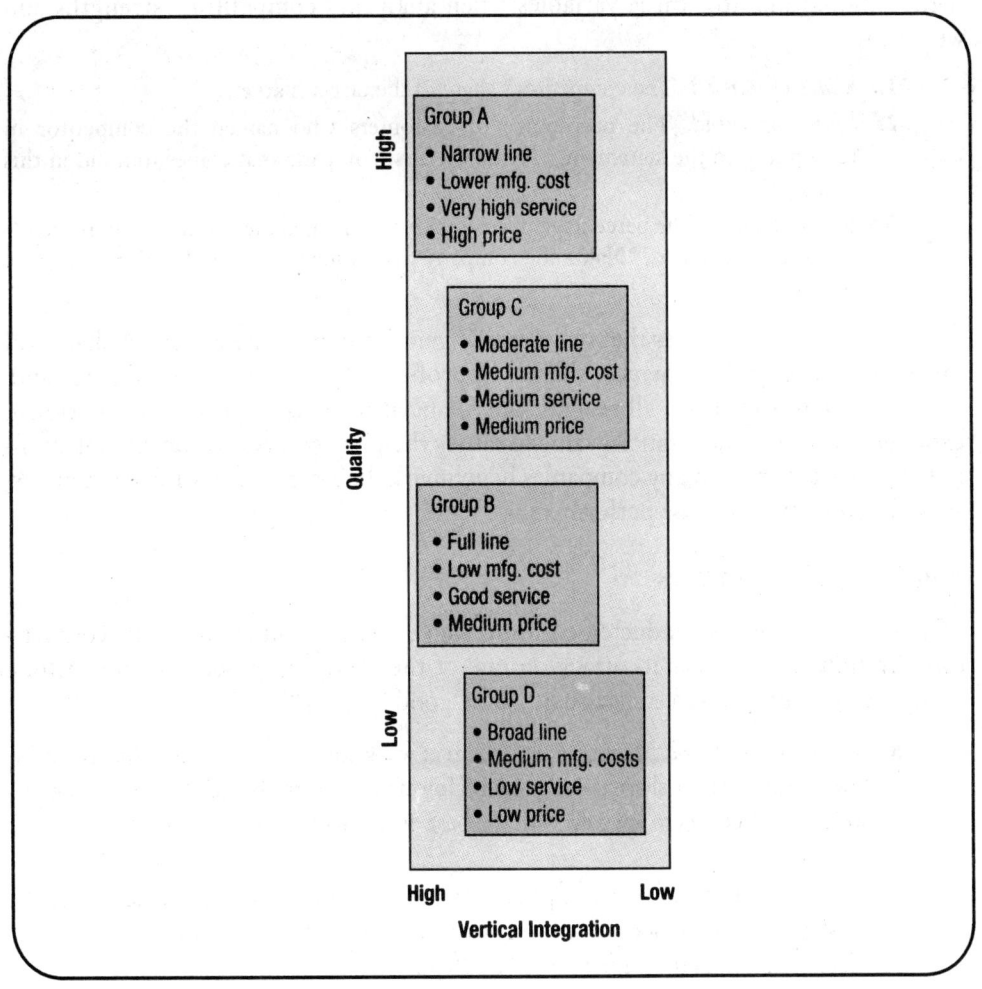

Objectives

Once a company has identified its main competitors and their strategies, it must ask: What is each competitor seeking in the marketplace? What drives each competitor's behavior? Many factors shape a competitor's objectives, including size, history, current management, and financial situation. If the competitor is a division of a larger company, it's important to know whether the parent company is running it for growth, profits, or milking it.

Note that companies differ in the emphasis they put on short- versus long-term profits. Many U.S. firms have been criticized for operating on a short-run model, largely because current performance is judged by stockholders who might lose confidence, sell their stock, and cause the company's cost of capital to rise. Japanese firms operate largely on a market-share-maximization model. They receive much of their funds from banks at a lower interest rate and in the past have readily accepted lower profits. So another reliable assumption is that each competitor pursues some mix of objectives: current profitability, market share growth, cash flow, technological leadership, and service leadership.[27] Finally, a company must monitor competitors' expansion plans.

Strengths and Weaknesses

A firm should monitor three variables when analyzing competitors' strengths and weaknesses:

1. *Share of market.* The competitor's share of the target market.
2. *Share of mind.* The percentage of customers who named the competitor in responding to the statement, "Name the first company that comes to mind in this industry."
3. *Share of heart.* The percentage of customers who named the competitor in responding to the statement, "Name the company from which you would prefer to buy the product."

In general, companies that make steady gains in mind share and heart share will inevitably make gains in market share and profitability. Firms such as Timberland, Wegmans, and Toyota are all reaping the financial benefits of providing emotional, experiential, social, and financial value to satisfy their customers and constituents.[28] To improve market share, many companies benchmark their most successful competitors, as well as other world-class performers.

Selecting Competitors

After the company has conducted customer value analysis and examined its competitors carefully, it can focus its attack on one of the following classes of competitors: strong versus weak, close versus distant, and "good" versus "bad."

- *Strong versus weak.* Most companies aim at weak competitors, because this requires fewer resources per share point gained. However, the firm should also compete with strong competitors to keep up with the best. Even strong competitors have some weaknesses.
- *Close versus distant.* Most companies compete with the rivals that resemble them the most, yet it's also important to recognize distant competitors. Coca-Cola recognizes that its top competitor is tap water, not Pepsi.

- *"Good" versus "bad."* Every industry contains "good" and "bad" competitors.[29] Good competitors play by the industry's rules; make realistic assumptions about the industry's growth potential; set prices in reasonable relationship to costs; and favor a healthy industry. Bad competitors try to buy share rather than earn it; take large risks; invest in overcapacity; and upset industrial equilibrium. A company may find it necessary to attack bad competitors to reduce or end their dysfunctional practices.

COMPETITIVE STRATEGIES

A company can gain further insight by classifying its competitors and itself according to role in the target market: leader, challenger, follower, or nicher. On the basis of this classification, the company can take specific actions in line with its current and desired roles.

Market-Leader Strategies

Many industries contain one firm that is the acknowledged market leader, such as Microsoft (computer software) and McDonald's (fast food). This firm has the largest share in the relevant product market and usually leads the others in price changes, new-product introductions, distribution coverage, and promotional intensity. Although marketers assume well-known brands are distinctive in consumers' minds, unless the leader enjoys a legal monopoly, it must avoid missing key developments. A product innovation may hurt the leader; a competitor might unexpectedly find a fresh marketing angle or make a major marketing investment; or the leader might find its costs spiraling upward.

Companies that offer both low prices and high quality are capturing customers all over the world. As value-driven companies change the way they compete, traditional players in many industries are feeling new pressure. Often the value-driven rivals focus on one or a handful of segments; deliver the basic product better (or add a valued benefit); and boost efficiency to keep costs and prices down. To compete with value-based rivals, established firms must contain costs, emphasize differentiation, and manage prices carefully. In value-based markets, companies need to focus more intensely on their strategies and execute them flawlessly.[30]

To remain number one, the firm must find ways to expand total market demand. It must also protect its current market share through good defensive and offensive actions. Finally, the firm can try to increase its market share, even if market size remains constant.

Expanding the Total Market When the total market expands, the dominant firm usually gains the most. If U.S. consumers increase their consumption of ketchup, Heinz stands to gain the most because it sells almost two-thirds of the country's ketchup. If it can convince more people to use ketchup, or use ketchup with more meals, or use more ketchup on each occasion, Heinz will benefit. In general, the market leader should look for new customers or more usage from existing customers. It can try to attract buyers who are unaware of the product or resist it because of price or lack of certain features. A firm can search for new users among buyers who might use the product but don't (*market-penetration strategy*), those who have never used it (*new-market segment strategy*), or those who live elsewhere (*geographical-expansion strategy*).

To stimulate more usage, marketers can try to increase the amount, level, or frequency of consumption. Consumption can sometimes be increased through packaging or product design; for example, larger package sizes increase the amount that consumers use at one time.[31] Increasing frequency of use requires either identifying additional opportunities to use the brand in the same basic way or identifying completely new and different ways to use the brand. Product development can also spur new uses. For example, targeting the market for "nutraceutical" products with health benefits, Coca-Cola has introduced vitamin-enhanced Diet Coke Plus.[32]

Defending Market Share While trying to expand total market size, the dominant firm must also defend its current business against domestic and foreign rivals: Boeing against Airbus; Google against Yahoo! and Microsoft; MySpace against Facebook and specialized social network sites like Dogster for dog owners.[33] The most constructive response to defending market share is *continuous innovation*. The leader should lead the industry in new offerings, distribution effectiveness, and cost cutting. It keeps increasing its competitive strength and value to customers.

Even when it doesn't launch offensives, the market leader must leave no major flanks exposed. It must consider what segments to defend (even at a loss) and what segments to surrender. The aim of defensive strategy is to reduce the probability of attack, divert attacks to less threatening areas, and lessen their intensity. The leader can use six defense strategies.[34]

1. *Position defense*. This means occupying the most desirable market space in consumers' minds, making the brand almost impregnable, as Procter & Gable has done with Tide.
2. *Flank defense*. The market leader should also erect outposts to protect a weak front or possibly serve as an invasion base for counterattack. When Heublein's Smirnoff, which had 23% of the U.S. vodka market, was attacked by the low-priced competitor Wolfschmidt, Heublein raised Smirnoff's price and increased its advertising. It also launched one brand to compete with Wolfschmidt and a second brand to sell for less, protecting its flanks.
3. *Preemptive defense*. A more aggressive maneuver is to attack before a rival starts its offense. A company can hit one competitor here and another there, keeping everyone off balance, or it can try to achieve a grand market envelopment. Bank of America's 17,000 ATMs and 5,700 branches provide steep competition to local and regional banks and send out a signal to dissuade competitors from attacking.[35] A firm can also introduce a stream of new products supported by *preannouncements*—deliberate communications regarding future actions.[36]
4. *Counteroffensive defense*. When attacked, most leaders will counterattack. One effective counteroffensive is to invade the attacker's main market, forcing the rival to defend itself. Another is to use economic or political clout. For example, the leader may subsidize lower prices for a vulnerable product with revenue from more profitable products or lobby legislators to take political action that would inhibit the competition.
5. *Mobile defense*. Here, the leader stretches its domain over new territories that can serve as future centers for defense and offense, using market broadening and market diversification. *Market broadening* shifts focus from the current product to the underlying generic need. The company gets involved in R&D across the whole range of technology associated with that need. This is how "petroleum" firms such as BP recast themselves as "energy" companies to enter oil, nuclear, hydroelectric, and other industries. *Market*

diversification shifts into unrelated industries. Altria Group, which owns the tobacco company Philip Morris, has diversified into beer by taking a stake in SABMiller.

6. *Contraction defense.* Large companies sometimes must recognize that they can no longer defend all their territory. The best course of action then appears to be *planned contraction* (also called *strategic withdrawal*), giving up weaker territories and reassigning resources to stronger territories. As an example, Verizon spun off its Yellow Pages directories so it could concentrate on its core telecommunications businesses.[37]

Expanding Market Share In many markets, one share point is worth tens of millions of dollars. No wonder competition has turned so fierce in such markets—and much depends on the company's strategy.[38] Because the cost of buying market share may far exceed its revenue value, a company should consider four factors before pursuing increased share.

1. *The possibility of provoking antitrust action.* Jealous competitors may cry "monopoly" if a dominant firm makes further inroads. Microsoft, for example, has faced great scrutiny for its market leadership and practices.
2. *Economic cost.* After a certain level, profitability might fall, not rise, with further market-share gains. "Holdout" customers may dislike the company, be loyal to competitors, have unique needs, or prefer dealing with smaller suppliers. And the costs of legal work, public relations, and lobbying rise with market share. Pushing for higher market share is less justified when there are few scale or experience economies, unattractive market segments exist, buyers want multiple supply sources, and exit barriers are high. Some leaders have increased profitability by selectively decreasing market share in weaker areas.[39]
3. *Pursuing the wrong marketing activities.* Firms that gain share typically outperform rivals in new-product activity, relative product quality, and marketing expenditures.[40] Firms that cut prices more deeply than competitors typically don't achieve significant gains because enough rivals meet the price cuts and others offer values so buyers don't switch.
4. *The effect of increased market share on actual and perceived quality.*[41] Too many customers can strain the firm's resources, hurting product value and service delivery. If "exclusivity" is a key brand benefit, existing customers may resent additional new customers.

Other Competitive Strategies

Firms that are not market leaders in an industry are often called runner-up or trailing firms. Some, such as Ford and Avis, are quite large in their own right. These firms can either attack the leader and other competitors in an aggressive bid for further market share (*market challengers*), or they can choose not to "rock the boat" (*market followers*).

Market-Challenger Strategies Many market challengers have gained ground or even overtaken the leader.[42] A market challenger must first define its strategic objective; most aim to increase market share. Then the challenger must decide whom to attack. Attacking the leader is a high-risk but potentially high-payoff strategy if the leader isn't serving the market well. The challenger can attack firms of its own size that are underperforming and underfinanced, have aging products, charge excessive prices, or aren't satisfying customers in other ways. Or it can attack small local and regional firms.

Given clear opponents and objectives, five attack strategies are:

1. *Frontal attack.* Match the opponent's product, advertising, price, and distribution. The side with the greater resources will win. This can work if the leader doesn't retaliate and if the competitor convinces the market that its product is equal to the leader's product.
2. *Flank attack.* In a geographical attack, the challenger spots areas where a rival is underperforming. A second flanking strategy is to serve uncovered market needs. A flanking strategy is another name for identifying shifts in market segments that cause gaps to develop, then filling the gaps and developing them into strong segments. Flank attacks are particularly attractive to a challenger with fewer resources and are more likely to succeed than frontal attacks.
3. *Encirclement attack.* The encirclement maneuver is used to capture a wide slice of the enemy's territory through a blitz, launching a grand offensive on several fronts. Encirclement makes sense when the challenger commands superior resources and believes a swift encirclement will break the opponent's will.
4. *Bypass attack.* The most indirect strategy is to bypass the enemy and attack easier markets to broaden the firm's resource base. Three lines of approach are diversifying into unrelated products, diversifying into new geographical markets, and leapfrogging into new technologies to supplant existing products. For example, PepsiCo used a bypass when it bought Tropicana and then Quaker Oats (owner of Gatorade) as weapons against Coca-Cola. *Technological leapfrogging* is often used in high-tech industries.
5. *Guerilla warfare.* This consists of small, intermittent attacks to harass and demoralize the opponent and eventually secure permanent footholds. The challenger uses conventional and unconventional tactics, such as selective price cuts and intense promotional campaigns (see "Marketing Skills: Guerrilla Marketing"). Challengers must continue with stronger attacks if they hope to beat the leader—and all activities must be both legal and ethical.

Now the challenger must develop more specific strategies, such as lower-priced or discounted products; new or improved offerings; and innovative distribution.

MARKETING SKILLS: GUERRILLA MARKETING

Who needs guerrilla marketing skills? Any marketer who wants to attack and grab share from the leader without risking the higher cost and provocation of a frontal attack. Guerrilla marketers must think creatively about how to attract maximum customer attention and achieve marketing goals with minimal investment. They must test the idea internally and/or locally to spot potential problems before going national, and be prepared to change or drop a nonperforming guerilla campaign. Finally, guerilla marketers should anticipate stakeholders' reactions to controversial techniques or messages and be sensitive to legal and ethical concerns.

Consider the unintended consequences of the Cartoon Network's guerrilla marketing for *Aqua Teen Hunger Force*. The marketing firm hired by the Cartoon Network placed dozens of battery-powered lighted signs in public locations such as buildings and bridges around Boston and nine other U.S. cities. The promotion backfired when Boston police and officials closed roads and bridges for hours to investigate the seemingly suspicious devices. Amid the bad publicity, the Cartoon Network's general manager resigned; parent company Turner Broadcasting quickly apologized and paid $2 million to cover Boston's police costs.[43]

Market-Follower Strategies Theodore Levitt has argued that a strategy of *product imitation* might be as profitable as a strategy of *product innovation*.[44] The innovator bears the expense of developing the new product, getting it into distribution, and educating the market. The reward for all this work and risk is normally market leadership—even though another firm can then copy or improve on the new product. Although it probably won't overtake the leader, the follower can achieve high profits because it didn't bear any of the innovation expense.

Many companies prefer to follow rather than challenge the leader. This pattern is common in industries such as steel and chemicals, where few opportunities exist for product and image differentiation, service quality is often comparable, and price sensitivity is high. Short-run grabs for market share provoke retaliation, so most firms present similar offers to buyers, usually by copying the leader; this keeps market shares highly stable.

One broad strategy for followers is to be a *counterfeiter*, duplicating the leader's product and package and selling it on the black market or through disreputable dealers. Counterfeiters have plagued both Apple Computer and Rolex, especially in Asia. A second strategy is to be a *cloner*, emulating the leader's products, name, and packaging with slight variations. Ralcorp Holding sells imitations of name-brand cereals in lookalike boxes at lower prices. A third is to be an *imitator*, copying some things from the leader but maintaining differentiation of packaging, pricing, and so on. The leader doesn't mind as long as the imitator doesn't attack aggressively. A fourth strategy is to be an *adapter*, improving the leader's products, perhaps for different markets. S&S Cycle, for example, supplies engines to firms that build Harley-like cruiser bikes. It buys a new Harley-Davidson bike every year and takes the engine apart to see what it can improve upon.[45]

Normally, a follower earns less than the leader. For example, a study of food processing companies found that only the top two firms were profitable. Thus, followership is not always a rewarding path.

Market-Nicher Strategies An alternative to being a follower in a large market is to be a leader in a small market, or niche. Smaller firms normally avoid competing with larger firms by targeting small markets of little or no interest to the larger firms. Even large, profitable firms are now setting up business units or brands for specific niches. The key idea in nichemanship is specialization. Table 9.3 shows the specialist roles open to nichers. Because niches can weaken, the firm must continually create new niches, expand niches, and protect its niches. By developing strength in two or more niches, the company increases its chances for survival.

Balancing Customer and Competitor Orientations

Although a company can position itself competitively as a market leader, challenger, follower, or nicher, it must not spend all its time focusing on competitors. A *competitor-centered company* looks at what competitors are doing (increasing distribution, cutting prices, introducing new services) and then formulates competitive reactions (increasing promotion expenditures, meeting price cuts). This kind of planning has both pluses and minuses. On the positive side, the company develops a fighter orientation, training its marketers to be alert for weaknesses in its competitors' and its

TABLE 9.3   Specialized Niche Roles

Niche Specialty	Description
End-user specialist	The firm specializes in serving one type of end-use customer.
Vertical-level specialist	The firm specializes at some vertical level of the production-distribution value chain.
Customer-size specialist	The firm concentrates on selling to small, medium, or large customers.
Specific-customer specialist	The firm limits its selling to one or a few customers.
Geographic specialist	The firm sells only in a certain locality, region, or area of the world.
Product or product-line specialist	The firm carries or produces only one product line or product.
Product-feature specialist	The firm specializes in producing a certain type of product or product feature.
Job-shop specialist	The firm customizes its products for individual customers.
Quality-price specialist	The firm operates at the low- or high-quality ends of the market.
Service specialist	The firm offers one or more services not available from competitors.
Channel specialist	The firm specializes in serving only one channel of distribution.

own position. On the negative side, the company is too reactive: It determines its moves based on its competitors' moves rather than its own goals.

A *customer-centered company* focuses more on customer developments in formulating its strategies. Its marketers might learn, for example, that the total market is growing at 4% annually, while the quality-sensitive segment is growing at 8% annually. They might also find that the deal-prone customer segment is growing fast, but these customers don't stay with any supplier for very long. Additionally, they might find more customers asking for a 24-hour hotline, which no one else offers. In response, this firm could put more effort into reaching and satisfying the quality segment, avoid cutting prices, and research the possibility of a hotline.

Clearly, the customer-centered company is better able to identify new opportunities and set a strategy toward long-run profits. By monitoring customer needs, it can decide which customer groups and emerging needs are the most important to serve, given its resources and objectives.

EXECUTIVE SUMMARY

A good brand positioning helps guide marketing strategy by clarifying the brand's essence, what goals it helps the consumer achieve, and how it does so in a unique way. To craft a positioning, marketers must determine a frame of reference by identifying the target market, the competition, and category membership as well as the ideal points-of-parity and points-of-difference brand associations. Marketers must start with the belief that any offering can be differentiated. Moreover, customers must see any competitive advantage as a customer advantage. Differentiation can be created through the product and the service as well as through personnel, channel, and image.

A company is more likely to be hurt by emerging competitors or new technologies than by current competitors. Once a company identifies its main competitors, it must ascertain their strategies, objectives, strengths, and weaknesses. A market leader has the largest share in the relevant product market. The leader looks for ways to expand total market demand, protect its current share, and increase its market share. A challenger attacks the leader and other rivals in an aggressive bid for more share. A follower is a runner-up firm willing to maintain its market share and not rock the boat. A market nicher serves small segments not being served by larger firms. Companies should maintain a good balance of consumer and competitor monitoring.

NOTES

1. Joseph B. Treaster, "One-Stop Car Insurance Service, Body Work Included," *New York Times*, May 26, 2007, p. C6; Allan Sloan, "A New Dividend Idea for Rain or Shine," *Newsweek*, April 24, 2006, p. 22; Louise Lee, "Can Progressive Stay in Gear?" *BusinessWeek*, August 8, 2004, p. 44; Carol J. Loomis, "Sex. Reefer? And Auto Insurance," *Fortune*, August 7, 1995, p. 76; Robert J. Dolan and Hermann Simon, "Power Pricers," *Across the Board*, May 1997, pp. 18–19; www.progressive.com.

2. For a detailed academic treatment of various aspects of competition, see the Special Issue on Competitive Responsiveness, *Marketing Science* 24 (Winter 2005).

3. Al Ries and Jack Trout, *Positioning: The Battle for Your Mind*, 20th Anniversary Edition (New York: McGraw-Hill, 2000).

4. Claudia H. Deutsch, "U.P.S. Embraces High-Tech Delivery Methods," *New York Times*, July 12, 2007, www.nytimes.com; Daniel Machalaba and Corey Dade, "Freight-Carrier Weakness Shows Retailer Uncertainty," *Wall Street Journal*, April 26, 2007, p. A4; "Up With Brown," *Brandweek*, January 27, 2003; Brian O'Reilly, "They've Got Mail!" *Fortune*, February 7, 2000, p. 100; Charles Haddad, "Ground Wars," *BusinessWeek*, May 21, 2001, p. 64; UPS Annual Report, 2002 and 2005.

5. Kevin Lane Keller, Brian Stenthal, and Alice Tybout, "Three Questions You Need to Ask About Your Brand," *Harvard Business Review* (September 2002): 80–89.

6. Thomas A. Brunner and Michaela Wänke, "The Reduced and Enhanced Impact of Shared Features on Individual Brand Evaluations," *Journal of Consumer Psychology* 16 (April 2006): 101–111.

7. Gregory S. Carpenter, Rashi Glazer, and Kent Nakamoto, "Meaningful Brands from Meaningless Differentiation: The Dependence on Irrelevant Attributes," *Journal of Marketing Research*, August 1994: 339–50; Susan M. Broniarczyk and Andrew D. Gershoff, "The Reciprocal Effects of Brand Equity and Trivial Attributes," *Journal of Marketing Research* 40 (May 2003): 161–175.

8. Patrick Barwise, *Simply Better: Winning and Keeping Customers By Delivering What Matters Most* (Boston: Harvard Business School Press, 2004).

9. Some of these bases are discussed in David A. Garvin, "Competing on the Eight Dimensions of Quality," *Harvard Business Review* (November–December 1987): 101–109.

10. Paul Kedrosky, "Simple Minds," *Business 2.0*, April 2006, p. 38; Debora Viana Thompson, Rebecca W. Hamilton, and Roland Rust, "Feature Fatigue: When Product Capabilities Become Too Much of a Good Thing," *Journal of Marketing Research* 42 (November 2005): 431–442.

11. James H. Gilmore and B. Joseph Pine, *Markets of One: Creating Customer-Unique Value through Mass Customization* (Boston: Harvard Business School Press, 2000).

12. Bernd Schmitt and Alex Simonson, *Marketing Aesthetics: The Strategic Management of Brand, Identity, and Image* (New York: Free Press, 1997).

13. Bruce Nussbaum, "The Power of Design," *BusinessWeek*, May 17, 2004, pp. 88–94; "Masters of Design," *Fast Company*, June 2004, pp. 61–75. Also see Philip Kotler, "Design: A Powerful but Neglected Strategic Tool," *Journal of Business Strategy* (Fall 1984): pp. 16–21.

14. For a comprehensive discussion of Cemex, see Adrian J. Slywotzky and David J. Morrison, *How Digital Is Your Business?* (New York: Crown Business, 2000), ch. 5.
15. Mark Sanchez, "Herman Miller Offers Training to Its Furniture Users," *Grand Rapids Business Journal*, December 2, 2002, p. 23.
16. For a comprehensive treatment of product returns, see James Stock and Thomas Speh, "Managing Product Returns for Competitive Advantage," *MIT Sloan Management Review*, Fall 2006, pp. 57–62.
17. Leslie Earnest and Adrian G. Uribarri, "Costco Halts Liberal Electronics Return Policy," *Los Angeles Times*, February 28, 2007, p. C.1.
18. Sarah Ellison, "Taste Buds: After Making Beer Ever Lighter, Anheuser Faces a New Palate," *Wall Street Journal*, April 26, 2006, p. A1.
19. Michael E. Porter, *Competitive Strategy* (New York: Free Press, 1980), pp. 22–23.
20. Tarun Khanna and Krishna G. Palepu, "Emerging Giants," *Harvard Business Review* (October 2006): 60–69.
21. Allan D. Shocker, "Determining the Structure of Product-Markets: Practices, Issues, and Suggestions," in *Handbook of Marketing*, edited by Barton A. Weitz and Robin Wensley (London: Sage Publications, 2002), pp. 106–125. See also Bruce H. Clark and David B. Montgomery, "Managerial Identification of Competitors," *Journal of Marketing* 63 (July 1999): 67–83.
22. "What Business Are You In? Classic Advice from Theodore Levitt," *Harvard Business Review* (October 2006): 127–137. See also Theodore Levitt's seminal article, "Marketing Myopia," *Harvard Business Review* (July–August 1960): 45–56.
23. Jeffrey F. Rayport and Bernard J. Jaworski, *E-Commerce* (New York: McGraw-Hill, 2001), p. 53.
24. W. Chan Kim and Renée Mauborgne, *Blue Ocean Strategy: How to Create Uncontested Market Space and Make the Competition Irrelevant* (Boston: Harvard Business School Press, 2005); W. Chan Kim and Renée Mauborgne, "Value Innovation: The Strategic Logic of High Growth," *Harvard Business Review* (January–February 1997): 102ff; W. Chan Kim and Renée Mauborgne, "Creating New Market Space, *Harvard Business Review* (January–February 1999): 83.
25. Richard A. D'Aveni, "Competitive Pressure Systems: Mapping and Managing Multimarket Contact," *MIT Sloan Management Review*, Fall 2002, pp. 39–49.
26. Porter, *Competitive Strategy*, ch. 7.
27. For some of the long-term implications of marketing activities, see Koen Pauwels, "How Dynamic Consumer Response, Competitor Response, Company Support, and Company Inertia Shape Long-Term Marketing Effectiveness," *Marketing Science* 23 (Fall 2004): 596–610; Koen Pauwels, Dominique M. Hanssens, and S. Siddarth, "The Long-Term Effects of Price Promotions on Category Incidence, Brand Choice, and Purchase Quantity," *Journal of Marketing Research* 34 (November 2002): 421–439; and Marnik Dekimpe and Dominique Hanssens, "Sustained Spending and Persistent Response: A New Look at Long-term Marketing Profitability," *Journal of Marketing Research* 36 (November 1999): 397–412.
28. Rajendra S. Sisodia, David B. Wolfe, and Jagdish N. Sheth, *Firms of Endearment: How World Class Companies Benefit Profit from Passion & Purpose* (Upper Saddle River, NJ: Wharton School Publishing, 2007).
29. Porter, *Competitive Strategy*, ch. 7.
30. Robert J. Frank, Jeffrey P. George, and Laxman Narasimhan, "When Your Competitor Delivers More for Less," *McKinsey Quarterly* (Winter 2004): 48–59; Nirmalya Kumar, "Strategies to Fight Low-Cost Rivals," *Harvard Business Review*, (December 2006): 104–112.
31. Brian Wansink, "Can Package Size Accelerate Usage Volume?" *Journal of Marketing* 60 (July 1996): 1–14. See also Valerie Folkes and Shashi Matta, "The Effect of Package Shape on Consumers' Judgments of Product Volume: Attention as a Mental Contaminant," *Journal of Consumer Research* 31 (September 2004): 390–401; and Priya Raghubir and Eric A. Greenleaf, "Ratios in Proportion: What Should the Shape of the Package Be?" *Journal of Marketing* 70 (April 2006): 95–107.
32. Andrew Martin, "Makers of Sodas Try a New Pitch: They're Healthy," *New York Times*, March 7, 2007.
33. Robert D. Hof, "There's Not Enough 'Me' in MySpace," *BusinessWeek*, December 4, 2006, p. 40; Patricia Sellers, "MySpace Cowboys," *Fortune*, September 4, 2006, pp. 66–74; Aaron Pressman, "MySpace for Baby Boomers," *BusinessWeek*, October 16, 2006, pp. 120–122; George Stalk, Jr. and Rob Lachanauer, "Hardball: Five Killer Strategies for Trouncing the Competition," *Harvard Business Review* (April 2004): 62–71; Richard D'Aveni, "The Empire Strikes Back: Counter-revolutionary Strategies for Industry Leaders," *Harvard Business Review* (November 2002): 66–74.

Chapter 9 Crafting the Brand Positioning and Dealing with Competition

34. These six defense strategies, as well as the five attack strategies, are taken from Philip Kotler and Ravi Singh, "Marketing Warfare in the 1980s," *Journal of Business Strategy* (Winter 1981): 30–41. For additional reading, see Gerald A. Michaelson, *Winning the Marketing War: A Field Manual for Business Leaders* (Lanham, MD: Abt Books, 1987); Al Ries and Jack Trout, *Marketing Warfare* (New York: McGraw-Hill, 1990); Jay Conrad Levinson, *Guerrilla Marketing* (Boston: Houghton-Mifflin, 1984); and Barrie G. James, *Business Wargames* (Harmondsworth, England: Penguin Books, 1984).

35. Porter, *Competitive Strategy*, ch. 4; Jaideep Prabhu and David W. Stewart, "Signaling Strategies in Competitive Interaction: Building Reputations and Hiding the Truth," *Journal of Marketing Research* 38 (February 2001): 62–72.

36. Jehoshua Eliashberg and Thomas S. Robertson, "New Product Preannouncing Behavior: A Market Signaling Study," *Journal of Marketing Research* 25 (August 1988): 282–292; Roger J. Calantone and Kim E. Schatzel, "Strategic Foretelling: Communication-Based Antecedents of a Firm's Propensity to Preannounce," *Journal of Marketing* 64 (January 2000): 17–30.

37. Kenneth Hein, "Yellow Pages Publisher Has Its Own Story to Tell," *Brandweek*, March 26, 2007, p. 19.

38. Stuart E. Jackson, *Where Value Hides: A New Way to Uncover Profitable Growth for Your Business* (New York: John Wiley & Sons, 2006); J. Scott Armstrong and Kesten C. Green, "Competitor-oriented Objectives: The Myth of Market Share," *International Journal of Business* 12 (1) (2007): 115–134.

39. Philip Kotler and Paul N. Bloom, "Strategies for High Market-Share Companies," *Harvard Business Review* (November–December 1975): 63–72. See also Porter, *Competitive Strategy*, pp. 221–226.

40. Robert D. Buzzell and Frederick D. Wiersema, "Successful Share-Building Strategies," *Harvard Business Review* (January–February 1981): 135–144.

41. Linda Hellofs and Robert Jacobson, "Market Share and Customer's Perceptions of Quality: When Can Firms Grow Their Way to Higher Versus Lower Quality?" *Journal of Marketing* 63 (January 1999): 16–25.

42. Jon Birger, "Second-Mover Advantage," *Fortune*, March 20, 2006, pp. 20–21.

43. Michael Levenson, "Network Boss Quits, Apologizes for Stunt," *Boston Globe*, February 10, 2007, p. A1; Bill Wolpin, "Spilling the Beans: Guerilla Marketing, Turner Broadcasting," *American City & County*, February 1, 2007; Cary Hatch, "When Should You Try Guerilla Marketing?" *ABA Bank Marketing*, March 2005, p. 53; Shari Caudron, "Guerrilla Tactics," *IndustryWeek*, July 16, 2001, pp. 53ff; "If You Can't Stand the Heat, Stay Out of the Streets," *Brandweek*, November 12, 2001, p. 36.

44. Theodore Levitt, "Innovative Imitation," *Harvard Business Review* (September–October 1966): 63ff. Also see Steven P. Schnaars, *Managing Imitation Strategies: How Later Entrants Seize Markets from Pioneers* (New York: Free Press, 1994).

45. Stuart F. Brown, "The Company That Out-Harleys Harley," *Fortune*, September 28, 1998, pp. 56–57.

PART IV Shaping the Market Offerings

CHAPTER 10

Setting Product Strategy and Marketing through the Life Cycle

In this chapter, we will address the following questions:

1. What are the characteristics of products, and how do marketers classify products?
2. How can a company build and manage its product mix and product lines?
3. How can companies use packaging, labeling, warranties, and guarantees as marketing tools?
4. What are the main stages in developing and managing new products?
5. What factors affect the rate of diffusion and consumer adoption of new products?
6. What marketing strategies are appropriate at each product life-cycle stage?

MARKETING MANAGEMENT AT CATERPILLAR

Caterpillar has become a major force in the construction-equipment industry by maximizing total customer value, despite challenges from able competitors. First, Caterpillar produces high-performance equipment known for reliability and durability—key purchase considerations in the choice of heavy industrial equipment. The firm offers a full line of construction equipment, from backhoes and road graders to lift trucks and gas turbines, along with a wide range of financial terms for customer convenience. Just as important, Caterpillar's global network of independent construction-equipment dealers is the industry's largest. And it has a highly efficient worldwide parts and service system to keep all its products in good repair.

Chapter 10 Setting Product Strategy and Marketing through the Life Cycle

Annual sales have surged past $44 billion as industrial customers have responded to the value of Caterpillar's offerings and shown their willingness to pay premium prices for the brand. In fact, demand for the firm's construction equipment is so strong in Indonesia, Chile, South Africa, and other nations that an entire year's worth of production can sell out in just six months, at times leaving some Caterpillar dealers scrambling for inventory. To serve its international customers, the company continues to open production facilities within high-growth markets.[1]

At the heart of a great brand is a great product, a key element in the market offering. When customers judge an offering like Caterpillar equipment, they consider three basic elements: (1) product features and quality; (2) services mix and quality; and (3) price appropriateness for the value. This chapter examines the concept of product; basic product decisions; new product development and adoption; and the product life cycle. Chapter 11 looks at services and Chapter 12 explores price. All three elements must be meshed into a competitively attractive offering.

PRODUCT CHARACTERISTICS AND CLASSIFICATIONS

A **product** is anything that can be offered to a market to satisfy a want or need, including physical goods, services, experiences, events, persons, places, properties, organizations, information, and ideas.

Product Levels

Marketers plan their market offering at five levels, as shown in Figure 10.1.[2] Each level adds more customer value, and together the levels constitute a **customer value hierarchy**. The most basic level is the **core benefit**: the fundamental service or benefit that the customer is really buying. A hotel guest is buying "rest and sleep." The purchaser of a drill is buying "holes." Marketers must see themselves as benefit providers.

FIGURE 10.1 Five Product Levels

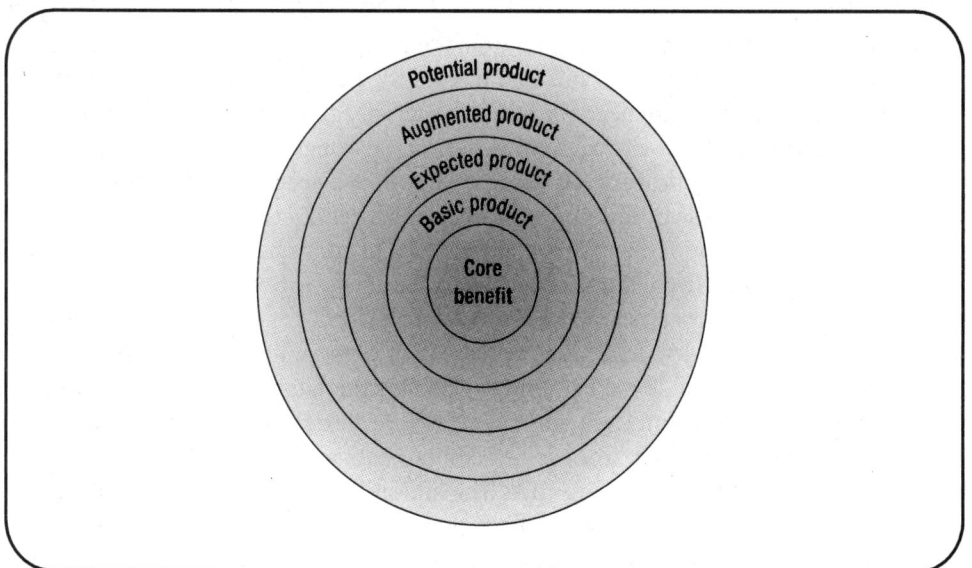

At the second level, the marketer has to turn the core benefit into a **basic product**. Thus, a hotel room includes a bed, bathroom, and towels. At the third level, the marketer prepares an **expected product**, a set of attributes and conditions that buyers normally expect when they buy this product. Hotel guests expect a clean bed, fresh towels, and so on. At the fourth level, the marketer prepares an **augmented product** that exceeds customer expectations. In developed countries, brand positioning and competition take place at this level. (In less-developed countries, competition takes place mostly at the expected product level.) At the fifth level is the **potential product**, all the possible augmentations and transformations the product might undergo in the future. Here is where firms search for new ways to satisfy customers and distinguish offerings.

Differentiation arises and competition increasingly occurs on the basis of product augmentation, which leads the marketer to look at the user's total **consumption system:** the way the user performs the tasks of getting and using products and related services.[3] Each augmentation adds cost, and augmented benefits soon become expected benefits, which means that competitors have to search for still other features and benefits. As some firms raise the price of their augmented product, others offer a "stripped-down" version at a much lower price. "Breakthrough Marketing: Toyota" shows how that company differentiates its vehicles through product augmentation.

Product Classifications

Marketers have traditionally classified products on the basis of three characteristics: durability, tangibility, and consumer or industrial use. Each product classification is associated with a different marketing-mix strategy.[4]

- *Durability and tangibility.* *Nondurable goods* are tangible goods normally consumed in one or a few uses (such as beer and soap). Because these goods are consumed quickly and purchased frequently, the appropriate strategy is to make them available

BREAKTHROUGH MARKETING: TOYOTA

Toyota may have gotten its start in automaking by being a fast follower, but it's now the innovator. It offers a full line of cars for the U.S. market, from family sedans to sport utility vehicles to trucks to minivans, and was the first to launch a hybrid electric-gasoline car, the Prius. Toyota also has products for different price points, from the lower-cost Scion to the mid-priced Camry to the luxury Lexus. Designing these different products means listening to different customers, building the cars they want, and using marketing to convey each product's image.

For example, Toyota spent four years carefully listening to teens before launching the Scion for first-time car buyers. It learned, for instance, that Scion's target age group of 16- to 21-year-olds wants personalization. To meet that preference, Toyota builds the car "mono-spec" at the factory with just one well-equipped trim level but lets customers at dealerships choose from over 40 customization elements, from stereo components to wheels. Careful differentiation helped Toyota earn more than $11 billion in 2006—more than all other major automakers *combined*. In the first quarter of 2007, it edged past General Motors to become the world's largest carmaker.[5]

in many locations, charge a small markup, and advertise heavily to induce trial and build preference. *Durable goods* are tangible goods that survive many uses (such as appliances). These normally require more personal selling and service, command a higher margin, and require more seller guarantees. *Services* are intangible, inseparable, variable, and perishable products (such as haircuts or legal advice), so they require more quality control, supplier credibility, and adaptability.

- *Consumer-goods classification.* Classified according to consumer shopping habits, these products include **convenience goods** (such as newspapers) that are usually purchased frequently, immediately, and with little effort; **shopping goods** (such as furniture) that the consumer compares on the basis of suitability, quality, price, and style; **specialty goods** (such as cars) with unique characteristics or brand identification for which a sufficient number of buyers are willing to make a special purchasing effort; and **unsought goods** (such as smoke detectors) that consumers don't know about or don't normally think of buying.

- *Industrial-goods classification.* *Materials and parts* are goods that enter the manufacturer's product completely. Raw materials can be *farm products* (wheat) or *natural products* (lumber). Farm products are sold through intermediaries; natural products are sold through long-term supply contracts, with price and delivery as key purchase factors. *Manufactured materials and parts* are either *component materials* (iron) or *component parts* (small motors); again, price and supplier reliability are important factors. **Capital items** are long-lasting goods that facilitate developing or managing the finished product, including *installations* (factories) and *equipment* (trucks), both sold through personal selling. **Supplies and business services** are short-term goods and services that facilitate developing or managing the finished product; these include *maintenance and repair services* and *business advisory services*.

PRODUCT AND BRAND RELATIONSHIPS

A **product system** is a group of diverse but related items that function in a compatible manner. A **product mix** (also called a **product assortment**) is the set of all products and items a particular marketer offers for sale. A product mix consists of various **product lines**, each a group of products within a product class that is closely related because they perform a similar function, are sold to the same customer groups, are marketed through the same outlets or channels, or fall within given price ranges. A product line may be composed of different brands, a single family brand, or an individual brand that has been line extended. A **product type** is a group of items within a line that share one of several possible forms of the product, while an *item* is a distinct unit within a line distinguishable by size, appearance, or another attribute.

A company's product mix can be described in terms of width, length, depth, and consistency. The *width* refers to how many different product lines the company carries. The *length* is the total number of items in the mix. The *depth* is how many variants of each product are offered. The *consistency* is how closely related the various product lines are in end use, production requirements, distribution, or some other way. These four dimensions permit the company to expand its business by adding new product lines (widening its product mix); lengthening each product line; deepening the product mix (adding more variants); and pursuing more product-line consistency. Marketers need to conduct product-line analysis to support these decisions.

Product-Line Analysis

In offering a product line, the company normally develops a basic platform and modules that can be expanded to meet different customer requirements. Homebuilders show a model home to which buyers can add more features, a modular approach that enables them to offer variety while lowering production costs. Product-line managers need to know the sales and profits of each item so they can determine which items to build, maintain, harvest, or divest.[6] The manager must calculate each item's percentage contribution to total sales and profits. A high concentration of sales in a few items means line vulnerability. Also, the firm may consider eliminating items that deliver a low percentage of sales and profits—unless these exhibit strong growth potential.

The manager must also review how the line is positioned against competitors' lines. A useful tool is a *product map* showing which competitive products compete against the company's products. This helps identify market segments and indicates how well the firm is positioned to serve the needs of each. These analyses set the stage for decisions about product-line length.

Product-Line Length

Companies seeking high market share and market growth will carry longer lines; companies emphasizing high profitability will carry shorter lines of carefully chosen items. **Line stretching** occurs when a firm lengthens its product line beyond the current range. A down-market stretch—introducing a lower-priced line—can be risky. With an up-market stretch, a company enters the high end of the market for more growth, higher margins, or to position itself as a full-line manufacturer. The leading Japanese automakers all have separate upscale brands: Toyota has Lexus; Nissan has Infiniti; and Honda has Acura. Firms serving the middle market can stretch their product lines in both directions, as Holiday Inn has done with its upscale Crowne Plaza, traditional Holiday Inn, budget Holiday Inn Express, and business-oriented Holiday Inn Select.

The relative position of a brand and its competitor context will affect consumer acceptance. Research shows that a high-end model of a low-end brand is favored over a low-end model of a high-end brand, even when information about competing categories is made available.[7] A firm can also lengthen its product line by adding more items within the present range. There are several motives for *line filling*: seeking incremental profits, satisfying dealers who complain about lost sales because of missing items in the line, trying to utilize excess capacity, seeking to be the leading full-line company, and plugging holes to keep out competitors.

Line Modernization, Featuring, and Pruning

Product lines need to be modernized. Modernization happens continuously in rapidly changing product markets. The product-line manager may showcase one or a few items in the line to attract customers, lend prestige, or achieve other goals. If one end of the line is selling well and the other end is not, the company may use featuring to boost demand for the slower sellers. In addition, managers must periodically review the entire line for pruning, identifying weak items through sales and cost analysis. One study found that for a big Dutch retailer, a major assortment reduction led to a short-term drop in category sales, caused mainly by fewer category purchases by former buyers—yet it attracted new category buyers at the same time. These new buyers partially offset the sales losses among former buyers of the pruned items.[8]

Co-Branding and Ingredient Branding

Sometimes products feature more than one brand. In **co-branding**—also called dual branding or brand bundling—two or more well-known brands are combined into a joint product and/or marketed together in some fashion.[9] Co-branding can take the form of *same-company co-branding*, as when General Mills advertises Trix and Yoplait yogurt. Another form is *joint-venture co-branding*, as in the case of the Citibank AAdvantage credit card. Other forms are *retail co-branding*, in which two retail establishments use the same location to optimize space and profits (such as jointly owned Pizza Hut and KFC restaurants) and *multiple-sponsor co-branding*.[10]

Co-branding's main advantage is that a product may be convincingly positioned by virtue of the multiple brands, generating greater sales from the existing target market and opening more opportunities for new consumers and channels. It can reduce the cost of product introduction because two well-known images are combined, and it may help marketers learn more about consumers and how other companies approach them. The potential disadvantages are the risks and lack of control in becoming aligned with another brand in the minds of consumers. For co-branding to succeed, the two brands must separately have brand equity. Most important is a logical fit between the brands. Research shows that consumers are more apt to perceive co-brands favorably if the two brands are complementary rather than similar.[11]

Ingredient branding is a special case of co-branding that involves creating brand equity for materials, components, or parts that are necessarily contained within other branded products.[12] One example is Gore-Tex water-resistant fibers. An interesting take on ingredient branding is "self-branding" in which companies advertise and even trademark their own branded ingredients, the way Westin Hotels advertises its "Heavenly Bed." Done well, self-branded ingredients give the firm more control to develop the ingredient to suit its purposes.[13]

PACKAGING, LABELING, WARRANTIES, AND GUARANTEES

Most physical products have to be packaged and labeled. Some packages—such as the Coke bottle—are world famous. Many marketers call packaging a fifth P, along with price, product, place, and promotion; however, packaging and labeling are usually treated as an element of product strategy. Warranties and guarantees can also be important to a firm's product strategy.

Packaging

Packaging refers to all the activities of designing and producing a product's container. The package might include up to three levels of material. Cool Water cologne comes in a bottle (*primary package*) inside a cardboard box (*secondary package*) within a corrugated box (*shipping package*) containing six dozen boxes.

Effective packaging pays off: Kleenex tissues' seasonally themed, oval-shaped boxes and Domino sugar's easy-to-store plastic canister have both led to sales increases.[14] Several factors contribute to packaging's growing use as a potent marketing tool:

- *Self-service.* The typical supermarket shopper walks past some 300 items per minute. An effective package will attract attention, describe features, inspire confidence, and make a favorable impression.
- *Consumer affluence.* Rising consumer affluence means consumers are willing to pay a little more for the convenience, appearance, dependability, and prestige of better packages.
- *Company and brand image.* Packages contribute to instant recognition of the firm or brand.
- *Innovation opportunity.* Innovative packaging can benefit consumers and ring up profits for producers.

From the perspective of both the firm and consumers, packaging must achieve a number of objectives.[15] It must identify the brand, convey descriptive and persuasive information, facilitate product transportation and protection, assist at-home storage, and aid product consumption. All packaging elements must be in harmony and must fit with the product's pricing, advertising, and other marketing elements. The company should also test to ensure that the package stands up under normal conditions; the script is legible and the colors harmonious; dealers find the packages attractive and easy to handle; and buyers respond favorably.

Labeling

The label may be a simple tag attached to the product or an elaborately designed graphic that is part of the package. A label performs several functions. First, it *identifies* the product or brand—for instance, the name Sunkist stamped on oranges. It may also *grade* the product, the way canned peaches are grade labeled A, B, and C. It may *describe* the product: who made it, where it was made, when it was made, what it contains, how it is to be used, and how to use it safely. Finally, the label might *promote* the product through attractive graphics.

Labels eventually need freshening up. Ivory soap's label has been redone 18 times since the 1890s, with gradual changes in the lettering. Legal and regulatory requirements are another consideration. For instance, the Food and Drug Administration (FDA) requires processed foods to carry nutritional labeling that clearly states the amounts of protein, fat, carbohydrates, and calories, plus vitamin and mineral content as a percentage of the recommended daily allowance.[16]

Warranties and Guarantees

All sellers are legally responsible for fulfilling a buyer's normal or reasonable expectations. **Warranties** are formal statements of expected product performance by the manufacturer; whether expressed or implied, warranties are legally enforceable. Products under warranty can be returned to the manufacturer or designated repair center for repair, replacement, or refund. For example, ten years ago, Shoes for Crews began offering a $5,000 performance warranty reassuring customers that its work shoes, priced at $50–$75 per pair, will not slip. Today, nine of the ten largest U.S. restaurant chains either buy the shoes for their workers or urge them to do so.[17]

Many sellers offer either general guarantees or specific guarantees.[18] The purpose is to reduce the buyer's perceived risk and provide assurances that the company and its offerings are dependable. This can be especially helpful when the brand or product is not well known or when the product's quality is superior to that of competitors.

MANAGING NEW PRODUCTS

A company can add new products in two ways: through acquisition (buying another company, buying other firms' patents, or buying a license or franchise) or organically through development (using its own laboratories, hiring independent researchers, or hiring a new-product development firm).[19] There is a range or continuum with new products, from new-to-the-world products that create an entirely new market at one end, to minor improvements or revisions of existing products at the other end.[20] Actually, most new products are improvements of existing products. Some of the most successful new consumer products in recent years have been brand extensions, such as Tide with Febreze. In contrast, new-to-the-world products involve the greatest cost and risk because they are new to both the company and the marketplace.[21]

Most established companies focus on *incremental innovation*. Many high tech firms strive for radical innovation.[22] Newer companies create *disruptive technologies* that are cheaper and more likely to alter the competitive space. Established companies can be slow to react or invest in these disruptive technologies because they threaten their investment. Then they suddenly find themselves facing formidable new competitors, and many fail.[23] To ensure that they don't fall into this trap, incumbent firms must monitor customers' and prospects' preferences over time and uncover evolving, difficult-to-articulate needs.[24]

Why New Products Fail—and Succeed

New products are failing at a disturbing rate. Recent studies put the rate at as much as 95% in the United States and 90% in Europe.[25] New products fail for many reasons: ignoring or misinterpreting market research; overestimating market size; high development costs; poor design; incorrect positioning, ineffective advertising, or wrong price; insufficient distribution support; and competitors who fight back hard. On the other hand, Cooper and Kleinschmidt found that unique, superior products succeed 98% of the time, compared with products with a moderate advantage (58% success) and those with a minimal advantage (18% success). The company must carefully define and assess the target market, product requirements, and benefits before proceeding with a new product. Other success factors include technological and marketing synergy, quality execution, and market attractiveness.[26]

New Product Development

Continuous innovation is a necessity in an economy of rapid change. Innovative firms create a positive attitude toward innovation and risk taking, systematically develop innovative new products, and allow their people to experiment and even fail. The stages in the new-product development process are shown in Figure 10.2. Many firms have multiple, parallel product-development projects, each at a different stage in the process.[27]

FIGURE 10.2 The New-Product Development Decision Process

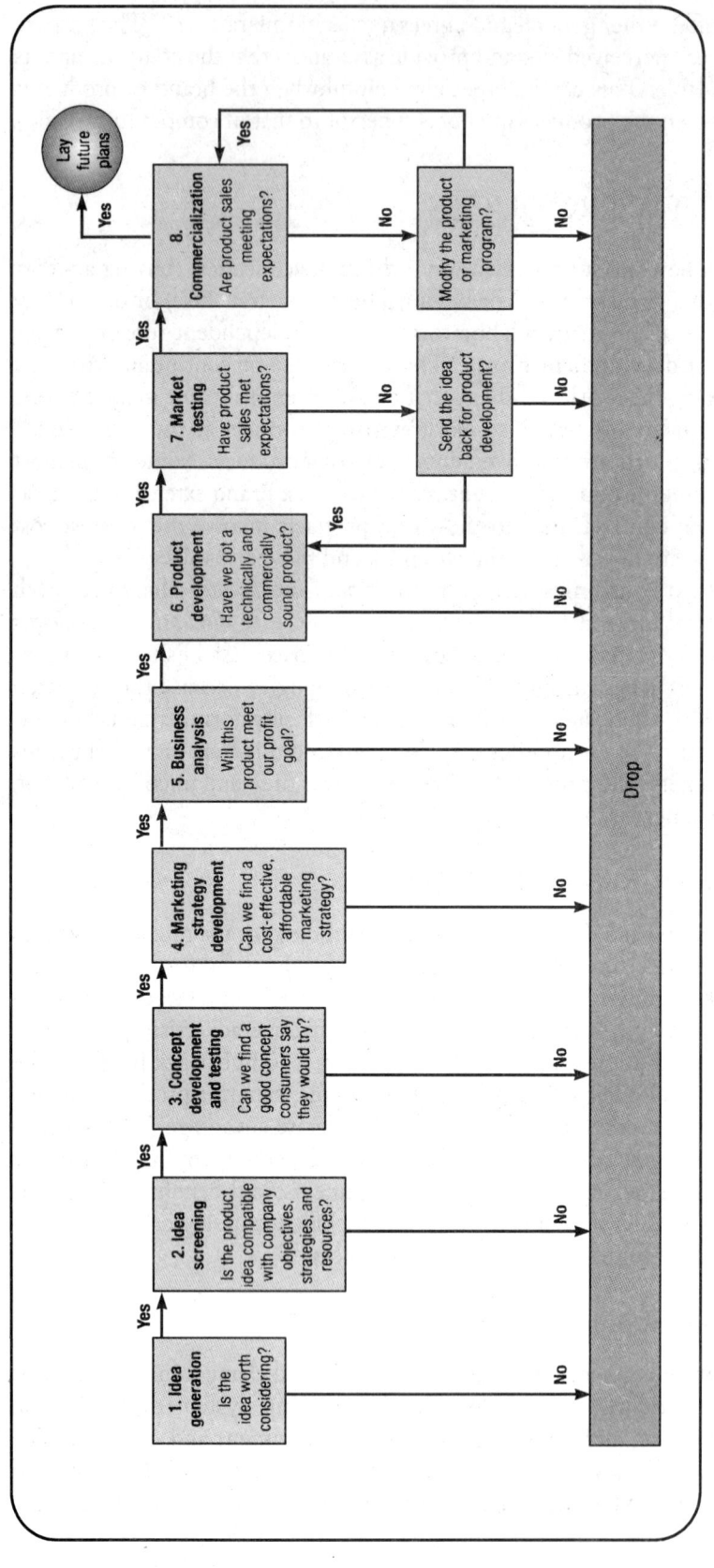

Idea Generation The process starts with the search for ideas (see "Marketing Skills: Finding New Product Ideas"). Some marketing experts believe that the greatest opportunities and highest leverage with new products are found by uncovering the best possible set of unmet customer needs or technological innovation.[28] Ideas can come from interacting with others (customers, scientists, competitors, employees, channel members, top management) and from using creativity-generating techniques (listing attributes; identifying relationships; listing combinations of dimensions related to a problem; reversing normal assumptions; finding new contexts; mind-mapping). Toyota says its employees submit 2 million ideas every year for improving products, production, and services, over 85% of which are implemented.

Idea Screening The second step is to screen out poor ideas early, because product-development costs rise substantially with each successive development stage. Most companies require ideas to be described on a standard form for review by a new-product committee. The description states the product idea, target market, and competition, along with estimates of market size, product price, development time and costs, manufacturing costs, and rate of return. The committee reviews each idea against criteria such as: Does the product meet a need and offer superior value? Will it deliver the expected sales volume, sales growth, and profit? Customer input may be needed to understand marketplace reality.[29] The company also estimates each idea's overall probability of success and determines which are high enough to warrant continued development.

Concept Development A *product idea* is a possible product the company might offer to the market. In contrast, a *product concept* is an elaborated version of the idea expressed

MARKETING SKILLS: FINDING NEW PRODUCT IDEAS

How do marketers find promising new product ideas? First, view every customer contact as an opportunity to identify unmet or changing needs, spark new ways to solve old problems, or innovatively apply old technology and techniques to new problems. A company can observe how customers use its products and competing products; ask customers what they would like the firm's product to do (even if it sounds impossible); use Web sites to invite customer ideas and feedback; interact with brand enthusiasts; and tap into feedback gathered by customer-contact employees such as salespeople and technicians. Marketers should document and keep new-product ideas in an "idea vault" that can be easily accessed at any time.

For example, Procter & Gamble searches for ideas by identifying the top ten customer needs, investigating product adjacencies that leverage brand equity, and mapping cross-category flow of technology adoption. Also, it taps into networks of individuals, organizations, and experts; consults government, private labs, and research institutions; and talks with suppliers, retailers, partners, venture-capital firms, and entrepreneurs. Thanks to these connections, P&G has launched 100 new products in two years. For example, it used ink-jet technology for printing edible images on cakes—invented by a professor in Italy—to put jokes and pictures on Pringles potato chips. The result was a speedy product introduction and double-digit growth for the Pringles brand.[30]

in consumer terms. A product idea can be turned into several concepts by asking: Who will use this product? What primary benefit will it provide? When will people consume or use it? By answering such questions, a company can often form several product concepts, select the single most promising concept, and create a *product-positioning map* for it. Figure 10.3a shows the positioning of a product concept, a low-cost instant breakfast drink, compared to other breakfast foods already on the market. These contrasts can be used in communicating and promoting the concept to the market.

Next, the product concept is turned into a *brand concept*. To transform the low-cost instant breakfast drink concept into a brand concept, the company must decide how much to charge and how calorific to make its drink. Figure 10.3b shows the positions of three instant breakfast drink brands. The new brand concept would have to be distinctive in the medium-price, medium-calorie market or the high-price, high-calorie market.

Concept Testing Concept testing involves presenting the product concept to appropriate target consumers and getting their reactions. The concepts can be presented symbolically or physically. The more the tested concepts resemble the final product or experience, the more dependable concept testing is. In the past, creating physical prototypes was costly and time-consuming, but computer-aided design and manufacturing programs have changed that. Today firms use *rapid prototyping* to design products on a computer and create rough models to obtain feedback from potential consumers. This can bring ideas to life quickly when marketers see promising opportunities to exploit.[31] Companies are also using *virtual reality* to test product concepts.

Consumer preferences for alternative product concepts can be measured through **conjoint analysis**, a method for deriving the utility values that consumers attach to varying levels of a product's attributes.[32] Respondents are shown different hypothetical offers formed by combining varying levels of the attributes, then asked to rank the various offers. Management can identify the most appealing offer and the estimated market share and profit the company might realize. Note that the most customer-appealing offer is not always the most profitable for the firm.

Marketing Strategy After a successful concept test, the new-product manager will draft a three-part preliminary marketing strategy for introducing the new product.

FIGURE 10.3 Brand-Positioning Map

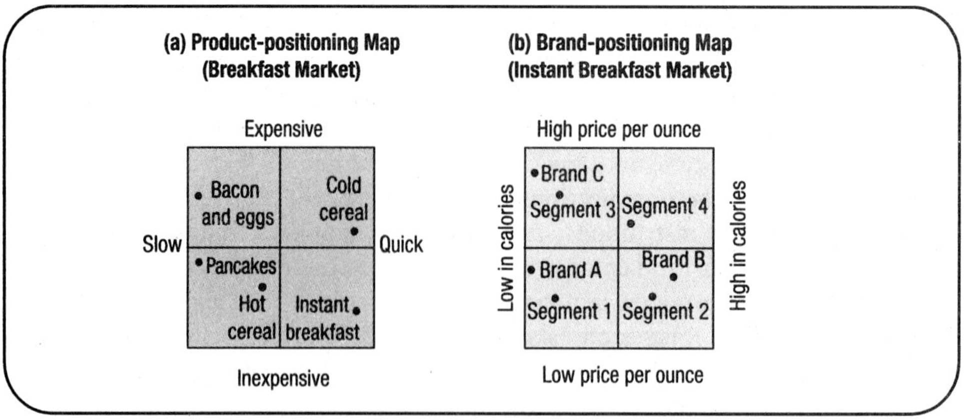

The first part describes the target market's size, structure, and behavior; the planned product positioning; and the sales, market share, and profit goals sought in the first few years. The second part outlines the planned price, distribution strategy, and marketing budget for the first year. The third part describes the long-run sales and profit goals and marketing-mix strategy over time. This plan forms the basis for the business analysis that is conducted before management makes a final decision on the new product.

Business Analysis The company evaluates the proposed new product's business attractiveness by preparing sales, cost, and profit projections to determine whether these satisfy company objectives. If they do, the concept can move to the development stage. As new information emerges, the business analysis must be revised and expanded accordingly.

Total estimated sales are the sum of estimated first-time sales, replacement sales, and repeat sales. For one-time purchased products such as a retirement home, sales rise at the beginning, peak, and later approach zero as the number of potential buyers is exhausted; if new buyers keep entering the market, the curve will not drop to zero. Infrequently purchased products, such as cars, exhibit replacement cycles dictated by physical wearing out or by obsolescence due to changing styles, features, and performance; therefore, sales forecasting calls for estimating first-time sales and replacement sales separately. For frequently purchased products such as soap, the number of first-time buyers initially increases and then decreases as fewer buyers are left (assuming a fixed population). Repeat purchases occur soon, providing the product satisfies some buyers. The sales curve eventually plateaus, representing a level of steady repeat-purchase volume; by this time, the product is no longer a new product.

Management also analyzes expected costs and profits based on estimates prepared by research and development (R&D), manufacturing, marketing, and finance departments. Companies use other financial measures to evaluate new-product proposals. The simplest is **break-even analysis**, in which management estimates how many units of the product the company will have to sell to break even with the given price and cost structure. A more complex method is **risk analysis**, in which three estimates (optimistic, pessimistic, and most likely) are obtained for each uncertain variable affecting profitability under an assumed marketing environment and strategy for the planning period. The computer simulates possible outcomes and computes a rate-of-return probability distribution showing the range of possible rates of returns and their probabilities.[33]

Product Development Up until now, the product has existed only as a word description, a drawing, or a prototype. The next step involves a jump in investment that dwarfs the costs incurred in the earlier stages. At this stage the company will determine whether the product idea can be translated into a technically and commercially feasible product.

The job of translating target customer requirements into a working prototype is helped by a set of methods known as *quality function deployment* (QFD). The methodology takes the list of desired *customer attributes* (CAs) generated by market research and turns them into a list of *engineering attributes* (EAs) that the engineers can use. For example, customers of a proposed truck may want a certain acceleration rate (CA). Engineers can turn this into the required horsepower and other engineering equivalents

(EAs). QFD allows marketers to measure the trade-offs and costs of providing customer requirements; it also improves communication between marketers, engineers, and the manufacturing people.[34]

The R&D department will develop one or more physical versions of the product concept, looking for one that embodies the key attributes described in the concept statement, performs safely under normal use, and can be produced within the budget. The Web and sophisticated virtual-reality technology are speeding this process.

When the prototypes are ready, they undergo rigorous functional tests and customer tests. *Alpha testing* means testing the product within the firm to check its performance in different applications. After refining the prototype further, the company moves to *beta testing*, enlisting customers to use the prototype and give feedback. Consumer testing can take a variety of forms, from bringing consumers into a laboratory to giving them samples to use in their homes. In-home placement tests are common with many consumer products. For example, when DuPont developed new synthetic carpeting, it installed free carpeting in several homes in exchange for the homeowners' willingness to report their likes and dislikes about the product.

Market Testing After management is satisfied with a product's functional and psychological performance, it can use market testing to gauge the size of the market and see how consumers and dealers react to handling, using, and repurchasing the product. Not all firms use market testing; the extent of such testing is influenced by the investment cost and risk on the one hand and the time pressure and research cost on the other. In testing consumer products, the company seeks to estimate four variables: trial, first repeat purchase, adoption, and purchase frequency. Table 10.1 shows four methods of consumer-goods testing.

Business goods also benefit from market testing. Expensive industrial goods and new technologies will normally undergo both alpha and beta testing. New business products are sometimes market-tested at trade shows to check buyer interest, see reaction to various features and terms, and see how many buyers express purchase intentions or place orders. New industrial products can be tested in distributor and dealer

TABLE 10.1 Four Methods of Consumer-Goods Market Testing

Method	Description
Sales-wave research	Consumers who initially try the product at no cost are reoffered the product, or a competitor's product, at reduced prices in three to five sales waves. The firm notes how many customers select its product again and their reported level of satisfaction.
Simulated test marketing	Researchers ask buyers about brand familiarity and preferences in a specific product category. After consumers view ads, they're invited into a store and given money to shop. Researchers note how many buy the new brand and competing brands and ask why consumers bought or didn't buy. Nonbuyers get a new-product sample and are reinterviewed later to determine attitudes, usage, satisfaction, and repurchase intention.
Controlled test marketing	A research firm tests the firm's new product in a certain number of stores and geographic locations. Researchers deliver the product and control shelf position, facings, displays, point-of-purchase promotions, and pricing, then measure results using checkout scanner data.
Test markets	The firm chooses a few representative cities, sells intermediaries on carrying the product, and mounts a full marketing campaign in these areas. Marketers must decide on the number and location of test cities, length of the test, what to track, and what action to take.

display rooms, where they may be next to the manufacturer's other products and possibly competitors' products. This yields preference and pricing information in the product's normal selling atmosphere; however, customers will not be able to place early orders and those who come in might not represent the target market.

Commercialization If the company goes ahead with commercialization, it will face its largest costs to date.[35] The firm will have to contract for manufacture or build or rent a full-scale manufacturing facility. Another major cost is marketing. To introduce a major new consumer packaged good into the national market, the firm may have to spend from $25 million to as much as $100 million in advertising, promotion, and other communications in the first year.

In addition to promotion, major decisions during this stage include timing, geographic strategy, target-market prospects, and introductory market strategy. Market-entry timing is critical. If a firm learns that a competitor is readying a new product, it can choose *first entry* (being first to market, locking up key distributors and customers, and gaining reputational leadership; but if the product is not thoroughly debugged, this can backfire); *parallel entry* (launching at the same time as a rival may gain both products more attention[36]); or *late entry* (waiting until a rival has borne the cost of educating the market and revealed problems to avoid).

The company must also decide whether to launch the new product in one locality, one region, several regions, the national market, or the international market. Small companies often select one city for a blitz campaign, entering other cities one at a time; large companies usually launch within a whole region and then move to the next region, although companies with national distribution generally launch new models nationally. More firms are rolling out new products simultaneously around the globe or using a sequential rollout across countries.[37]

Within the rollout markets, the company must target its initial distribution and promotion to the best prospect groups. Presumably, the company has already profiled the prime prospects—who would ideally be early adopters, heavy users, and opinion leaders who can be reached at a low cost.[38] The company should rate the various prospect groups on these characteristics and target the best group to generate strong sales as soon as possible and attract further prospects.

Finally, the firm needs an action plan for introducing the new product. It's important to allocate sufficient time and resources (without over-spending) as the new product gains traction in the marketplace.[39] Management can use network-planning techniques such as *critical path scheduling (CPS)*, which uses a master chart to show the simultaneous and sequential activities that must take place to launch the product. By estimating how much time each activity takes, the planners can estimate the project's completion time. A delay in any activity on the critical path will delay the entire project.[40]

THE CONSUMER ADOPTION PROCESS

Adoption is an individual's decision to become a regular user of a product. How do potential customers learn about new products, try them, and adopt or reject them? In the past, companies used a mass-market approach to introduce new products, on the assumption that most people are potential adopters. Yet consumers have different levels of interest in new products and brands. The theory of innovation diffusion and consumer adoption helps firms identify and target people who adopt products before the majority of consumers in a market.

Stages in the Adoption Process

An **innovation** refers to any good, service, or idea that is *perceived* by someone as new. The idea may have a long history, but it is an innovation to the person who sees it as new. Innovations take time to spread through the social system. Rogers defines the **innovation diffusion process** as "the spread of a new idea from its source of invention or creation to its ultimate users or adopters."[41] The adoption process focuses on the mental process through which a consumer passes from first hearing about an innovation to adoption.[42]

An adopter of a new product moves through five stages: (1) *awareness* (consumer becomes aware of the innovation but has no information about it); (2) *interest* (consumer is stimulated to seek information); (3) *evaluation* (consumer considers whether to try the innovation); (4) *trial* (consumer tries the innovation to estimate its value); and (5) *adoption* (consumer decides to make full and regular use of the innovation).

Factors Influencing Adoption

Rogers defines a person's innovativeness as "the degree to which an individual is relatively earlier in adopting new ideas than the other members of his social system." As Figure 10.4 shows, innovators are the first to adopt something new, while laggards are the last. Because people differ in their readiness to try new products, there are pioneers and early adopters for each product.[43] After a slow start, an increasing number of people adopt the innovation, the number reaches a peak, and then it diminishes as fewer nonadopters remain.

Personal influence is the effect one person has on another's attitude or purchase probability. Although personal influence is greater in some situations and for some individuals, it is more important in the evaluation stage of the adoption process

FIGURE 10.4 Adopter Categorization on the Basis of Relative Time of Adoption of Innovations

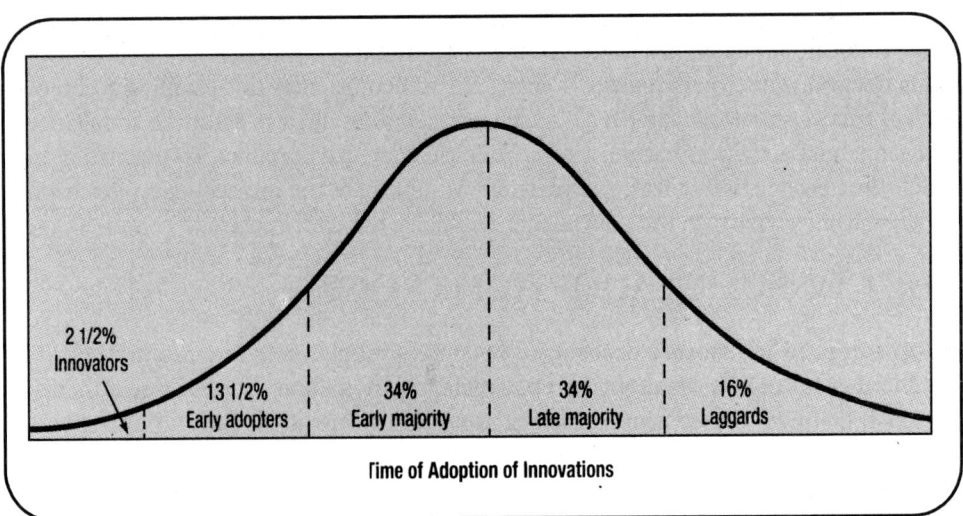

Source: Redrawn from Everett M. Rogers, *Diffusion of Innovations* (New York: The Free Press, 1983).

than in the other stages. It generally has more influence on late adopters and is more important in risky situations, as well.

Five characteristics influence adoption rate. The first is *relative advantage*—the degree to which the innovation appears superior to existing products. The second is *compatibility*, the degree to which the innovation matches consumers' values and experiences. Third is *complexity*, the degree to which the innovation is relatively difficult to understand or use. Fourth is *divisibility*—the degree to which consumers can try the innovation on a limited basis. Fifth is *communicability*, the degree to which the benefits are observable or describable to others. Marketers must research and consider these factors in designing a new product and its marketing program.[44]

Finally, adoption is associated with variables in the organization's environment, the organization itself (size, profits, pressure to change), and its managers. Other forces come into play when trying to get a product adopted into organizations that receive most of their funding from the government. And a controversial or innovative product can be squelched by negative public opinion.

MARKETING THROUGH THE PRODUCT LIFE CYCLE

A company's positioning and differentiation strategy must change as the product, market, and competitors change over the *product life cycle* (PLC). To say that a product has a life cycle is to assert that: (1) products have a limited life; (2) product sales pass through distinct stages with different challenges, opportunities, and problems for the seller; (3) profits rise and fall at different stages of the product life cycle; and (4) products require different marketing, financial, manufacturing, purchasing, and human resource strategies in each stage.

Product Life Cycles

Most product life-cycle curves are portrayed as a bell-shape (Figure 10.5). This curve is typically divided into four stages.[45] In *introduction*, sales grow slowly as the product

FIGURE 10.5   Sales and Profit Life Cycles

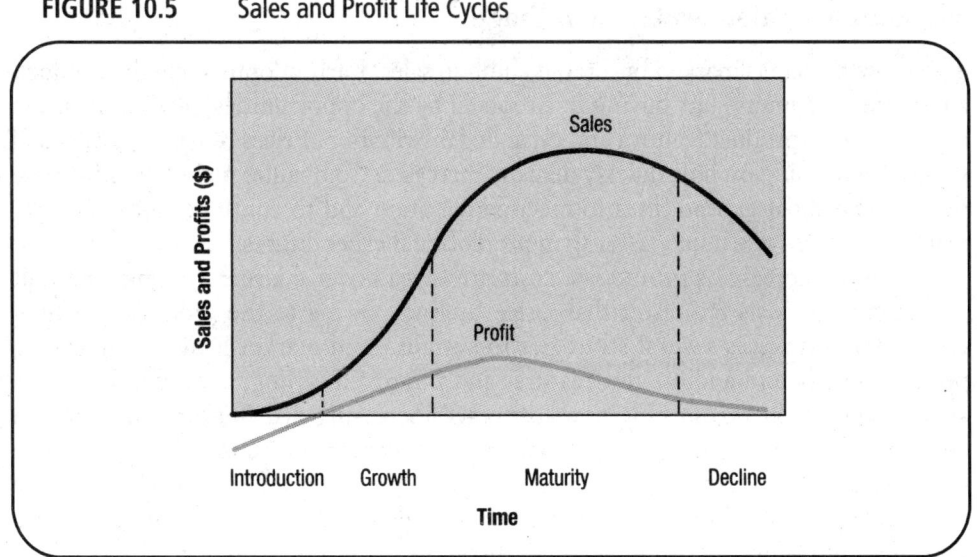

enters the market; profits are nonexistent due to the heavy expenses of introduction. *Growth* is a period of rapid market acceptance and substantial profit improvement. In *maturity*, sales growth slows because the product has achieved acceptance by most potential buyers, and profits stabilize or decline due to higher competition. In *decline*, sales drift downward and profits erode.

Marketing Strategies: Introduction Stage and the Pioneer Advantage

Because it takes time to roll out a new product, work out the technical problems, fill dealer pipelines, and gain consumer acceptance, sales growth tends to be slow in the introduction stage.[46] Profits are negative or low in this stage, while promotional costs are at their highest ratio to sales because of the need to (1) inform potential consumers, (2) induce product trial, and (3) secure retail distribution.[47] Firms focus on buyers who are the most ready to buy, usually in higher-income groups. Prices tend to be high because costs are high.

Companies must decide when to enter the market with a new product. Being first can be rewarding, but risky and expensive; entering later makes sense if the firm can bring superior technology, quality, or brand strength. Yet most studies indicate that the pioneer gains the most advantage.[48] Such pioneers as Amazon.com have developed sustained market dominance.

The pioneer advantage is not inevitable. Studying 28 industries in which the imitators surpassed the innovators, Schnaars found several weaknesses among the failing pioneers, including new products that were too crude, were improperly positioned, or appeared before there was strong demand; product-development costs that exhausted the innovator's resources; a lack of resources to compete against entering larger firms; and managerial incompetence or complacency. Successful imitators offered lower prices, improved the product more continuously, or used brute market power to overtake the pioneer.[49] Golder and Tellis raise further doubts about the pioneer advantage; they say long-term market leadership is supported by vision of a mass market; persistence; relentless innovation; financial commitment; and asset leverage.[50]

Marketing Strategies: Growth Stage

The growth stage is marked by a rapid climb in sales. Early adopters like the product, and more consumers start buying it. Attracted by the opportunities, new competitors enter with new product features and expanded distribution. Prices remain steady or fall slightly, depending on how quickly demand increases. Companies maintain or increase their promotional expenditures to meet competition and to continue to educate the market, but sales rise much faster than promotional expenditures.

Profits increase as promotion costs are spread over a larger volume, and unit manufacturing costs fall faster than price declines, owing to the producer learning effect. The firm uses several strategies to sustain rapid market growth: improving product quality and adding new features and improved styling; adding new models and flanker products; entering new segments; increasing distribution coverage and entering new channels; shifting from product-awareness to product-preference advertising; and lowering prices to attract the next layer of price-sensitive buyers. The growth stage involves a trade-off between high market share and high current profit. By spending on product improvement, promotion, and distribution, the firm can capture a dominant position. It forgoes maximum current profit in the hope of making even greater profits in the next stage.

Marketing Strategies: Maturity Stage

At some point, the rate of sales growth slows, and the product enters a stage of relative maturity, which normally lasts longer than the previous stages and poses formidable marketing challenges. Most products are in the maturity stage of the life cycle.

Three ways to change a brand's course in the maturity stage are market, product, and marketing program modification. With market modification, the company tries to expand the market for its mature brand by increasing the number of brand users and increasing usage rates among users. To expand the number of users, the firm can convert nonusers, enter new segments, or attract competitors' customers. To increase usage rates, the firm can convince current customers to use the product on more occasions, use more on each occasion, or use the product in new ways.

With product modification, managers try to stimulate sales by improving quality, feature, or style. *Quality improvement* increases the product's functional performance. *Feature improvement* adds new features that build the company's image as an innovator and win the loyalty of market segments that value these features. However, feature improvements are easily imitated; unless there's a permanent gain from being first, the improvement might not pay off in the long run.[51] *Style improvement* increases the product's esthetic appeal. This may provide a unique market identity, but it's difficult to predict whether people—and which people—will like a new style, and the company risks losing customers when an old style is discontinued. Another way to stimulate sales is to modify other marketing program elements such as prices, distribution, advertising, sales promotion, personal selling, and services.

Marketing Strategies: Decline Stage

Sales decline for a number of reasons, including technological advances, shifts in consumer tastes, and increased competition. All can lead to overcapacity, increased price-cutting, and profit erosion. As sales and profits decline, some firms withdraw from the market. Those remaining may reduce the number of products they offer. They may withdraw from smaller segments and weaker channels, cut promotion budgets, and further reduce prices.

To identify weak products, many firms appoint a product-review committee to review all available information and make a recommendation for each product—leave it alone, modify its marketing strategy, or drop it.[52] The appropriate decline strategy depends on the industry's barriers to exit and relative attractiveness as well as the company's competitive strength. Companies that successfully rejuvenate a mature product often do so by adding value to the original offering.

Harvesting calls for gradually reducing a product's or business's costs while trying to maintain its sales. The first step is to cut costs for R&D, plant, and equipment. The company might also reduce product quality, sales force size, marginal services, and advertising expenditures without letting customers, competitors, and employees know what is happening. Harvesting is difficult to execute, but it can substantially increase the company's current cash flow.[53] If a company wants to divest, it can probably sell the product to another firm if the offering has strong distribution and residual goodwill; if not, it must decide whether to liquidate quickly or slowly.

Critique of the Product Life-Cycle Concept

The PLC concept helps firms interpret product and market dynamics and conduct marketing planning and control. Recent research suggests that slowdown occurs at 34% penetration on average, well before most households own a new product; product categories with large sales increases at takeoff tend to have larger sales declines at slowdown.[54]

Critics claim that life-cycle patterns are too variable in shape and duration to be generalized and that marketers can seldom tell what stage the product is in. A product may appear to be mature when actually it's reached a plateau prior to another upsurge. One final criticism is that the PLC pattern is the result of marketing strategies rather than an inevitable course that sales must follow—and skillful marketing can spur continued growth.[55] See Table 10.2 for a summary of PLC characteristics, objectives, and strategies.

TABLE 10.2 Summary of Product Life-Cycle Characteristics, Objectives, and Strategies

	Introduction	Growth	Maturity	Decline
Characteristics				
Sales	Low sales	Rapidly rising sales	Peak sales	Declining sales
Costs	High cost per customer	Average cost per customer	Low cost per customer	Low cost per customers
Profits	Negative	Rising profits	High profits	Declining profits
Customers	Innovators	Early adopters	Middle majority	Laggards
Competitors	Few	Growing number	Stable number beginning to decline	Declining number
Marketing Objectives	Create product awareness and trial	Maximize market share	Maximize profit while defending market share	Reduce expenditure and milk the brand
Strategies				
Product	Offer a basic product	Offer product extensions, service, warranty	Diversify brands and items	Phase out weak
Price	Charge cost-plus	Price to penetrate market	Price to match or best competitors	Cut price
Distribution	Build selective distribution	Building intensive distribution	Build more intensive distribution	Go selective: phase out unprofitable outlets
Advertising	Build product awareness among early adopters and dealers	Build awareness and interest in the mass market	Stress brand differences and benefits	Reduce to level needed to retain hard-core loyals
Sales Promotion	Use heavy sales promotion to entice trial	Reduce to take advantage of heavy consumer demand	Increase to encourage brand switching	Reduce to minimal level

Sources: Chester R. Wasson, *Dynamic Competitive Strategy and Product Life Cycles* (Austin. TX: Austin Press, 1978); John A. Weber, "Planning Corporate Growth with Inverted Product Life Cycles," *Long Range Planning* (October 1976): 12–29: Peter Doyle, "The Realities of the Product Life Cycle," *Quarterly Review of Marketing* (Summer 1976).

EXECUTIVE SUMMARY

Marketers plan a market offering at five levels, each of which adds value: the core benefit, basic product, expected product, augmented product, and potential product. Products can be classified in terms of durability, reliability, and consumer or industrial use. By changing the width, length, depth, and consistency of the product mix, firms can expand their business. Product-line managers analyze sales, profits, and market profile when deciding which items to build, maintain, harvest, or divest. Physical products must be packaged and labeled, have well-designed packages, and may come with warranties and guarantees.

The new product development process consists of idea generation; screening; concept development and testing; marketing strategy development; business analysis; product development; market testing; and commercialization. The adoption process—by which customers learn about, evaluate, and try new products, then adopt or reject them—is influenced by many factors.

The product life cycle typically covers introduction, growth, maturity, and decline; most products are in the maturity stage. Each stage calls for different marketing strategies. The introduction stage is marked by slow growth and minimal profits. The growth stage is marked by rapid sales growth and increasing profits, followed by a maturity stage in which sales growth slows and profits stabilize. In the decline stage, the challenge is to identify weak products and decide whether to rejuvenate, harvest, or divest each.

NOTES

1. "In Brief: Caterpillar," *Wall Street Journal*, August 29, 2007, p. A8; Ilan Brat and Lavonne Kuykendall, "Caterpillar Net Slides on U.S. Results," *Wall Street Journal*, July 21, 2007, p. A3; Bruce Upbin, "Sharpening the Claws," *Forbes*, July 26, 1999, pp. 102–105.
2. This discussion is adapted from Theodore Levitt, "Marketing Success through Differentiation—of Anything," *Harvard Business Review* (January–February 1980): 83–91. The first level, core benefit, has been added to Levitt's discussion.
3. See Harper W. Boyd Jr. and Sidney Levy, "New Dimensions in Consumer Analysis," *Harvard Business Review* (November–December 1963): 129–140.
4. For some definitions, see *Dictionary of Marketing Terms*, ed. Peter D. Bennett (Chicago: American Marketing Association, 1995). Also see Patrick E. Murphy and Ben M. Enis, "Classifying Products Strategically," *Journal of Marketing* (July 1986): 24–42.
5. Royal Ford, "Scion, the Next Generation," *Boston Globe*, September 23, 2007, www.boston.com; Martin Zimmerman, "Toyota's First Quarter Global Sales Beat GM's Preliminary Numbers," *Los Angeles Times*, April 24, 2007; Charles Fishman, "No Satisfaction at Toyota," *Fast Company*, December 2006/January 2007, pp. 82-90; Stuart F. Brown, "Toyota's Global Body Shop," *Fortune*, February 9, 2004, p. 120; James B. Treece, "Ford Down; Toyota Aims for No. 1," *Automotive News*, February 2, 2004, p.1; Brian Bemner and Chester Dawson, "Can Anything Stop Toyota?" *BusinessWeek*, November 17, 2003, pp. 114–122.
6. Robert Bordley, "Determining the Appropriate Depth and Breadth of a Firm's Product Portfolio," *Journal of Marketing Research* 40 (February 2003): 39–53; Peter Boatwright and Joseph C. Nunes, "Reducing Assortment: An Attribute-Based Approach," *Journal of Marketing* 65 (July 2001): 50–63.
7. France Leclerc, Christopher K. Hsee, and Joseph C. Nunes, "Narrow Focusing: Why the Relative Position of a Good in Its Category Matters More Than It Should," *Marketing Science* 24 (Spring 2005): 194–205.
8. Laurens M. Sloot, Dennis Fok, and Peter Verhoef, "The Short- and Long-Term Impact of an Assortment Reduction on Category Sales," *Journal of Marketing Research* 43 (November 2006): 536–548.

9. Akshay R. Rao and Robert W. Ruekert, "Brand Alliances as Signals of Product Quality," *Sloan Management Review* (Fall 1994): 87–97; Akshay R. Rao, Lu Qu, and Robert W. Ruekert, "Signaling Unobservable Quality through a Brand Ally," *Journal of Marketing Research* 36, no. 2 (1999): 258–268.
10. Bernard L. Simonin and Julie A. Ruth, "Is a Company Known by the Company It Keeps? Assessing the Spillover Effects of Brand Alliances on Consumer Brand Attitudes," *Journal of Marketing Research* (February 1998): 30–42; see also C. W. Park, S. Y. Jun, and A. D. Shocker, "Composite Branding Alliances: An Investigation of Extension and Feedback Effects," *Journal of Marketing Research* 33 (1996): 453–466.
11. Lance Leuthesser, Chiranjier Kohli, and Rajneesh Suri, "2 + 2 = 5? A Framework for Using Co-Branding to Leverage a Brand," *Journal of Brand Management* 2, no. 1 (September 2003): 35–47.
12. For more about successful ingredient branding, see: Kevin Lane Keller, *Strategic Brand Management*, 3rd ed. (Upper Saddle River, NJ: Prentice Hall, 2008); Paul F. Nunes, Stephen F. Dull, and Patrick D. Lynch, "When Two Brands Are Better than One," *Outlook*, No. 1 (2003): 14–23; Philip Kotler and Waldemar Pfoertsch, *B2B Brand Management* (New York: Springer, 2006).
13. Kalpesh Kaushik Desai and Kevin Lane Keller, "The Effects of Brand Expansions and Ingredient Branding Strategies on Host Brand Extendibility," *Journal of Marketing* 66 (January 2002): 73–93; D. C. Denison, "Ingredient Branding Puts Big Names in the Mix," *Boston Globe*, May 26, 2002, p. E2.
14. Susanna Hamner, "Packaging That Pays," *Business 2.0*, July 2006, pp. 68–69.
15. Susan B. Bassin, "Value-Added Packaging Cuts through Store Clutter," *Marketing News*, September 26, 1988, p. 21.
16. Siva K. Balasubramanian and Catherine Cole, "Consumers' Search and Use of Nutrition Information: The Challenge and Promise of the Nutrition Labeling and Education Act," *Journal of Marketing* 66 (July 2002): 112–127; John C. Kozup, Elizabeth H. Creyer, and Scot Burton, "Making Healthful Food Choices: The Influence of Health Claims and Nutrition Information on Consumers' Evaluations of Packaged Food Products and Restaurant Menu Items," *Journal of Marketing* 67 (April 2003): 19–34.
17. Dee Gill, ". . . or Your Money Back," *Inc.*, September 2005, p. 46.
18. "More Firms Pledge Guaranteed Service," *Wall Street Journal*, July 17, 1991, pp. B1, B6; Barbara Ettore, "Phenomenal Promises Mean Business," *Management Review* (March 1994): 18–23. Also see Christopher W. L. Hart, *Extraordinary Guarantees* (New York: Amacom, 1993); Sridhar Moorthy and Kannan Srinivasan, "Signaling Quality with a Money-Back Guarantee: The Role of Transaction Costs," *Marketing Science* 14, no. 4 (1995): 442–446.
19. Stephen J. Carson, "When to Give Up Control of Outsourced New Product Development," *Journal of Marketing* 71 (January 2007), pp. 49-66. For some scholarly reviews of new product development, see Ely Dahan and John R. Hauser, "Product Development: Managing a Dispersed Process," in *Handbook of Marketing*, edited by Bart Weitz and Robin Wensley (London: Sage Publications, 2002), pp. 179–222; Dipak Jain, "Managing New Product Development for Strategic Competitive Advantage," Chapter 6 in *Kellogg on Marketing*, Dawn Iacobucci (ed). (New York: John Wiley, 2001), pp. 130–148.
20. For an academic discussion of how new product introductions affect markets, see Harald J. Van Heerde, Carl F. Mela, and Puneet Manchanda, "The Dynamic Effect of Innovation on Market Structure," *Journal of Marketing Research* 41 (May 2004): 166–183.
21. Sungwook Min, Manohar U. Kalwani, and William T. Robinson, "Market Pioneer and Early Follower Survival Risks: A Contingency Analysis of Really New versus Incrementally New Product-Markets," *Journal of Marketing* 70 (January 2006): 15–33; C. Page Moreau, Arthur B. Markman, and Donald R. Lehmann, "'What Is It?' Category Flexibility and Consumers' Response to Really New Products," *Journal of Consumer Research* 27 (March 2001): 489–498.
22. Ashish Sood and Gerard J. Tellis, "Technological Evolution and Radical Innovation," *Journal of Marketing* 69 (July 2005): 152–168.
23. Clayton M. Christensen, *The Innovator's Dilemma: When New Technologies Cause Great Firms to Fail* (Boston: Harvard University Press, 1997).
24. Ely Dahan and John R. Hauser, "Product Development: Managing a Dispersed Process," in *Handbook of Marketing*, edited by Bart Weitz and Robin Wensley (London: Sage Publications, 2002), pp. 179–222.
25. Susumu Ogama and Frank T. Piller, "Reducing the Risks of New Product Development," *MIT Sloan Management Review* (Winter 2006): 65–71;

Deloitte and Touche, "Vision in Manufacturing Study," Deloitte Consulting and Kenan-Flagler Business School, March 6, 1998; A. C. Nielsen, "New Product Introduction—Successful Innovation/Failure: Fragile Boundary," A. C. Nielsen BASES and Ernst & Young Global Client Consulting, June 24, 1999.

26. Robert G. Cooper and Elko J. Kleinschmidt, *New Products: The Key Factors in Success* (Chicago: American Marketing Association, 1990).

27. Ely Dahan and John R. Hauser, "Product Development: Managing a Dispersed Process," in *Handbook of Marketing*, edited by Weitz and Robin Wensley (Thousand Oaks, CA: Sage, 2002) pp. 179–222.

28. John Hauser, Gerard J. Tellis, and Abbie Griffin, "Research on Innovation: A Review and Agenda for Marketing Science," *Marketing Science* 25 (November–December 2006): 687–717.

29. Olivier Toubia and Laurent Florès, "Adaptive Idea Screening Using Consumers," *Marketing Science* 26 (May–June 2007): 342–360; Melanie Wells, "Have It Your Way," *Forbes*, February 14, 2005.

30. "Will She, Won't She?—Procter & Gamble," *The Economist*, August 11, 2007, p. 61; Philip Kotler, "Drawing New Ideas from Your Customers," unpublished paper, 2007; Robert Cooper, *Product Leadership: Creating and Launching Superior New Products* (New York: Perseus Books, 1998); Steve Hamm, "Speed Demons," *BusinessWeek*, March 27, 2006, pp. 69–76; Larry Huston and Nabil Sakkab, "Connect and Develop: Inside Procter & Gamble's New Model for Innovation," *Harvard Business Review* (March 2006): 58–66.

31. Hamm, "Speed Demons."

32. For more information, see David Bakken and Curtis L. Frazier, "Conjoint Analysis: Understanding Consumer Decision Making," in Rajiv Grover and Marco Vriens (ed.), *The Handbook of Marketing Research* (Thousand Oaks, CA: Sage Publications, 2006); Jordan J. Louviere, David A. Hensher, and Joffre D. Swait, *Stated Choice Models: Analysis and Applications* (New York: Cambridge University Press, 2000); Paul E. Green and V. Srinivasan, "Conjoint Analysis in Marketing: New Developments with Implications for Research and Practice," *Journal of Marketing* (October 1990): 3–19; Dick R. Wittnick, Marco Vriens, and Wim Burhenne, "Commercial Uses of Conjoint Analysis in Europe: Results and Critical Reflections," *International Journal of Research in Marketing* (January 1994): 41–52.

33. See David B. Hertz, "Risk Analysis in Capital Investment," *Harvard Business Review* (January–February 1964): 96–106.

34. John Hauser, "House of Quality," *Harvard Business Review* (May–June 1988): 63–73. Customer-driven engineering is also called "quality function deployment." See Lawrence R. Guinta and Nancy C. Praizler, *The QFD Book: The Team Approach to Solving Problems and Satisfying Customers through Quality Function Deployment* (New York: AMACOM, 1993); V. Srinivasan, William S. Lovejoy, and David Beach, "Integrated Product Design for Marketability and Manufacturing," *Journal of Marketing Research* (February 1997): 154–163.

35. Rajesh Chandy, Brigette Hopstaken, Om Narasimhan, and Jaideep Prabhu, "From Invention to Innovation: Conversion Ability in Product Development," *Journal of Marketing Research* 43 (August 2006): 494–508.

36. Remco Prins and Peter C. Verhoef, "Marketing Communication Drivers of Adoption Timing of a New E-Service among Existing Customers," *Journal of Marketing* 71 (April 2007): 169–183.

37. Katrijn Gielens and Jan-Benedict E.M. Steenkamp, "What Drives New Product Success? An Investigation across Products and Countries," Marketing Science Institute Working Paper 04-108, Cambridge, MA; Katrijn Gielens and Jan-Benedict E.M. Steenkamp, "Drivers of Consumer Acceptance of New Packaged Goods: An Investigation across Products and Countries," *International Journal of Research in Marketing* 24 (June 2007): 97–111; Marc Fischer, Venkatesh Shankar, and Michael Clement, "Can a Late Mover Use International Market Entry Strategy to Challenge the Pioneer?" Marketing Science Institute Working Paper 05-118, Cambridge, MA; Venkatesh Shankar, Gregory S. Carpenter, and Lakshman Krishnamukthi, "Late Mover Advantages: How Innovative Late Entrants Outsell Pioneers," *Journal of Marketing Research* 35 (February 1998): 54–70.

38. Philip Kotler and Gerald Zaltman, "Targeting Prospects for a New Product," *Journal of Advertising Research* (February 1976): 7–20.

39. Mark Leslie and Charles A. Holloway, "The Sales Learning Curve," *Harvard Business Review* (July–August 2006): 114–123.

40. For details, see Keith G. Lockyer, *Critical Path Analysis and Other Project Network Techniques* (London: Pitman, 1984). Also see Arvind Rangaswamy and Gary L. Lilien, "Software Tools for New Product Development," *Journal of Marketing Research* (February 1997): 177–184.

41. The following discussion leans heavily on Everett M. Rogers, *Diffusion of Innovations* (New York: Free Press, 1962). Also see his third edition, published in 1983.
42. C. Page Moreau, Donald R. Lehmann, and Arthur B. Markman, "Entrenched Knowledge Structures and Consumer Response to New Products," *Journal of Marketing Research* 38 (February 2001): 14–29.
43. Michal Herzenstein, and Steven S. Posavac, and J. Joškon Brakuz, "Adoption of New and Really New Products: the Effects of Self-Regulation Systems and Risk Salience," *Journal of Marketing Research* 44 (May 2007): 251–260; Christophe Van den Bulte and Yogesh V. Joshi, "New Product Diffusion with Influentials and Imitators," *Marketing Science* 26 (May–June 2007): 400–421; Steve Hoeffler, "Measuring Preferences for Really New Products," *Journal of Marketing Research* 40 (November 2003): 406–420; Rogers, *Diffusion of Innovations*, p. 192.
44. See Hubert Gatignon and Thomas S. Robertson, "A Propositional Inventory for New Diffusion Research," *Journal of Consumer Research* (March 1985): 849–867; Vijay Mahajan, Eitan Muller, and Frank M. Bass, "Diffusion of New Products: Empirical Generalizations and Managerial Uses," *Marketing Science* 14, no. 3, part 2 (1995): G79–G89; Fareena Sultan, John U. Farley, and Donald R. Lehmann, "Reflection on 'A Meta-Analysis of Applications of Diffusion Models,'" *Journal of Marketing Research* (May 1996): 247–249; Minhi Hahn, Sehoon Park, and Andris A. Zoltners, "Analysis of New Product Diffusion Using a Four-Segment Trial-Repeat Model," *Marketing Science* 13, no. 3 (1994): 224–247.
45. Some authors distinguished additional stages. Wasson suggested a stage of competitive turbulence between growth and maturity; see Chester R. Wasson, *Dynamic Competitive Strategy and Product Life Cycles* (Austin, TX: Austin Press, 1978). Maturity describes a stage of sales growth slowdown and saturation, a stage of flat sales after sales have peaked.
46. Robert D. Buzzell, "Competitive Behavior and Product Life Cycles," in *New Ideas for Successful Marketing*, edited by John S. Wright and Jack Goldstucker (Chicago: American Marketing Association, 1956), p. 51.
47. Rajesh J. Chandy, Gerard J. Tellis, Deborah J. MacInnis, and Pattana Thaivanich, "What to Say When: Advertising Appeals in Evolving Markets," *Journal of Marketing Research* 38 (November 2001): 399–414.
48. William T. Robinson and Claes Fornell, "Sources of Market Pioneer Advantages in Consumer Goods Industries," *Journal of Marketing Research* (August 1985): 305–317; Glen L. Urban et al., "Market Share Rewards to Pioneering Brands: An Empirical Analysis and Strategic Implications," *Management Science* (June 1986): 645–659.
49. Steven P. Schnaars, *Managing Imitation Strategies* (New York: Free Press, 1994).
50. Gerald Tellis and Peter Golder, *Will & Vision: How Latecomers Can Grow to Dominate Markets* (New York: McGraw-Hill, 2001); Peter N. Golder and Gerald J. Tellis, "Pioneer Advantage: Marketing Logic or Marketing Legend?" *Journal of Marketing Research* (May 1992): 34–46; Peter N. Golder, "Historical Method in Marketing Research with New Evidence on Long-Term Market Share Stability," *Journal of Marketing Research* 37 (May 2000): 156–172. See also Rajesh K. Chandy and Gerald J. Tellis, "The Incumbent's Curse? Incumbency, Size, and Radical Product Innovation," *Journal of Marketing Research* (July 2000): 1–17.
51. Stephen M. Nowlis and Itamar Simmonson, "The Effect of New Product Features on Brand Choice," *Journal of Marketing Research* (February 1996): 36–46.
52. Rajan Varadarajan, Mark P. DeFanti, and Paul S. Busch, "Brand Portfolio, Corporate Image, and Reputation: Managing Brand Deletions," *Journal of the Academy of Marketing Science* 34 (Spring 2006), 195-205; Stephen J. Carlotti, Jr., Mary Ellen Coe, and Jesko Perrey, "Making Brand Portfolios Work," *McKinsey Quarterly*, No. 4, 2004, pp. 24–36; Nirmalya Kumar, "Kill a Brand, Keep a Customer," *Harvard Business Review*, 81 (December 2003): 86–95; Philip Kotler, "Phasing Out Weak Products," *Harvard Business Review* (March–April 1965): 107–118; George J. Avlonitis, "Product Elimination Decision Making: Does Formality Matter," *Journal of Marketing* (Winter 1985): 41–52.
53. See Philip Kotler, "Harvesting Strategies for Weak Products," *Business Horizons*, August 1978, pp. 15–22; and Laurence P. Feldman and Albert L. Page, "Harvesting: The Misunderstood Market Exit Strategy," *Journal of Business Strategy* (Spring 1985): 79–85.
54. Peter N. Golder and Gerard J. Tellis, "Growing, Growing, Gone: Cascades, Diffusion, and Turning Points in the Product Life Cycle," *Marketing Science*, 23 (Spring 2004): 207–218.
55. Youngme Moon, "Break Free from the Product Life Cycle," *Harvard Business Review* (May 2005): 87–94.

CHAPTER 11

Designing and Managing Services

> In this chapter, we will address the following questions:
>
> 1. How are services defined and classified?
> 2. How are services marketed, and how can service quality be improved?
> 3. How do services marketers create strong brands?
> 4. How can goods marketers improve customer support services?

MARKETING MANAGEMENT AT THE MAYO CLINIC

The Mayo Clinic, the world's first and largest integrated not-for-profit medical group practice, has set new service standards in the health care industry by considering all aspects of the patient experience. The clinic's founders, William and Charles Mayo, championed two interrelated core values that have guided the organization for more than a century. First, place the patient's interests above all others. Second, practice teamwork.

The clinic plans every detail of the patient experience. From public exam rooms to laboratories, Mayo facilities have been designed so that, in the words of the architect of one of the buildings, "patients feel a little better before they see their doctors." The 20-story Gonda Building in Rochester, Minnesota, has spectacular wide-open spaces, and the lobby of the Mayo Clinic hospital in Scottsdale, Arizona, has an indoor waterfall and a mountain view. In pediatric exam rooms, resuscitation equipment is hidden behind cheery pictures. Hospital rooms feature microwave ovens and chairs that really do convert to beds because, as one staff member explained, "People don't come to the hospital alone."[1]

As companies find it harder and harder to differentiate their physical products, they turn to service differentiation. Many in fact find significant profitability in delivering superior service, whether that means on-time delivery, faster response to inquiries, or speedier resolution of complaints.[2] Because marketers in all industries need to understand the special nature of services, this chapter systematically analyzes services and discusses how to market them most effectively.

THE NATURE OF SERVICES

Service industries are everywhere. The *government sector* has courts, employment services, hospitals, loan agencies, military services, police and fire departments, post office, regulatory agencies, and schools. Services in the *private nonprofit sector* include museums, charities, churches, colleges, foundations, and hospitals. A good part of the *business sector*, with its airlines, banks, hotels, insurance firms, law firms, consulting firms, medical practices, and real estate firms, is in the service business. Many workers in the *manufacturing sector*, such as computer operators, accountants, and legal staff, are really service providers, making up a "service factory" that provides services to the "goods factory." Those in the *retail sector*, such as cashiers, clerks, salespeople, and customer service representatives, are also providing a service.

A **service** is any act or performance that one party can offer to another that is essentially intangible and does not result in the ownership of anything. Its production may or may not be tied to a physical product. Many services include no physical products, and some service firms are purely online, with no physical presence (the career site Monster.com is a good example).

Categories of Service Mix

A company's offerings often include some services. Five categories of offerings are:

1. *Pure tangible good*. The offering is a tangible good such as soap, not accompanied by services.
2. *Tangible good with accompanying services*. The offering consists of a tangible good accompanied by one or more services. General Motors, for example, offers repairs, warranty fulfillment, and other services along with its vehicles.
3. *Hybrid*. The offering consists of equal parts of goods and services. For example, people patronize restaurants for both food and service.
4. *Major service with accompanying minor goods and services*. The offering consists of a major service along with additional services or supporting goods. For example, airline passengers are buying transportation service, although they get snacks and drinks as well.
5. *Pure service*. The offering consists primarily of a service; examples include babysitting and psychotherapy.

Customers cannot judge the technical quality of some services even after they have received them, as shown in Figure 11.1.[3] At the left are goods high in *search qualities*—characteristics the buyer can evaluate before purchase. In the middle are goods and services high in *experience qualities*—characteristics the buyer can evaluate after purchase. At the right are services high in *credence qualities*—characteristics the buyer finds hard to evaluate even after consumption.[4]

FIGURE 11.1 Continuum of Evaluation for Different Types of Products

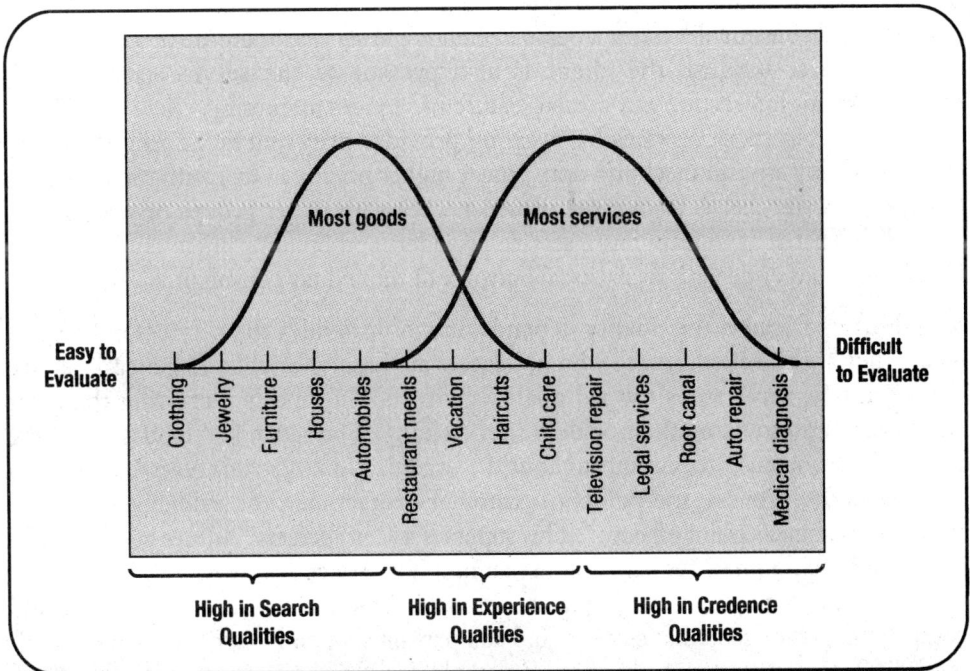

Source: Valarie A. Zeithaml, "How Consumer Evaluation Processes Differ between Good and Services," in *Marketing of Services*, ed. James H. Donnelly and William M. George (Chicago: American Marketing Association, 1981). Reprinted with permission of the American Marketing Association.

Because services are generally high in experience and credence qualities, there is more risk in purchase. As a result, service consumers generally rely on word of mouth rather than on advertising. They also rely heavily on price, personnel, and physical cues to judge quality, and are highly loyal to service providers who satisfy them. And because switching costs are high, consumer inertia can make it challenging to entice a customer away from a competitor.

Distinctive Characteristics of Services

Services have four major characteristics that greatly affect the design of marketing programs: *intangibility, inseparability, variability,* and *perishability*.[5]

Intangibility Unlike physical products, services cannot be seen, tasted, felt, heard, or smelled before they are bought. The person getting cosmetic surgery cannot see the results before the purchase, just as the patient in the psychiatrist's office cannot know the exact outcome of the treatment. To reduce uncertainty, buyers will look for signs or evidence of the service quality, drawing inferences from the place, people, equipment, communication material, symbols, and price they see. Therefore, the service provider's task is to "manage the evidence," to "tangibilize the intangible."[6]

Service firms can try to demonstrate their service quality through *physical evidence* and *presentation*.[7] A hotel will develop a look and a style of dealing with customers that realizes its intended customer value proposition, whether it's cleanliness, speed, or some other benefit. Service marketers must be able to transform intangible services into concrete benefits and a well-defined experience.[8] The Disney Company is a master at tangibilizing the intangible and creating magical fantasies in its theme parks, for instance.[9]

Inseparability Services are typically produced and consumed simultaneously, unlike physical goods, which are manufactured, put into inventory, distributed through resellers, and consumed later. If a person renders the service, then the provider is part of the service. Because the client is also present as the service is produced, provider–client interaction is a special feature of services marketing.

Often, buyers of services have strong provider preferences. Several strategies exist for getting around this limitation. One is higher pricing in line with the provider's limited time. Another is having the provider work with larger groups or work faster. A third alternative is to train more service providers and build up client confidence, as H&R Block has done with its national network of trained tax consultants.

Variability Because the quality depends on who provides the services, when and where they are provided, and to whom, services are highly variable. In general, service firms can take three steps toward quality control. The first is recruiting the right employees and providing them with proper training. The second is standardizing the service-performance process throughout the organization. A *service blueprint* can map out the service process, the points of customer contact, and the evidence of service from the customer's point of view.[10] This supports a "zero defects" culture and is helpful both in developing new services and in planning for service recovery.

The third step is monitoring customer satisfaction through suggestion and complaint systems, customer surveys, and comparison shopping. General Electric sends out 700,000 response cards yearly, asking households to rate its service people's performance. Firms can also develop customer information databases and systems to permit more personalized service, especially online.[11] Finally, some firms offer *service guarantees* to reduce consumer perceptions of risk.[12]

Perishability Services cannot be stored, so their perishability is a problem when demand fluctuates. For example, public-transportation companies have to own much more equipment because of higher rush-hour demand than if demand were even throughout the day. Service providers can deal with perishability in a number of ways. Table 11.1 shows some strategies for matching demand and supply in a service business.[13]

For example, Club Med cultivates nonpeak demand using midweek e-mails to pitch unsold weekend packages to consumers in its database, offering discounts of 30% to 40% off the standard price.[14] Another example is Disney's Fastpass, which allows visitors to reserve a spot in line and eliminate the wait at its theme parks. A Disney vice president says: "We have been teaching people how to stand in line since 1955, and now we are telling them they don't have to. Of all the things we can do and all the marvels we can create with the attractions, this is something that will have a profound effect on the entire industry."[15]

MARKETING STRATEGIES FOR SERVICE FIRMS

Although service firms once lagged behind manufacturers in their use of marketing, this has certainly changed. Not all companies, however, have invested in providing superior service, at least not to all customers. Customers complain about inaccurate information; unresponsive, rude, or poorly trained personnel; and long wait times. Even worse, many complaints never actually reach a live human being because of slow or faulty phone or online customer service. When Forrester Research had its analysts contact 16 top

TABLE 11.1 Improving the Match between Service Demand and Supply

Demand-Side Strategies	Supply-Side Strategies
Differential pricing will shift some demand from peak to off-peak periods. Example: Low early-evening movie prices.	*Part-time employees* can serve peak demand. Example: Stores hire extra clerks during holiday periods.
Nonpeak demand can be cultivated. Example: McDonald's promotes breakfast service.	*Peak-time efficiency* routines allow employees to perform only essential tasks during peak periods. Example: Paramedics assist physicians during busy periods.
Complementary services can provide alternatives for waiting customers. Example: Banks offer automatic teller machines.	*Increased consumer participation* can be encouraged. Example: Consumers bag their own groceries.
Reservation systems can manage the demand level. Example: Airlines and hotels use these extensively.	*Facilities for future expansion* can be a good investment. Example: A theme park buys surrounding land for later development.
	Shared services can improve offerings. Example: Several hospitals can share medical-equipment purchases.

Source: Adapted from W. Earl Sasser, "Match Supply and Demand in Service Industries," *Harvard Business Review* (November–December 1976): 133–140.

companies via their Web sites, phone agents, interactive voice response (IVR), and e-mail to assess customer service, their experiences were not all positive.[16] At the other end of the service spectrum, Butterball Turkey has 55 operators handling the 100,000 calls it receives annually on its toll-free phone number—10,000 on Thanksgiving Day alone—answering questions about how to prepare, cook, and serve turkeys.[17]

A Shifting Customer Relationship

Firms are raising fees and lowering service to those customers who barely pay their way, while they coddle big spenders with special discounts, promotional offers, and lots of special service to retain their patronage. For instance, Charles Schwab's best customers get their calls answered in 15 seconds; other customers can wait 10 minutes or more.[18] Companies that provide differentiated levels of service, however, must be careful about claiming superior service—the customers who receive poor treatment will bad-mouth the company and injure its reputation. Delivering services that maximize both customer satisfaction and company profitability can be challenging. "Breakthrough Marketing: Southwest Airlines" describes how that airline successfully challenged established carriers.

Customers are becoming more sophisticated about buying support services and are pressing for "services unbundling." They want separate prices for each service element and the right to select the elements they want. Customers also increasingly dislike having to deal with a multitude of service providers handling different types of equipment. Most important, the Internet has empowered customers by letting them vent about bad service or reward good service and, with a mouse click, send their comments around the world.

> ### BREAKTHROUGH MARKETING: SOUTHWEST AIRLINES
>
> Southwest Airlines began flying in 1971 with little money, lots of personality, and low fares thanks to unusually efficient operations. It only flies one type of aircraft, which saves time and money: training is simplified for pilots, flight attendants, and mechanics; and management can substitute aircraft, reschedule flight crews, or transfer mechanics quickly. Also, Southwest flies to smaller airports that have lower gate fees and less congestion, which speeds aircraft turnaround and allows each plane to complete more flights every day.
>
> Even though Southwest is a low-cost airline, it has pioneered services such as same-day freight service and consistently wins customer-service kudos. *Fortune* magazine has ranked it the most-admired U.S. airline since 1997 (and one of the top five best places to work). Southwest's financial results also shine: It has been profitable every year since 1973. "Our fares can be matched; our airplanes and routes can be copied. But we pride ourselves on our customer service," said Sherry Phelps, director of corporate employment. A sense of humor is one of the selection criteria Southwest uses when it hires new employees. As one employee explained, "We can train you to do any job, but we can't give you the right spirit."[19]

The reality is that customers do not merely buy and use services, they play an active role in service delivery every step of the way.[20] Their words and actions affect the quality of their service experiences and those of others, and the productivity of front-line employees. One study estimated that one-third of all service problems are caused by the customer.[21] Preventing service failures from ever happening to begin with is crucial, as service recovery is always challenging.

Many firms have excellent procedures to deal with their own failures, yet they find that managing customer failures is more difficult. Figure 11.2 shows four categories of root causes for customer failures (note that multiple causes may be at work). Some of the ways firms deal with these failures are to redesign processes and customer roles to simplify service encounters; use technology to aid customers and employees; and encourage customers to help each other.[22]

Holistic Marketing for Services

A host of variables influence the service outcome and whether customers will remain loyal to a service provider. One study identified more than 800 critical behaviors that cause customers to switch services.[23] These behaviors fall into eight categories (see Table 11.2).

Holistic marketing for services requires external, internal, and interactive marketing (see Figure 11.3).[24] *External marketing* is the normal work of preparing, pricing, distributing, and promoting the service to customers. *Internal marketing* is training and motivating employees to serve customers well. The most important contribution the marketing department can make is to be "exceptionally clever in getting everyone else in the organization to practice marketing."[25]

Interactive marketing is the employees' skill in serving clients. Clients judge service not only by its *technical quality* (Was the surgery successful?), but also by its

FIGURE 11.2 Root Causes of Customer Failure

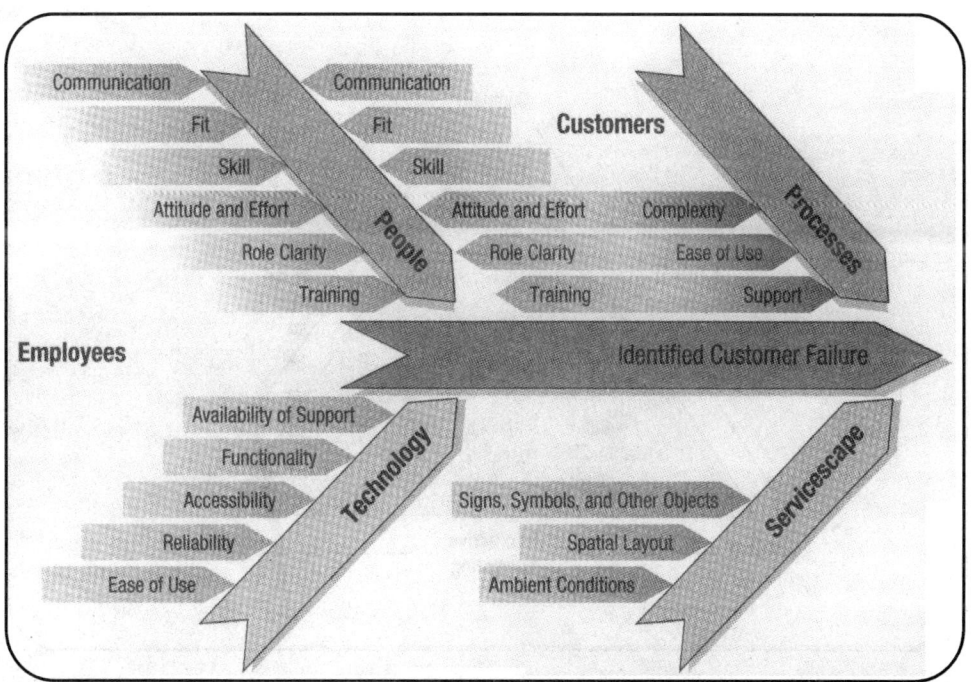

TABLE 11.2 Factors Leading to Customer Switching Behavior

Pricing	Response to Service Failure
■ High price	■ Negative response
■ Price increases	■ No response
■ Unfair pricing	■ Reluctant response
■ Deceptive pricing	
Inconvenience	**Competition**
■ Location/hours	■ Found better service
■ Wait for appointment	
■ Wait for service	
Core Service Failure	**Ethical Problems**
■ Service mistakes	■ Cheat
■ Billing errors	■ Hard sell
■ Service catastrophe	■ Unsafe
	■ Conflict of interest
Service Encounter Failures	**Involuntary Switching**
■ Uncaring	■ Customer moved
■ Impolite	■ Provider closed
■ Unresponsive	
■ Unknowledgeable	

Source: Susan M. Keaveney, "Customer Switching Behavior in Service Industries: An Exploratory Study," *Journal of Marketing* (April 1995): 71–82.

FIGURE 11.3 Three Types of Marketing in Service Industries

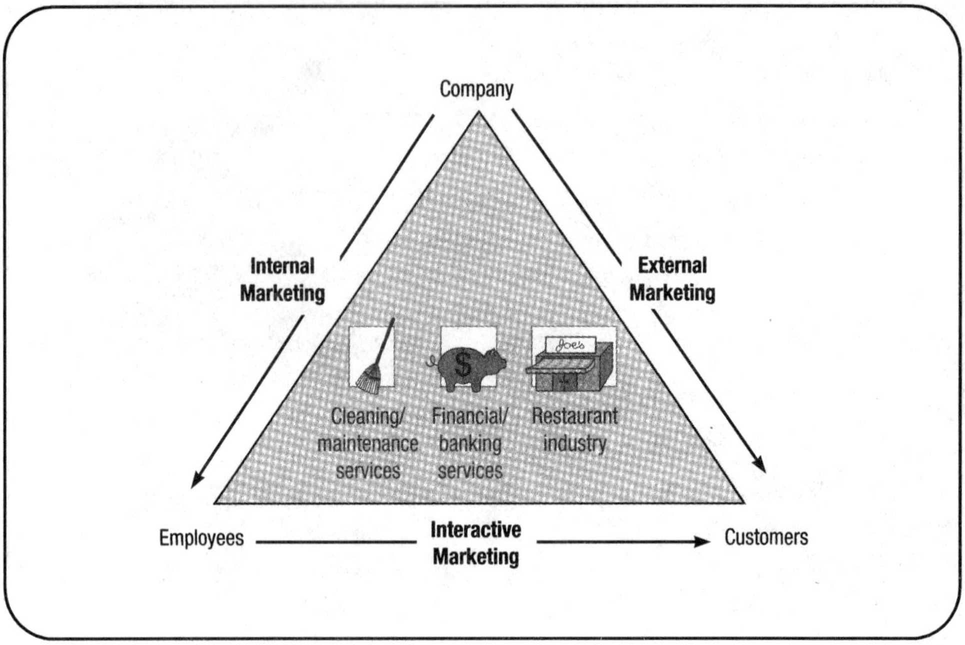

functional quality (Did the surgeon show concern and inspire confidence?).[26] Technology can make service workers much more productive. Staff members at Potomac Hospital in Woodbridge, Virginia, use handheld computers to schedule and track patient transport between hospital rooms and testing departments, saving both time and money.[27] Companies must avoid pushing productivity so hard, however, that they reduce perceived quality. Service must be "high-touch" as well as "high-tech." This is why Charles Schwab offers innovative portfolio analysis tools for customers to use online as well as in-person investment consultations and educational seminars.[28]

The Internet lets firms improve their service offerings and strengthen customer relationships by allowing for true interactivity, personalization, and real-time adjustments of the firm's offerings.[29] As companies collect, store, and use more information, they must also incorporate safeguards and reassure their customers about data security and privacy.[30]

MANAGING SERVICE QUALITY

The service quality of a firm is tested at each service encounter. If service personnel are bored, uninformed, or too busy to wait on customers, customers will think twice about doing business again with that seller.

Customer Expectations

Customers form service expectations from many sources, such as past experiences, word of mouth, and advertising. In general, customers compare the *perceived service* with the *expected service*.[31] If the perceived service falls below the expected service, customers are disappointed. Successful companies add benefits that not only satisfy customers but also delight them. The service-quality model in Figure 11.4 identifies five gaps that cause unsuccessful service delivery:[32]

1. *Gap between consumer expectation and management perception.* Management does not always correctly perceive what customers want. Hospital administrators may think that patients want better food, but patients may be more concerned with nurse responsiveness.
2. *Gap between management perception and service-quality specification.* Management might correctly perceive the customers' wants but not set a performance standard. Hospital administrators may tell the nurses to give "fast" service without specifying it quantitatively.
3. *Gap between service-quality specifications and service delivery.* Personnel might be poorly trained, or incapable or unwilling to meet the standard; or they may be held to conflicting standards, such as taking time to listen to customers and serving them fast.

FIGURE 11.4 Service Quality Model

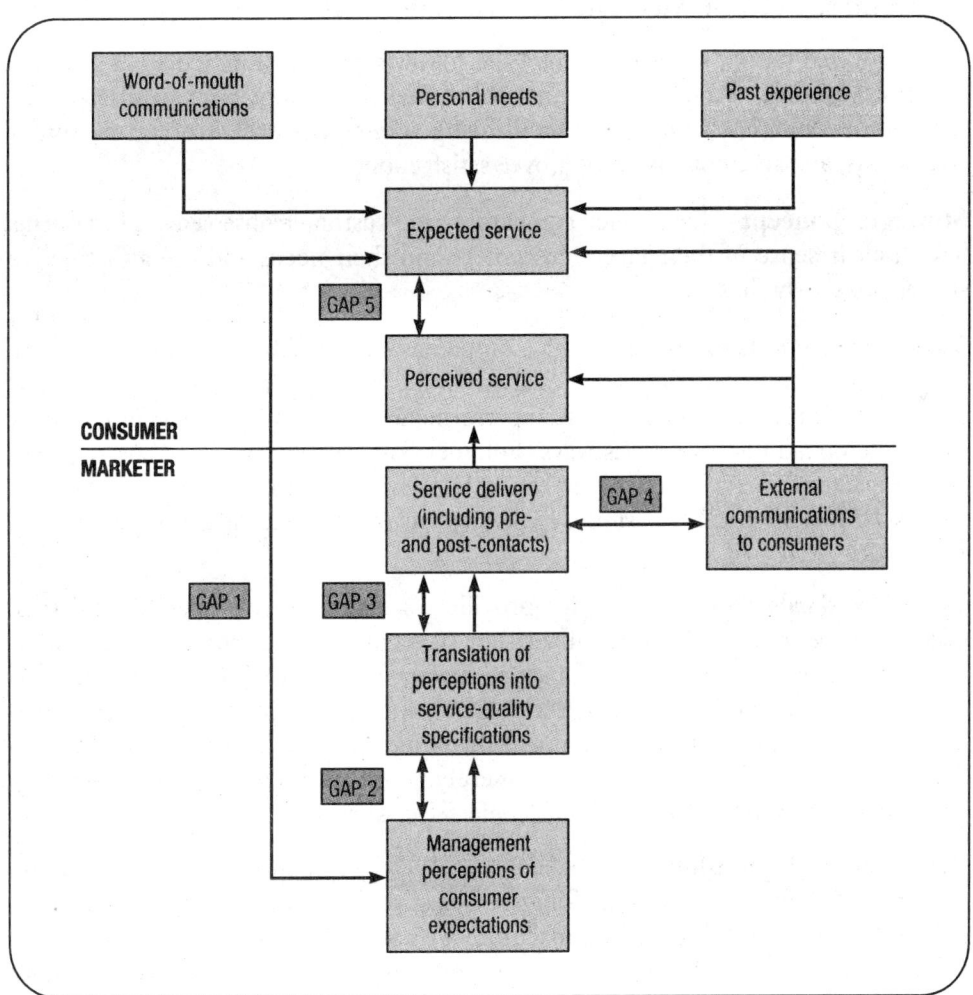

Source: A. Parasuraman, Valarie A. Zeithaml, and Leonard L. Berry, "A Conceptual Model of Service Quality and Its Implications for Future Research," *Journal of Marketing* (Fall 1985): 44. Reprinted with permission of the American Marketing Association. The model is more fully discussed or elaborated in Valarie Zeithaml, Mary Jo Bitner and Dwayne D. Gremler, *Services Marketing: Integrating Customer Focus across the Firm,* 4th ed. (New York: McGraw-Hill, 2006).

4. *Gap between service delivery and external communications.* Statements made by company representatives and ads affect customer expectations. If a hospital brochure shows an attractive room, but the patient finds an unappealing room, communications have distorted the customer's expectations.
5. *Gap between perceived service and expected service.* This gap occurs when the consumer misperceives the service quality. The physician may keep visiting the patient to show care, but the patient may interpret this as an indication that something really is wrong.

Based on the service-quality model, researchers identified five determinants of service quality. In order of importance, they are reliability, responsiveness, assurance, empathy, and tangibles.[33] There is also a *zone of tolerance* or range in which customer perceptions of a service dimension would be deemed satisfactory, anchored by the minimally acceptable level and the level that customers believe can and should be delivered.

Best Practices of Service-Quality Management

Well-managed service companies share the following common practices: a strategic concept, a history of top-management commitment to quality, high standards, self-service technologies, systems for monitoring service performance and customer complaints, and an emphasis on employee satisfaction.

Strategic Concept Top service companies are "customer obsessed." These firms have a clear sense of their target customers and their needs and use a distinctive strategy to satisfy these needs.

Top-Management Commitment Companies such as Marriott and Disney are thoroughly committed to service quality. Every month, their executives look at service performance as well as financial performance. Top-management commitment can be demonstrated in various ways. Founder Sam Walton of Wal-Mart required employees to pledge: "I solemnly swear and declare that every customer that comes within 10 feet of me, I will smile, look them in the eye, and greet them, so help me Sam."

High Standards The best service providers set high service-quality standards. Citibank aims to answer phone calls within 10 seconds and customer letters within two days. Service standards must be set *appropriately* high. A 98% accuracy standard may sound good, but it would result in FedEx losing 64,000 packages a day; 400,000 misfilled prescriptions daily; and unsafe drinking water eight days a year. We can distinguish between firms offering "merely good" service and those offering "breakthrough" service aiming at 100% defect-free service.[34]

Self-Service Technologies Consumers value convenience in services.[35] Many person-to-person service interactions are being replaced by self-service technologies.[36] To the traditional vending machines we can add automated teller machines (ATMs), hotel self-checkout, and online self-customization of products, among others. Not all such technologies improve service quality, but they can make transactions more accurate, convenient, and faster. For example, Borders deployed Title Sleuth self-service kiosks so customers can do their own title searches. The kiosks handle up to 1.2 million customer searches per week, and customers using these machines spend 50% more per visit.[37] For such technologies to succeed, customers must understand their role in the process, see a clear benefit, and feel they can actually use the system.[38]

Monitoring Systems Top firms regularly audit service performance, both their own and their competitors'. They collect *voice of the customer (VOC) measurements* to probe customer satisfiers and dissatisfiers. And they use a number of measurement devices: comparison shopping, ghost shopping, customer surveys, suggestion and complaint forms, service-audit teams, and letters to the president. Mystery shopping—the use of undercover shoppers who are paid to report back to the company—is now big business, used by fast-food chains, major retailers, and even large government agencies to pinpoint and fix customer service problems.

Satisfying Customer Complaints Firms that encourage disappointed customers to complain—and empower employees to remedy the situation on the spot—have been shown to achieve higher revenues and profits than firms that do not systematically address service failures.[39] Pizza Hut prints its toll-free number on all pizza boxes. When a customer complains, Pizza Hut sends voice mail to the store manager, who must call the customer within 48 hours and resolve the complaint (see "Marketing Skills: Service Recovery" for more about recovering from service missteps).

Satisfying Employees as Well as Customers Excellent service companies know that positive employee attitudes promote stronger customer loyalty. Sears found a high correlation between customer satisfaction, employee satisfaction, and store profitability. Employees are a key factor in the success of Paychex, Inc., a leading provider

MARKETING SKILLS: SERVICE RECOVERY

With good service recovery skills, marketers can turn a bad service experience into an opportunity for strengthening customer ties. Service recovery starts with an intense focus on understanding and meeting customers' needs. This allows marketers to identify potential problems and appropriate solutions. In planning for service recovery, consider cross-training and empowerment so employees can solve problems without bouncing customers from one department to another. The ability to listen carefully and tactfully ask questions (of the customer and the employees involved) will help clarify the problem. Apologize when appropriate and offer a solution that is acceptable to the customer and fits with the company's objectives. Finally, tell the customer what will happen and when, and then follow through to see that the customer is satisfied.

Consider how Ocado, a U.K. online grocery delivery company, planned for service recovery to back up its promise of excellent customer service. After identifying elements that influence customers' perception of service quality, such as on-time delivery, Ocado set and communicated high service standards. Customers can call at any time with questions or concerns; call-center employees are trained to resolve complaints quickly and to the customer's satisfaction. To show that it's serious about service, Ocado offers an on-time delivery guarantee. Thanks to its superior service, Ocado has expanded rapidly and now delivers 77,000 customer orders every week.[40]

of payroll and human resources services with 43,000 clients nationwide. Paychex regularly appears on *Fortune*'s very competitive "100 Best Companies to Work For" list because it's a place where, in the words of its CEO, ". . . employees can't wait to get to work—a place where employees are genuinely valued and where their opinions matter."[41]

MANAGING SERVICE BRANDS

Some of the world's strongest brands are services—consider financial service leaders such as Citigroup, American Express, and HSBC. To build their brands, marketers must be skillful at differentiating their services and developing appropriate brand strategies.

Differentiating Services

Service marketers frequently complain about the difficulty of differentiating their services. The deregulation of major service industries—communications, transportation, energy, and banking—has resulted in intense price competition. To the extent that customers view a service as fairly homogeneous, they care less about the provider than the price.

Marketers can differentiate service offerings in many ways. One way is to offer innovative features that go beyond the *primary service package* that the customer expects. Vanguard, the second-largest no-load mutual fund company, has a unique client ownership structure that lowers costs and permits better fund returns. Strongly differentiated from many competitors, the brand grew through word of mouth, public relations, and viral marketing.[42]

The firm can add *secondary service features* to its offering. In the hotel industry, various chains have introduced such secondary service features as merchandise for sale, free breakfast buffets, and loyalty reward programs. Many companies use the Web to offer secondary service features that were never possible before. Conversely, other service providers are adding a human element to combat competition from online businesses. Sometimes the firm achieves differentiation through the sheer range of its service offerings and the success of its cross-selling efforts. The major challenge is that most service offerings and innovations are easily copied. Still, the firm that regularly innovates will gain a succession of temporary advantages over competitors.

Developing Brand Strategies for Services

Marketers of service offerings must pay special attention to choosing brand elements, establishing image dimensions, and devising the branding strategy.

Choosing Brand Elements Because services are intangible, and because customers often make decisions and arrangements about them away from the actual service location itself (at home or at work), brand recall becomes critically important. Therefore, an easy-to-remember name is essential. Logos, symbols, characters, and slogans can complement the name to build awareness and image. These other elements often attempt to make the service and some of its key benefits more tangible, concrete, and real, as the "good hands" do for Allstate insurance.

In addition, the physical facilities of the service provider—its signage, environmental design and reception area, apparel, collateral material, and so on—are especially important. All aspects of the service delivery process can be branded, which is why UPS has developed such strong equity with its brown trucks.

Establishing Image Dimensions Given the human nature of services, it's no surprise that brand personality is an important image dimension for services. Starwood trains its hotel employees and call center operators to convey different experiences for the different hotel chains: Sheraton is positioned as warm, comforting, and casual; Westin is positioned in terms of renewal and is a little more formal; Four Points by Sheraton is designed to be all about honest, uncomplicated comfort.[43] Service firms can also design marketing communication and information programs so that consumers learn more about the brand than the information they get from service encounters alone.

Devising Branding Strategy Finally, services also must consider developing a brand hierarchy and brand portfolio that permit positioning and targeting of different market segments. Marketers can brand classes of service vertically on the basis of price and quality. Vertical extensions often require sub-branding strategies that combine the corporate name with an individual brand name or modifier. To illustrate, Hilton Hotels has a portfolio of brands that includes Hilton Garden Inns to target budget-conscious business travelers and compete with the Courtyard by Marriott chain, as well as DoubleTree, Embassy Suites, and Hampton Inn.

Cirque du Soleil (French for "circus of the sun") has successfully built its brand by breaking loose from circus convention. It showcases talented trapeze artists, clowns, and other performers in a nontraditional circus setting with lavish costumes, New Age music, and spectacular stage designs. Each production is tied together with a theme such as "a phantasmagoria of urban life" (*Saltimbanco*). Now Cirque du Soleil has grown into a half-billion dollar enterprise and put its brand on a record label, a retail operation, and other ventures.[44]

MANAGING PRODUCT SUPPORT SERVICES

Among product marketers, *product support services* have become a major battleground for competitive advantage. Some equipment companies, such as John Deere, make over 50% of their profits from these services. In the global marketplace, companies that make a good product but provide poor local service support are seriously disadvantaged.

Identifying and Satisfying Customer Needs

In general, customers have three worries.[45] First, they worry about reliability and *failure frequency*. A farmer may tolerate a combine that breaks down once a year, but not more often. The second issue is *downtime*. The longer the downtime, the higher the cost, which is why customers count on *service dependability*—the seller's ability to fix the product quickly or at least provide a loaner.[46] The third issue is *out-of-pocket costs*. How much will maintenance and repairs cost?

A buyer considers all of these factors and tries to estimate the **life-cycle cost**, which is the product's purchase cost plus the discounted cost of maintenance and repair less the discounted salvage value. To provide the best support, a manufacturer must identify which services its customers value the most and their relative importance.

Manufacturers of medical equipment, for example, offer *facilitating services* such as installation, repairs, and financing. They may also add *value-augmenting services* that extend beyond the product's functioning and performance.

A manufacturer can offer and charge for enhanced product support services in different ways. One specialty organic chemical company provides a standard offering plus a basic level of services. If an industrial customer wants additional services, it can pay extra or increase its annual purchases to a higher level, in which case additional services would be included. Many companies offer *service contracts* (also called *extended warranties*), agreeing to provide free maintenance and repair services for a specified period at a specified contract price.

Product companies must understand their strategic intent and competitive advantage in developing services. Are service units supposed to support or protect existing product businesses or to grow as an independent platform? Are the sources of competitive advantage based on economies of scale or economies of skill?[47]

Post-Sale Service Strategy

In providing post-sale service, most companies progress through a series of stages. Manufacturers usually start out by running their own parts and service department because they want to stay close to their products and learn about problems right away. They also find it expensive and time consuming to train others. Often, they discover that they can make good money running the parts-and-service business—especially if they're the only supplier of the needed parts and can charge premium prices. In fact, many equipment manufacturers price their equipment low and compensate by charging high prices for parts and service.

Over time, manufacturers switch more maintenance and repair services to authorized distributors and dealers. These intermediaries are closer to customers, operate in more locations, and can offer quicker service. Still later, independent service firms emerge. Independent service organizations handle computers, telecommunications products, and other items, typically offering lower prices or faster service.

Customer service choices are increasing rapidly, however, and equipment manufacturers have to find new ways of making money on their products, independent of service contracts. Some new car warranties cover 100,000 miles before servicing. The increase in disposable or never-fail equipment makes customers less inclined to pay from 2% to 10% of the purchase price every year for a service. Some business customers may find it cheaper to have their own service personnel handle maintenance and repair.

EXECUTIVE SUMMARY

A service is any act or performance, offered to one party by another, that is essentially intangible and does not result in the ownership of anything. It may or may not be tied to a physical product. Services are intangible, inseparable, variable, and perishable. Marketers must find ways to give tangibility to intangibles; increase the productivity of service providers; increase and standardize service quality; and match the supply of services with demand. Delivering services that maximize both customer satisfaction and company profitability can be challenging.

Holistic marketing of services requires: external marketing; internal marketing to motivate employees; and interactive marketing for both "high-tech" and "high-touch" emphasis. Customers' expectations play a critical role in their service experiences and evaluations. Firms must manage service quality by understanding the effects of each service encounter. Top service companies have a strategic concept, top-management commitment to quality, high standards, self-service technologies, systems for monitoring service performance and customer complaints, and an emphasis on employee and customer satisfaction. A service brand is differentiated through primary and secondary service features as well as appropriate brand strategies, often including multiple brand elements, brand hierarchies and portfolios, and image dimensions to reinforce or complement service offerings. Even product-based firms must provide support services, identify the most valued services, understand their relative importance, and plan for post-sale services.

NOTES

1. Leonard L. Berry and Kent D. Seltman, "Building a Strong Services Brand: Lessons from Mayo Clinic," *Business Horizons* 50 (May 2007): 199–209; Leonard L. Berry and Neeli Bendapudi, "Clueing in Customers," *Harvard Business Review* (February 2003): 100–106; John La Forgia, Kent Seltman, and Scott Swanson, "Mayo Clinic: Sustaining a Legacy Brand and Leveraging its Equity in the 21st Century Market," Presentation at the Marketing Science Institute's Conference on Brand Orchestration, Orlando, FL, December 4–5, 2003; Leonard L. Berry, "Leadership Lessons from Mayo Clinic," *Organizational Dynamics*, 33 (August 2004): 228–242.

2. Leonard L. Berry, *On Great Service: A Framework for Action* (New York: The Free Press, 2006); Leonard L. Berry, *Discovering the Soul of Service: The Nine Drivers of Sustainable Business Success* (New York: The Free Press, 1999); Fred Wiersema, ed., *Customer Service: Extraordinary Results at Southwest Airlines, Charles Schwab, Lands' End, American Express, Staples, and USAA* (New York: HarperBusiness, 1998). For a thorough review of academic research into services, see Roland T. Rust and Tuck Siong Chung, "Marketing Models of Service and Relationships," *Marketing Science* 25 (November–December 2006): 560–580.

3. See Valarie A. Zeithaml, "How Consumer Evaluation Processes Differ between Goods and Services," in J. Donnelly and W. R. George, eds., *Marketing of Services* (Chicago: American Marketing Association, 1981), pp. 186–190.

4. Amy Ostrom and Dawn Iacobucci, "Consumer Trade-Offs and the Evaluation of Services," *Journal of Marketing* (January 1995): 17–28.

5. For discussion of how the blurring of the line distinguishing products and services changes the meaning of this taxonomy, see Christopher Lovelock and Evert Gummesson, "Whither Services Marketing? In Search of a New Paradigm and Fresh Perspectives," *Journal of Service Research* 7 (August 2004): 20–41 and Stephen L. Vargo and Robert F. Lusch, "Evolving to a New Dominant Logic for Marketing," *Journal of Marketing* 68 (January 2004): 1–17.

6. See Theodore Levitt, "Marketing Intangible Products and Product Intangibles," *Harvard Business Review* (May–June 1981): 94–102; Leonard L. Berry, "Services Marketing Is Different," *Business* (May–June 1980): 24–30.

7. B. H. Booms and M. J. Bitner, "Marketing Strategies and Organizational Structures for Service Firms," in J. Donnelly and W. R. George, eds., *Marketing of Services* (Chicago: American Marketing Association, 1981), pp. 47–51.

8. Lewis P. Carbone and Stephan H. Haeckel, "Engineering Customer Experiences," *Marketing Management* 3 (Winter 1994): 17.

9. Bernd H. Schmitt, *Customer Experience Management* (New York: John Wiley & Sons, 2003).

10. The material in this paragraph is based in part on Chapter 9 of Valarie Zeithaml, Mary Jo Bitner, and Dwayne D. Gremler, *Services Marketing: Integrating Customer Focus across the Firm*, 4th ed. (New York: McGraw-Hill, 2006).

11. Jeffrey F. Rayport, Bernard J. Jaworski, and Ellie J. Kyung, "Best Face Forward: Improving Companies' Service Interface with Customers," *Journal of Interactive Marketing* 19 (Autumn 2005): 67–80; Asim Ansari and Carl F. Mela, "E-customization," *Journal of Marketing Research* 40 (May 2003): 131–145.

12. Gila E. Fruchter and Eitan Gerstner (1999) "Selling with 'Satisfaction Guaranteed,'" *Journal of Service Research* 1 (4): 313–323. See also Rebecca J. Slotegraaf and J. Jeffrey Inman, "Longitudinal Shifts in the Drivers of Satisfaction with Product Quality: The Role of Attribute Resolvability," *Journal of Marketing Research* 41 (August 2004): 269–280.
13. W. Earl Sasser, "Match Supply and Demand in Service Industries," *Harvard Business Review* (November–December 1976): 133–140.
14. Carol Krol, "Case Study: Club Med Uses E-Mail to Pitch Unsold, Discounted Packages," *Advertising Age*, December 14, 1998, p. 40; www.clubmed.com.
15. Seth Godin, "If It's Broke, Fix It," *Fast Company*, October 2003, p. 131.
16. Kenneth Hein, "Communications Breakdown: Why Brands Can't Connect," *Brandweek*, February 19, 2007, p. 10.
17. Mary Clingman, "Turkey Talker," *Fortune*, November 27, 2006, p. 70.
18. Bruce Horovitz, "Whatever Happened to Customer Service?" *USA Today*, September 26, 2003, p. A1.
19. "Southwest Airlines to Cut 'Cattle Call,'" *BusinessWeek*, September 19, 2007, businessweek.com; "Southwest's Kelleher Sets Deal to Stay On at Airline," *Wall Street Journal*, July 20, 2007, p. B4; Barney Gimbel, "Southwest's New Flight Plan," *Fortune*, May 16, 2005, pp. 93–98; Eva Kaplan-Leiserson, "Strategic Service," *Training and Development* (November 2003): 14–16; Andy Serwer, "Southwest Airlines: The Hottest Thing in the Sky," *Fortune*, March 8, 2004.
20. Stephen S. Tax, Mark Colgate, and David Bowen, "How to Prevent Your Customers from Failing," *MIT Sloan Management Review* (Spring 2006): 30–38; Mei Xue and Patrick T. Harker (2002), "Customer Efficiency: Concept and Its Impact on E-Business Management," *Journal of Service Research* 4 (4): 253–267; Matthew L. Meuter, Amy L. Ostrom, Robert I. Roundtree, and Mary Jo Bitner (2000), "Self-Service Technologies: Understanding Customer Satisfaction with Technology-Based Service Encounters," *Journal of Marketing* 64 (3): 50–64.
21. Valarie Zeithaml, Mary Jo Bitner, and Dwayne D. Gremler, *Services Marketing: Integrating Customer Focus Across the Firm*, 4th ed. (New York: McGraw-Hill, 2006).
22. Tax, Colgate, and Bowen, "How to Prevent Your Customers from Failing."
23. Susan M. Keaveney, "Customer Switching Behavior in Service Industries: An Exploratory Study," *Journal of Marketing* (April 1995): 71–82. See also Michael D. Hartline and O. C. Ferrell, "The Management of Customer-Contact Service Employees: An Empirical Investigation," *Journal of Marketing* (October 1996): 52–70; Lois A. Mohr, Mary Jo Bitner, and Bernard H. Booms, "Critical Service Encounters: The Employee's Viewpoint," *Journal of Marketing* (October 1994): 95–106; Linda L. Price, Eric J. Arnould, and Patrick Tierney, "Going to Extremes: Managing Service Encounters and Assessing Provider Performance," *Journal of Marketing* (April 1995): 83–97; Jaishankar Ganesh, Mark J. Arnold, and Kristy E. Reynolds, "Understanding the Customer Base of Service Providers: An Examination of the Differences between Switchers and Stayers," *Journal of Marketing* 64 (July 2000): 65–87.
24. Christian Gronroos, "A Service Quality Model and Its Marketing Implications," *European Journal of Marketing* 18, no. 4 (1984): 36–44.
25. Leonard Berry, "Big Ideas in Services Marketing," *Journal of Consumer Marketing* (Spring 1986): 47–51. See also Walter E. Greene, Gary D. Walls, and Larry J. Schrest, "Internal Marketing: The Key to External Marketing Success," *Journal of Services Marketing* 8, no. 4 (1994): 5–13; John R. Hauser, Duncan I. Simester, and Birger Wernerfelt, "Internal Customers and Internal Suppliers," *Journal of Marketing Research* (August 1996): 268–280; Jagdip Singh, "Performance Productivity and Quality of Frontline Employees in Service Organizations," *Journal of Marketing* 64 (April 2000): 15–34.
26. Gronroos, "A Service Quality Model and Its Marketing Implications," pp. 38–39; Michael D. Hartline, James G. Maxham III, and Daryl O. McKee, "Corridors of Influence in the Dissemination of Customer-Oriented Strategy to Customer Contact Service Employees," *Journal of Marketing* (April 2000): 35–50.
27. "Hospital Uses PDA App for Patient Transport," *Health Data Management*, June 2007, p. 14.
28. Betsy Morris, "Charles Schwab's Big Challenge," *Fortune*, May 30, 2005; John Batelle, "Charles Schwab, Back from the Brink," *Business 2.0*, March 2006; "Q&A with Becky Saeger, CMO, Charles Schwab," *ANA Marketing Musings*, September 11, 2006.

29. Roland T. Rust and Katherine N. Lemon (2001), E-Service and the Consumer," *International Journal of Electronic Commerce* 5 (3): 83–99. See also Balaji Padmanabhan and Alexander Tuzhilin (2003), "On the Use of Optimization for Data Mining: Theoretical Interactions and eCRM opportunities," *Management Science* 49 (10): 1327–1343; B. P. S. Murthi and Sumit Sarkar, "The Role of the Management Sciences in Research on Personalization," *Management Science*, 49 (10): 1344–1362.
30. Roland T. Rust, P. K. Kannan and Na Peng (2002), "The Economics of Internet Privacy," *Journal of the Academy of Marketing Science* 30 (4): 455–464.
31. Glenn B. Voss, A. Parasuraman, and Dhruv Grewal, "The Role of Price, Performance, and Expectations in Determining Satisfaction in Service Exchanges," *Journal of Marketing* 62 (October 1998): 46–61.
32. Michael K. Brady and J. Joseph Cronin Jr., "Some New Thoughts on Conceptualizing Perceived Service Quality," *Journal of Marketing* 65 (July 2001): 34–49; A. Parasuraman, Valarie A. Zeithaml, and Leonard L. Berry, "A Conceptual Model of Service Quality and Its Implications for Future Research," *Journal of Marketing* (Fall 1985): 41–50. See also Susan J. Devlin and H. K. Dong, "Service Quality from the Customers' Perspective," *Marketing Research: A Magazine of Management and Applications* (Winter 1994): 4–13; William Boulding, Ajay Kalra, and Richard Staelin, "A Dynamic Process Model of Service Quality: From Expectations to Behavioral Intentions," *Journal of Marketing Research* (February 1993): 7–27.
33. Leonard L. Berry and A. Parasuraman, *Marketing Services: Competing Through Quality* (New York: The Free Press, 1991), p. 16.
34. James L. Heskett, W. Earl Sasser, Jr., and Christopher W. L. Hart, *Service Breakthroughs* (New York: Free Press, 1990).
35. Leonard L. Berry, Kathleen Seiders, and Dhruv Grewal, "Understanding Service Convenience," *Journal of Marketing* 66 (July 2002): 1–17.
36. Mary Jo Bitner, "Self-Service Technologies: What Do Customers Expect?" *Marketing Management* (Spring 2001): 10–11; Matthew L. Meuter, Amy L. Ostrom, Robert J. Roundtree, and Mary Jo Bitner, "Self-Service Technologies: Understanding Customer Satisfaction with Technology-Based Service Encounters," *Journal of Marketing* 64 (July 2000): 50–64.
37. Jeffrey F. Rayport and Bernard J. Jaworski, "Best Face Forward," *Harvard Business Review*, 82 (December 2004): 47–58; Jeffrey F. Rayport and Bernard J. Jaworski, *Best Face Forward* (Boston, MA: Harvard Business School Press, 2005); Jeffrey F. Rayport, Bernard J. Jaworski, and Ellie J. Kyung, "Best Face Forward," *Journal of Interactive Marketing* 19 (Autumn 2005): 67–80.
38. Matthew L. Meuter, Mary Jo Bitner, Amy L. Ostrom, and Stephen W. Brown, "Choosing among Alternative Service Delivery Modes: An Investigation of Customer Trial of Self-Service Technologies," *Journal of Marketing* 69 (April 2005): 61–83.
39. Claes Fornell and Birger Wernerfelt, "A Model for Customer Complaint Management," *Marketing Science* 7 (Summer 1988): 271–286; Stephen S. Tax and Stephen W. Brown, "Recovering and Learning from Service Failures," *Sloan Management Review* (Fall 1998): 75–88; Jeffrey G. Blodgett and Ronald D. Anderson (2000), "A Bayesian Network Model of the Customer Complaint Process," *Journal of Service Research* 2 (4): 321–338.
40. "Ocado Ups Its Game in Bid to Compete with Supermarkets," *Grocer*, July 7, 2007, p. 6; Claire Armitt, "Strategic Play—Ocado," *New Media Age*, August 11, 2005, pp. 16+; "Customer Service: Disaffected Nation," *Marketing*, June 8, 2005, p. 32; Julie Demers, "Service Drives a New Program," *CMA Management*, May 2002, pp. 36+; Robert Geier, "How to Create Disaster Recovery Plans for Customer Contact Operations," *Customer Contact Management Report*, January 2002, pp. 1+; Don Merit, "Dealing with Irate Customers," *American Printer*, October 2001, p. 66.
41. Philip Walzer, " 'Best to Work for' Companies Have Happy, and Loyal, Employees," *Knight Ridder Tribune Business News*, January 28, 2007, p. 1.
42. Amy Barrett, "Vanguard Gets Personal," *BusinessWeek*, October 3, 2005, pp. 115–118; Carolyn Marconi and Donna MacFarland, "Growth by Marketing under the Radar," presentation made at Marketing Science Institute Board of Trustees Meeting: Pathways to Growth, November 7, 2002.
43. Mike Beirne and Javier Benito, "Starwood Uses Personnel to Personalize Marketing," *Brandweek*, April 24, 2006, p. 9.
44. Linda Tischler, "Join the Circus," *Fast Company*, July 2005, 53–58; Cirque du Soliel, *America's Greatest Brands*, Vol III, 2004; Geoff Keighley, "The Phantasmagoria Factory," *Business 2.0*, February 2004, p. 102; Robin D. Rusch, "Cirque du Soleil—Contorts," brandchannel.com, December 1, 2003.

45. Mark Vandenbosch and Niraj Dawar, "Beyond Better Products: Capturing Value in Customer Interactions," *MIT Sloan Management Review* 43 (Summer 2002), 35–42; Milind M. Lele and Uday S. Karmarkar, "Good Product Support Is Smart Marketing," *Harvard Business Review* (November–December 1983): 124–132.
46. Research on the effects of service delays on service evaluations: Shirley Taylor, "Waiting for Service: The Relationship between Delays and Evaluations of Service," *Journal of Marketing* (April 1994): pp. 56–69; Michael K. Hui and David K. Tse, "What to Tell Customers in Waits of Different Lengths," *Journal of Marketing* (April 1996): 81–90.
47. Byron G. Auguste, Eric P. Harmon, and Vivek Pandit, "The Right Service Strategies for Product Companies," *McKinsey Quarterly*, Number 1, 2006, 41–51.

CHAPTER 12

Developing Pricing Strategies and Programs

> In this chapter, we will address the following questions:
>
> 1. How do consumers process and evaluate prices?
> 2. How should a company set prices initially for its offerings?
> 3. How should a company adapt prices to meet varying circumstances and opportunities?
> 4. How should a company initiate a price change and respond to a competitor's price change?

MARKETING MANAGEMENT AT GILLETTE

Gillette has a long tradition of product innovation, beginning when King C. Gillette invented the safety razor in 1901. That tradition continues to generate impressive revenues and profits for Gillette, now owned by Procter & Gamble. For instance, sales of Gillette's Mach 3, the first triple blade system, have topped $16 billion since the razor debuted in 1998. In 2006, the company introduced the Fusion—with five blades in the front for regular shaving and one in the back for trimming—in both power and non-power versions. Within four weeks, the Fusion (backed by strong advertising and distribution) had captured a 55% market share. Gillette's newest Venus razors for women are increasingly popular, as well.

Although Gillette invests heavily in research and development as well as in marketing, the payoff is enormous: It holds an impressive 70% share of the global market for razors and blades. Moreover, its products command sizable price premiums. A four-pack of blades for the

Fusion Power costs $14, compared to $5.29 for a five-pack of Sensor Excel blades. The bottom line for smart pricing is significant, sustained profitability for Gillette and parent P&G.[1]

As Gillette's marketers know, price is the one marketing-mix element that produces revenue; the others produce costs. Price is perhaps the easiest element to adjust; changing product features, channels, and promotions take more time. Price also communicates the product or brand's intended value positioning to the market. Yet pricing decisions are complex and difficult—and many marketers neglect their pricing strategies.[2] Holistic marketers must take into account numerous factors when making pricing decisions, including the company, customers, competition, and marketing environment. This chapter discusses how marketers set and adjust prices.

UNDERSTANDING PRICING

Price is not just a number on a tag. Price comes in many forms and performs many functions, whether it's called rent, tuition, fare, or interest. Throughout most of history, prices were set by negotiation between buyers and sellers. Setting one price for all buyers arose with the development of large-scale retailing at the end of the 19th century, when many stores followed a "strictly one-price policy" because they carried so many items and had so many employees.

A Changing Pricing Environment

Today, the Internet is partially reversing the fixed pricing trend. As one industry observer noted, "We are moving toward a very sophisticated economy. It's kind of an arms race between merchant technology and consumer technology."[3] The Internet allows sellers to discriminate between buyers and buyers to discriminate between sellers in a variety of ways. Buyers can get instant price comparisons from thousands of vendors; name their price and have it met; and get products free. Sellers can monitor customer behavior and tailor offers to individuals as well as giving certain customers access to special prices. And both buyers and sellers can negotiate prices in online auctions and exchanges.[4] See "Marketing Skills: Giving It Away" for a discussion of how companies can profit when marketers give some offerings away.

How Companies Price

In small companies, the boss often sets prices. In large companies, division and product-line managers handle pricing. Even here, top management sets general pricing objectives and policies and often approves the prices proposed by lower levels of management. In industries where pricing is a key factor (aerospace, railroads, oil companies), companies will often establish a pricing department to set or assist others in determining appropriate prices. This department reports to the marketing department, finance department, or top management. Others who can influence pricing include sales managers, production managers, finance managers, and accountants.

Executives complain that pricing is a big headache. Some firms focus on costs and strive for the industry's traditional margins. Other common mistakes are not revising price often enough to capitalize on market changes; setting price independently rather than as an intrinsic element of market-positioning strategy; and not varying price enough for different products, segments, channels, and purchase occasions.

MARKETING SKILLS: GIVING IT AWAY

More and more firms are using a "freemium" strategy, giving some of their offerings away for free while profiting from extras that are priced appropriately. Skype, for instance, offers its Internet calling software for free but charges for calls that customers make to non-Internet phones. Planning to give something away is actually trickier than it sounds: "Only one in ten companies will succeed at pulling this off," says Howard Anderson of the MIT Entrepreneurship Center. How can marketers do a good job of planning to give goods or services away? First, the offering must be superior and the fee-based extras should be part of the plan from the beginning. Second, never change a free product to a fee product, because that will alienate loyal customers. Finally, have a number of revenue sources to cover the cost of the free offering.

The European discount airline Ryanair has profited by charging for almost—but not quite—everything. A quarter of Ryanair's seats are free today, and the ultimate goal is for all seats to be free, with passengers paying only taxes and fees (which means an average one-way fare of roughly $52). Passengers pay extra for nearly everything else: checked luggage, snacks, and merchandise such as digital cameras. Ryanair also generates revenue by turning its planes into giant billboards for Hertz and others. With this pricing strategy, Ryanair enjoys net margins of 18%, more than double the 7% margins of Southwest Airlines.[5]

Now companies like General Electric are implementing more disciplined approaches to pricing. At GE, the CMO leads the pricing initiative and each business unit has a head of pricing who reports to the CMO. In addition, a Global Pricing Council helps pricing leaders from each unit spread best practices across the company.[6]

Effectively designing and implementing pricing strategies requires a thorough understanding of consumer psychology and a systematic approach to setting, adapting, and changing prices.

Consumer Psychology and Pricing

Many economists assume that consumers accept prices as given. Marketers recognize that consumers often actively process price information, interpreting prices in terms of their knowledge from prior purchasing experience, formal communications (advertising, sales calls, and brochures), informal communications (friends, colleagues, or family members), point-of-purchase or online resources, and other factors.[7] Purchase decisions are based on how consumers perceive prices and what they consider to be the current actual price—*not* the marketer's stated price. Customers may have a lower price threshold below which prices signal inferior or unacceptable quality, as well as an upper threshold above which offerings are seen as not worth the money.

- *Reference prices.* Although consumers may have fairly good knowledge of the price range involved, surprisingly few can recall specific product prices accurately.[8] Consumers often employ a **reference price**, comparing a product's price to an internal reference price they remember or an external frame of reference such as a posted "regular retail price."[9] Sellers may manipulate these reference prices by situating a product among expensive products to imply that it belongs in the same class; stating a high manufacturer's suggested price; or pointing to a rival's high price.[10] Consumer expectations also play a key role. In the case of online auction sites such as eBay, when consumers know similar goods will be available in future auctions, they will bid less in the current auction.[11]

- *Price-quality inferences.* Many consumers use price as an indicator of quality. Image pricing is especially effective with ego-sensitive products such as perfumes and expensive cars. A $100 bottle of perfume might contain $10 worth of scent, but gift givers pay $100 to communicate their high regard for the receiver. Price and quality perceptions of cars interact.[12] Higher-priced cars are perceived to be high quality; higher-quality cars are perceived to be higher priced than they actually are. When alternative information about true quality is available, price becomes a less significant indicator of quality. And for luxury-goods buyers who desire uniqueness, demand may actually increase with higher prices, as they may believe that fewer others will be able to afford the product.[13]

- *Price cues.* Consumers tend to process prices in a "left-to-right" manner rather than by rounding.[14] Thus, many will see an item priced at $299 as in the $200 price range rather than the $300 range. Price encoding in this fashion is important if there is a mental price break at the higher, rounded price. Prices ending in odd numbers also may convey the idea of a discount or bargain, so firms with high-price images should avoid this tactic.[15]

SETTING THE PRICE

A company must consider many factors in setting a product's price.[16] A firm must set a price when it introduces a new product, launches its regular product into a new distribution channel or geographical area, or bids on contract work. The six-step procedure for setting pricing policy is: (1) select the pricing objective; (2) determine demand; (3) estimate costs; (4) analyze competitors' costs, prices, and offers; (5) select a pricing method; and (6) select the final price.

Step 1: Selecting the Pricing Objective

A company can pursue any of five major objectives through pricing: survival, maximum current profit, maximum market share, maximum market skimming, or product-quality leadership. *Survival* is a short-term objective that is appropriate for companies plagued with overcapacity, intense competition, or changing consumer wants. As long as prices cover variable costs and some fixed costs, the company stays in business.

To gain the *maximum current profit*, companies estimate the demand and costs associated with alternative prices and then choose the price that produces maximum current profit, cash flow, or return on investment. However, by emphasizing current profits, the company may sacrifice long-run performance by ignoring the effects of other marketing-mix variables, competitors' reactions, and legal restraints on price.

Some firms want *maximum market share*, believing that higher sales volume will lead to lower unit costs and higher long-run profit. With **market-penetration pricing**, the firm sets the lowest price, assuming the market is price sensitive. This is appropriate when the market is highly price sensitive and a low price stimulates market growth; production and distribution costs fall with accumulated production experience; and a low price discourages competition.

Other companies favor setting high prices to "skim" the market. **Market-skimming pricing,** in which prices start high and slowly drop over time, makes sense when enough buyers have high current demand; the unit costs of producing a small volume are not so high that they cancel the advantage of charging what the traffic will bear; the high initial price does not attract more competitors; and the high price communicates the image of a superior product.

Companies that aim to be *product-quality leaders* can either offer affordable luxuries at prices just high enough not to be out of reach (such as Starbucks coffee) or products combining quality, luxury, and premium prices (such as Absolut super-premium vodka). Nonprofit and public organizations may adopt other pricing objectives. A university aims for *partial cost recovery*, knowing it must rely on private gifts and public grants to cover the remaining costs, while a nonprofit theater company sets prices to fill the maximum number of seats.

Step 2: Determining Demand

Each price will lead to a different level of demand and will have a different impact on a company's marketing objectives. A demand curve shows the relationship between price and demand. Normally, demand and price are inversely related: The higher the price, the lower the demand. For prestige goods, the demand curve sometimes slopes upward because some consumers take the higher price to signify a better product. Yet if the price is too high, demand may fall.

Influences on Price Sensitivity The demand curve shows the market's probable purchase quantity at alternative prices, summing the reactions of many individuals who have different price sensitivities. The first step in estimating demand is to understand what affects price sensitivity. Generally speaking, customers are less price-sensitive to low-cost items or items they buy infrequently. On the other hand, a seller can charge a higher price than competitors and still get the business if the customer perceives that it offers the lowest *total cost of ownership* (TCO).

Companies, of course, prefer customers who are less price-sensitive. Table 12.1 shows some factors associated with less price sensitivity. Firms need to understand customers' and prospects' price sensitivity and the trade-offs people are willing to make between price and product characteristics. Targeting only price-sensitive consumers may mean "leaving money on the table."

TABLE 12.1   Some Factors Leading to Less Price Sensitivity

- The expenditure is small relative to the buyer's income.
- Others pay part of the purchase price.
- The cost of switching suppliers is high.
- The buyer can't easily compare suppliers.
- The cost of not getting the expected benefits is high.
- The product is a small part of the cost to obtain an important benefit.
- The price is a proxy for the product's likely quality.
- The price is within the range buyers perceive as "fair" or "reasonable."

Source: Adapted from Thomas T. Nagle and John E. Hogan, *The Strategy and Tactics of Pricing*, 4th ed. (Upper Saddle River, NJ: Pearson Prentice Hall, 2006), Exhibit 7-2, p. 130.

Estimating Demand Curves Companies can use one of three basic methods to estimate their demand curves. First, they can use surveys to explore about how many units consumers would buy at different proposed prices. However, consumers might understate their purchase intentions at higher prices to discourage the company from setting higher prices. Second, they can experiment by setting different prices in similar territories to see how sales are affected or test different prices online, being careful not to alienate customers.[17] A third method is to statistically analyze past prices, quantities sold, and other factors to reveal their relationships. However, building a model and fitting the data with the proper techniques calls for considerable skill.

In measuring the price–demand relationship, the marketer must control for various factors that will influence demand, such as competitive response.[18] Also, if the company changes other marketing-mix factors besides price, the effect of the price change itself will be hard to isolate.

Price Elasticity of Demand Marketers need to know how responsive, or elastic, demand would be to a change in price. If demand hardly changes with a small change in price, the demand is *inelastic*; if it changes considerably, it is *elastic*. The higher the elasticity, the greater the volume growth resulting from a 1% price reduction. If demand is elastic, sellers will consider cutting price to raise total revenue, especially when their costs for more units don't increase disproportionately.[19]

Price elasticity depends on the magnitude and direction of the contemplated price change. It may be negligible with a small price change and substantial with a large price change; it may differ for a price cut versus a price increase. Also, long-run price elasticity may differ from short-run elasticity. Buyers may continue to buy from a supplier after a price increase but they may eventually switch suppliers. The distinction between short-run and long-run elasticity means that sellers won't know the total effect of a price change until time passes.

One study reviewing a 40-year period of academic research projects investigating price elasticity found that price elasticity magnitudes were higher for durable goods than for other goods, and higher for products in the introduction/growth stages of the product life cycle than in the mature/decline stages. In addition, promotional price elasticities were higher than actual price elasticities in the short-run (although the reverse was true in the long-run).[20]

Step 3: Estimating Costs

Whereas demand sets a ceiling on the price of a company's product, costs set the floor. The company wants to charge a price that covers its cost of producing, distributing, and selling the product, including a fair return for its effort and risk.

Types of Costs and Levels of Production A company's costs take two forms. **Fixed costs** (also known as **overhead**) are costs that don't vary with production or sales revenue, such as payments for rent, heat, salaries, and other bills that must be paid regardless of output. **Variable costs** vary directly with the level of production. For example, each calculator produced by Texas Instruments (TI) incurs the cost of plastic, microprocessor chips, and packaging. These costs tend to be constant per unit produced, but they're called variable because their total varies with the number of units produced. **Total costs** are the sum of the fixed and variable costs for a given level of production. **Average cost** is the cost per unit at that level of production; it equals total costs divided by production. Management wants to charge a price that will at least cover the total production costs at a given level of production.

To price intelligently, management needs to know how its costs vary with different levels of production. The cost per unit is high if few units are produced every day, but as production increases, the average cost falls because the fixed costs are spread over more units. At some point, however, average cost may increase because the plant becomes inefficient (due to problems such as machines breaking down more often). By calculating costs for different-sized plants, a company can identify the optimal size and production level to achieve economies of scale and lower average cost.

To estimate the real profitability of selling to different retailers or customers, the manufacturer needs to use **activity-based cost (ABC) accounting** instead of standard cost accounting. ABC accounting tries to identify the real costs (both variable and overhead) associated with serving each customer. Companies that fail to measure their costs correctly are not measuring their profit correctly, and they are likely to misallocate their marketing effort.

Accumulated Production Suppose TI runs a plant that produces 3,000 hand calculators per day. As TI gains experience producing calculators, its methods improve. Workers learn shortcuts, materials flow more smoothly, and procurement costs fall. Then the average cost falls with accumulated production experience. Assume the average cost of producing the first 100,000 hand calculators is $10 per calculator. When TI has produced the first 200,000 calculators, the average cost falls to $9. After its accumulated production rises to 400,000, the average cost is $8. This decline in the average cost with accumulated production experience is called the **experience curve** or **learning curve**.

Now suppose TI competes against firms A and B in this industry, as shown in Figure 12.1. TI is the lowest-cost producer at $8, having produced 400,000 units in the past. If all three firms sell the calculator for $10, TI makes $2 profit per unit, A makes $1 per unit, and B breaks even. The smart move for TI would be to lower its price to $9 to drive B out of the market; even A will consider leaving. TI will pick up the business that would have gone to B (and possibly A). Also, price-sensitive customers will enter

FIGURE 12.1 Cost Per Unit as a Function of Accumulated Production: The Experience Curve

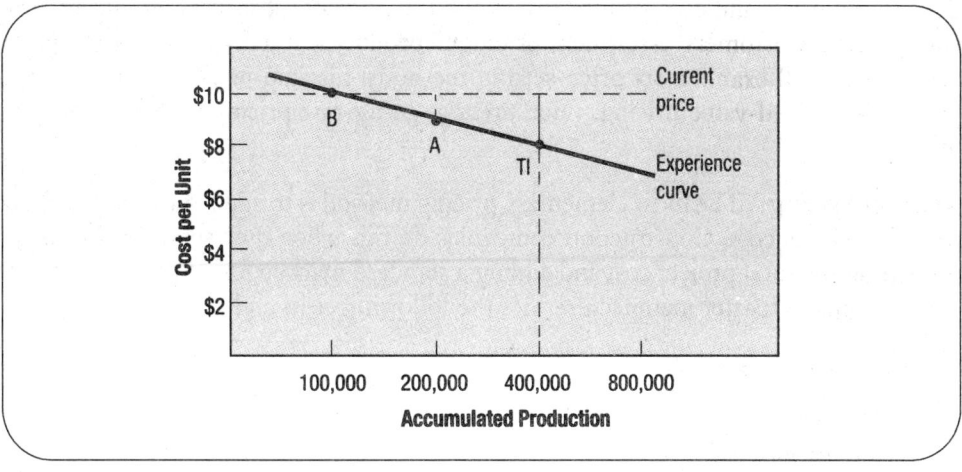

the market at the lower price. As production increases beyond 400,000 units, TI's costs will drop further, restoring profits even at a price of $9. TI has used this pricing strategy repeatedly to gain market share and drive others out of the industry.

Experience-curve pricing is risky because aggressive pricing may give the product a cheap image. The strategy also assumes that rivals are weak followers, and it may lead the firm into building more plants to meet demand. If a competitor innovates with a lower-cost technology, the leader will be stuck with the old technology.

Target Costing Costs change with production scale and experience. They can also change as a result of a concentrated effort by the company's designers, engineers, and purchasing agents to reduce them through **target costing**.[21] Market research establishes a new product's desired functions and the price at which it will sell, given its appeal and competitors' prices. Deducting the desired profit margin from this price leaves the target cost the marketer must achieve. The firm must examine each cost element—design, engineering, manufacturing, sales—and consider different ways to bring the final cost projections into the target cost range. If this is not possible, the firm should not develop the product because it can't sell for the target price and make the target profit.

Step 4: Analyzing Competitors' Costs, Prices, and Offers

Within the range of possible prices determined by market demand and company costs, the firm must take into account competitors' costs, prices, and possible price reactions. If the firm's offer contains features not offered by the nearest competitor, the marketer should evaluate their worth to the customer and add that value to the competitor's price. If the competitor's offer contains some features not offered by the firm, the marketer should subtract their value from its own price. Now the firm can decide whether it can charge more, the same, or less than the competitor, remembering that competitors can change their prices at any time.

Step 5: Selecting a Pricing Method

The three Cs—the customers' demand schedule, the cost function, and competitors' prices—are major considerations in selecting a price (see Figure 12.2). Costs set a floor to the price, and competitors' prices and the price of substitutes provide an orienting point. Customers' assessment of unique product features establishes the price ceiling. We will examine six price-setting methods: markup pricing, target-return pricing, perceived-value pricing, value pricing, going-rate pricing, and auction-type pricing.

Markup Pricing The most elementary pricing method is to add a standard **markup** to the product's cost. Construction companies do this when they submit job bids by estimating the total project cost and adding a standard markup for profit.

Suppose a toaster manufacturer has the following costs and sales expectations:

Variable cost per unit	$10
Fixed cost	$300,000
Expected unit sales	50,000

FIGURE 12.2 The Three Cs Model for Price Setting

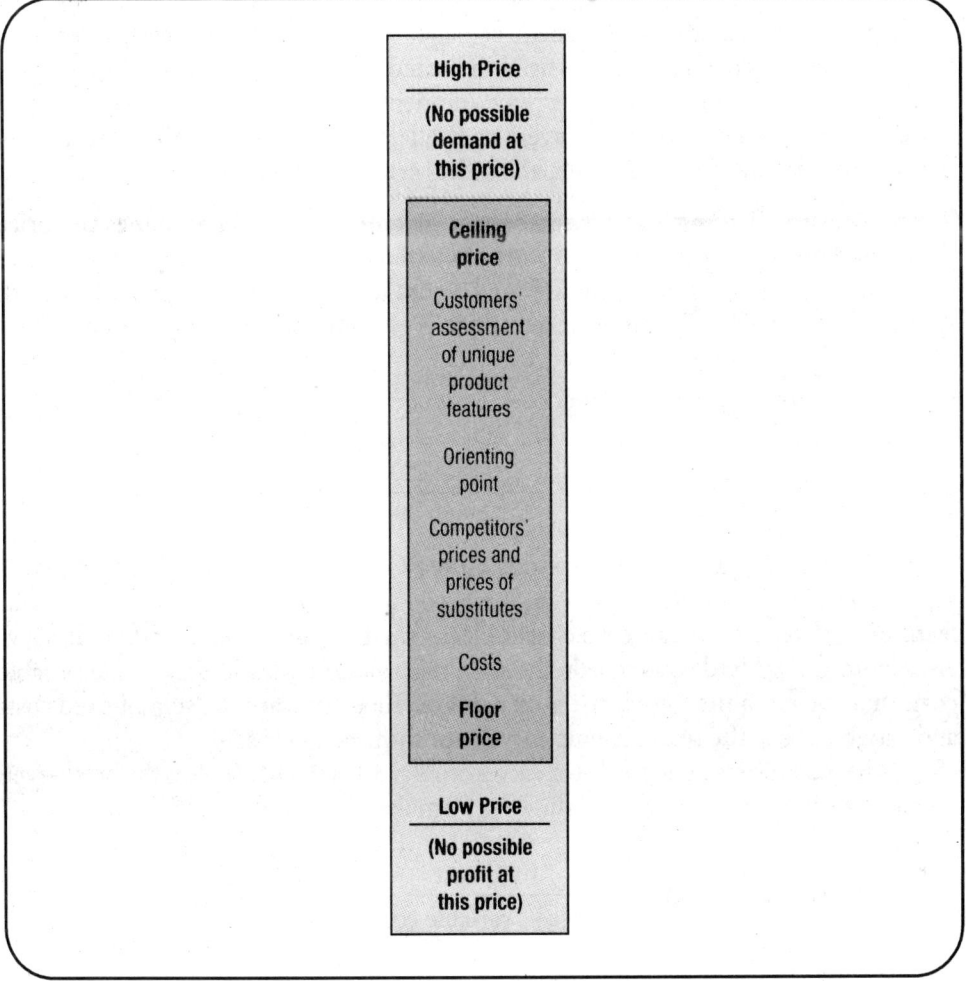

The manufacturer's unit cost is given by:

$$\text{Unit cost} = \text{variable cost} + \frac{\text{fixed costs}}{\text{unit sales}} = \$10 + \frac{\$300,000}{50,000} = \$16$$

If the manufacturer wants to earn a 20% markup on sales, its markup price is given by:

$$\text{Markup price} = \frac{\text{unit cost}}{(1 - \text{desired return on sales})} = \frac{\$16}{1 - 0.2} = \$20$$

The manufacturer charges dealers $20 per toaster and makes a profit of $4 per unit. If the dealers want to earn 50% on their selling price, they mark up the toaster 100% to $40.

Do standard markups make logical sense? Generally, no. Any pricing method that ignores current demand, perceived value, and competition is not likely to lead to the optimal price. Markup pricing works only if the price actually brings in the expected level of sales. Still, markup pricing remains popular because sellers can determine costs much more easily than they can estimate demand. By tying the price to cost, sellers simplify the pricing task. Also, where all firms in the industry use this pricing method, prices tend to be similar, which minimizes price competition. Finally, many people feel that markup pricing is fairer to both buyers and sellers. Sellers do not take advantage of buyers when demand becomes acute, and sellers earn a fair return on investment.

Target-Return Pricing In **target-return pricing**, the firm determines the price that would yield its target rate of return on investment (ROI). Suppose the toaster manufacturer has invested $1 million and wants to set a price to earn a 20% ROI, specifically $200,000. The target-return price is given by the following formula:

$$\text{Target-return price} = \text{unit cost} + \frac{\text{desired return} \times \text{invested capital}}{\text{unit sales}}$$

$$= \$16 + \frac{.20 \times \$1,000,000}{50,000} = \$20$$

The manufacturer will realize this 20% ROI provided its costs and estimated sales turn out to be accurate, but what if sales do not reach 50,000 units? The manufacturer can prepare a break-even chart to learn what would happen at other sales levels (Figure 12.3). Fixed costs remain the same regardless of sales volume, while variable costs (not shown in the figure) rise with volume. Total costs are the sum of fixed costs and variable costs; the total revenue curve rises with each unit sold.

The total revenue and total cost curves cross at 30,000 units. This is the break-even volume. It can be verified by the following formula:

$$\text{Break-even volume} = \frac{\text{fixed cost}}{(\text{price} - \text{variable cost})} = \frac{\$300,000}{\$20 - \$10} = 30,000$$

FIGURE 12.3 Break-Even Chart for Determining Target Return Price and Break-Even Volume

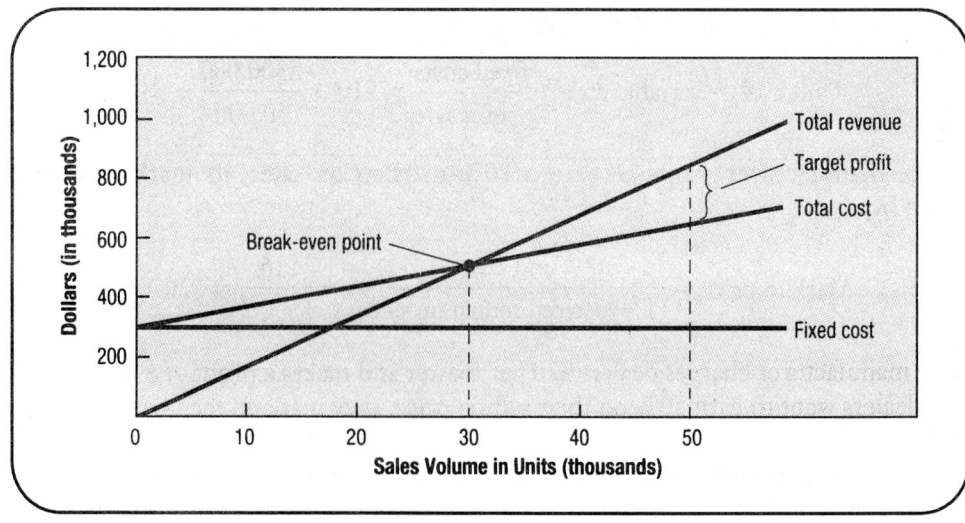

If the manufacturer sells 50,000 units at $20, it earns a $200,000 profit on its $1 million investment. However, much depends on price elasticity and competitors' prices, two elements ignored by target-return pricing. The manufacturer needs to consider different prices and estimate their probable impacts on sales volume and profits. It should also find ways to lower fixed or variable costs, because lower costs will decrease its required break-even volume.

Perceived Value Pricing An increasing number of firms now base their price on customers' *perceived value*. Perceived value is made up of several elements: the buyer's image of the product performance, the channel deliverables, warranty quality, customer support, and softer attributes such as the supplier's reputation and trustworthiness. Companies must deliver the value promised by their value proposition, and the customer must perceive this value. Firms use the other marketing-mix elements, such as advertising, to communicate and enhance perceived value in buyers' minds.[22]

Yet even when a company claims that its offering delivers more total value, not all customers will respond positively. A segment of buyers will always care only about the price. Other buyers suspect the company is exaggerating its product quality and services. One company installed its software system in a customer's plant to demonstrate the substantial cost savings—which convinced the customer to buy the software for its other plants.

The key to perceived-value pricing is to deliver more value than competitors and demonstrate this to buyers. A firm must understand the customer's decision-making process and the value of its offering, which it can do through managerial judgments, assessing similar products' value, focus groups, surveys, experimentation, analysis of historical data, and conjoint analysis.[23]

Value Pricing **Value pricing** is a method in which the firm wins loyal customers by charging a fairly low price for a high-quality offering. IKEA, Southwest Airlines, and Target practice value pricing. This is not a matter of simply setting lower prices; it means reengineering operations to become a low-cost producer without sacrificing quality, to attract a large number of value-conscious customers.

An important type of value pricing is **everyday low pricing (EDLP)**, which takes place at the retail level. Retailers using EDLP pricing charge a constant low price with few or no price promotions and special sales. These constant prices eliminate week-to-week price uncertainty and the "high-low" pricing of promotion-oriented competitors. In **high-low pricing**, the retailer charges higher prices on an everyday basis but then runs frequent promotions in which prices are temporarily lowered below the EDLP level.[24]

The most important reason retailers adopt EDLP is that constant sales and promotions are costly and erode consumer confidence in the credibility of everyday prices. Consumers also have less time and patience for such time-honored traditions as watching for specials and clipping coupons. Yet promotions do create excitement and draw shoppers. For this reason, EDLP is not a guarantee of success. As supermarkets face heightened competition from store rivals and alternative channels, many are drawing shoppers using a combination of high-low and EDLP strategies, with increased advertising and promotions.

Going-Rate Pricing In **going-rate pricing**, the firm bases its price largely on competitors' prices. The firm might charge the same, more, or less than major competitor(s).

In oligopolistic industries that sell a commodity such as steel or paper, all firms normally charge the same price. The smaller firms "follow the leader," changing prices when the leader's prices change rather than when their own demand or costs change. Some firms may charge a slight premium or discount, but they preserve the amount of difference. When costs are difficult to measure or competitive response is uncertain, firms adopt the going price because it seems to reflect the industry's collective wisdom.

Auction-Type Pricing Auction-type pricing is growing more popular, especially online. One major use is to dispose of excess inventories or used goods; another is to obtain goods and services at lower prices. "Breakthrough Marketing: eBay" discusses that company's pioneering of online auctions.

In *English auctions* (*ascending bids*), a seller offers to sell a product (such as an antique), and buyers raise their bids until the top price is reached. In *Dutch auctions* (*descending bids*), one seller may propose pricing to many buyers or one buyer may solicit bids from many sellers. In the first kind, an auctioneer announces a high price for a product and then decreases the price until a bidder accepts the price. In the other kind, buyers announce what they want to buy and potential sellers compete by offering the lowest price.

In *sealed-bid auctions*, each would-be supplier submits only one bid and cannot know the other bids. A supplier won't bid below its cost but can't bid too high for fear of losing the job. The net effect can be described in terms of the bid's *expected profit*. Using expected profit for setting price makes sense for the seller that makes many bids. It's not appropriate for the seller that bids only occasionally or needs a particular contract badly because it doesn't distinguish between a $1,000 profit with a 0.10 probability and a $125 profit with a 0.80 probability. Yet a firm that wants to keep production going would prefer the second contract to the first. Industrial firms also need to recognize how online auctions may affect their suppliers. If the increased savings a firm obtains in an online auction reduces profit margins for an incumbent supplier, the supplier may feel its customer is opportunistically squeezing out price concessions.[25]

BREAKTHROUGH MARKETING: EBAY

Pierre Omidyar started eBay as a way to help his girlfriend sell and trade Pez candy dispensers online. Soon eBay was hosting auctions for both consumers and businesses and later began offering a fixed-price "buy it now" option to those willing to pay the seller's price. Yet eBay doesn't buy any inventory or own the products featured on its site. Its $7.3 billion in annual sales come from auction fees and commissions plus revenues from acquired companies such as Skype (Internet communication), PayPal (online payments), shopping.com (comparison shopping), StubHub (online ticket resales), and rent.com (online apartment listings).

Recently, Yahoo! closed its North American auction business rather than try to compete with eBay. Germany is one of eBay's best markets, yet the firm is weak in Eastern Europe and has struggled in Asia. In fact, eBay withdrew from Japan, where Yahoo! Japan dominates, and its first venture into China failed. Now eBay is reentering the China market with a local partner, where it will seek to win trust by holding payments in escrow until buyers receive their purchases. What new pricing ideas will eBay use to keep profits flowing?[26]

Step 6: Selecting the Final Price

Pricing methods narrow the range from which the company selects its final price. In selecting that price, the company must consider factors such as the impact of other marketing activities, company pricing policies, gain-and-risk-sharing pricing, and the impact of price on other parties.

Impact of Other Marketing Activities The final price must take into account the brand's quality and advertising relative to competition. When Farris and Reibstein examined the relationships among relative price, relative quality, and relative advertising for 227 consumer businesses, they found that brands with average relative quality but high relative advertising budgets were able to charge premium prices. Consumers seemed willing to pay higher prices for known products than for unknown products. Also, brands with high relative quality and high relative advertising brought the highest prices, while brands with low quality and advertising had the lowest prices. The positive relationship between high prices and high advertising held most strongly late in the product life cycle for market leaders.[27]

Company Pricing Policies The price must be consistent with company pricing policies. General Electric and other firms have a pricing department to develop policies and establish or approve decisions. The aim is to ensure that salespeople quote prices that are reasonable to customers and profitable to the company. Some firms have initiated the policy of charging fees to raise revenue without really raising prices. For example, credit card companies now collect more than $17 billion annually in late payment fees and over-the-limit penalty fees.[28]

Gain-and-Risk-Sharing Pricing Buyers may resist a seller's proposal because of a high perceived level of risk. The seller has the option of offering to absorb part or all of the risk if it doesn't deliver the promised value. Baxter Healthcare, a medical products firm, was able to secure a contract for an information management system from Columbia/HCA, a health care provider, by guaranteeing several million dollars in savings over an eight-year period. An increasing number of firms, especially business marketers who promise great savings, may have to stand ready to guarantee promised savings, and possibly participate if the gains are much greater than expected.

Impact of Price on Other Parties Management must also consider the reactions of other parties to the contemplated price, including distributors, dealers, and the sales force. How will competitors react? Will suppliers raise their prices when they see the company's price? Will the government intervene and prevent this price from being charged? Moreover, marketers need to know the laws regulating pricing. Sellers can't talk to competitors about pricing and can't use deceptive pricing practices. For example, a company can't set artificially high "regular" prices, and then announce a "sale" at prices close to previous everyday prices.

ADAPTING THE PRICE

Companies usually don't set a single price but rather establish a pricing structure that reflects variations in geographical demand and costs, market-segment requirements, purchase timing, order levels, delivery frequency, guarantees, service contracts, and other factors. As a result of discounts, allowances, and promotions, a firm rarely realizes the same profit from each unit sold. Here we examine the price-adaptation strategies of geographical pricing, price discounts and allowances, promotional pricing, differentiated pricing, and product-mix pricing.

Geographical Pricing

In geographical pricing, the company decides how to price its products to different customers in different locations and countries. For example, should the company charge distant customers more to cover higher shipping costs or set a lower price to win additional business? Another issue is how to get paid. This is particularly critical when foreign buyers lack sufficient hard currency to pay for their purchases. Many buyers want to offer other items in payment; this is **countertrade**, which accounts for 15% to 25% of world trade and takes several forms:[29]

- *Barter.* The direct exchange of goods, with no money and no third party involved.
- *Compensation deal.* The buyer pays partly in cash and partly in products. A British aircraft company used this approach to sell planes to Brazil for 70% cash and the rest in coffee.
- *Buyback arrangement.* The seller sells a plant, equipment, or technology to another country and accepts as partial payment products manufactured with the supplied equipment. A U.S. chemical firm built a plant for an Indian company and accepted partial payment in cash and the remainder in chemicals manufactured at the plant.
- *Offset.* The seller receives full cash payment but agrees to spend much of the cash in that country within a stated period. For example, PepsiCo sells its cola syrup to Russia for rubles and buys Russian vodka at a certain rate for sale in the United States.

Price Discounts and Allowances

Most companies will adjust their list price and give discounts and allowances for early payment, volume purchases, and off-season buying, as shown in Table 12.2.[30] Companies must do this carefully or their profits will be much less than planned.[31] Sales executives need to monitor the proportion of customers who are receiving discounts, the average discount, and the particular salespeople who are overrelying on discounting. Higher levels of management should conduct a *net price analysis* to arrive at the offering's "real price," which is affected by discounts and many other expenses that reduce the realized price.

Promotional Pricing

Companies can use several pricing techniques to stimulate early purchase:

- *Loss-leader pricing.* Stores often cut the price of well-known brands to attract more shoppers, which pays off if the additional revenue compensates for loss-leader items' lower margins.
- *Special-event pricing.* Sellers will establish special prices in certain seasons to draw in more customers; an example is the back-to-school sale.
- *Cash rebates.* Auto companies and others offer cash rebates to encourage purchase of their products within a specified period, clearing inventories without cutting the stated list price.

Chapter 12 Developing Pricing Strategies and Programs

TABLE 12.2 Price Discounts and Allowances

Cash Discount	A price reduction to buyers who pay bills promptly. A typical example is "2/10, net 30," which means that payment is due within 30 days and that the buyer can deduct 2% by paying the bill within 10 days.
Quantity Discount	A price reduction to those who buy large volumes. A typical example is "$10 per unit for less than 100 units; $9 per unit for 100 or more units." Quantity discounts must be offered equally to all customers and must not exceed the cost savings to the seller. They can be offered on each order placed or on the number of units ordered over a given period.
Functional Discount	Discount (also called *trade discount*) offered by a manufacturer to trade-channel members if they will perform certain functions, such as selling, storing, and recordkeeping. Manufacturers must offer the same functional discounts within each channel.
Seasonal Discount	A price reduction to those who buy merchandise or services out of season. Hotels, motels, and airlines offer seasonal discounts in slow selling periods.
Allowance	An extra payment designed to gain reseller participation in special programs. *Trade-in allowances* are granted for turning in an old item when buying a new one. *Promotional allowances* reward dealers for participating in advertising and sales support programs.

- *Low-interest financing*. Rather than cut price, the firm offers customers low- or no-interest financing.
- *Longer payment terms*. Sellers, especially mortgage banks and auto companies, stretch loans over longer periods and thus lower the monthly payments. Consumers often worry less about the cost (the interest rate) and more about whether they can afford the monthly payment.
- *Warranties and service contracts*. Companies promote sales with a free or low-cost warranty or service contract.
- *Psychological discounting*. The firm sets an artificially high price and then offers the product at substantial savings; for example, "Was $359, now $299." The Federal Trade Commission and Better Business Bureaus fight illegitimate discount tactics.

Promotional-pricing strategies are often a zero-sum game. If they work, competitors copy them and they lose their effectiveness. If they don't work, they waste money that could have been put into other marketing tools, such as improving product quality and service or strengthening product image through advertising.

Differentiated Pricing

Companies often adjust their basic price to accommodate differences in customers, products, locations, and so on. **Price discrimination** occurs when a company sells a product or service at two or more prices that do not reflect a proportional difference in costs. In first-degree price discrimination, the seller charges a separate price based on the intensity of each customer's demand. In second-degree price discrimination, buyers who buy in larger volume receive lower prices. In third-degree price discrimination, the seller sets different prices for different classes of buyers:

- *Customer-segment pricing*. Different customer groups pay different prices for the same offering. For example, museums often set lower admission fees for students and senior citizens.

- *Product-form pricing.* Different versions of the product are priced differently but not proportionately to their respective costs. Evian may price a 48-ounce bottle of water at $2 and its 1.7-ounce moisturizer spray at $6.
- *Image pricing.* Some firms price the same product at two different levels based on image differences. Perfume in one bottle with a particular brand and image might be priced at $10 an ounce, whereas the same perfume in another bottle with a different name and image could be priced at $30 an ounce.
- *Channel pricing.* Coca-Cola carries a different price depending on whether it is purchased in a fine restaurant, fast-food restaurant, or vending machine.
- *Location pricing.* The same product is priced differently at different locations even though the costs are the same; for example, theaters often vary seat prices according to audience preferences for different locations.
- *Time pricing.* Prices are varied by season, day, or hour. Utilities vary energy rates to commercial users by time of day and weekend versus weekday. Airlines use **yield pricing** to offer lower prices on unsold inventory before it expires.[32]

The phenomenon of offering different pricing schedules to different consumers and dynamically adjusting prices is exploding.[33] Price discrimination works when (1) the market is segmentable and the segments show different intensities of demand; (2) members in the lower-price segment can't resell the product to the higher-price segment; (3) competitors can't undersell the firm in the higher-price segment; (4) the cost of segmenting and policing the market doesn't exceed the extra revenue derived from price discrimination; (5) the practice doesn't breed customer resentment and ill will; and (6) the particular form of price discrimination isn't illegal.[34]

Product-Mix Pricing

Price-setting logic must be modified when marketing a product mix. In **product-mix pricing,** the firm searches for a set of prices that maximizes profits on the total mix. Pricing is difficult because the demand and cost of the various products are interrelated and are subject to different degrees of competition. Six product-mix pricing situations are:

- *Product-line pricing.* Many sellers use well-established price points (such as $200, $400, and $600 for suits) to distinguish the products in their line. The seller's task is to create perceived-quality differences that justify the price differences.
- *Optional-feature pricing.* Automakers and other firms offer optional products, features, and services along with their main product. Pricing options is a sticky problem because companies must decide which to include in the standard price and which to offer as options.
- *Captive-product pricing.* Some products require the use of ancillary, or **captive**, products. Razor manufacturers often price their razors low and set high markups on blades. There's a danger in pricing the captive product too high in the aftermarket, however. If parts and service are too expensive, counterfeiting and substitutions can erode sales.
- *Two-part pricing.* Many service firms use **two-part pricing**, which consists of a fixed fee plus a variable usage fee. Telephone customers pay a monthly fee plus charges for calls beyond a certain area. The challenge is to price the basic service or fee low enough to induce purchase and then price the variable usage for profitability.

- *By-product pricing.* The production of certain goods—meats, chemicals, and so on—often results in by-products, which can be priced according to their value to customers. Any income earned on the by-products will make it easier for the company to charge less for the main product if competition forces it to do so.
- *Product-bundling pricing. Pure bundling* occurs when a firm only offers its products as a bundle. With *mixed bundling*, a seller offers bundles (at a lower price than if items were purchased separately) and individual products. A theater company will price a season subscription lower than the cost of buying tickets to all performances separately. Because customers may not have planned to buy all of the components, the savings on the price bundle must be substantial enough to induce them to buy the bundle.[35]

INITIATING AND RESPONDING TO PRICE CHANGES

Marketers often need to cut or raise prices in certain situations.

Initiating Price Cuts

Several circumstances might lead a firm to cut prices. One is excess plant capacity: The firm needs more business but can't generate it through increased sales effort or other efforts. Companies sometimes cut prices in a drive to dominate the market through lower costs. Either the firm starts with lower costs than those of its competitors or it initiates price cuts in the hope of gaining market share and lower costs. Four possible traps of price-cutting are: (1) customers assume quality is low; (2) a low price buys market share but not loyalty because the same customers will shift to any lower-price firm; (3) higher-priced competitors match the lower prices but have longer staying power because of deeper cash reserves; and (4) a price war may be triggered.

Initiating Price Increases

A successful price increase can raise profits considerably. If the company's profit margin is 3% of sales, a 1% price increase will increase profits by 33% if sales volume doesn't drop. In many cases, firms increase prices due to *cost inflation*, when rising costs—unmatched by productivity gains—squeeze profit margins. In fact, companies often raise their prices by more than the cost increase in anticipation of further inflation or government price controls, a practice called *anticipatory pricing*.

Another factor leading to price increases is *overdemand*. When a company cannot supply all of its customers, it can use one of the following pricing techniques:

- *Delayed quotation pricing.* The firm doesn't set a final price until the product is finished or delivered. This is prevalent in industries with long production lead times.
- *Escalator clauses.* The firm requires the customer to pay today's price and all or part of any inflation increase that occurs before delivery, based on some specified price index.
- *Unbundling.* The firm maintains its price but removes or prices separately one or more elements that were part of the former offer, such as free delivery or installation.
- *Reduction of discounts.* The firm no longer offers its usual cash and quantity discounts.

Marketers should decide whether to raise the price sharply one time or raise it by small amounts several times (consumers prefer the latter). In passing along price increases, the firm must avoid looking like a price gouger.[36] The more similar a company's offerings, the more likely consumers are to interpret any pricing differences as unfair. Thus, clarifying differences through product customization and communications is critical.[37]

Responding to Competitors' Price Changes

How should a firm respond to a price cut initiated by a competitor? London Business School's Nirmalya Kumar, who has studied the threats posed by disruptive, low-cost competitors, offers three possible responses, depending on the factors shown in Figure 12.4.

In markets characterized by high product homogeneity, a firm should find ways to enhance its augmented product; otherwise, it may have to meet the price reduction. If the competitor raises its price in a homogeneous product market, the other firms might not match it unless the increase will benefit the industry as a whole. Then the leader will have to roll back the increase. In nonhomogeneous product markets, a firm can ask: Why did the competitor change the price? Was it to steal the market, utilize excess capacity, meet changing cost conditions, or lead an industry-wide price change? Is the competitor's

FIGURE 12.4 A Framework for Responding to Low–Cost Rivals

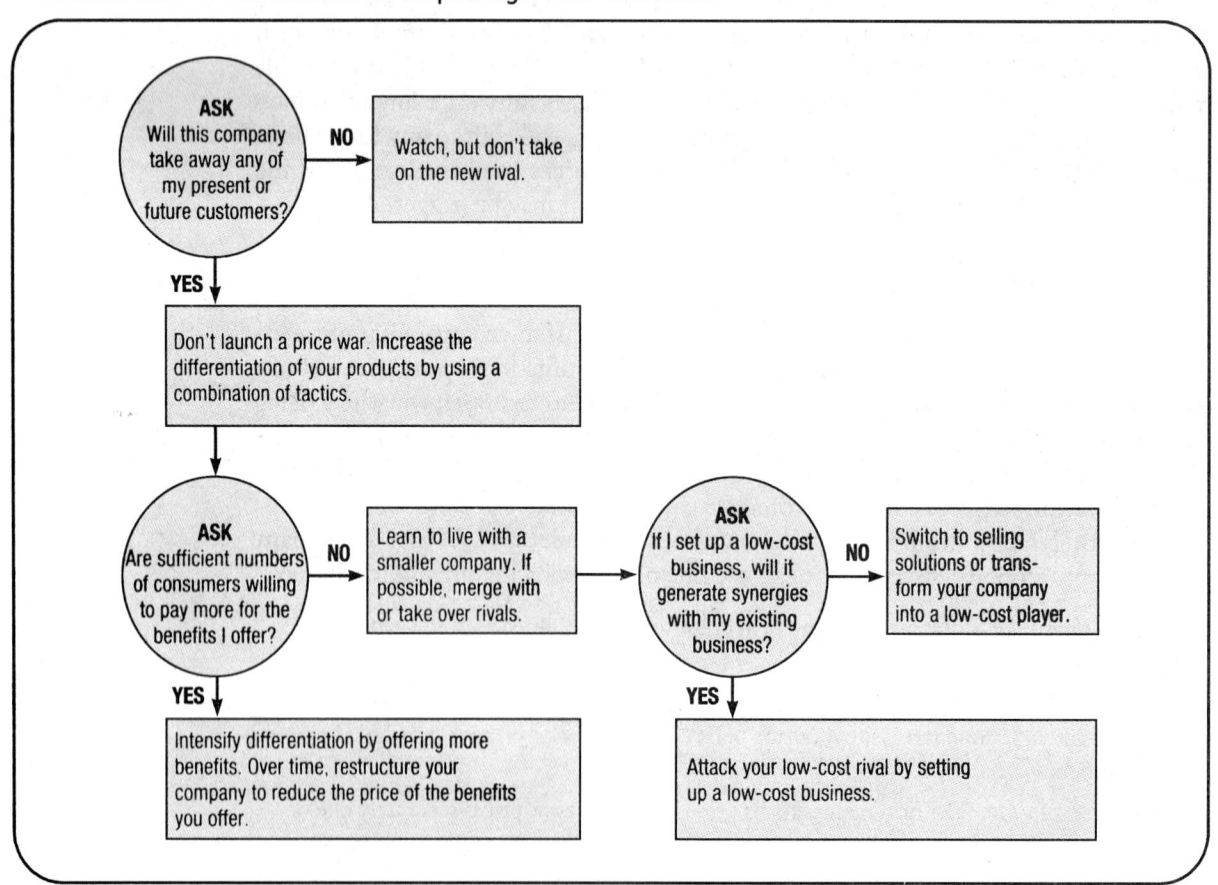

Source: Nirmalya Kumar, "Strategies to Fight Low-Cost Rivals," *Harvard Business Review* (December 2006):104–12.

price change temporary or permanent? What will happen to the company's market share and profits if it doesn't respond? Are other firms going to respond? What are the competitor's and other firms' likely responses to each possible reaction?

EXECUTIVE SUMMARY

Price is the only marketing element that produces revenue; the others produce costs. In setting pricing policy, a firm follows six steps: (1) select the pricing objective; (2) determine demand; (3) estimate costs; (4) analyze competitors' costs, prices, and offers; (5) select a pricing method; and (6) select the final price. To adapt prices, firms use geographical pricing, discounts and allowances, promotional pricing, differentiated pricing, and product-mix pricing.

After developing pricing strategies, firms often face situations in which they must change prices. In raising prices, firms must carefully manage customer perceptions. In addition, firms need to anticipate competitor price changes and prepare contingent responses. A number of responses are possible in terms of maintaining or changing price or quality. Pricing strategy often depends on whether the product market is homogeneous or nonhomogeneous.

NOTES

1. "Gillette Razor Sales Bolster Profit at P&G," *New York Times*, August 4, 2007, p. C3; Christina Veiders, "The Top 10: 6, A.G. Lafley," *Supermarket News*, July 23, 2007; Mary Ellen Lloyd, "Gillette's Razor Makes Big Gains in Market Share," *Wall Street Journal*, March 6, 2006, p. 1; Jenn Abelson, "And Then There Were Five," *Boston Globe*, September 15, 2005, pp. C1–C2; Jack Neff, "Six-Blade Blitz," *Advertising Age*, September 19, 2005, pp. 3, 53; Editorial, "Gillette Spends Smart on Fusion," *Advertising Age*, September 26, 2005, p. 24; Dan Beucke, "A Blade Too Far," *BusinessWeek*, August 14, 2006.
2. "The Price Is Wrong," *The Economist*, May 25, 2002.
3. Jack Neff, "It Worked: Ad Boost Pays Off for Colgate; Unilever Also Sees Sales and Share Uptick, But Both Still Lag Behind P&G," *Advertising Age*, August 8, 2005, pp. 3+; Susanna Howard, "P&G, Unilever Court the World's Poor," *Wall Street Journal*, June 1, 2005, pp. 1+; "Procter & Gamble Poses Competitive Threat to India Detergent Nirma," *The Economic Times*, December 20, 2004; Eric Bellman and Deborah Ball, "Unilever, P&G Wage Price War for Edge in India," *Wall Street Journal*, August 11, 2004, p. B1.
4. Paul Markillie, "A Perfect Market: A Survey of E-Commerce," *The Economist*, May 15, 2004, pp. 3–20; David Kirpatrick, "How the Open-Source World Plans to Smack Down Microsoft, and Oracle, and . . .", *Fortune*, February 23, 2004, pp. 92–100; Amy E. Cortese, "Good-Bye to Fixed Pricing?" *BusinessWeek*, May 4, 1998, pp. 71–84; Michael Menduno, "Priced to Perfection," *Business 2.0*, March 6, 2001, pp. 40–42; Faith Keenan, "The Price Is Really Right," *BusinessWeek*, March 31, 2003, pp. 61–67. For a discussion of some of the academic issues involved, see Florian Zettelmeyer, "Expanding to the Internet: Pricing and Communication Strategies when Firms Compete on Multiple Channels," *Journal of Marketing Research* 37 (August 2000): 292–308; John G. Lynch Jr. and Dan Ariely, "Wine Online: Search Costs Affect Competition on Price, Quality, and Distribution," *Marketing Science* (Winter 2000): 83–103; Rajiv Lal and Miklos Sarvary, "When and How Is the Internet Likely to Decrease Price Competition?" *Marketing Science* 18, no. 4 (1999): 485–503.
5. Jonathan Saul, "Ryanair Keeps Goals, Eyes Expansion Beyond Europe," *Reuters UK*, September 20, 2007, http://today.reuters.co.uk/news; Peter J. Howe, "The Next Pinch: Fees to Check Bags," *Boston Globe*, March 8, 2007, pp. A1, A18; Katherine Heires, "Why It Pays to Give Away the Store," *Business 2.0*, October 2006, pp. 36–37; Kerry Capel, " 'Wal-Mart with Wings'," *BusinessWeek*, November 27, 2006, pp. 44–45; Matthew Maier, "A Radical Fix for Airlines: Make Flying Free," *Business 2.0*, April 2006, pp. 32–34;

Gary Stoller, "Would You Like Some Golf Balls with That Ticket," *USA Today*, October 30, 1996, pp. B1–B2.

6. "Pricing Benchmarks for the Future: How General Electric Does It," white paper, Simon-Kucher Partners, March 6, 2007; "Growth as a Process," interview with Jeffrey Immelt, *Harvard Business Review* (June 2006).

7. For a thorough review of pricing research, see Chezy Ofir and Russell S. Winer, "Pricing: Economic and Behavioral Models," in Bart Weitz and Robin Wensley, eds. *Handbook of Marketing*, (New York: Sage Publications, 2002), 5–86.

8. Peter R. Dickson and Alan G. Sawyer, "The Price Knowledge and Search of Supermarket Shoppers," *Journal of Marketing* (July 1990): 42–53. For a methodological qualification, however, see Hooman Estalami, Alfred Holden, and Donald R. Lehmann, "Macro-Economic Determinants of Consumer Price Knowledge: A Meta-Analysis of Four Decades of Research," *International Journal of Research in Marketing* 18 (December 2001): 341–355.

9. For a comprehensive review, see Tridib Mazumdar, S. P. Raj, and Indrajit Sinha, "Reference Price Research: Review and Propositions," *Journal of Marketing* 69 (October 2005): 84–102. For a different point of view, see Chris Janiszewski and Donald R. Lichtenstein, "A Range Theory Account of Price Perception," *Journal of Consumer Research* (March 1999): 353–368.

10. Christina Binkley, "The Psychology of the $14,000 Handbag," *Wall Street Journal*, August 9, 2007, p. D8. For a discussion of how "incidental" prices outside the category can serve as contextual reference prices, see Joseph C. Nunes and Peter Boatwright, "Incidental Prices and Their Effect on Willingness to Pay," *Journal of Marketing Research* 41 (November 2004): 457–466. Also see K. N. Rajendran and Gerard J. Tellis, "Contextual and Temporal Components of Reference Price," *Journal of Marketing* (January 1994): 22–34.

11. Ribert Ziethammer, "Forward-Looking Buying in Online Auctions," *Journal of Marketing Research* 43 (August 2006): 462–476.

12. Gary M. Erickson and Johny K. Johansson, "The Role of Price in Multi-Attribute Product-Evaluations," *Journal of Consumer Research* (September 1985): 195–199.

13. Wilfred Amaldoss and Sanjay Jain, "Pricing of Conspicuous Goods: A Competitive Analysis of Social Effects," *Journal of Marketing Research* 42 (February 2005): 30–45; Angela Chao and Juliet B. Schor (1998) "Empirical Tests of Status Consumption: Evidence from Women's Cosmetics," *Journal of Economic Psychology* 19 (1): 107–131.

14. Mark Stiving and Russell S. Winer, "An Empirical Analysis of Price Endings with Scanner Data," *Journal of Consumer Research* (June 1997): 57–68.

15. Eric Anderson and Duncan Simester (2003), "Effects of $9 Price Endings on Retail Sales: Evidence from Field Experiments," *Quantitative Marketing and Economics* 1(1): 93–110.

16. Shantanu Dutta, Mark J. Zbaracki, and Mark Bergen, "Pricing Process as a Capability: A Resource-Based Perspective," *Strategic Management Journal* 24, no. 7 (2000): 615–630.

17. Walter Baker, Mike Marn, and Craig Zawada, "Price Smarter on the Net," *Harvard Business Review* (February 2001): 122–127.

18. See Thomas T. Nagle and John E. Hogan, *The Strategy and Tactics of Pricing*, 4th ed. (Upper Saddle River, NJ: Pearson Prentice Hall, 2006).

19. For a summary of elasticity studies, see Dominique M. Hanssens, Leonard J. Parsons, and Randall L. Schultz, *Market Response Models: Econometric and Time Series Analysis* (Boston: Kluwer Academic Publishers, 1990), pp. 187–191.

20. Tammo H.A. Bijmolt, Harald J. Van Heerde, and Rik G. M. Pieters, "New Empirical Generalizations on the Determinants of Price Elasticity," *Journal of Marketing Research* 42 (May 2005): 141-156.

21. "Japan's Smart Secret Weapon," *Fortune*, August 12, 1991, p. 75.

22. Tung-Zong Chang and Albert R. Wildt, "Price, Product Information, and Purchase Intention: An Empirical Study," *Journal of the Academy of Marketing Science* (Winter 1994): 16–27. See also G. Dean Kortge and Patrick A. Okonkwo, "Perceived Value Approach to Pricing," *Industrial Marketing Management*, May 1993, pp. 133–140.

23. James C. Anderson, Dipak C. Jain, and Pradeep K. Chintagunta, "Customer Value Assessment in Business Markets: A State-of-Practice Study," *Journal of Business-to-Business Marketing* 1, no. 1 (1993): 3–29.

24. Stephen J. Hoch, Xavier Dreze, and Mary J. Purk, "EDLP, Hi-Lo, and Margin Arithmetic," *Journal of Marketing* (October 1994): 16–27; Rajiv Lal and R. Rao, "Supermarket Competition: The Case of Everyday Low Pricing," *Marketing Science* 16, no. 1 (1997): 60–80.

25. Sandy D. Jap, "The Impact of Online Reverse Auction Design on Buyer-Supplier Relationships," *Journal of Marketing*, 71 (January 2007): 146–159;

Sandy D. Jap, "An Exploratory Study of the Introduction of Online Reverse Auctions," *Journal of Marketing*, 67 (July 2003): 96–107.

26. Victoria Shannon, "EBay Is Preparing to Re-enter the China Auction Business," *New York Times*, June 22, 2007, p. C2; Malia Wollan, "Auctions Remain a Challenge for eBay," *Wall Street Journal*, July 19, 2007, p. A2; "Adam Lashinsky, "Building eBay 2.0," *Fortune*, October 16, 2006, pp. 161–164; Glen L. Urban, Matthew Creamer, "A Million Marketers," *Advertising Age*, June 26, 2006, pp. 1, 71; Clive Thompson, "eBay Heads East," *Fast Company*, July/August 2006, pp. 87–89.

27. Paul W. Farris and David J. Reibstein, "How Prices, Expenditures, and Profits Are Linked," *Harvard Business Review* (November–December 1979): 173–184. See also Makoto Abe, "Price and Advertising Strategy of a National Brand against Its Private-Label Clone: A Signaling Game Approach," *Journal of Business Research* (July 1995): 241–250.

28. Kathy Chu, "Credit Card Fees Can Suck You In," *USA Today*, December 15, 2006.

29. Michael Rowe, *Countertrade* (London: Euromoney Books, 1989); P. N. Agarwala, *Countertrade: A Global Perspective* (New Delhi: Vikas Publishing House, 1991); and Christopher M. Korth, ed., *International Countertrade* (New York: Quorum Books, 1987).

30. For an interesting discussion of a quantity surcharge, see David E. Sprott, Kenneth C. Manning, and Anthony Miyazaki, "Grocery Price Settings and Quantity Surcharges," *Journal of Marketing* 67 (July 2003): 34–46.

31. Michael V. Marn and Robert L. Rosiello, "Managing Price, Gaining Profit," *Harvard Business Review* (September–October 1992): 84–94. See also Gerard J. Tellis, "Tackling the Retailer Decision Maze: Which Brands to Discount, How Much, When, and Why?" *Marketing Science* 14, no. 3, pt. 2 (1995): 271–299; Kusum L. Ailawadi, Scott A. Neslin, and Karen Gedenk, "Pursuing the Value-Conscious Consumer: Store Brands versus National Brand Promotions," *Journal of Marketing*, 65 (January 2001): 71–89.

32. Robert E. Weigand, "Yield Management: Filling Buckets, Papering the House," *Business Horizons*, September–October 1999, pp. 55–64.

33. Peter Coy, "The Power of Smart Pricing," *BusinessWeek*, April 10, 2000, pp. 160–164; Charles Fishman, "Which Price Is Right?" *Fast Company*, March 2003, pp. 92–102; Bob Tedeschi, "E-Commerce Report," *New York Times*, September 2, 2002, p. C5; Faith Keenan, "The Price Is Really Right," *BusinessWeek*, March 31, 2003, pp. 62–67. For a review of recent and seminal work linking pricing decisions with operational insights, see Moritz Fleischmann, Joseph M. Hall, and David F. Pyke, "Research Brief: Smart Pricing," *MIT Sloan Management Review* (Winter 2004): 9–13.

34. For more information on illegal price discrimination, see Henry Cheesman, *Business Law*, 6th ed. (Upper Saddle River, NJ: Prentice Hall, 2007).

35. Gerald J. Tellis, "Beyond the Many Faces of Price: An Integration of Pricing Strategies," *Journal of Marketing* (October 1986): 155. This article also analyzes and illustrates other pricing strategies.

36. Margaret C. Campbell, "Perceptions of Pricing Unfairness: Antecedents and Consequences," *Journal of Marketing Research* 36 (May 1999): 187–199.

37. Lan Xia, Kent B. Monroe, and Jennifer L. Cox, "The Price is Unfair! A Conceptual Framework of Price Fairness Perceptions," *Journal of Marketing* 68 (October 2004): 1–15.

PART V Delivering Value

CHAPTER 13

Designing and Managing Integrated Marketing Channels

> In this chapter, we will address the following questions:
>
> 1. What are marketing channel systems and value networks?
> 2. What functions do marketing channels perform?
> 3. What decisions do companies face in designing, managing, and integrating their channels?
> 4. What key issues do companies face in e-commerce?

MARKETING MANAGEMENT AT ROYAL PHILIPS ELECTRONICS

Royal Philips Electronics of the Netherlands is one of the world's biggest electronics companies and Europe's largest, with annual sales of over $36 billion. The company offers a broad range of products, from flat screen TVs and electric razors for consumers to medical imaging equipment and professional lighting systems for hospitals and businesses. Philips uses local distributors in some countries but relies mainly on its company sales force and its own Web sites to handle orders from institutional and industrial buyers. A hospital purchasing agent can log on, compare product specifications, enter a purchase order, check the delivery status of a previous order, or access service and support databases.

On the consumer side, Philips products reach buyers worldwide through a diverse distribution model that includes mass merchants, retail chains, independent stores, and small specialty stores. Philips has created an organization designed around these retail customers, with dedicated Global Key Account Managers serving leading retailers such as Best Buy, Carrefour, Costco, Dixons, and Tesco. The company also sells to consumers via its own online store as well as through other online retailers.[1]

Successful value creation needs successful value delivery. Holistic marketers are increasingly taking a value network view of their businesses, examining the whole supply chain that links raw materials, components, and manufactured goods and shows how they move toward the final consumers. This chapter discusses the strategic and tactical issues of marketing channels and value networks; Chapter 14 will examine marketing channel issues from the perspective of retailers, wholesalers, and physical-distribution agencies.

MARKETING CHANNELS AND VALUE NETWORKS

Most producers don't sell their goods directly to the final users; between them stands a set of intermediaries performing a variety of functions. These intermediaries constitute **marketing channels** (also called trade channels or distribution channels), sets of interdependent organizations involved in the process of making a product or service available for use or consumption. They're the set of pathways a product or service follows after production, culminating in purchase and use by the final end user.[2]

The Importance of Channels

A **marketing channel system** is the particular set of marketing channels employed by a firm. Decisions about the marketing channel system are among the most critical facing management. In the United States, channel members collectively earn margins that account for 30% to 50% of the ultimate selling price, whereas advertising typically accounts for less than 7% of the final price.[3] Marketing channels also represent a substantial opportunity cost because they don't just *serve* markets, they must also *make* markets.[4]

The channels chosen affect all other marketing decisions. The company's pricing depends on whether it uses mass merchandisers or high-quality boutiques. The firm's sales force and advertising decisions depend on how much training and motivation dealers need. In addition, channel decisions involve relatively long-term commitments to other firms. When an automaker signs up independent dealers to sell its automobiles, it can't buy them out the next day and replace them with company-owned outlets. Holistic marketers ensure that marketing decisions in all these different areas are made to collectively maximize value.

Today's successful companies are also multiplying the number of "go-to-market" or **hybrid channels** in any one area. For example, Hewlett-Packard uses its sales force to sell to large accounts, outbound telemarketing to sell to medium-sized accounts, direct mail with an inbound number for small accounts, retailers for still smaller accounts and consumers, and the Internet to sell specialty items. Consumers may choose their preferred channels based on price, product assortment, and convenience, as well as their economic, social, or experiential shopping goals.[5]

The firm must decide how much effort to devote to push versus pull marketing. A **push strategy** uses the manufacturer's sales force and trade promotion to induce intermediaries to carry, promote, and sell the product to end users. This is appropriate where there is low brand loyalty in a category, brand choice is made in the store, the product is an impulse item, and product benefits are well understood. In a **pull strategy,** the manufacturer uses advertising and promotion to persuade consumers to ask intermediaries for the product, thus inducing the intermediaries to order it. This is appropriate when there is high brand loyalty and high involvement in the category, people perceive differences between brands, and people choose the brand before they shop. Top marketing firms such as Nike and Intel skillfully employ both push and pull strategies.

Value Networks

The company should first think of the target market and then design the supply chain backward from that point, a view called **demand-chain planning**. Northwestern's Don Schultz says: "A demand chain management approach doesn't just push things through the system. It emphasizes what solutions consumers are looking for, not what products we are trying to sell them." He suggests replacing the marketing "four Ps" with a new acronym, SIVA, which stands for solutions, information, value, and access.[6]

The concept of a **value network**—a system of partnerships and alliances that a firm creates to source, augment, and deliver its offerings—takes an even broader view. A value network includes a firm's suppliers and its suppliers' suppliers, and its immediate customers and their end customers. The value network includes valued relations with others such as university researchers and regulatory agencies.

Demand chain planning yields several insights. First, the firm can estimate whether more money is made upstream or downstream, in case it might want to integrate backward or forward. Second, the company is more aware of disturbances anywhere in the supply chain that might cause costs, prices, or supplies to change suddenly. Third, companies can go online with business partners for faster, more accurate, and less costly communications, transactions, and payments.

THE ROLE OF MARKETING CHANNELS

Why would a producer delegate some of the selling job to intermediaries? Delegation means relinquishing some control over how and to whom the products are sold. But producers can often gain effectiveness and efficiency by using intermediaries. It's impractical for the William Wrigley Jr. Company to establish small retail gum shops throughout the world or to sell gum by mail order. It would have to sell gum along with many other small products and would end up in the drugstore and grocery store business. Wrigley finds it easier to work through the extensive network of privately owned distribution organizations. Even General Motors would be hard-pressed to replace all the tasks handled by its 8,000 dealers.

Channel Functions and Flows

A marketing channel performs the work of moving products from producers to consumers, overcoming the time, place, and possession gaps that separate goods and services from those who need or want them. Members of the marketing channel perform a number of key functions (see Table 13.1). Some functions (physical, title, and promotion) constitute a *forward flow* of activity from the company to the customer; other functions (ordering and payment) constitute a *backward flow* from customers to the company.

Still others (information, negotiation, finance, and risk taking) occur in both directions. If the flows for forklift trucks shown in Figure 13.1 were superimposed in one diagram, the complexity of even simple marketing channels would be apparent.

The question is not *whether* these channel functions need to be performed—they must be—but rather *who* is to perform them. All channel functions have three things in common: They use up scarce resources; they can often be performed better through specialization; and they can be shifted among channel members. If a manufacturer shifts some functions to intermediaries, its costs and prices go down, but the intermediaries must add a charge to cover their work. Still, if the intermediaries are more efficient than the manufacturer, prices to consumers should be lower. If consumers

TABLE 13.1 Channel Member Functions

- Gather information about potential and current customers, competitors, and other actors and forces in the marketing environment.
- Develop and disseminate persuasive communications to stimulate purchasing.
- Reach agreements on price and other terms so that transfer of ownership or possession can be effected.
- Place orders with manufacturers.
- Acquire the funds to finance inventories at different levels in the marketing channel.
- Assume risks connected with carrying out channel work.
- Provide for the successive storage and movement of physical products.
- Provide for buyers' payment of their bills through banks and other financial institutions.
- Oversee actual transfer of ownership from one organization or person to another.

FIGURE 13.1 Five Marketing Flows in the Marketing Channel for Forklift Trucks

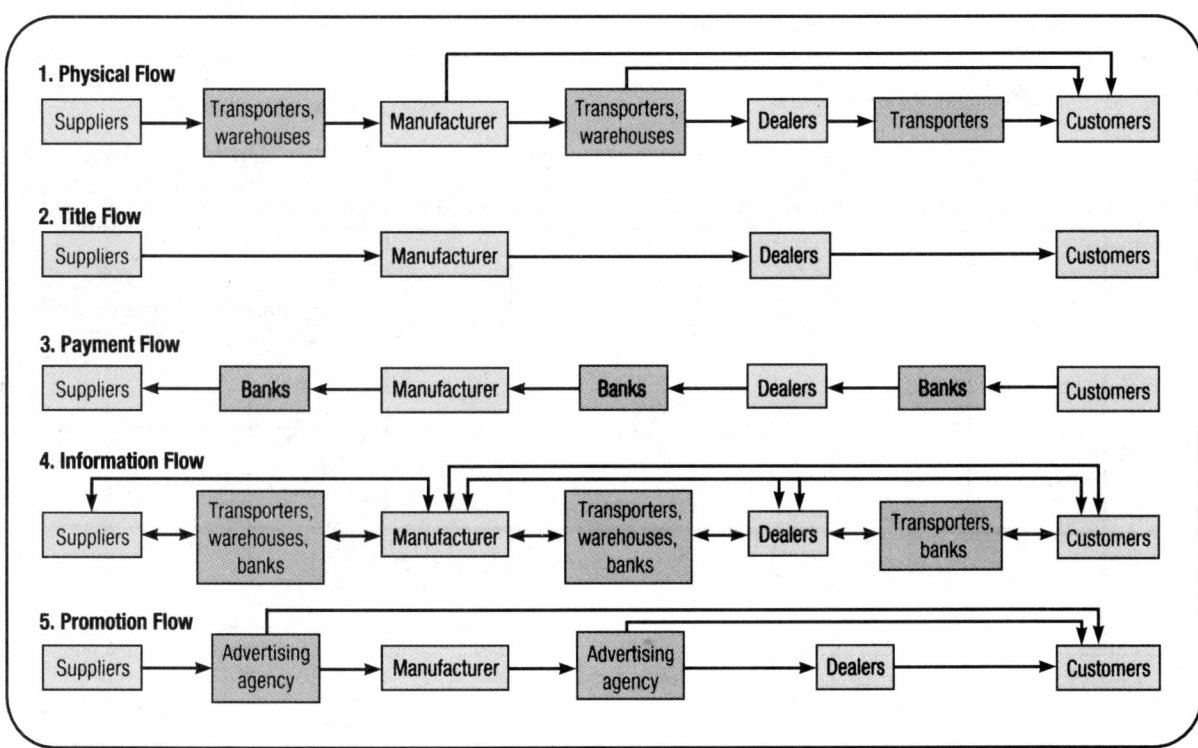

perform some functions themselves, they should enjoy still lower prices. Changes in channel institutions thus reflect the discovery of more efficient ways to combine or separate the economic functions that provide assortments of products to target customers.

Channel Levels

The producer and the final customer are part of every channel. We'll use the number of intermediary levels to designate the length of a channel. Figure 13.2a illustrates consumer-goods marketing channels of different lengths, while Figure 13.2b illustrates industrial marketing channels.

A **zero-level channel** (also called a **direct-marketing channel**) consists of a producer selling directly to final customers through door-to-door sales, Internet selling, mail order, telemarketing, home parties, TV selling, manufacturer-owned stores, and other methods. A *one-level channel* contains one intermediary, such as a retailer. A *two-level channel* contains two intermediaries; a *three-level channel* contains three intermediaries. From the producer's perspective, obtaining information about end users and exercising control becomes more difficult as the number of channel levels increases.

Channels normally describe a forward movement of products, but there are also *reverse-flow channels*, important for bringing products back for reuse (such as refillable bottles); refurbishing items for resale; recycling products; and disposing of products and packaging. Several intermediaries play a role in these channels, including manufacturers' redemption centers, community groups, traditional intermediaries such as trash-collection specialists, recycling centers, trash-recycling brokers, and central-processing warehousing.[7]

FIGURE 13.2 Consumer and Industrial Marketing Channels

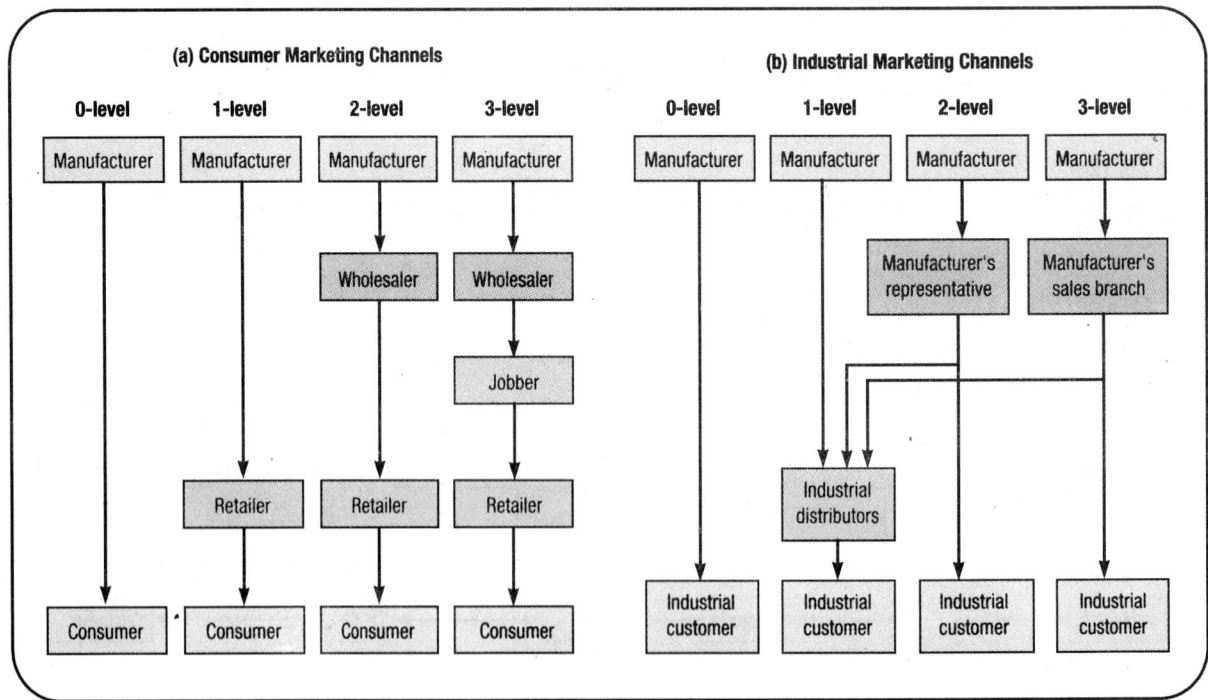

Service Sector Channels

Producers of services and ideas also face the problem of making their output available and accessible to target populations. Schools develop "educational-dissemination systems" and hospitals develop "health-delivery systems." These institutions must determine agencies and locations for reaching a population that is spread out over an area. Marketing channels are also changing in "person" marketing. Besides live and programmed entertainment, entertainers can reach fans online in many ways—via their own Web sites, social community sites such as MySpace, and third-party Web sites. And as Internet technology advances, service industries such as banking, travel, and insurance are operating through new channels. Kodak offers its customers four ways to print their digital photos—minilabs in retail outlets, home printers, the Kodak Gallery Web site, and self-service kiosks.[8]

CHANNEL-DESIGN DECISIONS

Designing a marketing channel system involves analyzing customer needs, establishing channel objectives, identifying major channel alternatives, and evaluating major channel alternatives.

Analyzing Customers' Desired Service Output Levels

The marketer must understand the service output levels its target customers want. Channels produce five service outputs:

1. *Lot size.* The number of units the channel permits a typical customer to purchase on one occasion. In buying for its fleet, Hertz wants a channel from which it can buy a large lot size; a household wants a channel that permits buying a lot size of one.
2. *Waiting and delivery time.* The average time customers of that channel wait for receipt of the goods. Customers normally prefer fast delivery channels.
3. *Spatial convenience.* The degree to which the marketing channel makes it easy for customers to purchase the product.
4. *Product variety.* The assortment breadth provided by the channel. Normally, customers prefer a greater assortment, which increases the chance of finding what they need.
5. *Service backup.* The add-on services (credit, delivery, installation, repairs) provided by the channel.

Providing greater service outputs means increased channel costs and higher prices for customers. The success of discount resellers (online and offline) indicates that many consumers will accept lower outputs if they can save money.

Establishing Objectives and Constraints

Marketers should state their channel objectives in terms of targeted service output levels. Under competitive conditions, channel institutions should arrange their functional tasks to minimize total channel costs and still provide desired levels of service outputs.[9] Usually, planners can identify several market segments that want different service levels. Effective planning requires determining which market segments to serve and the best channels for each.

Channel objectives vary with product characteristics. Perishable products require more direct marketing. Bulky products, such as building materials, require channels that minimize the shipping distance and the amount of handling. Nonstandard products, such as custom-built machinery, are sold directly by company sales representatives. Products requiring installation or maintenance services, such as heating systems, are usually sold and maintained by the company or franchised dealers. High-unit-value products such as turbines are often sold through a company sales force rather than intermediaries.

Channel design is also influenced by such environmental factors as competitors' channels, economic conditions, and legal regulations and restrictions. U.S. law looks unfavorably on channel arrangements that substantially lessen competition or create a monopoly.

Identifying Major Channel Alternatives

Companies can choose from a wide variety of channels for reaching customers, each of which has unique strengths as well as weaknesses. Each channel alternative is described by (1) the types of available intermediaries; (2) the number of intermediaries needed; and (3) the terms and responsibilities of each channel member.

Types of Intermediaries A firm needs to identify the types of intermediaries available to carry on its channel work. Some intermediaries—*merchants* such as wholesalers and retailers—buy, take title to, and resell the merchandise. *Agents* such as brokers, manufacturers' representatives, and sales agents search for customers and may negotiate on the producer's behalf but don't take title to the goods. *Facilitators*, including transportation companies, independent warehouses, banks, and advertising agencies, assist in the distribution process but neither take title to goods nor negotiate purchases or sales. Companies should identify innovative marketing channels. For instance, seeing its printed catalog as out of date, commercial lighting company Display Supply & Lighting developed an interactive online catalog that cost less, sped up the sales process, and increased revenue.[10]

Number of Intermediaries In deciding how many intermediaries to use, companies can use one of three strategies: exclusive, selective, or intensive distribution. **Exclusive distribution** means severely limiting the number of intermediaries. Firms such as automakers use this approach to maintain control over the service level and service outputs offered by the resellers. Often it involves *exclusive dealing* arrangements, in which resellers agree not to carry competing brands.

Selective distribution relies on more than a few but less than all of the intermediaries willing to carry a particular product. The company doesn't have to worry about too many outlets; it can gain adequate market coverage with more control and less cost than intensive distribution. In **intensive distribution**, the manufacturer places the goods or services in as many outlets as possible. This strategy is generally used for items such as snack foods, newspapers, and gum, products the consumer seeks to buy frequently or in a variety of locations.

Terms and Responsibilities of Channel Members Each channel member must be treated respectfully and given the opportunity to be profitable.[11] The main elements in the "trade-relations mix" are price policy, conditions of sale, territorial rights, and specific services to be performed by each party.

Price policy calls for the producer to establish a price list and schedule of discounts and allowances that intermediaries see as equitable and sufficient. *Conditions of sale* are payment terms and producer guarantees. Most producers grant cash discounts to distributors for early payment. Producers might also provide distributors a guarantee against defective merchandise or price declines. A guarantee against price declines gives distributors an incentive to buy more.

Distributors' territorial rights define the distributors' territories and the terms under which the producer will enfranchise other distributors. Distributors normally expect to receive full credit for all sales in their territory, whether or not they did the selling. *Mutual services and responsibilities* must be carefully spelled out, especially in franchised and exclusive-agency channels. McDonald's provides franchisees with a building, promotional support, a recordkeeping system, training, and general administrative and technical assistance. In turn, franchisees must satisfy company standards for the physical facilities, cooperate with promotional programs, furnish requested information, and buy supplies from specified vendors.

Evaluating the Major Alternatives

The company must evaluate each alternative against appropriate economic, control, and adaptive criteria. Figure 13.3 shows the value added per sale and cost per transaction of six different sales channels. The firm should determine whether its own sales force or a sales agency will produce more sales; next, it estimates the costs of selling different volumes through each channel.

FIGURE 13.3 The Value-Adds versus Costs of Different Channels

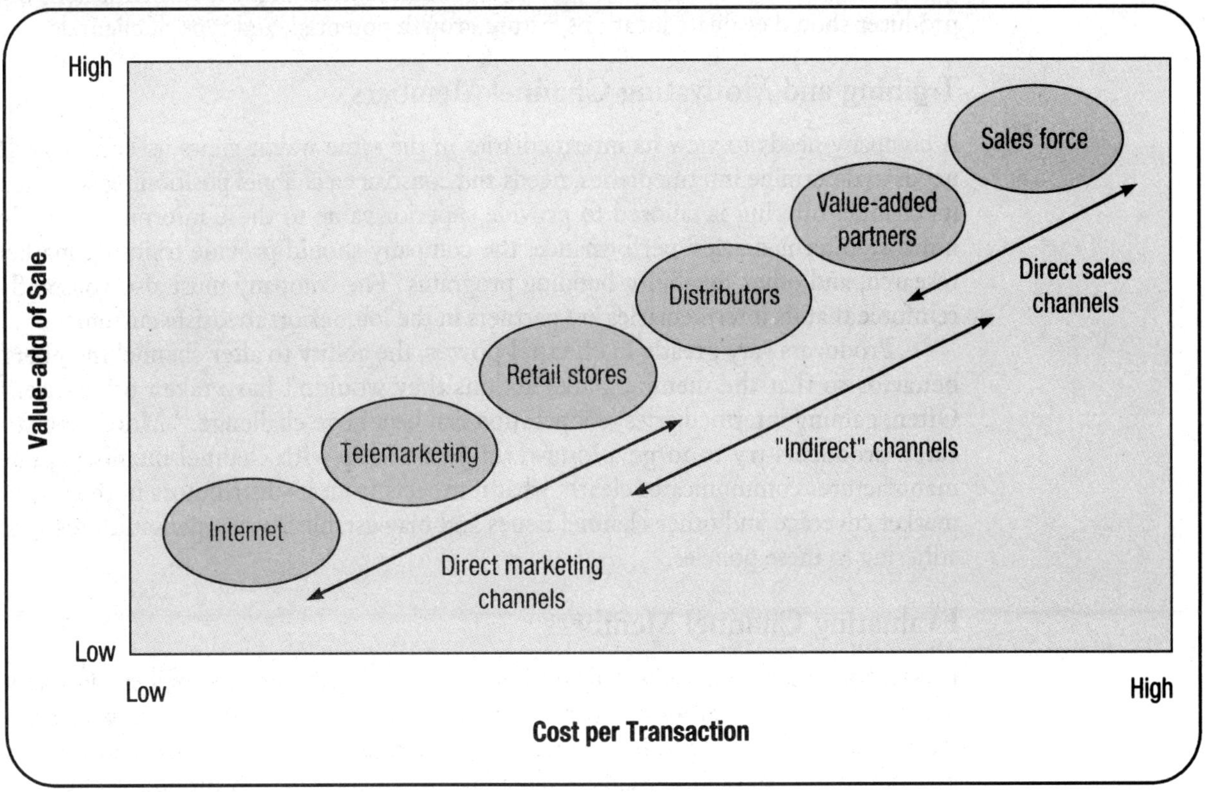

Source: Oxford Associates, adapted from Dr. Rowland T. Moriarity, Cubex Corp.

Using a sales agency poses a control problem because the agency is an independent firm seeking to maximize its profits. Agents may concentrate on customers who buy the most, but not necessarily of the producer's goods. Furthermore, agents might not master the details of every product they carry or handle all promotion materials effectively. To develop a channel, the members must make some mutual commitments for a specified period; this reduces the producer's ability to respond to a changing marketplace. In dynamic, volatile, or uncertain environments, producers need channels and policies that provide high adaptability.

CHANNEL-MANAGEMENT DECISIONS

After a firm has chosen a channel system, it must select, train, motivate, and evaluate individual intermediaries for each channel. It must also modify channel design and arrangements over time.

Selecting Channel Members

Companies need to select their channel members carefully because to customers, the channels are the company. Producers should determine what characteristics distinguish the better intermediaries and examine the number of years in business, other lines carried, growth and profit record, financial strength, cooperativeness, and service reputation of potential channel members. If the intermediaries are sales agents, producers should evaluate the number and character of other lines carried and the size and quality of the sales force. If the intermediaries want exclusive distribution, the producer should evaluate locations, future growth potential, and type of clientele.

Training and Motivating Channel Members

A company needs to view its intermediaries in the same way it views its end users. It needs to determine intermediaries' needs and construct a channel positioning such that its channel offering is tailored to provide superior value to these intermediaries. To improve intermediaries' performance, the company should provide training, market research, and other capability-building programs. The company must also constantly reinforce that its intermediaries are partners in the joint effort to satisfy customers.

Producers vary greatly in **channel power**, the ability to alter channel members' behavior so that the members take actions they wouldn't have taken otherwise.[12] Often, gaining intermediaries' cooperation can be a huge challenge.[13] More sophisticated producers try to forge a long-term partnership with channel members. The manufacturer communicates clearly what it expects from its distributors in the way of market coverage and other channel issues and may establish a compensation plan for adhering to these policies.

Evaluating Channel Members

Producers must periodically evaluate intermediaries' performance against such standards as sales-quota attainment, average inventory levels, customer delivery time, treatment of damaged and lost goods, and cooperation in promotional and training programs (see "Marketing Skills: Evaluating Intermediaries"). A producer will occasionally discover that it is paying particular intermediaries too much for what they are

MARKETING SKILLS: EVALUATING INTERMEDIARIES

How important is it for marketers to evaluate and manage suppliers, wholesalers, retailers, and other intermediaries? One company found that unpredictable supplier deliveries were causing it to hold $200 million in excess inventory. By evaluating suppliers on standards such as on-time delivery, this company slashed its costs. To start, determine how suppliers (and their suppliers) as well as distributors can influence the company's performance. Also, translate companywide strategic goals and measurements into specific targets and measures for channel partners. Finally, continually measure and reward performance to keep channels efficient, reactive, and reliable.

A key criterion for toymaker Cranium is how well an intermediary can support the company's drive for growth. To get an edge in its highly competitive industry, the company often works with channel members that typically don't carry toys and games. Early on, it arranged to sell its Cranium game in Starbucks outlets, an innovative deal that built Cranium's brand. Today its games are still sold in Starbucks but now they're also in Whole Foods Market, Barnes & Noble, and thousands of other stores in 30 countries.[14]

actually doing. One manufacturer compensating a distributor for holding inventories found that the stock was actually held in a public warehouse at its own expense. Producers should set up functional discounts in which they pay specified amounts for the intermediary's performance of each agreed-upon service. Underperformers need to be counseled, retrained, remotivated, or terminated.

Modifying Channel Arrangements

Channel arrangements must be reviewed periodically and modified when distribution isn't working as planned, consumer buying patterns change, the market expands, new competition arises, innovative distribution channels emerge, and the product moves into later stages in the product life cycle. No marketing channel remains effective over the entire product life cycle. Early buyers might be willing to pay for high-cost value-added channels, but later buyers will switch to lower-cost channels. In competitive markets with low entry barriers, the optimal channel structure will change over time; the firm may add or drop individual channel members, add or drop particular market channels, or develop a new way to sell goods.

Adding or dropping an individual channel member requires an incremental analysis to determine what the firm's profits would look like with and without this intermediary. Increasingly, marketers are using datamining to analyze customer shopping data as input for channel decisions.[15] The most difficult decision is whether to revise the overall channel strategy.[16] Channels can become outmoded as a gap arises between the existing distribution system and the ideal system to satisfy customers' (and producers') requirements. This is why Avon's door-to-door system for selling cosmetics had to be modified as more women entered the workforce, for example.

CHANNEL INTEGRATION AND SYSTEMS

Distribution channels don't stand still. New wholesaling and retailing institutions emerge, and new channel systems evolve. We look next at the recent growth of vertical, horizontal, and multichannel marketing systems and see how these systems cooperate, conflict, and compete.

Vertical Marketing Systems

One of the most significant channel developments is the rise of vertical marketing systems. A **conventional marketing channel** comprises an independent producer, wholesaler(s), and retailer(s). Each is a separate business seeking to maximize its own profits, even if this goal reduces profit for the system as a whole. No channel member has complete or substantial control over other members.

A **vertical marketing system (VMS)**, by contrast, comprises the producer, wholesaler(s), and retailer(s) acting as a unified system. One channel member, the *channel captain*, owns the others, franchises them, or has so much power that they all cooperate. The channel captain can be the producer, the wholesaler, or the retailer. *Channel stewardship* is the ability of a given participant (steward) in a distribution channel to create a go-to-market strategy that simultaneously addresses customers' best interests and drives profits for all channel partners. An effective channel steward considers the channel from the customer's point of view and advocates for change among all participants, transforming disparate entities into partners with a common purpose.[17]

VMSs arose as a result of strong channel members' attempts to control channel behavior and eliminate conflict from independent channel members pursuing their own objectives. They achieve economies through size, bargaining power, and elimination of duplicated services. VMSs have become the dominant distribution mode in the U.S. consumer marketplace, serving between 70% and 80% of the total market. There are three types of VMSs: corporate, administered, and contractual.

A *corporate VMS* combines successive stages of production and distribution under single ownership. Companies that desire a high level of control over their channels favor vertical integration. Sherwin-Williams, for example, makes paint but also owns and operates 3,200 retail outlets.[18] An *administered VMS* coordinates successive stages of production and distribution through one member's size and power. Manufacturers of a dominant brand are able to secure strong trade cooperation and support from resellers. Thus Campbell Soup can command cooperation from its resellers in connection with displays, shelf space, promotions, and price policies.

A *contractual VMS* consists of independent firms at different levels of production and distribution, integrating their programs on a contractual basis to obtain more economies or sales impact than they could achieve alone. Johnston and Lawrence call them "value-adding partnerships" (VAPs).[19] Contractual VMSs are of three types:

1. *Wholesaler-sponsored voluntary chains* organize groups of independent retailers to better compete with large chains through standardized selling practices and buying economies.
2. *Retailer cooperatives* arise when the stores take the initiative and organize a new business entity to carry on wholesaling and possibly some production. Members of retail cooperatives concentrate their purchases through the co-op, jointly plan their advertising, and share in profits in proportion to their purchases.

3. *Franchise organizations* are created when a *franchisor* links several successive stages in the production–distribution process. Franchises include manufacturer-sponsored retailer franchises (Honda and its dealers); manufacturer-sponsored wholesaler franchises (Coca-Cola and its bottlers); and service-firm-sponsored retailer franchises (Ramada Inn and its motel franchisees). Some franchising uses dual distribution: vertical integration (franchisor owns and operates the units) and market governance (franchisor licenses units to franchisees).[20]

The New Competition in Retailing

The new competition in retailing is no longer between independent business units but between whole systems of centrally programmed networks (corporate, administered, and contractual) competing against one another to achieve the best cost economies and customer response. Other developments include horizontal marketing systems and multichannel marketing systems.

Horizontal Marketing Systems   In the **horizontal marketing system**, two or more unrelated companies put together resources or programs to exploit an emerging marketing opportunity. Each company lacks the capital, know-how, production, or marketing resources to venture alone, or it is afraid of the risk. The companies might work with each other on a temporary or permanent basis or create a joint venture company. Many supermarket chains have arrangements with local banks to offer in-store banking, the way Citizens Bank has placed 500 branches inside New England supermarkets.

Integrating Multichannel Marketing Systems   Most companies have adopted **multichannel marketing**, which occurs when a single firm uses two or more marketing channels to reach one or more customer segments. An **integrated marketing channel system** is one in which the strategies and tactics of selling through one channel reflect the strategies and tactics of selling through other channels.

By adding more channels, companies can gain three important benefits. The first is increased market coverage. Not only are more customers able to shop for the company's products in more places, but customers who buy in more than one channel are often more profitable than single-channel customers.[21] The second is lower channel cost—selling by phone is cheaper than personal visits to small customers. The third is more customized selling—such as adding a technical sales force to sell more complex equipment. However, new channels typically introduce conflict and control problems. Different channels may end up competing for the same customers, and, as the new channels become more independent, cooperation becomes more difficult.

Conflict, Cooperation, and Competition

No matter how well channels are designed and managed, there will be some conflict, if for no other reason than that the interests of independent business entities don't always coincide. **Channel conflict** is generated when one channel member's actions prevent another channel from achieving its goal. **Channel coordination** occurs when channel members are brought together to advance the goals of the channel, as opposed to their own potentially incompatible goals.[22] Here we examine three questions: What types of conflict arise in channels? What causes channel conflict? What can be done to resolve conflict situations?

Types of Conflict and Competition *Vertical channel conflict* means conflict between different levels within the same channel. General Motors came into conflict with its dealers in trying to enforce policies on service, pricing, and advertising. *Horizontal channel conflict* is conflict between members at the same level within the channel. Some Pizza Inn franchisees complained that other Pizza Inn franchisees were cheating on ingredients, maintaining poor service, and hurting the brand image.

Multichannel conflict exists when the manufacturer has established two or more channels that sell to the same market. It's likely to be especially intense when the members of one channel get a lower price (based on larger volume purchases) or work with a lower margin. Independent dealers were angered when Goodyear began selling its popular tire brands through Sears, Wal-Mart, and Discount Tire. Goodyear eventually placated them by offering exclusive tire models not sold in other retail outlets. Other strategies to reduce multichannel conflict are creating and enforcing rules of engagement beforehand and compensating both parties that participate in a sale regardless of which one books the order.[23]

Causes of Channel Conflict One major cause of channel conflict is *goal incompatibility*. For example, the manufacturer may want to achieve rapid market penetration through a low-price policy. Dealers, in contrast, may prefer to work with high margins for short-run profitability. Sometimes conflict arises from *unclear roles and rights*. HP may sell PCs to large accounts through its own sales force, but its licensed dealers may also be trying to sell to large accounts. Territory boundaries and credit for sales often produce conflict.

Conflict can also stem from *differences in perception*, as when the producer is optimistic about the short-term economic outlook and wants dealers to carry more inventory, while dealers are more pessimistic. At times, conflict can arise because of the intermediaries' *dependence* on the manufacturer. The fortunes of exclusive dealers, such as auto dealers, are greatly affected by the manufacturer's product and pricing decisions, creating high potential for conflict.

Managing Channel Conflict Some channel conflict can be constructive and lead to more dynamic adaptation in a changing environment.[24] Too much conflict can be dysfunctional, however, so the challenge is not to eliminate conflict but to manage it better. There are several mechanisms for effective conflict management (see Table 13.2).[25] One is the adoption of superordinate goals, with channel members agreeing on the fundamental goal they jointly seek, whether it's survival, market share, high quality, or customer satisfaction. Members usually come to agreement when the channel faces an outside threat such as a more efficient competing channel, an adverse piece of legislation, or a shift in consumer desires.

TABLE 13.2 Strategies for Managing Channel Conflict

- Adoption of superordinate goals
- Exchange of employees
- Joint membership in trade associations
- Co-optation
- Diplomacy, mediation, or arbitration
- Legal recourse

Source: Excerpted from Hallie Mummert, "Multi-Channel Marketers Earn a 'C+' on Returns," *Target Marketing*, October 2003, p. 158.

A useful step is to exchange persons between two or more channel levels. General Motors executives might work briefly in some dealerships, and some dealership owners might work in GM's dealer policy department, to help participants appreciate the other's viewpoint. Marketers can accomplish much by encouraging joint membership in and between trade associations. *Co-optation* is an effort by one organization to win the support of another organization's leaders by including them in advisory councils, boards of directors, and the like. As long as the initiating organization treats the leaders and their ideas seriously, co-optation can reduce conflict.

Diplomacy takes place when each side sends a person or group to meet with its counterpart to resolve the conflict. *Mediation* means having a skilled, neutral third party reconcile the two parties' interests. *Arbitration* occurs when the two parties agree to present their arguments to an arbitrator and accept the arbitration decision. When none of these methods proves effective, a company or channel partner may choose to file a lawsuit.

Dilution and Cannibalization Marketers must also avoid diluting their brands through inappropriate channels. This is especially a concern with luxury brands whose images are built on the basis of exclusivity and personalized service. To reach affluent shoppers who work long hours and have little time to shop, high-end fashion brands such as Dior and Louis Vuitton now sell through e-commerce sites. These luxury makers also see their Web sites as a way for customers to research items before walking into a store and a means to help combat fakes sold over the Internet.[26]

Legal and Ethical Issues in Channel Relations

For the most part, companies are legally free to develop whatever channel arrangements suit them. In fact, the law seeks to prevent companies from using exclusionary tactics that might keep competitors from using a channel. Here we briefly consider the legality of exclusive dealing, exclusive territories, tying agreements, and dealers' rights.

With exclusive dealing, the seller allows only certain outlets to carry its products and requires that these dealers not handle competitors' products. Both parties benefit from exclusive arrangements: The seller obtains more loyal and dependable outlets, and the dealers obtain a steady source of supply of special products and stronger seller support. Exclusive arrangements are legal as long as they don't substantially lessen competition or tend to create a monopoly, and both parties have voluntarily entered into the agreement.

Exclusive dealing often includes exclusive territorial agreements. The producer may agree not to sell to other dealers in a given area, or the dealer may agree to sell only in its own territory. The first practice increases dealer enthusiasm and commitment and is perfectly legal—a seller has no legal obligation to sell through more outlets than it wishes. The second practice, whereby the producer tries to keep a dealer from selling outside its territory, is a major legal issue.

The producer of a strong brand sometimes sells it to dealers only if they will take some or all of the rest of the line, a practice called full-line forcing. Such **tying agreements** aren't necessarily illegal, but they do violate U.S. law if they tend to lessen competition substantially. Note that a producer's right to terminate dealers is somewhat restricted. In general, sellers can drop dealers "for cause," but not if, for instance, the dealers refuse to cooperate in a doubtful legal arrangement, such as exclusive dealing or tying agreements.

E-COMMERCE MARKETING PRACTICES

E-business describes the use of electronic means and platforms to conduct a company's business. **E-commerce** means that the company or site transacts or facilitates the online selling of products and services. E-commerce has given rise to e-purchasing and e-marketing. **E-purchasing** means companies decide to buy goods, services, and information from various online suppliers. **E-marketing** describes company efforts to inform buyers, communicate, promote, and sell its offerings online.

We can distinguish between **pure-click** companies, those that have launched a Web site without any previous existence as a firm, and **brick-and-click** companies, existing companies that have added an online site for information and/or e-commerce. M-commerce (m for mobile) is another emerging trend in e-commerce.

Pure-Click Companies

There are several kinds of pure-click companies: search engines, Internet service providers (ISPs), commerce sites, transaction sites, content sites, and enabler sites. Commerce sites sell all types of products and services, notably books, music, toys, insurance, travel services, clothes, and so on. "Breakthrough Marketing: Amazon" describes that quintessential commerce site.

Although the popular press has given the most attention to business-to-consumer (B2C) Web sites, even more activity is being conducted on business-to-business (B2B) sites, which make markets more efficient. In the past, buyers had to exert a lot of effort to gather information on worldwide suppliers. With the Internet, buyers have easy access to information from (1) supplier Web sites; (2) *infomediaries*, third parties that add value by aggregating information about alternatives; (3) *market makers*, third

BREAKTHROUGH MARKETING: AMAZON

Amazon started as the "world's largest bookstore" in July 1995 and has blazed a trail of e-commerce innovations ever since. It set out to create personalized storefronts for each customer by providing more useful information and more choices than neighborhood stores. Amazon invites readers to review books, evaluate them on a one- to five-star rating system, and vote on how helpful each review is. Readers can browse and search pages from thousands of books, receive personal recommendations based on their buying patterns, and buy with just one click. And, to overcome the lag between purchase and delivery, Amazon offers fast, inexpensive shipping.

Today Amazon generates $10 billion in annual revenue from its Web sites in Canada, the United Kingdom, Germany, Austria, France, China, and Japan, offering everything from clothing and kitchen items to downloadable movies and music. It also profits from serving as an electronic marketplace, enabling all kinds of merchants to sell on Amazon.com. Its Amazon Web project opened its databases to more than 65,000 programmers and businesses that, in turn, have created moneymaking Web sites, online shopping interfaces, and services for Amazon's 800,000 sellers. Recently Amazon began renting excess data storage capacity to businesses, the first in a new series of technology offerings. What will Amazon sell next?[27]

parties that create markets linking buyers and sellers; and (4) *customer communities*, sites where buyers can swap stories about suppliers' offerings.

The net impact of these mechanisms is to make prices more transparent.[28] In the case of undifferentiated products, price pressure will increase. For highly differentiated products, buyers will gain a better picture of the items' true value. Suppliers of superior products will be able to offset price transparency with value transparency; suppliers of undifferentiated products will have to drive down their costs to compete.

Brick-and-Click Companies

Many brick-and-mortar companies debated adding an e-commerce channel, fearing that channel conflict would arise from competing with their offline retailers, agents, or company-owned stores.[29] Most eventually added the Internet as a distribution channel after seeing how much business their online competitors were generating.

The question is how to sell both through intermediaries and online. There are at least three strategies for trying to gain acceptance from intermediaries: (1) offer different brands or products on the Internet; (2) offer offline partners higher commissions to cushion the negative impact on sales; and (3) take orders on the Web site but have retailers deliver and collect payment. Harley-Davidson asks customers who want to order accessories online to select a participating dealer. The dealer, in turn, fulfills the order, adhering to Harley's standards for prompt shipping.[30]

M-Commerce

Consumers and businesspeople no longer need to be near a computer to go online. All they need is a cellular phone or personal digital assistant to wirelessly connect to the Internet so they can check the weather, sports scores, and more; send and receive e-mail messages; and place online orders. Many see a big future in what is now called *m-commerce* (m for mobile).[31] M-commerce success will be driven, in part, by convenience, ease of use, trust, and widespread availability.[32]

For example, in Japan, millions of teenagers carry DoCoMo phones from NTT (Nippon Telephone and Telegraph). In addition to voice and text communication, they can use their phones to order goods or make purchases at participating outlets like McDonald's. Subscribers receive a monthly bill from NTT listing the subscriber fee, usage fee, and cost of all other transactions—and they can pay the bill at any 7-Eleven convenience store.[33]

EXECUTIVE SUMMARY

Most producers don't sell their goods directly to final users. Between producers and final users stands one or more marketing channels, a host of marketing intermediaries performing a variety of functions. Companies use intermediaries when they lack the financial resources to carry out direct marketing, when direct marketing isn't feasible, and when they can earn more by doing so. The most important functions performed by intermediaries are information, promotion, negotiation, ordering, financing, risk taking, physical possession, payment, and title.

Manufacturers can reach a market by selling direct or using one-, two-, or three-level channels, depending on customer needs, channel objectives, and their identification and evaluation of major channel alternatives. Effective channel management calls for selecting intermediaries, then training and motivating them to build a long-term, mutually profitable partnership. Three key channel trends are the growth of vertical marketing systems, horizontal marketing systems, and multichannel marketing systems. All channels have the potential for conflict and competition. Marketers have to consider legal and ethical issues relating to practices such as exclusive dealing or territories, tying agreements, and dealers' rights. As e-commerce has grown in importance, channel integration must recognize the distinctive strengths of online and offline selling to maximize their joint contributions.

NOTES

1. Leila Abboud, "New Treatment: Electronics Giant Seeks a Cure in Health Care," *Wall Street Journal*, July 11, 2007, p. A1; Kerry Capell, "Thinking Simple at Philips," *BusinessWeek*, December 11, 2006, p. 50; "Philips—Unfulfilled," brandchannel.com, June 20, 2005; *Royal Philips Electronics Annual Report*, 2006; Jennifer L. Schenker, "Fine-Tuning a Fuzzy Image," TIMEeurope.com, Spring 2002.
2. Anne T. Coughlan, Erin Anderson, Louis W. Stern, and Adel I. El-Ansary, *Marketing Channels*, 6th ed. (Upper Saddle River, NJ: Prentice Hall, 2001).
3. Louis W. Stern and Barton A. Weitz, "The Revolution in Distribution: Challenges and Opportunities," *Long Range Planning* 30, no. 6 (1997): 823–829.
4. For a summary of academic research, see Erin Anderson and Anne T. Coughlan, "Channel Management: Structure, Governance, and Relationship Management," in Bart Weitz and Robin Wensley, eds., *Handbook of Marketing* (London: Sage Publications, 2001), pp. 223–247 and Gary L. Frazier, "Organizing and Managing Channels of Distribution," *Journal of the Academy of Marketing Sciences* 27, no. 2 (1999): 226–240.
5. Asim Ansari, Carl F. Mela, and Scott A. Neslin, "Customer Channel Migration," *Journal of Marketing*, 2007, forthcoming; Jacquelyn S. Thomas and Ursula Y. Sullivan, "Managing Marketing Communications," *Journal of Marketing* 69 (October 2005): 239–251; Edward J. Fox, Alan L. Montgomery, and Leonard M. Lodish (2004), "Consumer Shopping and Spending Across Retail Formats," *The Journal of Business* 77 (2): S25–S60; Sridhar Balasubramanian, Rajagopal Raghunathan, and Vijay Mahajan (2005), "Consumers in a Multichannel Environment: Product Utility, Process Utility, and Channel Choice," *Journal of Interactive Marketing* 19 (2): 12–30.
6. Chekitan S. Dev and Don E. Schultz, "In the Mix: A Customer-Focused Approach Can Bring the Current Marketing Mix into the 21st Century," *Marketing Management* 14 (January/February 2005).
7. For additional information on reverse-flow channels, see Marianne Jahre, "Household Waste Collection as a Reverse Channel—A Theoretical Perspective," *International Journal of Physical Distribution and Logistics* 25, no. 2 (1995): 39–55; and Terrance L. Pohlen and M. Theodore Farris II, "Reverse Logistics in Plastics Recycling," *International Journal of Physical Distribution and Logistics* 22, no. 7 (1992): 35–37.
8. Katherine Boehret, "The Mossberg Solution: How the Big Photo-Sharing Sites Stack Up," *Wall Street Journal*, August 1, 2007, p. D8; William M. Bulkeley, "Kodak Revamps Wal-Mart Kiosks," *Wall Street Journal*, September 6, 2006; Faith Keenan, "Big Yellow's Digital Dilemma," *BusinessWeek*, March 24, 2003, pp. 80–81.
9. Louis P. Bucklin, *A Theory of Distribution Channel Structure* (Berkeley: Institute of Business and Economic Research, University of California, 1966).
10. Allison Enright, "Shed New Light," *Marketing News*, May 1, 2006, pp. 9–10.
11. For more on relationship marketing and the governance of marketing channels, see Jan B. Heide, "Interorganizational Governance in Marketing Channels," *Journal of Marketing* (January 1994): 71–85.
12. Anderson and Coughlan, "Channel Management: Structure, Governance, and Relationship Management," pp. 223–247.
13. Bert Rosenbloom, *Marketing Channels: A Management View*, 5th ed. (Hinsdale, IL: Dryden, 1995).
14. Bruce Horovitz, "Cranium Guys Have Their Inner Child on Speed Dial," *USA Today*, May 8, 2006, p. 7B; Christopher Palmeri, "March of the Toys—Out of the Toy Section," *BusinessWeek*, November 29, 2004,

p. 37; Miles Cook and Rob Tyndall, "Lessons from the Leaders," *Supply Chain Management Review*, November–December 2001, pp. 22+.
15. Thomas H. Davenport and Jeanne G. Harris, *Competing on Analytics: the New Science of Winning* (Boston: Harvard Business School Press, 2007).
16. For an excellent report on this issue, see Howard Sutton, *Rethinking the Company's Selling and Distribution Channels*, research report no. 885, Conference Board, 1986, p. 26.
17. V. Kasturi Rangan, *Transforming Your Go-to-Market Strategy: The Three Disciplines of Channel Management* (Boston: Harvard Business School Press, 2006).
18. Parker Howell, "Columbia Paint Takeover Set," *Spokesman-Review (Spokane)*, August 29, 2007.
19. Russell Johnston and Paul R. Lawrence, "Beyond Vertical Integration—The Rise of the Value-Adding Partnership," *Harvard Business Review* (July–August 1988): 94–101. See also Judy A. Siguaw, Penny M. Simpson, and Thomas L. Baker, "Effects of Supplier Market Orientation on Distributor Market Orientation and the Channel Relationship: The Distribution Perspective," *Journal of Marketing* (July 1998): 99–111; Narakesari Narayandas and Manohar U. Kalwani, "Long-Term Manufacturer–Supplier Relationships: Do They Pay Off for Supplier Firms?" *Journal of Marketing* (January 1995): 1–16.
20. Raji Srinivasan, "Dual Distribution and Intangible Firm Value: Franchising in Restaurant Chains," *Journal of Marketing* 70 (July 2006): 120–135.
21. Rajkumar Venkatesan, V. Kumar, and Nalini Ravishanker, "Multichannel Shopping: Causes and Consequences," *Journal of Marketing* 71 (April 2007): 114–132.
22. Anne T. Coughlan and Louis W. Stern, "Marketing Channel Design and Management," in Dawn Iacobucci, ed., *Kellogg on Marketing* (New York: John Wiley, 2001), pp. 247–269.
23. Alberto Sa Vinhas and Erin Anderson, "How Potential Conflict Drives Channel Structure: Concurrent (Direct and Indirect) Channels," *Journal of Marketing Research* 42 (November 2005): 507–515.
24. For an example of when conflict can be viewed as helpful, see Anil Arya and Brian Mittendorf, "Benefits of Channel Discord in the Sale of Durable Goods," *Marketing Science* 25 (January-February 2006): 91–96 and Nirmalya Kumar, "Living with Channel Conflict," *CMO Magazine*, October 2004.
25. This section draws on Coughlan, Anderson, Stern, and El-Ansary, *Marketing Channels*, ch. 6. See also Jonathan D. Hibbard, Nirmalya Kumar, and Louis W. Stern, "Examining the Impact of Destructive Acts in Marketing Channel Relationships," *Journal of Marketing Research* 38 (February 2001): 45–61; Kersi D. Antia and Gary L. Frazier, "The Severity of Contract Enforcement in Interfirm Channel Relationships," *Journal of Marketing* 65 (October 2001): 67–81; James R. Brown, Chekitan S. Dev, and Dong-Jin Lee, "Managing Marketing Channel Opportunism: The Efficiency of Alternative Governance Mechanisms," *Journal of Marketing* 64 (April 2001): 51–65.
26. Christina Passriello, "Fashionably Late? Designer Brands Are Starting to Embrace E-Commerce," *Wall Street Journal*, May 19, 2006, pp. B1, B4.
27. Mylene Mangalindan, "Amazon's MP3 Store Takes Aim at Apple," *Wall Street Journal*, September 26, 2007, p. B3; Jim Carlton, "Amazon Looks to Keep Sales Momentum," *Wall Street Journal*, July 25, 2007, p. A3; Riva Richmond, "Amazon Offer: Its Gigabytes Now for Sale," *Wall Street Journal*, June 27, 2007, p. B5D; "Click to Download," *The Economist*, August 19, 2006, pp. 57–58; Robert D. Hof, "Jeff Bezos' Risky Bet," *BusinessWeek*, November 13, 2006; Erick Schonfield, "The Great Giveaway," *Business 2.0*, April 2005, 80–86.
28. For an in-depth academic examination, see John G. Lynch, Jr. and Dan Ariely, "Wine Online: Search Costs and Competition on Price, Quality, and Distribution," *Marketing Science* 19 (Winter 2000): 83–103.
29. Described in *Inside 1-to-1*, Peppers and Rogers Group newsletter, May 14, 2001.
30. Bob Tedeschi, "How Harley Revved Online Sales," *Business 2.0*, December 2002/January 2003, p. 44.
31. Douglas Lamont, *Conquering the Wireless World: The Age of M-Commerce* (New York: Wiley, 2001); Marc Weingarten, "The Medium Is the Instant Message," *Business 2.0*, February 2002, pp. 98–99.
32. Gordon Xu and Jairo A. Gutierrez, "An Exploratory Study of Killer Applications and Critical Success Factors in M-commerce," *Journal of Electronic Commerce in Organizations* 4.3 (July-September 2006): 63+.
33. Kanako Takahara, "McDonald's, DoCoMo Team Up on Marketing," *Japan Times*, February 27, 2007.

CHAPTER 14

Managing Retailing, Wholesaling, and Logistics

In this chapter, we will address the following questions:

1. What are the major types of marketing intermediaries?
2. What marketing decisions do these marketing intermediaries make?
3. What are the major trends in retailing, wholesaling, and logistics?

MARKETING MANAGEMENT AT ZARA

Spain's Zara has become Europe's leading apparel retailer by offering "fast fashion" at affordable prices. Owned by Inditex, Zara can introduce 20,000 different items in a year, about triple what The Gap would do. The company distributes all its merchandise, regardless of origin, from Spain, and management will tolerate occasional shortages to preserve an image of exclusivity. Unlike some other retailers, Zara doesn't spend lavishly on advertising or deals with designers. Instead, it invests more in its locations, opening spacious stores—over 90% of which it owns—in heavily trafficked, high-end retail zones.

These practices help Zara sell more at full price—85% of its merchandise—than the industry average of 60%. By controlling all aspects of the supply chain, Zara can take a new product from idea to production to store floor in about five weeks, compared to the months needed by a typical clothing manufacturer. With more than 1,000 stores and a varied product line that includes men's and women's clothing as well as home fashions, Zara is a fierce competitor, and so successful that it accounts for three-quarters of parent Inditex's revenue.[1]

In the previous chapter, we examined intermediaries from the viewpoint of manufacturers and service providers who build and manage marketing channels. In this chapter, we view retailers like Zara as well as wholesalers and logistical organizations as requiring and forging their own marketing strategies. While former U.S. stars like The Gap have struggled, innovative retailers like Zara have thrived through skillful strategic planning, targeting and positioning, and the use of sophisticated marketing tools to implement plans and measure performance.

RETAILING

Retailing includes all of the activities involved in selling goods or services directly to final consumers for personal, nonbusiness use. A **retailer** or **retail store** is any business enterprise whose sales volume comes primarily from retailing. Any organization that sells to final consumers—whether a manufacturer, wholesaler, or retailer—is engaged in retailing. It doesn't matter *how* the goods or services are sold (by person, mail, telephone, vending machine, or Internet) or *where* they are sold (in a store, on the street, or in the consumer's home).

Types of Retailers

Retailers exhibit great variety, and new forms keep emerging. Table 14.1 shows the most important types.

Like products, retail-store types pass through stages of growth and decline that can be described as the *retail life cycle*.[2] A type emerges, enjoys a period of accelerated growth, reaches maturity, and then declines. Department stores took 80 years to reach maturity, whereas warehouse retail outlets reached maturity in 10 years. New store types emerge, according to the *wheel-of-retailing hypothesis*, after conventional stores increase services and raise prices to cover the cost. These higher costs provide an

TABLE 14.1   Major Retailer Types

Specialty store: Narrow product line. Athlete's Foot, The Limited, The Body Shop.

Department store: Several product lines. JCPenney, Nordstrom.

Supermarket: Large, low-cost, low-margin, high-volume, self-service store designed to meet total needs for food and household products. Kroger, Jewel, Food Emporium.

Convenience store: Small store in residential area, often open 24/7, limited line of high-turnover convenience products plus takeout. 7-Eleven, Circle K.

Discount store: Standard or specialty merchandise; low-price, low-margin, high-volume stores. Wal-Mart, Circuit City.

Off-price retailer: Leftover goods, overruns, irregular merchandise sold at less than retail. Factory outlets, independent off-price retailers. T.J. Maxx, warehouse clubs Sam's Clubs, Costco, BJ's Wholesale.

Superstore: Huge selling space, routinely purchased food and household items, plus services (laundry, shoe repair, dry cleaning). Category killer (deep assortment in one category) such as Petsmart, Staples, Home Depot; combination store such as Osco; hypermarket (combining supermarket, discount, and warehouse retailing) such as France's Carrefour.

Catalog showroom: Broad selection of high-markup, fast-moving, brand-name goods sold by catalog at discount. Customers pick up merchandise at the store. Inside Edge Ski and Bike.

opportunity for new retail forms to emerge with lower prices and less service.[3] Retailers can position themselves as offering one of four levels of service:

1. *Self-service:* The cornerstone of all discount stores, self-service allows customers to save money by carrying out their own locate-compare-select process.
2. *Self-selection:* Customers find their own goods, although they can ask for help.
3. *Limited service:* These retailers carry more shopping goods and offer more services such as credit and merchandise-return privileges. Customers need more information and assistance.
4. *Full service:* Salespeople are ready to assist in the locate-compare-select process. The high staffing cost, the higher proportion of specialty goods, slower-moving items, and more services, add up to high-cost retailing.

By combining these different service levels with different assortment breadths, we can distinguish four broad retail positioning strategies:

1. *Bloomingdale's:* Stores with a broad product assortment and high value added; they pay attention to store design, product quality, service, and image, and they enjoy high margins.
2. *Tiffany:* Stores with a narrow product assortment and high value added; they cultivate an exclusive image and tend to operate on high margin and low volume.
3. *Sunglass Hut:* With a narrow line and low value added, these stores keep costs and prices low by centralizing buying, merchandising, advertising, and distribution.
4. *Wal-Mart:* With a broad line and low value added, these stores keep prices low to create an image of being a place for bargains, and they make up for low margin with high volume.

Although the overwhelming majority of goods and services is sold through stores, *nonstore retailing* has been growing much faster than store retailing. Nonstore retailing falls into four major categories: (1) *direct selling,* a $9-billion industry with more than 600 companies (such as Avon) selling door-to-door or at home; (2) *direct marketing,* with roots in direct-mail and catalog marketing (L.L. Bean) and encompassing telemarketing (1-800-FLOWERS), television direct-response marketing (QVC), and electronic shopping (Amazon.com); (3) *automatic vending,* used for items such as soft drinks, candy, and newspapers; and (4) *buying service,* a storeless retailer serving a specific clientele—usually employees of large organizations—who are entitled to buy from retailers that provide discounts in return for membership.

Many stores remain independently owned, but an increasing number are part of some form of **corporate retailing** (see Table 14.2). Such organizations achieve economies of scale and have greater purchasing power, wider brand recognition, and better-trained employees.

The New Retail Environment

Retail-store assortments have grown more alike as national-brand manufacturers place their branded goods in more places. Service differentiation also has eroded. Many department stores have trimmed services, and many discounters have increased theirs. Facing stiffer competition from discounters and specialty stores, department stores like JCPenney and Kohl's are waging a comeback war with updated ambiance and products.[4] JCPenney and others now sell online, through mail-order catalogs, and

TABLE 14.2 Major Types of Corporate Retail Organizations

Corporate chain store: Two or more outlets owned and controlled, employing central buying and merchandising, and selling similar lines of merchandise. GAP, Pottery Barn, Hold Everything.

Voluntary chain: A wholesaler-sponsored group of independent retailers engaged in bulk buying and common merchandising. Independent Grocers Association (IGA).

Retailer cooperative: Independent retailers using a central buying organization and joint promotion efforts. Unified Grocers, ACE Hardware.

Consumer cooperative: A retail firm owned by its customers. Members contribute money to open their own store, vote on its policies, elect a group to manage it, and receive dividends.

Franchise organization: Contractual association between a franchiser and franchisees, popular in a number of product and service areas. McDonald's, Subway, Jiffy Lube.

Merchandising conglomerate: A corporation that combines several diversified retailing lines and forms under central ownership, with some integration of distribution and management.

---

phone orders.[5] Some stores are trying limited-time-only "pop-up" outlets to reach seasonal shoppers in busy areas and create brand buzz.[6] As big discounters add grocery sections, supermarkets are battling back with specialty products and customer-focused services.[7] And global competition is growing, with U.S. retailers like Wal-Mart expanding internationally while foreign firms like Tesco's enter U.S. markets.[8]

Retailer Marketing Decisions

In this new retail environment, effective differentiation requires savvy marketing decisions about target market, product assortment and procurement, prices, services and store atmosphere, store activities and experiences, communications, and location.

Target Market Until it defines and profiles its target market, the retailer can't make consistent decisions on product assortment, store decor, advertising messages and media, price, and service levels. Some retailers are slicing the market into finer segments and introducing new store chains for specific niches, the way Hot Topic launched the Torrid chain offering fashions for plus-sized teen girls.

Product Assortment and Procurement The retailer's product assortment—*breadth* and *depth*—must match the target market's shopping expectations. A restaurant can offer a narrow and shallow assortment (small lunch counters), a narrow and deep assortment (delicatessen), a broad and shallow assortment (cafeteria), or a broad and deep assortment (large restaurant). Next, the retailer must develop a product-differentiation strategy. It might feature national brands not available at competing stores (like Saks); feature mostly private branded merchandise (like Benetton); feature the latest or newest items first (like Hot Topic); feature surprise or ever-changing merchandise (like T.J. Maxx); offer customizing services (like Harrod's of London); or offer a highly targeted assortment (like Brookstone).

Some stores use **direct product profitability (DPP)** to measure a product's handling costs (receiving, moving to storage, paperwork, selecting, checking, loading, and space cost) from the time it reaches the warehouse until a customer buys it in the store. Users learn to their surprise that the gross margin on a product often has little relation to the direct product profit. Some high-volume products may have such high handling costs that they are less profitable and deserve less shelf space than some low-volume products. Retailers rarely know which third of their products generates profit, which third breaks even, and which third doesn't yield an economic profit.[9]

Price Price is a key positioning factor and must be decided in relation to the target market, the mix of products and services, and the competition.[10] All retailers would like to achieve both high volumes and high gross margins, but the two don't usually go together. Most retailers fall into the *high-markup, lower-volume group* (fine specialty stores) or the *low-markup, higher-volume group* (mass merchandisers and discount retailers). As noted in Chapter 12, some retailers offer everyday low pricing (EDLP) while others use high-low sale pricing; EDLP can be more profitable for supermarkets in certain situations.[11] "Breakthrough Marketing: Target" describes how Target hits the retail sweet spot with low prices and differentiated products.

Services and Store Atmosphere The *services mix* is a key tool for differentiating a particular store. For example, a store may offer prepurchase services such as telephone and mail orders, advertising, window and interior display, fitting rooms, fashion shows, and trade-ins. Postpurchase services can include shipping and delivery, gift wrapping, adjustments and returns, alterations and tailoring, and installation. Ancillary services include restaurants, repairs, interior decorating, credit, and baby-attendant service.

Atmosphere is another differentiation tool. Every store has a physical layout that makes it hard or easy to move around, as well as a "look." The store must embody a planned atmosphere that matches the shopper's basic motivations: If target consumers are more likely to be in a task-oriented and functional mindset, then a simpler, more restrained in-store environment may be better.[12] The Kohl's department store chain uses a racetrack model to convey customers past all the merchandise in the store, along with a middle aisle for shoppers in a hurry. This loop yields higher per-square-foot revenues than other retailers.[13] Fragrance also

BREAKTHROUGH MARKETING: TARGET

With an innovative merchandising approach and world-class marketing, Target has polished its "upscale discounter" image and achieved annual sales of $59 billion. The first step to successful differentiation was to focus on unique and contemporary merchandise from around the world. The store also arranged to carry exclusive products from star designers such as Michael Graves, Isaac Mizrahi, and Mossimo Giannulli. To differentiate the look of its stores and minimize "visual clutter," Target switched to lower shelves, wider aisles, and halogen and track lighting.

In 1999, the company unveiled what has become a long-running campaign featuring "Bulls-Eye World," full of "funky, retro pop culture" settings where its bulls-eye logo dominates the landscape. Target also developed experiential marketing efforts that generate buzz both locally and globally. It built a 220-foot floating shop, called the *U.S.S. Target*, at a pier on Manhattan's West Side during one holiday season; in one fashion show, its models appeared in climbing gear to move down a vertical "runway" attached to the side of a skyscraper. In the coming decade, Target plans to expand into fast-growing markets such as China and India, helping push annual revenues well beyond $100 billion.[14]

contributes to atmosphere. Bloomingdales uses baby powder fragrance in the baby store; suntan lotion in the bathing suit area; lilacs in lingerie; and cinnamon and pine scent during the holiday season.[15]

Store Activities and Experiences The growth of e-commerce has forced traditional brick-and-mortar retailers to respond. Now retailers also provide a shopping experience as a strong differentiator, in addition to natural advantages such as products that shoppers can actually see, touch, and test; real-life customer service; and no delivery lag time for many purchases.[16] The change can be noticed in practices as simple as calling each shopper a "guest" and as grandiose as building an indoor amusement park. For instance, retailers such as Bass Pro Shops are providing a place to congregate and in-store entertainment for customers who want fun and excitement.[17] See "Marketing Skills: Experience Marketing" for more on this development.

Communications Retailers use a wide range of communication tools to generate traffic and purchases: advertising, special sales, money-saving coupons, frequent shopper rewards, in-store sampling, in-store couponing, point-of-sale displays featuring name brands.[18] Fine stores place tasteful ads in high-fashion magazines and carefully train salespeople to greet customers, interpret their needs, and handle complaints. Off-price retailers promote the idea of bargains and large savings, while conserving on service and sales assistance.

Location The three keys to retail success are "location, location, and location." Stores have five major location choices, as shown in Table 14.3. Given the relationship between high traffic and high rents, retailers need to support location decisions with assessment methods such as traffic counts, surveys of shoppers' habits, and analysis of competitive locations.[19] Several software models for site location have also been formulated.[20] Retailers can assess a particular location's sales effectiveness by

MARKETING SKILLS: EXPERIENCE MARKETING

Experience marketing is a good way for a store to set itself apart. Experts advise starting with a thorough understanding of what customers value and expect. Think about enhancing the sensory experience (feel, look, sound, smell, or taste) in unique, brand appropriate, and memorable ways. A basic experience might be built around a particular sense; for example, the scent of fresh coffee or baked goods in a food store. The Starbucks store experience includes a rich coffee aroma (smell), soft jazz (sound), and comfortable seating (feel). The aim is to create an in-store experience that's "entertaining, educational, aesthetic, and escapist all at once," says one marketer.

The REI retail chain is well known for applying experience marketing to outdoor gear and clothing products. Shoppers can rely on salespeople in any of the 80 stores for informed advice about the best products and services for their needs. Then customers are invited to try before they buy: test climbing equipment on 25-foot walls, wear a Gore-Tex raincoat under a simulated rain shower, test the roominess of a tent. REI stores feature exciting displays, huge product selection, special events, and a division that sells adventure vacations. Thanks to its experience in experience marketing, REI sells $1.2 billion worth of goods and services every year.[21]

TABLE 14.3 Location Options for Retailers

Location	Description
General business district	"Downtown," the oldest and most heavily trafficked city areas.
Regional shopping center	Large suburban mall containing 40 to 200 stores and one or more anchor stores such as JCPenney; or a combination of big box stores such as Circuit City and many smaller stores, including franchise operations.
Community shopping center	Smaller mall with one anchor store and 20 to 40 smaller stores.
Shopping strip	A cluster of stores, usually in one long building, serving a neighborhood's needs for groceries, hardware, dry cleaning, and more.
Location within a larger store	Concession space rented by McDonald's or other retailers within a larger store or an operation such as an airport.

checking the number of people who pass by on an average day; the percentage who enter the store; the percentage of those entering who buy; and the average amount spent per sale.

PRIVATE LABELS

A **private label brand** (also called reseller, store, house, or distributor brand) is one developed by retailers and wholesalers. Retailers such as Benetton, The Body Shop, and Marks and Spencer carry mostly own-brand merchandise. In Britain, the largest food chains, Sainsbury and Tesco, sell 50% and 45% store-label goods, respectively. In the United States, store brands now account for one of every five items sold, a $65 billion business, according to the Private Label Manufacturers' Association.[22] Many manufacturers of branded products are concerned because private labels are rapidly gaining ground (see Table 14.4). Kraft's CEO acknowledges losing sales to private-label competitors—even as supermarkets launch additional private-label foods.[23] Some experts say 50% is the natural limit for carrying private brands, because consumers prefer certain national brands, and many categories aren't feasible or attractive as private labels.[24]

House Brands

Why do intermediaries bother to sponsor their own brands? First, they are more profitable. Intermediaries search for manufacturers with excess capacity to produce the private label at a low cost. Other costs, such as research and development,

TABLE 14.4 Private Labels in Action

Retailer	Example of Private Brands
JCPenney	Arizona apparel, American Living apparel
Kroger	Private Selection foods, Naturally Preferred organics
Macy's	Charter Club apparel, Style & Co bed and bath items
Wal-Mart	Ol'Roy dog food, Great Value paper goods

advertising, sales promotion, and physical distribution, are also much lower, so private labels can sell for less yet generate a higher profit margin. Second, retailers develop exclusive store brands to differentiate themselves. Some retailers are implementing a "no branding" strategy. Japanese retailer Mujirushi Ryohin (the name means "no-brand quality products"), which operates 387 stores in 15 countries, targets 20- to 30-year-olds who want a change from designer goods and like low prices.[25]

Generics are unbranded, plainly packaged, less expensive versions of common products such as spaghetti, paper towels, and canned peaches. They offer standard or lower quality at a price that may be as much as 20% to 40% lower than national brands and 10% to 20% lower than retailer's private label brands. The lower price of generics is made possible by lower-quality ingredients, lower-cost labeling and packaging, and minimal advertising.

The Private Label Threat

In the confrontation between manufacturers' and private brands, retailers have many advantages and increasing market power.[26] Because shelf space is scarce, many supermarkets charge a *slotting fee* for accepting a new brand; often, retailers also charge for special display space and in-store advertising space. They typically display their own brands more prominently and make sure these are well stocked.

The growing power of store brands is not the only factor weakening national brands. Consumers are more price sensitive, trained in part by the continuous barrage of coupons and price specials. The fact that companies have reduced advertising to 30% of their total promotion budget has weakened their brand equity. A steady stream of brand extensions and line extensions has blurred brand identity at times and led to a confusing amount of product proliferation.

Leading manufacturers are responding by investing significantly in R&D for new product development. Also, many are investing in strong "pull" advertising programs to maintain high brand recognition and preference and overcome the in-store marketing advantage of private labels. Top brand marketers are also seeking partnerships with major mass distributors to build economies of scale and cost-saving competitive strategies. Steenkamp and Kumar recommend that manufacturers enhance their brands with symbolic imagery as well as ensuring that functional quality is superior to that of the private labels.[27]

WHOLESALING

Wholesaling includes all the activities in selling goods or services to those who buy for resale or business use. Wholesaling excludes manufacturers and farmers (because they are engaged primarily in production) and retailers. The major types of wholesalers are described in Table 14.5.

Wholesalers (also called *distributors*) differ from retailers in several ways. First, wholesalers pay less attention to promotion, atmosphere, and location because they deal with business customers rather than final consumers. Second, wholesale transactions are usually larger than retail transactions, and wholesalers usually cover a larger trade area than retailers. Third, wholesalers and retailers comply with different legal regulations and taxes.

TABLE 14.5   Major Wholesaler Types

Merchant wholesalers: Independently owned businesses that take title to the merchandise they handle. They are full-service and limited-service jobbers, distributors, mill supply houses.

Full-service wholesalers: Carry stock, maintain a sales force, offer credit, make deliveries, and provide management assistance. Wholesale merchants sell primarily to retailers. Some carry several merchandise lines, some carry one or two lines, others carry only part of a line. Industrial distributors sell to manufacturers and provide services like credit and delivery.

Limited-service wholesalers: Cash-and-carry wholesalers sell a limited line of fast-moving goods to small retailers for cash. *Truck wholesalers* sell and deliver a limited line of semi-perishable goods to supermarkets, grocery stores, hospitals, restaurants, hotels. *Drop shippers* serve bulk industries such as coal, lumber, and heavy equipment, assuming title and risk from the time an order is accepted to its delivery. *Rack jobbers* serve grocery retailers in nonfood items. Delivery people set up displays, price goods, and keep inventory records; they retain title to goods and bill retailers only for goods sold to end of year. *Producers' cooperatives* assemble farm produce to sell in local markets. *Mail-order wholesalers* send catalogs to retail, industrial, and institutional customers; orders are filled and sent by mail, rail, plane, or truck.

Brokers and agents: Facilitate buying and selling, on commission of 2% to 6% of the selling price; limited functions; generally specialize by product line or customer type. *Brokers* bring buyers and sellers together and assist in negotiation, paid by the party hiring them. Food brokers, real estate brokers, insurance brokers. *Agents* represent buyers or sellers on a more permanent basis. Most manufacturers' agents are small businesses with a few skilled salespeople. Selling agents are authorized to sell a manufacturer's entire output; purchasing agents make purchases for buyers and may also receive, inspect, warehouse, and ship merchandise; commission merchants negotiate sales and take physical possession of products.

Manufacturers' and retailers' branches and offices: Wholesaling operations conducted by sellers or buyers themselves rather than through independent wholesalers. Separate branches and offices are dedicated to sales or purchasing. Many retailers set up buying offices in major markets.

Specialized wholesalers: Agricultural assemblers buy the agricultural output of many farms; petroleum bulk plants and terminals consolidate the output of many wells; auction companies auction cars, equipment, etc., to businesses.

Why don't manufacturers sell directly to retailers or final consumers rather than through wholesalers? The main reason is efficiency: Wholesalers are often better at handling one or more of these functions:

- *Selling and promoting.* Wholesalers provide a sales force that helps manufacturers reach many small business customers at a relatively low cost.
- *Buying and assortment building.* Wholesalers can select items and build the assortments their customers need, which saves customers considerable work.
- *Bulk breaking.* Wholesalers achieve savings for their customers through buying in large lots and breaking the bulk into smaller units.
- *Warehousing.* Wholesalers hold inventories, reducing the inventory costs and risks to suppliers and customers.
- *Transportation.* Wholesalers can often provide quicker delivery because they're closer to buyers.
- *Financing.* Wholesalers finance customers by granting credit and finance suppliers by ordering early and paying bills on time.
- *Risk bearing.* Wholesalers absorb some risk by taking title and bearing the cost of theft, damage, spoilage, and obsolescence.

- *Market information.* Wholesalers supply information to suppliers and customers regarding competitors' activities, new products, price developments, and so on.
- *Management services and counseling.* Wholesalers often help retailers train staff, plan store layouts and displays, and set up accounting and inventory-control systems. They may help industrial customers with training and technical services.

Trends in Wholesaling

Wholesaler-distributors have faced mounting pressures in recent years from new sources of competition, demanding customers, new technologies, and more direct-buying programs by large buyers. Manufacturers complain that wholesalers don't aggressively promote their products; act more like order takers; carry insufficient inventory and, therefore, fail to fill customers' orders quickly; fail to supply up-to-date market, customer, and competitive information; fail to bring down their own costs; and charge too much.

Recognizing they must add value to the channel, wholesalers have rallied to the challenge. They're revisiting decisions on target markets, products and services, price, communications, and distribution; increasing asset productivity by better managing inventories and receivables; and cutting costs by investing in materials-handling technology and information systems. For example, with annual sales of $5.9 billion, W. W. Grainger is the leading supplier of facilities maintenance products that help 1.8 million North American businesses and institutions stay up and running. It serves customers through more than 500 branches and state-of-the-art distribution centers in North America. Supported by more than 1,300 suppliers, Grainger offers an assortment of 800,000 supplies and parts available by catalog, direct mail, Web site, and in branches.[28]

Strengthening Channel Relationships

Interviewing leading industrial distributors, Narus and Anderson identified four ways wholesalers can strengthen relationships with manufacturers: (1) seek a clear agreement with manufacturers about their expected functions in the channel; (2) gain insight into manufacturers' requirements by visiting plants and attending conventions and trade shows; (3) fulfill commitments by meeting volume targets, paying promptly, and providing feedback of customer information to manufacturers; and (4) offer value-added services to help suppliers.[29]

Still, the wholesaling industry faces fierce resistance to price increases and the winnowing out of suppliers based on cost and quality. Also, the trend toward vertical integration, in which manufacturers try to control or own their intermediaries, is still strong.

MARKET LOGISTICS

Physical distribution starts at the factory, where managers choose warehouses and transportation carriers that will deliver products to final destinations in the desired time or at the lowest cost. Physical distribution has been expanded into the broader concept of **supply chain management (SCM)**. Supply chain management starts before physical distribution, covering procurement of inputs (raw materials, components, and equipment); conversion into finished products; and product movement to final destinations. An even broader perspective calls for studying the suppliers' suppliers. The supply chain perspective can help a company identify superior suppliers and distributors and help them improve productivity, which ultimately brings down the company's costs.

Market logistics includes planning the infrastructure to meet demand, then implementing and controlling the physical flows of materials and final goods from points of origin to points of use to meet customer needs at a profit. Market logistics planning has four steps, as shown in Figure 14.1, which lead to examining the most efficient way to deliver value.

Integrated Logistics Systems

The market logistics task calls for **integrated logistics systems (ILS)**, which include materials management, material flow systems, and physical distribution, aided by information technology. Third-party suppliers, such as FedEx Global Supply Chain Services, often participate in designing or managing these systems. For example, on behalf of General Motors, FedEx manages the movement of components and parts from 1,125 suppliers to 27 automotive assembly plants throughout North America.[30]

FIGURE 14.1 Steps in Market Logistics Planning

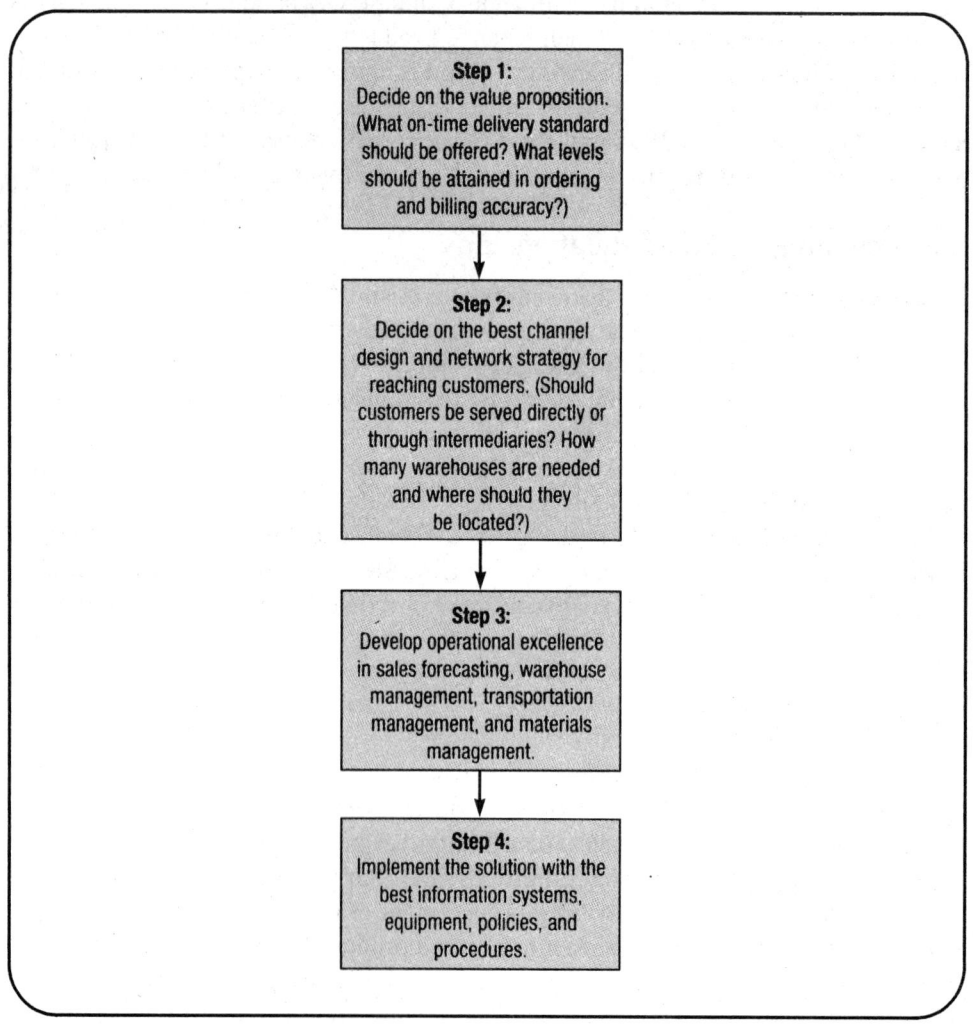

Market logistics link several activities, starting with sales forecasting, which helps the company schedule distribution, production, and inventory levels. In turn, production plans indicate the materials the purchasing department must order. These materials arrive through inbound transportation, enter the receiving area, and are stored in raw-material inventory, to be converted into finished goods. Finished-goods inventory is the link between customer orders and manufacturing activity. Customers' orders draw down the finished-goods inventory level, and manufacturing activity builds it up. Finished goods flow off the assembly line and pass through packaging, in-plant warehousing, shipping-room processing, outbound transportation, field warehousing, and customer delivery and servicing.

Management has become concerned about the total cost of market logistics, which can amount to 30% to 40% of the product's cost. The grocery industry alone thinks it can decrease its annual operating costs by 10%, or $30 billion, by revamping market logistics. A typical box of breakfast cereal spends 104 days chugging through a labyrinth of intermediaries to reach the supermarket.[31] No wonder experts call market logistics "the last frontier for cost economies." In 1982, logistics represented 14.5% of U.S. GDP; by 2006, the share had dropped to just over 8%.[32] Lower logistics costs permit lower prices, higher profit margins, or both. Although market logistics can be costly, a well-planned program can be a potent tool in competitive marketing.

Market-Logistics Objectives

Many companies state their market-logistics objective as "getting the right goods to the right places at the right time for the least cost." Unfortunately, no market-logistics system can simultaneously maximize customer service and minimize distribution cost. Maximum customer service implies large inventories, premium transportation, and multiple warehouses, which can be costly.

Given that market-logistics activities involve strong trade-offs, managers must make decisions on a total system basis. The starting point is to study what customers require and what competitors offer. Customers want on-time delivery, supplier willingness to meet emergency needs, careful handling of merchandise, and supplier willingness to take back defective goods and resupply them quickly. The company must research the relative importance of these service outputs. For example, service-repair time is very important to buyers of copying equipment. Xerox developed a service-delivery standard that "can put a disabled machine anywhere in the continental United States back into operation within three hours after receiving the service request." It then designed a service division of personnel, parts, and locations to deliver on this promise.

The company must also consider competitors' service standards, seeking to match or exceed those levels. Still, the objective is to maximize profits, not sales, which means looking at the costs of providing higher service levels. Some companies offer less service and charge a lower price; others offer more service and charge a premium price. In the end, the company must establish some service promise to the market. One appliance manufacturer set these service standards: to deliver at least 95% of the dealer's orders within seven days of order receipt, to fill the dealer's orders with 99% accuracy, to answer dealer inquiries on order status within three hours, and to ensure that damage to merchandise in transit doesn't exceed 1%.

Now the company must design a system that will minimize the cost of achieving its logistical objectives. Each possible market-logistics system will lead to the following cost:

$$M = T + FW + VW + S$$

where

M = total market-logistics cost of proposed system;
T = total freight cost of proposed system;
FW = total fixed warehouse cost of proposed system;
VW = total variable warehouse costs (including inventory) of proposed system;

and

S = total cost of lost sales due to average delivery delay under proposed system.

Choosing a market-logistics system calls for examining the total cost (M) associated with different systems and selecting the system that minimizes it. If S is hard to measure, the company should aim to minimize $T + FW + VW$ for a target level of customer service.

Market-Logistics Decisions

Managers face four major decisions with regard to market logistics: (1) How should orders be handled? (2) Where should stocks be located? (3) How much stock should be held? (4) How should goods be shipped?

Order Processing Most companies want to shorten the *order-to-payment cycle*—the elapsed time between an order's receipt, delivery, and payment. This cycle has many steps, including order transmission by the salesperson, order entry and customer credit check, inventory and production scheduling, order and invoice shipment, and receipt of payment. The longer this cycle, the lower the customer's satisfaction and the lower the company's profits. General Electric's information system checks the customer's credit standing upon receipt of an order and determines whether and where the items are in stock. The system issues an order to ship, bills the customer, updates inventory records, orders new stock, and notifies the sales representative that the order is on the way—all in less than 15 seconds.

Warehousing Every manufacturer has to store finished goods until they are sold because production and consumption cycles rarely match. The storage function helps to smooth discrepancies between production and quantities desired by the market. The company must decide on the number of inventory stocking locations. Having more stocking locations means that goods can be delivered to customers more quickly, but it also means higher warehousing costs. To reduce warehousing and inventory duplication costs, the company might centralize its inventory in one place and use fast transportation to fill orders.

Some inventory is kept at or near the plant, and the rest is located in warehouses in other locations. The company might own private warehouses and also rent space in public warehouses. *Storage warehouses* store goods for moderate to long periods of time. *Distribution warehouses* receive goods from various company plants and suppliers and move them out as soon as possible. *Automated warehouses* employ advanced materials-handling systems under the control of a central computer. When the Helene Curtis Company replaced its six antiquated warehouses with a new $32 million facility, it cut its distribution costs by 40%.[33]

Inventory Inventory levels represent a major cost. Salespeople would like companies to carry enough stock to fill all customer orders immediately, but this isn't cost-effective. *Inventory cost increases at an accelerating rate as the customer service level approaches 100%.* Management needs to know how much sales and profits would increase as a result of carrying larger inventories and promising faster order fulfillment times, and then make a decision.

Inventory management requires knowing when and how much to order. As inventory draws down, management must know at what stock level to place a new order. This stock level is called the *order* (or *reorder*) *point*. An order point of 20 means reordering when the stock falls to 20 units. The order point should balance the risks of stockout against the costs of overstock. The other decision is how much to order. Here, the company is balancing order-processing costs against inventory-carrying costs. *Order-processing costs* for a manufacturer consist of *setup costs* and *running costs* (operating costs when production is running). If setup costs are low, the manufacturer can produce the item often, and the average cost per item is stable and equal to the running costs. If setup costs are high, however, the manufacturer can cut the average cost per unit by producing a long run and carrying more inventory.

Order-processing costs must be compared with *inventory-carrying costs*. The larger the average stock carried, the higher the inventory-carrying costs, including storage charges, cost of capital, taxes and insurance, depreciation, and obsolescence. This means that marketing managers who want their companies to carry larger inventories must show that the larger inventories would produce incremental gross profit that exceeds incremental carrying costs.

The optimal order quantity can be determined by analyzing the sum of order-processing costs and inventory-carrying costs at different order levels. Figure 14.2 shows that the order-processing cost per unit decreases with the number of units ordered because the costs are spread over more units. Inventory-carrying charges per unit increase with the number of units ordered because each unit remains longer in inventory. The two cost curves are summed vertically into a total-cost curve. The lowest point on the total-cost curve is projected down on the horizontal axis to find the optimal order quantity, Q^*.[34]

FIGURE 14.2 Determining Optimal Order Quantity

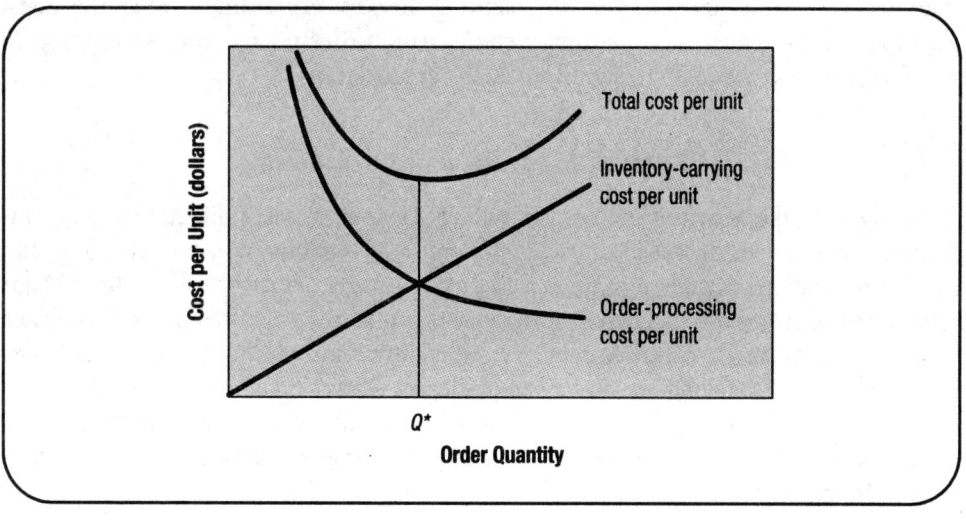

Companies are reducing their inventory costs by treating inventory items differently, positioning them according to risk and opportunity. They distinguish between bottleneck items (high risk, low opportunity), critical items (high risk, high opportunity), commodities (low risk, high opportunity), and nuisance items (low risk, low opportunity).[35] They're also keeping slow-moving items in a central location while carrying fast-moving items in warehouses closer to customers. The ultimate answer to carrying *near-zero inventory* is to build for order, not for stock.

Transportation   Transportation choices affect product pricing, on-time delivery performance, and the condition of the goods on arrival, all of which influence customer satisfaction. In shipping goods to its warehouses, dealers, and customers, the company can choose among rail, air, truck, waterway, and pipeline, using such criteria as speed, frequency, dependability, capability, availability, traceability, and cost. For speed, air and truck are the prime contenders; for low cost, waterway and pipeline are appropriate.

Shippers are increasingly combining two or more transportation modes, thanks to containerization. **Containerization** consists of putting the goods in boxes or trailers that are easy to transfer between two transportation modes. *Piggyback* describes the use of rail and trucks; *fishyback*, water and trucks; *trainship*, water and rail; and *airtruck*, air and trucks. Each coordinated mode offers specific advantages. For example, piggyback is cheaper than trucking alone, yet provides flexibility and convenience.

Shippers can choose from private, contract, and common carriers. If the shipper owns its own truck or air fleet, it becomes a *private carrier*. A *contract carrier* is an independent organization that sells transportation services to others on a contract basis. A *common carrier* provides services between predetermined points on a schedule and is available to all shippers at standard rates. In Europe, P&G uses a three-tier logistics system to schedule deliveries of fast- and slow-moving goods, bulky and small items in the most efficient way.[36]

Market Logistics Lessons

Market-logistics strategies must be derived from business strategies, rather than solely from cost considerations. The logistics system must be information-intensive and establish electronic links among all the significant parties. Finally, the company should set its logistics goals to match or exceed competitors' service standards and should involve members of all relevant teams in the planning process. For example, after the Pepsi Bottling Group overhauled its supply chain, from order taking to truck loading to store deliveries, it was able to significantly lower stock outs.[37]

EXECUTIVE SUMMARY

Retailing is all the activities involved in selling goods or services directly to final consumers for personal, nonbusiness use, including store retailing, nonstore retailing, and retail organizations. Retail-store types pass through stages of growth and decline. Major types of retail stores are specialty stores, department stores, supermarkets, convenience stores, discount stores, off-price retailers, superstores, and catalog showrooms. Major types of nonstore retailing are direct selling, direct marketing, automatic vending, and buying services. Many retailers achieve economies of scale as part of corporate retailing. Retailing firms face decisions about target markets, product assortment and procurement, services and store atmosphere, price, promotion, and location.

Wholesaling covers all the activities involved in selling goods or services to those who buy for resale or business use. Wholesalers can perform certain functions better and more cost effectively than producers can, such as selling and promoting, buying and assortment building, bulk breaking, warehousing, transportation, financing, risk bearing, dissemination of market information, and training and consulting. Successful wholesalers add value by adapting their services to meet suppliers' and target customers' needs. Producers manage market logistics by planning the infrastructure to meet demand, then implementing and controlling the physical flows of materials and final goods from points of origin to points of use to meet customer needs at a profit. This involves managing supply chain activities to process orders, warehouse goods, manage inventory, and transport goods in line with market logistics objectives.

NOTES

1. Robert Murphy, "Inditex Lists 33% Earnings Gain," *WWD*, June 14, 2007, p. 15; Kerry Capell, "Fashion Conquistador," *BusinessWeek*, September 4, 2006, pp. 38–39; Rachel Tipaldy, "Zara: Taking the Lead in Fast-Fashion, *BusinessWeek*, April 4, 2006; Vivian Manning-Schaffel, "Zara-Zesty," brandchannel.com, August 23, 2004; Kasra Ferdows, Michael A. Lewis, and Jose A.D. Machuca, "Zara's Secret for Fast Fashion," *Harvard Business School Working Knowledge*, February 21, 2005.
2. William R. Davidson, Albert D. Bates, and Stephen J. Bass, "Retail Life Cycle," *Harvard Business Review* (November–December 1976): 89–96.
3. Stanley C. Hollander, "The Wheel of Retailing," *Journal of Marketing* (July 1960): 37–42.
4. Cheryl Lu-Lien Tan, "Hot Kohl's," *Wall Street Journal*, April 16, 2007, p. R3.
5. Robert Berner, "J. C. Penney Gets the Net," *BusinessWeek*, May 7, 2007, p. 70; Anne D'Innocenzio, "Penney's Uses Net to Boost Traffic and Image," *Marketing News*, April 1, 2006, pp. 29–30.
6. Theresa Howard, "Retail Stores Pop Up for Limited Time Only," *USA Today*, May 28, 2004, p. 1B.
7. Charles Fishman, "The Anarchist's Cookbook," *Fast Company*, July 2004, pp. 70–78.
8. Dale Kasler and Jon Ortiz, "Retail Giant Thinking Smaller," *Sacramento Bee*, August 28, 2007, p. A1.
9. Uta Werner, John McDermott, and Greg Rotz, "Retailers at the Crossroads: How to Develop Profitable New Growth Strategies," *Journal of Business Strategy* 25, no. 2 (2004): 10–17.
10. Venkatesh Shankar and Ruth N. Bolton, "An Empirical Analysis of Determinants of Retailer Pricing Strategy," *Marketing Science* 23 (Winter 2004): 28–49.
11. Frank Feather, *The Future Consumer* (Toronto: Warwick Publishing, 1994), p. 171. Also see Stephen J. Hoch, Xavier Dreeze, and Mary E. Purk, "EDLP, Hi-Lo, and Margin Arithmetic," *Journal of Marketing* (October 1994): 1–15; David R. Bell and James M. Lattin, "Shopping Behavior and Consumer Preference for Retail Price Format: Why 'Large Basket' Shoppers Prefer EDLP," *Marketing Science* 17 (Spring 1998): 66–68.
12. Velitchka D. Kaltcheva and Barton Weitz, "When Should a Retailer Create an Exciting Store Environment," *Journal of Marketing* 70 (January 2006): 107–118.
13. Cametta Coleman, "Kohl's Retail Racetrack," *Wall Street Journal*, March 1, 2000, pp. B1+; Lu-Lien Tan, "Hot Kohl's," p. R3.
14. Maria Puente, "Top Fashion Designers Go Down-Market," *USA Today*, September 25, 2007, www.usatoday.com; Ann Zimmerman, "Staying on Target," *Wall Street Journal*, May 7, 2007, p. B1; Katherine Bowers, "Target Eyes Overseas Expansion," *Daily News Record*, April 16, 2007, p. 49; Michelle Conlin, "Mass with Class," *Forbes*, January 11, 1999, p. 50; Shelly Branch, "How Target Got Hot," *Fortune*, May 24, 1999, p. 169; Julie Schlosser, "How Target Does It," *Fortune*, October 18, 2004, p. 100; Target.com.
15. Mindy Fetterman and Jayne O'Donnell, "Just Browsing at the Mall? That's What *You* Think," *USA Today*, September 1, 2006, pp. 1B, 2B.
16. Kenneth T. Rosen and Amanda L. Howard, "E-tail: Gold Rush or Fool's Gold?" *California Management Review* (April 1, 2000): 72–100; "Reinventing the Store," *The Economist*, November 22, 2003, pp. 65–68.
17. For more discussion, see Philip Kotler, "Atmospherics as a Marketing Tool," *Journal of*

Retailing (Winter 1973–1974): 48–64. Also see B. Joseph Pine II and James H. Gilmore, *The Experience Economy* (Boston: Harvard Business School Press, 1999).

18. Jeff Cioletti, "Super Marketing," *Beverage World*, November 2006, pp. 60–61.
19. R. L. Davies and D. S. Rogers, eds., *Store Location and Store Assessment Research* (New York: John Wiley, 1984).
20. See Sara L. McLafferty, *Location Strategies for Retail and Service Firms* (Lexington, MA: Lexington Books, 1987).
21. Bethany Clough, "Ready for Battle," *Fresno Bee*, August 1, 2007, www.fresnobee.com; Bethany Clough, "REI Considers Fresno, Calif., for New Store," *Fresno Bee*, August 23, 2005, www.fresnobee.com; Stephane Fitch, "Uphill Battle," *Forbes*, April 25, 2005, p. 62; Tim Palmer, "Sensing a Winner," *Grocer*, January 26, 2002, pp. 40+ "Go Live with a Big Brand Experience," *Marketing*, October 26, 2000, pp. 45+.
22. www.plma.com (May 2007).
23. Ann Zimmerman, David Kesmodel, and Julie Jargon, "From Cheap Stand-in to Shelf Star," *Wall Street Journal*, August 29, 2007, p. B1.
24. Kusum Ailawadi and Bari Harlam, "An Empirical Analysis of the Determinants of Retail Margins: The Role of Store-Brand Share," *Journal of Marketing* 68 (January 2004): 147–165.
25. Kenji Hall, "Zen and the Art of Selling Minimalism," *Business Week*, April 9, 2007, p. 45; Rob Walker, "Museum Quality," *The New York Times Magazine*, January 9, 2005, p. 25.
26. Michael Felding, "No Longer Plain, Simple," *Marketing News*, May 15, 2006, pp. 11–13; Rob Walker, "Shelf Improvement," *New York Times*, May 7, 2006.
27. Nirmalya Kumar and Jan-Benedict E.M. Steenkamp, *Private Label Strategy: How to Meet the Store Brand Challenge* (Boston, MA: Harvard Business School Press, 2007).
28. Kate Maddox, Sean Callahan, and Carol Krol, "Top Trends," *B to B*, June 13, 2005, pp. 22+; "Annual Meetings: Grainger Out to Build Distribution Efficiency," *Crain's Chicago Business*, May 6, 2002, p. 12.
29. J.A. Narus and J.C. Anderson, "Contributing as a Distributor to Partnerships with Manufacturers," *Business Horizons* (September-October 1987). Also see James D. Hlavecek and Tommy J. McCuistion, "Industrial Distributors—When, Who, and How," *Harvard Business Review* (March–April 1983): 96–101.
30. "FedEx Honored as a 2006 Supplier of the Year," *Traffic World*, April 2, 2007.
31. Ronald Henkoff, "Delivering the Goods," *Fortune*, November 28, 1994, pp. 64–78.
32. "Cargo Cults," *The Economist: A Survey of Logistics*, June 17, 2006, pp. 9–14.
33. Rita Koselka, "Distribution Revolution," *Forbes*, May 25, 1992, pp. 54–62.
34. The optimal order quantity is given by the formula $Q^* = 2DS/IC$, where D = annual demand, S = cost to place one order, and I = annual carrying cost per unit. Known as the economic-order quantity formula, it assumes a constant ordering cost, a constant cost of carrying an additional unit in inventory, a known demand, and no quantity discounts. For more, see Richard J. Tersine, *Principles of Inventory and Materials Management*, 4th ed. (Upper Saddle River, NJ: Prentice Hall, 1994).
35. William C. Copacino, *Supply Chain Management* (Boca Raton, FL: St. Lucie Press, 1997), pp. 122–123.
36. "Manufacturing Complexity," *The Economist: A Survey of Logistics*, June 17, 2006, pp. 6–9.
37. Chad Terhune, "Pepsi's Supply-Chain Fix," *Wall Street Journal*, June 6, 2006.

PART VI Communicating Value

CHAPTER 15

Designing and Managing Integrated Marketing Communications

In this chapter, we will address the following questions:

1. What is the role of marketing communications?
2. What are the major steps in developing effective communications?
3. What is the communications mix and how should it be set?
4. What is an integrated marketing communications program and how is it managed?

MARKETING MANAGEMENT AT DOVE

Until recently, Dove was a Unilever stalwart backed by traditional advertising touting the brand's benefit of one-quarter moisturizing cream and exhorting women to take the seven-day Dove test to test its effects. Then came the launch of Dove's Real Beauty campaign celebrating "real women" of all shapes, sizes, ages, and colors, based on research revealing that only 2% of women worldwide considered themselves beautiful. Ads featuring candid and confident images of full-bodied women—not traditional models—promoted Dove skin products such as Intensive Firming Cream, Lotion, and Body Wash.

The multimedia campaign was thoroughly integrated, combining TV and print ads with new media such as real-time voting for models on cell phones and tabulated displays of results on giant billboards. Dove's "Campaign for Real Beauty" Web site included ad videos like the "Evolution," a rapid-motion view of an ordinary-looking woman transformed by makeup artists, hairdressers, lighting, and digital retouching to look like a model. Uploaded to YouTube, it became an instant viral hit, drawing 2.5 million views. The campaign boosted Dove sales and share in every country in which it was launched—and received the American Marketing Association's Grand EFFIE for the most effective marketing campaign in 2006.[1]

Modern marketing calls for more than developing a good product, pricing it attractively, and making it accessible. Firms must also communicate with stakeholders and the general public. The question is not whether to communicate but what to say, how to say it, to whom, and how often—difficult decisions as marketers clamor for the consumer's increasingly divided attention. This chapter describes how communications work, what they can do for a company, and how holistic marketers integrate marketing communications. Chapter 16 examines mass communications (advertising, sales promotion, events and experiences, public relations, and publicity); Chapter 17 discusses personal communications (direct marketing, e-commerce, personal selling).

THE ROLE OF MARKETING COMMUNICATIONS

Marketing communications are the means by which firms attempt to inform, persuade, and remind consumers—directly or indirectly—about the products and brands they sell. They represent the "voice" of the company and brand and are a good way to establish a dialogue and build relationships with consumers. Marketing communications are used to tell or show how and why a product is used, by what kind of person, and where and when; explain what the company and brand stand for; and offer an incentive for trial or usage. Companies use marketing communications to link brands to other people, places, events, brands, experiences, feelings, and things. And they contribute to brand equity by establishing the brand in memory and creating a brand image; they can drive sales and even affect shareholder value.[2]

The Changing Marketing Communications Environment

Although marketing communications can play a number of crucial roles, they must do so in an increasingly tough communication environment. Technology and other factors have profoundly changed the way consumers process communications, and even whether they choose to process them. The rapid diffusion of broadband Internet connections, ad-skipping digital video recorders, multipurpose cell phones, and portable music and video players have forced marketers to rethink a number of their traditional practices.[3] These dramatic changes have eroded the effectiveness of the mass media.[4] In fact, consumers not only have more media choices, they also have a choice about whether and how they want to receive commercial content.[5]

Commercial clutter is rampant, and it seems the more consumers tune out marketing appeals, the more marketers try to dial them up. Supermarket eggs have been stamped with the name of CBS; Chinese food cartons promote Continental

Airlines; and USAirways is selling ads on its motion sickness bags. Ads in almost every medium and form have been on the rise, causing some consumers to feel that advertising is increasingly invasive.[6]

Marketing Communications, Brand Equity, and Sales

Although advertising is often a central element of a marketing communications program, it's not the only one—or even the most important one—in terms of building brand equity and driving sales. The **marketing communications mix** consists of eight major modes of communication:[7]

1. *Advertising.* Any paid form of nonpersonal presentation and promotion of ideas, goods, or services by an identified sponsor.
2. *Sales promotion.* Short-term incentives to encourage trial or purchase of a product or service.
3. *Events and experiences.* Company-sponsored activities and programs designed to create brand-related interactions.
4. *Public relations and publicity.* Programs promoting or protecting company or product image.
5. *Direct marketing.* Use of mail, telephone, fax, e-mail, or Internet to communicate directly with or solicit response or dialogue from specific customers and prospects.
6. *Interactive marketing.* Online activities and programs to engage customers or prospects and directly or indirectly raise awareness, improve image, or elicit sales.
7. *Word-of-mouth marketing.* People-to-people oral, written, or electronic communications related to the merits or experiences of purchasing or using products or services.
8. *Personal selling.* Face-to-face interaction with prospective purchasers for the purpose of making presentations, answering questions, and procuring orders.

Company communication actually goes beyond the specific platforms listed in Table 15.1. The product's styling and price, the package shape and color, the salesperson's manner and dress, and the store or dealership decor all communicate something to buyers. Every *brand contact* delivers an impression that can strengthen or weaken a customer's view of the company.[8]

As Figure 15.1 shows, communications contribute to brand equity by creating brand awareness, linking the brand image with the right associations, eliciting positive brand responses, and/or facilitating a stronger consumer-brand connection. And all marketing communications activities must be integrated to deliver a consistent message and achieve the strategic positioning.

Communications Process Models

Marketers should understand the fundamental elements of effective communications. Two models are useful: a macromodel and a micromodel. Figure 15.2 shows a communications macromodel with nine elements. Two represent the major parties in a communication—*sender* and *receiver*. Two represent the major communication tools—*message* and *media*. Four represent major functions—*encoding, decoding, response,* and *feedback*. The last element in the system is *noise* (random and competing messages that may interfere with the intended communication).[9]

TABLE 15.1 Common Communication Platforms

Advertising	Sales Promotion	Events/ Experiences	Public Relations	Personal Selling	Direct Marketing
Print and broadcast ads	Contests, games, sweepstakes, lotteries	Sports	Press Kits	Sales presentations	Catalogs
Packaging-outer		Entertainment	Speeches	Sales meetings	Mailings
Packaging inserts	Premiums and gifts	Festivals	Seminars	Incentive programs	Telemarketing
Motion pictures	Sampling	Arts	Annual reports	Samples	Electronic shopping
Brochures and booklets	Fairs and trade shows	Causes	Charitable donations	Fairs and trade shows	TV shopping
Posters and leaflets	Exhibits	Factory tours	Publications		Fax mail
Directories	Demonstrations	Company museums	Community relations		E-mail
Reprints of ads	Coupons	Street activities	Lobbying		Voice mail
Billboards	Rebates		Identity media		
Display signs	Low-interest financing		Company magazine		
Point-of-purchase displays	Entertainment				
Audiovisual material	Trade-in allowances				
Symbols and logos	Continuity programs				
Videotapes	Tie-ins				

Micromodels of marketing communications concentrate on consumers' specific responses to communications. Figure 15.3 summarizes four classic *response hierarchy models*. These models assume that the buyer passes through a cognitive, affective, and behavioral stage, in that order. This "learn-feel-do" sequence is appropriate when the audience has high involvement with a product category perceived to have high differentiation, as in purchasing a car. An alternative sequence, "do-feel-learn," is relevant when the audience has high involvement but perceives little or no differentiation within the product category, as in purchasing an airline ticket. A third sequence, "learn-do-feel," is relevant when the audience has low involvement and perceives little differentiation within the product category, as in purchasing salt. By choosing the right sequence, the marketer can do a better job of planning communications.[10]

DEVELOPING EFFECTIVE COMMUNICATIONS

Developing effective communications requires eight steps. The first five steps are (1) identify the target audience; (2) determine the objectives; (3) design the communications; (4) select the channels; and (5) establish the budget. The final three steps will be examined later in this chapter: (6) decide on the media mix; (7) measure the results; and (8) manage integrated marketing communications.

Chapter 15 Designing and Managing Integrated Marketing Communications

FIGURE 15.1 Integrating Marketing Communications to Build Brand Equity

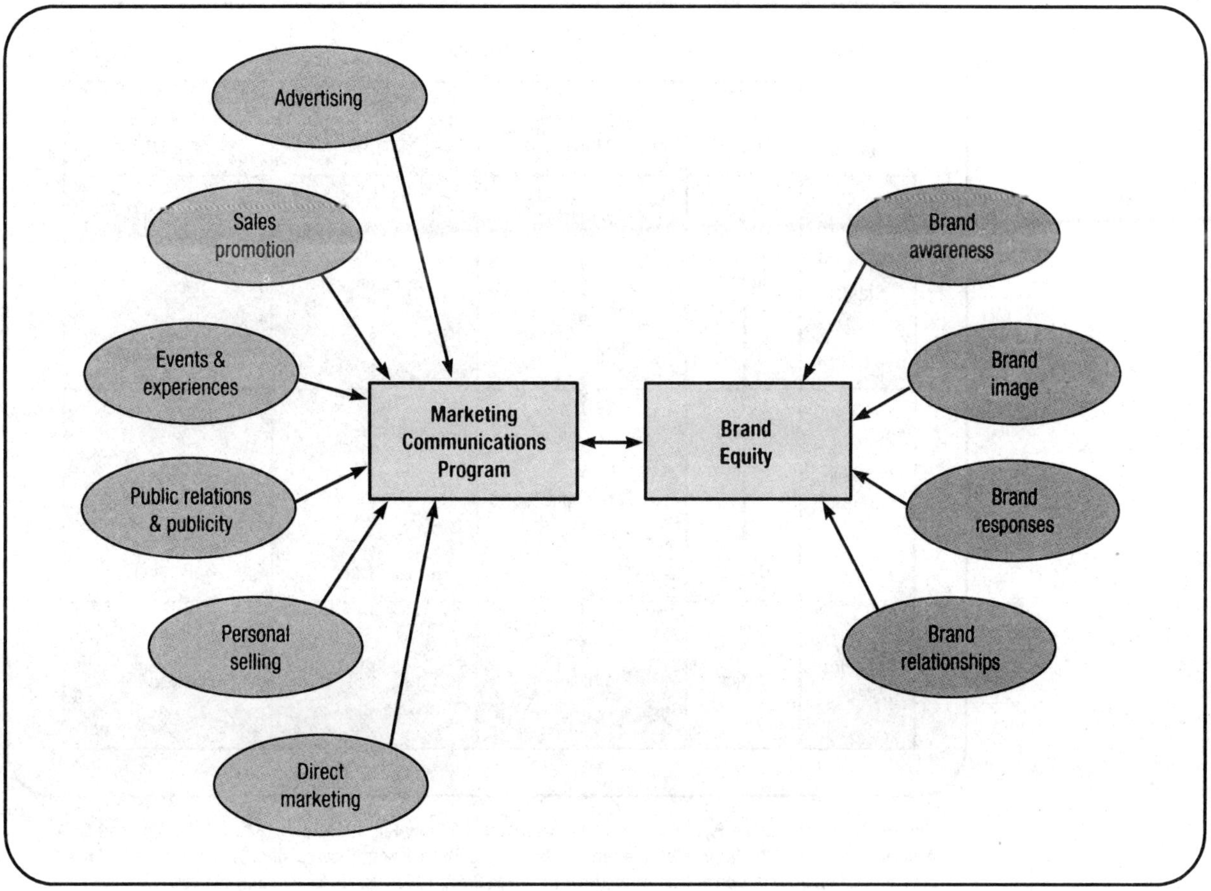

FIGURE 15.2 Elements in the Communication Process

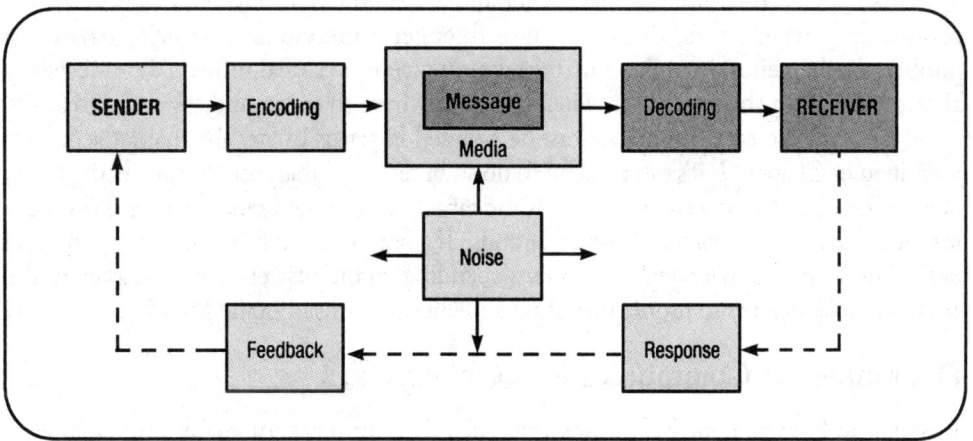

FIGURE 15.3 Response Hierarchy Models

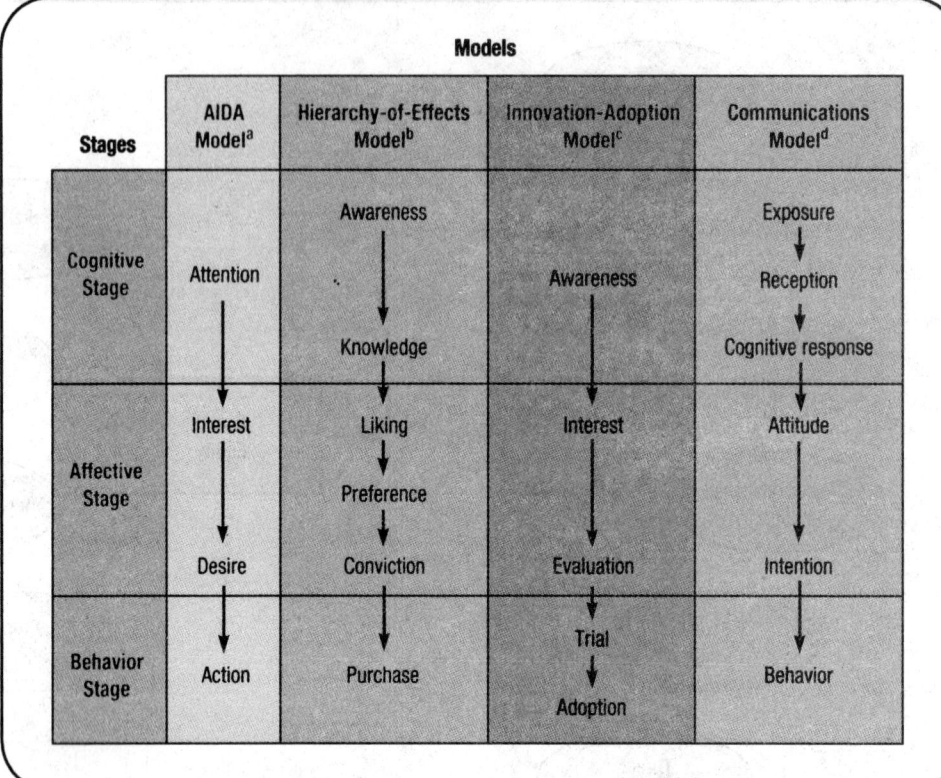

Sources: [a] E. K. Strong, *The Psychology of Selling* (New York: McGraw-Hill, 1925), p. 9; [b] Robert J. Lavidge and Gary A. Steiner, "A Model for Predictive Measurements of Advertising Effectiveness," *Journal of Marketing* (October 1961): 61; [c] Everett M. Rogers, *Diffusion of Innovation* (New York: Free Press, 1962), pp. 79–86; [d] Various sources.

Identify the Target Audience

The first step is to identify a clear target audience: potential buyers of the company's products, current users, deciders, or influencers; individuals, groups, particular publics, or the general public. The target audience is a critical influence on decisions about what to say, how to say it, when to say it, where to say it, and to whom to say it.

Though the target audience can be profiled in terms of any the market segments identified in Chapter 7, it's often useful to do so in terms of usage and loyalty. Is the target new to the category or a current user? Is the target loyal to the brand, loyal to a competitor, or someone who switches between brands? If a brand user, is he or she a heavy or light user? Communication strategy will differ depending on the answers. Many marketers also conduct *image analysis* to profile the target audience in terms of brand knowledge.

Determine the Communications Objectives

Rossiter and Percy identify four possible objectives for marketing communications, as follows:[11]

1. *Category need.* Establish a product or service category as necessary to remove or satisfy a perceived discrepancy between a current motivational state and a desired emotional state.

Chapter 15 Designing and Managing Integrated Marketing Communications

2. *Brand awareness.* Ability to recognize or recall the brand within the category in sufficient detail to make a purchase. Recognition is easier to achieve than recall, but recall is important outside the store, whereas brand recognition is important inside the store. Brand awareness provides a foundation for brand equity.
3. *Brand attitude.* Evaluation of the brand's perceived ability to meet a currently relevant need. Relevant brand needs may be negatively oriented (problem removal or avoidance, incomplete satisfaction, normal depletion) or positively oriented (sensory gratification, intellectual stimulation, or social approval).
4. *Brand purchase intention.* Self-instructions to buy the brand or take buying-related action.

The most effective communications often can achieve multiple objectives.

Design the Communications

Formulating the communications to achieve the desired response will require solving three problems: what to say (message strategy), how to say it (creative strategy), and who should say it (message source).

Message Strategy In determining message strategy, management searches for appeals, themes, or ideas that tie into the brand positioning and help establish points-of-parity or points-of-difference. Some of these may relate directly to product or service performance (the quality, economy, or value of the brand), whereas others may relate to more extrinsic considerations (the brand as being contemporary, popular, or traditional). John Maloney saw buyers as expecting one of four types of reward from a product: rational, sensory, social, or ego satisfaction.[12] Buyers might visualize these rewards from results-of-use experience, product-in-use experience, or incidental-to-use experience.

Creative Strategy *Creative strategies*, how marketers translate their messages into a specific communication, can be classified as either informational appeal or transformational appeal.[13] An **informational appeal** elaborates on attributes or benefits. Examples in advertising are problem-solution ads (Excedrin stops headache pain quickly), product demonstration ads (Thompson Water Seal can withstand intense rain, snow, and heat), product comparison ads (DirecTV offers better HD options than cable operators), and testimonials (NBA star LeBron James pitching Sprite and Nike). Such appeals assume the consumer is processing the communication very rationally.

The best ads with informational appeals ask questions and allow consumers to form their own conclusions.[14] If Honda had hammered away that the Element was for young people, this strong definition might have kept older consumers away. Some stimulus ambiguity can lead to a broader market definition and more spontaneous purchases. A one-sided presentation praising a product might seem to be more effective than two-sided arguments that also mention shortcomings. Yet two-sided messages may be more appropriate, especially when a negative association must be overcome. In this spirit, Heinz ran the message "Heinz ketchup is slow good."[15] Two-sided messages are more effective with more educated audiences and those who are initially opposed.[16]

The order in which arguments are presented is also important.[17] In a one-sided message, presenting the strongest argument first establishes audience attention and interest. This is important in newspapers and other media where the audience often does not attend to the whole message. With a captive audience, a climactic presentation might be more effective. In a two-sided message, if the audience is initially opposed, the communicator might start with the other side's argument and conclude with the strongest argument.[18]

A **transformational appeal** elaborates on a nonproduct-related benefit or image. It might depict what kind of person uses a brand (VW advertised to active, youthful people with its "Drivers Wanted" campaign) or what kind of experience results from using the brand (Pringles advertised "Once You Pop, The Fun Doesn't Stop"). Transformational appeals often attempt to stir up emotions that will motivate purchase. Communicators use negative appeals such as fear, guilt, and shame to get people to do things (brush their teeth) or stop doing things (smoking). Also, communicators use positive emotional appeals such as humor, love, pride, and joy, sometimes employing "borrowed interest" devices such as frisky puppies or sex appeal to attract interest and raise involvement in the ad. The challenge here is to avoid detracting from comprehension and overshadowing the product.[19]

Message Source Because messages delivered by attractive or popular sources can achieve higher attention and recall, advertisers often use celebrities as spokespeople. Celebrities are likely to be effective when they're credible or personify a key product attribute. Thus, consumers saw self-proclaimed overweight actress Kirstie Alley's ads for the Jenny Craig weight-loss system as a good fit.[20]

Three factors underlying source credibility are expertise, trustworthiness, and likability.[21] *Expertise* is the specialized knowledge the communicator possesses to back the claim. *Trustworthiness* is related to perceptions of the source's objectivity and honesty. Friends are trusted more than strangers or salespeople, and people who aren't paid to endorse a product are seen as more trustworthy than people who are paid.[22] *Likability* describes the source's attractiveness; qualities like candor, humor, and naturalness make a source more likable. The most credible source would score high on all three factors.

Multinational companies wrestle with several challenges in developing global communications. First, they must decide whether the product is appropriate for a country. Second, they must make sure the targeted market segment is both legal and customary. Third, they must decide if the style of the ad is acceptable. Fourth, they must decide whether ads should be created at headquarters or locally.[23]

Select the Communications Channels

Selecting efficient channels to carry the message becomes more difficult as communication channels become more fragmented and cluttered. For example, pharmaceutical salespeople can rarely wrest more than five minutes' time from a busy physician. Because personal selling is expensive, the industry has added multiple communications channels, including ads in medical journals, direct mail, sampling, telemarketing, Web sites, and conferences.[24]

There are two kinds of communication channels: personal and nonpersonal.

Personal Communications Channels **Personal communications channels** let two or more persons communicate face-to-face, person-to-audience, over the telephone, or through e-mail. Instant messaging and independent sites to collect consumer reviews are also growing in importance. Personal channels derive their effectiveness through individualized presentation and feedback.

A study by Burson-Marsteller and Roper Starch Worldwide found that one influential person's word of mouth can affect the buying attitudes of two other people, on average. Online, that circle of influence jumps to eight. Online visitors also increasingly

MARKETING SKILLS: PERMISSION MARKETING

Permission marketing is important because it's a highly targeted and cost-effective way to build ongoing relationships with customers and prospects. How do marketers develop this skill? According to Seth Godin, the first step is to calculate a customer's worth over the duration of a typical relationship and decide on a budget for customer acquisition. Then the marketer creates messages to educate customers about the value of the company's offers and get their permission to engage in ongoing dialogue. Messages should be customizable as the company learns more about the customer and should provide incentives (such as more information or a discount) for continuing the relationship. Finally, the marketer should always ask for a response to learn how customers are reacting to the communications and to measure the results.

Hewlett-Packard, for example, uses permission marketing to reach business customers in specific market segments with timely information relevant to their jobs and industries. Before subscribers receive one of HP's e-mail newsletters, they answer a few basic questions so the company can customize newsletter content accordingly. Thanks to permission marketing, HP has boosted response to its e-mail offers and generated millions of dollars in new sales.[26]

---

create product information, not just consume it. They join Internet interest groups to share information, so that "word of Web" is joining "word of mouth" as an important buying influence. As one marketer noted, "You don't need to reach 2 million people to let them know about a new product—you just need to reach the right 2,000 people in the right way and they will help you reach 2 million."[25] So marketers must reach out carefully to consumers (see "Marketing Skills: Permission Marketing").

Nonpersonal Communications Channels *Nonpersonal communications channels* are directed to more than one person and include media, sales promotions, events and experiences, and publicity.

- *Media* consist of print media (newspapers, magazines); broadcast media (radio, television); network media (telephone, cable, satellite, wireless); electronic media (audiotape, videotape, DVD, CD, Web page); and display media (billboards, signs, posters). Most nonpersonal messages come through paid media.
- *Sales promotions* consist of consumer promotions (such as samples, coupons, and premiums); trade promotion (such as advertising and display allowances); and business and sales-force promotion (contests for sales reps).
- *Events and experiences* include sports, arts, entertainment, and cause events as well as less formal activities that create novel brand interactions with consumers.
- *Public relations* include communications directed internally to the company's employees or externally to consumers, other firms, the government, and media.

Much of the recent growth of nonpersonal channels has taken place through events and experiences. A company can build its brand image through creating or sponsoring events. Events marketers who once favored sports events are now using other venues such as museums and zoos to entertain clients and employees. IBM sponsors symphony performances and art exhibits, Visa is a sponsor of the Olympics, and Harley-Davidson sponsors annual motorcycle rallies.

Integration of Communications Channels Although personal communication is often more effective than mass communication, mass media might be the major means of stimulating personal communication. Mass communications affect personal attitudes and behavior through a two-step process. Ideas often flow from media sources to opinion leaders and from these to the less media-involved population groups. This two-step flow has several implications. First, the influence of mass media on public opinion is mediated by opinion leaders, people whose opinions are sought or who carry their opinions to others. Second, the two-step flow shows that people interact primarily within their own social groups and acquire ideas from their group's opinion leaders. Third, two-step communication suggests that mass communicators should direct messages specifically to opinion leaders and let them carry the message to others.

Establish the Total Marketing Communications Budget

Industries and companies vary considerably in how much they spend on promotion. Expenditures might amount to 40% to 45% of sales in the cosmetics industry but only 5% to 10% in the industrial-equipment industry, with company-to-company variations. Four common methods for deciding on a budget include:

1. *Affordable method.* Many managers set the promotion budget at what they think the firm can afford. This method ignores promotion as an investment and the immediate impact of promotion on sales volume; it also leads to an uncertain budget, complicating long-range planning.
2. *Percentage-of-sales method.* Many firms set promotion expenditures at a specified percentage of current sales, anticipated sales, or the sales price. Supporters say this method links promotion expenditures to the movement of corporate sales over the business cycle; focuses attention on the interrelationship of promotion cost, selling price, and unit profit; and encourages stability when rivals spend approximately the same percentage. On the other hand, this method views sales as the determiner of promotion rather than as the result; it leads to a budget set by funds availability rather than by market opportunities; and it discourages experimentation with countercyclical promotion or aggressive spending. Finally, it offers no logical basis for choosing the specific percentage, nor does it allow for determining the promotion budget each product and territory deserves.
3. *Competitive-parity method.* Some companies set their promotion budget to achieve share-of-voice parity with competitors. Although proponents say that competitors' expenditures represent the collective wisdom of the industry and that maintaining competitive parity prevents promotion wars, neither argument is valid. Company reputations, resources, opportunities, and objectives differ so much that promotion budgets are hardly a guide. And there's no evidence that competitive parity discourages promotional wars.
4. *Objective-and-task method.* Here, marketers develop promotion budgets by defining specific objectives, determining the tasks that must be performed to achieve these objectives, and estimating the costs of performing these tasks. The sum of these costs is the proposed promotion budget. This method has the advantage of requiring firms to spell out assumptions about the relationship among dollars spent, exposure levels, trial rates, and regular usage.

BREAKTHROUGH MARKETING: OCEAN SPRAY

Ocean Spray faced a tough situation in 2004. Domestic sales had been flat for five years and household penetration had been declining for some time. Sales in the juice category as a whole suffered from concerns over sugar, increased competition, and growing consumer interest in beverages such as water and sports drinks. Then Ocean Spray, an agricultural cooperative of cranberry growers, hired Arnold Worldwide to guide its marketing communications. Working closely with Ocean Spray COO and experienced marketer Ken Romanzi, the agency set out to "reintroduce the cranberry" as the "surprisingly versatile little fruit that supplies modern day benefits," through an innovative campaign to reach consumers in a variety of settings and promote the full range of products—cranberry sauce, fruit juices, and dried cranberries.

Arnold's experts realized that the heart of the brand was the cranberry bog, so their "Straight from the Bog" campaign focused on the bog and reinforced two benefits: Ocean Spray products taste good and are good for you. Miniature bogs brought to Manhattan were featured on an NBC *Today* show segment; the event reached 23 million people through related media pickup. Television and print ads featured two natural-looking and sounding growers (depicted by actors) standing in a bog talking, often humorously, about what they did; the ads improved both awareness and persuasion for the brand's benefits. The campaign also included a Web site, in-store displays, and special events for consumers and members of the growers' cooperative. The result: Ocean Spray's brand exposure rose and sales increased by 10%.[27]

DECIDING ON THE MARKETING COMMUNICATIONS MIX

Companies must allocate the marketing communications budget over the eight major modes of communication—advertising, sales promotion, public relations and publicity, events and experiences, direct marketing, interactive marketing, word-of-mouth marketing, and the sales force. Within the same industry, companies can differ considerably in their media and channel choices. Avon concentrates its promotional funds on personal selling, whereas Revlon spends heavily on advertising. "Breakthrough Marketing: Ocean Spray" shows how that company has used its communications mix to great effect.

Characteristics of the Marketing Communications Mix

Each communication tool has its own unique characteristics and costs.

- *Advertising.* Advertising reaches geographically dispersed buyers, can build a long-term image for a product (Coca-Cola ads), or trigger quick sales (a Sears ad for a weekend sale). It offers opportunities for amplified expressiveness, is pervasive, and serves as a monologue in front of, rather than a dialogue with, the audience.
- *Sales promotion.* Sales-promotion tools—coupons, contests, premiums, and the like—offer three key benefits: (1) communication (gaining attention to lead

consumers to the product); (2) incentive (a concession or an inducement that gives value to consumers); and (3) invitation (a distinct invitation to engage in the transaction now). Sales promotion can be used for short-run effects such as highlighting product offers and boosting sagging sales.

- *Public relations and publicity.* The appeal of public relations and publicity is based on three qualities: (1) high credibility (news stories and features are more authentic and credible than ads); (2) ability to catch buyers off guard (reaching prospects who prefer to avoid salespeople and advertisements); and (3) dramatization (the potential for dramatizing a firm or product).
- *Events and experiences.* A well-chosen event or experience seen as highly relevant can get the consumer personally involved. Because events and experiences are live, consumers find them more actively engaging. Also, events are an indirect "soft sell."
- *Direct and interactive marketing.* All forms of direct and interactive marketing share three characteristics: They're (1) customized (for the addressed individual); (2) up to date (can be prepared very quickly); and (3) interactive (can be changed depending on response).
- *Word-of-mouth marketing.* Noteworthy characteristics of online or off-line word-of-mouth marketing are that it's (1) credible (which makes it influential); (2) personal (reflecting personal opinions and experiences); and (3) timely (occurring when people are most interested).
- *Personal selling.* Personal selling is the most effective tool at later stages of the buying process, particularly in building up buyer preference, conviction, and action. Qualities of personal selling are (1) personal interaction (an immediate and interactive relationship between two or more persons); (2) cultivation (all kinds of relationships can spring up, from a matter-of-fact selling relationship to a deep personal friendship); and (3) response (the buyer feels under some obligation for having listened to the sales talk).

Factors in Setting the Marketing Communications Mix

In developing their communications mix, firms must consider the type of product market, consumer readiness to make a purchase, and product life-cycle stage; market rank is also a factor. First, consumer and business markets tend to require different allocations. Although advertising is used less than sales calls in business markets, it plays a significant role in introducing the firm and its products, explaining product features, generating sales leads, legitimizing the firm and its products, and reassuring customers about purchases. Personal selling can also be effective in consumer markets, by helping to persuade dealers to take more stock and display more of the product, build dealer enthusiasm, sign up more dealers, and grow sales at existing accounts.

Second, promotional tools vary in cost effectiveness at different stages of buyer readiness (see Figure 15.4). Advertising and publicity are most important in the awareness-building stage. Customer comprehension is affected primarily by advertising; customer conviction is influenced mostly by personal selling. Closing the sale is influenced mostly by personal selling and sales promotion. Reordering is also affected mostly by personal selling and sales promotion, and somewhat by reminder advertising.

Third, promotional tools vary in cost effectiveness at different stages of the product life cycle. Advertising, events and experiences, and publicity are most cost effective in the introduction stage, followed by personal selling to gain distribu-

FIGURE 15.4 Cost Effectiveness of Three Different Communication Tools at Different Buyer-Readiness Stages

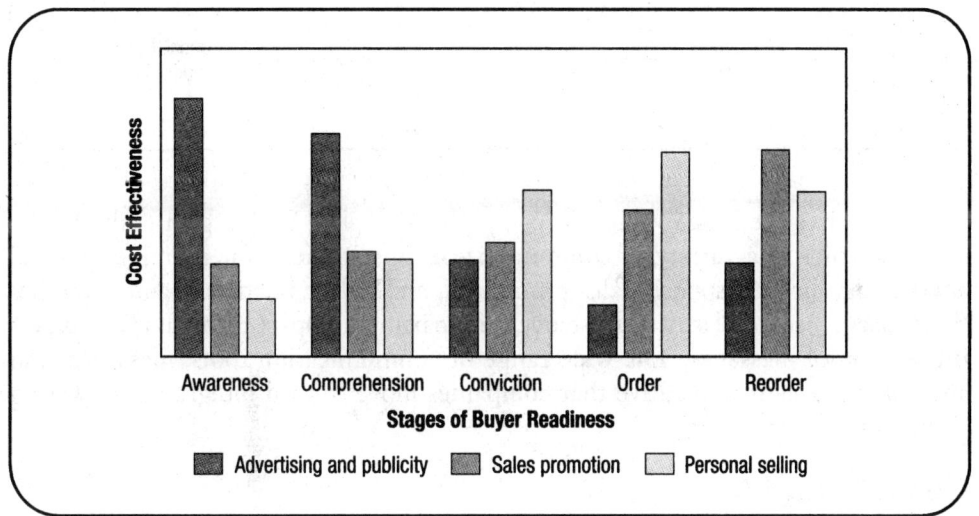

tion and sales promotion and direct marketing to induce trial. In the growth stage, demand has its own momentum through word of mouth. Sales promotion, advertising, and events and experiences, and personal selling grow more important in the maturity stage. In the decline stage, sales promotion continues strong, other communication tools are reduced, and salespeople give the product minimal attention.

Measuring Communication Results

After implementing the communications plan, the company must measure its impact by asking members of the target audience whether they recognize or recall the message, how many times they saw it, what points they recall, how they felt about the message, and their previous and current attitudes toward the product and company. The communicator should also collect behavioral measures of audience response, such as how many people bought the product, liked it, and talked to others about it.

Suppose 80% of the targeted customers are aware of the brand, 60% have tried it, and only 20% who tried it are satisfied. The communications program has effectively created awareness, but the product failed to meet consumer expectations. However, if 40% of the targeted customers are aware of the brand and only 30% have tried it—but 80% of those who tried it are satisfied—communications should be strengthened to take advantage of the brand's power.

MANAGING THE INTEGRATED MARKETING COMMUNICATIONS PROCESS

As defined by the American Association of Advertising Agencies, **integrated marketing communications (IMC)** is a concept of marketing communications planning

FIGURE 15.5 Example of Multiple Vehicle, Multiple-Stage Communication Campaign

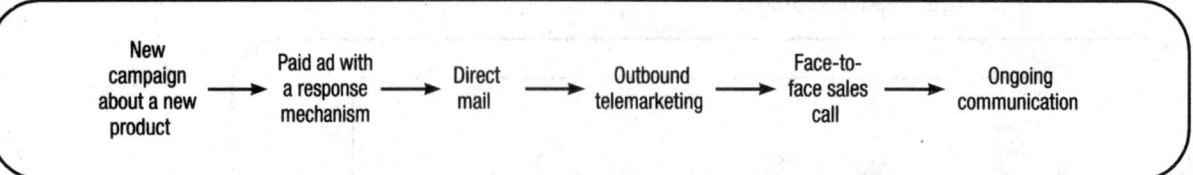

that recognizes the added value of a comprehensive plan. Such a plan evaluates the strategic roles of a variety of communications disciplines—for example, general advertising, direct response, sales promotion, and public relations—and combines these disciplines for clarity, consistency, and maximum impact through the seamless integration of messages. The wide range of communication tools, messages, and audiences makes it imperative that companies move toward integrated marketing communications.[28]

Coordinating Media

Although media coordination can occur across and within media types, marketers should combine personal and nonpersonal communications channels for maximum impact. Instead of using a single tool in a "one-shot" effort, a more powerful approach is the *multiple-vehicle, multiple-stage campaign* such as the sequence in Figure 15.5.

Multiple media deployed within a tightly defined time frame can increase message reach and impact. Research has also shown that promotions can be more effective when combined with advertising.[29] The awareness and attitudes created by advertising campaigns can improve the success of more direct sales pitches. Many companies are coordinating their online and offline communications activities. Listing Web addresses in ads (especially print) and on packages allows people to explore a company's offerings, find store locations, and get more information. Dannon uses communications to drive traffic to its homepage so it can build customer relationships and strengthen loyalty through targeted coupons, e-mail newsletters, and other activities.[30]

Implementing IMC

Integrated marketing communications can produce stronger message consistency, help to build brand equity, and create greater sales impact.[31] It forces management to think about every way the customer comes in contact with the company, how the company communicates its positioning, the relative importance of each vehicle, and timing issues. It also gives someone responsibility to unify the various brand images and messages, and it improves the firm's ability to reach the right customers with the right messages at the right time and in the right place.[32]

To determine whether communications are truly integrated, management must look at coverage of the target audience; contribution to creating the desired response; commonality of associations reinforced across communications options; complementarity, the extent to which different associations and linkages are emphasized across communication options; versatility, so a marketing communication works for consumers who have or have *not* seen other communications; and cost for the most effective and efficient communications program.[33]

Chapter 15 Designing and Managing Integrated Marketing Communications

EXECUTIVE SUMMARY

The marketing communications mix includes advertising, sales promotion, public relations and publicity, events and experiences, direct marketing, interactive marketing, word-of-mouth marketing, and personal selling. The communications process includes sender, receiver, message, media, encoding, decoding, response, feedback, and noise. Developing effective communications involves eight steps: (1) identify the target audience; (2) determine communications objectives; (3) design the communications; (4) select communications channels; (5) establish the total communications budget; (6) decide on the communications mix; (7) measure the results; and (8) manage the integrated marketing communications process.

Communications objectives may involve category need, brand awareness, brand attitude, or brand purchase intention. Marketers formulate the communication through message strategy, creative strategy, and message source. Communications channels may be personal or nonpersonal. The objective-and-task method of setting the promotion budget is the most desirable. In deciding on the marketing communications mix, marketers must examine each tool's advantages and costs, company market rank, type of product market, buyer readiness, and product life-cycle stage. To measure the mix's effectiveness, marketers ask members of the target audience whether they recognize or recall the communication, how many times they saw it, what they recall, how they felt about it, and their previous and current attitudes. Integrated marketing communications (IMC) recognizes the added value of a comprehensive plan that evaluates the strategic roles of a variety of communications disciplines and combines these disciplines to provide clarity, consistency, and maximum impact through the seamless integration of discrete messages.

NOTES

1. Louise Story, "The Campaign Is Clean, the Stunts Fairly Dirty," *New York Times*, September 28, 2007, p. C4; Jack Neff, "The Force Behind Digital at Unilever," *Advertising Age*, July 9, 2007, p. 31; Randall Rothenberg, "Dove Effort Gives Packaged-Goods Marketers Lessons for the Future," *Advertising Age*, March 5, 2007; Theresa Howard, "Ad Campaign Tell Women to Celebrate Who They Are," *USA Today*, July 8, 2005; Jack Neff, "In Dove Ads, Normal is the New Beautiful," *Advertising Age*, September 27, 2004; www.campaignforrealbeauty.com.
2. Xueming Luo and Naveen Donthu, "Marketing's Credibility: A Longitudinal Investigation of Marketing Communication Productivity and Shareholder Value," *Journal of Marketing* 70 (October 2006): 70–91.
3. Catherine Holahan, "The Sell-Phone Revolution," *BusinessWeek*, April 23, 2007, pp. 94-97; David Kiley, "Hey Advertisers, TiVo is Your Friend," *BusinessWeek*, October 17, 2005, pp. 97–98; Linda Kaplan Thaler and Robin Koval with Delia Marshall, *Bang! Getting Your Message Heard in a Noisy World* (New York: Currency, 2003).
4. Noreen O'Leary, "The 30-Second Spot Is Dead, Long Live the 30-Second Spot," *Adweek*, November 17, 2003, pp. 12–21; Anthony Bianco, "The Vanishing Mass Market," *Business Week*, July 12, 2004, pp. 60–68; Susan Thea Posnock, "It Can Control Madison Avenue," *American Demographics*, February 2004, pp. 28–33.
5. Louise Story, "Viewers Fast-Forwarding Past Ads? Not Always," *New York Times*, February 16, 2007.
6. Louise Story, "Anywhere the Eye Can See, It's Likely to See an Ad," *New York Times*, January 15, 2007; Laura Petrecca, "Product Placement—You Can't Escape It," *USA Today*, October 11, 2006, pp. 1B, 2B.
7. Some of these definitions adapted from Peter D. Bennett, ed., *Dictionary of Marketing Terms* (Chicago: American Marketing Association, 1995).
8. Tom Duncan and Sandra Moriarty, "How Integrated Marketing Communication's 'Touchpoints' Can Operationalize the Service-Dominant Logic,"

in Robert F. Lusch and Stephen L. Vargo, eds., *The Service Dominant Logic of Marketing: Dialog, Debate, and Directions* (Armonk, NY: M.E. Sharpe, 2006); Tom Duncan, IMC: *The New Principles of Advertising and Promotion*, 2nd ed. (McGraw-Hill/Irwin, 2005).

9. For an alternate communications model developed specifically for advertising communications, see Barbara B. Stern, "A Revised Communication Model for Advertising: Multiple Dimensions of the Source, the Message, and the Recipient," *Journal of Advertising* (June 1994): 5–15. For additional perspectives, see Tom Duncan and Sandra E. Moriarity, "A Communication-Based Marketing Model for Managing Relationships," *Journal of Marketing* (April 1998): 1–13.

10. Demetrios Vakratsas and Tim Ambler, "How Advertising Works: What Do We Really Know?" *Journal of Marketing* 63, no. 1 (January 1999): 26–43.

11. This section is based on the excellent text John R. Rossiter and Larry Percy, *Advertising and Promotion Management*, 2d ed. (New York: McGraw-Hill, 1997).

12. James F. Engel, Roger D. Blackwell, and Paul W. Minard, *Consumer Behavior*, 9th ed. (Fort Worth, TX: Dryden, 2001).

13. Rossiter and Percy, *Advertising and Promotion Management*.

14. Engel, Blackwell, and Minard, *Consumer Behavior*, 9th ed.

15. Ayn E. Crowley and Wayne D. Hoyer, "An Integrative Framework for Understanding Two-Sided Persuasion," *Journal of Consumer Research* (March 1994): 561–574.

16. See C. I. Hovland, A. A. Lumsdaine, and F. D. Sheffield, *Experiments on Mass Communication*, vol. 3 (Princeton, NJ: Princeton University Press, 1948), ch. 8; and Crowley and Hoyer, "An Integrative Framework." For an alternative viewpoint, see George E. Belch, "The Effects of Message Modality on One- and Two-Sided Advertising Messages," in Richard P. Bagozzi and Alice M. Tybout, eds., *Advances in Consumer Research* (Ann Arbor, MI: Association for Consumer Research, 1983), pp. 21–26.

17. Curtis P. Haugtvedt and Duane T. Wegener, "Message Order Effects in Persuasion: An Attitude Strength Perspective," *Journal of Consumer Research* (June 1994): 205–218; H. Rao Unnava, Robert E. Burnkrant, and Sunil Erevelles, "Effects of Presentation Order and Communication Modality on Recall and Attitude," *Journal of Consumer Research* (December 1994): 481–490.

18. Brian Sternthal and C. Samuel Craig, *Consumer Behavior: An Information Processing Perspective* (Upper Saddle River, NJ: Prentice Hall, 1982), pp. 282–284.

19. Some recent research on humor in advertising, for example, includes: Haseeb Shabbir and Des Thwaites, "The Use of Humor to Mask Deceptive Advertising: It's No Laughing Matter," *Journal of Advertising* 36 (Summer 2007): 75–85; Thomas W. Cline and James J. Kellaris, "The Influence of Humor Strength and Humor Message Relatedness on Ad Memorability: A Dual Process Model," *Journal of Advertising* 36 (Spring 2007): 55–67; H. Shanker Krishnan and Dipankar Chakravarti (2003), "A Process Analysis of the Effects of Humorous Advertising Executions on Brand Claims Memory," *Journal of Consumer Psychology* 13 (3): 230–245.

20. NPD Celebrity Influence Study 2005, NPD Group.

21. Herbert C. Kelman and Carl I. Hovland, "Reinstatement of the Communication in Delayed Measurement of Opinion Change," *Journal of Abnormal and Social Psychology* 48 (1953): 327–335.

22. David J. Moore, John C. Mowen, and Richard Reardon, "Multiple Sources in Advertising Appeals: When Product Endorsers Are Paid by the Advertising Sponsor," *Journal of the Academy of Marketing Science* (Summer 1994): 234–243.

23. Richard C. Morais, "Mobile Mayhem," *Forbes*, July 6, 1998, p. 138; "Working in Harmony," *Soap Perfumery & Cosmetics*, July 1, 1998, p. 27; Rodger Harrabin, "A Commercial Break for Parents," *Independent*, September 8, 1998, p. 19; Naveen Donthu, "A Cross-Country Investigation of Recall of and Attitude Toward Comparative Advertising," *Journal of Advertising* 27 (June 1998): 111; "EU to Try Again on Tobacco Advertising Ban," Associated Press, May 9, 2001.

24. "Rebirth of a Salesman," *The Economist*, April 14, 2001.

25. Ian Mount, "Marketing," *Business 2.0*, August/September 2001, p. 84.

26. "How HP Made Its E-mail More Relevant to Customers," *B to B*, April 3, 2006, p. 59; John Lehmann, "Permission Marketing Personalizes the Sales Pitch," *Crain's Cleveland Business*, September 13, 2004, p. 23; Karin Connelly, "Effective E-mailing," *Inside Business*, June 2003, pp. 59+; Gina Bernacchi, "Permission Marketing: A New Path for Your Appeals," *Non-Profit Times*, March 15, 2002, p. 23; L. Erwin, "The Secret Behind Permission-Based Marketing," *Point of Purchase*, February 2001, p. 41; Seth Godin, "Permission Marketing," *Credit Union Executive*, January 2001, pp. 42+.

27. Sonia Reyes, "Ocean Spray Bogs Make Bank," *BrandWeek*, March 26, 2007, p. R7; Laurie Peterson, "Breakaway Brands: Ocean Spray Tells it Straight from the Bog," *MediaPost*, October 9, 2006; Francis J. Kelly III and Barry Silverstein, *The Breakaway Brand* (New York: McGraw-Hill, 2005).
28. Prasad A. Naik and Kalyan Raman, "Understanding the Impact of Synergy in Multimedia Communications," *Journal of Marketing Research* 40 (November 2003): 375–388. See also Prasad A. Naik, Kalyan Raman, and Russell S. Winer, "Planning Marketing-Mix Strategies in the Presence of Interaction Effects," *Marketing Science* 24 (January 2005): 25–34.
29. Scott Neslin, *Sales Promotion*, MSI Relevant Knowledge Series (Cambridge, MA: Marketing Science Institute, 2002).
30. Gerry Khermouch, "The Top 5 Rules of the Ad Game," *BusinessWeek*, January 20, 2003, pp. 72–73.
31. Sreedhar Madhavaram, Vishag Badrinarayanan, and Robert E. McDonald, "Integrated Marketing Communication (IMC) and Brand Identity as Critical Components of Brand Equity Strategy," *Journal of Advertising* 34 (Winter 2005):. 69–80; Mike Reid, Sandra Luxton, and Felix Mavondo, "The Relationship between Integrated Marketing Communication, Market Orientation, and Brand Orientation," *Journal of Advertising* 34 (Winter 2005): 11–23.
32. Don E. Schultz, Stanley I. Tannenbaum, and Robert F. Lauterborn, *Integrated Marketing Communications: Putting It Together and Making It Work* (Lincolnwood, IL: NTC Business Books, 1992); Don E. Schultz and Heidi Schultz, *IMC, The Next Generation: Five Steps For Delivering Value and Measuring Financial Returns* (New York: McGraw-Hill, 2003).
33. Kevin Lane Keller, *Strategic Brand Management*, 3rd ed. (Upper Saddle River, NJ: Prentice Hall, 2008).

CHAPTER 16

Managing Mass Communications

> In this chapter, we will address the following questions:
>
> 1. What are the steps in developing an advertising program?
> 2. How should sales promotion decisions be made?
> 3. What are the guidelines for effective brand-building events and experiences?
> 4. How can companies exploit the potential of public relations and publicity?

MARKETING MANAGEMENT AT GEICO

Has the $600 million Geico spent on television advertising been worth it? In eight years, Geico has nearly quadrupled its sales, from slightly under $3 billion in 1998 to more than $11 billion. Now Geico is the fastest-growing U.S. car insurance company, with brand recognition in the high 90% range. According to Ted Ward, vice president of marketing, Geico's success is due to three things: great employees, breakthrough call-to-action advertising, and a strong brand personality that evolves on TV and video sites such as youtube.com.

Because Geico targets a broad audience, it runs several ad campaigns simultaneously. The popular TV spots advertising Geico's claim that its Web site is "so easy a caveman can use it" feature offended Neanderthals, often dressed improbably in suits, who appeared in additional ads to express frustration and indignation at the prejudice they face. The gecko series establishes Geico's brand personality as hip and urbane. A third campaign features celebrities like Little Richard and Charo paraphrasing the stories of Geico's real-life satisfied customers. The multiple campaigns build on each other's success; the company dominates the TV airwaves with so many varied car insurance messages that any competitor's ads are lost.[1]

Although Geico clearly has found great success with its advertising, other marketers are trying to come to grips with how to best use mass media in the new communication environment.[2] This chapter examines the nature and use of four mass communication tools: advertising; sales promotion; events and experiences; and public relations and publicity.

DEVELOPING AND MANAGING AN ADVERTISING PROGRAM

Advertising is any paid form of nonpersonal presentation and promotion of ideas, goods, or services by an identified sponsor. Ads can be a cost-effective way to disseminate messages, whether to build a brand preference or to educate people. In developing an advertising program, marketing managers must always start by identifying the target market and buyer motives. Then they make five major decisions, known as the five Ms: *Mission:* What are the advertising objectives? *Money:* How much can be spent? *Message:* What message should be sent? *Media:* What media should be used? *Measurement:* How should the results be evaluated? These decisions are summarized in Figure 16.1 and described in the following sections.

Setting the Objectives

An **advertising goal** (or **objective**) is a specific communication task and achievement level to be accomplished with a specific audience in a specific period. Advertising objectives can be classified according to their aim: to inform, persuade, remind, or reinforce. They aim at different stages in the hierarchy of effects discussed in Chapter 15.

Informative advertising aims to create awareness and knowledge of new products or new features of existing products. *Persuasive advertising* aims to create liking, preference, conviction, and purchase. Some persuasive advertising is comparative

FIGURE 16.1 The Five Ms of Advertising

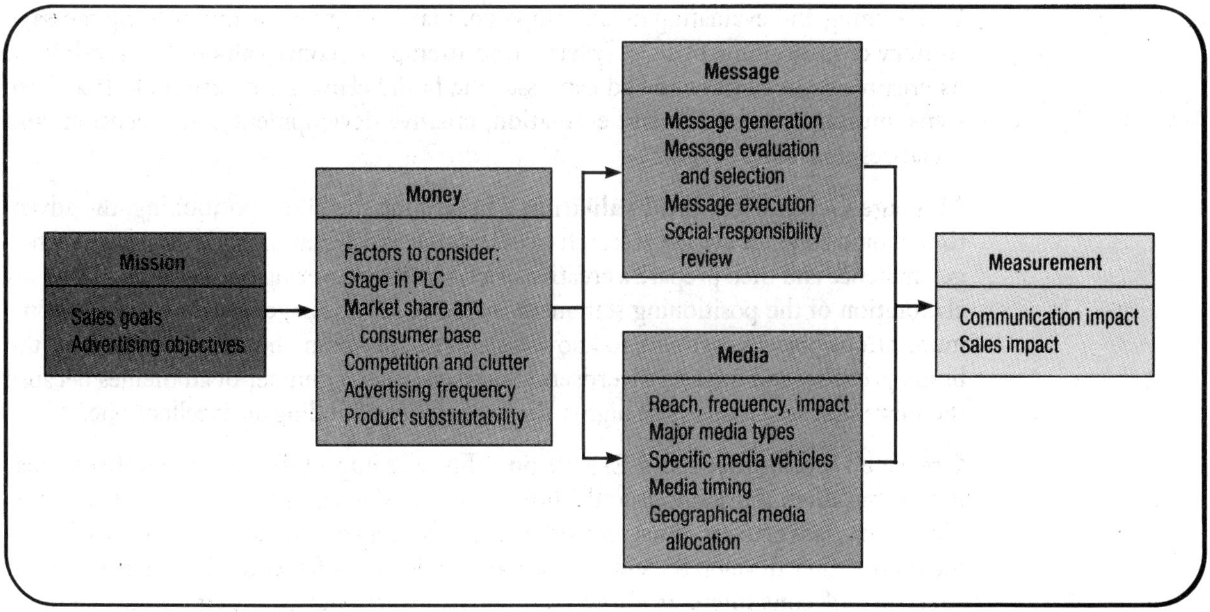

Mission	Money	Message	Media	Measurement
Sales goals Advertising objectives	Factors to consider: Stage in PLC Market share and consumer base Competition and clutter Advertising frequency Product substitutability	Message generation Message evaluation and selection Message execution Social-responsibility review	Reach, frequency, impact Major media types Specific media vehicles Media timing Geographical media allocation	Communication impact Sales impact

advertising, which explicitly compares two or more brands; this advertising works best when it elicits cognitive and affective motivations simultaneously and consumers are processing advertising in a detailed, analytical mode.[3] *Reminder advertising* aims to stimulate repeat purchase of products (Coca-Cola ads do this). *Reinforcement advertising* seeks to convince current purchasers that they made the right choice. Car ads often depict satisfied customers enjoying special features of their new vehicle.

The advertising objective should emerge from a thorough analysis of the current marketing situation. If the product class is mature, the company is the market leader, and brand usage is low, the objective is to stimulate more usage. If the product class is new and the company is not the market leader, but the brand is superior to the leader, the objective is to convince the market of the brand's superiority.

Deciding on the Advertising Budget

Management should consider these five factors when setting the advertising budget:[4]

1. *Product life cycle stage.* New products typically merit large budgets to build awareness and gain trial, whereas established brands are supported with lower budgets as a ratio to sales.[5]
2. *Market share and consumer base.* High-market-share brands usually require less advertising expenditure as a percentage of sales to maintain share. To build share by increasing market size requires larger expenditures.
3. *Competition and clutter.* In a market with many competitors and high advertising spending, a brand must advertise more heavily to be heard. Even ad clutter from noncompetitors creates a need for heavier advertising.
4. *Advertising frequency.* The number of repetitions needed to convey the brand's message to customers has an obvious impact on the advertising budget.
5. *Product substitutability.* Brands in a commodity class (beer, soft drinks) require heavy advertising to establish a differential image.

Developing the Advertising Campaign

In designing and evaluating an ad campaign, marketers must distinguish the message strategy or positioning of an ad (what the ad attempts to convey about the brand) from its creative strategy (how the ad expresses the brand claims). Advertisers follow three steps: message generation and evaluation, creative development and execution, and social-responsibility review.

Message Generation and Evaluation In refining the brand positioning, the advertiser should conduct market research to determine which appeal works best with its target audience and then prepare a creative brief, typically covering one or two pages. This elaboration of the positioning statement includes: key message, target audience, communications objectives (to do, to know, to believe), key brand benefits, supports for the brand promise, and media. Advertisers should consider a number of ad themes because the more that are created, the higher the probability of finding an excellent one.

Creative Development and Execution The ad's impact depends not only on what it says, but often more importantly, how it says it. Message execution can be decisive. Therefore, advertisers must consider the advantages and disadvantages of each medium as they develop the creative strategy. Television, for example, reaches a broad spectrum of consumers at a low cost per exposure, but producing and placing a commercial can be expensive. Print ads can provide detailed product information, yet print media are fairly passive. Radio, an inexpensive and flexible medium, reaches 94% of all Americans age 12 and older.[6] Disadvantages are the lack of visual images and the relatively passive nature of the consumer processing.[7]

Legal and Social Issues Advertisers and their agencies must be sure advertising does not overstep social and legal norms. Public policy makers have developed a substantial body of laws and regulations to govern advertising. Under U.S. law, for example, companies must avoid false or deceptive advertising and cannot use bait-and-switch advertising to attract buyers under false pretenses. To be socially responsible, advertisers try not to offend the general public, as well as any ethnic groups, racial minorities, or special-interest groups.[8] For example, every year, the nonprofit trade group Advertising Women of New York singles out ads it says portray particularly negative images of women. Pizza Hut's recent ad starring singer Jessica Simpson wearing short shorts and feeding a "Cheesy Bite" to a teenage boy won a Grand Ugly.[9]

Deciding on Media and Measuring Effectiveness

The advertiser's next task is to choose media to carry the message. The steps here are (1) deciding on reach, frequency, and impact; (2) choosing among media types; (3) selecting specific media vehicles; (4) deciding on media timing; and (5) deciding on geographical media allocation. Then the company evaluates the results of these decisions.

Deciding on Reach, Frequency, and Impact Media selection is finding the most cost-effective media to deliver the desired number and type of exposures to the target audience. More specifically, the advertiser seeks a certain advertising objective and response from the target audience—for example, a target level of product trial—which depends, among other things, on level of brand awareness. The effect of exposures on audience awareness depends on reach, frequency, and impact:

- *Reach (R).* The number of different persons or households that are exposed to a particular media schedule at least once during a specified period.
- *Frequency (F).* The number of times within the specified period that an average person or household is exposed to the message.
- *Impact (I).* The qualitative value of an exposure through a given medium (thus a food ad in *Good Housekeeping* would have a higher impact than in *Fortune* magazine).

Although audience awareness will be greater with higher reach, frequency, and impact, there are important trade-offs here. Reach is most important when launching new products, flanker brands, extensions of well-known brands, or infrequently purchased brands; or when going after an undefined target market. Frequency is most important where there are strong competitors, a complex story to tell, high consumer resistance, or a frequent-purchase cycle.[10]

Many advertisers believe a target audience needs a large number of exposures for the advertising to work. Those who doubt the value of high frequency believe that after people see the same ad a few times, they either act on it, get irritated by it, or stop noticing it.[11] Another reason for repetition is forgetting. The higher the forgetting rate associated with a brand, product category, or message, the higher the warranted

TABLE 16.1 Profiles of Major Media Types

Medium	Advantages	Limitations
Newspapers	Flexibility; timeliness; good local market coverage; broad acceptance; high believability	Short life; poor reproduction quality; small "pass-along" audience
Television	Combines sight, sound, and motion; appealing to the senses; high attention; high reach	High absolute cost; high clutter; fleeting exposure; less audience selectivity
Direct mail	Audience selectivity; flexibility; no ad competition within the same medium; personalization	Relatively high cost; "junk mail" image
Radio	Mass use; high geographic and demographic selectivity; low cost	Audio presentation only; lower attention than television; nonstandardized rate structures; fleeting exposure
Magazines	High geographic and demographic selectivity; credibility and prestige; high-quality reproduction; long life; good pass-along readership	Long ad purchase lead time; some waste circulation; no guarantee of position
Outdoor	Flexibility; high repeat exposure; low cost; low competition	Limited audience selectivity; creative limitations
Yellow Pages	Excellent local coverage; high believability; wide reach; low cost	High competition; long ad purchase lead time; creative limitations
Newsletters	Very high selectivity; full control; interactive opportunities; relative low costs	Costs could run away
Brochures	Flexibility; full control; can dramatize messages	Overproduction could lead to runaway costs
Telephone	Many users; opportunity to give a personal touch	Relative high cost unless volunteers are used
Internet	High selectivity; interactive possibilities; relatively low cost	Relatively new media with a low number of users in some countries

level of repetition. However, advertisers shouldn't coast on a tired ad—they need fresh executions of the message.[12]

Choosing Among Major Media Types The media planner has to know the capacity of the major media types to deliver reach, frequency, and impact. The costs, advantages, and limitations of the major media are profiled in Table 16.1.

Media planners make choices by considering four main variables. One is the target audience's media habits. For example, radio, television, and the Internet are effective media for reaching teenagers. A second is the product. Media types have different potentials for demonstration, visualization, explanation, believability, and color. Third is the message. A message announcing a major sale tomorrow will require radio, TV, or newspaper; a message containing technical data might require specialized magazines or mailings. The final variable is cost. Television is relatively expensive, whereas newspaper and radio are relatively inexpensive. What counts is the cost per thousand exposures.

Given the abundance of media, the planner must decide on how to allocate the budget to the major media types, with the awareness that people are increasingly time-starved. Attention is a scarce currency, and advertisers need strong devices to capture people's attention.[13]

Alternative Advertising Options In recent years, researchers have noticed reduced effectiveness for television due to increased commercial clutter, more "zipping and zapping" of commercials, and lower viewing owing to the growth in cable and satellite TV and DVD/VCRs.[14] Because television advertising costs have risen faster than other media costs, many firms are now seeking alternative advertising media.[15]

Place advertising, or out-of-home advertising, is a broad category including many creative and unexpected forms to grab consumers' attention where they work, play, and, of course, shop. Some of the options include billboards (many with digitally produced graphics and even three-dimensional images), public spaces (such as sports arenas, parking meters, and bus shelters), product placement (in movies and on TV), and **point-of-purchase**, where consumers make purchases (on shopping carts, aisles, shelves, floor space, in-store TV, and more).[16]

Ads now can appear virtually anywhere consumers have a few spare minutes or even seconds and thus enough time to notice them. The main advantage is that a very precise and—because of the nature of the setting—captive audience often can be reached in a cost-effective manner with a simple and direct message. A key challenge is demonstrating the reach and effectiveness of new media through credible, independent research. Another concern: consumers may perceive as invasive and obtrusive the unique ad placements that successfully break through clutter. For more on using alternative media effectively, see "Marketing Skills: Advertising in Hard Times."

Selecting Specific Vehicles Media planners search for the most cost-effective vehicles within each chosen media type, relying on measurement services for estimates of audience size, composition, and media cost. Audience size can be measured according to *circulation*, the number of physical units carrying the advertising; *audience*, the number of people exposed to the vehicle; *effective audience*, the number of people with target audience characteristics exposed to the vehicle; and *effective ad-exposed audience*, the number of people with target audience characteristics who actually saw the ad.

MARKETING SKILLS: ADVERTISING IN HARD TIMES

Getting through to the target audience can be difficult even in the best of times. That's why marketers who can plan effective advertising for hard times will be better able to plan ads for any kind of economic climate. When other companies are cutting back on advertising, advertisers who make their messages stand out will gain an important advantage. Be sure the messages offer insight into what the brand stands for; don't make decisions solely based on marketing research, because people often reject original or unconventional ideas simply for being different. Finally, target carefully to reach influential customer groups, and use creative, engaging approaches.

Innovative communications need not to be expensive to be effective. Honda developed an online game in which players choose a Honda and zoom around city streets plastered with Honda logos. In the first three months, 78,000 people played for an average of eight minutes. The cost per thousand (CPM) of $7 compared favorably to a prime time TV commercial CPM of $11.65. As another example, Cisco Systems, T-Mobile, Toyota, Coca-Cola, and other companies are using reasonably-priced placement opportunities in virtual communities such as Second Life to communicate with hard-to-reach 18- to 34-year-olds.[17]

Knowing the audience size, media planners can calculate the cost-per-thousand persons a vehicle reaches. If a full-page color ad in *Newsweek* costs $200,000, and the estimated readership is 3.1 million people, the cost of exposing the ad to 1,000 persons is approximately $65. The same ad in *BusinessWeek* may cost $70,000 but reach only 970,000 persons—at a cost per thousand of about $72. The media planner ranks each magazine by cost per thousand and favors magazines with the lowest cost per thousand for reaching target consumers. The magazines themselves often put together a "reader profile" summarizing the characteristics of the magazine's readers with respect to age, income, residence, marital status, and leisure activities.

Deciding on Media Timing and Allocation In choosing media, the advertiser faces both a macroscheduling and a microscheduling problem. The *macroscheduling problem* involves scheduling advertising in relation to seasons and the business cycle. Suppose 70% of a product's sales occur between June and September. The firm can vary its advertising expenditures to follow the seasonal pattern, oppose the seasonal pattern, or be constant throughout the year.

The *microscheduling problem* calls for allocating advertising expenditures within a short period to obtain maximum impact. Over a given period, advertising messages can be concentrated ("burst" advertising), dispersed continuously, or dispersed intermittently. The firm must also decide to schedule ad messages with a level, increasing, decreasing, or alternating frequency.

In launching a new product, the advertiser can choose among ad continuity, concentration, flighting, and pulsing. **Continuity** means exposures appear evenly throughout a given period. Generally, advertisers use this method in an expanding market, with frequently purchased items, and in tightly defined buyer categories. **Concentration** calls for spending all advertising dollars in a single period, which makes sense for products with one selling season or holiday. **Flighting** calls for advertising for a period, followed by a period with no advertising, followed by a second period of advertising activity. It's useful when funding is limited, the purchase cycle is relatively infrequent, or items are seasonal. **Pulsing** is continuous advertising at low-weight levels reinforced periodically by waves of heavier activity.[18] Those who favor pulsing say the audience will learn the message more thoroughly at a lower cost to the firm.

A company has to decide how to allocate its advertising budget over space as well as over time. The company makes "national buys" when it places ads on national TV networks or in nationally circulated magazines. It makes "spot buys" when it buys TV time in just a few markets or in regional editions of magazines. The company makes "local buys" when it advertises in local newspapers, on radio, or on outdoor sites.

Evaluating Advertising Effectiveness Most advertisers try to measure an ad's communication effect—its potential effect on awareness, knowledge, or preference—as well as its sales effect. **Communication-effect research** called *copy testing* seeks to determine whether an ad is communicating effectively. This can be done before an ad is placed (pretesting) and after it is placed (posttesting). Advertisers also need to posttest the overall impact of a completed campaign.

An ad's sales effect is easiest to measure in direct-marketing situations and hardest to measure in brand or corporate image-building advertising. In general, the fewer or more controllable other factors like features and price are, the easier it is to measure the effect on sales. One approach is shown in Figure 16.2. A company's *share of*

FIGURE 16.2 Formula for Measuring Sales Impact of Advertising

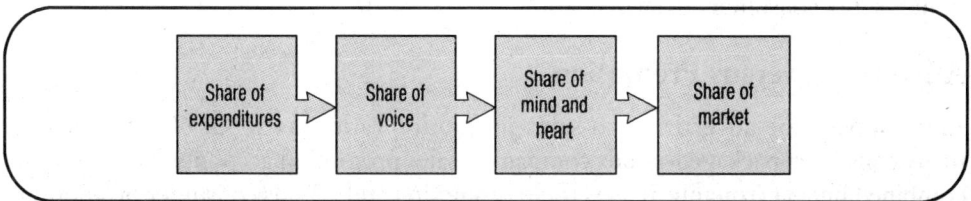

advertising expenditures produces a *share of voice* that earns a *share of consumers' minds and hearts* and ultimately a *share of market*.

Researchers try to measure the sales impact through analyzing historical or experimental data. The *historical approach* involves correlating past sales to past advertising expenditures using advanced statistical techniques.[19] Other researchers use an *experimental design* to measure advertising's sales impact. A growing number of researchers are striving to measure the sales effect of advertising expenditures instead of settling for communication-effect measures.[20]

SALES PROMOTION

Sales promotion, a key ingredient in marketing campaigns, consists of a collection of incentive tools, mostly short term, designed to stimulate quicker or greater purchase of particular products or services by consumers or the trade.[21] Whereas advertising offers a *reason* to buy, sales promotion offers an *incentive* to buy. Sales promotion includes tools for *consumer promotion* (samples, coupons, cash refund offers, prices off, premiums, prizes, patronage rewards, free trials, warranties, tie-in promotions, cross-promotions, point-of-purchase displays, and demonstrations); *trade promotion* (prices off, advertising and display allowances, and free goods); and *business* and *sales-force promotion* (trade shows and conventions, sales contests, and specialty advertising).

Sales Promotion Objectives

Sales promotion can be used to achieve a variety of objectives. Sellers use incentive-type promotions to attract new triers, reward loyal customers, and increase the repurchase rates of occasional users. Sales promotions often attract brand switchers looking for low price, good value, or premiums. If some of them would not have otherwise tried the brand, promotion can yield long-term increases in market share.[22] Sales promotions used in markets of high brand similarity produce a high sales response in the short run but little permanent gain in market share. In markets of high brand dissimilarity, promotions may alter market shares permanently. In addition to brand switching, consumers may engage in stockpiling—buying earlier than usual or buying extra quantities—but sales may then hit a postpromotion dip.[23]

A number of sales promotion benefits flow to manufacturers and consumers.[24] Manufacturers can adjust to short-term variations in supply and demand; test how high a list price they can charge (because they can always discount); sell more than they would normally at the list price; and adapt programs to different consumer segments. Promotions induce consumers to try new products and make consumers more aware of prices. Also, promotions lead to more varied retail formats, such as everyday-low-pricing and promotional-pricing. For retailers, promotions may increase sales of complementary categories (cake mix promotions may drive frosting sales), as well as induce some consumers to switch stores.

Advertising versus Promotion

In years past, the advertising-to-sales-promotion ratio was about 60:40. Today, in many consumer-packaged-goods companies, sales promotion accounts for 75% of the combined budget (roughly 50% is trade promotion and 25% is consumer promotion). Several factors have shaped this trend, particularly in consumer markets.[25] Top management now accepts promotion as an effective sales tool; the number of brands has increased; competitors use promotions frequently; many brands are seen as similar; consumers became more price-oriented; the trade demanded more deals from manufacturers; and advertising efficiency declined.

Sales promotion, with its incessant coupons, deals, premiums, and percentages off, may devalue the product offering in the buyers' minds. There is risk in putting a well-known brand leader on promotion over 30% of the time.[26] Advertising appears to be more effective at deepening brand loyalty, although added-value promotions can be distinguished from price promotions.[27] Also, loyal brand buyers tend not to change their buying patterns as a result of competitive promotions. And price promotions may not build permanent total-category volume. One study of more than 1,000 promotions concluded that only 16% paid off.[28]

Small-share competitors find it advantageous to use sales promotion because they can't match the market leaders' large advertising budgets; nor can they obtain shelf space without offering trade allowances or stimulate consumer trial without offering incentives. Price competition is often used by a small brand seeking to enlarge its share, but it's less effective for a category leader whose growth lies in expanding the entire category.[29] The upshot is that many consumer-packaged-goods companies feel forced to use more sales promotion than they wish.

Major Decisions

In using sales promotion, a company establishes its objectives, selects the tools, develops the program, pretests the program, implements and controls it, and evaluates the results.

Establishing Objectives Sales-promotion objectives derive from broader promotion objectives, which are derived from more basic marketing objectives for the product. Targeting consumers, objectives include encouraging purchase of larger-size units, building trial among nonusers, and attracting switchers away from competitors' brands. Targeting retailers, objectives include persuading retailers to carry new items and higher inventory levels, encouraging off-season buying, offsetting competitive promotions, building brand loyalty, and gaining entry into new outlets. Targeting the sales force, objectives include encouraging support of a new product or model, encouraging more prospecting, and stimulating off-season sales.[30]

Selecting Consumer Promotion Tools Table 16.2 shows the main consumer promotion tools. *Manufacturer promotions* are, for example in the auto industry, rebates and gifts to motivate test-drives and purchases; *retailer promotions* include price cuts, feature advertising, retailer coupons, and retailer contests or premiums.[31]

We can also distinguish between sales-promotion tools that are *consumer-franchise building* and those that are not. The former imparts a selling message along

TABLE 16.2 Major Consumer-Promotion Tools

Samples: Offer of a free amount of a product or service delivered door-to-door, sent in the mail, picked up in a store, attached to another product, or featured in an advertising offer.

Coupons: Certificates entitling the bearer to a stated saving on the purchase of a specific product: mailed, enclosed in other products or attached to them, or inserted in magazine and newspaper ads.

Cash Refund Offers (rebates): Provide a price reduction after purchase rather than at the retail shop: consumer sends a specified "proof of purchase" to the manufacturer who "refunds" part of the purchase price by mail.

Price Packs (cents-off deals): Offers to consumers of savings off the regular price of a product, flagged on the label or package. *A reduced-price pack* is a single package sold at the reduced price (such as two for the price of one). *A banded pack* is two related products banded together (such as a toothbrush and toothpaste).

Premiums (gifts): Merchandise offered at a relatively low cost or free as an incentive to purchase a particular product. A *with-pack premium* accompanies the product inside or on the package. A *free in-the-mail premium* is mailed to consumers who send in a proof of purchase, such as a box top or UPC code. A *self-liquidating premium* is sold below its normal retail price to consumers who request it.

Frequency Programs: Programs providing rewards related to the consumer's frequency and intensity in purchasing the company's products or services.

Prizes (contests, sweepstakes, games): *Prizes* are offers of the chance to win cash, trips, or merchandise as a result of purchasing something. A *contest* calls for consumers to submit an entry to be examined by a panel of judges who will select the best entries. A *sweepstakes* asks consumers to submit their names in a drawing. A *game* presents consumers with something every time they buy—bingo numbers, missing letters—which might help them win a prize.

Patronage Awards: Values in cash or in other forms that are proportional to patronage of a certain vendor or group of vendors.

Free Trials: Inviting prospective purchasers to try the product without cost in the hope that they will buy.

Product Warranties: Explicit or implicit promises by sellers that the product will perform as specified or that the seller will fix it or refund the customer's money during a specified period.

Tie-in Promotions: Two or more brands or companies team up on coupons, refunds, and contests to increase pulling power.

Cross-Promotions: Using one brand to advertise another noncompeting brand.

Point-of-Purchase (POP) Display and Demonstrations: POP displays and demonstrations take place at the point-of-purchase or sale.

TABLE 16.3 Major Trade Promotion Tools

Price-Off (off-invoice or off-list): A straight discount off the list price on each case purchased during a stated time period.

Allowance: An amount offered in return for the retailer's agreeing to feature the manufacturer's product in some way. An *advertising allowance* compensates retailers for advertising the manufacturer's product. A *display allowance* compensates them for carrying a special product display.

Free Goods: Offers of extra cases of merchandise to intermediaries who buy a certain quantity or who feature a certain flavor or size.

Source: For more information, see Betsy Spethman, "Trade Promotion Redefined," *Brandweek*, March 13, 1995, pp. 25–32.

---

with the deal, such as coupons that include a selling message. Sales promotion tools that typically are *not* brand-building include price-off packs, consumer premiums not related to a product, contests and sweepstakes, consumer refund offers, and trade allowances. Sales promotion used with advertising seems most effective: In one study, a price promotion alone increased sales by 15%. Promotion combined with feature advertising boosted sales volume by 19%; when point-of-purchase display was added, sales volume increased by 24%.[32]

Selecting Trade Promotion Tools Manufacturers use a number of trade-promotion tools (see Table 16.3) to (1) persuade an intermediary to carry the product;

(2) persuade an intermediary to carry more units; (3) induce retailers to promote the brand by featuring, display, and price reduction; and (4) stimulate retailers and their salespeople to push the product.[33] Today, giant retailers have more power to demand trade promotion at the expense of consumer promotion and advertising.[34] Yet trade promotions are often complex to administer, difficult to manage, and may even lead to lost revenues.

Selecting Business and Sales-Force Promotion Tools Companies spend billions of dollars on business and sales-force promotion tools (see Table 16.4) to gather business leads, impress and reward customers, and motivate the sales force to greater effort. The budget for each promotion tool typically remains fairly constant from year to year. For many new businesses that want to make a splash to a targeted audience, trade shows are an important tool, but the cost per contact is the highest of all communication options.

Developing the Program In deciding to use a particular incentive, marketers must consider (1) the *size* of the incentive (a certain minimum is necessary if the promotion is to succeed); (2) the *conditions* for participation (whether to offer the incentive to everyone or to select groups); (3) the *duration*; (4) the *distribution vehicle* (each will have a different level of reach, cost, and impact); (5) the *timing*; and (6) the *total sales-promotion budget* (including administrative costs and incentive costs).

Pretesting, Implementing, Controlling, and Evaluating the Program Although most sales promotion programs are designed on the basis of experience, pretests can determine whether the tools are appropriate, the incentive size is optimal, and the presentation method efficient. Marketers can ask consumers to rate or rank different possible deals or they can run trial tests in limited geographic areas. Implementation planning must cover *lead time* (to prepare the program before the launch) and *sell-in time* (beginning with the launch and ending when about 95% of the deal merchandise is in the hands of consumers).

Manufacturers can use sales data, consumer surveys, and experiments to evaluate a promotion. Sales (scanner) data can show who took advantage of the promotion, what they used to buy, and how they behaved toward the brand and other brands. Sales promotions work best when they attract competitors' customers who then switch. Surveys can help determine recall, attitude, behavior, and subsequent brand-choice behavior among the target audience.[35] When running experiments that vary attributes such as incentive value, duration, and distribution media, marketers can use scanner data to determine whether more people bought the product and when.

TABLE 16.4 Major Business Promotion and Sales-Force Promotion Tools

Trade Shows and Conventions: Industry associations organize annual trade shows and conventions where firms selling products and services to this industry set up booths and display their products. Participating vendors expect several benefits, including generating new sales leads, maintaining customers contacts, introducing new products, meeting new customers, selling more to present customers and educating customers with publications, videos, and other audiovisual materials.

Sales Contests: A sales contest aims at inducing the sales force or dealers to increase their sales results over a stated period, with prizes (money, trips, gifts, or points) going to those who succeed.

Specialty Advertising: Specialty advertising consists of useful, low-cost items bearing the company's name and address, and sometimes an advertising message, that salespeople give to prospects and customers. Common items are ballpoint pens, calendars, key chains, flashlights, tote bags, and memo pads.

EVENTS AND EXPERIENCES

Becoming part of a personally relevant moment in consumers' lives can broaden and deepen a company's relationship with the target market. For example, American Express has benefited from being a sponsor of the U.S. Open tennis tournament, achieving high levels of awareness and engaging thousands of consumers with the brand.[36] Daily encounters with brands may also affect consumers' brand attitudes and beliefs. *Atmospheres* are "packaged environments" that create or reinforce leanings toward product purchase. Law offices decorated with oriental rugs and oak furniture communicate "stability" and "success."[37] A five-star hotel will use elegant chandeliers, marble columns, and other tangible signs of luxury.

Events Objectives

Marketers report a number of reasons why they sponsor events:

1. *To identify with a particular target market or life style.* Customers can be targeted geographically, demographically, psychographically, or behaviorally according to events. Old Spice sponsors college sports and motor sports to highlight product relevancy and sample among its target audience of 16- to 24-year-old males.[38]
2. *To increase awareness of company or product name.* Sponsorship often offers sustained exposure to a brand, a necessary condition for building brand recognition. Frito-Lay used balloon festivals and street parades to sample its Flat Earth crisps, build awareness, and drive retail traffic.[39]
3. *To create or reinforce perceptions of key brand image associations.* Events themselves have associations that help to create or reinforce brand associations.[40] To toughen its image and appeal to America's heartland, Toyota Tundra has sponsored bass-fishing tournaments.[41]
4. *To enhance corporate image.* Sponsorship can improve perceptions that the company is likable and prestigious. Although Visa views its Olympic sponsorship as a means of enhancing international brand awareness and increasing usage and volume, it also engenders patriotic goodwill and taps into the emotional Olympic spirit.[42]
5. *To create experiences and evoke feelings.* The feelings engendered by an exciting or rewarding event may indirectly link to the brand, as Visa has found with its Olympic sponsorship.
6. *To express commitment to the community or on social issues.* Cause-related marketing sponsors nonprofit organizations and charities. Firms such as Stoneyfield Farm, Starbucks, American Express, and Tom's of Maine have made cause-related marketing an important cornerstone of their marketing programs.
7. *To entertain key clients or reward key employees.* Many events include lavish hospitality tents and other special services or activities only for sponsors and their guests, to engender goodwill and establish valuable business contacts. The financial services firm BB&T Corp. uses its NASCAR Busch Series sponsorship to entertain business customers and its minor league baseball sponsorship to generate excitement among employees.[43]
8. *To permit merchandising or promotional opportunities.* Many marketers tie in contests or sweepstakes, in-store merchandising, direct response, or other marketing activities with an event, the way Coca-Cola has done with the hit TV show *American Idol*.

Despite these potential advantages, an event's success can still be unpredictable and beyond the sponsor's control. Although many consumers will credit sponsors for providing the financial assistance to make an event possible, some may resent the commercialization of events.

Major Sponsorship Decisions

Successful sponsorships require choosing the appropriate events; designing the optimal sponsorship program; and measuring the effects of sponsorship.[44]

- *Choosing event opportunities.* The event must meet the brand's marketing objectives and communication strategy, attract the desired target market, generate favorable attention, be unique but not encumbered with many sponsors, lend itself to ancillary marketing activities, and reflect or enhance sponsor's brand or corporate image.[45] More firms are also using their names to sponsor the arenas, stadiums, and other venues that hold the events.[46]
- *Designing sponsorship programs.* Many marketers believe that it's the marketing program accompanying an event sponsorship that ultimately determines its success. At least two to three times the amount of the sponsorship expenditure should be spent on related marketing activities. When Jamba Juice sponsors running races, it displays its brand banners all around and offers samples of smoothies to competitors and spectators.[47]
- *Event creation.* This is a key skill in publicizing fund-raising drives for nonprofit organizations. Fund-raisers have developed a large repertoire of special events, including anniversary celebrations, art exhibits, auctions, benefit evenings, bingo games, book sales, cake sales, contests, dances, dinners, fairs, fashion shows, parties in unusual places, rummage sales, tours, and walkathons. No sooner is one type of event created, such as a walkathon, than competitors spawn new versions, such as readathons, bikeathons, and jogathons.[48]
- *Measuring sponsorship activities.* Measuring the effects of events can be difficult. The *supply-side* method focuses on potential brand exposure by assessing the extent of media coverage; the *demand-side* method focuses on reported exposure from consumers. Some experts say that positive editorial coverage can be worth five to ten times the equivalent advertising value; however, sponsorship rarely gets such favorable treatment.[49] On the demand side, surveying spectators can show the effect on brand knowledge, attitudes, and intentions.

Creating Experiences

A large part of local, grassroots marketing is experiential marketing, which not only communicates features and benefits, but also connects a product or service with unique and interesting experiences. "The idea is not to sell something, but to demonstrate how a brand can enrich a customer's life."[50] Consultants and authors Pine and Gilmore argue that we're on the threshold of the "Experience Economy," in which all businesses must orchestrate memorable events for their customers.[51] Companies can even create a strong image by inviting prospects and customers to visit their headquarters and factories. Ben & Jerry's, Boeing, Hershey's, and Crayola all sponsor excellent company tours that draw millions of visitors a year.[52]

PUBLIC RELATIONS

Not only must the company relate constructively to customers, suppliers, and dealers, it must also relate to a large number of interested publics. A **public** is any group that has an actual or potential interest in or impact on a company's ability to achieve its objectives. **Public relations (PR)** includes a variety of programs to promote or protect a company's image or individual products.

The wise company takes concrete steps to manage successful relations with its key publics. PR departments perform five functions: (1) *press relations* (presenting news and information about the organization in the most positive light); (2) *product publicity* (publicizing specific products); (3) *corporate communication* (promoting understanding of the organization through internal and external communications); (4) *lobbying* (dealing with legislators and government officials to promote or defeat legislation and regulation); and (5) *counseling* (advising management about public issues and company positions and image, during good times and bad). The more strongly brand equity and corporate image have been established—especially corporate credibility and trustworthiness—the more likely that the firm can weather the storm, especially with preparation and a crisis management program.[53]

Marketing Public Relations

Many companies are turning to **marketing public relations (MPR)** to support corporate or product promotion and image making. MPR, like financial PR and community PR, serves a special constituency, the marketing department.[54] MPR was once called **publicity,** the task of securing editorial space—as opposed to paid space—in print and broadcast media to promote a product, a service, an idea, a place, a person, or an organization. MPR goes beyond simple publicity and plays an important role in:

- *Launching new products.* The success of toys such as Leap Frog owes much to strong publicity.
- *Repositioning a mature product.* New York City had bad press in the 1970s until the "I Love New York" campaign.
- *Building interest in a product category.* Companies and industry groups use MPR to rebuild interest in commodities such as eggs and expand consumption of products such as tea.
- *Influencing specific target groups.* McDonald's sponsors special neighborhood events in Latino and African American communities to build goodwill.
- *Defending products that have encountered public problems.* PR professionals must be adept at managing crises, such as the JetBlue Valentine Day's fiasco in 2007 when two inches of ice led to 1,000 cancelled flights, massive delays, and passengers stuck on planes for hours.[55]
- *Building the corporate image in a way that reflects favorably on its products.* Steve Jobs's dramatic product announcements have helped to create an innovative image for Apple.

As the power of mass advertising weakens, marketing managers are turning to MPR to build awareness and brand knowledge in a cost-effective manner and to reach local communities and specific audiences. Nevertheless, it must be planned jointly

BREAKTHROUGH MARKETING: VIRGIN GROUP

Virgin, the brainchild of Sir Richard Branson, shows the power of strong traditional and non-traditional marketing communications. Branson roared onto the British stage in the 1970s with his upstart Virgin Records, beginning a marathon of publicity that continues to this day. Although he sold Virgin Records, he's created over 200 companies worldwide, with combined revenues exceeding $5 billion. Virgin—the third most respected brand in Britain—and Branson's personality help sell diverse offerings such as air and train transportation, financial services, soft drinks, music, mobile phones, cars, wines, publishing, even bridal wear. Despite the diversity, all the lines connote value for money, quality, innovation, fun, and a sense of competitive challenge.

Branson is a master of the strategic publicity stunt. In the 1980s, when he announced Virgin Atlantic Airways as a competitor to stodgy, overpriced British Airways, Branson wore World War I-era flying gear. More recently, Branson invited Comedy Central star Stephen Colbert to help launch Virgin America on the first flight aboard the brightly-painted "Air Colbert" jet. Although heavy rain and a nearby tornado prevented Colbert from getting to the airport, his missing the flight was almost as newsworthy as Branson's high-profile appearance. Remembering a friend's advice about publicity—"If you don't give them a photograph that will get them on the front page, they won't turn up at your next event"—Branson always gives them a reason.[56]

with advertising.[57] "Breakthrough Marketing: Virgin Group" focuses on Sir Richard Branson, an accomplished user of MPR.

Major Decisions in Marketing PR

In considering when and how to use MPR, management must establish the marketing objectives, choose the messages and vehicles, implement the plan carefully, and evaluate the results. The main tools of MPR are described in Table 16.5.[58]

TABLE 16.5 Major Tools in Marketing PR

Publications: Companies rely extensively on published materials to reach and influence their target markets. These include annual reports, brochures, articles, company newsletters and magazines, and audiovisual materials.

Events: Companies can draw attention to new products or other company activities by arranging special events like news conferences, seminars, outings, trade shows, exhibits, contests and competitions, and anniversaries that will reach the target publics.

Sponsorships: Companies can promote their brands and corporate name by sponsoring sports and cultural events and highly regarded causes.

News: One of the major tasks of PR professionals is to find or create favorable news about the company, its products, and its people and get the media to accept press releases and attend press conferences.

Speeches: Increasingly, company executives must field questions from the media or give talks at trade associations or sales meetings, all these appearances can build the company's image.

Public-Service Activities: Companies can build goodwill by contributing money and time to good causes.

Identity Media: Companies need a visual identity that the public immediately recognizes. The visual identity is carried by company logos, stationary, brochures, signs, business forms, business cards, buildings, uniforms, and dress codes.

- *Establishing the marketing objectives.* MPR can build *awareness* of a product, a service, a person, an organization, or an idea; add *credibility* by communicating a message in an editorial context; boost sales force and dealer *enthusiasm*; and hold down *promotion cost* because it costs less than media advertising. Whereas PR reaches target publics through the mass media, MPR is increasingly borrowing direct-response marketing techniques and technology to reach target audience members one-on-one.

- *Choosing messages and vehicles.* The MPR manager must identify or develop interesting stories about the product. If there are few stories, the manager should propose newsworthy events to sponsor as a way of stimulating media coverage. For instance, smart MPR has helped Sweden's Vattenfall, Europe's largest heating firm, reach key audiences in several nations and improve its financials. In addition to sponsorships of the National Geographic Society and the World Childhood Foundation, Vattenfall has garnered publicity by sponsoring local events such as Germany's Brandenburg Gate commemorations.[59]

- *Implementing and evaluating the plan.* MPR's contribution to the bottom line is difficult to measure because it's used along with other promotional tools. The easiest measure is the number of *exposures* carried by the media. A better measure would be the *change in product awareness, comprehension, or attitude* resulting from the MPR campaign (after allowing for the effect of other promotional tools).

EXECUTIVE SUMMARY

Advertising is any paid form of nonpersonal presentation and promotion of ideas, goods, or services by an identified sponsor. To develop an advertising program, (1) set advertising objectives; (2) establish a budget; (3) choose the advertising message and creative strategy; (4) decide on the media; and (5) evaluate communication and sales effects. Sales promotion consists of a diverse collection of incentive tools, mostly short term, to stimulate quicker or greater purchase of particular products or services by consumers or the trade. Sales promotion includes tools for consumer promotion, trade promotion, and business and sales-force promotion.

Events and experiences are a means to become part of special and more personally relevant moments in consumers' lives. Involvement with properly managed events can broaden and deepen the relationship of the sponsor with its target market. Public relations (PR) involves a variety of programs to promote or protect a company's image or its individual products. Today marketing public relations (MPR) is used to support the marketing department in corporate or product promotion and image making. MPR can affect public awareness at a fraction of the cost of advertising and is often much more credible. The main tools of MPR are publications, events, news, speeches, public service activities, and identity media.

NOTES

1. "Geico Gets 'Scoop' on Pop Icons," *Adweek Online*, August 29, 2007, www.adweek.com; Lewis Lazare, "Martin Agency Comes Up with More Winners for Geico," *Chicago Sun-Times*, September 5, 2007, http://www.suntimes.com/business/lazare/541924,CST-FIN-lew05.article; Adam Armbruster, "Geico Takes Varied Roads to Consumers," *Television Week*, March 12, 2007, p. 10;

Rob Walker, "Pop-Culture Evolution," *The New York Times Magazine*, April 15, 2007.
2. Paul F. Nunes and Jeffrey Merrihue, "The Continuing Power of Mass Advertising, *Sloan Management Review*, Winter 2007, pp. 63–69.
3. William L. Wilkie and Paul W. Farris, "Comparison Advertising: Problem and Potential," *Journal of Marketing* (October 1975): 7–15; Debora Viana Thompson and Rebecca W. Hamilton, "The Effects of Information Processing Mode on Consumers' Responses to Comparative Advertising," *Journal of Consumer Research* 32 (March 2006): 530–540; Randall L. Rose, Paul W. Miniard, Michael J. Barone, Kenneth C. Manning, and Brian D. Till, "When Persuasion Goes Undetected: The Case of Comparative Advertising," *Journal of Marketing Research* (August 1993): 315–330; Dhruv Grewal, Sukumar Kavanoor, and James Barnes, "Comparative versus Noncomparative Advertising: A Meta-Analysis," *Journal of Marketing* (October 1997): 1–15.
4. See Donald E. Schultz, Dennis Martin, and William P. Brown, *Strategic Advertising Campaigns* (Chicago: Crain Books, 1984), pp. 192–197.
5. Rajesh Chandy, Gerard J. Tellis, Debbie MacInnis, and Pattana Thaivanich, "What to Say When: Advertising Appeals in Evolving Markets," *Journal of Marketing Research* 38, no. 4 (November 2001); Gerard J. Tellis, Rajesh Chandy, and Pattana Thaivanich, "Decomposing the Effects of Direct Advertising: Which Brand Works, When, Where, and How Long?" *Journal of Marketing Research* 37 (February 2000): 32–46.
6. http://www.stateofthenewsmedia.org/2007/narrative_radio_audience.asp?cat=2&media=9.
7. David Ogilvy, *Ogilvy on Advertising* (New York: Vintage Books, 1983).
8. Kim Bartel Sheehan, *Controversies in Contemporary Advertising* (Thousand Oaks, CA: Sage Publications, 2003).
9. Eleftheria Parpis, "Dove's 'Evolution' Is All to the Good," *Adweek*, April 25, 2007; http://www.awny.org/.
10. Schultz, et al., *Strategic Advertising Campaigns*, p. 340.
11. Herbert E. Krugman, "What Makes Advertising Effective?" *Harvard Business Review* (March–April 1975): 98.
12. Prashant Malaviya, "The Moderating Influence of Advertising Context on Ad Repetition Effects: The Role of Amount and Type of Elaboration," *Journal of Consumer Research* 34 (June 2007): 32–40.
13. Thomas H. Davenport and John C. Beck, *The Attention Economy: Understanding the New Currency of Business* (Boston, MA: Harvard Business School Press, 2000).
14. Susan Thea Posnock, "It Can Control Madison Avenue," *American Demographics* (February 2004): 29–33.
15. James Betzold, "Jaded Riders Are Ever-Tougher Sell," *Advertising Age*, July 9, 2001, p. S2; Michael McCarthy, "Ads Are Here, There, Everywhere," *USA Today*, June 19, 2001, www.usatoday.com; Kipp Cheng, "Captivating Audiences," *Brandweek*, November 29, 1999, p. 64; Michael McCarthy, "Critics Target 'Omnipresent' Ads," *USA Today*, April 16, 2001, www.usatoday.com.
16. Sam Jaffe, "Easy Riders," *American Demographics* (March 2004): 20–23; http://www.prwebdirect.com/releases/2007/3/prweb511540.htm; Matthew Boyle, "Hey Shoppers: Ads on Aisle 7!" *Fortune*, November 24, 2003; Laura Petrecca, "Wal-Mart TV Sells Marketers Flexibility," *USA Today*, March 29, 2007, p. B3.
17. "Virtual Worlds Generate Real-Life Benefits for Properties, Sponsors," *IEG Sponsorship Report*, June 11, 2007, pp. 1, 8; Allison Fass, "Sex, Pranks and Reality," *Forbes*, July 2, 2007, p. 48; David Radd, "Advergaming: You Got It," *BusinessWeek*, October 11, 2006; Warren Berger, "Just Do It Again," *Business 2.0*, September 2002, p. 81; Brian Steinberg, "Marketing Folks' New Medium May Be Your PC's Hard Drive," *Wall Street Journal*, May 2, 2005, p. B8.
18. Hani I. Mesak, "An Aggregate Advertising Pulsing Model with Wearout Effects," *Marketing Science*, Summer 1992, pp. 310–326; and Fred M. Feinberg, "Pulsing Policies for Aggregate Advertising Models," *Marketing Science*, Summer 1992, pp. 221–234.
19. Kristian S. Palda, *The Measurement of Cumulative Advertising Effect* (Upper Saddle River, NJ: Prentice Hall, 1964), p. 87; David B. Montgomery and Alvin J. Silk, "Estimating Dynamic Effects of Market Communications Expenditures," *Management Science* (June 1972): 485–501.
20. In addition to the sources cited below, see David Walker and Tony M. Dubitsky, "Why Liking Matters," *Journal of Advertising Research* (May–June 1994): 9–18; Abhilasha Mehta, "How Advertising Response Modeling (ARM) Can Increase Ad Effectiveness," *Journal of Advertising Research* (May–June 1994): 62–74; Karin Holstius, "Sales Response to Advertising," *International Journal of Advertising* 9, no. 1 (1990): 38–56; John Deighton, Caroline Henderson, and Scott Neslin,

"The Effects of Advertising on Brand Switching and Repeat Purchasing," *Journal of Marketing Research* (February 1994): 28–43; Anil Kaul and Dick R. Wittink, "Empirical Generalizations About the Impact of Advertising on Price Sensitivity and Price," *Marketing Science* 14, no. 3, pt. 1 (1995): G151–160; Ajay Kalra and Ronald C. Goodstein, "The Impact of Advertising Positioning Strategies on Consumer Price Sensitivity," *Journal of Marketing Research* (May 1998): 210–224; Gerard J. Tellis, Rajesh K. Chandy, and Pattana Thaivanich, "Which Ad Works, When, Where, and How Often? Modeling the Effects of Direct Television Advertising," *Journal of Marketing Research* 37 (February 2000): 32–46.

21. From Robert C. Blattberg and Scott A. Neslin, *Sales Promotion: Concepts, Methods, and Strategies* (Upper Saddle River, NJ: Prentice Hall, 1990). A comprehensive review of academic work on sales promotions can be found in Scott Neslin, "Sales Promotion," in Bart Weitz and Robin Wensley, eds., *Handbook of Marketing*, (London: Sage Publications, 2002), pp. 310–338.

22. Kusum Ailawadi, Karen Gedenk, and Scott A. Neslin, "Heterogeneity and Purchase Event Feedback in Choice Models: An Empirical Analysis with Implications for Model Building," *International Journal of Research in Marketing* 16 (1999): 177–198. See also Kusum L. Ailawadi, Karen Gedenk, Christian Lutzky, and Scott A. Neslin, "Decomposition of the Sales Impact of Promotion-Induced Stockpiling," *Journal of Marketing Research* 44 (August 2007); Praveen Kopalle, Carl F. Mela, and Lawrence Marsh, "The Dynamic Effect of Discounting on Sales: Empirical Analysis and Normative Pricing Implications," *Marketing Science* 18 (Summer 1999): 317–332; Eric T. Anderson and Duncan Simester, "The Long-Run Effects of Promotion Depth on New Versus Established Customers: Three Field Studies," *Marketing Science* 23, no. 1 (Winter 2004): 4–20; Luc Wathieu, A. V. Muthukrishnan and Bart J. Bronnenberg. "The Asymmetric Effect of Discount Retraction on Subsequent Choice," *Journal of Consumer Research* 31 (December 2004): 652–665.

23. Carl Mela, Kamel Jedidi, and Douglas Bowman, "The Long Term Impact of Promotions on Consumer Stockpiling," *Journal of Marketing Research* 35, no. 2 (May 1998): 250–262; Harald J. Van Heerde, Peter S. H. Leeflang, and Dick Wittink, "The Estimation of Pre- and Postpromotion Dips with Store-Level Scanner Data," *Journal of Marketing Research* 37, no. 3 (August 2000): 383–395; Harald J. Van Heerde, Sachin Gupta, and Dick Wittink, "Is 75% of the Sales Promotion Bump Due to Brand Switching? No, Only 33% Is," *Journal of Marketing Research* 40 (November 2003): 481–491.

24. Paul W. Farris and John A. Quelch, "In Defense of Price Promotion," *Sloan Management Review* (Fall 1987): 63–69.

25. Roger A. Strang, "Sales Promotion—Fast Growth, Faulty Management," *Harvard Business Review* (July–August 1976): 116–119.

26. For a summary of research on whether promotion erodes the consumer franchise of leading brands, see Blattberg and Neslin, *Sales Promotion: Concepts, Methods, and Strategies*.

27. Robert George Brown, "Sales Response to Promotions and Advertising," *Journal of Advertising Research* (August 1974): 36–37. Also see Carl F. Mela, Sunil Gupta, and Donald R. Lehmann, "The Long-Term Impact of Promotion and Advertising on Consumer Brand Choice," *Journal of Marketing Research* (May 1997): 248–261; Purushottam Papatla and Lakshman Krishnamurti, "Measuring the Dynamic Effects of Promotions on Brand Choice," *Journal of Marketing Research* (February 1996): 20–35; Kamel Jedidi, Carl F. Mela, and Sunil Gupta, "Managing Advertising and Promotion for Long-Run Profitability," *Marketing Science* 18, no. 1 (1999): 1–22.

28. Magid M. Abraham and Leonard M. Lodish, "Getting the Most Out of Advertising and Promotion," *Harvard Business Review* (May–June 1990): 50–60. See also Shuba Srinivasan, Koen Pauwels, Dominique Hanssens, and Marnik Dekimpe, "Do Promotions Benefit Manufacturers, Retailers, or Both?" *Management Science*, vol. 50, no. 5 (May 2004): 617–629.

29. F. Kent Mitchel, "Advertising/Promotion Budgets: How Did We Get Here, and What Do We Do Now?" *Journal of Consumer Marketing* (Fall 1985): 405–447.

30. A model for setting sales promotions objectives can be found in David B. Jones, "Setting Promotional Goals: A Communications Relationship Model," *Journal of Consumer Marketing* 11, no. 1 (1994): 38–49.

31. Kusum L. Ailawadi, Bari A. Harlam, Jacques Cesar, and David Trounce, "Promotion Profitability for a Retailer: The Role of Promotion, Brand, Category, and Store Characteristics," *Journal of Marketing Research* 43 (November 2006): 518–536.

32. See John C. Totten and Martin P. Block, *Analyzing Sales Promotion: Text and Cases*, 2d ed. (Chicago: Dartnell, 1994), pp. 69–70.
33. Miguel Gomez, Vithala Rao, and Edward McLaughlin, "Empirical Analysis of Budget and Allocation of Trade Promotions in the U.S. Supermarket Industry," *Journal of Marketing Research* 44 (August 2007); Norris Bruce, Preyas S. Desai, and Richard Staelin, "The Better They Are, the More They Give: Trade Promotions of Consumer Durables," *Journal of Marketing Research* 42 (February 2005): 54–66.
34. Kusum L. Ailawadi (2001), "The Retail Power-Performance Conundrum: What Have We Learned?" *Journal of Retailing* 77 (3): 299–318; Kusum L. Ailawadi and Bari Harlam, "An Empirical Analysis of the Determinants of Retail Margins: The Role of Store Brand Share," *Journal of Marketing* 68 (January 2004): 147–166; Paul W. Farris and Kusum L. Ailawadi, "Retail Power: Monster or Mouse?" *Journal of Retailing* (Winter 1992): 351–369; Koen Pauwels, "How Retailer and Competitor Decisions Drive the Long-term Effectiveness of Manufacturer Promotions," *Journal of Retailing*, in press.
35. Joe A. Dodson, Alice M. Tybout, and Brian Sternthal, "Impact of Deals and Deal Retraction on Brand Switching," *Journal of Marketing Research* (February 1978): 72–81.
36. From internal company sources.
37. Philip Kotler, "Atmospherics as a Marketing Tool," *Journal of Retailing* (Winter 1973–1974): 48–64.
38. "Personal Care Marketers: Who Does What," *IEG Sponsorship Report*, April 16, 2007, p. 4.
39. "New Frito-Lay Brand Seeks to Rise Above Pack with Event Ties," *IEG Sponsorship Report*, April 16, 2007, p. 7.
40. Bettina Cornwell, Michael S. Humphreys, Angela M. Maguire, Clinton S. Weeks, Cassandra Tellegen, "Sponsorship-Linked Marketing: The Role of Articulation in Memory," *Journal of Consumer Research* 33 (December 2006): 312–321.
41. Mark Rechtin, "To Pitch New Tundra, Toyota Turns to NASCAR, Fishing," *Automotive News*, September 18, 2006, p. 4.
42. Hilary Cassidy, "So You Want to Be an Olympic Sponsor?" *Brandweek*, November 7, 2005, pp. 24–28.
43. "Bank's New Department, Deals Reflect Elevated Sponsorship Status," *IEG Sponsorship Report*, April 16, 2007, pp. 1, 8.
44. The Association of National Advertisers has a useful source: *Event Marketing: A Management Guide*, which is available at www.ana.net/bookstore.
45. T. Bettina Cornwell, Michael S. Humphreys, Angela M. Maguire, Clinton S. Weeks, Cassandra L. Tellegen, "Sponsorship-Linked Marketing: The Role of Articulation in Memory," *Journal of Consumer Research* 33 (December 2006): 312–321.
46. Constantine von Hoffman, "Buying Up the Bleachers," *Brandweek*, February 19, 2007, pp. 18–21.
47. Kelley Gates, "Wild in the Streets," *Brand Marketing*, February 2001, p. 54.
48. Dwight W. Catherwood and Richard L. Van Kirk, *The Complete Guide to Special Event Management* (New York: John Wiley, 1992).
49. William L. Shankin and John Kuzma, "Buying That Sporting Image," *Marketing Management*, Spring 1992, p. 65.
50. Peter Post, "Beyond Brand—The Power of Experience Branding," *ANA/The Advertiser* (October/November 2000).
51. B. Joseph Pine and James H. Gilmore, *The Experience Economy: Work Is Theatre and Every Business a Stage* (Boston: Harvard Business School Press, 1999).
52. Ethan Gilsdorf, "10 Things Not to Miss," *Boston Globe*, June 10, 2007, p. M.7.
53. Harald Van Heerde, Kristiaan Helsen, and Marnik G. Dekimpe, "The Impact of a Product Harm Crisis on Marketing Effectiveness," *Marketing Science* 26 (March-April 2007): 230–245; Jill Klein and Niraj Dawar (2004), "Corporate Social Responsibility and Consumers' Attributions and Brand Evaluations in a Product-Harm Crisis," *International Journal of Research in Marketing*, 21(3): 203–217; Michelle L. Roehm and Alice M. Tybout, "When Will a Brand Scandal Spill Over and How Should Competitors Respond?" *Journal of Marketing Research* 43 (August 2006): 366–373.
54. For an excellent account, see Thomas L. Harris, *The Marketer's Guide to Public Relations* (New York: John Wiley, 1991). Also see Thomas L. Harris, *Value-Added Public Relations* (Chicago: NTC Business Books, 1998).
55. Chuck Salter, "Lessons from the Tarmac," *Fast Company*, May 2007, pp. 31–32.
56. Suzanne Marta, "Virgin America Takes off with Inaugural Flights," *Dallas Morning News*, August 9, 2007; Alan Deutschman, "The Enlightenment of Richard Branson," *Fast Company*, September 2006, p. 49; Sam Hill and Glenn Rifkin, *Radical Marketing* (New York: Harper Business, 1999); Melanie Wells, "Red Baron," *Forbes*, July 3, 2000,

pp. 151–160; Kerry Capell with Wendy Zellner, "Richard Branson's Next Big Adventure," *BusinessWeek*, March 8, 2004, pp. 44–45; Andy Serwer, "Do Branson's Profits Equal His *Joie de Vivre?*" *Fortune*, October 17, 2005, p. 57.

57. "Do We Have A Story For You!" *The Economist*, January 21, 2006, pp. 57–58; Al Ries and Laura Ries, *The Fall of Advertising and the Rise of PR* (New York: HarperCollins, 2002).

58. For more on cause-related marketing, see P. Rajan Varadarajan and Anil Menon, "Cause-Related Marketing: A Co-Alignment of Marketing Strategy and Corporate Philanthropy," *Journal of Marketing* (July 1988): 58–74.

59. Stefan Nurpin, "From Brand Out of Mind to Brand in Hand: Brand Unification By Icons, Totems and Titans," talk given at IEG's 24th Annual Sponsorship Conference, March 13, 2007.

CHAPTER 17

Managing Personal Communications

In this chapter, we will address the following questions:

1. How can companies use integrated direct marketing for competitive advantage?
2. How can companies use interactive marketing and word of mouth most effectively?
3. How can personal selling be used to build profitable customer relationships?
4. What decisions do companies face in designing and managing a sales force?

MARKETING MANAGEMENT AT COCA-COLA

Coca-Cola, with global sales of $24 billion per year, has a long history of reaching out to consumers through eye-catching television and magazine ads, colorful billboard ads, store displays, and other mass communications. Now the company is using the Internet to get consumers more actively involved with its iconic brand. It changed Coke.com from a typical corporate Web site, complete with facts, figures, and annual reports, to an interactive community for consumers to share their creativity. Its MyCoke.com site invites visitors to participate in a virtual world, play games, mix music tracks, read or write blog entries, download screen savers, and more. Knowing that not every online feature will gain an audience right away, Coca-Cola—like other advertisers—has been experimenting to discover which site activities will draw audiences most effectively.

The company is also inviting interaction through activities inside Second Life, the popular online community. For example, it invited consumers to design a virtual vending machine that could dispense the essence of Coca-Cola—entertainment, adventure, or happiness—as well as satisfy curiosities and fulfill virtual wishes. And it used Second Life for the high-profile premiere of "Happiness Factory—the Movie," the follow-up to its award-winning commercial. "Through the short film and other promotional elements, including authentically designed movie posters, movie-style trailers, an interactive digital program, promotions, and packaging, we were able to extend the life of this campaign," says a Coca-Cola spokesperson.[1]

Marketing communications are increasingly seen as an interactive dialogue between the company and its customers. Marketers must ask not only "How can we reach our customers?" but also "How can our customers reach us?" It's critical to personalize messages and create dialogues by communicating with the right person at the right time. This chapter discusses direct marketing, interactive marketing, word-of-mouth marketing, and personal selling and the sales force.

DIRECT MARKETING

Direct marketing is the use of consumer-direct channels to reach and deliver goods and services to customers without marketing middlemen. These channels include direct mail, catalogs, telemarketing, interactive TV, kiosks, Web sites, and mobile devices. Direct marketers seek a measurable response, typically a customer order, through **direct-order marketing**.[2] Many firms use direct marketing to build long-term customer relationships by sending birthday cards, information, small premiums, or loyalty rewards to strengthen bonds over time.[3]

More marketers have turned to direct marketing in response to the high and increasing costs of reaching business markets through a sales force. Today companies spend $161 billion annually on direct marketing, accounting for 10.3% of GDP.[4] Direct sales include sales to the consumer market (53%), B2B (27%), and charitable fundraising (20%).[5]

The Benefits of Direct Marketing

Time-pressured customers appreciate the convenience, ease, and speed of ordering from home or office. Moreover, they can buy specialty items not available in local stores through direct marketing. Direct marketers benefit as well: They can buy mailing lists for almost any segment (left-handed people, millionaires); customize and personalize messages; build relationships; reach the most interested prospects at the right moment; easily test alternative media and messages; and easily measure campaign results.

Direct Mail

Direct-mail marketing involves sending an offer, announcement, reminder, or other item to a person. Using highly targeted mailing lists, direct marketers send out millions of mail pieces each year—letters, flyers, and other "salespeople with wings." Direct mail is popular because it permits target market selectivity, can be personalized, is flexible, and allows early testing and response measurement. Although the cost per thousand people reached is higher than with mass media, the people reached are better prospects.

In constructing a direct-mail campaign, marketers must decide on objectives, target markets, and prospects; offer elements; means of testing the campaign; and measures of campaign success.

- *Objectives.* A campaign's success is judged by the response rate. An order-response rate of 2% is normally considered good (this number varies with product category and price). Direct mail can also generate prospect leads, strengthen customer relationships, inform and educate customers, remind customers of offers, and reinforce customer purchase decisions.
- *Target markets and prospects.* Direct marketers apply the R-F-M formula (*recency, frequency, monetary amount*) to select customers according to how much time has

passed since their last purchase, how many times they have purchased, and how much they've spent as a customer. Marketers also identify prospects on the basis of age, sex, income, education, and previous mail-order purchases; occasions; and consumer lifestyle. In B2B direct marketing, the prospect is often a group of people that includes decision makers and influencers.

- *Offer elements.* The offer strategy consists of five elements—the *product*, the *offer*, the *medium*, the *distribution method*, and the *creative strategy*—all of which can be tested.[6] In addition, the marketer has to choose five components of the mailing itself: the outside envelope, sales letter, circular, reply form, and reply envelope. Direct mail can be followed up by e-mail, which is less expensive and less intrusive than telemarketing.

- *Testing elements.* One of the great advantages of direct marketing is the ability to test, under real marketplace conditions, elements such as products and features, copy platform, mailer type, envelope, prices, and mailing lists. Response rates typically understate a campaign's long-term impact; this is why some firms measure the impact of direct marketing on awareness, intention to buy, and word of mouth.

- *Measuring success: lifetime value.* By adding up the planned costs, the direct marketer can determine the needed break-even response rate (net of returned merchandise and bad debts). Even when a campaign fails to break even in the short run, it can be profitable in the long run if customer lifetime value is factored in. Calculate the average customer longevity, average customer annual expenditure, and average gross margin, minus the average cost of customer acquisition and maintenance (discounted for the opportunity cost of money).[7]

Catalog Marketing

In catalog marketing, companies may send full-line merchandise catalogs, specialty consumer catalogs, and business catalogs, usually in print form but also sometimes as CDs, videos, or online. JCPenney sends consumers general merchandise catalogs; IKEA sends consumers furniture catalogs. Grainger sends industrial and office supply catalogs to businesses. Many direct marketers have found that combining catalogs and Web sites can be an effective way to sell.

Catalogs are a huge business—about 71% of U.S. consumers shop from home using catalogs by phone, mail, and Internet.[8] For successful catalog marketing, marketers manage customer lists carefully to minimize duplication and bad debts; control inventory; offer quality goods so few items are returned; and project a distinctive image. Some companies add literary or information features, send swatches of materials, operate a special hot line to answer questions, send gifts to their best customers, and donate some profits to good causes for social responsibility purposes.

Telemarketing

Telemarketing is the use of the telephone and call centers to attract prospects, sell to existing customers, and provide service by taking orders and answering questions. Companies use call centers for *inbound telemarketing* (receiving calls from customers) and *outbound telemarketing* (initiating calls to prospects and customers). Effective telemarketing depends on choosing the right telemarketers, training them well, and providing performance incentives.

Although telemarketing is a major direct-marketing tool, its sometimes intrusive nature led to the Federal Trade Commission's establishment of a National Do Not Call Registry. In the first four years, more than 140 million U.S. consumers registered to prevent telemarketers from calling them at home. Only political organizations, charities, telephone surveyors, or firms with existing relationships with consumers are exempt.[9]

Other Media for Direct-Response Marketing

Direct marketers use all the major media. Newspapers and magazines carry abundant print ads offering books, clothing, vacations, and other goods and services that individuals can order via toll-free numbers. Radio ads present offers to listeners 24 hours a day. Some companies have used 30- and 60-minute *infomercials*, commercials combining selling with information and entertainment, to present offers that are complicated, technologically advanced, or require a great deal of explanation. Marketers also reach consumers through at-home shopping television channels, taking orders on a toll-free number and delivering within 48 hours.

Public and Ethical Issues in Direct Marketing

Direct marketers and their customers usually enjoy mutually rewarding relationships. Occasionally, however, a darker side emerges. Many people are irritated by hard-sell direct-marketing solicitations and computerized calls. Unscrupulous direct marketers take advantage of impulsive, less sophisticated, or vulnerable consumers, especially the elderly.[10] Some direct marketers create mailers and copy intended to mislead; the Federal Trade Commission receives thousands of complaints each year about fraudulent investment scams or phony charities. Critics worry about invasion of privacy, saying marketers may know too much about consumers. People in the direct-marketing industry have been addressing these issues. Most want what consumers want: honest, well-designed marketing offers targeted only to those who appreciate hearing about the offer.

INTERACTIVE MARKETING

The newest channels for direct marketing are electronic. The Internet provides marketers and consumers with opportunities for much greater *interaction* and *individualization*. Few campaigns are considered complete without a prominent online component. Companies can send tailored messages that engage consumers by reflecting their special interests and behavior. The Internet is highly accountable and its effects can be easily traced. Online advertisers can gauge response instantaneously by noting how many unique visitors click on a page or ad, how long they spend with it, where they go afterwards, and so on.[11]

The Web offers the advantage of *contextual placement* and buying ads on sites that are related to the marketer's offerings. Marketers can also place advertising based on keywords from search engines, to reach people when they've actually started the buying process. And advertisers can use rich media ads that combine animation, video, and sound with interactive features.[12]

However, consumers can screen out most online advertising. Moreover, advertisers lose some control over what consumers do with online marketing messages and activity. For example, consumers might place a marketer's video in undesirable or unseemly places. Still, many feel the pros outweigh the cons, and the Web is attracting

BREAKTHROUGH MARKETING: YAHOO!

Yahoo! has grown from a tiny upstart search engine to a powerful force in Internet media. Today the company proudly proclaims itself: "The only place anyone needs to go to find anything, communicate with anyone, or buy anything." Its wide range of Web services includes e-mail, news, weather, music, photos, games, shopping, auctions, travel, and more. Users can personalize the experience by creating a My Yahoo! page with features chosen from among the company's hundreds of content partners. Each month more than 475 million people worldwide visit one of its myriad sites, with billions of page views per day.

Thanks to a database showing where its millions of registered users live and what their interests are, Yahoo! can present users with more relevant search results and more relevant advertising. And the Yahoo! Mobile Web service allows advertisers to reach consumers around the globe on their mobile phones. One of the first advertisers to participate was Pepsi. "We've had exceptional results reaching our consumers on Yahoo! online," notes John Vail, director of interactive marketing, Pepsi-Cola North America. "Now we can reach consumers when they're on the move and communicate with them in a way we haven't before."[13]

---

marketers of all kinds. "Breakthrough Marketing: Yahoo" describes that company's online efforts.

Marketers must decide which forms of interactive marketing will be most cost-effective in achieving communication and sales objectives. Popular forms include:

- *Web sites.* A key challenge is designing a site that's attractive on first viewing and interesting enough to encourage repeat visits.[14] As shown in Table 17.1, Rayport and Jaworski propose that effective Web sites feature the 7 *C*s specific design elements.[15] And to bring visitors back again and again, marketers must embrace another *C*—constant change.[16] Visitors judge site performance based on ease of use (quick downloads, first page easy to understand, easy navigation) and physical attractiveness (pages clean and not crammed, readable fonts and typefaces, good use of color and sound).

TABLE 17.1 Elements of Effective Web Design

Design Element	Description
Context	Layout and design.
Content	Text, pictures, sound, and video on the site.
Community	How the site enables user-to-user communication.
Customization	Site's ability to tailor itself to different users or allow users to personalize the site.
Communication	How the site enables site-to-user, user-to-site, or two-way communication.
Connection	Degree to which the site is linked to other sites.
Commerce	Site's capabilities to enable commercial transactions.

Source: Jeffrey F. Rayport and Bernard J. Jaworski, *E-Commerce* (New York: McGraw-Hill, 2001), p. 116.

- *Microsites.* A **microsite** is a limited area on the Web, managed and paid for by an external advertiser/company, designed to supplement a primary site. Burger King's ad agency, for example, promoted the TenderCrisp sandwich with a microsite featuring a "subservient chicken," an actor in a chicken costume who seemed to perform wacky actions such as playing air guitar, based on a user's typed commands (the moves were prerecorded). In the microsite's first week, 54 million people checked out the chicken.[17]

- *Search-related ads.* **Paid-search** or **pay-per-click ads** now represent 40% of all online ads.[18] The search terms are a proxy for the consumer's consumption interests and trigger relevant links to product or service offerings alongside search results from Google or other search sites. Advertisers pay only if people click on the links; the cost depends on how high the link is ranked and the popularity of the keyword.[19] One Samsung executive estimated it was 50 times cheaper to reach 1,000 people online than on TV, so the firm shifted 10% of its advertising budget to the Internet.[20]

- *Display ads.* **Display ads** or **banner ads** are small, rectangular boxes containing text and perhaps a picture that companies pay to place on relevant Web sites. The larger the audience, the more costly the placement. In the early days of the Internet, viewers clicked on 2% to 3% of the banner ads they saw, but that percentage quickly plummeted and advertisers began to explore other forms of communication.[21] Still, display ads can be useful if they're attention-getting and influential, well targeted, and closely tracked.[22]

- *Online videos and ads.* With user-generated content sites like YouTube, MySpace Video, and Google Video, consumers and advertisers can upload ads and videos to be shared virally by millions of people. Online videos, sometimes edgy, can be a cost-effective way to reach large audiences.

- *Sponsorships.* Many companies get their name on the Internet by paying to be named as the sponsor of special content on Web sites that carry news, financial information, and so on. A popular vehicle for targeted sponsorship is *podcasts*, digital media files created for playback on portable MP3 players, laptops, or PCs. Sponsors pay about $25 per thousand listeners to run a brief audio ad at the beginning of the podcast.[23]

- *Alliances.* When one Internet company works with another, they end up advertising each other through alliances and *affiliate programs*. AOL has created many successful alliances. Amazon has almost 1 million affiliates that post its banners on their Web sites.

- *Online communities.* Many companies get useful, hard-to-get information by sponsoring online communities where members communicate through postings, instant messaging, and chat discussions about special interests related to the company's products and brands. Members of Kraft's online community said they wanted to control how much they ate, giving rise to 100-calorie bags and $100 million in sales. Successful online communities create activities that encourage bonds among community members.[24]

- *E-mail.* E-mail campaigns cost a fraction of what "d-mail," or direct mail, campaigns cost. Microsoft used to spend about $70 million yearly on mail campaigns; now it spends significantly less and still sends 20 million e-mails a month. However, many consumers use spam filters to screen out unwanted e-mails. Productive e-mail campaigns give customers a reason to respond, personalize the content, make offers not available via direct mail, and allow customers to "unsubscribe" easily.[25]

- *Mobile marketing*. Mobile ad spending was an estimated $871 million worldwide in 2006, most spent on text messages. Given the number of cell phones in use and the ability to personalize messages based on demographics, the appeal of mobile marketing is obvious; still, some wonder how consumers will react to ads on the "third screen."[26]

WORD OF MOUTH

Social networks such as MySpace and FaceBook have become an important force in both business-to-consumer and business-to-business marketing.[27] A key aspect of social networks is *word of mouth* and the number and nature of conversations and communications between different parties. Consumers talk about dozens of brands each day. Although many are media and entertainment products like movies, TV shows, and publications, other offerings such as food products, travel services, and retail stores are often mentioned, as well.

Niche social networks offer access to targeted segments that are more likely to spread the brand message. Consider CaféMom, started by CMI Marketing, with several thousand members who participate in dozens of forums for moms. When the site started a forum for discussing developmentally appropriate play activities, toymaker Playskool sent toy kits to 2,500 members and encouraged them to share their experiences with each other. "The great thing is you get direct feedback from actual moms," says an executive at Hasbro, Playskool's parent company.[28]

Buzz and Viral Marketing

Some marketers highlight two particular forms of word of mouth—buzz and viral marketing.[29] *Buzz marketing* generates excitement, creates publicity, and conveys new relevant brand-related information through unexpected or even outrageous means.[30] *Viral marketing* is another form of word of mouth, or "word of mouse," that encourages consumers to pass along company-developed products and services or audio, video, or written information to others online.[31] Both try to showcase a brand and its noteworthy features by creating a splash in the marketplace.

Agencies have been created solely to help clients create buzz. P&G has 225,000 teens enlisted in Tremor and 600,000 mothers enrolled in Vocalpoint. Both groups are built on the premise that certain individuals want to learn about products, receive samples and coupons, share their opinions with companies, and, of course, talk up their experiences with others. P&G chooses well-connected people—the Vocalpoint moms have big social networks and generally speak to 25 to 30 other women during the day, compared to an average of five for other moms—and their messages carry a strong reason to share product information with a friend.[32] See Figure 17.1 for BzzAgent's Word-of-Mouth Dos and Don'ts.

Opinion Leaders

Communication researchers propose a social-structure view of interpersonal communication.[33] They see society as consisting of *cliques*, small groups whose members interact frequently. Clique members are similar, and their closeness facilitates effective

FIGURE 17.1   BzzAgent's Word-of-Mouth Dos and Don'ts

"PAY" WITH FEEDBACK

You don't need to pay cash to get someone to say something about your product—they're already doing it. Find a way to let your customers communicate with you, then listen to them and provide them real support and appreciation. They'll volunteer to help a brand that lets them be part of the process.

INSIST ON OPENNESS

Campaign success—and perhaps your company's reputation— hinges on the openness of your word-of-mouth participants. If you're creating an organized word-of-mouth program, require that your volunteers are aboveboard.

DEMAND HONESTY

If you listen closely, you'll realize that honest opinions influence purchasing decisions more so than questionably positive opinions.

HELP CUSTOMERS TELL STORIES

Consumers place products in the context of their daily lives. If a runner's footwear helps her set a personal best in a marathon, she doesn't exclaim, "Just do it!" Rather, she talks about how the sneakers benefited her stride. In a word-of-mouth campaign for Levi's Dockers, participants described the pride of being dressed sharply at social events. Provide your customers with tools to help them share their real stories more effectively.

DON'T SCRIPT

For years marketers have delivered their messages as taglines that make every product sound perfect. Forcing word-of-mouth participants to repeat these messages is awkward and unnatural. Worse still is asking participants to repeat a marketing script of a perfect opinion that's not their own. Communicate the history, benefits, and unique attributes of your product to those who volunteer to experience and discuss it—and then get out of the way.

DON'T PLAN

Word of mouth is a spontaneous event. It can happen at anytime or anywhere—and yes, it can not happen, even when you want it to. If you try to force word of mouth to take place when it's not appropriate or comfortable, the result will no longer resemble real word of mouth. The key is to help people become more conscious of their opinions. They'll share them when others are really listening.

DON'T SELL

Odds are your company employs a trained and qualified sales force. Let them do their job ... and let word-of-mouth volunteers do theirs. No one likes to be forcibly sold a product. We like to learn about the pros and cons and then arrive at our own decision. Your word-of-mouth volunteers are not salespeople. They are siblings, friends, coworkers, and accidental acquaintances.

DON'T IGNORE

Listening to word of mouth about your product can be like a trip to the dentist: It's uncomfortable for a moment, but the benefits last a lifetime. However difficult the feedback may be to hear, it is even more powerful to incorporate. Honest word of mouth provides you with a unique opportunity to use real opinions as an incredible feedback loop; and the more you listen and perfect your product, the better your word of mouth will become.

Source: Dave Balter, "Rules of the Game," *Advertising Age Point* (December 2005): 22–23.

communication but also insulates the clique from new ideas. The challenge is to create more openness so that cliques exchange information with others in the society. This openness is helped by people who function as liaisons and connect two or more cliques without belonging to either, and *bridges*, people who belong to one clique and are linked to a person in another.

Author Malcolm Gladwell sees three factors working to ignite public interest in an idea.[34] The first is reaching the three types of people who can spread an idea like an epidemic: *mavens*, knowledgeable people; *connectors*, who know and communicate with many others; and *salesmen*, who possess natural persuasive power. Any idea that catches the interest of mavens, connectors, and salesmen is likely to be broadcast far and wide. The second factor is "stickiness," expressing an idea so it motivates people to act. The third, "the power of context," controls whether those spreading an idea are able to organize groups and communities around it. "Marketing Skills: How to Start a Buzz Fire" discusses the skill of generating buzz.

Blogs

Blogs, regularly updated online journals or diaries, have become an important outlet for word of mouth because they bring together people with common interests. Some are personal for close friends and families, while others are designed to reach and influence a vast audience. Blog networks such as Gawker Media offer marketers a portfolio of choices. Online celebrity gossip blog PopSugar has spawned other blogs on fashion (FabSugar), fitness (FitSugar), and humor (GiggleSugar), attracting college-educated women aged 18 to 44 making more than $60,000.[35]

Corporations such as Ford are creating their own blogs and carefully monitoring those of others.[36] Especially popular blogs are creating influential opinion leaders. Bloggers at the Treehugger site track green consumer products, offering video and

MARKETING SKILLS: HOW TO START A BUZZ FIRE

Although many word-of-mouth effects are beyond a company's control, marketers can develop their skills to improve the likelihood of starting a positive buzz. The first step is to identify influential individuals and companies and devote extra attention to them. Next, supply these key people with product samples to encourage word of mouth. Also cultivate contacts with community influentials such as local radio personalities, class presidents, and heads of local organizations. Develop word of mouth referral channels to build business. Finally, provide compelling information that people want to pass along—information that's original and useful.

Several television networks are generating buzz using Twitter, a social-networking site that draws a young audience. Twitter's special appeal is the ability to send very short messages via e-mail, instant messaging, or posted on Twitter's Web page. MTV promoted the MTV Music Awards and the MTV Video Music Awards using Twitter messages sent by MTV personalities as they walked the red carpet. CW is also looking at ways to get buzz going through Twitter. Its executive vice president of marketing stresses that the messages must ". . . be of value. It can't be just 'watch Gossip Girl at 9.' It's got to be more fun."[37]

reference guides in frequent posts.[38] Yet consumers may still see information from corporate Web sites or professional review sites such as Edmunds.com as more trustworthy.[39]

Measuring the Effects of Word of Mouth[40]

Marketers are exploring various measures to capture word-of-mouth effects. Research and consulting firm Keller Fay notes that although 80% of word of mouth occurs offline, many marketers focus on easy-to-track online effects. When Intuit measured the viral success of its jackrabbit.intuit.com site for small business owners, it identified blogs that either picked up stories from influential bloggers given a special preview or that carried their own stories. Intuit classified each blog according to *velocity* (whether it took a month or happened in a few days), *share of voice* (how much talk occurred in the blogosphere), *voice quality* (what was said and how positive or negative it was) and *sentiment* (how meaningful the comments were).

PERSONAL SELLING AND THE SALES FORCE

The original and oldest form of direct marketing is the field sales call. Today most industrial firms rely heavily on a professional sales force to locate prospects, develop them into customers, and grow the business; or they hire manufacturers' representatives and agents to carry out the direct-selling task. In addition, consumer companies such as Avon, Allstate, and Tupperware use a direct-selling force. U.S. firms spend over a trillion dollars annually on sales forces and sales force materials—more than on any other promotional method. Nearly 12% of the total workforce works full-time in sales occupations, in nonprofit as well as for-profit organizations.[41] Hospitals and museums, for example, use fundraisers to solicit donations.

The term *sales representative* covers six positions, ranging from the least to the most creative types of selling:[42]

1. *Deliverer.* A salesperson whose major task is the delivery of a product (water, fuel).
2. *Order taker.* An inside order taker (behind a counter) or outside order taker (calling on supermarket managers).
3. *Missionary.* A salesperson not expected or permitted to take an order but rather to build goodwill or educate users (the medical "detailer" representing a pharmaceutical firm).
4. *Technician.* A salesperson with a high level of technical knowledge (the engineering salesperson who is primarily a consultant to client companies).
5. *Demand creator.* A salesperson who relies on creative methods for selling tangible products (vacuum cleaners or siding) or intangibles (insurance or education).
6. *Solution vendor.* A salesperson whose expertise lies in solving a customer's problem, often with a system of the firm's goods and services (such as computer systems).

Personal Selling and Relationship Marketing

The best salespeople have more than instinct; they're trained in methods of analysis, customer management, and the principles of personal selling so they're active order getters, not passive order takers. The major steps involved in any effective sales process are shown in Table 17.2.[43]

TABLE 17.2 Major Steps in Effective Selling

Sales Step	Application in Industrial Selling
Prospecting and qualifying	Firms generate leads and then qualify them by mail or phone to assess level of interest and financial capacity. Hot prospects are turned over to the field sales force; warm prospects receive telemarketing follow-up.
Preapproach	The sales rep researches what the prospect needs, who is involved in buying decisions, and the buyers' personal characteristics and buying styles. The rep also sets call objectives to qualify the prospect, gather information, or make an immediate sale; decides whether to visit, call, or write; plans the timing of the approach; and sets an overall sales strategy.
Presentation and demonstration	The rep tells the product "story" to the buyer, using a *features, advantages, benefits*, and *value* approach. Reps should guard against spending too much time on product features (product orientation) and not enough on benefits and value (customer orientation).
Overcoming objections	Salespeople must handle objections posed by customers during the presentation or when asked for the order. Here, the rep must maintain a positive approach, ask for clarification, ask questions that lead the buyer to answer his or her own objection, deny the validity of the objection, or turn objection into a reason for buying.
Closing	Attempting to close the sale, the rep can ask for the order, recapitulate points of agreement, offer to help write up the order, ask whether the buyer wants A or B, get the buyer to make minor choices such as color or size, or show what the buyer will lose by not ordering now. The rep might offer the buyer an inducement to close, such as a special price or a token gift.
Follow-up and maintenance	To ensure customer satisfaction and repeat business, the rep should cement details such as delivery time and purchase terms immediately after closing. Also, the rep should schedule a follow-up call to check on proper installation and training after delivery. This helps detect problems, shows interest, and reduces any cognitive dissonance. Further, each account needs a maintenance and growth plan.

Although the principles of personal selling may be applied in a transaction situation to close a specific sale, often the company wants to build a long-term supplier–customer relationship. Today's customers prefer suppliers who can sell and deliver a coordinated set of products and services to many locations, quickly solve problems in different locations, and work closely with customer teams to improve products and processes. Reps should monitor key accounts, know customers' problems, and be ready to serve them in a number of ways. They must be adaptive and respond to different customer needs or situations.[44]

With a properly implemented relationship management program, the firm begins to focus as much on managing its customers as on managing its products. However, relationship marketing is not effective in all situations. Ultimately, companies must judge which segments and customers will respond profitably to relationship management.

Designing the Sales Force

Companies are sensitive to the high and rising costs of maintaining a sales force (including salaries, commissions, bonuses, travel expenses, and benefits). Because the average cost of a personal sales call ranges from $200 to $300, and closing a sale typically requires four calls, the total cost of a sale can range from $800 to $1,200.[45] Not surprisingly, companies are trying to increase the productivity of the sales force through better selection, training, supervision, motivation, and compensation. Figure 17.2 shows the basic steps in designing a sales force.

FIGURE 17.2 Designing a Sales Force

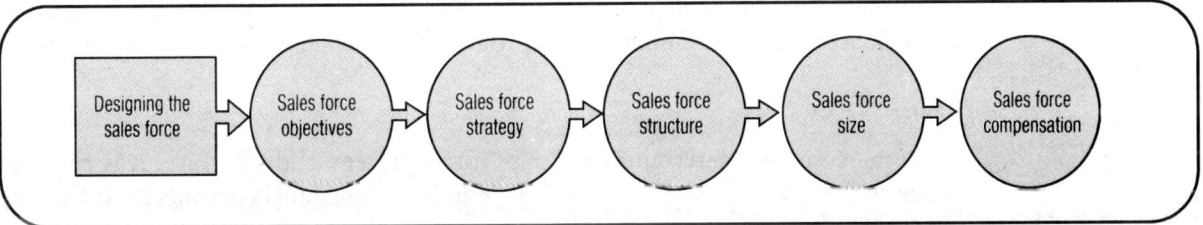

Sales Force Objectives and Strategy

Companies need to define specific sales force objectives. For example, a company might want its sales representatives to spend 80% of their time with current customers and 20% with prospects, and 85% of their time on established products and 15% on new products. Salespeople perform one or more of the following tasks: prospecting (for prospects or leads); targeting (allocating time among prospects and customers); communicating (information about the company's offerings); selling (approaching, presenting, overcoming objections, and closing sales); servicing (consulting on problems, rendering technical assistance, arranging financing, expediting delivery); information gathering (market research, market intelligence); and allocating (deciding which customers will get scarce products during shortages).

Today's sales representatives act as "account managers," arranging fruitful contact among people in the buying and selling organizations. Increasingly, effective sales requires teamwork and the support of other personnel, such as top management, especially when national accounts or major sales are at stake; technical people, who supply technical information and service to customers; customer service representatives, who provide installation, maintenance, and other services; and an office staff of sales analysts, order expediters, and assistants.

Once the company decides on an approach, it can use either a direct or contractual sales force. A **direct (company) sales force** consists of full- or part-time paid employees who work exclusively for the firm. Inside sales personnel conduct business from the office (using the telephone, fax, and e-mail) and receive visits from prospective buyers; field sales personnel travel and visit customers. A **contractual sales force** consists of manufacturers' reps, sales agents, and brokers who earn a commission based on sales.

Sales Force Structure

The sales force strategy has implications for sales force structure. A company that sells one product line to one end-using industry with customers in many locations would use a territorial structure. A company that sells many products to many types of customers might need a product or market structure. Some firms need a more complex structure. Motorola, for example, has four types of sales forces: (1) a strategic market sales force of technical, applications, and quality engineers and service personnel for major accounts; (2) a geographic sales force calling on customers in different territories; (3) a distributor sales force calling on and coaching Motorola distributors; and (4) an inside sales force doing telemarketing and taking orders by phone and fax.

Companies typically single out major accounts (also called key accounts, national accounts, global accounts, or house accounts) for special attention. The largest accounts may have a strategic account management team with cross-functional personnel to cover all aspects of the relationships. For example, Procter & Gamble has a 300-person strategic account team stationed at Wal-Mart's Bentonville, Arkansas, headquarters.[46]

Sales Force Size

After the company determines the sales force strategy and structure, it is ready to establish the sales force size, based on the number of customers it wants to reach. One method is the five-step *workload approach*: (1) group customers into size classes by annual sales volume; (2) establish call frequencies (number of calls on an account per year) for each customer class; (3) multiply the number of accounts in each size class by the call frequency to arrive at the total workload, in sales calls per year; (4) determine the average number of calls a sales rep can make per year; and (5) divide the total annual calls (calculated in step 3) by the average annual calls made by a rep (in step 4) to see how many reps are needed.

Suppose the firm has 1,000 A accounts and 2,000 B accounts; A accounts require 36 calls a year (36,000 calls yearly), and B accounts require 12 calls a year (24,000 calls). This company needs a sales force that can make 60,000 sales calls a year. If the average rep can make 1,000 calls a year, the company would need 60 representatives.

Sales Force Compensation

To attract top-quality sales reps, the company needs an attractive compensation package. The four components of sales force compensation are a fixed amount, a variable amount, expense allowances, and benefits. The *fixed amount*, a salary, is intended to satisfy the need for income stability. The *variable amount*, which might be commissions, a bonus, or profit sharing, is intended to stimulate and reward greater effort. *Expense allowances* enable sales reps to meet the expenses involved in travel and entertaining. *Benefits*, such as paid vacations and life insurance, provide security and job satisfaction.

Fixed compensation receives more emphasis in jobs with a high ratio of non-selling to selling duties and when the selling task is technically complex and requires teamwork. Variable compensation works where sales are cyclical or depend on individual initiative. Fixed and variable compensation give rise to three basic types of compensation plans—straight salary, straight commission, and combination salary and commission. One survey revealed that more than half of sales reps receive at least 40% of their compensation in variable pay.[47]

Straight-salary plans provide sales reps with a secure income, make them more willing to perform nonselling activities, and give them less incentive to overstock customers. These plans are easy to administer and they lower turnover. Straight-commission plans attract higher sales performers, provide more motivation, require less supervision, and control selling costs; however, they emphasize getting the sale over building the relationship. Combination plans offer the benefits of both plans while reducing their disadvantages.

MANAGING THE SALES FORCE

Sales force management covers the steps in recruiting and selecting, training, supervising, motivating, and evaluating representatives (see Figure 17.3).

FIGURE 17.3 Managing the Sales Force

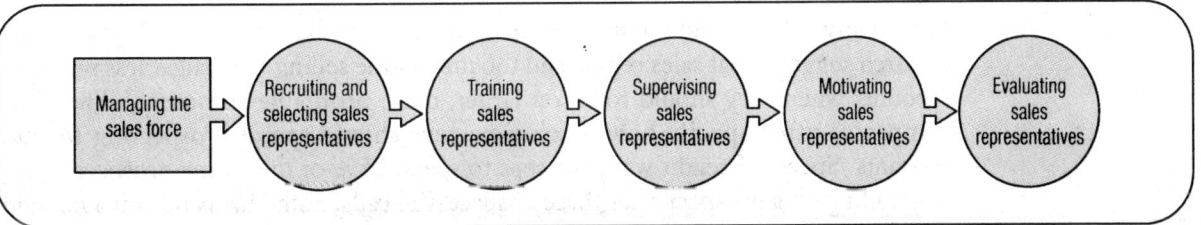

Recruiting and Selecting Sales Representatives

At the heart of any successful sales force is the selection of effective representatives. One survey revealed that the top 27% of the sales force brought in over 52% of the sales. Conversely, it's a great waste to hire the wrong people. The average annual turnover rate for all industries is almost 20%. Turnover leads to lost sales, costs of finding and training replacements, and a strain on existing salespeople to pick up the slack. Numerous studies have shown little relationship between sales performance on one hand, and background and experience variables, current status, lifestyle, attitude, personality, and skills on the other. More effective predictors have been composite tests and assessment centers that simulate the working environment.[48]

After management develops selection criteria, the next step is to recruit applicants by soliciting names from current sales reps, using employment agencies, placing job ads, and contacting college students. Selection procedures can vary from an informal interview to prolonged testing and interviewing. Although test scores are only one information element in a set that includes personal characteristics, references, past employment history, and interviewer reactions, they are weighted quite heavily by some companies. Gillette says that tests have reduced turnover and scores correlated well with the progress of new reps.

Training and Supervising Sales Representatives

Today's customers expect salespeople to have deep product knowledge, add ideas to improve the customer's operations, and be efficient and reliable. This requires companies to make a much higher investment in sales training. New reps may spend a few weeks to several months in training. The median training period is 28 weeks in industrial-products companies, 12 in service companies, and 4 in consumer-products companies. Training time and method varies with the complexity of the selling task and the type of person recruited for sales. Training may involve role-playing, audio- and videotapes, CD-ROMs, and distance learning. Altera, which makes reprogrammable chips, has invested in personality testing to form the right sales teams and empathy training to help reps better understand customers' problems.[49]

Companies vary in how closely they supervise sales reps. Reps paid mostly on commission generally receive less supervision. Those who are salaried and must cover definite accounts are likely to receive substantial supervision. With multilevel selling, used by Avon and others, independent distributors are also in charge of their own sales force selling company products. These independent contractors or reps are paid a commission not only on their own sales, but also on the sales of people they recruit and train.[50]

Sales Rep Productivity

How many calls should a company make on a particular account each year? Some research suggests that sales reps spend too much time selling to smaller, less profitable accounts when they should focus on larger, more profitable accounts.[51] Therefore, companies often specify how much time reps should spend prospecting for new accounts. Spector Freight wants its reps to spend 25% of their time prospecting and stop calling on a prospect after three unsuccessful calls. Some firms rely on a missionary sales force to open new accounts.

The best sales reps manage their time efficiently. *Time-and-duty analysis* helps reps understand how they spend their time and how they might increase their productivity. In general, sales reps spend time planning, traveling, waiting, selling, and in administrative tasks (report writing and billing, attending sales meetings, and talking to others in the company about production, delivery, billing, sales performance, and other matters). No wonder face-to-face selling time amounts to as little as 29% of total working time![52]

To cut costs, reduce time demands on their outside sales force, and take advantage of computer and telecommunications innovations, many firms have increased the size and responsibilities of their inside sales force. Inside salespeople are of three types. *Technical support people* provide technical data and answer customers' questions. *Sales assistants* provide clerical backup for outside reps by confirming appointments, checking credit, following up on deliveries, and answering customers' questions. *Telemarketers* find new leads, qualify them, and sell to them.

The company Web site is a valuable tool for reps, especially for prospecting. Company Web sites can help define the firm's relationships with individual accounts and identify those whose business warrants a personal sales call. The site can provide an introduction to self-identified potential customers and might even receive the initial order. For more complex transactions, the site provides a way for buyers to contact the seller. Selling over the Internet supports relationship marketing by solving problems that don't require live intervention so reps can spend more time on issues best addressed face-to-face.

Motivating Sales Representatives

The majority of sales representatives require encouragement and special incentives, especially those in field selling.[53] Most marketers believe that the higher the salesperson's motivation, the greater the effort and the resulting performance, rewards, and satisfaction—all of which further motivation. Marketers reinforce performance with intrinsic and extrinsic rewards of all types. One study found that the sales reward with the highest value was pay, followed by promotion, personal growth, and sense of accomplishment.[54] The least-valued rewards were liking and respect, security, and recognition. In other words, salespeople are highly motivated by pay and the chance to get ahead and satisfy their intrinsic needs, and less motivated by compliments and security.

Many firms set annual sales quotas for dollar sales, unit volume, margin, selling effort or activity, and product type. Compensation is often tied to degree of quota fulfillment. Sales quotas are developed from the annual marketing plan. Management first prepares a sales forecast that becomes the basis for planning production, workforce size, and financial requirements. Then the firm can establish quotas for regions and territories, often setting the total higher than the sales forecast to encourage managers and salespeople to perform at their best. If they fail to make their quotas, the firm might still make its sales forecast.

Each area sales manager divides the area's quota among its sales reps. A rep's quota can be set high to spur extra effort or more modestly to build confidence. One general view is that a salesperson's quota should be at least equal to the person's last year's sales, plus some fraction of the difference between territory sales potential and last year's sales. The more favorably the salesperson reacts to pressure, the higher the fraction should be.

Evaluating Sales Representatives

We have been describing the *feed-forward* aspects of sales supervision—how management communicates what sales reps should be doing and motivates them to do it. However, good feed-forward requires good *feedback*, which means getting regular information from reps to evaluate their performance. Information about reps can come from sales reports, self-reports, personal observation, customer letters and complaints, customer surveys, and conversations with other sales reps. Many firms require their reps to develop an annual territory marketing plan for developing new accounts and increasing business from existing accounts.

Sales reps write up completed activities on *call reports* and, in addition, submit expense reports, new-business reports, lost-business reports, and reports on local conditions. These reports provide raw data from which sales managers can check sales performance: (1) average number of sales calls per rep per day; (2) average sales call time per contact; (3) average revenue per sales call; (4) average cost per sales call; (5) entertainment cost per sales call; (6) percentage of orders per hundred sales calls; (7) number of new customers per period; (8) number of lost customers per period; and (9) sales force cost as a percentage of total sales.

Sales reports, along with other observations, supply the raw materials for evaluation. There are several approaches to conducting evaluations. One type of evaluation compares current performance to past performance. These comparisons help management pinpoint specific areas for improvement. For example, if a rep's average gross profit per customer is lower than the company's average, that rep could be concentrating on the wrong customers or not spending enough time with each customer. A rep's performance can be related to both internal factors (effort, ability, and strategy) and external factors (task and luck).[55]

EXECUTIVE SUMMARY

Direct marketing is the use of consumer-direct channels to reach and deliver goods and services to customers without marketing intermediaries. Direct marketers plan campaigns by deciding on objectives, target markets and prospects, offers, and prices; then they test and establish measures to determine success. Major channels for direct marketing include face-to-face selling, direct mail, catalog marketing, telemarketing, television, kiosks, Web sites, and mobile devices. Interactive marketing offers more opportunities for dialogue and individualization through well-designed Web sites, as well as online ads, promotions, and other approaches. Two notable forms of word-of-mouth marketing are buzz marketing, which gets people talking about a brand by ensuring that the offer or how it is marketed is out of the ordinary, and viral marketing, which encourages people to exchange online information related in some way to a product or service.

Designing the sales force requires decisions about objectives, strategy, structure, size, and compensation. There are five steps to managing the sales force: (1) recruiting and selecting representatives; (2) training representatives in sales techniques and in the company's products, policies, and customer-satisfaction orientation; (3) supervising the sales force and helping reps use their time efficiently; (4) motivating the sales force and balancing quotas, monetary rewards, and supplementary motivators; and (5) evaluating individual and group sales performance. Personal selling entails six steps: (1) prospecting and qualifying; (2) preapproach; (3) presentation and demonstration; (4) overcoming objections; (5) closing; (6) follow-up and maintenance. Relationship marketing is often an important part of personal selling.

NOTES

1. Brian Morrissey, "Why Some Brands Seem Anti-Social," *Adweek*, August 27, 2007, http://www.adweek.com/aw/magazine/article_display.jsp?vnu_content_id=1003627780; Kamau High, "'Happiness' Is . . . Coca-Cola in Second Life," *Adweek.com*, August 16, 2007, www.adweek.com; Andrew Martin, "Does Coke Need a Refill?" *New York Times*, May 27, 2007, sec. 3, pp. 1ff; Kenneth Hein, "Coke's Web Formula Is a Work in Progress," *Brandweek*, September 4, 2006, p. 9; "Coke.com Finds Its Inner YouTube," *Adweek*, July 10, 2006, p. 7.

2. The terms *direct-order marketing* and *direct-relationship marketing* were suggested as subsets of direct marketing by Stan Rapp and Tom Collins in *The Great Marketing Turnaround* (Upper Saddle River, NJ: Prentice Hall, 1990).

3. Ran Kivetz and Itamar Simonson, "Earning the Right to Indulge: Effort as a Determinant of Customer Preferences Toward Frequency Program Rewards," *Journal of Marketing Research* 39 (May 2002): 155–170; Ran Kivetz and Itamar Simonson, "The Idiosyncratic Fit Heuristic: Effort Advantage as a Determinant of Consumer Response to Loyalty Programs," *Journal of Marketing Research* 40 (November 2003): 454–467.

4. "DMA's 2006 'Power of Direct Marketing' Reports," *Direct Marketing Association*, June 5, 2007; Carol Krol, "Direct Hits It Big," *B to B*, October 10, 2005, pp. 29–31; "Direct Marketing's Growth Rate to Cushion Cooling U.S. Economy," *Direct Marketing Association*, October 17, 2006.

5. Figures supplied by *Direct Marketing Magazine*, phone 516-716-6700.

6. Edward L. Nash, *Direct Marketing: Strategy, Planning, Execution*, 4th ed. (New York: McGraw-Hill, 2000).

7. The *average customer longevity* (N) is related to the *customer retention rate* (CR). Suppose the company retains 80% of its customers each year. Then the average customer longevity is given by: $N = 1/(1 - CR) = 1/.2 = 5$.

8. Lorie Grant, "Niche Catalogs' Unique Gifts Make Money Less of an Object," *USA Today*, November 20, 2003, p. 3B; Olivia Barker, "Catalogs Are Complementary with Online Sales, Purchases," *USA Today*, December 4, 2002, p. 4E.

9. Ryan Kim, "Telemarketers Getting Through," *San Francisco Chronicle*, April 16, 2007, p. C1; www.ftc.gov.

10. Charles Duhigg, "Telemarketing Thieves Sharpen Their Focus on the Elderly," *New York Times*, May 20, 2007.

11. Emily Steel, "Advertising's Brave New World," *Wall Street Journal*, May 25, 2007, pp. B1, B3; Johnnie L. Roberts, "How to Count Eyeballs," *Newsweek*, November 27, 2006, p. 42.

12. Daniel Michaels and J. Lynn Lunsford, "Ad-Sales Woes Likely to Continue," *Wall Street Journal*, December 4, 2006, p. B6; Byron Acohido, "Rich Media Enriching PC Ads," *USA Today*, February 25, 2004, p. 3B

13. Olga Kharif, "AOL's Mobile Ambitions," *BusinessWeek Online*, September 27, 2007, www.businessweek.com/technology; Catherine Holahan, "Yahoo's Bid to Think Small," *BusinessWeek*, February 26, 2007, p. 94; Kevin J. Delaney, "As Yahoo Falters, Executive's Memo Calls

for Overhaul," *Wall Street Journal*, November 18, 2006; Justin Hibbard, "How Yahoo! Gave Itself a Face-lift," *BusinessWeek*, October 9, 2006, pp. 74–77; "Yahoo!'s Personality Crisis," *The Economist*, August 13, 2005, pp. 49–50; Fred Vogelstein, "Yahoo's Brilliant Solution," *Fortune*, August 8, 2005, pp. 42–55; Ben Elgin, "Yahoo's Boulevard of Broken Dreams," *Business Week*, March 13, 2006, pp. 76–77.

14. Peter J. Danaher, Guy W. Mullarkey, and Skander Essegaier, "Factors Affecting Web Site Visit Duration: A Cross-Domain Analysis," *Journal of Marketing Research* 43 (May 2006): 182–914.

15. Jeffrey F. Rayport and Bernard J. Jaworski, *E-Commerce* (New York: McGraw-Hill, 2001), p. 116.

16. Bob Tedeschi, "E-Commerce Report," *New York Times*, June 24, 2002, p. C8.

17. Allison Fass, "A Kingdom Seeks Magic," *Forbes*, October 16, 2006, pp. 68–70; David Kiley, "The Craziest Ad Guys in America," *BusinessWeek*, May 22, 2006, pp. 72–80; www.subservientchicken.com.

18. "Prime Clicking Time," *The Economist*, May 31, 2003, p. 65; Ben Elgin, "Search Engines Are Picking Up Steam," *BusinessWeek*, March 24, 2003, pp. 86–87.

19. "Global Click-Through Rates Level Off in 2004 After Year of Decline," *New Media Age*, November 25, 2004, p. 10; Ned Desmond, "Google's Next Runaway Success," *Business 2.0*, November 2002, p. 73.

20. Heather Green, "Online Ads Take Off Again," *BusinessWeek*, May 5, 2003, p. 75.

21. Puneet Manchanda, Jean-Pierre Dubé, Khim Yong Goh, and Pradeep K. Chintagunta, "The Effects of Banner Advertising on Internet Purchasing," *Journal of Marketing Research* 43 (February 2006): 98–108; "Pay Per Sale," *The Economist*, October 1, 2005, p. 62.

22. Paul Sloan, "The Quest for the Perfect Online Ad," *Business 2.0*, March 2007, pp. 88–93; Catherine Holahan, "The Promise of Online Display Ads," *BusinessWeek*, May 1, 2007.

23. Heather Green, "Searching for the Pod of Gold," *BusinessWeek*, November 14, 2005, pp. 88–90.

24. Heather Green, "It Takes a Web Village," *BusinessWeek*, September 4, 2006, p. 66; Paul Dwyer, "Measuring the Value of Word of Mouth and Its Impact in Consumer Communities," MSI Report No. 06-118, *Marketing Science Institute*, Cambridge, MA.

25. Seth Godin, *Permission Marketing: Turning Strangers into Friends and Friends into Customers* (New York: Simon & Schuster, 1999).

26. Amol Sharma, "Companies Vie for Ad Dollars on Mobile Web," *Wall Street Journal*, January 17, 2007, pp. A1, A17; Amol Sharma, "T-Mobile Readies New Web Phones and Hangs Up on a Star Pitchwoman," *Wall Street Journal*, September 26, 2006, pp, B1, B6.

27. For a thorough review of relevant academic literature see Christophe Van Den Bulte and Stefan Wuyts, *Social Networks and Marketing*, Marketing Science Institute Relevant Knowledge Series, Cambridge, MA, 2007.

28. Brian Morrisey, "Niche Social Networks Offer Target Practice," *Adweek*, April 9, 2007, p. 11.

29. Dave Balter and John Butman, "Clutter Cutter," *Marketing Management*, July/August 2006, pp. 49–50.

30. Emanuel Rosen, *The Anatomy of Buzz* (New York: Doubleday Currency, 2000).

31. Rosen, *The Anatomy of Buzz*, ch. 12; "Viral Marketing," *Sales & Marketing Automation* (November 1999): 12–14; George Silverman, *The Secrets of Word-of-Mouth Marketing* (New York: Amacom, 2001).

32. Robert Berner, "I Sold It Through the Grapevine," *BusinessWeek*, May 29, 2006, pp. 32–34.

33. Peter H. Riengen and Jerome B. Kernan, "Analysis of Referral Networks in Marketing: Methods and Illustration," *Journal of Marketing Research* (November 1986): 37–78; J. Johnson Brown and Peter Reingen, "Social Ties and Word-of-Mouth Referral Behavior," *Journal of Consumer Research* 14 (1987): 350–362; Jacqueline Johnson Brown, Peter M. Reingen, and Everett M. Rogers, *Diffusion of Innovations*, 4th ed. (New York: The Free Press, 1995).

34. Malcolm Gladwell, *The Tipping Point: How Little Things Can Make a Big Difference* (Boston: Little, Brown & Company, 2000).

35. Claire Cain Miller, "The Sweet Spot," *Forbes*, April 23, 2007, p. 41.

36. David Kiley, "Ford on the Web, Warts and All," *BusinessWeek*, October 30, 2006, pp. 68–71.

37. Stephanie Kang and Suzanne Vranica, "Networks Try 'Twittering' to Spread Their Message," *Wall Street Journal*, July 16, 2007, p. B2; Sarit Moldovan, Jacob Goldenberg, and Amitava Chattopadhyay, "What Drives Word of Mouth? The Roles of Product Originality and Usefulness," *MSI Report No. 06-111*, (Cambridge, MA: Marketing Science Institute, 2006); Karen J. Bannan, "Online Chat Is a Grapevine That Yields Precious Fruit," *New York Times*, December 25, 2006; John Batelle, "The Net of Influence," *Business 2.0*, March 2004, p. 70;

Malcolm Macalister Hall, "Selling by Stealth," *Business Life*, November 2001, pp. 51–55; Ann Meyer, "Word-of-Mouth Marketing Speaks Well for Small Business," *Chicago Tribune*, July 28, 2003.

38. Heather Green, "The Big Shots of Blogdom," *BusinessWeek*, May 7, 2007.
39. Todd Wasserman, "Report: Consumers Don't Trust Blogs," *Brandweek*, September 4, 2006, p. 10. For an academic discussion of chat rooms, recommendation sites, and online customer review sections, see Dina Mayzlin, "Promotional Chat on the Internet," *Marketing Science* 25 (March-April 2006): 155–163 and Judith Chevalier and Dina Mayzlin, "The Effect of Word of Mouth on Sales: Online Book Reviews," *Journal of Marketing Research* 43 (August 2006): 345–354.
40. This section is based on an excellent summary, "Is There a Reliable Way to Measure Word-of-Mouth Marketing," *Marketing NPV*, Vol. 3, Issue 3, 2006, pp. 3–9 available at www.marketingnpv.com.
41. http://www.bls.gov/oco/reprints/ocor012.pdf.
42. Adapted from Robert N. McMurry, "The Mystique of Super-Salesmanship," *Harvard Business Review* (March–April 1961): 114. Also see William C. Moncrief III, "Selling Activity and Sales Position Taxonomies for Industrial Salesforces," *Journal of Marketing Research* (August 1986): 261–270.
43. Some of this discussion of personal selling is based on W. J. E. Crissy, William H. Cunningham, and Isabella C. M. Cunningham, *Selling: The Personal Force in Marketing* (New York: John Wiley, 1977), pp. 119–129.
44. George R. Franke and Jeong-Eun Park, "Salesperson Adaptive Selling Behavior and Customer Orientation: A Meta-Analysis," *Journal of Marketing Research* 43 (November 2006): 693–702; Richard G. McFarland, Goutam N. Challagalla, and Tasadduq A. Shervani, "Influence Tactics for Effective Adaptive Selling," *Journal of Marketing* 70 (October 2006): 103–117.
45. Bill Keenan, "Cost-per-call Data Deserve Scrutiny," *Industry Week*, January 10, 2000.
46. Clare Doyle, Brad McPhee, and Ian Harris, "Marketing, Sales, and Major Account Management: Managing Enterprise Customers as a Portfolio of Opportunities," talk at Marketing Science Institute's *Marketing, Sales, and Customers* conference, December 7, 2005; Noel Capon, *Key Account Management and Planning* (New York: Free Press, 2001); Sallie Sherman, Joseph Sperry, and Samuel Reese, *The Seven Keys to Managing Strategic Accounts* (New York: McGraw-Hill Trade, 2003); Jack Neff, "Bentonville or Bust," *Advertising Age*, February 24, 2003.
47. "Sales Performance Benchmarks," *Go-to-Market Strategies*, June 5, 2007.
48. Sonke Albers, "Salesforce Management—Compensation, Motivation, Selection, and Training," in *Handbook of Marketing*, edited by Bart Weitz and Robin Wensley (London: Sage Publications, 2002), pp. 248–266.
49. Cliff Edwards, "Death of a Pushy Salesman," *BusinessWeek*, July 3, 2006, pp. 108–109.
50. Nanette Byrnes, "Avon Calling—Lots of New Reps," *BusinessWeek*, June 2, 2003, pp. 53–54.
51. Michael R. W. Bommer, Brian F. O'Neil, and Beheruz N. Sethna, "A Methodology for Optimizing Selling Time of Salespersons," *Journal of Marketing Theory and Practice* (Spring 1994): 61–75. See also Lissan Joseph, "On the Optimality of Delegating Pricing Authority to the Sales Force," *Journal of Marketing* 65 (January 2001): 62–70.
52. Dartnell Corporation, 30th Sales Force Compensation Survey. Other breakdowns show that 12.7% is spent in service calls, 16% in administrative tasks, 25.1% in telephone selling, and 17.4% in waiting/traveling.
53. Willem Verbeke and Richard P. Bagozzi, "Sales Call Anxiety: Exploring What It Means When Fear Rules a Sales Encounter," *Journal of Marketing* 64 (July 2000): 88–101.
54. Eric G. Harris, John C. Mowen, and Tom J. Brown, "Re-examining Salesperson Goal Orientations: Personality Influencers, Customer Orientation and Work Satisfaction," *Journal of the Academy of Marketing Science* 33 (1), 2005: 19–35; Gilbert A. Churchill, Jr., Neil M. Ford, and Orville C. Walker, Jr., *Sales Force Management: Planning, Implementation and Control*, 4th ed. (Homewood, IL: Irwin, 1993). Also see Jhinuk Chowdhury, "The Motivational Impact of Sales Quotas on Effort," *Journal of Marketing Research* (February 1993): 28–41; Murali K. Mantrala, Prabhakant Sinha, and Andris A. Zoltners, "Structuring a Multiproduct Sales Quota-Bonus Plan for a Heterogeneous Sales Force: A Practical Model-Based Approach," *Marketing Science* 13, no. 2 (1994): 121–144; Wujin Chu, Eitan Gerstner, and James D. Hess, "Costs and Benefits of Hard-Sell," *Journal of Marketing Research* (February 1995): 97–102; Manfred Krafft, "An Empirical Investigation of the Antecedents of Sales Force Control Systems," *Journal of Marketing* 63 (July 1999): 120–134.

55. Philip M. Posdakoff and Scott B. MacKenzie, "Organizational Citizenship Behaviors and Sales Unit Effectiveness," *Journal of Marketing Research* (August 1994): 351–363. See also, Andrea L. Dixon, Rosann L. Spiro, and Magbul Jamil, "Successful and Unsuccessful Sales Calls: Measuring Salesperson Attributions and Behavioral Intentions," *Journal of Marketing* 65 (July 2001): 64–78; Willem Verbeke and Richard P. Bagozzi, "Sales Call Anxiety: Exploring What It Means When Fear Rules a Sales Encounter," *Journal of Marketing* 64 (July 2000): 88–101.

PART VII Creating Successful Long-Term Growth

CHAPTER 18

Managing Marketing in the Global Economy

> In this chapter, we will address the following questions:
>
> 1. What factors should a company review before deciding to market internationally?
> 2. What are the major ways of entering foreign markets?
> 3. What are the keys to effective internal marketing?
> 4. How can a company improve its marketing implementation?
> 5. How can companies be responsible social marketers?

MARKETING MANAGEMENT AT STONYFIELD FARM

Stonyfield Farm's roots go back to the mid-1980s, when local farms were disappearing in New England. Gary Hirshberg sat on the board of directors of an organic dairy farming school and convinced its founder there was a business opportunity in selling organic dairy products while "restoring the environment." Social responsibility has been at the core of the company from the start. In Hirshberg's words: "Profits . . . are a means to an end. My highest goal is to save the planet for my children."

Stonyfield is willing to pay more for organic ingredients and is strongly committed to eco-friendly operations. After calculating how much energy it needs to run its plant, for instance, Stonyfield made an equivalent investment in environmental projects like reforestation. The company no longer puts plastic lids on its yogurt, saving about a million pounds of plastic a year, and its packaging carries messages about global warming, farmland protection, and genetically modified foods. Being acquired by France's Groupe Danone hasn't changed Stonyfield's core values or products. In fact, its sales continue to increase by roughly 20% every year, making it the number three U.S. yogurt brand. Now the company is going international, bringing its products and values to France, the United Kingdom, and beyond.[1]

Healthy long-term growth for a brand requires that the marketing organization be managed properly. Holistic marketers must plan, implement, and control a range of interconnected marketing activities and satisfy a broad set of constituents.[2] Despite risks, growth can also come from international marketing. In this chapter, we explore how companies expand into global markets; how they organize their marketing efforts; and how they manage, control, and evaluate marketing implementation. We also discuss the long-term importance of socially responsible marketing.

COMPETING ON A GLOBAL BASIS

Many firms have marketed internationally for decades—Nestlé, Shell, Bayer, and Toshiba are familiar to consumers around the world. However, as global competition intensifies, domestic companies that never thought about foreign rivals suddenly find them in their backyards. In a **global industry**, competitors' strategic positions in major geographic or national markets are fundamentally affected by their overall global positions.[3] A **global firm** operates in two or more countries and captures R&D, production, logistics, marketing, and finance advantages not available to purely domestic competitors. "Breakthrough Marketing: Samsung" describes the marketing strength of this fast-growing global firm.

Global firms plan, operate, and coordinate their activities on a worldwide basis. Otis Elevator uses door systems from France, small geared parts from Spain, electronics from Germany, and special motor drives from Japan; systems integration happens in the United States. Small- and medium-sized firms can practice global nichemanship. The Poilane Bakery sells 15,000 loaves of old-style bread each day in Paris—2.5% of all bread sold in that city—via company-owned delivery trucks. The company also ships its breads via FedEx to loyal customers in 20 countries.[4]

For a company of any size to go global, it must make a series of decisions (see Figure 18.1).

BREAKTHROUGH MARKETING: SAMSUNG

Korea's Samsung has made a remarkable transformation from marketing value-priced commodity products to marketing premium-priced Samsung-branded consumer electronics like flat-screen televisions, digital cameras, and cell phones. In the past, it stressed volume and market domination rather than profitability. Today it focuses on product quality and manufacturing flexibility; bringing innovative new items to global markets takes months rather than years.

Over the years, Samsung has invested more than $6 billion in marketing to upgrade its image. Among its high-profile activities are Olympic sponsorships and ad campaigns framing the brand's message in terms of "technology," "design," and "sensation" (human). Samsung needed only 12 years to became the world's second-largest seller of cell phones—and it's aiming to overtake market-leader Nokia in the near future. In 2005, Interbrand determined that the Samsung brand was for the first time more valuable than the Sony brand. To maintain its momentum, Samsung must continue to successfully expand via new products and new markets.[5]

FIGURE 18.1 Major Decisions in International Marketing

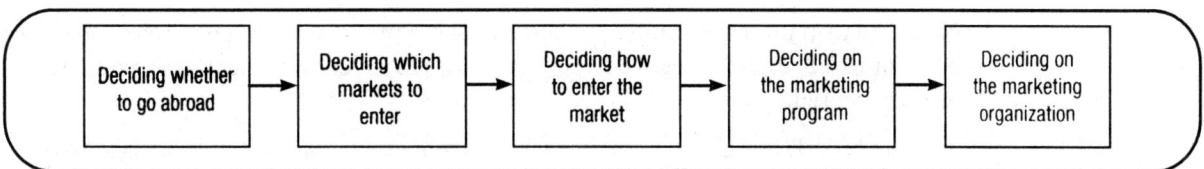

Deciding Whether to Go Abroad

Several factors are drawing companies into the international arena. Some foreign markets offer higher profit opportunities than the domestic market. A company may need a larger customer base to achieve economies of scale or want to reduce dependence on any one market. Sometimes a firm decides to counterattack global competitors in their home markets; or its customers are going abroad and require international service.

Before making a decision to go abroad, the company must weigh several risks. First, the company might not understand foreign preferences and could fail to offer a competitively attractive product. Second, it might not understand the other country's business culture or know how to deal effectively with foreign regulations. Third, it may lack managers with international experience. Finally, the other country might change its commercial laws, devalue its currency, or undergo a political revolution and expropriate foreign property.

Deciding Which Markets to Enter

In deciding to go abroad, the company needs to define its marketing objectives and policies. What proportion of international to total sales will it seek? Most companies start small when they venture abroad, but others have bigger plans. Increasingly, firms—especially technology-intensive firms—are *born global* and market to the entire world from the outset.[6]

The company must also decide on the countries to consider. The product, geography, income and population, political climate, and other factors influence attractiveness. Developed nations and the prosperous parts of developing nations account for about 20% of the world's population. Can marketers serve the other 80%, which has much less purchasing power? Marketers need a special set of skills and plans to successfully enter developing regions. For instance, Fiat created a "third-world car," the Palio, for developing nations and produces it in Brazil, India, Turkey, and other countries.[7] Some firms have succeeded by changing their conventional marketing practices to sell offerings more effectively.[8]

How does a company evaluate potential markets? Many prefer to sell to neighboring countries because they understand these countries better and can control their costs more effectively. At other times, *psychic proximity* determines choices. Many U.S. firms prefer to sell in Canada, England, and Australia because they feel comfortable with the language, laws, and culture. By choosing markets according to cultural distance, a firm may overlook potentially better markets; perform superficial analysis of the very real differences among countries; or adopt predictable marketing actions that put it at a disadvantage.[9]

Deciding How to Enter the Market

Next, the firm must determine the best mode of entry for a foreign market. As shown in Figure 18.2, each successive strategy involves more commitment, risk, control, and profit potential.

- *Indirect and direct exporting.* Companies typically start with indirect exporting, working through independent intermediaries. This involves less investment and less risk. Eventually companies may decide to handle their own exports; this entails higher investment and risk but also offers higher potential return.[10] Companies may exhibit at overseas trade shows or set up country-specific Web sites for key markets.

- *Licensing.* Here, the licensor issues a license to a foreign firm to use a manufacturing process, trademark, patent, trade secret, or other item of value for a fee or royalty. The licensor gains entry at little risk; the licensee gains production expertise or a well-known product or brand name. However, the licensor has less control than it does over its own production and marketing; if the licensee is very profitable, the firm has given up profits. If and when the contract ends, the company might find it has created a competitor.

- *Joint ventures.* Foreign investors may join with local investors to create a **joint venture** company in which they share ownership and control, sometimes desirable for political or economic reasons. One drawback is that the partners might disagree over investment, marketing, or other policies. Or one partner might want to reinvest earnings for growth, but the other wants to declare more dividends. Joint ownership can also prevent a multinational company from carrying out specific manufacturing and marketing policies on a worldwide basis.

- *Direct investment.* The ultimate form of foreign involvement is direct investment, when a firm buys all or part of a local company or builds its own facilities. General Motors has invested heavily in auto manufacturers around the world, including Daewoo and Saab.[11] This strategy leads to cost economies, like cheaper labor or raw materials, government investment incentives, and freight savings. It helps the company strengthen its image in the host country by creating jobs. Also, it leads to deeper relationships with government, customers, local suppliers, and distributors, enabling the firm to adapt its products better to the local environment. However, it entails currency risks and expropriation risks; in addition, reducing or eliminating operations may be expensive because of government-required severance pay to employees.

FIGURE 18.2   Five Modes of Entry into Foreign Markets

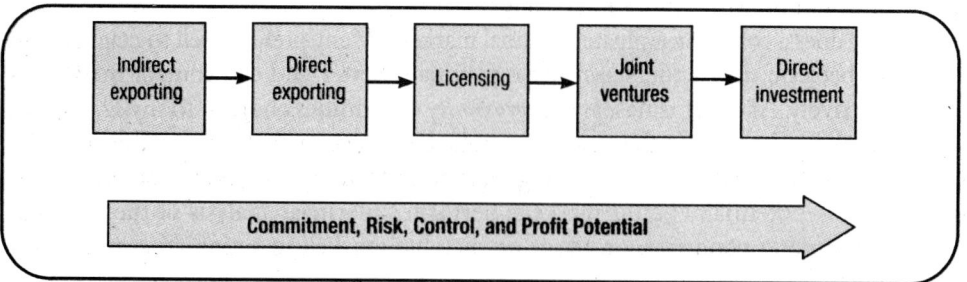

Deciding on the Marketing Program

International companies must decide how much to adapt their marketing strategy to local conditions.[12] At one extreme are companies that use a globally *standardized marketing mix* worldwide, which keeps costs low, allows for brand image consistency, and enables the firm to leverage ideas quickly and efficiently. At the other extreme is an *adapted marketing mix*, where the marketing program is adjusted to each target market. Most brands are adapted to some extent to reflect significant differences in consumer behavior, brand development, competitive forces, and the legal or political environment.[13] Even global brands undergo some changes in product features, packaging, channels, pricing, or communications in different global markets.[14] Warren Keegan has distinguished five strategies for adapting product and communications to a foreign market (see Figure 18.3).[15]

Product Some types of products travel better across borders than others; food and beverage marketers, for instance, must contend with widely varying tastes.[16] **Straight extension** introduces the product in the foreign market without any change, a successful strategy with cameras, consumer electronics, and many machine tools that may be costly in the long run. **Product adaptation** alters the product to meet local conditions or preferences. The company might develop a *regional version* of its product, a *country version*, a *city version*, or different *retailer versions*.

Product invention consists of creating something new, in one of two forms. *Backward invention* is reintroducing earlier product forms that are well adapted to a foreign country's needs. *Forward invention* is creating a new product to meet a need in another country. Product invention is costly, but the payoffs can be great, particularly if the innovation can be launched elsewhere. Häagen-Dazs originally developed the dulce de leche flavor, named for the locally popular caramelized milk, for sale in Argentina. Then the company launched it internationally; very quickly, dulce de leche became one of the top 10 flavors in America.[17]

Communications Companies can run the same marketing communications programs used in the home market or change them for each local market, a process called **communication adaptation.** If a company adapts both the product and the communications, it's using **dual adaptation.**

Consider the message. One approach is to use the same message everywhere, varying the language, name, and colors.[18] Another is to use one creative theme globally but adapt the execution for local markets. As an example, Apple created

FIGURE 18.3 Five International Product and Communication Strategies

Communications	Product: Do Not Change Product	Product: Adapt Product	Product: Develop New Product
Do Not Change Communications	Straight extension	Product adaptation	Product invention
Adapt Communications	Communication adaptation	Dual adaptation	

"Mac vs. PC" ads and dubbed them for Spain, France, Germany, and Italy. Its U.K. ads followed a similar formula but with jokes tweaked for British humor; its Japanese ads avoided direct comparisons.[19] The third approach is to develop a global pool of ads, from which each country selects the most appropriate. Some companies allow their country managers to create country-specific ads—within guidelines, of course.

The use of media also requires international adaptation because media availability varies from country to country. Personal selling tactics may have to change too. The direct, no-nonsense approach favored by Americans may not work as well in Europe, Asia, and other places where a more indirect, subtle approach can be more effective.[20]

Price When a company sells abroad, it faces a **price escalation** problem because it must add the cost of transportation, tariffs, importer margin, wholesaler margin, and retailer margin to the product's factory price. Depending on these added costs, as well as currency-fluctuation risk, the product might have to sell for two to five times as much in another country to make the same profit for the manufacturer. So the company can set a uniform price in all markets, a market-based price in each market, or a cost-based price in each market.

Many multinationals are dealing with problems of the **gray market,** in which branded products are diverted from normal or authorized distribution channels in the country of product origin or across international borders. Dealers in the low-price country earn more by selling their products in higher-price countries. Multinationals fight back by policing the distributors, raising their prices to lower-cost distributors, and altering the product characteristics or service warranties for different countries. Fakes and imitations have also become a costly concern for brand marketers. Online, firms are using technology to search for counterfeit storefronts and sales by detecting domain names similar to legitimate brands and unauthorized Web sites that plaster brand trademarks and logos on their home pages.[21]

Distribution Companies must consider how to get products to the borders of other nations as well as how the channels within each country get products to final users. Distribution channels within countries vary considerably, as do the size and character of retail units. Large-scale retail chains dominate the U.S. scene, but much foreign retailing is in the hands of small, independent retailers. Although their markups are high, the real price is brought down through haggling. Incomes are low, and people must shop daily for small amounts, limited to what they can carry home on foot or on a bicycle. Breaking bulk remains an important function and helps perpetuate the long channels of distribution, a major obstacle to the expansion of large-scale retailing in developing countries. When entering a country, the multinational must choose the right distributors, invest in them, and agree on suitable performance goals.[22]

Country-of-Origin Effects

In an increasingly connected, competitive global marketplace, governments and companies are concerned about *country-of-origin perceptions*, distinct attitudes and beliefs about brands or products from particular countries.[23] Government officials want to strengthen their country's image to help domestic firms that export and to attract foreign firms and investors; marketers want positive country-of-origin perceptions to sell their products and services. In the domestic market, these perceptions may stir consumers' patriotic notions or remind them of their past. As international trade grows, consumers may view certain brands as symbolically important to their own cultural heritage and identity.

INTERNAL MARKETING

Internal marketing requires that everyone in the organization buy into the concepts and goals of marketing and engage in choosing, providing, and communicating customer value. Over the years, marketing has evolved as it has grown from work done by the sales department into a complex group of activities spread through the organization.[24] Let's look at how marketing departments are being organized and how they can work effectively with other departments.

Organizing the Marketing Department

Modern marketing departments may be organized in a number of different, sometimes overlapping ways:[25] functionally, geographically, by product or brand, by market, in a matrix, and/or by corporate/division.

Functional Organization   The most common marketing organization consists of functional specialists (such as the sales manager and marketing research manager) reporting to a marketing vice president, who coordinates their activities. The main advantage is administrative simplicity, although this form loses effectiveness as products and markets increase. A functional organization often leads to inadequate planning for specific products and markets. Also, each functional group competes with others for budget and status. The marketing vice president constantly has to weigh the claims of competing functional specialists and faces a difficult coordination problem.

Geographic Organization   A company selling in a national market often organizes its sales force (and sometimes other functions, including marketing) along geographic lines. The national sales manager may supervise four regional sales managers, who each supervise six zone managers, who in turn supervise eight district sales managers, who supervise ten salespeople. Some firms are adding *area market specialists* (regional or local marketing managers) to support sales efforts in high-volume markets.

Product- or Brand-Management Organization   Companies producing a variety of products and brands often establish a product- (or brand-) management organization, not to replace the functional organization but as another layer of management. A product manager supervises product category managers, who in turn supervise specific product and brand managers. Such an organization makes sense if the firm's products are quite different or it has too many products for a functional organization to handle.

The product-management organization lets the product manager concentrate on developing a cost-effective marketing mix and react more quickly to marketplace changes; it also gives the firm's smaller brands a product advocate. On the other hand, product managers may have insufficient authority to carry out their responsibilities or be experts in their product but rarely achieve functional expertise. Appointing product managers for major and even minor products can be costly. Brand managers may expect to be with a brand for a short time, leading to short-term thinking instead of taking a long-term view. Fragmentation of markets means brand managers must increasingly please regional and local sales groups. Finally, product and brand managers often focus on building market share rather than on building customer relationships.

A second alternative is *product teams*. Some firms assign each major brand to a *brand-asset management team* (*BAMT*) with representatives from functions affecting the brand's performance. These BAMTs report to a BAMT Directors Committee, which itself reports to a Chief Branding Officer. Another approach to the product-management organization is to eliminate product manager positions for minor products and assign two or more products to each remaining manager. This is feasible where two or more products appeal to a similar set of needs.

A fourth alternative is to introduce *category management*, in which a company focuses on product categories to manage its brands. Procter & Gamble, a brand-management pioneer, and several other top firms have shifted to category management.[26] P&G wanted to ensure that all categories received adequate resources. Further, because retailers have tended to think in terms of profitability from product categories, P&G wanted to deal with the trade along similar lines. Category management is not a panacea, because it's still product-driven. Colgate has moved from brand management (Colgate toothpaste) to category management (toothpaste category) to customer-need management (mouth care), focusing the organization on a basic customer need.[27]

Market-Management Organization When a company sells to customers who fall into different user groups with distinct buying preferences and practices, a *market management organization* is desirable. Market managers supervise several market-development managers, market specialists, or industry specialists and draw on functional services as needed. Market managers are staff (not line) people, with duties similar to those of product managers. The main advantage here is organizing marketing activity to meet the needs of distinct customer groups. Many firms are reorganizing along market lines and becoming *market-centered organizations*. In a *customer-management organization*, companies organize to deal with individual customers rather than with mass market or market segments.[28]

Matrix-Management Organization Companies that produce many products flowing into many markets may adopt a *matrix organization*. DuPont was a pioneer in developing the matrix structure. Matrix management gained advocates because companies provide the context in which a matrix can thrive—flat, lean team organizations focused around business processes that cut horizontally across functions.[29] A matrix organization seems desirable in a multiproduct, multimarket company. However, it's costly and can create conflicts as well as questions about authority and responsibility.[30] Some corporate marketing groups assist top management with overall opportunity evaluation, provide divisions with consulting assistance, and promote the marketing concept throughout the company.

Global Organization Companies just going global usually start with an export department, staffed by a sales manager and a few assistants, and add various marketing services as needed. As global activities expand, the company creates an international division with marketing specialists and other functional departments. Firms that become truly global have top corporate management and staff who plan worldwide operations, marketing policies, financial flows, and logistical systems. The global operating units report to top management, not to the head of an international division.

Relations with Other Departments

In the typical organization, each business function has a potential impact on customer satisfaction. Under the marketing concept, all departments need to "think customer" and work together to satisfy customer needs and expectations. The marketing department must drive this point home. The marketing vice president, or CMO, has two tasks: (1) to coordinate the company's internal marketing activities and (2) to coordinate marketing with finance, operations, and other company functions to serve the customer. Many companies avoid the problems of departmental politics by appointing process leaders to manage cross-disciplinary teams that include marketing and sales people, among other functional representatives.[31]

Although it's *necessary* to be customer-oriented, it's not *enough*. The organization must also be creative. Ulster University's Stephen Brown says marketers make too much of researching and satisfying consumers—and risk losing marketing imagination and significant consumer impact.[32] Market leaders tend to miss trends when they are risk-averse, obsessed about protecting existing markets and resources, and more interested in efficiency than innovation.[33]

MANAGING THE MARKETING PROCESS

Marketing implementation is the process that turns marketing plans into action assignments and ensures that they accomplish the plan's stated objectives.[34] A brilliant strategic marketing plan counts for little if implemented improperly. Whereas strategy addresses the *what* and *why* of marketing activities, implementation addresses the *who, where, when,* and *how*. Strategy and implementation are closely related, in that one layer of strategy implies certain tactical implementation assignments at a lower level. For example, top management's strategy to "harvest" a product must be translated into specific actions and assignments.

Companies today are striving to make marketing operations more efficient and return on marketing investment more measurable, because marketing costs can amount to 20% to 40% of the total operating budget. As a result, they're using more and better marketing metrics to evaluate and control marketing performance (see Table 18.1).[35] Many firms use *marketing resource management (MRM)* software to automate, integrate, and manage marketing activities and budgets, manage brands, and manage customer relationships. Some systems include marketing dashboards to display key data for decision makers.[36] The goal is to improve marketing investment decisions, speed new products to market, and cut decision time and costs.

Evaluation and Control

Companies need four types of marketing control: annual-plan control, profitability control, efficiency control, and strategic control (see Table 18.2). Annual-plan control

Part VII Creating Successful Long-Term Growth

TABLE 18.1 Marketing Metrics

Sales Metrics
- Sales growth
- Market share
- Sales from new products

Customer Readiness to Buy Metrics
- Awareness
- Preference
- Purchase intention
- Trial rate
- Repurchase rate

Customer Metrics
- Customer complaints
- Customer satisfaction
- Number of promoters to detractors
- Customer acquisition costs
- New customer gains
- Customer loses
- Customer churn
- Retention rate
- Customer lifetime value
- Customer equity
- Customer profitability
- Return on customer

Distribution Metrics
- Number of outlets
- Share in shops handling
- Weighted distribution
- Distribution gains
- Average stocks volume (value)
- Stocks cover in days
- Out of stock frequency
- Share of shelf
- Average sales per point of sale

Communication Metrics
- Spontaneous (unaided) brand awareness
- Top of mind brand awareness
- Prompted (aided) brand awareness
- Spontaneous (unaided) advertising awareness
- Prompted (aided) advertising awareness
- Effective reach
- Effective frequency
- Gross rating points (GRP)
- Response rate

shows whether the company achieved the sales, profits, and other goals established in its annual plan. At its heart is management by objectives: Management sets monthly or quarterly goals, monitors marketplace performance, determines the cause of serious performance deviations, and takes corrective action to close gaps between goals and performance (see Figure 18.4).

Suppose a profitability analysis reveals the company is earning poor profits in certain products, territories, or markets. Are there more efficient ways to manage the sales force, advertising, sales promotion, and distribution in connection with these marketing entities? Some companies have established a *marketing controller* position to improve marketing efficiency. At companies such as Johnson & Johnson, marketing

FIGURE 18.4 The Control Process

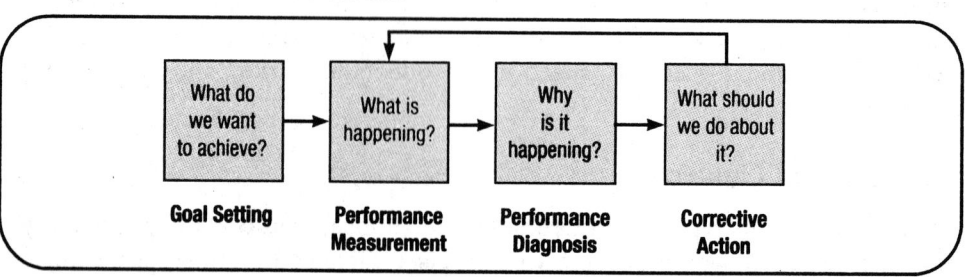

TABLE 18.2 Types of Marketing Control

Types of Control	Prime Responsibility	Purpose of Control	Approaches
I. Annual-plan control	Top management Middle management	To examine whether the planned results are being achieved	■ Sales analysis ■ Market share analysis ■ Sales-to-expense ratios ■ Financial analysis ■ Market-based scorecard analysis
II. Profitability control	Marketing controller	To examine where the company is making and losing money	Profitability by: ■ product ■ territory ■ customer ■ segment ■ trade channel ■ order size
III. Efficiency control	Line and staff management Marketing controller	To evaluate and improve the spending efficiency and impact of marketing expenditures	Efficiency of: ■ sales force ■ advertising ■ sales promotion ■ distribution
IV. Strategic control	Top management Marketing auditor	To examine whether the company is pursuing its best opportunities with respect to markets, products, and channels	■ Marketing-effectiveness rating instrument ■ Marketing audit ■ Marketing excellence review ■ Company ethical and social responsibility review

controllers perform sophisticated financial analyses of marketing expenditures and results, examining adherence to profit plans, helping prepare brand managers' budgets, measuring the efficiency of promotions, checking media production costs, evaluating customer and geographic profitability, and educating marketing personnel on the financial implications of their decisions.[37]

The Marketing Audit

The average U.S. corporation loses half its customers in five years, half its employees in four years, and half its investors in less than one year. Clearly, this points to some weaknesses. Companies that uncover weaknesses should reassess their strategic approach to the marketplace with a marketing audit. A **marketing audit** is a comprehensive, systematic, independent, and periodic examination of a company's (or business unit's) marketing environment, objectives, strategies, and activities to identify problems and opportunities and to recommend improvements.[38] The marketing audit examines six major marketing components: (1) the macroenvironment and task environment;

(2) marketing strategy; (3) marketing organization; (4) marketing systems; (5) marketing productivity; and (6) marketing function.

SOCIALLY RESPONSIBLE MARKETING

Companies also need to evaluate whether they're practicing ethical and socially responsible marketing. A number of forces are contributing to the drive for corporate social responsibility and sustainability: rising customer expectations, evolving employee goals and ambitions, tighter government legislation and pressure, developing investor interest in social criteria, relentless media scrutiny, and changing business procurement practices.[39] One benefit of being seen as a socially responsible company is the ability to attract employees, especially younger people, who want to work for companies they feel good about. The world's most admired—and increasingly most successful—companies abide by a code of serving people's interests, not only their own.

Ethical, Legal, and Social Responsibility Behavior

Socially responsible marketing calls for proper legal, ethical, and social responsibility behavior.

- *Legal behavior.* Every employee must know and observe relevant laws; they can't lie to customers, offer bribes to purchasing agents, or steal competitors' secrets.[40]
- *Ethical behavior.* Certain practices are clearly unethical or illegal: bribery, false and deceptive advertising, quality or safety defects, false warranties, inaccurate labeling, price-fixing or undue discrimination, predatory competition. Other ethical issues are less clear. When Kraft stopped advertising some less-healthy products like Oreos on television programs targeted to children less than 11 years old, critics wanted even more restrictions.[41]
- *Social responsibility behavior.* Individual marketers must practice a "social conscience" in dealings with customers and stakeholders. Yet once a firm touts an environmental initiative, it may become a target for criticism. More firms are coming to the belief that corporate social responsibility (cash donations, in-kind contributions, cause marketing, and employee volunteerism programs) is the not just the "right thing" but also the "smart thing to do."[42] However, good deeds can be overlooked or resented if the firm is seen as exploitive or fails to live up to a "good guy" image.[43]

Cause-Related Marketing

Many firms blend corporate social responsibility initiatives with marketing activities. **Cause-related marketing** links the firm's contributions to a designated cause with customers' engaging directly or indirectly in revenue-producing transactions with the firm.[44] Cause marketing is part of *corporate societal marketing (CSM)*, which Drumwright and Murphy define as marketing efforts ". . . that have at least one noneconomic objective related to social welfare and use the resources of the company and/or of its partners."[45]

Cause-related marketing can produce a number of benefits: improving social welfare; creating differentiated brand positioning; building strong consumer bonds;

enhancing the company's public image and market value; creating goodwill; boosting internal morale and galvanizing employees; and driving sales.[46] Consumers may develop a strong, unique bond with the firm that transcends normal marketplace transactions.[47] (For more about marketing and social responsibility, see "Marketing Skills: Cause-Related Marketing").

Sustainability

Sustainability, the importance of meeting humanity's needs without harming future generations, has risen to the top of many corporate agendas. Major corporations now outline in great detail how they're trying to improve the long-term impact of their actions on communities and the environment. As one sustainability consultant put it, "There is a triple bottom line—People, Planet, and Profit—and the people part of the equation must come first. Sustainability means more than being eco-friendly; it also means you are in it for the long haul."[48] Sustainability ratings exist, although there is little agreement about appropriate metrics.[49]

EXECUTIVE SUMMARY

In deciding to go abroad, a company needs to define its international marketing objectives and policies; determine how many and which countries to enter; and determine the mode of entry (indirect or direct exporting, licensing, joint ventures, or direct

---

MARKETING SKILLS: CAUSE-RELATED MARKETING

To develop cause-related marketing skills, marketers first learn to choose the cause(s) to support. The cause should fit the company's or brand's image and be meaningful to employees and other stakeholders. For assistance, seek out non-governmental organizations with expertise on social issues and access to opinion leaders. Next, prepare to brand the program, perhaps with a new self-branded organization associated with the cause, such as the Ronald McDonald House Charities. The aim is to enhance existing consumer associations via emotional and imagery appeals. Another approach is to co-brand the program as sponsor or supporter, which complements the brand's image with specific associations "borrowed" or "transferred" from the cause. A third option is to partner with a cause and brand the program linked to the cause. Finally, cause-related marketing should be planned and managed as carefully as all other marketing activities.

(RED), championed by U2 singer and activist Bono and Bobby Shriver, Chairman of DATA, was created to raise awareness and money for the Global Fund to help women and children affected by HIV/AIDS in Africa. Iconic products like American Express cards, Motorola phones, Gap T-shirts, Apple iPods, and Armani sunglasses have produced (PRODUCT)RED branded products, giving up to half of the profits to the Global Fund. The parentheses in the logo signify "the embrace"; each participating firm places its logo in this embrace and is "elevated to the power of red," tapping the positive associations of the (RED) brand. In its first 18 months, (RED) raised more than $36 million for the Global Fund.[50]

investment). Each succeeding strategy involves more commitment, risk, control, and profit potential. Firms going global can pursue a product strategy of straight extension, product adaptation, or product invention and a communication strategy of adaptation or dual adaptation. Price escalation and gray markets may be issues. Firms should also take a whole-channel view of distribution to final users. Country-of-origin effects can affect consumers and business alike.

Companies can organize marketing by function, geography, product and brand, market segment, or a matrix organization. To market abroad, a firm can create an export department, an international division, or a global organization. Effective marketing requires the company's departments to cooperate and exhibit a customer focus. Marketing control helps management ensure that the marketing plan's objectives are achieved. Companies can apply annual-plan control, profitability control, efficiency control, and strategic control. Today firms are practicing social responsibility through legal, ethical, and social responsibility behavior, as well as cause-related marketing and sustainability initiatives.

NOTES

1. "Stonyfield Farm and Environmental Defense Launched a Petition Drive Last Month," *Dairy Field*, July 2007, p. 8; Tara Weiss, "Special Report: Going Green," *Forbes.com*, July 3, 2007; Matthew Grimm, "Progressive Business," *Brandweek*, November 28, 2005, pp. 16–26.
2. Keith Fox, Katherine Jocz, and Bernard Jaworski, "A Common Language," *Marketing Management* (May/June 2003): 14–17.
3. Michael E. Porter, *Competitive Strategy* (New York: The Free Press, 1980), p. 275.
4. Ron Lieber, "Give Us This Day Our Global Bread," *Fast Company*, March 2001, p. 158.
5. Moon Ihlwan, "What's Propelling Korea's Growth," *BusinessWeek Online*, September 28, 2007, www.businessweek.com; Stephanie Mehta, "Samsung Moves Up the Ranks," *Fortune*, September 3, 2007, p. 20; Moon Ihlwan, "Samsung Is Having a Sony Moment," *BusinessWeek*, July 30, 2007, pp. 38; Martin Fackler, "Raising the Bar at Samsung," *The New York Times*, April 25, 2006; John Quelch and Anna Harrington, "Samsung Electronics Company: Global Marketing Operations," Harvard Business School Case 9-504-051; Heidi Brown and Justin Doeble, "Samsung's Next Act," *Forbes*, July 26, 2004; "Brand New," *The Economist*, January 15, 2005, pp. 10–11; Patricia O'Connell, "Samsung's Goal: Be Like BMW," *BusinessWeek*, August 1, 2005.
6. For a thorough review of academic research on global marketing, see Johny K. Johansson, "Global Marketing: Research on Foreign Entry, Local Marketing, Global Management," in *Handbook of Marketing*, edited by Bart Weitz and Robin Wensley (London: Sage Publications, 2002), pp. 457–483. Also see Johny K. Johansson, *Global Marketing*, 2nd ed. (New York: McGraw–Hill, 2003). For some global marketing research issues, see Susan Douglas and Samuel R. Craig, *International Marketing Research*, 2nd ed. (Upper Saddle River, NJ: Prentice Hall, 2000).
7. Adapted from Vijay Mahajan, Marcos V. Pratini De Moraes, and Jerry Wind, "The Invisible Global Market," *Marketing Management* (Winter 2000): 31–35. See also Tarun Khanna and Krishna G. Palepu, "Emerging Giants: Building World-Class Companies in Developing Countries," *Harvard Business Review*, October 2006, pp. 60–69.
8. C. K. Prahalad, *The Fortune at the Bottom of the Pyramid: Eradicating Poverty through Profits* (Upper Saddle River, NJ: Wharton School Publishing, 2005); Niraj Dawar and Amitava Chattopadhyay, "Rethinking Marketing Programs for Emerging Markets," *Long Range Planning* 35 (October 2002): 457–474.
9. Johny K. Johansson, "Global Marketing: Research on Foreign Entry, Local Marketing, Global Management," in *Handbook of Marketing*, edited by Bart Weitz and Robin Wensley (London: Sage Publications, 2002), pp. 457–483.
10. For an academic review, see Leonidas C. Leonidou, Constantine S. Katsikeas, and Nigel F. Piercy, "Identifying Managerial Influences on Exporting: Past Research and Future Directions," *Journal of International Marketing* 6, no. 2 (1998): 74–102.

11. Joann Muller, "Global Motors," *Forbes*, January 12, 2004, pp. 62–68.
12. "Burgers and Fries a la Francaise," *The Economist*, April 17, 2004, pp. 60–61; Shaoming Zou and S. Tamer Cavusgil, "The GMS: A Broad Conceptualization of Global Marketing Strategy and Its Effect on Firm Performance," *Journal of Marketing* 66 (October 2002): 40–56; David M. Szymanski, Sundar G. Bharadwaj, and P. Rajan Varadarajan, "Standardization versus Adaptation of International Marketing Strategy: An Empirical Investigation," *Journal of Marketing* (October 1993): 1–17; Johny K. Johansson, "Global Marketing: Research on Foreign Entry, Local Marketing, Global Management," in *Handbook of Marketing*, edited by Bart Weitz and Robin Wensley (London: Sage Publications, 2002), pp. 457–483.
13. For some recent treatments of branding in other nations, see: S. Ramesh Kumar, *Marketing & Branding: The Indian Scenario* (Delhi: Pearson Education, 2007); Martin Roll, *Asian Brand Strategy: How Asia Builds Strong Brands* (New York: Palgrave MacMillan, 2006); Paul Temporal, *Branding in Asia: The Creation, Development and Management of Asian Brands for the Global Market* (Singapore: John Wiley & Sons, 2001).
14. Pankaj Ghemawat, "Globalization: The Strategy of Differences," *Harvard Business School Working Knowledge*, November 10, 2003; Pankaj Ghemawat, "The Forgotten Strategy," *Harvard Business Review* 81 (November 2003): 76–84.
15. Warren J. Keegan, *Global Marketing Management*, 7th ed. (Upper Saddle River, NJ: Prentice Hall, 2002); Walter J. Keegan and Mark C. Green, *Global Marketing*, 4th ed. (Upper Saddle River, NJ: Prentice Hall, 2005).
16. Arundhati Parmar, "Dependent Variables: Sound Global Strategies Rely on Certain Factors," *Marketing News*, September 16, 2002, p. 4.
17. David Leonhardt, "It Was a Hit in Buenos Aires—So Why Not Boise?" *BusinessWeek*, September 7, 1998, pp. 56–58; Marlene Parrish, "Taste Buds Tango at New Squirrel Hill Café," *Pittsburgh Post-Gazette*, February 6, 2003.
18. For an interesting distinction based on the concept of global consumer culture positioning, see Dana L. Alden, Jan-Benedict E.M. Steenkamp, and Rajeev Batra, "Brand Positioning through Advertising in Asia, North America, and Europe: The Role of Global Consumer Culture," *Journal of Marketing* 63 (January 1999): 75–87.
19. Geoffrey Fowler, Brian Steinberg, and Aaron O. Patrick, "Globalizing Apple's Ads," *Wall Street Journal*, March 1, 2007, p. B1.
20. John L. Graham, Alma T. Mintu, and Waymond Rogers, "Explorations of Negotiations Behaviors in Ten Foreign Cultures Using a Model Developed in the United States," *Management Science* 40 (January 1994): 72–95.
21. Carol Matlack, "Fed Up with Fakes," *BusinessWeek*, October 9, 2006, pp. 56–57; Deborah Kong, "Smart Tech Fights Fakes," *Business 2.0*, March 2007, p. 30; Eric Shine, "Faking Out the Fakers," *BusinessWeek*, June 4, 2007, pp. 76–80.
22. David Arnold, "Seven Rules of International Distribution," *Harvard Business Review*, (November–December 2000): 131–137.
23. Zeynep Gurhan-Canli and Durairaj Maheswaran, "Cultural Variations in Country of Origin Effects," *Journal of Marketing Research* 37 (August 2000): 309–317.
24. For a broad historical treatment of marketing thought, see D. G. Brian Jones and Eric H. Shaw, "A History of Marketing Thought," in *Handbook of Marketing*, edited by Barton A. Weitz and Robin Wensley (London: Sage Publications, 2002), pp. 39–65.
25. Frederick E. Webster Jr., "The Role of Marketing and the Firm," in *Handbook of Marketing*, edited by Barton A. Weitz and Robin Wensley (London: Sage Publications, 2002), pp. 39–65.
26. Zachary Schiller, "The Marketing Revolution at Procter & Gamble," *BusinessWeek*, July 25, 1988, pp. 72–76; Laurie Freeman, "P&G Widens Power Base: Adds Category Managers," *Advertising Age*, October 12, 1987, pp. 1+; Michael J. Zenor, "The Profit Benefits of Category Management," *Journal of Marketing Research*, 31 (May 1994): 202–213; Gerry Khermouch, "Brands Overboard," *Brandweek*, August 22, 1994, pp. 25–39.
27. For further reading, see Robert Dewar and Don Shultz, "The Product Manager, an Idea Whose Time Has Gone," *Marketing Communications* (May 1998): 28–35; George S. Low and Ronald A. Fullerton, "Brands, Brand Management, and the Brand Manager System: A Critical Historical Evaluation," *Journal of Marketing Research* (May 1994): 173–190; Michael J. Zanor, "The Profit Benefits of Category Management," *Journal of Marketing Research* (May 1994): 202–213.
28. Larry Selden and Geoffrey Colvin, *Angel Customers & Demon Customers* (New York: Portfolio, 2003).

29. Richard E. Anderson, "Matrix Redux," *Business Horizons*, November–December 1994, pp. 6–10.
30. Frederick E. Webster Jr., "The Role of Marketing and the Firm," in *Handbook of Marketing*, edited by Barton A. Weitz and Robin Wensley (London: Sage Publications, 2002), pp. 39–65.
31. Ranjay Gulati, "Silo Busting: How to Execute on the Promise of Customer Focus," *Harvard Business Review*, May 1, 2007, pp. 98ff.
32. Stephen Brown, *Marketing—The Retro Revolution* (Thousand Oaks, CA: Sage Publications, 2001).
33. Jagdish N. Sheth, *The Self-Destructive Habits of Good Companies . . . And How to Break Them* (Upper Saddle River, NJ: Wharton School Publishing, 2007).
34. For more on developing and implementing marketing plans, see Marian Burk Wood, *The Marketing Plan Handbook*, 3rd ed. (Upper Saddle River, NJ: Pearson Prentice Hall, 2008); and H. W. Goetsch, *Developing, Implementing, and Managing an Effective Marketing Plan* (Lincolnwood, IL: NTC Business Books, 1993).
35. For other examples of marketing metrics, see Paul W. Farris, Neil T. Bendle, Phillip E. Pfeifer, and David J. Reibstein, *Marketing Metrics: 50+ Metrics Every Executive Should Master* (Upper Saddle River, NJ: Wharton School Publishing, 2006); Marion Debruyne and Katrina Hubbard, "Marketing Metrics," working paper series, Conference Summary, Marketing Science Institute, Report No. 00-119, 2000.
36. Richard Karpinski, "Making the Most of a Marketing Dashboard," *B to B*, March 13, 2006, p. 18; C. Marcus, "Marketing Resource Management: Key Components," *Gartner Research Note*, August 22, 2001.
37. Sam R. Goodman, *Increasing Corporate Profitability* (New York: Ronald Press, 1982), ch. 1. Also see Bernard J. Jaworski, Vlasis Stathakopoulos, and H. Shanker Krishnan, "Control Combinations in Marketing: Conceptual Framework and Empirical Evidence," *Journal of Marketing* (January 1993): 57–69.
38. See Philip Kotler, William Gregor, and William Rodgers, "The Marketing Audit Comes of Age," *Sloan Management Review* (Winter 1989): 49–62; Frederick Reichheld, *The Loyalty Effect* (Boston: Harvard Business School Press, 1996) discusses attrition figures.
39. William L. Wilkie and Elizabeth S. Moore, "Marketing's Relationship to Society," in *Handbook of Marketing*, edited by Barton A. Weitz and Robin Wensley (London: Sage Publications, 2002), pp. 1–38; "Special Report: Corporate Social Responsibility," *The Economist*, December 14, 2002, pp. 62–63.
40. For further reading, see Dorothy Cohen, *Legal Issues in Marketing Decision Making* (Cincinnati, OH: South-Western, 1995).
41. Sarah Ellison, "Kraft Limits on Kids' Ads May Cheese Off Rivals," *Wall Street Journal*, January 13, 2005, p. B3.
42. Craig N. Smith, "Corporate Social Responsibility: Whether or How?" *California Management Review* 45 (4), 2003, pp. 52–76; Robert Berner, "Smarter Corporate Giving, *BusinessWeek*, November 28, 2005, pp. 68–76.
43. Michael E. Porter and Mark R. Kramer, "The Competitive Advantage of Corporate Philanthropy," *Harvard Business Review* (December 2002): 5–16; Dwane Hal Deane, "Associating the Corporation with a Charitable Event through Sponsorship: Measuring the Effects on Corporate Community Relations," *Journal of Advertising* (Winter 2002): 77–87.
44. Rajan Varadarajan and Anil Menon, "Cause-Related Marketing: A Co-alignment of Marketing Strategy and Corporate Philanthropy," *Journal of Marketing* 52 (1988): 58–74.
45. Minette Drumwright and Patrick E. Murphy, "Corporate Societal Marketing," in *Handbook of Marketing and Society*, edited by Paul N. Bloom and Gregory T. Gundlach (Thousand Oaks, CA: Sage Publications, 2001), pp. 162–183. See also Minette Drumwright, "Company Advertising with a Social Dimension: The Role of Noneconomic Criteria," *Journal of Marketing* 60 (October 1996): 71–87.
46. Pat Auger, Paul Burke, Timothy Devinney, and Jordan J. Loviere, "What Will Consumers Pay for Social Product Features?" *Journal of Business Ethics* 42 (2003): 281–304; Xueming Luo and C. B. Bhattacharya, "Corporate Social Responsibility, Customer Satisfaction, and Market Value," *Journal of Marketing* 70 (October 2006): 1–18.
47. C. B. Bhattacharya and Sankar Sen, "Consumer-Company Identification: A Framework for Understanding Consumers' Relationships with Companies," *Journal of Marketing* 67 (April 2003): 76–88; Sankar Sen and C. B. Bhattacharya, "Does Doing Good Always Lead to Doing Better? Consumer Reactions to Corporate Social Responsibility," *Journal of Marketing Research* 38, no. 2 (2001): 225–244; Dennis B. Arnett, Steve D. German, and Shelby D. Hunt, "The Identity Salience Model of Relationship Marketing

Success: The Case of Nonprofit Marketing," *Journal of Marketing* 67 (April 2003): 89–105.
48. Sandra O'Loughlin, "The Wearin' o' the Green," *Brandweek*, April 23, 2007, pp. 26–27. For a critical response, see also John R. Ehrenfield, "Feeding the Beast," *Fast Company*, December 2006/January 2007, pp. 42–43.
49. Pete Engardio, "Beyond the Green Corporation," *BusinessWeek*, January 29, 2007, pp. 50–64.
50. Kamau High, "Bobby Shriver Sees (Product) Red," *Adweek Online*, September 24, 2007, www.adweek.com; Michelle Conlin, "Shop (In the Name of Love)," *BusinessWeek*, October 2, 2006; Carol L. Cone, Mark A. Feldman, and Alison T. DaSilva, "Cause and Effects," *Harvard Business Review* (July 2003): 95–101; Pat Auger, Paul Burke, Timothy Devinney, and Jordan J. Loviere, "What Will Consumers Pay for Social Product Features?" *Journal of Business Ethics* 42 (2003): 281–304; Hamish Pringle and Marjorie Thompson, *How Cause-Related Marketing Builds Brands* (New York: John Wiley & Sons, 1999); Christine Bittar, "Seeking Cause and Effect," *Brandweek*, November 11, 2002, pp. 19–24; "Marketing, Corporate Social Initiatives, and the Bottom Line," Marketing Science Institute Conference Summary, *MSI Report No. 01-106*, 2001.

Glossary

Activity-Based Cost (ABC) Accounting procedures that can quantify the true profitability of different activities by identifying their actual costs, 215.

Adoption an individual's decision to become a regular user of a product, 181.

Advertising any paid form of nonpersonal presentation and promotion of ideas, goods, or services, by an identified sponsor, 283.

Advertising Goal or Objective a specific communication task and achievement level to be accomplished with a specific audience in a specific period of time, 283.

Aspirational Groups groups a person hopes to join, 78.

Associative Network Memory Model a conceptual representation that views memory as consisting of a set of nodes and interconnecting links where nodes represent stored information or concepts and links represent the strength of association between this information or concepts, 83.

Attitude person's enduring favorable or unfavorable evaluation, emotional feeling, and action tendencies toward some object or idea, 87.

Augmented Product a product that includes features that go beyond consumer expectations and differentiate the product from competitors, 170.

Available Market the set of consumers who have interest, income, and access to a particular offer, 46.

Average Cost the cost per unit at a given level of production; it is equal to total costs divided by production, 214.

Banner Ads on the Internet, small, rectangular boxes containing text and perhaps a picture, 307.

Basic Product what specifically the actual product is, 170.

Belief descriptive thought that a person holds about something, 87.

Brand name, term, sign, symbol, or design, or a combination of these, intended to identify the goods or services of one seller or group of sellers and to differentiate them from those of the competitors, 129.

Brand Associations all brand-related thoughts, feelings, perceptions, images, experiences, beliefs, attitudes, and so on that become linked to the brand node, 84.

Brand Audit a consumer-focused exercise that involves a series of procedures to assess the health of the brand, uncover its sources of brand equity, and suggest ways to improve and leverage its equity, 135.

Brand Contact any information-bearing experience a customer or prospect has with the brand, the product category, or the market that relates to the offering, 133.

Brand Dilution when consumers no longer associate a brand with a specific product or highly similar products or start thinking less favorably about the brand, 139.

Brand Elements those trademarkable devices that serve to identify and differentiate the brand such as a brand name, logo, or character, 132.

Brand Equity the added value endowed to products and services, 130.

Brand Extension a company's use of an established brand to introduce a new product, 137.

Brand Knowledge all the thoughts, feelings, images, experiences, beliefs, and so on, that become associated with the brand, 131.

Brand Line all products sold under a particular brand, 137.

Brand Mix the set of all brand lines that a firm offers to buyers (also known as brand assortment), 137.

Brand Personality the specific mix of human traits that may be attributed to a particular brand, 79.

Brand Portfolio the set of all brands and brand lines a particular firm offers for sale to buyers in a particular category, 140.

Brand Promise the marketer's vision of what the brand must be and do for consumers, 131.

Brand Valuation an estimate of the total financial value of the brand, 136.

Branded Variants specific brand lines supplied to particular retailers or channels, 137.

Branding endowing products and services with the power of a brand, 129.

Branding Strategy the number and nature of common and distinctive brand elements applied to the different products sold by the firm, 137.

Break-Even Analysis a means by which management estimates how many units of the product the company would have to sell to break even with the given price and cost structure, 179.

Brick-and-Click existing companies that have added an online site for information and/or e-commerce, 244.

Business Database complete information about business customers' past purchases; past volumes, prices, and profits; and related data, 71.

Business Market all the organizations that acquire goods and services used in the production of other products or services that are sold, rented, or supplied to others, 95.

Buying Center several participants with differing interests, authority, status, and persuasiveness who are the decision-making unit of a buying organization, 98.

Capital Items long-lasting goods that facilitate developing or managing the finished product, 171.

Captive Products products that are necessary to the use of other products, such as razor blades or film, 224.

Category Membership the products or sets of products with which a brand competes and which function as close substitutes, 149.

Channel Conflict when one channel member's actions prevent the channel from achieving its goal, 241.

Channel Coordination when channel members are brought together to advance the goals of the channel, as opposed to their own potentially incompatible goals, 241.

Channel Power the ability to alter channel members' behavior so that they take actions they would not have taken otherwise, 238.

Co-Branding when two or more existing brands are combined into a product or are marketed together, 173.

Communication Adaptation changing marketing communications programs for each local market, 327.

Glossary

Communication-Effect Research determining whether an ad is communicating effectively, 288.

Company Demand company's estimated share of market demand at alternative levels of company marketing effort in a given time period, 48.

Company Sales Forecast expected level of company sales based on a chosen marketing plan and an assumed marketing environment, 48.

Competitive Advantage a company's ability to perform in one or more ways that competitors cannot or will not match, 152.

Conformance Quality the degree to which all the produced units are identical and meet the promised specifications, 152.

Conjoint Analysis a method for deriving the utility values that consumers attach to varying levels of a product's attributes, 178.

Consumer Behavior the behavior consumers display in searching for, purchasing, using, evaluating, and disposing of goods, services, and ideas, 77.

Consumerist Movement an organized movement of citizens and government to strengthen the rights and powers of buyers in relation to sellers, 56.

Consumption System the way the user performs the tasks of getting and using products and related services, 170.

Containerization putting the goods in boxes or trailers that are easy to transfer between two transportation modes, 262.

Contractual Sales Force manufacturers' reps, sales agents, and brokers, who are paid a commission based on sales, 313.

Convenience Goods products purchased frequently, immediately, and with a minimum of effort, 171.

Conventional Marketing Channel an independent producer, wholesaler(s), and retailer(s), 240.

Core Benefit the service or benefit the customer is really buying, 169.

Core Competency attribute that (1) is a source of competitive advantage by contributing significantly to perceived customer benefits, (2) has applications in a wide variety of markets, (3) is difficult for competitors to imitate, 23.

Core Values the belief systems that underlie consumer attitudes and behavior, and that determine people's choices and desires over the long term, 80.

Corporate Culture the shared experiences, stories, beliefs, and norms that characterize an organization, 29.

Countertrade when buyers offer other items as payment because they lack sufficient hard currency to pay for their purchases, 222.

Cues stimuli that determine when, where, and how a person responds, 83.

Culture the fundamental determinant of a person's wants and behavior, 77.

Customer Churn high rate of customer defection, 68.

Customer Database organized collection of comprehensive data about individual customers, prospects, or suspects that is current, accessible, and actionable for marketing purposes, 70.

Customer Equity the sum of lifetime values of all customers for a brand, 141.

Customer Lifetime Value (CLV) the net present value of the stream of future profits expected over the customer's lifetime purchases, 66.

Customer Perceived Value (CPV) difference between total customer's evaluation of all the benefits and the total customer cost, 60.

Customer Performance Scorecard how well the company is doing year after year on particular customer-based measures, 34.

Customer Profitability Analysis (CPA) a means of assessing and ranking customer profitability through accounting techniques such as Activity-Based Costing (ABC), 65.

Customer Relationship Management (CRM) process of managing detailed information about individual customers and managing all customer encounters to maximize customer loyalty, 67.

Customer Value Hierarchy five product levels that must be addressed by marketers in planning a market offering, 169.

Customerization combination of operationally driven mass customization with customized marketing in a way that empowers consumers to design the offering of their choice, 113.

Data mining use of statistical and mathematical techniques to extract information about individuals, trends, and segments, 71.

Data Warehouse a collection of current data captured, organized, and stored in a company's contact center, 71.

Database Marketing process of building, maintaining, and using customer databases and other databases (products, suppliers, resellers) for marketing purposes, 71.

Demand-Chain Planning designing the supply chain based on adopting a target market perspective and working backward, 232.

Direct (Company) Sales Force number of full- or part-time paid sales employees who work exclusively for the company, 313.

Direct Product Profitability (DPP) a way of measuring a product's handling costs from the time it reaches the warehouse until a customer buys it in the retail store, 251.

Dissociative Groups those groups whose values or behavior an individual rejects, 78.

Drive a strong internal stimulus impelling action, 83.

Dual Adaptation adapting both the product and the communications to the local market, 327

Durability a measure of a product's expected operating life under natural or stressful conditions, 152.

E-Business the use of electronic means and platforms to conduct a company's business, 244.

E-Commerce a company or site offers to transact or facilitate the selling of products and services online, 244.

E-Marketing company efforts to inform buyers, communicate, promote, and sell its offerings online, 244.

Environmental Threat challenge posed by an unfavorable external trend or development that would lead, in the absence of defensive marketing action, to deterioration in sales or profit, 30.

E-Purchasing purchase of goods, services, and information from online suppliers, 244.

Everyday Low Pricing (EDLP) in retailing, a constant low price with few or no price promotions and special sales, 219.

Exclusive Distribution severely limiting the number of intermediaries to maintain control over the service level and outputs offered by resellers, 236.

Expectancy-Value Model consumers evaluate products and services by combining their brand beliefs—positive and negative—according to their weighted importance, 87.

Expected Product a set of attributes and conditions buyers normally expect when they purchase a particular product, 170.

Experience Curve (learning curve) a decline in the average cost that occurs with accumulated production experience, 215.

Fad a craze that is unpredictable, short-lived, and without social, economic, and political significance, 50.

Family Brand a parent brand that is associated with multiple brand extensions, 137

Glossary

Family of Orientation parents and siblings, 78.

Family of Procreation spouse and children, 78.

Features characteristics that enhance the basic function of a product, 152.

Fixed Costs costs that do not vary with production or sales revenue, 214.

Flexible Market Offering the product and service elements that all segment members value, plus discretionary options that some segment members value, 111.

Focus Group a gathering of six to ten people who are carefully selected based on certain demographic, psychographic, or other considerations and brought together to discuss various topics of interest, 43.

Forecasting the art of anticipating what buyers are likely to do under a given set of conditions, 50.

Form the size, shape, or physical structure of a product, 152.

Frequency Programs (FPs) programs to reward customers who buy frequently and/or in substantial amounts, 70.

Generics unbranded, plainly packaged, less expensive versions of common products, 255.

Global Firm a firm that operates in more than one country and captures R&D, production, logistical, marketing, and financial advantages in its costs and reputation that are not available to purely domestic competitors, 324

Global Industry an industry in which the strategic positions of competitors in major geographic or national markets are fundamentally affected by their overall global positions, 324

Goal Formulation the process of developing specific goals for the planning period, 31.

Going-Rate Pricing price based largely on competitors' prices, 219.

Gray Market branded products diverted from normal or authorized distribution channels in the country of product origin or across international borders, 328

High-Low Pricing charging higher prices on an everyday basis but then running frequent promotions and special sales, 219.

Holistic Marketing a concept based on the development, design, and implementation of marketing programs, processes, and activities that recognizes their breadth and interdependencies, 12.

Horizontal Marketing System two or more unrelated companies put together resources or programs to exploit an emerging market opportunity, 241.

Hybrid Channels use of multiple channels of distribution to reach customers in a defined market, 231.

Industry a group of firms that offer a product or class of products that are close substitutes for one another, 155.

Ingredient Branding a special case of co-branding that involves creating brand equity for materials, components, or parts that are necessarily contained within other branded products, 173.

Innovation any good, service, or idea that is perceived by someone as new, 182.

Innovation Diffusion Process the spread of a new idea from its source of invention or creation to its ultimate users or adopters, 182.

Institutional Market schools, hospitals, nursing homes, prisons, and other institutions that must provide goods and services to people in their care, 95.

Integrated Logistics Systems (ILS) materials management, material flow systems, and physical distribution, abetted by information technology (IT), 258.

Integrated Marketing mixing and matching marketing activities to maximize their individual and collective efforts, 133.

Integrated Marketing Channel System channel system in which strategies and tactics of one system reflect the strategies and tactics of selling through other channels, 241.

Integrated Marketing Communications (IMC) a concept of marketing communications planning that recognizes the added value of a comprehensive plan, 277.

Intensive Distribution the manufacturer placing the goods or services in as many outlets as possible, 236.

Internal Branding activities and processes that help to inform and inspire employees, 134.

Joint Venture a company in which multiple investors share ownership and control, 326.

Learning changes in an individual's behavior that arise from experience, 83.

Learning Curve the decline in the average cost with accumulated production experience, 215.

Licensed Product using the brand name licensed from one firm on a product made by another firm, 137.

Life-Cycle Cost the product's purchase cost plus the discounted cost of maintenance and repair less the discounted salvage value, 203.

Lifestyle person's pattern of living in the world as expressed in activities, interests, and opinions, 80.

Line Extension using the parent brand to brand a new product that targets a new market segment within a category currently served by the parent brand, 137.

Line Stretching lengthening the product line beyond its current range, 172.

Loyalty a customer's commitment to re-buy or re-patronize a preferred product or service, 62.

Market-Buildup Method identifying all the potential buyers in each market and estimating their potential purchases, 49.

Market Demand total volume that would be bought by a defined customer group in a defined geographical area, within a given period, in a defined marketing environment under a defined marketing program, 47.

Market Forecast the market demand corresponding to the level of industry marketing expenditure, 48.

Market Logistics planning the infrastructure to meet demand, then implementing and controlling the physical flows or materials and final goods from points of origin to points of use, to meet customer requirements at a profit, 258.

Market Potential limit approached by market demand as industry marketing expenditures approach infinity for a given marketing environment, 48.

Market Share level of selective demand for the company's product, 47.

Market-Penetration Pricing pricing strategy where prices start low to drive higher sales volume from price-sensitive customers and produce productivity gains, 212.

Market-Skimming Pricing pricing strategy where prices start high and are slowly lowered over time to maximize profits from less price-sensitive customers, 213.

Marketer someone who seeks a response (attention, a purchase, a vote, a donation) from another party, called the prospect, 5.

Marketing process of planning and executing the conception, pricing, promotion, and distribution of ideas, goods, and services to create exchanges that satisfy individual and organizational goals, 2.

Glossary

Marketing Audit comprehensive, systematic, independent, and periodic examination of a company's (or SBUs) marketing environment, objectives, strategies, and activities, 333.

Marketing Channel System the particular set of marketing channels employed by a firm, 231.

Marketing Channels sets of interdependent organizations involved in the process of making a product or service available for use or consumption, 231.

Marketing Communications the means by which firms attempt to inform, persuade, and remind consumers—directly or indirectly—about products and brands that they sell, 266.

Marketing Communications Mix advertising, sales promotion, events and experiences, public relations and publicity, direct marketing, and personal selling, 267.

Marketing Information System (MIS) people, equipment, and procedures that gather, sort, analyze, evaluate, and distribute information to marketing decision makers, 39.

Marketing Intelligence System set of procedures and sources used by managers to obtain everyday information about developments in the marketing environment, 40.

Marketing Management the art and science of choosing target markets and getting, keeping, and growing customers through creating, delivering, and communicating superior customer value, 3.

Marketing Metrics the set of measures that helps firms to quantify, compare, and interpret their marketing performance, 34.

Marketing Network the company and its supporting stakeholders, with whom it has built mutually profitable business relationships, 12.

Marketing Opportunity area of buyer need in which a company can perform profitably, 30.

Marketing Plan written document that summarizes what the marketer has learned about the marketplace, indicates how the firm plans to reach its marketing objectives, and helps direct and coordinate the marketing effort, 26, 33.

Marketing Public Relations (MPR) publicity and other activities that build corporate or product image to facilitate achievement of marketing goals, 295.

Marketing Research systematic design, collection, analysis, and reporting of data and findings that are relevant to a specific marketing situation facing the company, 40.

Markup pricing an item by adding a standard increase to the product's cost, 216.

Media Selection finding the most cost-effective media to deliver the desired number and type of exposures to the target audience, 285.

Megamarketing the strategic coordination of economic, psychological, political, and public relations skills, to gain the cooperation of a number of parties in order to enter or operate in a given market, 124.

Membership Groups groups having a direct influence on a person, 78.

Microsales Analysis examination of specific products and territories that failed to produce expected sales, 34.

Microsite a limited area on the Web managed and paid for by an external advertiser/company, 307.

Mission Statement statement of why the organization exists, which is shared with managers, employees, and (in many cases) customers, 27.

Motive a need that is sufficiently pressing to drive a person to act, 81.

Opinion Leader the person in informal, product-related communications who offers advice or information about a specific product or category, 78.

Organization a company's structures, policies, and corporate culture, 29.

Organizational Buying decision-making process by which formal organizations establish the need for purchased products and services and identify, evaluate, and choose among alternative brands and suppliers, 95.

Overall Market Share the company's sales expressed as a percentage of total market sales, 34.

Overhead costs that do not vary with production or sales revenue, 214.

Packaging designing and producing the container for a product, 173.

Parent Brand an existing brand that gives birth to a brand extension or sub-brand, 137.

Partner Relationship Management (PRM) activities to build mutually satisfying long-term relations with key partners such as suppliers, distributors, ad agencies, and marketing research suppliers, 31.

Penetrated Market the set of consumers who are buying a company's product, 47.

Perception process by which an individual selects, organizes, and interprets information inputs to create a meaningful picture of the world, 82.

Performance Quality the level at which the product's primary characteristics operate, 152.

Personal Communications Channels two or more persons communicating directly face-to-face, person-to-audience, over the telephone, or through e-mail, 272.

Personal Influence the effect one person has on another's attitude or purchase probability, 182.

Personality distinguishing psychological characteristics that lead to relatively consistent and enduring responses to environmental stimuli, 79.

Place Advertising ads that appear outside of home and where consumers work and play, 287.

Point-of-Purchase the location where a purchase is made, typically in a retail setting, 287.

Positioning act of designing the company's offering and image to occupy a distinctive place in the target market's mind, 148.

Potential Market the set of consumers who profess a sufficient level of interest in a market offer, 46.

Potential Product all the possible augmentations and transformations the product or offering might undergo in the future, 170.

Price Discrimination pricing approach in which a company sells a product or service at two or more prices that do not reflect a proportional difference in costs, 223.

Private Label Brand brands developed and marketed by retailers and wholesalers, 254.

Product anything that can be offered to a market to satisfy a want or need, 169.

Product Adaptation altering the product to meet local conditions or preferences, 327.

Product Invention creating something new via product development or other means, 327.

Product Mix (Assortment) set of all products and items that a particular marketer offers for sale, 171.

Product System group of diverse but related items that function in a compatible manner, 171.

Profitable Customer a person, household, or company that over time yields a revenue stream that exceeds by an acceptable amount the company's cost stream of attracting, selling, and servicing that customer, 69.

Glossary

Prospect an individual or group from whom a marketer seeks to get a response such as a purchase, a vote, or donation, 64.

Public any group that has an actual or potential interest in or impact on a company's ability to achieve its objectives, 295.

Public Relations (PR) variety of programs that are designed to promote or protect a company's image or its individual products, 295.

Publicity the task of securing editorial space—as opposed to paid space—in print and broadcast media to promote something, 295.

Pull Strategy when the manufacturer uses advertising and promotion to persuade consumers to ask intermediaries for the product, thus inducing the intermediaries to order it, 232.

Pure-Click companies that have launched a Web site without any previous existence as a firm, 244.

Push Strategy when the manufacturer uses its sales force and trade promotion money to induce intermediaries to carry, promote, and sell the product to end users, 231.

Quality the totality of features and characteristics of a product or service that bear on its ability to satisfy stated or implied needs, 64.

Reference Groups all the groups that have a direct or indirect influence on a person's attitudes or behavior, 78.

Reference Price pricing information a consumer retains in memory which is used to interpret and evaluate a new price, 211.

Relationship Marketing building mutually satisfying long-term relationships with key parties, in order to earn and retain their business, 12.

Relative Market Share market share in relation to a company's largest competitor, 35.

Retailer (Retail Store) any business enterprise whose sales volume comes primarily from retailing, 249.

Retailing all activities involved in selling goods or services directly to final consumers for personal, nonbusiness use, 260.

Risk Analysis a method by which possible rates of returns and their probabilities are calculated by obtaining estimates for uncertain variables affecting profitability, 179.

Role the activities a person is expected to perform, 78.

Sales Analysis measuring and evaluating actual sales in relation to goals, 34.

Sales Budget conservative estimate of the expected sales volume; used primarily for making current purchasing, production, and cash-flow decisions, 48.

Sales Promotion collection of incentive tools, mostly short term, designed to stimulate quicker or greater purchase of particular products or services by consumers or the trade, 289.

Sales Quota sales goal set for a product line, company division, or sales representative, 48.

Sales-Variance Analysis a measure of the relative contribution of different factors to a gap in sales performance, 34.

Satisfaction a person's feelings of pleasure or disappointment resulting from comparing a product's perceived performance (or outcome) in relation to his or her expectations, 62.

Scenario Analysis developing plausible representations of a firm's possible future that make different assumptions about forces driving the market and include different uncertainties, 29.

Selective Attention the mental process of screening out certain stimuli while noticing others, 82.

Selective Distribution the use of more than a few but less than all of the intermediaries who are willing to carry a particular product, 236.

Served Market all the buyers who are able and willing to buy a company's product, 34.

Served Market Share a company's sales expressed as a percentage of the total sales to its served market, 34.

Service any act or performance that one party can offer to another that is essentially intangible and does not result in the ownership of anything, 192.

Shopping Goods products that the customer, in the process of selection and purchase, characteristically compares on the basis of suitability, quality, price, and style, 171.

Social Classes homogeneous and enduring divisions in a society, which are hierarchically ordered and whose members share similar values, interests, and behavior, 77.

Specialty Goods products with unique characteristics or brand identification for which a sufficient number of buyers are willing to make a special purchasing effort, 171.

Stakeholder-Performance Scorecard a measure to track the satisfaction of various constituencies who have a critical interest in and impact on the company's performance, 34.

Status one's position within his or her own hierarchy or culture, 78.

Straight Extension introducing a product in a foreign market without any change in the product, 327.

Strategic Business Unit (SBU) a business that can be planned separately from the rest of the company, with its own set of competitors and a manager who is responsible for strategic planning and profit performance, 28.

Strategic Group firms pursuing the same strategy directed to the same target market, 31, 157.

Strategic Marketing Plan laying out the target markets and the value proposition that will be offered based on analysis of the best market opportunities, 26.

Strategy a company's game plan for achieving its goals, 31.

Subbrand combining a new brand with an existing brand, 137.

Subculture subdivisions of a culture that provide more specific identification and socialization, such as nationalities, religions, racial groups, and geographical regions, 54.

Supersegment a set of segments sharing some exploitable similarity, 123.

Supplies and Business Services short-term goods and services that facilitate developing or managing the finished product, 171.

Supply Chain the partnerships a firm forges with suppliers and distributors to deliver value to customers; also known as a value delivery network, 23.

Supply Chain Management (SCM) plan specifying the firm's procuring the right inputs (raw materials, components, and capital equipment); converting them efficiently into finished products; and dispatching them to the final destinations, 257.

Tactical Marketing Plan marketing tactics, including product features, promotion, merchandising, pricing sales channels, and services, 26.

Target Costing determining the cost that must be achieved to sell a new product, with the desired functions, at the price consumers are willing to pay, given the offering's appeal and competitors' prices, 216.

Target Market the part of the qualified available market the company decides to pursue, 46.

Target-Return Pricing determining the price that would yield the firm's target rate of return on investment (ROI), 218.

Telemarketing the use of telephone and call centers to attract prospects, sell to existing customers, and provide service by taking orders and answering questions, 304.

Total Costs the sum of the fixed and variable costs for any given level of production, 214.

Glossary

Total Customer Cost perceived monetary value of the bundle of costs that customers expect to incur in evaluating, obtaining, using, and disposing of the product or service, 60.

Total Customer Value bundle of benefits that customers expect from a given product or service, 60.

Trend direction or sequence of events that has some momentum and durability, 50.

Unsought Goods products that consumers do not know about or do not normally think of buying, 171.

Value Chain a group of strategically relevant activities that create value and cost in a specific business, 22.

Value-Delivery Network *see* supply chain, 23.

Value-Delivery System all the experiences the customer will have on the way to obtaining and using the offering, 62.

Value Network a system of partnerships and alliances that a firm creates to source, augment, and deliver its offerings, 232.

Value Pricing winning loyal customers by charging a fairly low price for a high-quality offering, 219.

Value Proposition the whole cluster of benefits the company promises to deliver, 7.

Variable Costs costs that vary directly with the level of production, 214.

Vertical Marketing System (VMS) producer, wholesaler(s), and retailer(s) acting as a unified system, 240.

Wholesaling all of the activities involved in selling goods or services to those who buy for resale or business use, 255.

Yield Pricing situation in which companies offer (1) discounted but limited early purchases, (2) higher-priced late purchases, and (3) the lowest rates on unsold inventory just before it expires, 224.

Zero-Level Channel a manufacturer selling directly to the final customer (also known as direct marketing channel), 234.

Index

1Up.com, 112
3M, 11, 34
7-Eleven, 249
7 Ss, 32
20th Century Fox Home Entertainment, 32
20–80 rule, 64
42 Below, 132

A

Aaker, David A., 109n31, 138, 144n34, 145n38, 145n42, 145n45
Aaker, Jennifer, 73n9, 79, 91n16, 91n17, 91n20
Abboud, Leila, 246n1
Abe, Makoto, 229n27
Abell, Derek, 36n15
Abelson, Jenn, 227n1
Abhijit, Roy, 127n36
Abita Brewing Co., 154
Abraham, Magid M., 92n30, 299n28
Absolut, 52
Accenture, 150, 155
Accountability, financial, 15
Accounting. *See* Activity-based costing
Accumulated production, 215–16
ACE Hardware, 251
Acohido, Byron, 318n12
Active information search, 85–86
Activity-based costing (ABC), 32, 35, 65, 215
Actual self-concept, 79
Acura, 172
Adamson, Alan P., 144n29
Adamy, Janet, 18n1
Adapted marketing mix, 327
Adaptors, 163
Add-on spending, 141
Adler, Jerry, 57n1
Administered VMS, 240
Adolescents. *See* Teens
Adoption, of products, 181–83
Advertising, 267, 268, 275
 budget, 284
 defining, 283
 frequency of, 284, 285–86
 media selection and effectiveness, 285–89
 objectives, 283–84
 online, 307
 sales promotion versus, 290
 search-related, 307
 specialty, 292

Advertising allowance, 291
Advertising campaigns, developing, 284–85
Advertising expenditures, share of, 288–89
Advertising Women of New York, 285
Advocates, for customers, 68, 69
Affiliate programs, 307
Affluence, 174
Affordable budget method, 274
Agarwal, Manoj K., 144n35
Age, 79, 114
Agents, 236, 256
Aggrawal, Pankaj, 73n9
Ahluwalia, R., 145n46
Ailawadi, Kusum L., 37n39, 143n12, 229n31, 264n24, 299n22, 299n31, 300n34
Airbus, 160
Aksoy, Lerzan, 74n22
Alba, Joseph W., 145n46
Albers, Sonke, 320n47
Alden, Dana L., 337n18
Allen, James, 19n23
Allenby, G., 126n29
Alley, Kirstie, 272
Alliances, 307
AlliedSignal, 104
Allison, Sarah, 126n18
Allowance, and price, 222, 223, 291
Allstate, 311
Alpha testing, 180
Altera, 315
Alternatives, evaluation of, 86, 87–88
Altria Group, 161
Amaldoss, Wilfred, 228n13
Amazon, 9, 184, 244, 307
Ambler, Tim, 37n36, 279n10
American Airlines, 41–42, 43, 44, 45
American Association of Advertising Agencies, 277
American Express, 52, 202, 292
American Idol, 292
American Marketing Association, 3, 18n3, 129, 266
Anand, Bharat N., 145n41
Anderson, Eric, 228n15, 299n22
Anderson, Erin, 246n2, 246n4, 246n12, 247n23, 247n25
Anderson, Eugene W., 73n6, 73n12, 73n14
Anderson, Howard, 211

Anderson, James C., 19n24, 107n2, 107n11, 108n16, 108n24, 111, 125n2, 126n12, 228n23, 264n29
Anderson, John R., 92n28
Anderson, Richard E., 338n29
Anderson, Ronald D., 207n39
Andrews, J., 145n43
Angwin, Julia, 108n21
Annual-plan control, 333
Ansari, Asim, 205n11, 246n5
Antia, Kersi D., 247n25
Anticipatory pricing, 225
Antitrust actions, 161
Antorini, Yun Mi, 144n33
AOL, 307
Apple, 3, 46, 150, 153, 163, 295, 327–28
Approvers, in buying center, 99
Aramark Corp., 96
Arbitration, 243
Area market potential, 49
Area market specialists, 329
Ariely, Dan, 227n4, 247n28
Armbruster, Adam, 297n1
Armitt, Claire, 207n40
Armstrong, J. Scott, 167n38
Arnett, Dennis B., 338n47
Arnold, David, 337n22
Arnold, Mark J., 206n23
Arnold, Thomas K., 37n32
Arnold Worldwide, 275
Arnould, Eric J., 57n8, 206n23
Arya, Anil, 247n24
Ascending bids, 220
Aspirational groups, 78
Asplund, Christer, 18n7
Asset turnover, 35
Association of National Advertisers, 14
Associations, secondary, 134–35
Associative network memory model, 83
Assortment. *See* Product assortment
AT&T, 46
Athlete's Foot, 249
Atkin, Thomas, 108n28
Atmosphere, 252–53, 292
Attention
 heightened, 85
 selective, 82–83
Attitudes, 87, 119
Attitudes of others, 88
Auction-type pricing, 220
Audience, 270, 287

Audit, 135–36
 brand, 135–36
 marketing audit, 333–34
Auger, Pat, 338n46, 339n48
Augmented product, 170
Auguste, Byron G., 208n47
Automated warehouses, 260
Automatic vending, 250
Automobile Association, 149
Available market, 46
Average cost, 214–15
Average customer longevity, 318n7
Avis, 112
Avlonitis, George J., 190n52
Avon, 239, 311, 315
Awareness, 297
Awareness set, 86, 87

B

Babcock, Charles, 57n2
Backward flow, of channel, 232
Backward invention, 327
Badrinarayanan, Vishag, 281n31
Bagley, Constance, 143n4
Bagozzi, Richard P., 280n16, 320n53, 320n55
Baker, Stephen, 58n28
Baker, Thomas L., 247n19
Baker, Walter, 228n17
Bakken, David, 189n32
Balachander, Subramanian, 145n40
Balasubramanian, Siva K., 188n16
Balasubramanian, Sridhar, 246n5
Ball, Deborah, 227n3
Ballantyne, David, 19n22
Balter, David, 309, 319n29
Bamford, Joanna, 75n45
Banerjee, Subhabrata Bobby, 58n31
Bank of America, 160
Bannan, Karen J., 319n35
Bargaining power, 155
Barker, Olivia, 318n8
Barletta, Marti, 126n21
Barnes & Noble, 239
Barnes, James, 298n3
Barone, Michael J., 298n3
Barrett, Amy, 207n42
Barter markets, 102
Bartering, 222
Barwise, Patrick, 145n47, 165n8
Basic product, 170
Bass, Frank M., 18n18, 190n44
Bass, Stephen J., 263n2

347

Index

Bassin, Susan B., 188n15
Bass Pro Shops, 253
Batelle, John, 206n28, 319n35
Bates, Albert D., 263n2
Batra, Rajeev, 144n34, 337n18
Bauer, Raymond A., 93n40
Baxter Healthcare, 221
Bayer, 324
Bayot, Jennifer, 91n13
BB&T Corp., 292
BBC, 70
Beach, David, 189n34
Bearden, William O., 145n39
Beatty, Sharon E., 91n8
Beck, John C., 298n13
Bed Bath & Beyond, 114
Behavior. *See* Consumer behavior
Behavioral data, 43
Behavioral segmentation, 115, 117–19
Beirne, Mike, 207n43
Belch, George E., 280n16
Beliefs, 87
Bell, David R., 263n11
Bellman, Eric, 227n3
Bello, D. C., 143n6
Bemner, Brian, 187n5
Ben & Jerry's, 293
Benchmarks, 22
Bendapudi, Neeli, 205n1
Bendle, Neil T., 37n37, 338n35
Benefits, 118, 314
Benet-Martinez, Veronica, 91n17
Benetton, 251, 254
Benito, Javier, 207n43
Bennett, Peter D., 187n4, 279n7
BenQ Corp., 20
Berelson, Bernard, 92n26
Berens, Guido, 144n34
Bergen, Mark, 228n16
Berger, Warren, 298n17
Bernacchi, Gina, 280n26
Berner, Robert, 143n8, 263n5, 319n32, 338n42
Berry, Leonard L., 75n38, 205n1, 205n2, 205n6, 206n25, 207n32, 207n33, 207n35
Best Buy, 40, 231
Best, R. J., 121, 127n34
Beta testing, 180
Better Business Bureau, 223
Bettman, James R., 90n2, 92n32
Betzold, James, 298n15
Beucke, Dan, 227n1
Bharadwaj, Sundar G., 337n12
Bhattacharya, C. B., 338n46, 338n47
Bianco, Anthony, 279n4
Bijmolt, Tammo H. A., 228n20
Billboards, 287
Binkley, Christina, 228n10
Biogenic needs, 81
Birger, Jon, 167n42
Bitner, Mary Jo, 205n7, 205n10, 206n20, 206n21, 206n23, 207n36, 207n38
Bittar, Christine, 339n48
BJ's Wholesale, 249
Blackwell, Roger D., 58n10, 92n32, 143n9, 280n12, 280n14
Blanket family names, 138

Blattberg, Robert C., 125n3, 146n51, 146n52, 299n21, 299n26
Blau, John, 57n7
Block, Martin P., 300n32
Blodgett, Jeffrey G., 207n39
Blogs, 310–11
Bloom, Paul N., 167n39, 338n45
Bloomingdale's, 250, 253
Blue ocean strategy, 156
Blue Ribbon Sports, 13
Boatwright, Peter, 187n6, 228n10
Body Shop, 249, 254
Boehret, Katherine, 246n8
Boeing, 160, 293
Bolton, Ruth N., 108n25, 263n10
Bommer, Michael R. W., 320n51
Bond, Sir John, 126n9
Bonoma, Thomas V., 120
Bonuses, 314
Booms, B. H., 205n7, 206n23
Borch, Fred J., 18n18
Borden, Neil H., 19n26
Borders, 200
Bordley, Robert, 187n6
Boston, William, 36n1
Bottomly, Paul A., 143n19
Boulding, William, 73n10, 207n32
Boutilier, Robert, 91n7
Bovée, Courtland L., 107n13
Bowen, David, 206n20, 206n22
Bowers, Katherine, 263n12
Bowman, Douglas, 92n31, 299n23
Boyd, Harper W., Jr., 187n3
Boyle, Matthew, 298n16
Brady, Michael K., 207n32
Brakuz, J. J., 190n43
Branch, Shelly, 263n12
Brand-asset management team (BAMT), 330
Brand associations, 84
Brand attitude, 271
Brand audits, 135–36
Brand awareness, 270–71
Brand bonding, 134
Brand concept, 178
Brand contact, 133, 267
Brand dilution, 139–40
Branded house, 138
Branded variants, 137
Brand elements, 132–33, 202–3
Brand equity, 128–29
  brand strategy and customer equity, 137–42
  building, 131–35
  defining, 129–31
  executive summary, 142
  marketing communications and, 267, 269
  measuring and managing, 135–37
Brand equity drivers, 132
Brand extension, 137, 139–40
Brand funnel, 118
Brand identity, 133
Brand image, 133, 174
Branding, 129–30, 143n7, 173
Brand knowledge, 131, 135
Brand line, 137
Brand-management organization, 329
Brand mix, 137
Brand personality, 79

Brand portfolios, 140–41
Brand positioning. *See* Positioning; Positioning strategy
Brand promise, 131
Brand purchase intention, 271
Brand reinforcement, 136
Brand revitalization, 136–37
Brands, 7, 9
  building, 16–17
  cult, 134
  defining, 129
  pricing and, 221
  private labels, 254–55
  product relationships, 171–73
  role of, 129
  service, 202–203
Brandt, John R., 18n10
Brand strategy, 137–41
Brand tracking, 135–36
Brand valuation, 136
Brandweek (magazine), 14
Branson, Sir Richard, 296
Brasel, S. Adam, 73n9
Brat, Ilan, 187n1
Break-even analysis, 179
Break-even volume, 218–19
Brick-and-click companies, 244, 245
Bridges, 310
Bright, Becky, 107n13
British Airways, 296
Brochures, 286
Broder, John M., 18n8
Brodie, Roderick J., 74n31
Brokers, 256
Broniarczyk, Susan M., 145n46, 165n7
Bronnenberg, Bart J., 299n22
Brookstone, 251
Brown, George H., 126n29
Brown, Heidi, 336n4
Brown, J. J., 319n33
Brown, John, 92n29
Brown, J. R., 247n25
Brown, Robert George, 299n27
Brown, Stephen W., 207n38, 207n39, 331, 338n42
Brown, Stuart F., 167n45, 187n5
Brown, Thomas J., 144n34, 320n54
Brown, William P., 298n4
Bruce, Norris, 300n33
Bruggen, Gerrit H. van, 144n34
Brunner, Thomas A., 165n6
Bucklin, Louis P., 246n9
Budget
  advertising, 284
  research and development, 55–56
  sales, 48
  sales promotion, 292
  total marketing communications, 274
Bulkeley, William M., 246n8
Bulk breaking, 256
Burger King, 307
Burhenne, Wim, 189n32
Burkan, Wayne, 58n18
Burke, Paul, 338n46, 339n48
Burnkrant, Robert E., 280n17
Burns, David J., 91n7

Burson-Mastellar and Roper Starch Worldwide Study, 272
Burton, Scott, 188n16
Busch, Paul S., 190n52
Business, defining the, 27–28
Business advisory services, 171
Business analysis, for new products, 179
Business buying. *See* Organizational buying
Business database, 71
Business legislation, 56
Business market, 95, 96
Business market segmentation, 113, 119–20
Business mission, 29, 30
Business promotion, 289, 292
Business relationships, 104–6
Business sector, 192
Business unit, on organizational level, 25, 26
Business unit strategic planning, 29–33
BusinessWeek, 288
Buss, Dale, 58n12, 126n7
Butman, John, 319n29
Butterball Turkey, 195
Buvik, Arnt, 109n32, 109n35
Buyback arrangement, 222
Buyclasses, 101
Buyer-readiness stage, 118–19
Buyers, 96, 99, 117, 154, 155
Buyers' intentions, survey of, 50
Buygrid framework, 101
Buying, by wholesalers, 256. *See also* Organizational buying
Buying alliances, 102
Buying center, 98–100
Buying decision process, consumer, 85–90
Buying situations, 97–98
Buyphases, 101
Buzz marketing, 308, 309
Buzzell, Robert D., 74n21; 167n40, 190n46
BzzAgent, 308, 309
Bypass attack, 162
By-product pricing, 225
Byrne, John A., 108n29
Byrnes, Nanette, 126n14, 320n49
Byron, Ellen, 143n8

C

Cadbury, 139
CaféMom, 308
Calantone, Roger J., 167n36
Calder, Bobby, 144n23
Callahan, Sean, 264n28
Call reports, 317
Calvin Klein, 151
Campaign. *See* Advertising
Campbell, Colin, 126n9
Campbell, Margaret C., 93n40, 229n36
Cannibalization, 140, 243
Cannon, Joseph P., 108n30
Capell, Kerry, 75n43, 91n21, 227n5, 246n1, 263n1, 300–301n57
Capital items, 171

Index

Capon, Noel, 320n46
Captive-product pricing, 224
Carbone, Lewis P., 205n8
Carey, John, 57n1
Carlotti, Stephen J., 190n52
Carlton, Jim, 247n27
Carmon, Ziv, 90n2
Carpenter, Gregory S., 165n7, 189n37
Carr, Coeli, 144n26
Carrefour, 231, 249
Carroll, Doug, 75n46
Carson, Stephen J., 188n19
Cartoon Network, 162
Cash-and-carry wholesalers, 256
Cash cows, 141
Cash discounts, 223
Cash rebates, 222
Cash refund offers, 291
Cassidy, Hilary, 300n42
Catalog marketing, 304
Catalog showrooms, 249
Catalog sites, 102. *See also* Internet, E-commerce marketing, Websites
Category benefits, 150
Category extension, 137
Category killers, 249
Category management, 330
Category membership, 149, 150–51
Category points-of-parity, 150
Caterpillar, 27, 46, 60–61, 95, 168–69
Catherwood, Dwight W., 300n48
Caudron, Shari, 167n43
Causal research, 42
Cause marketing, 16
Cause-related marketing, 16, 334–35
Cavusgil, S. Tamer, 337n12
CBS, 266
Cebrzynski, Gregg, 93n43
Celebrity marketing, 3
Celente, Gerald, 58n17
Cell phones. *See* M-commerce
Cemex, 153
Cents-off deals, 291
Cesar, Jacques, 299n31
Chakravarti, D., 280n19
Challagalla, G. N., 320n44
Chamberlain, Lisa, 58n13
Champy, James, 36n6
Chandy, Rajesh, 189n35, 190n47, 190n50, 298n5, 298–99n20
Chang, Dae Ryun, 144n28
Chang, Tung-Zong, 228n22
Channel arrangements, modifying, 239
Channel captain, 240
Channel conflict, 241–43
Channel coordination, 241, 242–43
Channel differentiation, 154
Channel members, 236–39
Channel power, 238
Channel pricing, 224
Channel specialist, 164
Channel stewardship, 240
Chao, Angela, 228n13
Charles Schwab, 195, 198
Chattopadhyay, Amitava, 319n35, 336n8

Cheesman, Henry, 229n34
ChemConnect.com, 102
Cheng, Kipp, 298n15
Chevalier, Judith, 320n39
Chevrolet, 141
Chicken of the Sea, 68
Chief Marketing Officer (CMO), 2, 5, 6, 331
Children, and consumer behavior, 78
China, 1–2, 10
Chintagunta, Pradeep K., 108n24, 228n23, 319n21
Choice set, 86, 87
Chowdhury, Jhinuk, 320n54
Christensen, Clayton M., 188n23
Christopher, Martin, 19n22
Chu, Kathy, 229n28
Chu, Wujin, 320n54
Chung, Tuck Siong, 205n2
Chura, Hillary, 91n9
Churchill, Gilbert A., Jr., 107n7, 320n54
Cimperman, John D., 93n43
Cioletti, Jeff, 126n23, 264n19
Circle K, 249
Circuit City, 249
Cirque du Soleil, 203
Cisco, 94, 95, 287
Citibank, 112, 173, 200
Citigroup, 202
Citizens Bank, 241
Clancy, Heather, 36n12
Clancy, Kevin J., 58n14
Claritas Inc., 114
Clark, Bruce H., 166n21
Clark, Don, 36n12
Clement, Michael, 189n37
Clients, 68, 69, 292
Clifton, Rita, 142n3
Cline, Thomas W., 280n19
Clingman, Mary, 206n17
Cliques, 308, 310
Cloners, 163
Closing, 312
Clough, Bethany, 264n18
Club Med, 194
Club membership programs, 70
Clustered preferences, 111
ClusterPlus, 126n16
Clutter, 284
CMI Marketing, 308
Coast, Rhonda, 107n13
Co-branding, 173
Coca-Cola, 11, 111, 124, 136, 155, 156, 158, 160, 162, 224, 241, 284, 287, 292, 302
Coe, Mary Ellen, 190n52
Cognitive space, 25
Cohen, Dorothy, 58n33, 338n40
Cohen, Joel B., 92n36
Cohn, Laura, 75n45
Cohorts, 52
Coke.com, 302
Colbert, Stephen, 296
Cole, Catherine, 188n16
Coleman, Cametta, 263n14
Coleman, Richard P., 91n5
Colgate, 330
Colgate, Mark, 206n20, 206n22
Colgate-Palmolive, 112, 125
Collaborative network, 24

Collins, Tom, 318n2
Columbia/HCA, 221
Colvin, Geoffrey, 108n29, 337n28
Combination stores, 249
Comer, James M., 108n20
Commercialization, 181
Commissions, 314
Commitment, expressing, 292
Common carrier, 262
Communicability, 183
Communication
  company capabilities and, 10
  positioning strategy and, 148–52
  value and, 17
Communication adaptation, 327
Communication channels, 8, 272–74
Communication-effect research, 288
Communication metrics, 332
Communication platforms, 268
Communications
  corporate, 295
  objectives, 270–71
  retailing and, 253
  See also Marketing communications; Mass communications; Personal communications
Community involvement, corporate, 16
Company capabilities, 10
Company demand, 48
Company image, 174
Company orientation, 10–16
Company sales force, 313
Company sales potential, 48
Company trust dimensions, 104–5
Compatibility, 183
Compensation deal, 222
Compensation, for sales force, 314
Competition, 8–9
  advertising and, 284
  global marketplace, 324–29
  industry and market views of, 155–56
  marketing channels, 241–43
  retailing, 241
  sales promotion and, 290
Competitive advantage, 23, 152
Competitive forces, 154–56
Competitive frame of reference, 149
Competitive-parity budget, 274
Competitive points-of-parity, 150
Competitive strategies, 159–64
Competitor-centered company, 163–64
Competitor orientations, 163–64
Competitors, 154–56
  acquiring, 28
  analyzing, 157–59
  executive summary, 165
  pricing and, 216, 225–26
  selecting, 158–59
Complaints, 201
Concentration and advertising, 288
Concentric diversification strategy, 28
Concept development, 177
Concept testing, 178
Conditions of sale, 236–37

Cone, Carol L., 339n48
Conformance quality, 64, 152
Conglomerate diversification strategy, 29
Conlin, Michelle, 263n12, 339n48
Connectors, 310
Connelly, Karin, 280n26
Consideration set, 86, 87
Constellation Wines U.S., 118
Constraints, on marketing channels, 235–36
Consumer adoption process, 181–83
Consumer affluence, 174
Consumer base, for advertising, 284
Consumer behavior, 76–77
  buying decision process, 85–90
  executive summary, 90
  factors affecting, 77–81
  psychological processes, 81–85
Consumer capabilities, 10
Consumer cooperatives, 251
Consumer-franchise building, 290–91
Consumer-goods classification, 171
Consumerist movement, 56
Consumer market, 95
Consumer marketing channels, 234
Consumer market segmentation, 113–20
Consumer promotion, 289
Consumer psychology, pricing and, 211–12
Consumers
  advertising and, 289
  savings, debt, and credit availability, 53
  See also Customers
Consumption chain method, 30
Consumption system, 170
Contact methods, 44, 45
Containerization, 262
Contests, 291, 292
Contextual placement, 305
Continental Airlines, 266–67
Continuity, 288
Continuous innovation, 160
Continuous replenishment programs, 104
Contract carrier, 262
Contraction defense, 161
Contractual sales force, 313
Contractual VMS, 240–41
Control, 30–33, 331–33
Controlled test marketing, 180
Convenience goods, 171
Convenience stores, 249
Conventional marketing channel, 240
Conventions, 292
Conversion Model, 119
Cook, Miles, 246–47n14
Cool Water, 173
Cooper, Lee G., 92n34
Cooper, Robert G., 175, 189n26, 189n30
Cooper, Robin, 37n28
Co-optation, 243
Copacino, William C., 264n35

Index

Copy testing, 288
Core benefit, 169
Core business processes, 23
Core competencies, 23, 24
Core values, persistence of, 54
Cornish, Edward, 58n18
Cornwell, Bettina, 300n40
Cornwell, T. Bettina, 300n45
Corporate chain stores, 251
Corporate communication, 295
Corporate community involvement, 16
Corporate credibility, 104–6
Corporate culture, 29
Corporate environmentalism, 54–55
Corporate expertise, 106
Corporate image, 292, 295
Corporate likability, 106
Corporate mission, defining, 26–27
Corporate philanthropy, 16
Corporate retailing, 250, 251
Corporate social marketing, 15, 16
Corporate societal marketing (CSM), 334
Corporate strategic planning, 26–29
Corporate trustworthiness, 104–6
Corporate VMS, 240
Cortese, Amy E., 227n4
Costco, 112, 153, 231, 249
Cost inflation, 225
Cost leadership, 31
Costs, pricing and, 214–16
Coughlan, Anne T., 246n2, 246n4, 246n12, 247n22
Counseling, 257, 295
Counterfeiters, 163
Counteroffensive defense, 160
Countertrade, 222
Country of origin perceptions, 328–29
Coupons, 291
Coviello, Nicole E., 74n31
Cox, Donald F., 93n40
Cox, Jennifer L., 229n37
Coy, Peter, 229n33
Craftsman, 138
Craig, C. Samuel, 280n18
Craig, Samuel R., 336n6
Craik, Fergus I. M., 92n29
Cranium, 239
Craven, Robert, 126n21
Crayola, 139, 293
Creamer, Matthew, 74n18, 228–29n25
Creative development and execution, in advertising, 284–85
Creative strategy, 271–72, 304
Credence qualities, 192, 193
Credibility, 104–6, 297
Credit availability, 53
Crest, 140
Creyer, Elizabeth H., 188n16
Cripps, John D., 93n45
Crissy, W. J. E., 320n43
Critical life events, and behavior, 79
Critical path scheduling (CPS), 181
Cronin, J. Joseph, Jr., 207n32

Cross-promotions, 291
Cross-selling, 141
Crowley, Ayn E., 280n15, 280n16
Crowne Plaza, 172
Cruz, Riza, 58n18
Csaba, Fabian F., 144n33
Cues, 83
Cult brands, 134
Cultural factors, influencing consumer behavior, 77
Culture, 77, 100
Cummings, Betsy, 107n13
Cuneo, Alice, 90n1
Cunningham, I. C. M., 320n43
Cunningham, William H., 320n43
Current demand, estimating, 48–50
Customer acquisition, 23, 67–68, 69, 141
Customer advantage, 152
Customer attributes, 179
Customer-based brand equity, 130–31
Customer-centered company, 164
Customer centricity, 13
Customer churn, 68
Customer communities, 245
Customer complaints, 201
Customer databases, 70–72
Customer equity, 141–42
Customer evangelists, 68, 70
Customer expectations, for service quality, 198–200
Customer failure, 196–197
Customer focus, 24
Customer-focused value proposition, 148
Customerization, 113
Customer lifetime value (CLV), 66–67
Customer loyalty, 62, 68, 69
Customer mailing lists, 71
Customer-management organization, 330
Customer metrics, 332
Customer needs, identifying and satisfying, 203–4
Customer orientations, 163–64
Customer perceived value (CPV), 60–62, 73n3
Customer performance scorecard, 34
Customer-product profitability analysis, 65
Customer profitability, 64–66
Customer profitability analysis (CPA), 65
Customer relationship management (CRM), 23, 67–70, 72, 141, 195–96, 197
Customer retention, 67–68, 69, 141
Customer retention rate, 318n7
Customers
  connecting with, 16
  interacting with, 68, 70
  marketing channels and, 235
  partnering with, 105
Customer satisfaction, 8, 60–64
Customer satisfaction ratings, 74n16

Customer-segment pricing, 223
Customer switching behavior, 197
Customer touch points, 67
Customer training, 153
Customer value, 21–26
  building, 60–64
  executive summary, 72–73
  lifetime, 64–67
Customer value assessment (CVA), 103
Customer value hierarchy, 169
Customization, 152
Customized marketing, 112

D

Dacin, Peter, 144n34
Dade, Corey, 165n4
Daewoo, 326
Dahan, Ely, 188n19, 188n24, 189n27
Dalgic, Tevfik, 125n4
Dalhoff, Denise, 144n35
Danaher, Peter J., 74n31, 319n14
Dannon, 278
Dant, Rajiv P., 108n30
Danziger, Pam, 126n27
Dartnell Corporation, 320n52
DaSilva, Alison T., 339n48
Database marketing, 70–72
Databases, customer, 70–72
Datamining, 40, 71–72
Data sources, 42–43
Data warehouses, 71–72
Daurairaj, M., 145n46
D'Aveni, Richard A., 166n25, 166n33
Davenport, Thomas H., 247n15, 298n13
David's Bridal, 77
Davidson, William R., 263n2
Davies, R. L., 264n20
Davis, John, 37n37, 126n21
Davis, Kirby Lee, 73n1
Davis, Scott, 143n6, 144n24
Davis, Stanley M., 37n30
Dawar, Niraj, 146n54, 208n45, 300n53, 336n8
Dawson, Chester, 187n5
Day, George S., 19n26, 23, 24, 36n8, 36n9, 108n21
Deal, Terrence E., 37n30
Deane, Dwayne Hal, 338n43
Debruyne, Marion, 338n35
Debt availability, 53
Deciders, 99, 117
Decision alternatives, 41–42
Decision making, 42, 45–46
  branding, 138
  market logistics, 260–62
  marketing channel design, 235–38
  marketing channel management, 238–39
  marketing communications mix, 275–77
  marketing public relations, 296–97
  new products, 176
  retailing, 251–54

sales promotion, 290–92
sponsorship, 293
Decline stage of product life cycle, 183, 184, 185–86
Decoding, 267
DeFanti, Mark P., 190n52
Deighton, John, 125n3, 146n51, 298n20
Dekimpe, Marnik, 166n27, 299n28, 300n53
Delaney, Kevin J., 318n13
Delayed quotation pricing, 225
Delivery, 153
Delivery time, 235
Delta Airlines, 45
Demand
  business markets and, 96
  pricing and, 213–14
  services, 195
  sponsorship and, 293
Demand-chain planning, 232
Demand curves, estimating, 214
Demand measurement, 46–50
Demands, 6–7
Demers, Julie, 207n40
Demographic environment, 51–53
Demographic segmentation, 114, 115, 116, 120
Demonstrations
  POP, 291
  sales, 312
Denison, D. C., 188n13
Department stores, 249
Deregulation, 9
Derived demand, 96
Desai, Kalpesh Kaushik, 188n13
Desai, P. S., 300n33
DeSarbo, Wayne S., 92n34
Descending bids, 220
Descriptive research, 42
Deshpande, Rohit, 18n20, 109n31
Design
  marketing channels, 235–38
  marketing communications, 271–72
  product differentiation, 153
  sales force, 312–13
Desmond, Ned, 319n19
Deutsch, Claudia H., 57n1, 165n4
Deutschman, Alan, 300n57
Dev, Chekitan S., 19n28, 246n6, 247n25
Devinney, Timothy, 338n46, 339n48
Devlin, Susan J., 207n32
Dewar, Robert, 337n27
Dhar, Ravi, 90n2
Dholakia, Utpal M., 75n40
Dickson, Peter R., 228n8
Differentiated goods, 10
Differentiated marketing, 124
Differentiation, 31, 152–54, 202, 223–24
Diffused preferences, 111
Digital River, 100
Dillon, William R., 126n33
Dilution, 243
D'Innocenzio, Anne, 263n5
Dior, 243
Diplomacy, 243
Direct exporting, 326

Index

Direct investment, 326
Direct mail, 286, 303–4
Direct marketing, 250, 267, 268, 276, 302–5
Direct marketing channels, 234, 237
Direct-order marketing, 303
Direct product profitability (DPP), 251
Direct purchasing, 96
Direct-response marketing, 305
Direct sales, 250
Direct sales channels, 237
Direct sales force, 313
Discounts, 222, 223, 225, 291
Discount stores, 249
Discount Tire, 242
Discretionary options, 111
Discrimination, and pricing, 83, 223,
Disintermediation, 9
Disney, 134, 140, 193, 194, 200
Display ads, 307
Display allowance, 291
Display Supply & Lighting, 236
Disruptive technologies, 175
Dissatisfiers, 82
Dissociative groups, 78
Distinctive capabilities, 23
Distribution
 direct mail, 304
 global marketing, 328
 sales promotion, 292
Distribution channels, 8
Distribution metrics, 332
Distribution warehouses, 260
Distributors
 acquiring, 28
 territorial rights of, 237
 wholesaling, 255–57
Diversification, market, 160–61
Diversification growth, 28–29
Diversification strategy, 28
Divisibility, 183
Division organizational level, 25, 26
Division strategic planning, 26–29
Dixon, Andrea L., 320n55
Dixons, 231
Dobscha, Susan, 75n47
Dr. Scholl's, 137
Dodes, Rachel, 143n15
Dodson, Joe A., 300n35
Doeble, Justin, 336n4
Dogster, 160
Dolan, Robert J., 165n1
Domino sugar, 174
Domino's, 148
Donath, Bob, 37n38
Doney, Patricia M., 108n30
Dong, H. K., 207n32
Donnelly, J., 93n44, 205n3, 205n7
Donthu, Naveen, 107n9, 279n2, 280n23
Douglas, Susan, 336n6
Dove, 265–66
Dow, 27
Dowling, Grahame R., 75n42, 93n40
Downtime, 203
Doyle, Clare, 320n46

Doyle, John R., 143n19
Doyle, Peter, 107n6, 186
Dreeze, Xavier, 228n24, 263n11
Drenth, P. J., 92n25
Drives, 83
Drolet, Aimee, 90n2
Drop shippers, 256
Drucker, Peter, 3, 18n4, 26, 33, 36n13
Drumwright, Minette, 334, 338n45
Du, Rex Y., 91n14
Dual adaptation, 327
Dubé, Jean-Pierre, 319n21
Dubitsky, Tony M., 298n20
Duhigg, Charles, 318n10
Dull, Stephen F., 188n12
Dun & Bradstreet, 102
Duncan, Tom, 279n8, 279n9
Dunn, Julie, 18n8
Dunn, Michael, 144n24
DuPont, 27, 56, 95, 104, 180
Durability, 152, 170–71
Durable goods, 171
Durante, Richard, 57n8
Dutch auctions, 220
Dutka, Elaine, 37n32
Dutta, Shantanu, 228n16
Dwyer, F. Robert, 108n28
Dwyer, Paul, 319n24

E

Earl, Peter E., 93n40
Earnest, Leslie, 166n17
EasyJet, 154
eBay, 2, 212, 220
E-business, 244
Eckert, James A., 108n28
Ecological lifestyles, 80
E-commerce marketing, 243–45. See also Internet, Websites
Economic circumstances, 79
Economic cost, 161
Economic environment, 53
Economic-order quantity formula, 264n34
Edmund's, 5
EDS, 155
Educational groups, 52
Edwards, Cliff, 36n12, 320n48
Edwards, Jim, 75n39
Effective ad-exposed audience, 287
Effective audience, 287
Efficiency control, 333
Eggert, Andreas, 108n26
Ehernfield, John, 19n34, 339n49
El-Ansary, Adel I., 246n2, 247n25
Elastic demand, 214
Electronic marketplaces, for business buying, 102
Elgin, Ben, 318–19n13, 319n18
Eliashberg, Jehoshua, 167n36
Ellison, Sarah, 166n18, 338n41
E-mail marketing, 307–8
E-marketing, 244
Emerson Electric, 100
Employees, rewards for, 292
Employee satisfaction, 201–2

Encirclement attack, 162
Encoding, 267
Engardio, Pete, 339n50
Engel, James F., 92n32, 280n12, 280n14
Engineering attributes, 179
English auctions, 220
Enis, Ben M., 187n4
Enright, Allison, 58n11, 107n12, 108n22, 246n10
Entrants, potential, 154, 155
Environment, marketing, 9
Environmental threat, 30
Environmentalism, 54–55
Epp, Amber, 57n8
Erdem, Tulin, 143n5, 143n10
Erevelles, Sunil, 280n17
Erickson, Gary M., 228n12
Erwin, L., 280n26
Escalator clauses, 225
ESPN, 128, 129
Essegaier, Skander, 319n14
Estalami, Hooman, 228n8
Ethical behavior, 334
Ethical issues
 channel relations, 243
 direct marketing, 305
 target markets, 124–25
 See also Social responsibility
Ethnic markets, 52
Ethnographic research, 43
Ettore, Barbara, 188n18
European Community, 56
Evaluation
 alternatives, 86, 87–88
 channel members, 238–39
 marketing process, 331–33
 message, 284
 sales reps, 317
 target markets, 122–24
Evans, Kenneth R., 108n30
Event marketing, 3, 267, 268, 273, 276, 293–94, 296
Everyday low pricing (EDLP), 219, 252
Evian, 224
Ewers, Justin, 19n23
Ewing, Jack, 36n1
Exchange markets, 102
Exclusive distribution, 236
Exemplars, 150–51
Expansible market, 47
Expectancy-value model, 87
Expectations, for service quality, 198–200
Expected bids, 220
Expected product, 170
Experience-curve pricing, 215–16
Experience qualities, 192, 193
Experiences, marketing of, 3, 267, 268, 273, 276, 293–94
Experimental advertising design, 289
Experimental research, 43
Expert opinion, 50
Expertise, 272
Exploratory research, 42
Exporting, 326
Extended warranties, 204
External environment analysis, 30
External marketing, 196, 198

F

FabSugar, 310
Facebook, 112, 160, 308
Facilitating services, 204
Facilitators, 236
Fader, Peter S., 74n30
Fads, 50
Failure frequency, 203
Fallon, Pat, 143n18
Family, and consumer behavior, 78
Family brand, 137
Family life cycle, 79
Family names, for brands, 138
Family of orientation, 78
Family of procreation, 78
Faris, Charles W., 107n5, 108n19
Farley, John U., 18n20, 93n38, 190n44
Farm products, 171
Farris, M. Theodore, II, 246n7
Farris, Paul W., 37n37, 145n49, 229n27, 298n3, 299n24, 300n34, 338n35
Fass, Allison, 298n17, 319n17
Fay, Keller, 311
Feather, Frank, 263n11
Feature improvement, 185
Features, 152
Featuring, 172–73
Federal Trade Commission, 223, 305
FedEx, 95, 138, 149, 200, 324
FedEx Global Supply Chain Services, 258
FedEx Kinko's, 138, 149
Feedback, 30, 32–33, 68, 70, 317
Feed-forward, 317
Feehan, Michael, 57n8
Feelings, evoking, 292
Fein, Adam J., 108n21
Feinberg, Fred M., 298n18
Felding, Michael, 264n26
Feldman, Laurence P., 190n53
Feldman, Mark A., 339n48
Ferdows, Kasra, 263n1
Fern, Edward F., 91n9
Ferrell, O. C., 206n23
Fetterman, Mindy, 263n15
Fialka, John J., 108n29
Fiat, 325
Fickler, Martin, 336n4
Fighter brands, 141
Final price, selection of, 221
Financial accountability, 15
Financial leverage, 35
Financial projections, 33
Financing, 223, 256
Findings, presenting, 42, 45
Finite nonrenewable resources, 55
First entry, 181
First-time customers, 68
Fischer, Marc, 189n37
Fishbein, Martin, 92n36, 93n39
Fisher, Daniel, 108n29
Fishman, Charles, 57n2, 187n5, 229n33, 263n7
Fishyback, 262
Fiske, Neil, 126n23
Fitch, Stephane, 264n18
FitSugar, 310

Index

Fixed compensation, 314
Fixed costs, 214
Flagship brands, 141
Flank attack, 162
Flank defense, 160
Flankers, 141
Fleischmann, Moritz, 229n33
Fletcher, Richard, 75n45
Flexible market offering, 111
Flighting, 288
Flint, Daniel J., 108n23
Florès, Laurent, 189n29
Flow, in channels, 232–34
Fluctuating demand, 96
Focus, as strategy, 31
Focus-group research, 43
Fok, Dennis, 187n8
Folkes, Valerie, 166n31
Follow-up, in sales, 312
Food and Drug Administration (FDA), 174
Food Emporium, 249
Ford (company), 103–4
Ford, Henry, 111
Ford, John B., 91n7
Ford, Neil M., 320n54
Ford, Royal, 187n5
Forecasting, 46–50
Form, 152
Fornell, Claes, 73n14, 190n48, 207n39
Forward flow, 232
Forward invention, 327
Four Points by Sheraton, 124
Four Ps, 13, 14. *See also* Marketing mix
Fournier, Susan, 73n8, 73n9, 75n47, 143n10
Fowler, Geoffrey, 18n16, 337n19
Fox, Edward J., 246n5
Fox, Keith, 336n2
Franc, Robert H., 58n26
Franchise organizations, 241, 251
Frank, Michael, 125n1
Frank, Robert J., 166n30
Franke, George R., 320n44
Frankel, Alex, 143n19
Fraud, 305
Frazier, Curtis L., 189n32
Frazier, Gary L., 246n4, 247n25
Free goods, 291
Freeman, Laurie, 337n26
"Freemium" strategy, 211
Free trials, 291
Frequency, of advertisements, 284, 285–86
Frequency programs (FPs), 70, 291
Freud, Sigmund, 81
Friedman, Phil, 63
Friedman, Richard A., 58n10
Friedman, Steve, 125n1
Frito-Lay, 54
Frontal attack, 162
Fruchter, Gila E., 206n12
Fulfillment management process, 23
Fullerton, Ronald A., 337n27
Full market coverage, 123–24
Full service, 250
Full-service wholesalers, 256
Functional discounts, 223

Functional hubs, 102
Functional organization, 329
Functional quality, 198
Functions, of marketing channel, 232–34
Future demand, estimating, 50
Future Industrial Technologies, 153

G

Gain-and-risk-sharing pricing, 221
Gale, Bradley T., 74n21
Galvin, John, 143n8
Games, as promotion, 291
Ganesan, Shankar, 108–9n30
Ganesh, Jaishankar, 206n23
Gap, 249, 251
Gardial, Sarah Fisher, 108n23
Garolera, Jordi, 91n17
Garvin, David A., 165n9
Gatekeepers, 99
Gates, Kelley, 300n47
Gather.com, 112
Gatignon, Hubert, 190n44
Gawker Media, 310
Gedenk, Karen, 229n31, 299n22
Geico, 282–83
Geier, Robert, 207n40
Gender, and consumer behavior, 78
Gender segmentation, 116
General Electric (GE), 95, 105, 138, 153, 157, 194, 211, 221, 260
General Mills, 138, 173
General Motors, 2, 104, 141, 232, 242, 258, 326
General need description, 101–2
Generation segmentation, 116
Generation Y, 116
Generics, 255
Geoclustering, 114
Geoffrey Beene, 151
Geographical-expansion strategy, 159
Geographical population shifts, 52–53
Geographical pricing, 222
Geographic organization, 329
Geographic segmentation, 114, 115
George, Jeffrey P., 166n30
George, W. R., 205n3, 205n7
Gerber, 27
German, Steve D., 338n47
Gershoff, Andrew D., 165n7
Gerstner, Eitan, 206n12, 320n54
Getz, Gary, 146n52
Ghemawat, Pankaj, 337n14
Ghose, Sanjoy, 145n40
Ghosh, Mrinal, 109n34
Giannulli, Mossimo, 252
Gielens, Katrijn, 189n37
Gift-giving occasions, 118
Gifts, as promotion, 291
GiggleSugar, 310
Gill, Dee, 188n17
Gillette, 130, 141, 209–10, 315
Gillette, King C., 209

Gilmore, James, 18n5, 165n11, 263–64n17, 294, 300n51
Gilsdorf, Ethan, 300n52
Gimbel, Barney, 19n30, 206n19
Gladwell, Malcolm, 310, 319n34
Glazer, Rashi, 165n7
Glenmick, David, 73n8
Global firm, 324
Global industry, 324
Globalization, 9
Global marketing
 competition, 324–29
 executive summary, 335–36
 internal marketing, 329–31
 socially responsible marketing, 334–35
Global marketing process, 331–34
Global organization, 330–31
Goal formulation, 30, 31
Goal incompatibility, 242
Godin, Seth, 206n15, 273, 280n26, 319n25
Goetsch, H. W., 338n34
Goh, Khim Yong, 319n21
Going-rate pricing, 219–20
Goldenberg, Jacob, 319n35
Golder, Peter N., 184, 190n50, 190n54
Goldstucker, Jack, 190n46
Gomez, Miguel, 300n33
Goodman, Sam R., 338n37
Goods
 differentiated, 10
 marketing of, 3
 See also Products
Goodstein, Ronald C., 93n40, 298–99n20
Goodyear, 242
Google, 23, 160, 307
Gopalakrishna, Srinath, 75n38
Gore-Tex, 151, 173
Government market, 96–97
Governments, 55
Government sector, 192
Graeff, Timothy R., 91n19
Graham, John L., 337n20
Grainger, 102, 257, 304
Grant, Alan W. H., 75n34
Grant, Lorie, 318n4
Grant, Robert M., 36n18
Grassroots marketing, 112
Graves, Michael, 252
Gray market, 328
Green, Heather, 319n20, 319n23, 319n24, 320n38
Green, Kesten C., 167n38
Green, Mark C., 337n15
Green, Paul, 75n46
Green, Paul E., 92n35, 189n32
Green, Stephen, 126n9
Greene, Walter E., 206n25
Greenleaf, Eric A., 166n31
Green programs, 55
Gregor, William, 338n38
Gregory, James R., 144n33
Gremler, Dwayne D., 205n10, 206n21
Grewal, Dhruv, 108n30, 207n31, 207n35, 298n3
Grewal, Rajdeep, 108n20, 108–9n30

Griffin, Abbie, 189n28
Griffin, Jill, 93n43
Grimm, Matthew, 336n1
Gronroos, Christian, 206n24, 206n26
Groupe Danone, 323
Grover, Rajiv, 57n8, 74n28, 75n46, 93n41, 126–27n33, 145–46n50, 189n32
Growth, long-term, 17
Growth Champions, 14–15
Growth opportunities, assessing, 28–29
Growth stage of product life cycle, 183, 184–85, 186
Gruca, Thomas S., 73n14
Guarantees, 174–75, 194
Gucci, 79
Guerrilla marketing, 162
Guinta, Lawrence R., 189n34
Gulati, Ranjay, 338n31
Gummesson, Evert, 19n22, 205n5
Gundlach, Gregory T., 338n45
Gunther, Marc, 57n1
Gupta, Mahendra, 74n23
Gupta, Sachin, 299n23
Gupta, Sunil, 66, 74n28, 299n27
Gürhan-Canli, Zeynep, 144n34, 145n46, 337n23
Gustafsson, Anders, 73n11
Gutierrez, Jairo A., 247n32
Gutman, Jonathan, 92n23

H

Häagen-Dazs, 327
Haddad, Charles, 165n4
Haeckel, Stephan H., 205n8
Haenlein, Michael, 74n30
Hahn, Minhi, 190n44
Haider, Donald H., 18n7
Haig, Matt, 144n28
Haiken, Melanie, 57n5
Hakansson, Hakan, 19n24, 107n3, 108n16
Hall, Joseph M., 229n33
Hall, Kenji, 264n25
Hall, Malcolm Macalister, 319n35
Hamel, Gary, 29, 36n7, 73n5
Hamilton, Booz Allen, 14, 19n31
Hamilton, Rebecca W., 165n10, 298n3
Hamm, Steve, 189n30, 189n31
Hammer, Michael, 36n6
Hamner, Susanna, 188n14
Handfield, Robert B., 108n28
H&R Block, 194
Hanson, Miles, 37n32
Hanssens, Dominique M., 166n27, 228n19, 299n28
Happenings data, 40
Harbison, John R., 37n27
Hardie, Bruce G. S., 74n30
Harkavy, Jerry, 125n6
Harker, Patrick T., 206n20
Harlam, Bari, 264n24, 299n31, 300n34
Harley-Davidson, 131, 163, 245, 274

Index

Harmon, Eric P., 208n47
Harrabin, Rodger, 280n23
Harrington, Anna, 336n4
Harris, Eric G., 320n54
Harris, Ian, 320n46
Harris, Jeanne G., 247n15
Harris, Thomas L., 300n54
Harrison, D., 108n16
Harrod's of London, 251
Hart, C. W. L., 188n18, 207n34
Hartline, Michael D., 206n23., 206n26
Hartman, Cathy L., 58n32
Harvesting, 185
Hasbro, 308
Hatch, Cary, 167n43
Hatch, Mary Jo, 144n33
Haugsted, Linda, 127n34
Haugtvedt, Curtis P., 280n17
Hauser, John R., 188n19, 188n24, 189n27, 189n28, 189n34, 206n25
Hayes, Jack, 74n19
Healthy lifestyles, 80
Heart, share of, 158, 289
Heckler, Susan, 143n19
Heide, Jan B., 107n2, 109n33, 109n36, 246n11
Heightened attention, 85
Heilman, Carrie M., 92n31
Hein, Kenneth, 126n9, 144n32, 167n37, 206n16, 318n1
Heinz, 138, 159, 271
Heires, Katherine, 227n5
Helene Curtis Company, 260
Hellofs, Linda, 167n41
Helsen, Kristiaan, 300n53
Henderson, Caroline, 298n20
Henkoff, Ronald, 264n31
Hensel, James S., 58n10
Hensher, David A., 189n32
Henthorne, Tony L., 91n7
Herbig, Paul, 145n38
Herman Miller, 51, 153
Hershey's, 293
Hertz, 211, 235
Hertz, David B., 189n33
Herzberg, Frederick, 81, 82, 92n25
Herzenstein, Michal, 190n43
Heskett, James L., 37n30, 207n34
Hess, James D., 320n54
Heublein, 160
Hewlett-Packard, 11, 83, 95, 102, 150, 231, 242, 273
Hibbard, Jonathan D., 247n25
Hibbard, Justin, 318–19n13
Hiebeler, Robert, 36n5
High, K., 318n1, 339n48
High-end prestige brand, 141
High-low pricing, 219
High-markup, low-volume group, 252
Hill, Sam, 300–301n57
Hilton Hotels, 114, 203
Hirschman, Albert O., 93n42
Hirshberg, Gary, 323
Hirshman, Elizabeth, 91n14
Historical advertising approach, 289
Hlavecek, James D., 264n29
Ho, Teck-Hua, 74n30
Hoch, Stephen J., 228n24, 263n11

Hoeffler, Steve, 190n43
Hof, Robert D., 125n5, 166n33, 247n27
Hogan, John E., 213, 228n18
Holahan, Catherine, 279n3, 318n13, 319n22
Holbrook, M. B., 143n6
Holbrook, Morris, 91n14
Hold Everything, 251
Holden, Alfred, 228n8
Holiday Inn, 172
Holidays, and segmentation, 118
Holistic marketing, 12
  activities, 133–34
  customer value and, 23–25
  services and, 196–98
Hollander, Stanley C., 263n3
Holloway, Charles A., 189n39
Holstein, William J., 144n36
Holtsius, Karin, 298n20
Homburg, Christian, 19n29, 73n13
Home Depot, 249
Homogeneous preferences, 111
Honda, 172, 241, 271, 287
Hong Kong and Shanghai Banking Corporation Limited, 113
Hopstaken, Brigette, 189n35
Horizontal channel conflict, 242
Horizontal diversification strategy, 28
Horizontal marketing system, 241
Horovitz, Bruce, 126n24, 144n22, 206n18, 246n14
Hosford, Christopher, 127n35
Hot Topic, 251
House brands, 254–55
House of brands, 138
Household patterns, 52
Houston, Mark B., 75n38
Houston, Michael J., 143n19
Hovland, C. I., 280n16, 280n21
Howard, Amanda L., 263n16
Howard, John A., 92n32, 93n38
Howard, Susanna, 227n3
Howard, Theresa, 263n6, 279n1
Howe, Peter J., 227n5
Howell, Parker, 247n18
Hoyer, Wayne D., 73n13, 280n15, 280n16
HSBC, 113, 202
Hsee, Christopher K., 187n7
Huba, J., 70, 75n41
Hubbard, Katrina, 338n35
Hui, Michael K., 208n46
Humphreys, Michael S., 300n40, 300n45
Hunt, Shelby D., 109n31, 338n47
Huston, Larry, 189n30
Hybrid channels, 231
Hyman, Mark, 18n5
Hypermarkets, 249
Hyundai, 64

I

Iacobucci, Dawn, 144n23, 146n52, 188n19, 205n4, 247n22
IBM, 95, 102, 112, 273–74

Idea generation, 177
Ideal self-concept, 79
Ideas, marketing of, 3, 4
Idea screening, 177
Identity media, 296
IDEO, 46
Ihlwan, Moon, 336n4
IKEA, 2–3, 23, 52, 81, 219, 304
Image differentiation, 154
Image dimensions, for service brands, 203
Image pricing, 224
Imitators, 163
Immelt, Jeffrey, 228n6
Impact, of advertisements, 285–86
Implementation, 30, 32
Implementation controls, 33
Inbound telemarketing, 304
Incentives, 105, 289
Income distribution, 53
Income segmentation, 116
Incremental innovation, 175
Independent Grocers Association (IGA), 251
Indirect exporting, 326
Indirect marketing channels, 237
Inditex, 248
Individual brand names, 138
Individual marketing, 112–13
Industrial-goods classification, 171
Industrializing economies, 53
Industrial marketing channels, 234
Industry competitors, 154
Industry conception of competition, 155–56
Industry convergence, 9
Industry-market relationship, 4–5
Inelastic demand, 96, 214
Infiniti, 172
Influencers, 99, 100, 117
Infomediaries, 244
Infomercials, 305
Informa Telecoms & Media, 76
Information, 3, 4, 13. See also Marketing information system
Informational appeal, 271
Information analysis, 42, 45
Information collection, 42, 44–45
Information flow, 233
Information search, 85–87
Information technology, 9
Informative advertising, 283
Infosys Technologies, 155
InfoUSA, 102
Ingredient branding, 173
Initiators, 98, 117
Inman, J. Jeffrey, 206n12
Innovation, 29
  consumer adoption process, 182
  continuous, 160
  incremental, 175
  technological environment and, 55
Innovation diffusion process, 182
Innovative packaging, 174
Inoue, Akihiro, 92n34
INSEAD, 156
Inseparability, and services, 194
Inside Edge Ski and Bike, 249
Installation, 153, 171
Institutional market, 95–97

Institutional ties, creating, 70
Intangibility, and services, 193
Integrated logistics systems (ILS), 258–59
Integrated marketing, 12, 13–14
Integrated marketing channel system, 241
Integrated marketing communications (IMC), 277–78
Integration, 133, 240–43
Integrative growth, 28
Intel, 2, 25, 95, 232
Intelligence. See Marketing intelligence system
Intensive distribution, 236
Intensive growth, 28
Interactive marketing, 196, 198, 267, 276, 305–8
Interbrand, 144n28, 324
Intermediaries, 236
Internal branding, 134
Internal environment analysis, 30–31
Internalization, 134
Internal marketing, 12, 14–15, 196, 198, 329–31
Internal records, 39–40
Internet, 10
  advertising, 286, 307
  dilution and cannibalization, 243
  e-commerce marketing practices, 243–45
  holistic marketing for services, 198
  interactive marketing, 305–8
  niche marketing and, 112
  personal communications channels, 272–73
  sales reps and, 316
  service sector channels, 235. See also E-commerce marketing, Microsites, Online videos and ads, Web sites
Internet purchasing, 102
Interviews, 45
Intrabrand shifts, 140
Introduction stage of product life cycle, 183–84, 186
Intuit, 311
Inventory, 261–62
Inventory-carrying costs, 261
Investments
  direct, to enter global market, 326
  specific, tied to partners, 106
iPod, 3
Ivancevich, John M., 93n44
Iyer, Easwar S., 58n31

J

Jackson, Barbara Bund, 108n28
Jackson, Stuart E., 167n38
Jacobson, Robert, 144n30, 167n41
Jacoby, Jacob, 143n4
Jacoby, Larry, 92n29
Jaffe, Sam, 298n16
Jahre, Marianne, 246n7
Jain, Dipak C., 108n24, 188n19, 228n23

Index

Jain, Sanjay, 228n13
James, Barrie G., 167n34
Jamil, Magbul, 320n55
Janiszewski, Chris, 228n9
Jap, Sandy D., 229n26
Jargon, Julie, 264n23
Jaworski, Bernard J., 18n20, 156, 166n23, 205n11, 207n37, 306, 319n15, 336n2, 338n37
JCPenney, 249, 250–51, 254, 304
Jedidi, Kamel, 92n34, 299n23, 299n27
Jenny Craig, 272
JetBlue, 295
Jewel, 249
Jiffy Lube, 251
Joachimsthaler, Erich, 138
Job-shop specialist, 164
Jobs, Steve, 295
Jocz, Katherine, 36n3, 336n2
Johanson, Jan, 19n24
Johansson, Johny K., 228n12, 336n6, 336n9, 337n12
John, Deborah Roedder, 144n27, 145n46
John, George, 109n32, 109n34, 109n35
Johnson, Jean L., 108–9n30
Johnson, Michael B., 73n11, 74n24, 74n25
Johnson, Richard D., 73n3
Johnson & Johnson, 332–33
Johnson, S. J., 37n18
Johnston, Russell, 240, 247n19
Johnston, Wesley J., 74n31
Joiner, Christopher, 145n46
Joint venture, 326
Joint-venture co-branding, 173
Jones, Conrad, 37n18
Jones, D. B., 299n30
Jones, D. G. Brian, 337n24
Jones, Thomas O., 73n15
Jones Soda, 134
Joseph, Lissan, 320n51
Joshi, Yogesh V., 190n43
Joyce, William, 37n31
Jun, S. Y., 188n10

K

Kalmenson, Stuart, 92n30
Kalra, Ajay, 73n10, 207n32, 298–99n20
Kaltcheva, Velitchka D., 263n13
Kalwani, Manohar U., 188n21, 247n19
Kamakura, Wagner A., 91n14, 126–27n33
Kamprad, Ingvar, 81
Kane, Courtney, 91n12
Kane, Kate, 126n15
Kang, Stephanie, 319n35
Kannan, P. K., 207n30
Kanuk, Leslie Lazar, 91n3, 91n6
Kaplan, Andreas M., 74n30
Kaplan, Andrew, 126n28
Kaplan, Robert S., 37n28, 37n41
Kaplan-Leiserson, Eva, 206n19
Karmarkar, Uday S., 208n45
Karpinski, Richard, 37n40, 338n36

Kashyap, Rajiv K., 58n31
Kasler, Dale, 263n8
Kassarjian, Hal, 108n15
Kassarjian, Harold H., 91n15, 92n35
Kassing, Jay, 93n43
Katsikeas, C. S., 336n10
Kaul, Anil, 298–99n20
Kavanoor, S., 298n3
Keaveney, Susan M., 197, 206n23
Kedrosky, Paul, 165n10
Keegan, Walter J., 337n15
Keegan, Warren J., 327, 337n15
Keenan, Bill, 320n45
Keenan, Faith, 227n4, 229n33, 246n8
Keighley, Geoff, 207n44
Keiningham, Timothy L., 74n22
Keith, Robert J., 18n18
Kellaris, James J., 280n19
Keller, Kevin Lane, 108n14, 109n31, 143n11, 143n19, 144n34, 145n38, 145n39, 145n42, 145n47, 146n53, 165n5, 188n12, 188n13, 281n33
Kellogg's, 138
Kelly, Francis J., III, 280n27
Kelly, Thomas B., 36n5
Kelman, Herbert C., 280n21
Kemmler, Tilman, 36n17
Kemp, Simon, 93n40
Kenmore, 138
Kennedy, Allan A., 37n30
Kenny, David, 145n43
Kernan, Jerome B., 319n33
Kesmodel, David, 264n23
Ketteman, Charles, 36n5
Key buying influencers, 100
KFC, 173
Khanna, Tarun, 166n20, 336n7
Kharif, Olga, 108n21, 318n13
Khermouch, Gerry, 281n30, 337n26
Kia, 62
Kiley, David, 279n3, 319n17, 320n37
Kilpatrick, David, 227n4
Kim, Byung-Do, 144n37
Kim, Kyeong-Heui, 144n27
Kim, Ryan, 318n9
Kim, W. Chan, 156, 166n24
King, Paul, 107n4
Kinko's, 138, 149
Kirsch, Michael, 74n19
Kivetz, Ran, 318n3
Klaasen, Abbey, 125n5
Klein, Jill, 300n53
Kleinschmidt, Elko J., 175, 189n26
Klingensmith, Dawn, 126n20
Knox, Simon, 144n25
Kodak, 2, 150, 235
Kohl's, 250
Kohli, Ajay K., 18n20, 107n9
Kohli, Chiranjier, 188n11
Komatsu, 60–61
Kong, Deborah, 337n21
Koopman-Iwerna, Agnes M., 92n25
Kopalle, Praveen K., 73n8, 299n22

Kortge, G. Dean, 228n22
Korth, Christopher M., 229n29
Koschate, Nichole, 73n13
Koselka, Rita, 264n33
Koss-Feder, Laura, 58n23
Kotler, Philip, 16, 18n5, 18n7, 37n24, 58n15, 107n8, 143n9, 145n47, 165n13, 167n34, 167n39, 188n12, 189n30, 189n38, 190n52, 190n53, 263n17, 300n37, 338n38
Kotter, John P., 37n30
Koval, Robin, 279n3
Kozup, John C., 188n16
Krafft, Manfred, 320n54
Kraft, 254, 307, 334
Kramer, Mark R., 19n35, 338n43
Kranhold, Kathryn, 108n29
Krauss, Michael, 75n41, 108n17
Krieg, Peter C., 58n14
Krishnamukthi, Lakshman, 189n37
Krishnamurti, Lakshman, 299n27
Krishnan, H. S., 145n42, 280n19, 338n37
Krishnan, M. S., 73n14
Kroger, 249, 254
Krohmen, Harley, 19n29
Krol, Carol, 206n14, 264n28, 318n4
Krugman, Herbert E., 298n11
Kubicová, 36n17
Kumar, Nirmalya, 22, 36n2, 108n27, 166n30, 190n52, 226, 247n24, 247n25, 255, 264n27
Kumar, S. Ramesh, 337n13
Kumar, V., 74n28, 74n29, 75n36, 75n44, 75n47, 247n21
Kuykendall, Lavone, 187n1
Kuzma, John, 300n49
Kyung, Ellie J., 205n11, 207n37

L

Labeling, 174
Labels, private, 254–55
Labich, Kenneth, 126n25
Labor, production concept and, 10
Lachanauer, Rob, 166n33
Laddering, 81–82
La Forgia, John, 205n1
Lal, Rajiv, 227n4, 228n24
Lamont, Douglas, 247n31
Lanning, Michael J., 73n6, 74n32
LaPointe, Patrick, 37n40
Larsen, Mogens Holten, 144n33
Las Vegas Convention & Tourism Authority, 4
Late entry, in new products, 181
LaTour, Michael S., 91n7
Lattin, James, 75n46, 263n11
Lauterborn, Robert F., 143n20, 281n32
Lawrence, Paul R., 240, 247n19
Lazardis, Mike, 29
Lazare, Lewis, 297n1
Lead time, 292
Leap Frog, 295
Learning, and consumer behavior, 83
Learning-curve pricing, 215–16

Leclerc, France, 187n7
Lee, Dong-Jin, 247n25
Lee, Ka Lok, 74n30
Lee, Louise, 165n1
Lee, Nancy, 16
Leeflang, Peter S. H., 299n23
Leeuw, Maarten, 125n4
Left-brain thinking skills, 6
Legal behavior, 334
Legal issues
  advertising, 285
  channel relations, 243
Lehmann, Donald R., 36n3, 37n39, 66, 73n8, 74n28, 143n12, 188n21, 190n42, 190n44, 228n8, 299n27
Lehmann, John, 280n26
Leislation, business, 56
Lele, Milind M., 208n45
Lemon, Katherine A., 145–46n50
Lemon, Katherine N., 207n29
Lenovo, 10
Leone, Robert, 146n53
Leonhardt, David, 58n26, 337n17
Leonidou, Leonidas C., 336n10
Lepisto, Lawrence, 91n14
Leslie, Mark, 189n39
Leung, Shirley, 126n23
Leuthesser, Lance, 188n11
Levenson, Michael, 167n43
Leverageable advantage, 152
Levey, Richard H., 57n4
Levi's, 2
Levin, Irwin P., 73n3
Levin, Paul, 110
Levinson, Jay Conrad, 167n34
Levitt, Theodore, 11, 18n19, 27, 36n16, 166n22, 167n44, 187n2, 205n6
Levy, Sidney, 187n3
Lewin, Jeffrey E., 107n9
Lewis, Jane, 19n30
Lewis, Jordan D., 37n27
Lewis, Michael, 75n35, 263n1
Lexus, 64, 150, 172
Licensed product, 137
Licensing, 326
Lichtenstein, Donald R., 228n9
Lieber, Ron, 336n5
Life-cycle cost, 203
Life-cycle stages, 79, 114
Life stage, 114, 116
Life styles, 80, 292
Lifetime value. *See* Customer lifetime value
Likability, of message source, 272
Lilien, Gary L., 58n15, 189n40
Limited, 249
Limited service, 250
Limited-service wholesalers, 256
Line extension, 137
Line filling, 172
Line managers, 6
Line modernization, featuring, and pruning, 172–73
Line organization, 6
Line stretching, 172
Listening, to customers, 68, 70
Livelsberger, Jeanne, 92n30
Liz Claiborne, 132
Lloyd, Mary Ellen, 227n1
Lobbying, 295

Local marketing, 112
Location, of retailers, 253–54
Location pricing, 224
Lockhart, Robert S., 92n29
Lockyer, Keith G., 189n40
Lodish, Leonard M., 92n30, 246n5, 299n28
Logistics, 257–62, 263
LOHAS (lifestyles of health and sustainability), 80
Loken, Barbara, 144n27, 145n46
Long-term growth, 17
Long-term memory (LTM), 83–84
Loomis, Carol J., 165n1
Lorange, Peter, 37n27
Loss-leader pricing, 222
Lot size, 235
Louis Vuitton, 243
Louviere, Jordan J., 189n32
Lovejoy, William S., 189n34
Lovelock, Christopher, 205n5
Loviere, Jordan J., 338n46, 339n48
Low, G. S., 145n43, 337n27
Low-end entry level, 141
Lowenstein, Michael W., 93n43
Low-interest financing, 223
Low-markup, higher volume group, 252
Lowry, Tom, 142n1
Loyalty, 62, 68, 69
Loyalty programs, 70
Loyalty status, 119
Lubetkin, Beth, 92n30
Luce, Mary Frances, 92n32
Lufthansa, 46
Lumsdaine, A. A., 280n16
Lunsford, J. Lynn, 318n12
Luo, Man, 146n53
Luo, X., 279n2, 338n46
Lusch, Robert F., 205n5, 279n8
Lustgarten, Abraham, 36n1
Lutz, Richard J., 91n7, 92n35
Lutzky, Christian, 299n22
Luxton, Sandra, 281n31
Lynch, John, 90n2, 227n4, 247n28
Lynch, Patrick D., 188n12

M

Macchiette, Bart, 127n36
MacFarland, Donna, 207n42
Machalaba, Daniel, 165n4
Machuca, Jose A. D., 263n1
MacInnis, Deborah J., 190n47, 298n5
MacKenzie, Scott B., 320n55
MacLachlan, Douglas L., 18n21
Macroenvironmental trends and forces, 50–56
Macroscheduling problem, 288
Macy's, 254
Maddox, Kate, 107n1, 264n28
Madhavaram, Sreedhar, 281n31
Magazine advertising, 286
Maguire, Angela M., 300n40, 300n45
Mahajan, Vijay, 190n44, 246n5, 336n7
Maheswaran, D., 337n23
Maier, Matthew, 227n5

Mail. *See* Direct mail
Mail Boxes Etc., 149
Mailing lists, 71
Mail-order wholesalers, 256
Mail questionnaire, 45
Maintenance, and products, 153, 312
Maintenance and repair services, 171
Maklan, Scott, 144n25
Malaviya, Prashant, 298n12
Maloney, John, 271
Management, of marketing channels, 238–39. *See also* Marketing management
Management services, 257
Manchanda, Puneet, 188n20, 319n21
Mangalindan, Mylene, 247n27
Manning, Kenneth C., 229n30, 298n3
Manning-Schaffel, Vivian, 263n1
Mantrala, Murali K., 320n54
Manufacturer promotions, 290
Manufacturers' branches and offices, 256
Manufacturing sector, 192
Mao, H., 145n42
Marcial, Gene G., 144n22
Marconi, Carolyn, 207n42
Marcus, C., 338n36
Market broadening, 160
Market-buildup method, 49
Market-centered organizations, 330
Market-challenger strategies, 161–62
Market conception of competition, 155–56
Market definitions, 27
Market demand, 46–50
Market-development strategy, 28
Market diversification, 160–61
Market entry, 326
Market-entry timing, 181
Marketer, 5
Market-follower strategies, 161, 163
Market forecast, 48
Market information, 257
Marketing
 company capabilities, 10
 company orientation, 10–16
 consumer capabilities, 10
 core concepts, 6–9
 database, 70–72
 defining, 2–3
 importance of, 2
 integrated, 12, 13–14
 internal, 12, 14–15, 329–31
 multicultural, 77
 new realities in, 9–10
 performance, 12, 15–16
 personalizing, 70
 product life cycles and, 183–86
 relationship, 12–13
 retailing and, 251–54
 scope of, 2–6
 societal forces, 9
 See also Global marketing; Target marketing
Marketing alliances, 31

Marketing audit, 333–34
Marketing channel integration, 240–43
Marketing channels, 8
 design decisions, 235–38
 e-commerce marketing practices, 243–45
 executive summary, 245–46
 management decisions, 238–39
 role of, 232–35
 value networks and, 231–32
 wholesaling and, 257
Marketing channel system, 231, 240–43
Marketing communications
 effective, 268, 270–75
 executive summary, 279
 global competition, 327–28
 integrated, 277–78
 role of, 266–68, 269–70
 See also Mass communications; Personal communications
Marketing communications mix, 275–77
Marketing concept, 11
Marketing control, 331–33
Marketing controller, 332
Marketing culture and structure, 6
Marketing dashboards, 34
Marketing department, organization of, 329–31
Marketing environment, 9
Marketing expense-to-sales ratio, 35
Marketing implementation, 331
Marketing information system (MIS), 39–40
Marketing insights, 16, 40
Marketing intelligence system, 40, 41
Marketing management
 Caterpillar, 168–69
 Cisco, 94
 Coca-Cola, 302
 Dove, 265–66
 ESPN, 128
 Geico, 282–83
 Gillette, 209–10
 Mayo Clinic, 191
 Procter & Gamble, 76
 Progressive Insurance, 147–48
 Ritz-Carlton, 59–60
 Royal Philips Electronics, 230–31
 Siemens AG, 20–21
 Signature Cycles, 110–11
 Starbucks, 1–2
 Stonyfield Farm, 323
 tasks, 16–17
 Wal-Mart, 38–39
 Zara, 248
Marketing metrics, 34, 332
Marketing mix, 13, 14, 327
Marketing myopia, 156
Marketing network, 12–13
Marketing opportunity, 30
Marketing organizations, types of, 14–15
Marketing performance, 33–35
Marketing plan, 26, 33–35. *See also* Marketing strategies and plans
Marketing process, 5–6

Marketing public relations (MPR), 295–97
Marketing research, 40
Marketing research system, 40–46
Marketing resource management (MRM), 331
Marketing strategies and plans, 31, 33
 business unit strategic planning, 29–33
 corporate and division strategic planning, 26–29
 customer value and, 21–26
 developing, 16
 executive summary, 35–36
 marketing performance and, 33–35
 new products, 178–79
 product life cycle, 184–86
 service firms, 194–98
Marketing system, 5
Marketing-mix strategy, 121
Market-leader strategies, 159
Market logistics, 257–62, 263
Market makers, 244–45
Market-management organization, 330
Market minimum, and demand, 47
Market-nicher strategies, 163, 164
Market offerings, 7, 17
Market opportunity analysis (MOA), 30
Market-penetration pricing, 212
Market-penetration strategy, 159
Marketplace, 4
Market potential, 47, 48–49
Markets
 business versus consumer, 95
 defining, 4–5
 electronic, 102
 ethnic, 52
 measuring, 46–47
 organizational and institutional, 95–97
 See also Business market segmentation; Consumer markets
Market segmentation
 consumer and business markets, 113–20
 executive summary, 125
 levels of, 111–13
 target marketing and, 120–25
Market segments, 80, 111
Market sensing process, 23
Market share, 47, 158
 advertising and, 284, 289
 defending, 160–61
 expanding, 161
 overall, 34
 pricing and, 212
 relative, 35
Market-skimming pricing, 213
Marketspace, 4
Market specialization, 123
Market testing, 180–81
Market-test method, 50
MarketTools Inc., 44
Markillie, Paul, 227n4
Markin, Rom J., 92n34
Markman, Arthur B., 188n21, 190n42
Marks and Spencer, 254

Index

Markup pricing, 216–18
Marn, Michael V., 229n31
Marn, Mike, 228n17
Marriott, 46, 200
Marriott International, 59
Marsh, Lawrence, 299n22
Marshall, Delia, 279n3
Marta, Suzanne, 300n57
Martin, Andrew, 166n32, 318n1
Martin, Dennis, 298n4
Maslow, Abraham, 81, 82, 92n24
Mass communications
　advertising program, 283–89
　events and experiences, 293–94
　executive summary, 297
　public relations, 295–97
　sales promotion, 289–92
Mass customization, 152
Mass marketing, 111
Materials, 171
Matlack, Carol, 337n21
Matrix-management organization, 330
Matsuno, Ken, 18n21
Matta, Shashi, 166n31
Maturity stage of product life cycle, 183, 184, 185, 186
Mauborgne, Renée, 156, 166n24
Maurey, Kiki, 126n21
Mavens, as opinion leaders, 310
Mavondo, Felix, 281n31
Maxham, James G., III, 206n26
Maximum current profit, 212
Maximum market share, 212
Maybelline, 150
Mayo, Charles, 191
Mayo Clinic, 46, 191
Mayo, William, 191
Maytag, 157
Mayzlin, Dina, 320n39
Mazumdar, Tridib, 228n9
Mazvancheryl, Sanal K., 73n14
McAlister, Leigh, 92n35, 146n53
McAlister's Deli, 63
McCarthy, E. Jerome, 13, 19n27, 37n22
McCarthy, Michael, 18n8, 298n15
McCarthy, M. S., 145n46
McConnell, Ben, 68, 70, 75n41
McCracken, Grant, 143n10
McCuistion, Tommy J., 264n29
McCulloch, R., 126n29
McDermott, John, 263n9
McDonald, Robert E., 281n31
McDonald's, 7, 15, 16, 159, 237, 251, 295
McFarland, Richard G., 320n44
McGovern, Gail, 5, 6, 18n14
McGregor, Jena, 37n21
McKay, Betsy, 144n32
McKee, Daryl O., 206n26
McKenna, Regis, 19n22
McKesson Corporation, 70
McKinsey & Company, 32
McKitterick, John B., 18n18
McLafferty, Sara L., 264n21
McLaughlin, Edward, 300n33
McManus, John, 37n34
McMurry, Robert N., 320n42
McNeil, Donald G., Jr., 58n19
M-commerce, 245, 308
McPhee, Brad, 320n46

McQuiston, Daniel H., 107n6
Media, 273, 278
　company capabilities and, 10
　direct mail and, 304
　direct-response marketing, 305
　global marketing communications, 328
Media selection, for advertising, 285–89
Mediation, 243
Meer, David, 126n32
Megamarketing, 124
Mehta, Abhilasha, 298n20
Mehta, Raj, 108n20
Mehta, Stephanie, 336n4
Mela, Carl F., 188n20, 205n11, 246n5, 299n22, 299n23, 299n27
Meloy, Margaret G., 92n27
Members, and loyalty, 68, 69
Membership groups, 78
Memory, 83–85
Memory encoding, 84–85
Memory retrieval, 85
Men. See Gender
Menduno, Michael, 227n4
Menon, Anil, 301n58, 338n44
Mentzer, John T., 18n21
Merchandising conglomerates, 251
Merchants, 236
Merchant wholesalers, 256
Merit, Don, 207n40
Merrick, David, 19n32
Merrihue, Jeffrey, 298n2
Mesak, Hani I., 298n18
Message generation and evaluation, 284
Message selection and vehicles, 297
Message source, 272
Message strategy, 271
Metamarket, 4–5
Metamediaries, 5
Metrics. See Marketing metrics
Meuter, Matthew L., 206n20, 207n36, 207n38
Meyer, Ann, 319n35
Michaels, Daniel, 318n12
Mick, David Glen, 75n47
Micromarketing, 111
Microsales analysis, 34
Microscheduling problem, 288
Microsites, 307
Microsoft, 2, 152, 155, 159, 160, 161, 307
Milberg, S. J., 145n46
Milewicz, John, 145n38
Miller, Charles, 73n4
Miller, Claire Cain, 320n36
Miller, Cyndee, 74n20
Miller, Jon, 143n1
Min, Sungwook, 188n21
Minard, Paul W., 280n12, 280n14, 298n3
Mind, share of, 158, 289
Miniard, Paul W., 92n32, 92n36
Mintu, Alma T., 337n20
Mission, of CMOs, 6
Missionary sales force, 97
Mission statement, 27
Mitchel, F. Kent, 299n29

Mitchell, Paul, 107n6
Mittal, Vikas, 73n6, 73n7, 73n12
Mittendorf, Brian, 247n24
Mixed bundling, 225
Miyazaki, Anthony, 229n30
Mizik, Natalie, 144n30
Mizrahi, Isaac, 252
Mobile defense, 160–61
Mobile marketing, 10, 308
Mobile phones 245, 308
Mobiltec, 44
Modernization, of product line, 172–73
Modified re-buy, 97
Moffett, Sebastian, 58n20
Mohr, Lois A., 206n23
Moldovan, Sarit, 319n35
Moncrief, William C., III, 320n42
Money-constrained lifestyles, 80
Monga, Alokparna Basu, 144n27
Monitoring systems, for service quality, 201
Monroe, Kent B., 142n2, 229n37
Montgomery, Alan L., 246n5
Montgomery, David B., 166n21, 298n19
Moon, Youngme, 190n54
Mooney, Loren, 125n1
Moore, David J., 280n22
Moore, Elizabeth S., 91n7, 338n39
Moorman, Christine, 109n31
Moorthy, K. Sridhar, 58n15, 188n18
Morais, Richard C., 280n23
Moreau, C. Page, 188n21, 190n42
Morgan, Neil A., 73n12, 74n17, 144n35
Morgan, Robert M., 109n31
Morgeson, Forrest V., III, 73n14
Moriarty, Sandra, 279n8, 279n9
Morrin, Maureen, 143n4, 145n43
Morris, Betsy, 206n28
Morrison, David J., 126n10, 166n14
Morrison, Pamela, 74n27
Morrison, Scott, 58n13
Morrissey, Brian, 318n1, 319n28
Mothers Against Drunk Driving (MADD), 54
Motivation, 81–82
　channel members, 238–39
　sales reps, 316–17
　VALS and, 117
Motives, 81
Motorola, 11, 104, 313
Mount, Ian, 280n25
Mowen, John C., 280n22, 320n54
MTV, 310
Muir, David, 143n13
Mujirushi Ryohin, 255
Mukherjee, Soumen, 126n33
Mullarkey, Guy W., 319n14
Mullen, Georgia, 57n9
Muller, Eitan, 190n44
Muller, Joann, 337n11
Mullins, Peter L., 37n43
Multichannel conflict, 242
Multichannel marketing systems, 241
Multicultural marketing, 77
Multilevel in-depth selling, 100

Multiple-sponsor co-branding, 173
Multiple-vehicle, multiple-stage campaign, 278
Mummert, Hallie, 242
Murphy, H. Lee, 18n6
Murphy, Patrick E., 187n4, 334, 338n45
Murphy, Robert, 263n1
Murthi, B. P. S., 207n29
Musselwhite, Robert, 36n17
Muthukrishnan, A. V., 299n22
MyBestSegments.com, 126n16
MyCoke.com, 302
Myers, Matthew B., 108n25
MySpace, 112, 160, 235, 307, 308

N

Nagle, Thomas T., 213, 228n18
Naik, Prasad A., 280n28, 280n28
Nakamoto, Kent, 165n7
Names, for brands, 138
Narasimhan, Chakravarthi, 74n23
Narasimhan, Laxman, 166n30
Narasimhan, Om, 189n35
Narayana, Chem L., 92n34
Narayandas, N., 247n19
Narus, James A., 107n2, 107n11, 108n16, 108n24, 111, 125n2, 126n12, 264n29
Narver, John C., 11, 18n20, 18n21
Nash, Edward L., 318n6
National Do Not Call Registry, 305
National Geographic Society, 297
Natural environment, 54–55
Natural products, 171
Nature, views of, 54
Near-zero inventory, 262
NEC, 27
Needs, 6–7, 81–82, 203–4
Needs-based segmentation, 121
Neff, Jack, 227n1, 227n3, 279n1, 320n46
Nelson, Charlie, 74n27
Neslin, Scott A., 37n39, 143n12, 229n31, 246n5, 280n29, 298n20, 299n21, 299n22, 299n26
Nestlé, 324
Netemeyer, Richard G., 145n46
Net price analysis, 222
Network information technology, 9
Neuromarketing, 44
New offering realization process, 23
New product launches, 295
New products, 175–81
New task, in business buying, 97
Newman, Bruce I., 18n17
New-market segment strategy, 159
Newsletters, 286
Newspaper advertising, 286
Newsweek, 288
Niche marketing, 111–12
Nicholson, Kate, 126n9
Nielsen Media Research, 40–41
Nike, 13, 23, 46, 112, 132, 232
Niraj, Rakesh, 74n23

Index

Nissan, 172
Nivea, 136
Nodes, 83–84
Nohria, Nitin, 37n31
Noise, 267
Nokia, 20, 136, 324
Nondurable goods, 170–71
Nonexpansible market, 47
Nonpersonal communications channels, 273–74
Nonprofit sector, 192
Nonstore retailing, 250
Nordstrom, 249
North American Industry Classification System (NAICS), 49
Norton, David P., 37n41
Nowlis, Stephen M., 90n2, 190n51
NPD Celebrity Influence Study 2005, 280n20
NTT, 245
Nucor, 8
Nunes, Joseph C., 187n6, 187n7, 228n10
Nunes, Paul F., 188n12, 298n2
Nurpin, Stefan, 301n59
Nussbaum, Bruce, 165n13

O

Objections, overcoming, 312
Objective-and-task budget, 274
Objectives, 158
　advertising, 283–84
　direct mail, 303
　events, 292
　marketing channels, 235–36
　marketing communications, 270–71
　marketing public relations, 297
　market logistics, 259–60
　pricing, 212–13
　sales force, 313
　sales promotion, 290
Observational research, 43
Ocado, 201
Occasions, 117–18
Occupation, 79
Ocean Spray, 275
O'Connell, Patricia, 336n4
O'Donnell, Jayne, 263n15
Offer elements, 304
Offerings, 304. *See* Market offerings
Off-invoice discounts, 291
Off-price retailers, 249
Offset, 222
Ofir, Chezy, 228n7
Ogama, Susumu, 188n25
Ogilvy, David, 298n7
Oh, Sejo, 108n28
Okonkwo, Patrick A., 228n22
Oldsmobile, 136
O'Leary, Noreen, 279n4
Oliva, Ralph A., 36n14
Oliver, Richard L., 93n41
O'Loughlin, Sandra, 339n49
Olympus, 150
Omidyar, Pierre, 220
O'Neil, Brian F., 320n51

One-level channel, 234
One-to-one marketing, 112
Online communities, 307
Online interview, 45
Online marketing. *See* E-commerce marketing, Internet, Web sites
Online videos and ads, 307
Operating variables, in business market segmentation, 120
Opinion leaders, 78, 308, 310
Opportunism, in business relationships, 106
Opportunity and threat analysis. *See* External environment analysis
Optional-feature pricing, 224
Order point, 261
Ordering, ease of, 153
Order processing, 260
Order-processing costs, 261
Order-routine specification, 104
Order-to-payment cycle, 260
O'Reilly, Brian, 165n4
Organization, 29
Organization, of marketing department, 329–31
Organizational buying, 95
　defining, 95–100
　executive summary, 106–7
　stages in, 101–6
Organizational culture, 29
Organizational levels, 25–26
Organizational market, 95–97
Organizations
　marketing of, 3, 4
　views of, 54
Orr, Deborah, 126n9
Ortiz, Jon, 263n8
Osco, 249
Ostenon, Tom, 75n34
Ostrom, Amy L., 205n4, 206n20, 207n36, 207n38
Others, views of, 54
Others' self-concept, 79
Otis Elevator, 324
Ottman, Jacquelyn A., 55, 58n32
Outbound telemarketing, 304
Outdoor advertising, 286
Out-of-pocket costs, 203
Out-suppliers, 104
Overall market share, 34
Overdemand, 225
Overhead, 214
Ozanne, Urban B., 107n7

P

Packaging, 173–74
Padmanabhan, Balaji, 207n29
Page, Albert L., 190n53
Page, Thomas J., Jr., 108n28
Paid-search, 307
Palan, Kay M., 91n8
Palda, Kristian S., 298n19
Palepu, Krishna G., 166n20, 336n7
Palmatier, Robert W., 75n38, 108n28
Palmer, Tim, 264n18
Palmeri, Christopher, 246n14

Pandit, Vivek, 208n47
Papatla, P., 299n27
Parallel entry, 181
Parasuraman, A., 75n38, 207n31, 207n32, 207n33
Parent brand, 137
Park, C. S., 144n28
Park, C. W., 145n39, 145n46, 188n10
Park, Jeong-Eun, 320n44
Park, Sehoon, 190n44
Park, Young-Hoon, 74n30
Parmar, Arundhati, 337n16
Parpis, E., 298n9
Parrish, Marlene, 337n17
Parsons, Leonard J., 228n19
Partial cost recovery, 213
Partner Relationship Management (PRM), 31
Partners, 68, 69
Passriello, Christina, 247n26
Past-sales analysis, 50
Pate, Kelly, 126n24
Patronage awards, 291
Paul, Pamela, 58n27
Pauwels, Koen, 166n27, 299n28, 300n34
Paychex, Inc., 201–2
Payment flow, 233
Payment terms, 223
Payne, Adrian, 19n22
Payne, John W., 92n32
PayPal, 220
Pay-per-click ads, 307
Pekar, Peter, Jr., 37n27
Pelham, A., 18n20
Penetrated market, 47
Peng, Na, 207n30
Peppers, Don, 74–75n33, 126n8
Pepsi Bottling Group, 262
PepsiCo, 27–28, 124, 137, 155, 162, 222
Pepsi-Cola North America, 306
Perceived risk, 88
Perceived service, 198–99
Perceived-value pricing, 219
Percentage-of-sales budget, 274
Perceptions, 82–83, 242, 328–29
Percy, Larry, 280n11, 280n13
Perdue, 148
Performance marketing, 12, 15–16
Performance quality, 64, 152
Performance review, 104
Performance. *See* Marketing performance
Perishability, of services, 194
Permission marketing, 273
Perreault, William D., 19n27
Perrey, Jesko, 190n52
Personal characteristics, in business market segmentation, 120
Personal communications
　direct marketing, 302–5
　executive summary, 317–18
　interactive marketing, 305–8
　personal selling and sales force, 311–14
　sales force management, 314–17
　word-of-mouth, 308–11
Personal communications channels, 272–73

Personal development, 80
Personal factors, influencing consumer behavior, 79–81
Personal influence, 182–83
Personal interview, in marketing research, 45
Personality, 6, 79
Personalization, 133, 134
Personal selling, 267, 268, 276, 311–14, 328
Personnel differentiation, 154
Persons, marketing of, 3
Persuasive advertising, 283–84
Pervasive advocacy, 105
Peters, Thomas J., 37n29
Peterson, Laurie, 280n27
Petrecca, Laura, 279n6, 298n16
Petro, Thomas M., 74n26
Petsmart, 249
Pew Internet and American Life Project Survey, 36n10
Pfeifer, Phillip E., 37n37, 338n35
Pfoertsch, Waldemar, 107n8, 188n12
Philanthropy, corporate, 16
Philip Morris, 161
Phillips, Michael B., 58n10
Physical distribution. *See* Market logistics
Physical flow, 233
Pier 1 Imports, 81
Piercy, Nigel F., 336n10
Pieters, Rig G. M., 228n20
Piggyback, 262
Piller, Frank T., 188n25
Pine, B. Joseph, II, 18n5, 165n11, 263–64n17, 294, 300n51
Pioneer advantage, 184
Pizza Hut, 173, 201, 285
Pizza Inn, 242
Place, 13, 14
Place advertising, 287
Place marketing, 3–4
Plank, Richard E., 109n31
Planned contraction, 161
Plastics.com, 102
Playskool, 308
Podcasts, 307
Pohlen, Terrance L., 246n7
Poilane Bakery, 324
Point-of-purchase advertising, 287
Point-of-purchase displays and demonstrations, 291
Points-of-difference (PODs), 149–50, 151–52
Points-of-parity (POPs), 149–50, 151–52
Political-action committees (PACs), 56
Political-legal environment, 56
PopSugar, 310
Population age mix, 52
Population growth, worldwide, 51–52
Population shifts, geographical, 52–53
Porsche, 122
Porter, Michael E., 19n35, 22, 31, 36n4, 154, 166n19, 166n26, 166n29, 167n35, 167n39, 336n3, 338n43
Posavac, Steven S., 190n43

Posdakoff, Philip M., 320n55
Position defense, 160
Positioning, 7, 22
Positioning strategy, 148
  developing and communicating, 148–52
  differentiation, 152–54
  executive summary, 164–65
Posnock, Susan Thea, 279n4, 298n14
Post, Peter, 300n50
Postpurchase behavior, 86, 88–90
Post-sale service strategy, 204
Potential entrants, 154, 155
Potential market, 46
Potential product, 170
Potentials, in customer development, 68, 69
Potomac Hospital, 198
Pottery Barn, 251
Prabhu, Jaideep, 189n35
Prada, 46, 79
Prahalad, C. K., 36n7, 336n8
Praizler, Nancy C., 189n34
Pratini De Moraes, Marcos V., 336n7
Preannouncements, 160
Preapproach, in sales, 312
Preemptive cannibalization, 140
Preemptive defense, 160
Premiums, 291
Presentation, sales, 312
Pressman, Aaron, 166n33
Press relations, 295
Pretesting, 292
Prezeau, Rodney, 36n17
Price, 13, 14. *See also* Pricing
Price, Linda L., 206n23
Price cues, 212
Price cuts, initiating, 225
Price discounts and allowances, 222, 223
Price discrimination, 223
Price elasticity of demand, 214
Price escalation, 328
Price increases, initiating, 225–26
Price packs, 291
Price policy, 236–37
Price pressures, 103
Price promotion. *See* Sales promotion
Price sensitivity, influences on, 213–14
Price-off discounts, 291
Price-quality inferences, 212
Pricing
  adapting, 221–25
  executive summary, 227
  global marketing, 328
  retailing and, 252
  setting, 212–21
  understanding, 210–12
Pricing changes, initiating and responding to, 225–27
Pricing environment, 210
Pricing method, selection of, 216–20
Pricing policies, 221
Primary data, 42
Primary demand, 47

Primary groups, 78
Primary package, 173
Primary service package, 202
Prime contractors, 98
Pringle, Hamish, 75n45, 339n48
Prins, Remco, 189n36
Prius, 3, 170
Private carrier, 262
Private exchanges, 102
Private Label Manufacturers' Association, 254
Private labels, 254–55
Private nonprofit sector, 192
Privatization, 9
Prizes, 291
PRIZM (Potential Rating Index by Zip Markets), 114
Proactive marketing orientation, 11
"Probe-and-learn" process, 11
Problem detection method, 30
Problem identification, 41–42
Problem recognition, 85, 86, 101
Procter & Gamble, 40, 46, 52, 76, 123, 130, 141, 151, 160, 177, 209, 210, 262, 308, 314, 330
Procurement, 251–52
Producers' cooperatives, 256
Product adaptation, 327
Product assortment, 171, 251–52, 256
Product-bundling pricing, 225
Product categories, building interest in, 295
Product comparisons and advice, 105
Product concept, 11
Product demonstration ads, 271
Product descriptors, 151
Product development, 160, 179–80
Product-development strategy, 28
Product differentiation, 152–53
Product-form pricing, 224
Product imitation, 163
Product innovation, 163
Product invention, 327
Production, accumulated, 215–16
Production concept, 10
Productivity, of sales reps, 316
Product levels, 169–70
Product life cycle, 183–86, 284
Product-line analysis, 172
Product-line length, 172
Product-line modernization, featuring, and pruning, 172–73
Product-line pricing, 224
Product-management organization, 329
Product map, 172
Product market expansion grid, 28
Product mix, 171
Product-mix pricing, 224
Product organizational level, 25, 26
Product placement, 287
Product-positioning map, 178
Product publicity, 295
Product quality, 64, 105
Product-quality leaders, 213

Products, 13, 14
  brand relationships, 171–73
  characteristics and classifications, 169–71
  consumer adoption process, 181–83
  consumer use and disposal of, 90
  direct mail and, 304
  executive summary, 187
  global marketing, 327
  labeling, 174
  new, 175–81, 295
  packaging, 173–74
  warranties and guarantees, 174–75
Product specialization, 123
Product specification, 101–2
Product substitutability, 284
Product support services, 203–4
Product system, 171
Product teams, 330
Product type, 171
Product value analysis (PVA), 101–2
Product variety, 235
Product warranties. *See* Warranties
Professional purchasing, 96
Profitability analysis, 35. *See* Customer profitability analysis
Profitability control, 333
Profitable customers, 64–66
Profit margin, 35
Profit sharing, 314
Program formulation, 30, 32
Progressive Insurance, 147–48
Promotion, 13, 14, 256. *See also* Sales promotion
Promotional allowances, 223
Promotional pricing, 222–23
Promotion cost, 297
Promotion flow, 233
Properties, marketing of, 3, 4
Proposal solicitation, 103
Prospecting, 312
Prospects, 5, 68, 69, 303–4
Prter, Michael E., 37n25, 37n26
Pruning, 172–73
Psychic proximity, 325
Psychogenic needs, 81
Psychographic segmentation, 115, 116–17
Psychological discounting, 223
Psychological life-cycle stages, 79
Psychological processes, in consumer behavior, 81–85
Public, and public relations, 295
Publications, 286, 296
Public issues. *See* Social issues
Publicity. *See* Public relations
Public relations, 267, 268, 273, 276, 295–97
Public-service activities, 296
Public space advertising, 287
Puente, Maria, 263n12
Pullig, Chris, 145n46
Pullins, Ellen Bolman, 109n31
Pull strategy, 232
Pulsing, 288
Purchase decision, 86, 88

Purchasing, 120. *See also* Organizational buying
Purchasing agents, 98
Pure bundling, 225
Pure-click companies, 244–45
"Pure play" auction sites, 102
Purk, Mary E., 263n11
Purk, Mary J., 228n24
Purple Haze, 154
Push strategy, 231–32
Putsis, William P., Jr., 92n33
Pyke, David F., 229n33

Q

Qu, Lu, 188n9
Quaker Oats, 162
Qualified available market, 46
Qualitative research techniques, 44
Quality
  conformance, 152
  functional, 198
  market share and, 161
  performance, 152
  service, 64, 105, 198–202
  technical, 196
  voice, 311
Quality function deployment, 179–80
Quality improvement, 185
Quality-price specialist, 164
Quantity discounts, 223
Quelch, John A., 5, 6, 18n14, 145n43, 299n24, 336n4
Questionnaires, 44–45

R

Rebates, 291
Rack jobbers, 256
Radd, David, 298n17
Radio advertising, 286
RadioShack, 78
Raghubir, Priya, 166n31
Raghunathan, Rajagopal, 246n5
Raikow, David, 107n1
Rainwater, Lee P., 91n5
Raj, S. P., 228n9
Rajendran, K. N., 228n10
Ralcorp Holding, 163
Ramada Inn, 241
Raman, Kalyan, 280n28
Rangan, V. Kasturi, 92n31, 247n17
Rangaswamy, A., 126n11, 189n40
Rao, Akshay R., 188n9
Rao, R., 228n24
Rao, Vithala R., 144n35, 146n53, 300n33
Rapid prototyping, 178
Rapp, Stan, 318n2
Rapport, Alfred, 37n42
Raskin, Andy, 58n10
Rate of return on net worth, 35
Ravishanker, N., 247n21
Rawlinson, Richard, 18n13
Raw-material-exporting economies, 53

Index

Raw materials, 55, 171
Rayport, Jeffrey, 18n11, 156, 166n23, 205n11, 207n37, 306, 319n15
Reach, 285–86
Reactive market orientation, 11
Real customer needs, 7
Reardon, Richard, 280n22
Recessions, 79
Rechtin, Mark, 126n8, 300n11
Records, internal, 39–40
Recruiting, for sales force, 315
Reese, Samuel, 320n46
Reference groups, 78
Reference prices, 211–12
Rego, Lopo L., 73n14, 74n17, 144n35
Regulation, of technological change, 56
REI, 253
Reibstein, David J., 37n37, 229n27, 338n35
Reichheld, Frederick, 63, 74n18, 75n37, 338n38
Reid, David A., 109n31
Reid, Mike, 281n31
Rein, Irving J., 18n7, 143n9
Reinartz, Werner, 75n36, 75n44, 75n47
Reinforcement advertising, 284
Reingen, Peter M., 319n33
Reintermediation, 9
Relationship marketing, 12–13, 311–12
Relationships. *See* Customer relationship management
Relative advantage, 183
Relative market share, 35
Reliability, 153
Reminder advertising, 284
Rendon, Jim, 126n19
Rent.com, 220
Reorder point, 261
Repairability, 153
Repairs, 153
Repeat customers, 68, 69
Repositioning, 295
Research. *See* Marketing research system
Research and development budgets, 55–56
Research approaches, 43
Research in Motion, 29
Research instruments, 43–44
Research objectives, 41–42
Research plan, 42–44
Resources, for SBUs, 28
Response, 267
Response hierarchy models, 268, 270
Responsibilities, of CMOs, 6
Results data, 40
Retail co-branding, 173
Retailer cooperatives, 240, 251
Retailer promotions, 290
Retailers, types of, 249–50, 251, 256
Retailing, 9, 249
  competition in, 241
  environment, 250–51

executive summary, 262
marketing decisions, 251–54
private labels, 254–55
retailer types, 249–50, 251
Retail life cycle, 249
Retail sector, 192
Retention. *See* Customer retention
Return on assets, 35
Reverse-flow channel, 234
Revlon, 275
Reyes, Sonia, 280n27
Reynolds, Christopher, 58n25
Reynolds, Kristy E., 206n23
Reynolds, Thomas J., 92n23
R-F-M formula, 303–4
Richardson, Bruce, 92n30
Richmond, Riva, 247n27
Riel, Cees B. M. van, 144n34
Riengen, Peter H., 319n33
Ries, Al, 139, 145n44, 165n3, 167n34, 300n56
Ries, Laura, 300n56
Riezebos, Rik, 142n3
Rifkin, Glenn, 300–301n57
Rigby, Elizabeth, 75n45
Right-brain thinking skills, 6
Rinehart, Lloyd M., 108n28
Ring, L. Winston, 93n38
Risk, 88, 106
Risk analysis, 179
Risk bearing, by wholesalers, 256
Ritz-Carlton, 59–60
Roberson, Bruce, 37n31
Roberts, John H., 66, 74n27
Roberts, Johnnie L., 318n11
Robertson, Thomas S., 91n15, 92n35, 145n47, 167n36, 190n44
Robertson, Tom, 108n15
Robinson, Patrick J., 107n5, 108n19
Robinson, William T., 188n21, 190n48
Rodgers, William, 338n38
Roehm, Michelle L., 300n53
Rogers, D. S., 264n20
Rogers, Everett M., 182, 190n41, 190n43, 319n33
Rogers, Martha, 74–75n33, 126n8
Rogers, Waymond, 337n20
Rohrlich, Marianne, 91n21
Rohwedder, Cecilie, 75n45
Rokkan, Akesel I., 109n33
Roles, 78
Rolex, 163
Roll, Martin, 337n13
Romanzi, Ken, 275
Roos, Johan, 37n27
Rose, Randall L., 298n3
Rosen, Emanuel, 319n30, 319n31
Rosen, Kenneth T., 263n16
Rosenbloom, Bert, 246n13
Rosiello, Robert L., 229n31
Ross, William T., 73n7
Rossi, Peter E., 126n29
Rossiter, John R., 280n11, 280n13
Rothenberg, Randall, 279n1
Rotz, Greg, 263n9
Roundtree, Robert, 206n20, 207n36

Rowe, Michael, 229n29
Royal Dutch/Shell Group, 29
Royal Philips Electronics, 230–31
Ruekert, Robert W., 188n9
Running costs, 261
Ruppersberger, Gregg, 108n21
Rusch, Robin D., 207n44
Russo, J. Edward, 92n27
Rust, Roland T., 145–46n50, 165n10, 205n2, 207n29, 207n30
Ruth, Julie A., 188n10
Ryanair, 211

S

Saab, 326
SABMiller, 161
Sainsbury, 254
St. Jude Medical, 27
Sakkab, Nabil, 189n30
Saks, 251
Salaries, 314
Sales, 267
Sales analysis, 34
Sales assistants, 316
Sales budget, 48
Sales contests, 292
Sales force
  management of, 314–17
  personal selling and, 311–14
Sales force opinions, composite of, 50
Sales force promotion, 289
Sales force promotion tools, 292
Sales forecast, 48
Sales forecast methods, 50
Salesmen, 310
Sales metrics, 332
Sales presentations and demonstrations, 312
Sales promotion, 267, 268, 273, 275–76, 289–92
Sales quota, 48
Sales reports, 317
Sales representatives, 311, 315–17
Sales-variance analysis, 34
Sales-wave research, 180
Sallies, James, 108–9n30
Salter, Chuck, 300n55
Same-company co-branding, 173
Samples, 291
Sample size, 44
Sampling plan, 44
Sampling procedure, 44
Sampling unit, 44
Sam's Clubs, 249
Samsung, 307, 324
Sanchez, Mark, 166n15
Sanders, Lisa, 37n35
Sarkar, Sumit, 207n29
Sarvaray, Miklos, 227n4
Sasser, W. Earl, 73n15, 195, 206n13, 207n34
Satisfaction, 8, 62. *See also* Customer satisfaction
Satisfiers, 82
Sattler, Henrik, 145n46

Saul, Jonathan, 227n5
Savings availability, 53
Sawhney, M., 18n12, 143n21
Sawyer, Alan G., 228n8
Sayrak, Akin, 73n6
Scenario analysis, 29
Schatzel, Kim E., 167n36
Schenker, Jennifer L., 246n1
Schieffer, Robert, 57n3
Schiffman, Leon G., 91n3, 91n6
Schiller, Zachary, 337n26
Schlesinger, Leonard A., 75n34
Schlosser, Julie, 263n12
Schmitt, Bernd, 18n5, 165n12, 205n9
Schnaars, Steven P., 167n44, 184, 190n49
Schoder, Detlef, 74n30
Schoemaker, Paul J. H., 24, 36n9, 37n23
Schonfield, Erick, 247n27
Schor, Juliet B., 228n13
Schrest, Larry J., 206n25
Schultz, Don E., 19n28, 143n20, 232, 246n6, 281n32, 298n4, 298n10
Schultz, Heidi, 143n20, 281n32
Schultz, Majken, 144n33
Schultz, Randall L., 228n19
Schurr, Paul, 108n28
Schwartz, Nelson D., 108n29
Sealed-bid auctions, 220
Search qualities, 192
Search-related ads, 307
Sears, 2, 138, 157, 201, 242
Seasonal discounts, 223
Second Life, 287, 302
Secondary associations, leveraging, 134–35
Secondary beliefs, 54
Secondary data, 42–43
Secondary groups, 78
Secondary package, 173
Secondary service features, 202
Secret needs, 7
Segment "acid test," 121
Segmentation, 7, 22. *See also* Market segmentation
Segment attractiveness, 121
Segment-by-segment invasions, 124
Segment identification, 121
Segment marketing, 111
Segment positioning, 121
Segment profitability, 121
Segment rivalry, 154–55
Seiders, Kathleen, 207n35
Selden, Larry, 19n25, 337n28
Selden, Yoko S., 19n25
Selective attention, 82–83
Selective demand, 47
Selective distortion, 83
Selective distribution, 236
Selective retention, 83
Selective specialization, 123
Self, views of, 53
Self-concept, 79
Self-liquidating premium, 291
Self-selection, 250
Self-service, 174, 250

Index

Self-service technologies, 200–201
Sellers, Patricia, 166n33
Selling, by wholesalers, 256. *See* Sales; Systems selling
Selling concept, 11
Sell-in time, 292
Selnes, Fred, 74n24, 74n25, 108–9n30
Seltman, Kent D., 205n1
Sen, Sankar, 338n47
Senior Counselors, 14
Senn, Fred, 143n18
"Sense-and-respond" philosophy, 11
Sentiment, 311
Served market, 34–35
Served market share, 34
Service backup, 235
Service blueprint, 194
Service brands, managing, 202–203
Service channels, 8
Service contracts, 204, 223
Service dependability, 203
Service firms, marketing strategies for, 194–98
Service guarantees, 194
Service mix, categories of, 192–93
Service Providers, 14
Service quality, 64, 105, 198–202
Service-quality management, best practices of, 200–202
Service recovery, 201
Services
  defining, 192
  executive summary, 204–5
  marketing of, 3
  nature of, 192–94
  product support, 203–4
  retailing and, 250, 252–53
Services differentiation, 153
Services mix, 252
Service sector channels, 235
Service specialist, 164
Serwer, Andrew E., 126n25, 206n19, 300–301n57
Sethna, B. N., 320n51
Setup costs, 261
Shabbir, Haseeb, 280n19
Shachar, Ron, 145n41
Shankar, Venkatesh, 189n37, 263n10
Shankin, William L., 300n49
Shannon, Victoria, 228n25
Shapiro, Benson P., 92n31, 120, 143n6
Shapiro, Carl, 18n9
Sharma, Amol, 319n26
Sharpe, Ashleye, 75n45
Shaw, Eric H., 337n24
Shaw, Robert, 19n32
Sheehan, Kim Bartel, 298n8
Sheehy, Gail, 91n14
Sheffet, Mary Jane, 91n15
Sheffield, F. D., 280n16
Shell, 324
Shelf space, 255
Sheraton, 203
Sherman, Erik, 36n12
Sherman, Sallie, 320n46

Shervani, T. A., 320n44
Sherwin-Williams, 240
Sheth, Jagdish N., 19n33, 92n32, 93n38, 166n28, 338n33
Shields, Ben, 143n9
Shine, Eric, 337n21
Shipping, 259, 262
Shocker, Allan D., 166n21, 188n10
Shoes for Crews, 174
Shopping.com, 220
Shopping goods, 171
Short-term memory (STM), 83
Shultz, Don, 337n27
Siddarth, S., 166n27
Siemens, 95
Siemens AG, 20–21
Siemens Electrical Apparatus Division, 111
Siemens Medical Systems, 4
Signature Cycles, 110–11, 113
Siguaw, Judy A., 247n19
Siklos, Richard, 108n29
Silk, Alvin J., 298n19
Silverman, George, 319n31
Silverstein, Barry, 280n27
Silverstein, Michael J., 126n23
Simester, Duncan I., 206n25, 228n15, 299n22
Simmons, Carolyn, 145n46
Simmons, John, 142n3
Simon, Hermann, 165n1
Simonin, Bernard L., 188n10
Simonson, Alex, 165n12
Simonson, Itamar, 90n2, 126n13, 190n51, 318n3
Simpson, Jessica, 285
Simpson, Penny M., 247n19
Simulated test marketing, 180
Singh, Jagdip, 206n25
Singh, Ravi, 167n34
Single-segment concentration, 122–23
Sinha, Indrajit, 228n9
Sinha, P., 320n54
Sirgy, M. Joseph, 91n18
Sisodia, Rajendra, 19n33, 166n28
Situational factors, 88, 120
Situation analysis, 33
SIVA, 13–14
Skype, 100, 220
Slater, Stanley F., 18n20
Sloan, Allan, 165n1
Sloan, Paul, 319n22
Slogans, 133
Sloot, Laurens M., 187n8
Slotegraaf, Rebecca J., 206n12
Slotting fee, 255
Slywotzky, Adrian J., 126n10, 143n6, 166n14
Smart, Tim, 19n23
Smith, Craig N., 338n42
Smith, Daniel C., 145n39
Smith, Terry, 89
Smith Corona, 137
Smith Kline Beecham, 124
Snehota, Ivan, 107n3
Social class, 77, 116
Social factors, influencing consumer behavior, 77–78

Social issues
  advertising, 285
  direct marketing, 305
  events and, 292
Social marketing, 4
Social networking, 10, 112
Social responsibility, 15, 16, 125, 285, 323, 334–35
Social responsibility behavior, 334
Societal forces, 9
Societal marketing concept, 15
Society, views of, 54
Socio-cultural environment, 53–54
Sohli, Ravipreet, 108–9n30
Solomon, Michael R., 92n37
Solution, and marketing, 13
Sony, 2, 150, 151, 155, 324
Sood, Ashish, 188n22
Sood, Sanjay, 145n39
Sourcing strategy, 31
Southwest Airlines, 15, 19, 211, 219
Spatial convenience, 235
Special-event pricing, 222
Special-interest groups, 56
Specialized wholesalers, 256
Specialty advertising, 292
Specialty goods, 171
Specialty stores, 249
Specific-customer specialist, 164
Specific investments, 106
Speece, Mark, 144n31
Speeches, 296
Speh, Thomas, 166n16
Spencer, Jane, 18n16
Sperry, Joseph, 320n46
Spethman, Betsy, 291
Spiro, Rosann L., 91n7, 320n55
Sponsorships, 292–93, 296, 307
Spot markets, 102
Sprott, David E., 229n30
SRI Consulting Business Intelligence (SRIC-BI). *See* VALS
Srinivasan, Kannan, 188n18
Srinivasan, Narasimhan, 92n33
Srinivasan, Raji, 247n20
Srinivasan, Shuba, 299n28
Srinivasan, V., 144n28, 189n32, 189n34
Srivatstava, Rajendra, 146n53
Srull, Thomas K., 92n28
Staelin, Richard, 73n10, 207n32, 300n33
Stafford, Edwin R., 58n32
Stakeholder-performance scorecard, 34
Stalk, George, Jr., 166n33
Standardized marketing mix, 327
Standards, for service quality, 200
Staples, 249
Starbucks, 1–2, 239, 253, 292
Starwood Hotels & Resorts, 124, 203
Stated needs, 7
State Farm, 84
Stathakopoulos, V., 338n37
Status, 78
Steel, Emily, 90n1, 318n11
Steenkamp, Jan-Benedict E. M., 189n37, 255, 264n27, 337n18

Steinberg, Brian, 298n17
Steiner, Gary A., 92n26
Stenthal, Brian, 165n5
Stepankowsky, Paula L., 19n23
Stephan, Tina, 143n9
Stephens, Christopher R., 75n46
Stern, Barbara B., 279n9
Stern, Louis W., 246n2, 246n3, 247n22, 247n25
Sternthal, Brian, 58n10, 280n18, 300n35
Stevens, Mary Ellen, 92n30
Stewart, David W., 167n35
Stiving, Mark, 228n14
Stock, James, 166n16
Stockless purchase plans, 104
Stoller, Gary, 227–28n5
Stoller, Martin, 18n6
Stonyfield Farm, 292, 323
Storage warehouses, 260
Store activities and experiences, 253
Store atmosphere, 252–53
Story, Louise, 142n1, 279n1, 279n5, 279n6
STP (segmentation, targeting, positioning), 22
Straight extension, 327
Straight re-buy, 97
Strang, Roger A., 299n25
Strategic brand management, 128–29
Strategic business unit, 28
Strategic concept, 200
Strategic control, 333
Strategic group, 31, 157
Strategic market definition, 27–28
Strategic marketing plan, 26
Strategic planning
  business unit, 29–33
  central role of, 25–26
  corporate and division, 26–29
Strategic withdrawal, 161
Strategy, 31
Strategy formulation, 30, 31
Strengths and weaknesses analysis. *See* Internal environment analysis
Stuart, Jennifer Ames, 74n28
StubHub, 220
Style, 153
Style improvement, 185
Su, Chenting, 91n9
Subaru, 52
Subbrand, 137
Subcultures, 54, 77
Subsistence economies, 53
Substitutes, 154, 155, 284
Subway, 251
Sukumar, R., 75n46
Sullivan, Mary W., 143n6, 144n37
Sullivan, Ursula Y., 246n5
Sultan, Fareena, 190n44
Sung, Yongjun, 91n17
Sunglass Hut, 250
Supermarkets, 249
Supersegment, 122
Superstores, 249
Supervision, of sales representatives, 315

Index

Supplier-customer relationship, 96
Suppliers
  acquiring, 28
  competitive forces and, 154, 155
  selection of, 103–4
Supplier search, 102
Supplies, 171
Supply, 195, 293
Supply chain, 8, 23, 105
Supply chain management (SCM), 257
Suri, Rajneesh, 142n2, 188n11
Survey research, 43
Surveys, of buyers' intentions, 50
Sustainability, 15, 335
Sustainable economy, 80
Sutton, Howard, 247n16
Sviokla, John, 18n11, 92n31
Swaddling, David C., 73n4
Swait, Joffre D., 189n32
Swanson, Scott, 205n1
Sweepstakes, 291
Swift and Company, 138
SWOT analysis, 30–31
Systems buying, 98
Systems contracting, 98
Systems selling, 98
Szymanski, David M., 337n12

T

Tactical marketing, 21
Tactical marketing plan, 26
Tadilamalla, Pandu, 73n6
Takahara, Kanako, 247n33
Talpade, Salil, 91n8
Tan, Cheryl Lu-Lien, 263n4, 263n14
Tangibility, 170–71
Tannenbaum, Stanley I., 143n20, 281n32
Target (store), 81, 219, 252
Target audience, 270
Target costing, 216
Target markets/target marketing, 7, 10, 22, 46, 120–21
  buying center, 100
  definition, 27
  direct mail, 303–4
  ethical choices, 124–25
  events and, 292
  executive summary, 125
  market segmentation criteria, 121
  market segmentation evaluation and selection, 122–24
  public relations and, 295
  retailing, 251
  segment-by-segment invasions, 124
Target-return pricing, 218–19
Task environment, 9
Tata Consultancy Services, 155
Tax, Stephen S., 206n20, 206n22, 207n39
Taylor, James W., 93n40
Taylor, Shirley, 208n46
Taylor, Valarie A., 145n39
Technical quality, 196

Technical support people, 316
Technological environment, 55–56
Technological leapfrogging, 162
Technology, 44. See also Internet
Technology strategy, 31
Tedeschi, Bob, 229n33, 247n30, 319n16
Teens, 78
Tejada, Carlos, 126n18
Telemarketers, 316
Telemarketing, 304–5
Telephone advertising, 286
Telephone interview, 45
Television advertising, 286
Tellegen, Cassandra, 300n40, 300n45
Tellis, Gerard J., 184, 188n22, 189n28, 190n47, 190n50, 190n54, 228n10, 229n31, 229n35, 298–99n20, 298n5
Temporal, Paul, 142n3, 337n13
Terhune, Chad, 264n37
Territorial rights, of distributors, 237
Tersine, Richard J., 264n34
Tesco, 4, 71, 231, 251, 254
Testimonials, 271
Testing elements, in direct-mail marketing, 304
Test markets, 180
Texas Instruments (TI), 214, 215–16
Thaivanich, Pattana, 190n47, 298–99n20, 298n5
Thaler, Linda Kaplan, 279n3
Thierry, Henk, 92n25
Thill, John V., 107n13
Thomas, Jacquelyn S., 75n36, 146n52, 246n5
Thompson, Clive, 228–29n25
Thompson, Debora Viana, 165n10, 298n3
Thompson, Marjorie, 75n45, 339n48
Thomson, Matthew, 143n9
Threat analysis. See External environment analysis
Three-level channel, 234
Thwaites, Des, 280n19
Tie-in promotions, 291
Tierney, Patrick, 206n23
Tiffany, 116, 250
Till, Brian D., 298n3
Timberland, 158
Time-and-duty analysis, 316
Time-constrained lifestyles, 80
Time pricing, 224
Time Warner Cable, 122
Tinkham, Spencer F., 91n17
Tipaldy, Rachel, 263n1
Tishler, Linda, 207n44
Title flow, 233
T.J. Maxx, 249, 251
T-Mobile, 287
Tommy Hilfiger, 150–51
Tom's of Maine, 112, 292
Top-management commitment, to service quality, 200
Toshiba, 324

Total cost of ownership (TCO), 213
Total costs, 214
Total customer cost, 60
Total customer satisfaction, 62
Total customer value, 60
Total market expansion, 159–60
Total marketing communications budget, 274
Total market orientation, 11
Total market potential, 48–49
Total set, and consumer buying, 86, 87
Totten, John C., 300n32
Toubia, Olivier, 189n29
Touchstone, 140
Toyota, 3, 158, 170, 172, 287, 292
Trade discounts, 223
Trade-in allowances, 223
Trade promotion, 289, 291–92
Trade shows, 292
Traditional physical process sequence, 21
Training
  channel members, 238
  customer, as service differentiation, 153
  sales representatives, 315
Transformational appeal, 272
Transitions, 79
Transparency, 105
Transportation, 256, 262
Treaster, Joseph B., 165n1
Treece, James B., 187n5
Treehugger, 310–11
Tremor, 308
Trends, 50–56, 257
Tropicana, 162
Trounce, David, 299n31
Trout, Jack, 139, 145n44, 145n48, 165n3, 167n34
Truck wholesalers, 256
Trust, corporate, 104–6
Trustworthiness, 272
Tse, David K., 208n46
Tsiros, Michael, 73n7
Tulving, Endel, 92n29
Tumbleweed Southwest Grill, 89
Tupperware, 311
Turbodog, 154
Turner Broadcasting, 162
Turnkey solution, 98
Turnover, in sales force, 315
Tuzhilin, Alexander, 207n29
TWA, 137
Twitter, 310
Two-level channel, 234
Two-part pricing, 224
Tybout, Alice M., 165n5, 280n16, 300n35, 300n53
Tying agreements, 243
Tyndall, Rob, 246–47n14

U

Ulaga, Wolfgang, 108n26
Unbundling, 225
Uncles, Mark, 75n42

Undifferentiated marketing, 123–24
Unified Grocers, 251
Unilever, 27, 265
U.S. Food and Drug Administration, 56
U.S. government, 96
U.S. Open, 292
U.S. Steel, 8–9
Universe, views of, 54
Unnava, H. Rao, 280n17
Unsought goods, 171
Unstated needs, 7
Upbin, Bruce, 187n1
UPS, 149, 203
UPS Store, 149
Urban, Glen L., 73n2, 105, 190n48, 228–29n25
Uribarri, Adrian G., 166n17
Usage rate, and segmentation, 118
USAirways, 267
Users, and consumer behavior, 98, 117
User status, 118
Ushikubo, Kasuaki, 36n11

V

Vail, John, 306
Vakratsas, D., 279n10
VALS, 116–17
Value, 8, 14, 17, 10, 21–26. See also Customer value
Value-adding partnerships, 240
Value-augmenting services, 204
Value chain, 22–23
Value creation, 24, 25
Value delivery, 21–22, 23, 24, 25
Value-developing process, 22
Value exploration, 24, 25
Value networks, 22, 231, 232
Value-price ratios, 73n3
Value pricing, 219
Value proposition, 7, 22, 62, 103
Values
  core, 54
  personal, 80
Value segment, 22
Van Bruggen, Gerrit H. See Bruggen, Gerrit H. van
Vandenbosch, Mark, 208n45
Van den Bulte, Christophe, 190n43, 319n27
Vanguard, 202
Van Heerde, Harald J., 188n20, 228n20, 299n23, 300n53
Van Hoffman, Constantine, 126n22
Van Kirk, Richard L., 300n48
Van Riel, Cees B. M. See Riel, Cees B. M. van
Van Rossum, Wouter, 108n16, 108n24
Van Stolk, Peter, 134
Varadarajan, P. R., 301n58, 337n12
Varadarajan, Rajan, 190n52, 338n44
Vargo, Stephen L., 205n5, 279n8

Index

Variability, 194
Variable compensation, 314
Variable costs, 214
Varian, Hal R., 18n9
Vattenfall, 297
Vavra, Terry G., 74n22
Veiders, Christine, 227n1
Velocity, 311
Vendor-managed inventory, 104
Venkatesan, Rajkumar, 74n28, 75n44, 247n21
Venkatesh, R., 107n9
Verbeke, Willem, 320n53, 320n55
Verhoef, Peter, 187n8, 189n36
Verizon, 161
Vertical channel conflict, 242
Vertical hubs, 102
Vertical marketing system (VMS), 240–41
Vertical markets, 102
Videos, online, 307
Vigilant organizations, 24
Vinhas, Alberto Sa, 247n23, 247n25
Violino, Bob, 109n31
Viral marketing, 266, 307, 308, 309
Virgin, 296
Virgin Atlantic Airways, 296
Virgin Records, 296
Virtual reality, 178
Visa, 274, 292
Vocalpoint, 308
Vogelstein, Fred, 318–19n13
Voice, share of, 289, 311
Voice of the customer (VOC) measurements, 201
Voice quality, 311
Völckner, Franziska, 145n46
Voluntary chains, and retailing, 251
Volvo, 7, 62, 131, 148
Von Hoffman, Constantine, 18n15, 19n31, 300n46
Voss, Glenn B., 207n31
Vranica, Suzanne, 319n35
Vriens, Marco, 57n8, 74n28, 75n46, 93n41, 126–27n33, 145–46n50, 189n32

W

Wagner, Cynthia G., 58n18
Walker, Chip, 126n30
Walker, David, 298n20
Walker, Orville C., Jr., 320n54
Walker, Rob, 91n4, 264n25, 264n26, 297–98n1
Wallard, Henri, 74n22
Walls, Gary D., 206n25
Wal-Mart, 2, 38–39, 102, 200, 242, 249, 250, 251, 254, 314
Walt Disney Company, 128
Walt Disney World's Magic Kingdom, 3
Walton, Sam, 200
Waluszewski, A., 108n16
Walzer, Philip, 207n41
Wänke, Michaela, 165n6
Wansink, Brian, 166n31
Wants, customer, 6–7
Ward, Sandra, 18n2
Ward, Scott, 108n15
Ward, Ted, 282
Warehousing, 256, 260
Warranties, 174–75, 204, 223, 291
Wasserman, Todd, 58n12, 320n39
Wasson, Chester R., 186, 190n45
Waterman, Robert H., Jr., 37n29
Wathieu, Luc, 299n22
Wathne, Kenneth H., 109n33, 109n36
Weaknesses analysis. See Internal environment analysis
Weber, John A., 186
Webster, Frederick E., Jr., 22, 36n3, 99, 107n3, 107n10, 107n11, 108n14, 108n15, 108n18, 337n25, 338n30
Web sites, 306. See also E-commerce marketing, Internet, Microsites, Online communities
Wedel, Michael, 126–27n33
Weeks, Clinton S., 300n40, 300n45
Wegener, Duane T., 280n17
Wegmans, 158
Weigand, Robert E., 229n32
Weight Watchers, 139
Weingarten, Marc, 247n31
Weiss, Michael J., 126n17
Weiss, Tara, 336n1
Weitz, Bart, 107n3, 166n21, 188n19, 188n24, 189n27, 228n7, 246n3, 246n4, 263n13, 299n21, 320n47, 336n6, 336n9, 337n12, 337n24, 337n25, 338n30, 338n39
Wells, Melanie, 144n22, 189n29, 300–301n57
Wenske, Paul, 58n29
Wensley, Robin, 107n3, 166n21, 188n19, 188n24, 189n27, 228n7, 246n4, 299n21, 320n47, 336n6, 336n9, 337n12, 337n24, 337n25, 338n30, 338n39
Werner, Uta, 263n9
Wernerfelt, Birger, 206n25, 207n39
Westin Hotels, 124, 173
Wheeler, Alina, 143n17
Wheel-of-retailing hypothesis, 249
Whirlpool, 157
White, Gregory L., 126n23
Whole-brain thinking, 6
Whole Foods Market, 239
Wholesaler-sponsored voluntary chains, 240
Wholesaling, 255–57, 263
Wiersema, Frederick D., 167n40, 205n2
Wildt, Albert R., 228n22
Wilkes, Robert E., 91n8
Wilkie, William L., 91n7, 298n3, 338n39
Wilks, T. J., 92n27
William Wrigley Jr. Company, 232
Williams, Christopher C., 144n22
Wilson, D., 18n20
Wilson, M., 126n24
Wind, Jerry, 126n11, 336n7
Wind, Yoram, 92n35, 107n3, 107n5, 107n10, 107n11, 108n18, 108n19
Winer, Russell S., 228n7, 228n14, 280n28
Witt, Louise, 58n10
Wittink, Dick R., 298–99n20, 299n22
Wittnick, Dick R., 189n32
Wolfe, David B., 19n33, 166n28
Wolfschmidt, 160
Wollan, Malia, 228n25
Wolpin, Bill, 167n43
Women, 78, 116, 285
Wood, Leslie, 74n19
Wood, Marian Burk, 37n33, 127n34, 338n34
Woodruff, Robert B., 108n23
Woodside, Arch G., 107n6
Word-of-mouth marketing, 267, 276, 308–11
Workload approach, 314
Workman, John P., Jr., 19n29
World Childhood Foundation, 297
Wright, Gordon P., 92n31
Wright, John S., 190n46
Wuyts, Stefan, 319n27
W. W. Grainger. See Grainger
Wyer, Robert S., Jr., 92n28

X

Xerox, 2, 63, 259
Xia, Lan, 229n37
Xu, Gordon, 247n32
Xue, Mei, 206n20

Y

Yahoo!, 160, 220, 306
Yankelovich, Daniel, 126n32
Ye, Keying, 91n9
Yellow pages, 286
Yield pricing, 224
YouTube, 266, 307

Z

Zabin, Jeff, 57n3
Zack, Ian, 125n6
Zaichkowsky, Judith, 143n4
Zaltman, Gerald, 58n10, 109n31, 189n38
Zanor, Michael J., 337n27
Zara, 248, 249
Zawada, Craig, 228n17
Zbaracki, Mark J., 228n16
Zeithaml, Valarie A., 145–46n50, 205n3, 205n10, 206n21, 207n32
Zellner, Wendy, 300–301n57
Zenith, 137
Zenor, Michael J., 337n26
Zero-level channels, 234
Zettelmeyer, Florian, 227n4
Zhou, Yong-Pin, 74n30
Ziethammer, Ribert, 228n11
Zimmerman, Ann, 263n12, 264n23
Zimmerman, Christine, 74n19
Zimmerman, Martin, 187n5
Zinn, Laura, 58n30
Zoltners, Andris A., 190n44, 320n54
Zone of tolerance, 200
Zook, Chris, 19n23
Zou, Shaoming, 337n12
Zyman, Sergio, 11

影印版教材可供书目

经济学精选教材·英文影印版/双语注释版

	书号	英文书名	中文书名	版次	编著者	定价
1	23793	Microeconomic Theory: Basic Principles and Extensions	微观经济理论:基本原理与扩展(双语版)	第11版	Walter Nicholson/著	75.00元
2	23654	Public Finance: A Contemporary Application of Theory to Policy	财政学:理论、政策与实践(双语版)	第10版	David N. Hyman/著	78.00元
3	24422	Economics: Principles and Policy	经济学:原理与政策	第11版	William J. Baumol 等/著	88.00元
4	12633	World Trade and Payments: An Introduction	国际贸易与国际收支	第10版	Richard E. Caves, Jeffrey A. Frankel 等/著	68.00元
5	09693	Macroeconomics: Theories and Policies	宏观经济学:理论与政策	第8版	Richard T. Froyen/著	48.00元
6	14529	Econometrics: A Modern Introduction	计量经济学:现代方法(上)	第1版	Michael P. Murray/著	54.00元
7	14530	Econometrics: A Modern Introduction	计量经济学:现代方法(下)	第1版	Michael P. Murray/著	41.00元

管理学精选教材·英文影印版/双语注释版

	书号	英文书名	中文书名	版次	编著者	定价
8	23303	Communicating at Work: Principles and Practices for Business and the Professions	商务沟通:原理与实践(双语版)	第10版	Ronald B. Adler 等/著	65.00元
9	24739	Excellence in Business Communication	卓越的商务沟通	第10版	John V. Thill 等/著	85.00元
10	22511	Management: Skills and Application	管理学:技能与应用(双语版)	第13版	Leslie W. Rue 等著	65.00元
11	12091	Operations Management: Goods, Services and Value Chains	运营管理:产品、服务和价值链	第2版	David A. Collier 等/著	86.00元
12	18239	Management Fundamentals: Concepts, Applications, Skill Development	管理学基础:概念、应用与技能提高	第4版	Robert N. Lussier/著	68.00元
13	06380	E-Commerce Management: Text and Cases	电子商务管理:课文和案例	第1版	Sandeep Krishnamurthy/著	47.00元

金融学精选教材·英文影印版/双语注释版

	书号	英文书名	中文书名	版次	编著者	定价
14	23025	International Corporate Finance	国际财务管理(双语版)	第11版	Jeff Madura/著	75.00元
15	23024	Financial Markets and Institutions	金融市场和金融机构	第10版	Jeff Madura/著	79.00元
16	21898	Money, Banking and Financial Markets	货币金融学(双语版)	第3版	Stephen G. Cecchetti/著	86.00元
17	20606	International Financial Management	国际金融管理(双语版)	第2版	Michael B. Connolly/著	49.00元
18	16314	Investments: Analysis and Behavior	投资学:分析与行为(双语版)	第1版	Mark Hirschey 等/著	68.00元
19	12306	Fundamentals of Futures and Options Markets	期货与期权市场导论	第5版	John C. Hull/著	55.00元
20	12040	Financial Theory and Corporate Policy	金融理论与公司决策	第4版	Thomas E. Copeland 等/著	79.00元
21	09657	Bond Markets: Analysis and Strategies	债券市场:分析和策略	第5版	Frank J. Fabozzi/著	62.00元
22	09767	Takeovers, Restructuring and Corporate Governance	接管、重组与公司治理	第4版	J. Fred Weston 等/著	69.00元
23	13206	Management of Banking	银行管理	第6版	S. Scott MacDonald 等/著	66.00元
24	05965	Principles of Finance	金融学原理(含CD-ROM)	第2版	Scott Besley 等/著	82.00元
25	10916	Risk Management and Insurance	风险管理和保险	第12版	James S. Trieschmann 等/著	65.00元

会计学精选教材·英文影印版

书号	英文书名	中文书名	版次	编著者	定价
26	17348	Advanced Accounting	高级会计学	第10版	Paul M. Fischer 等/著	79.00元
27	14752	Advanced Accounting	高级会计学	第9版	Joe Ben Hoyle 等/著	56.00元
28	17344	Management Decisions and Financial Accounting Reports	中级会计：管理决策与财务会计报告	第2版	Stephen P. Baginski 等/著	56.00元
29	13200	Financial Accounting: Concepts & Applications	财务会计：概念与应用	第10版	W. Steve Albrecht 等/著	75.00元
30	13201	Management Accounting: Concepts & Applications	管理会计：概念与应用	第10版	W. Steve Albrecht 等/著	55.00元
31	13202	Financial Accounting: A Reporting and Analysis Perspective	财务会计：报告与分析	第7版	Earl K. Stice 等/著	85.00元
32	12309	Financial Statement Analysis and Security Valuation	财务报表分析与证券价值评估	第3版	Stephen H. Penman/著	69.00元
33	12310	Accounting for Decision Making and Control	决策与控制会计	第5版	Jerold L. Zimmerman/著	69.00元
34	05416	International Accounting	国际会计学	第4版	Frederick D. S. Choi 等/著	50.00元
35	14536	Managerial Accounting	管理会计	第8版	Don R. Hansen 等/著	79.00元

营销学精选教材·英文影印版/双语注释版

书号	英文书名	中文书名	版次	编著者	定价
36	23015	Essentials of Marketing Management	营销管理精要（双语版）	第1版	Greg W. Marshall/著	56.00元
37	20285	Marketing for China's Managers: Current and Future	市场营销学	第2版	Noel Capon 等/著	56.00元
38	16713	Consumer Behavior	消费者行为学	第5版	Wayne D. Hoyer 等/著	64.00元
39	13205	Services Marketing: Concepts, Strategies, & Cases	服务营销精要：概念、战略与案例	第3版	K. Douglas Hoffman 等/著	63.00元
40	13203	Basic Marketing Research	营销调研基础	第6版	Gilbert A. Churchill, Jr. 等/著	66.00元
41	12305	Selling Today: Creating Customer Value	销售学：创造顾客价值	第10版	Gerald L. Manning, Barry L. Reece/著	52.00元
42	11213	Analysis for Marketing Planning	营销策划分析	第6版	Donald R. Lehmann 等/著	32.00元
43	09654	Market-based Management: Strategies for Growing Customer Value and Profitability	营销管理：提升顾客价值和利润增长的战略	第4版	Roger J. Best/著	48.00元
44	09655	Customer Equity Management	顾客资产管理	第1版	Roland T. Rust 等/著	55.00元
45	09662	Business Market Management: Understanding, Creating and Delivering Value	组织市场管理：理解、创造和传递价值	第2版	James C. Anderson 等/著	45.00元
46	24397	Marketing Strategy: A Decision Focused Approach	营销战略：以决策为导向的方法	第7版	Orville C. Walker, Jr., John W. Mullins/著	55.00元
47	10983	Principles of Marketing	市场营销学	第12版	Louis E. Boone 等/著	66.00元
48	11108	Advertising, Promotion, & Supplemental Aspects of Integrated Marketing Communication	整合营销传播：广告、促销与拓展	第7版	Terence A. Shimp/著	62.00元
49	11212	Marketing Research: Methodological Foundations	营销调研：方法论基础	第9版	Gilbert A. Churchill, Jr. 等/著	68.00元

人力资源管理精选教材 · 英文影印版

	书号	英文书名	中文书名	版次	编著者	定价
50	08536	Human Relations in Organizations: Applications and Skill Building	组织中的人际关系：技能与应用	第6版	Robert N. Lussier/著	58.00元
51	08131	Managerial Communication: Strategies and Applications	管理沟通：策略与应用	第3版	Geraldine E. Hynes/著	38.00元
52	07408	Human Resource Management	人力资源管理	第10版	Robert L. Mathis 等/著	60.00元
53	07407	Organizational Behavior	组织行为学	第10版	Don Hellriegel 等/著	48.00元

国际商务精选教材 · 英文影印版

	书号	英文书名	中文书名	版次	编著者	定价
54	14176	International Business	国际商务	第4版	John J. Wild 等/著	49.00元
55	12886	International Marketing	国际营销	第8版	Michael R. Czinkota 等/著	65.00元
56	06522	Fundamentals of International Business	国际商务基础	第1版	Michael R. Czinkota 等/著	45.00元
57	11674	International Economics: A Policy Approach	国际经济学：一种政策方法	第10版	Mordechai E. Kreinin/著	38.00元
58	06521	International Accounting: A User Perspective	国际会计：使用者视角	第2版	Shahrokh M. Saudagaran/著	26.00元

国际工商管理精选教材 · 英文影印版

	书号	英文书名	中文书名	版次	编著者	定价
59	25309	Analysis for Financial Management	财务管理分析	第9版	Robert C. Higgins/著	58.00元

MBA 精选教材 · 英文影印版

	书号	英文书名	中文书名	版次	编著者	定价
60	12838	Quantitative Analysis for Management	面向管理的数量分析	第9版	Barry Render 等/著	65.00元
61	18426	The Economics of Money, Banking, and Financial Markets	货币、银行和金融市场经济学	第8版	Frederic S. Mishkin/著	85.00元
62	21243	A Framework for Marketing Management	营销管理架构	第4版	Philip Kotler/著	49.00元
63	20916	Understanding Financial Statements	财务报表解析	第9版	Lyn M. Fraser 等/著	38.00元
64	10620	Principles of Operations Management	运作管理原理	第6版	Jay Heizer 等/著	72.00元
65	21546	Introduction to Financial Accounting	财务会计	第10版	Charles T. Horngren 等/著	79.00元
66	21781	Introduction to Management Accounting	管理会计	第15版	Charles T. Horngren 等/著	89.00元
67	11451	Management Communication: A Case-Analysis Approach	管理沟通：案例分析法	第2版	James S. O'Rourke/著	39.00元
68	10614	Management Information Systems	管理信息系统	第9版	Raymond McLeod 等/著	45.00元
69	10615	Fundamentals of Management	管理学基础：核心概念与应用	第4版	Stephen P. Robbins 等/著	49.00元
70	10874	Understanding and Managing Organizational Behavior	组织行为学	第4版	Jennifer M. George 等/著	65.00元
71	15177	Essentials of Entrepreneurship and Small Business Management	小企业管理与企业家精神精要	第5版	Thomas W. Zimmerer 等/著	68.00元
72	11224	Business	商务学	第7版	Ricky W. Griffin 等/著	68.00元
73	11452	Strategy and the Business Landscape: Core Concepts	战略管理	第2版	Pankaj Ghemawat/著	18.00元
74	13817	Managing Human Resources	人力资源管理	第5版	Luis R. Gomez-Mejia 等/著	60.00元
75	09663	Financial Statement Analysis	财务报表分析	第8版	John J. Wild 等/著	56.00元

经济学前沿影印丛书

	书号	英文名	中文书名	版次	编著者	定价
76	09218	Analysis of Panel Data	面板数据分析	第2版	Cheng Hsiao/著	48.00元
77	09236	Economics, Value and Organization	经济学、价值和组织	第1版	Avner Ben-Ner 等/著	59.00元
78	09217	A Companion to Theoretical Econometrics	理论计量经济学精粹	第1版	Badi H. Baltagi/著	79.00元
79	09680	Financial Derivatives: Pricing, Applications, and Mathematics	金融衍生工具:定价、应用与数学	第1版	Jamil Baz 等/著	45.00元

翻译版教材可供书目

重点推荐

	书号	英文名	中文书名	版次	编著者	定价
1	06693	The World Economy: A Millennial Perspective	世界经济千年史	第1版	安格斯·麦迪森(Angus Maddison)/著	58.00元
2	14751	The World Economy: Historical Statistics	世界经济千年统计	第1版	安格斯·麦迪森(Angus Maddison)/著	45.00元
3	14749	A Monetary History of The United States, 1867—1960	美国货币史(1867—1960)	第1版	米尔顿·弗里德曼(Milton Friedman)等/著	78.00元
4	18236	American Economic History	美国经济史	第7版	Jonathan Hughes 等/著	89.00元
5	10004	Fundamental Methods of Mathematical Economics	数理经济学的基本方法	第4版	蒋中一(Alpha C. Chiang)等/著	52.00元
6	23259	Essentials of Economics	经济学基础	第6版	曼昆(N. Gregory Mankiw)/著	68.00元
7	25690	Principles of Economics	经济学原理(微观经济学分册)	第7版	曼昆(N. Gregory Mankiw)/著	72.00元
8	25688	Principles of Economics	经济学原理(宏观经济学分册)	第7版	曼昆(N. Gregory Mankiw)/著	56.00元
9	25768	Study Guide for Principles of Economics	曼昆《经济学原理》学习指南	第7版	大卫·R.哈克斯(David R. Hakes)/著	58.00元(估)

国际经典教材中国版系列

	书号	英文名	中文书名	版次	编著者	定价
10	23120	Financial Statement Analysis and Security Valuation	财务报表分析与证券定价	第3版	Stephen H. Penman,林小驰,王立彦/著	85.00元
11	22803	Integrated Marketing Communication in Advertising and Promotion	整合营销传播:广告与促销	第8版	Terence A. Shimp,张红霞/著	82.00元
12	19263	Public Finance: A Contemporary Application of Theory to U.S. and Chinese Practice	财政学:理论在当代美国和中国的实践应用	第9版	David N. Hyman,张进昌/著	69.00元
13	14516	Investments: Analysis and Behavior	投资学:分析与行为	第1版	Mark Hirschey, John Nofsinger,林海/著	58.00元
14	11227	International Financial Management	国际金融管理	第1版	Michael B. Connolly,杨胜刚/著	38.00元

经济学精选教材译丛

	书号	英文名	中文书名	版次	编著者	定价
15	23322	Introduction to Spatial Econometrics	空间计量经济导论	第1版	James Lesage 等/著	45.00元
16	15917	Microeconomics	微观经济学	第1版	B. Douglas Bernheim 等/著	89.00元
17	13812	Macroeconomics: Theories and Policies	宏观经济学:理论与政策	第8版	Richard T. Froyen/著	49.00元
18	13815	World Trade and Payments: An Introduction	国际贸易与国际收支	第10版	Richard E. Caves 等/著	69.00元

	书号	英文书名	中文书名	版次	编著者	定价
19	13814	Macroeconomics	宏观经济学	第2版	Roger E. A. Farmer/著	46.00元
20	12289	Microeconomic Theory: Basic Principles and Extensions	微观经济理论:基本原理与扩展	第9版	Walter Nicholson/著	75.00元
21	11222	Economics: Principles and Policy	经济学:原理与政策(上、下册)	第9版	William J. Baumol 等/著	96.00元
22	24787	The History of Economic Thought	经济思想史	第8版	Stanley L. Brue 等/著	68.00元
23	13800	Urban Economics	城市经济学	第6版	Arthur O'Sullivan/著	49.00元

管理学精选教材译丛

	书号	英文书名	中文书名	版次	编著者	定价
24	24625	Innovation Management: Context, Strategies, Systems and Processes	创新管理:情境、战略、系统和流程	第1版	Pervaiz Ahmed 等/著	68.00元
25	22968	Management: Skills and Application	管理学:技能与应用	第13版	Leslie W. Rue 等/著	69.00元
26	14519	Operations Management: Goods, Services and Value Chains	运营管理:产品、服务和价值链	第2版	David A. Collier 等/著	79.00元
27	11210	Strategic Management of E-business	电子商务战略管理	第2版	Stephen Chen/著	39.00元
28	10005	Management Fundamentals: Concepts, Applications, Skill Development	管理学基础:概念、应用与技能提高	第4版	Robert N. Lussier/著	82.00元
29	16772	Applied Multivariate Statistical Analysis	应用多元统计分析	第2版	Wolfgang Härdel 等/著	65.00元

会计学精选教材译丛

	书号	英文书名	中文书名	版次	编著者	定价
30	25288	Financial Accounting: A Business Process Approach	财务会计:企业运营视角	第3版	Jane L. Reimers/著	76.00元
31	23288	Intermediate Accounting	中级会计学:基础篇	第17版	Earl Stice 等/著	79.00元
32	24454	Intermediate Accounting	中级会计学:应用篇	第17版	Earl Stice 等/著	78.00元
33	23159	Auditing Cases: An Interactive Learning Approach	审计案例:一种互动学习方法	第5版	Mark S. Beasley 等/著	54.00元
34	14531	Fundamentals of Financial Accounting	财务会计学原理	第2版	Fred Phillips 等/著	82.00元
35	14532	Managerial Accounting	管理会计	第8版	Don R. Hansen 等/著	99.00元
36	16780	Introduction to Management Accounting	管理会计	第14版	Charles T. Horngren 等/著	99.00元
37	20091	Advanced Accounting	高级会计学	第9版	Joe B. Hoyle 等/著	66.00元

金融学精选教材译丛

	书号	英文书名	中文书名	版次	编著者	定价
38	23074	Corporate Finance: A Focused Approach	公司金融:理论及实务精要	第4版	Michael C. Ehrhardt 等/著	89.00元
39	24817	International Corporate Finance	国际财务管理	第11版	Jeff Madura/著	89.00元
40	25314	Principles of Finance	金融学原理	第5版	Scott Besley 等/著	69.00元
41	12317	Management of Banking	银行管理	第6版	S. Scott MacDonald 等/著	78.00元
42	12316	Multinational Business Finance	跨国金融与财务	第11版	David K. Eiteman 等/著	78.00元
43	10007	Capital Budgeting and Long-Term Financing Decisions	资本预算与长期融资决策	第3版	Neil Seitz 等/著	79.00元
44	10609	Money, Banking, and Financial Markets	货币、银行与金融市场	第1版	Stephen G. Cecchetti/著	75.00元
45	11463	Bond Markets, Analysis and Strategies	债券市场:分析和策略	第5版	Frank J. Fabozzi/著	76.00元

	书号	英文书名	中文书名	版次	编著者	定价
46	10624	Fundamentals of Futures and Options Markets	期货与期权市场导论	第5版	John C. Hull/著	62.00元
47	09768	Takeovers, Restructuring and Corporate Governance	接管、重组与公司治理	第4版	J. Fred Weston 等/著	79.00元

营销学精选教材译丛

	书号	英文书名	中文书名	版次	编著者	定价
48	24879	Essentials of Marketing Management	营销管理精要	第1版	Greg W. Marshall 等/著	68.00元
49	24405	Marketing Strategy: A Decision-Focused Approach	营销战略:以决策为导向的方法	第7版	Orville C. Walker, Jr., John W. Mullins/著	64.00元
50	19303	Consumer Behavior	消费者行为	第5版	Wayne D. Hoyer 等/著	79.00元
51	13808	Basic Marketing Research	营销调研基础	第6版	Gilbert A. Churchill, Jr. 等/著	78.00元
52	12301	Principles of Marketing	市场营销学	第12版	Dave L. Kurtz 等/著	65.00元
53	15716	Selling Today: Creating Customer Value	销售学:创造顾客价值	第10版	Gerald L. Manning/著	62.00元
54	13795	Analysis for Marketing Planning	营销策划分析	第6版	Donald R. Lehmann/著	35.00元
55	13811	Services Marketing: Concepts, Strategies, & Cases	服务营销精要:概念、战略与案例	第2版	K. Douglas Hoffman 等/著	68.00元
56	12312	Customer Equity Management	顾客资产管理	第1版	Roland T. Rust 等/著	65.00元
57	16316	Marketing Research: Methodological Foundations	营销调研:方法论基础	第9版	Gilbert A. Churchill, Jr. 等/著	62.00元
58	11229	Market-based Management: Strategies for Growing Customer Value and Profitability	营销管理:提升顾客价值和利润增长的战略	第4版	Roger J. Best/著	58.00元
59	11226	Business Market Management: Understanding, Creating and Delivering Value	组织市场管理:理解、创造和传递价值	第2版	James C. Anderson 等/著	52.00元

人力资源管理精选教材译丛

	书号	英文书名	中文书名	版次	编著者	定价
60	16619	Human Relations in Organizations: Applications and Skill Building	组织中的人际关系:技能与应用	第6版	Robert N. Lussier/著	75.00元
61	10276	Human Resource Management	人力资源管理	第10版	Robert L. Mathis/著	68.00元
62	15982	Fundamentals of Organizational Behavior	组织行为学	第11版	Don Hellriegel 等/著	56.00元
63	09274	Managerial Communication: Strategies and Applications	管理沟通:策略与应用	第3版	Geraldine E. Hynes/著	45.00元
64	10275	Supervision: Key Link to Productivity	员工监管:提高生产力的有效途径	第8版	Leslie W. Rue 等/著	59.00元

国际商务精选教材译丛

	书号	英文书名	中文书名	版次	编著者	定价
65	16334	International Economics: A Policy Approach	国际经济学:政策视角	第10版	Mordechai E. Kreinin/著	45.00元
66	25306	International Business	国际商务	第7版	John J. Wild 等/著	69.00元
67	10001	Fundamentals of International Business	国际商务基础	第1版	Michael R. Czinkota 等/著	58.00元

国际工商管理精选教材·翻译版

	书号	英文书名	中文书名	版次	编著者	定价
68	25839	Managerial Economics: A Problem Solving Approach	管理经济学：一种问题解决方式	第3版	Luke M. Froeb 等/著	45.00元

全美最新工商管理权威教材译丛

	书号	英文书名	中文书名	版次	编著者	定价
69	24752	Excellence in Business Communication	卓越的商务沟通	第10版	John V. Thill, Courtland L. Bovée/著	89.00元
70	19036	Managing Human Resources	人力资源管理	第5版	Luis R. Gomez-Mejia 等/著	79.00元
71	18646	Contemporary Business Statistics with Microsoft Excel	基于Excel的商务与经济统计	第1版	Thomas A. Williams 等/著	76.00元
72	16318	Essentials of Managerial Finance	财务管理精要	第14版	John V. Thill 等/著	88.00元
73	16319	Understanding and Managing Organizational Behavior	组织行为学	第5版	Jennifer M. George 等/著	75.00元
74	13810	Crafting and Executing Strategy: Concepts and Cases	战略管理：概念与案例	第14版	Arthur A. Thompson 等/著	48.00元
75	14518	Management Communication: A Case-Analysis Approach	管理沟通：案例分析法	第3版	James S. O'Rourke/著	44.00元
76	16549	Quantitative Analysis for Management	面向管理的数量分析	第9版	Barry Render 等/著	85.00元
77	13790	Case Problems in Finance	财务案例	第12版	W. Carl Kester 等/著	88.00元
78	13807	Analysis for Financial Management	财务管理分析	第8版	Robert C. Higgins/著	42.00元
79	22456	Understanding Financial Statements	财务报表解析	第9版	Lyn M. Fraser 等/著	36.00元
80	13809	Strategy and the Business Landscape	战略管理	第2版	Pankaj Ghemawat/著	25.00元
81	16171	Principles of Operations Management	运作管理原理	第6版	Jay Heizer 等/著	86.00元
82	11609	Management: The New Competitive Landscape	管理学：新竞争格局	第6版	Thomas S. Bateman 等/著	76.00元
83	09690	Product Management	产品管理	第4版	Donald R. Lehmann 等/著	58.00元
84	12885	Entrepreneurial Small Business	小企业创业管理	第1版	Jerome A. Katz 等/著	86.00元
85	16780	Introduction to Management Accounting	管理会计	第14版	Charles T. Horngren 等/著	99.00元

增长与发展经济学译丛

	书号	英文书名	中文书名	版次	编著者	定价
86	05742	Introduction to Economic Growth	经济增长导论	第1版	Charles I. Jones/著	28.00元
87	05744	Development Microeconomics	发展微观经济学	第1版	Pranab Bardhan 等/著	35.00元
88	05743	Development Economics	发展经济学	第1版	Debraj Rag/著	79.00元
89	06905	Endogenous Growth Theory	内生增长理论	第1版	Philippe Aghion 等/著	75.00元

其他教材

	书号	英文书名	中文书名	版次	编著者	定价
90	21378	International and Comparative Employment Relations	国际与比较雇佣关系	第5版	Greg Bamber, 赵曙明 等/编	59.00元
91	24364	Management Innovation: A Casebook	管理创新案例集	第1版	Christopher Williams 等/编译	52.00元

北京培生信息中心	北京大学出版社
北京东城区北三环东路 36 号	经济与管理图书事业部
北京环球贸易中心 D 座 1208 室	北京市海淀区成府路 205 号 100871
邮政编码:100013	联系人：徐 冰 张 燕
电话:(8610)57355175	电话：010-62767312 / 62767348
传真:(8610)58257961	传真：010-62556201

尊敬的老师：

您好！

  为了确保您及时有效地申请教辅资源，请您务必完整填写如下教辅申请表，加盖学院的公章后传真给我们，我们将会为您开通属于您个人的唯一帐号以供您下载与教材配套的教师资源。

请填写所需教辅的开课信息：

采用教材				☐中文版 ☐英文版 ☐双语版	
作　　者			出版社		
版　　次			ISBN		
课程时间	始于　年　月　日		学生人数		
	止于　年　月　日		学生年级	☐专科 ☐研究生	☐本科 **1/2** 年级 ☐本科 **3/4** 年级

请填写您的个人信息：

学　　校			
院系/专业			
姓　　名		职　　称	☐助教 ☐讲师 ☐副教授 ☐教授
通信地址/邮编			
手　　机		电　　话	
传　　真			
official email (eg:XXX@crup.edu.cn)		**email** (eg:XXX@163.com)	
是否愿意接受我们定期的新书讯息通知：	☐是　　☐否		

系 / 院主任：＿＿＿＿＿＿＿＿（签字）

（系 / 院办公室章）

＿＿＿年＿＿＿月＿＿＿日

Please send this form to: em@pup.cn 或 Service.CN@pearson.com
Website: www.pearsonhighered.com/educator